D1068749

NETWORK CABLING HANDBOOK

ABOUT THE AUTHOR

Chris Clark is the president and founder of Clark Technology Group and NetCBT located in Roseville, California. Clark Technology Group provides network cabling and network design training courses and also provides telecommunications consulting. NetCBT develops and sells computer-based network cabling and network design training courses.

Chris holds both the RCDD and LAN Specialist credentials from BICSI. He is a licensed California Contractor with a C-7 license for low voltage systems. Chris is also a certified BICSI and Nordex/CDT IBDN instructor and a member of the BICSI Engineering and Methods Committee for Local Area Network and LAN cabling design.

ABOUT THE CONTRIBUTORS

Archi-Technology, LLC of Rochester, New York, is a "smart building" consulting firm that provides Web-based design and documentation services for telecommunication infrastructures based on the Division 17 organizational model. Using this model, we provide our clients with a telecommunications infrastructure design and documentation capable of supporting the technology services that are demanded in today's marketplace. For further information on web-based design and documentation services for telecommunication infrastructures, call 1-716-424-1952 or go to **www.architechnology.com** or **www.division17.com**.

Cable Management Solutions, Inc. of Deer Park, New York, is the manufacturer of Snake Tray™ and Snake Canyon™ cable trays. Snake tray is the only hand-bendable cable tray, which can create turns in ten seconds for use overhead, direct wall mount or installation below raised floors. Snake Canyon is a modular cable tray system that integrates the structural elements of a computer access floor with a high capacity cable tray into one easy to install drop-in element. For further information on Cable Management Solutions, products and services call 1-800-308-6788 or go to **www.snaketray.com**.

Fluke Networks™, Inc. of Everett, Washington, provides state-of-the-art network supervision solutions that support the installation, analysis, and monitoring of enterprise and telecommunications networks and the installation and certification of the fiber and copper network backbones. For more information on Fluke Networks, Inc.'s products and services go to www.flukenetworks.com.

Hubbell Premise Wiring of Stonington, Connecticut, manufactures high-performance structured cabling system-connecting hardware for voice, data, and video applications. Hubbell offers a comprehensive line of jacks, faceplates, panels, jumpers, raceway, power poles, cable management systems, and optical fiber interconnect solutions including rack- and wall-mounted patch panels/enclosures, multimedia outlets, connectors, adapters, patchcords, and termination tools. For more information on Hubbell Premise Wiring, call 1-800-626-0005 or go to **www.hubbell-premise.com**.

NETWORK CABLING HANDBOOK

CHRIS **CLARK**

McGraw-Hill/Osborne

New York   Chicago   San Francisco
Lisbon   London   Madrid   Mexico City   Milan
New Delhi   San Juan   Seoul   Singapore   Sydney   Toronto

McGraw-Hill/Osborne
2600 Tenth Street
Berkeley, California 94710
U.S.A.

To arrange bulk purchase discounts for sales promotions, premiums, or fund-raisers, please contact **McGraw-Hill**/Osborne at the above address. For information on translations or book distributors outside the U.S.A., please see the International Contact Information page immediately following the index of this book.

Network Cabling Handbook

Copyright © 2002 by The McGraw-Hill Companies. All rights reserved. Printed in the United States of America. Except as permitted under the Copyright Act of 1976, no part of this publication may be reproduced or distributed in any form or by any means, or stored in a database or retrieval system, without the prior written permission of the publisher, with the exception that the program listings may be entered, stored, and executed in a computer system, but they may not be reproduced for publication.

1234567890 DOC DOC 01987654321

ISBN 0-07-213233-7

Publisher
  Brandon A. Nordin
Vice President & Associate Publisher
  Scott Rogers
Editorial Director
  Tracy Dunkelberger
Production Manager
  Lisa Kent Bandini
Acquisitions Editor
  Michael Sprague
Senior Project Editor
  Betsy Manini

Acquisitions Coordinator
  Alex Corona
Technical Editor
  Allan Carole Anderson
Illustration Supervisor
  Lyssa Sieben-Wald
Photographer
  Ted Kurihara Photography
Full-Service Compositor
  MacAllister Publishing Services, LLC

This book was composed with QuarkXpress™.

Information has been obtained by **McGraw-Hill**/Osborne from sources believed to be reliable. However, because of the possibility of human or mechanical error by our sources, **McGraw-Hill**/Osborne, or others, **McGraw-Hill**/Osborne does not guarantee the accuracy, adequacy, or completeness of any information and is not responsible for any errors or omissions or the results obtained from use of such information.

This book is dedicated to
my wife Lauren and
my two children, Andy and Alecia.
It is your love and support that made this book possible.

AT A GLANCE

CONTENTS

Part I

Structured Cabling Systems and Standards

Part II

Installation and Testing

ACKNOWLEDGMENTS

I would like to acknowledge the following individuals for their hard work preparing the book for publication. My thanks go to Tracy Dunkelberger of McGraw Hill/Osborne for her hard work and organization skills in pulling this project together. I would also like to thank Molly Applegate of MacAllister Publishing Services for her hard work overseeing production of the book.

I would like to extend special thanks for Ted Kurihara of Ted Kurihara Photography of Mill Valley, California (415-285-3200). You are an exceptional artist and an extremely nice person. I enjoyed the time we spent taking the photographs for the book. I would also like to thank Archi-Technology, Cable Management Solutions, Fluke Networks, and Hubbell Premise Wiring for contributing images used in the book.

INTRODUCTION

Network Cabling Handbook is the most comprehensive book available today about network cabling. This book is designed for any individual who is involved with installing, terminating, or testing communication cabling systems for either voice and data communications systems. This book should be read by communication contractors, electrical contractors, network engineers, telephone contractors, network design engineers, cable designers, or any others involved with designing or installing communications cabling systems.

Network Cabling Handbook is organized into two sections. **Part I** will describe network cabling systems, different types of communication cables and components, communication cabling standards, and transmission fundamentals. **Part II** describes the specifics of pulling, securing, terminating and testing both copper and optical fiber communications cables. Network Cabling Handbook will provide all the information to handle any network cabling project correctly.

PART I

Structured Cabling Systems and Standards

CHAPTER 1

Communication Systems

Communication systems (voice, local area networks [LANs], or data systems) are a vital part of every business. In fact, most businesses rely on their communication systems to stay competitive, to streamline business operations, to improve communications, and to offer new services to their customers.

Communications systems cover a wide range of voice, information processing, and signaling systems used to connect users together or to share information. Every desk typically includes a phone and a data terminal. The two most popular types of communication systems that the average worker uses on a daily basis are the phone system and the LAN. The phone system enables users to make and receive phone calls. The LAN is a network that enables personal computers (PCs) to send and receive data files and e-mail messages. Today, most companies have connected their LAN to the Internet. This enables each network user to browse the Internet and send/receive data files and e-mail messages to anyone connected to the Internet.

The one characteristic that most communication systems share is the need for communications cables to distribute signals to system users or devices. All communication systems will typically use some form of communications cable to send these system signals to system users or devices. For example, a telephone requires a cable to be run from a phone switch to each user's desk. This cable is terminated on an outlet in the work area. The telephone cord is then plugged into the outlet. This cable connection is required to enable the phone to work. The cables supply power to the telephone and enables voice signals to be sent and received from the phone. Without the cables connecting the phone to the voice switch, the phone cannot work.

Five categories of communications systems in commercial buildings require communications cabling. These include

▼　Phone systems

■　Data systems

■　LANs

■　Building Automation and Control Systems (BACS)

▲　Sound systems

Phone systems require communications cabling to connect the individual phone on each user's desk to a centralized phone switch. Data systems usually consist of terminals that are connected to a centralized computer system, either a mainframe or minicomputer. A communications cable connects the terminal to the centralized computer system or a controller connected to the computer system. LANs enable PCs to share information with other PCs in a building or campus of buildings. PCs attach to a LAN by connecting a communications cable to a Network Interface Card (NIC) installed in the PC. The opposite end of the communication cable is connected to a LAN hub. BACS use communications cables to connect sensors to a central monitoring unit.

Each of these building communications systems is defined by the National Electrical Code (NEC) as a power-limited or communication system. Each system is referenced in different sections of the NEC. Each communication system also requires its own cabling system be installed to support system devices. Each communication system is usually specified in different sections of industry blueprints. As a result, the construction industry usually has each system bid and built by separate contractors.

NOTE: The specifications for most communications systems are specified in the mechanical and electrical sections of building blueprints. The construction industry is starting to integrate to specifications for all communication systems into Division 17. This will promote an integrated cabling system to support multiple communication systems, common pathways to support the cabling for multiple systems, and a single contractor to install and support these systems.

PHONE SYSTEMS

The term *phone system* is used to describe the different equipment and devices that provide telephone service. A phone system must consist of a minimum of three components: two telephones and a cable connecting them together. This is shown in Figure 1-1.

A telephone is a device that converts voice sounds (speech) into electrical communication signals. The communication signals are transmitted along the cable and are received by the second telephone. The receiving telephone will convert the electrical communication signals back into sound so the person using the phone can hear the original voice sounds. This simple phone system would enable only two users to talk together.

Most telephone systems are far more complex than this simple system because individuals need to talk to more than just one other person. In addition, many businesses and homes need more than two phones. A more complex phone system is created by using a

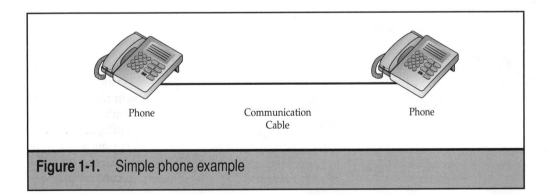

Phone   Communication   Phone
Cable

Figure 1-1.   Simple phone example

phone switch. A phone switch (see Figure 1-2) is a device that connects multiple phones together and connects to multiple phone lines. A phone switch enables any phone to connect to any other phone on the premises. It also enables any telephone to connect to an outside line to make or receive phone calls.

The basic operation of the phone system is the same as the simple phone example described earlier. A person picks up a telephone and dials a number. The phone switch will make a connection to another phone (sometimes this requires going through multiple phone switches). The person making the phone call speaks into the telephone. The telephone converts voice sounds (speech) into electrical communication signals. The communication signals are transmitted along the cable, through the phone switch to the second telephone. The receiving telephone will convert the electrical communication signals back into sound so the person using the phone can hear the original voice sounds.

Most homes and apartments only need a single phone line installed (see Figure 1-3). The phone line is provided by the local telephone company. The phone line originates from a phone switch in the telephone company's central office. Phones in a home or apartment are daisy chained together and connected to the signal phone line. The phone switch in the telephone company's central office will enable individuals to make and receive phone calls over the phone line.

Most commercial businesses require more than one phone line. It is very common for a commercial business to have multiple phone lines (see Figure 1-4) so the business employees can receive phone calls from customers while other employees are making phone

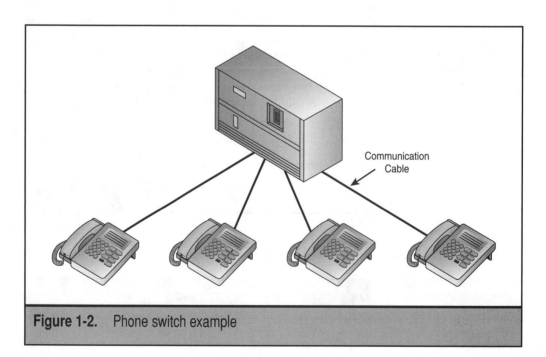

Figure 1-2. Phone switch example

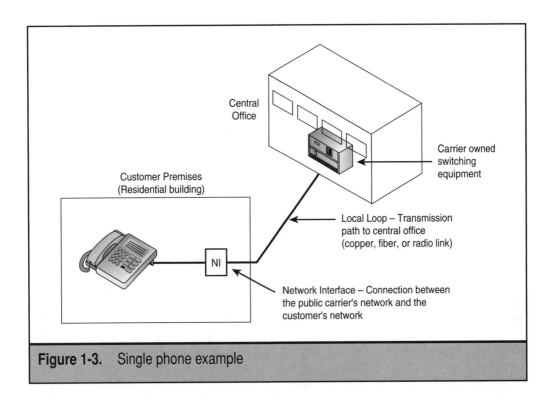

Central
Office

Carrier owned
switching
equipment

Customer Premises
(Residential building)

Local Loop – Transmission
path to central office
(copper, fiber, or radio link)

NI

Network Interface – Connection between
the public carrier's network and the
customer's network

Figure 1-3.   Single phone example

calls. A phone switch is required to support multiple phone lines. Each telephone is connected to the phone switch using UTP copper communication cable.

A business can either contract with the local telephone company to use their phone switch or purchase their own phone switch. The term *Centrex Service* (see Figure 1-5) is used to describe a business using the local telephone company's switch. The local phone company, called a Local Exchange Carrier (LEC), runs multiple cable pairs (in one or more cables) from the centralized phone switch to the business. Each cable pair will support a single telephone. The business would pay the LEC a monthly fee for the Centrex service based on the number of phones that need to be supported.

It is more common for a commercial business to purchase their own phone switch. Small businesses with a small number of employees requiring only a few phone lines would purchase a small phone switch. Small phone switches are called Key Service Units (KSUs). KSUs (see Figure 1-6) are typically designed to support a fixed number of phone lines and telephone extensions. For example, a typical KSU would support up to eight phone lines coming into the switch and up to 32 phones connected to the switch.

Large businesses with hundreds or thousands of employees requiring a large number of phone lines would purchase a large phone switch. Large phone switchs are called a Private Branch Exchange (PBX). PBXs (see Figure 1-7) are typically designed to be upgradable. They can grow as the user's needs grow. PBXs can be purchased to support

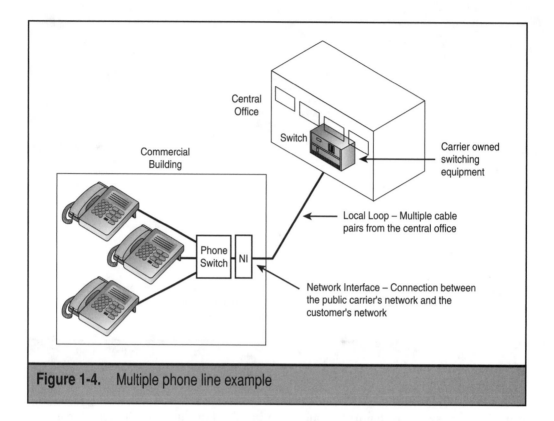

Figure 1-4.　Multiple phone line example

hundreds of phone lines and thousands of telephone extensions. These phone switches can cost hundreds of thousands of dollars.

Phone systems always require communication cables for passing control and communication signals between the system devices. Phone systems require that UTP cable be installed between the phone switch and the telephones. Phone switches are centralized devices. Each telephone must have a dedicated cable installed from the phone switch. Smaller phone switches are usually placed on the same floor as the telephones they serve. Larger phone switches are placed in centrally located equipment rooms. The larger the phone switch, the more extensive the cabling requirements. Every phone system requires the correct type and length of communication cable to be installed for the system to work correctly.

NOTE:　The only type of phone system that does not require communication cables is cellular (wireless) phones. This phone system uses radio signals transmitted through the air as the transmission medium.

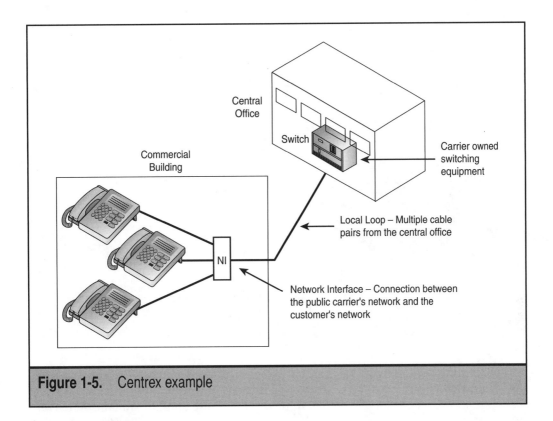

Figure 1-5.   Centrex example

DATA SYSTEMS

The term *data system* is typically used to describe a mainframe or minicomputer system. These systems were used extensively through the 1960s, 1970s, and 1980s. The mainframe and minicomputers predated the PCs used extensively today.

A mainframe (see Figure 1-8) is a large, centralized computer that performed all computing activities. All computer applications were installed on the mainframe computer, and all data was store on the mainframe computer's disk drives. Users interacted with the mainframe computer through terminals. The terminals were connected to a port on the mainframe's controller with a communication cable. A single mainframe computer was capable of supporting hundreds of terminals.

A mainframe computer is a large computer with a large processing capability. This means that mainframes can support large applications, large numbers of applications running concurrently, and large numbers of users connected to the mainframe. A mainframe computer was typically powerful enough to support the computing needs of an entire company.

A minicomputer (see Figure 1-9) is very similar to a mainframe computer. In fact, the minicomputer is a smaller version of the mainframe computer. Minicomputers were

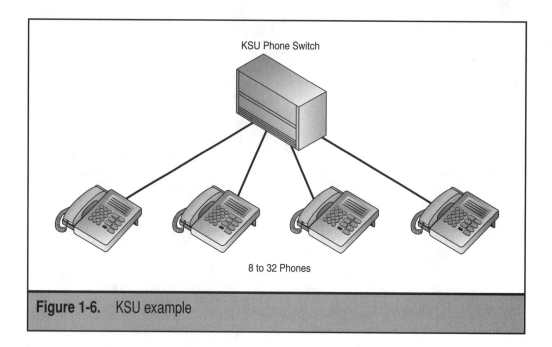

Figure 1-6. KSU example

created and introduced to the market in the 1970s. Minicomputers were less expensive than mainframe computers and made computer systems available to more companies.

From an architecture perspective, minicomputers are similar to mainframe computers. Minicomputers were characterized as having a single, centralized processor. All application programs ran on the centralized computer system and all data was stored on the computer's disk drives. Users interacted with the minicomputer through terminals. The terminals were connected to a port on the minicomputer with a communication cable.

The main difference between the minicomputer and the mainframe computer is that minicomputers are less powerful than mainframe computers. They are also smaller in size and support less terminal connections. This means that minicomputers cannot support large applications, large numbers of concurrent applications running, or large numbers of users connected to the system. They can only support a small number of terminals and are generally considered building serving devices. They can only support the terminals in a single building but not the entire company.

Both mainframe and minicomputers require communication cable to distribute data from the user terminals to the centralized processors and back again. A communication cable must be run to every terminal for it to communication with the mainframe or minicomputer system. Data systems have more stringent cabling requirements than voice systems because they use digital signaling. Digital signaling requires that all signals arrive at the receiving device without any errors. If any errors are detected, the entire data packet must be retransmitted.

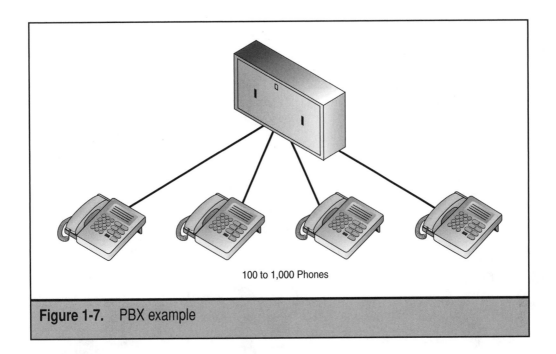

100 to 1,000 Phones

Figure 1-7. PBX example

The data transmitted between a terminal and the centralized mainframe or minicomputer is generally considered to be low speed data. The data transfer speeds of these connections range from 9,600 bits per second up to 2.5 Mb/s. Therefore, communication cables are very important to the overall performance, reliability, and speed of data systems.

LOCAL AREA NETWORKS (LANs)

A *local area network* (LAN) is a communication system that enables multiple computers to communicate together (see Figure 1-10). The IEEE defines a LAN as "a datacom system allowing a number of independent devices to communicate directly with each other and within a moderately sized geographic area."

LANs were created in the early 1980s. In 1980, IBM introduced the first PC to the market. The first LANs were created to link these new types of computers together. PCs have replaced the mainframe and minicomputer as the primary computing devices for most corporate users. Most users have a PC on their desk instead of a computer terminal. Computer applications are installed on the PC, and users store their data on the PC's disk drive.

NOTE: Mainframes and minicomputers still exist today. These systems are typically used for running legacy applications in companies. Most users interact with these computers by running a terminal emulation program on a PC and communicating with the computer through a LAN.

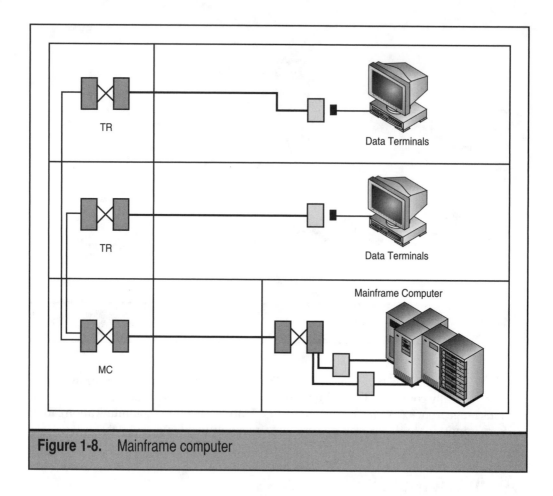

Figure 1-8.   Mainframe computer

PCs do not have the ability to communicate together. LANs are the primary means enabling PCs to be connected together and share information. LANs allow the individual PCs to share software applications and to share user created files. In addition, a LAN permits the sharing of peripheral devices such as CD-ROM drives, printers, and modems. Finally, LANs also provide a method of organizing the individual PC users into groups.

LANs are built using the following components:

▼ **Computers**   The devices that generate or receive information on a LAN. The computer can be a workstation or server connected to a hub.

■ **Network Interface Card (NIC)**   A hardware card installed in a computer. This card enables the computer to understand the rules of the network.

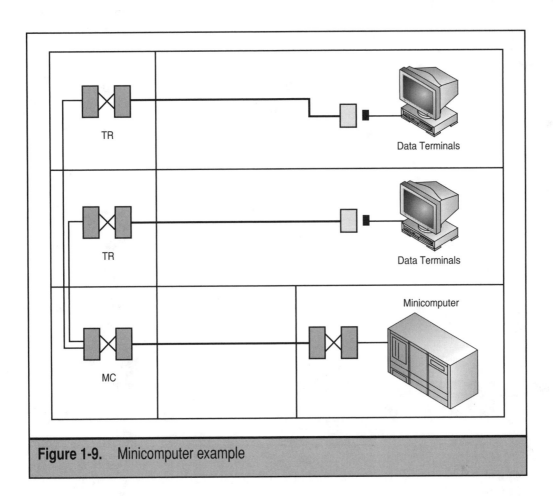

Figure 1-9. Minicomputer example

■ **Communication cable**   The transmission medium that distributes LAN signals from the NIC to the LAN hub. The media is usually copper twisted pair or optical fiber cable.

▲ **LAN hub**   A centralized hardware component that connects all network devices together. This network device is the center of the star topology. It repeats, amplifies, and broadcast LAN signals to all connected computers.

LANs are high-speed communication networks that transfer information at speeds that range from 10 Mb/s to 10 Gb/s. LANs use digital signaling like low-speed data systems. LANs also have the requirement that all signals must arrive at the receiving device without an error or the entire LAN frame must be retransmitted. LANs have the additional requirement of transmitting signals in the millions of bits per seconds (Mb/s) to billions of bits per second (Gb/s) speed range.

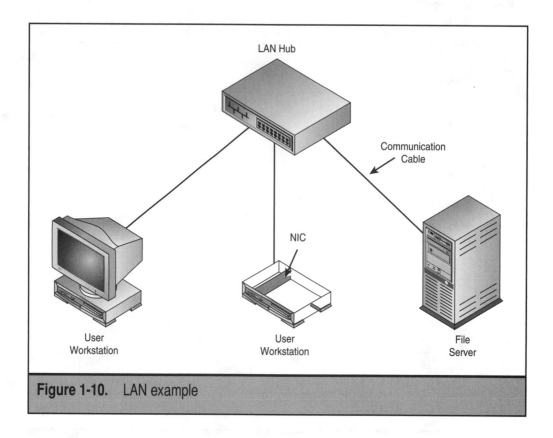

Figure 1-10.   LAN example

LANs support a small geographic area due to the high signaling rate. LANs are typically installed to support a single floor of a building. LANs can be expanded to support an entire building or cluster of buildings on a campus.

The communication cable is possibly the most important component of a LAN. It must pass data signals between devices and pass this information without imposing any errors to the data frames. Each station on the LAN must have a dedicated communication cable connection to a port on the hub. LANs require that high quality UTP or optical fiber cable be used for station connection. Low quality cabling will induce errors on the LAN, reduce system reliability, and reduce system throughput.

BUILDING AUTOMATION
AND CONTROL SYSTEMS (BACS)

The term *building automation and control systems* (BACS) is used to describe building systems that regulate a building's environment or monitor the building for safety or security purposes. BACS, also known as building automation systems (BAS), consist of the following important building systems:

▼ Heating, ventilating, and air conditioning (HVAC)

■ Energy management

■ Fire alarm

▲ Security, access control, and closed-circuit television

All of these building systems are power-limited systems and use a communications bus to transmit signals between system components. These systems also require communication cables be installed between system devices. The communication cables will enable system communication signals to pass between the system components. Communication cables will also enable these systems to share information and operate together.

All BACS usually follow a similar model of a centralized control unit and distributed system sensors or devices. Each sensor is connected to a port on the centralized control unit with a communication cable. The communication cable serves as the communication bus. The distributed sensors constantly monitor the environment and send this information back to the centralized control unit. The communication signals may be sent in the form of either analog or digital signals. The communication cable may also supply power from the centralized control unit to the distributed sensors.

Heating, Ventilating, and Air Conditioning (HVAC)

The HVAC systems provide building temperature, humidity, and environmental control. HVAC systems control the indoor building environment based on both indoor and outdoor conditions. The systems should provide a comfortable environment and limit energy usage.

The HVAC systems have a centralized control unit that controls system operation. Temperature thermostats are placed throughout the interior building spaces. These devices are wired back to the control unit with communication cable. Preset thresholds will trigger the centralized control unit to turn on a mechanical system. The result should be an environment that stays within narrow temperature and humidity levels.

The HVAC systems provide indoor temperatures by circulating chilled or heated water through a series of coils. Fans will blow building air over these coils to either cool or heat the building air. The HVAC control unit regulates air flow to adjust the following:

▼ Pressure

■ Rate of air flow (damper controls)

▲ Fan speeds

The communication cables are an important system component because they connect the system thermostats to the centralized control unit. The communication cables must be installed correctly for the system to work reliably. Incorrect cable selection or installation will result in the system not working correctly or experiencing intermittent system problems.

Energy Management

The emergency management system (EMS) is designed to make the HVAC system work efficiently and save energy costs (see Figure 1-11). The main purpose of the EMS system is to

▼   Enhance HVAC system efficiency

■   Achieve an integrated lighting control strategy

▲   Implement overall building schedules for HVAC and lighting systems

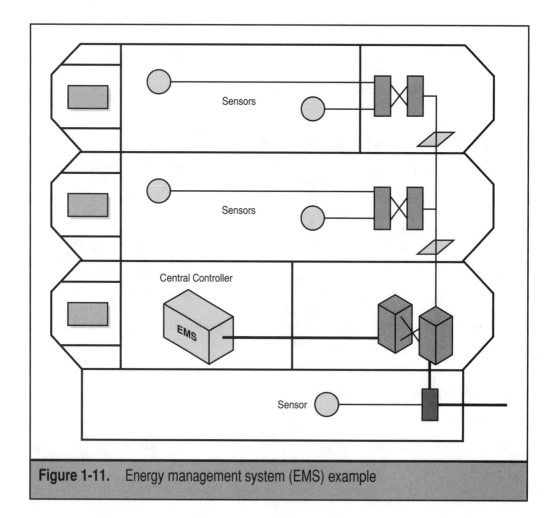

Figure 1-11.   Energy management system (EMS) example

The EMS consists of a central controller and multiple sensors placed throughout the building. The sensors are corrected to the central controller with communication cable.

The EMS consists of a series of sensors that are wired to a centralized control unit. The control unit is programmed with specific temperatures for different times of the day. Temperature sensors monitor ambient room temperature and humidity levels. If the temperature or humidity levels exceed preprogrammed levels, the EMS will turn on the air conditioning. Another example is to turn on lights in a room by means of a motion sensor.

The centralized controller can be programmed to provide scheduling and serves as a centralized scheduling location. Schedules can be created for

▼ **HVAC start and stop times**   This will provide the most efficient start and stop times for the entire HVAC system.

▲ **Lighting system tuning and control**   This provides the most efficient use of lighting energy to accommodate for occupancy levels, daylight levels, and overall power consumption.

Fire Alarm

The fire alarm system (see Figure 1-12) monitors a building for fire, smoke, or the build up of heat that could result in injury or the loss of life. A fire alarm system consists of three different systems working together:

▼ **Sensors**   Provide detection functions

■ **Sprinklers**   Provide suppression functions

▲ **Lights (strobes) and horns**   Provide notification for building occupants

A fire alarm system consists of a centralized fire alarm control panel and fire alarm sensors. The centralized fire alarm control panel is responsible for performing the following functions:

▼ Detection

■ Suppression

▲ Notification

Multiple fire alarm sensors serve a building zone. A building zone is typically one floor in a multistory building. The fire alarm sensors are connected to a port on the fire alarm control panel with a communication cable. Two wires are needed to attach sensors to ports on the fire alarm control panel. Multiple sensors are installed in a building zone and daisy chained together to provide complete zone coverage. Two control panel ports are needed to provide a fault tolerant configuration. Sensors can also be addressable or nonaddressable. Addressable sensors will enable system operators to identify the exact sensor responding to a fire or smoke condition in a building zone.

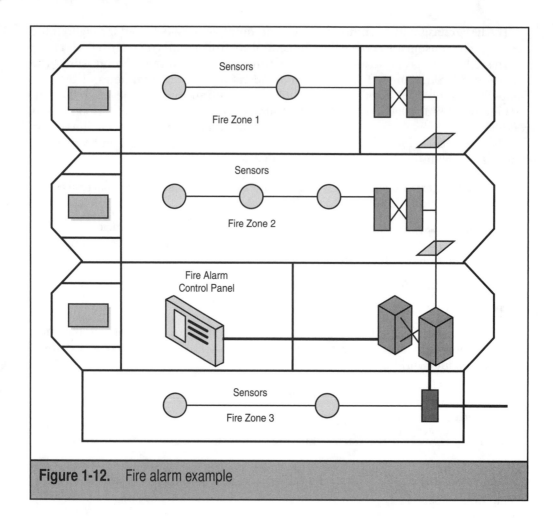

Figure 1-12. Fire alarm example

Fire alarm sensors use communication cable to communicate with the control panel. If fire alarm control panel receives a signal from a sensor indicating a fire condition, it may activate the suppression and notification devices.

The fire alarm system can be integrated with other building control systems to provide a safe environment. These include

▼ Integrating with the HVAC system to shut down fans and close dampers. This will prevent the spread of smoke, heat, and toxic gases through the ventilation system.

■ Integrating with the security system to unlock security doors and to enable automatic doors to be manually opened to provide additional escape routes from the building. The security system can also close but still enable manual operation for interior doors to prevent the spread of flames and smoke.

▲ Integrating with the electrical system to operate emergency lighting and perform elevator capture to prevent their use during a fire.

The communication cables of a fire alarm system are an extremely important system component because they tie the sensors to the central control panel. Faulty wiring can lead to sensors identifying fire dangers but not being able to notify the control panel. Fire alarm systems require that the correct type of cable being used and all cables must be terminated correctly. Incorrect cable selection or terminations will result in system errors and reliability problems.

Security, Access Control, and Closed Circuit Television

Security systems (see Figure 1-13) provide a safe and controlled operating environment in a building. Security systems include the following:

▼ Alarm systems to provide intruder detection

■ Control systems to provide restricted access to specific areas of a building

▲ Closed circuit television systems to provide 24-hour surveillance of building grounds and building spaces

The security and access control systems are often times integrated to provide notification of any unauthorized entries. The integrated system will also provide a complete log of all entries (authorized and unauthorized) into specific building spaces. The access log will include entry and exit time for a specific building space of all users or spaces visited by specific users.

The security system is made up of a centralized control unit, sensors, and magnetic contact points. The sensors and magnetic contacts are distributed throughout the building and wired back to the control unit with communication cable. Once the units are activated, the security system monitors all sensors for glass breaking, motion, or separation of the magnetic contact points on doors and windows. System activation will result in an audible or silent alarm and the system initiating an outgoing notification via a phone line to a monitoring service.

The access control system (see Figure 1-14) is made up of a centralized control unit and access points. The access points are wired back to the control unit with communication cable. The access points are magnetic card readers, key pads, or a type of biometric sensing device. The access point relays information from the user (card serial number, password, or thumbprint) and sends it back across the communication cable to the central control unit for verification. The control will send a signal to open a door once the user's identify and access status has been verified.

The communication cable for both security and access control systems creates the signaling path for system signals. The overall reliability of these systems depends on the communications cables being installed correctly and delivering system signals without errors to the centralized controller units.

A closed circuit television system (CCTV) system (see Figure 1-15) is a video network established for security purposes. The CCTV system is made up of multiple video cameras

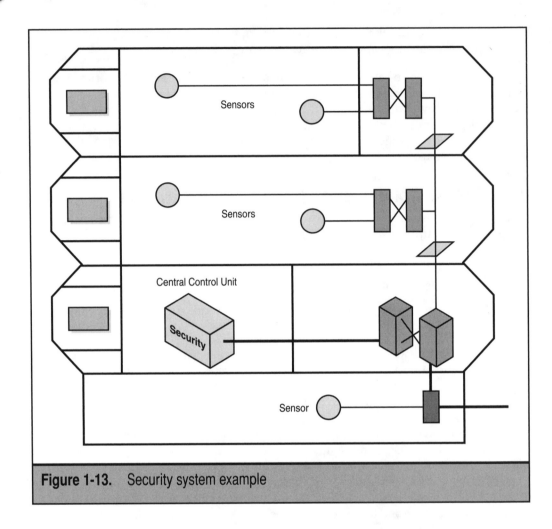

Figure 1-13. Security system example

distributed throughout a building or campus of buildings. The video cameras are connected with coaxial cable to a headend. The coaxial communication cable transmits the video signals to the headend device. The video signals from the headend are monitored by a series of television sets usually mounted in a security office.

The coaxial cable is an extremely important component of the CCTV system. The correct type of cable must be installed, and the correct termination procedures must be used for the cable to work correctly. CCTV systems that have cabling problems may not work at all or may experience intermittent system outages. In addition, video networks can experience signaling problems such as ghosting or fuzzy images if the wrong type of cable is used or the cables are not terminated correctly.

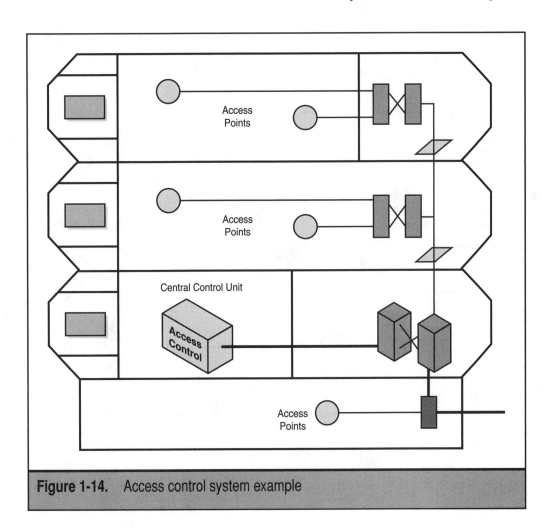

Figure 1-14.   Access control system example

SOUND SYSTEMS

Sound systems (see Figure 1-16) are another common type of communication system that is installed in many residential and commercial buildings. Sound systems can take the following forms of either an overhead paging or an audio system. The overhead paging system enables messages to be broadcast in a building or campus of buildings. Audio systems are often found in department stores and are used for distributing music and creating a pleasant environment.

All sound systems have four components:

▼   **Sound source**   This can be a microphone or a music source. The sound source represents the sound that needs to be distributed throughout the building.

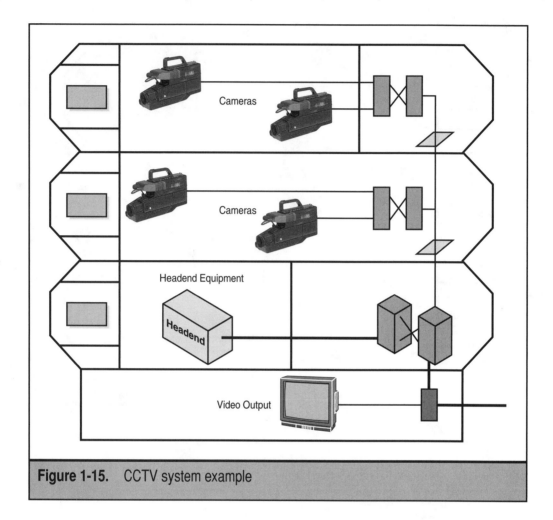

Figure 1-15. CCTV system example

- **Amplifier** The amplifier boosts the signal level and sends the signals out of each port. The sound source is inputted into the amplifier. If the sound has not been converted to an electrical format, the amplifier can form this function. The amplified electrical signals are sent out of each port.

- **Communication cable** Provides the path for the amplified communication signals to be transported to the speakers. Communication cable is usually stranded copper cable connecting the speakers to an amplifier port.

- ▲ **Speakers** The components that convert the electrical communication signals to an sound signal. Speakers are usually mounted on the ceiling or walls of a building and spaced to provide coverage for a desired floor area.

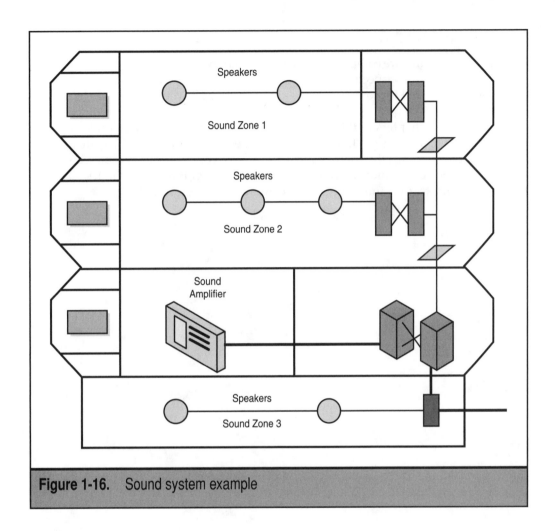

Figure 1-16.   Sound system example

Sound systems are necessary in buildings that support large numbers of individuals, such as airports, department stores, and sports stadiums. They are also necessary in environments that have high ambient noise levels and it is difficult to hear messages or people speaking.

The communication cable is an important element in a sound system. The correct cable and cable impedance must be used for the system components to work correctly. Using communication cable with the incorrect impedance will shorten the life of system amplifiers. In addition, the communication cables must also be the correct size to deliver the correct amount of power to the system speakers. Communication cables that are too small will result in the sound levels being too low.

CHAPTER SUMMARY

Commercial buildings are comprised of many different types of communication systems. Each system performs a specific function in a building. All systems have one common characteristic: the need for communication cables to connect system devices together and distribute system signals.

The following chapters of this book will investigate communication cables in more detail. The first half of this book will define the different types of cables that are used for communication systems, the components to terminate communication cables, and standards associated communication cables. The second half of this book will describe how to install, terminate, test, and troubleshoot communication cables.

CHAPTER 2

Network Media

Communications system signals are required to travel from some type of user device to a control module, device, or system. Communications signals must travel over some form of transmission medium. This transmission medium usually takes the form of some type of cable. This cable can be made of either copper for unshielded twisted-pair, screened twisted-pair, shielded twisted-pair, or coaxial cables. The cable can be made of either glass or plastic for optical fiber cables.

In the case of wireless signaling, the transmission medium is the air. Both microwave and satellite systems transmit radio waves through the air. Other types of wireless systems use light (visible or nonvisible) to transit communications system signals.

Signals from communications systems can travel in any of the following ways:

▼ As an electrical signal through a copper cable

■ As an optical signal through an optical fiber cable

■ As a radio signal through the air

▲ As a light signal through the air

The purpose of the transmission medium is to distribute communication system signals to user devices without interference or corruption of the system signals. The transmission medium should transmit signals reliably so the signal arrives at the receiving device of the communication system and can be interpreted without errors.

Communications systems typically use cables to distribute signals between system devices. Over the years, many different types of media have been used to support different types of systems.

Voice systems have always used unshielded twisted-pair (UTP) cable. Multipair UTP cable is used between voice switches to consolidate multiple phone connections at a voice switch. Four-pair UTP cables are run to the individual phones to supply dial tone and to carry voice signals to and from the voice switch.

Data systems have used a variety of media types to connect terminals to mainframe or minicomputers including

▼ UTP cable

■ Screened twisted-pair cable (ScTP)

▲ Coaxial (coax) cable

Local area network (LAN) has also used a variety of media types to support different types of LAN technologies. Ethernet LANs initially used either thick or thin coaxial cable. Today, Ethernet LANs are typically supported using either data grade (high quality) UTP cable, optical fiber cable, or a combination of both. Token Ring initially used 150-ohm, shielded twisted-pair (STP) cable. Today, Token Ring LANs can use STP-A cable, data grade UTP cable, optical fiber cable, or any combination of the three.

Building automation and control systems are the systems in a commercial or residential building that monitor or control various aspects of a building's environment. Building automation and control systems have sensors that communicate and provide information to a centralized processing and monitoring unit. Building automation and control systems include the following system types:

▼   Fire alarm system

■   Security system

■   Heating, ventilating, and air conditioning (HVAC) system

▲   Energy management system

These systems have traditionally used stranded 18 AWG or larger wires for device connections. The cables are not required to be a twisted-pair construction. Today, twisted-pair cables can support these systems.

Video systems are installed in both commercial and residential buildings. Video systems typically use coaxial cable to distribute system signals across a video network. The following media types are commonly used for video systems:

▼   RG-59 coaxial cable

■   RG-6 coaxial cable

■   RG-11 coaxial cable

▲   PIII-500 coaxial cable

Video systems continue to use coaxial cable for system connections because coaxial cable has a large bandwidth rating and can support long distances. Twisted-pair cables can be used for video systems, but this may result in limited system distances. Optical fiber cables can also be used, but this is only cost effective for backbone connections.

Audio and paging systems are the sound and audio systems installed in commercial and residential buildings to distribute voice pages and audio music. Audio and paging systems usually use a stranded 18 AWG conductor cable for speaker connections. The cables are not required to be a twisted-pair construction. Today, twisted-pair cables can support these systems connections.

CABLE DEFINITION

A cable is defined by the National Electrical Code (NEC) as: "A cable is a factory assembly of two or more insulated conductors having an overall covering."

A *cable* is the term used to describe the complete unit of multiple insulated conductors, strength members, and a cable jacket to keep all the cable elements together.

CABLE TYPES

There are many different types of cable that have been used for communications systems over the years. Cable can be divided into two general categories of copper cables and optical fiber cables. Copper cables have conductors that are constructed of some form of copper metal. All signals are transmitted across the copper conductors in the form of electrical energy. Optical fiber cables have conductors that are constructed of either glass or plastic. All signals are transmitted across the glass or plastic conductors in the form of light energy or pulses.

Some of the common types of cables used for communications systems include the following:

▼ Unshielded twisted-pair (UTP) cable
  - Category 3
  - Category 4
  - Category 5
  - Category 5e
  - Category 6

- Screened twisted-pair (ScTP) cable
  - Category 3
  - Category 4
  - Category 5

- Shielded twisted-pair (STP) cable
  - STP
  - STP-A

- Coaxial cable
  - RG-58 A/U Thinnet Ethernet
  - RG-8 thicknet ethernet
  - RG-6 video cable
  - RG-11 video cable
  - RG-59 video cable
  - RG-62

▲ Optical fiber cable
  - 50/125 μm multimode
  - 62.5/125 μm multimode
  - Singlemode

CABLE COMPONENTS

All cables share the same basic components in their construction (see Figure 2-1). All cables have a conductor for transmit signals, some form of insulation material over the conductor, and a cable sheath covering the insulated conductors and covering the entire cable configuration. Some cables include a cable shield. This protects the signals traveling along the cable from electrical interference and keeps electrical energy from emanating from the cable. Cable shields are an optional cable component and are only included in some types of cables.

Conductor

The cable conductor is the most important component of any communications cable. The conductor is responsible for carrying the transmitted communication signal.

The conductor of a copper cable is usually some form of copper metal material or copper metal composite material. The conductor can be any of the following:

▼ Copper

■ Copper covered steel

▲ Copper composite alloys (copper with other materials added for strength or durability)

Copper sets the standard for conductivity. It is typically used because of its excellent conductivity properties and low cost. Gold and silver are other metals with excellent conductivity properties but are rarely used due to their high costs.

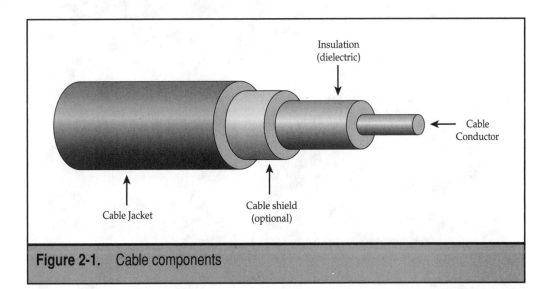

Figure 2-1.   Cable components

Aluminum can also be used for cable conductors. Aluminum is a lighter metal than copper but has lower conductivity characteristics than copper cable. This requires aluminum conductors to be larger in size to provide the same conductivity characteristics as copper conductors. In addition, aluminum conductors require special termination techniques because aluminum conductors suffer from galvanic corrosion when terminated with connectors made of copper or a copper alloy.

Solid Conductors versus Stranded Conductors

Copper cable conductors are generally available as either solid conductors or stranded conductors (see Figure 2-2). Solid conductors are round, solid metal conductors that run the entire length of the cable. Stranded conductors are constructed by twisting together many smaller conductors to create a larger conductor.

Solid conductors are easier and less costly to manufacture than stranded conductors. Solid conductors are also easier and less complex to terminate. Solid conductors provide better transmission performance at higher frequencies.

Stranded conductors are more flexible than solid conductors. Cables that have stranded conductors are preferred in environments where the cable must be bent at severe angles or moved and rearranged frequently. Stranded cables are specified for work areas

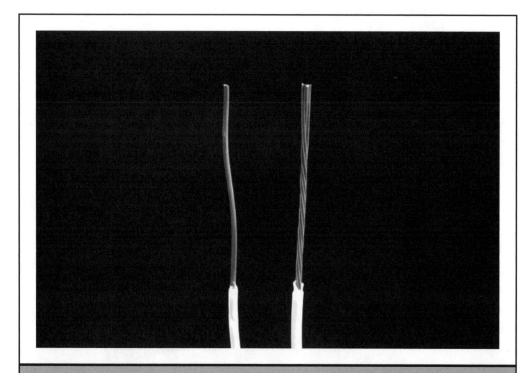

Figure 2-2.   Solid versus stranded conductors

where a flexible cord is desirable due to the possibility of sharp bends and frequent moving and rearranging of the cable around a desk. Because stranded conductor cables are more flexible, they can provide longer life in environments where they may be moved frequently.

Twisted-Pair Construction

Most copper cables that include multiple conductors twist the individual copper conductors together creating twisted pairs (see Figure 2-3). Therefore, an eight-conductor cable is manufactured to have four twisted pairs inside the cable jacket. The primary reason for twisting the individual conductors together into pairs is to minimize noise, called crosstalk, between the different cable pairs inside the cable. Twisting the individual conductors into pairs decreases mutual capacitance on each twisted pair. Twisted-pair construction also minimizes signal loss when the communication system equipment uses differential signaling.

Older twisted-pair cable primarily used for voice communication system use untwisted cable pairs to transmit voice signals. Older twisted-pair cable was called direct inside wire (DIW) or quad cable. These cables had the individual conductors twisted together but not into pairs. DIW cable was capable of supporting analog voice signals but

Figure 2-3.   Twisted-pair example

is not capable of supporting new digital voice signals or digital data signals. DIW cable is referred to as voice cable for this reason.

DIW cable is still found in many older residential buildings such as homes and apartment complexes. These cables can continue to provide analog telephone service to the residents of these buildings. However, these cables will not support new digital phone services such as digital subscriber line (DSL) services, Integrated Services Digital Network (ISDN), or other digital services. Twisted-pair cable must be installed to support these new digital services.

Research has proven that tighter pair twists reduce crosstalk coupling between cable pairs and reduce mutual capacitance within each cable pair. Therefore, data grade twisted-pair cables are manufactured with the individual conductors tightly twisted together. Data grade twisted-pair cables are capable of supporting high-speed LAN and other data processing signals. The installation specifications for data grade twisted-pair cables require that the individual cable pairs remain twisted up to 13 mm ($^1/_2$ in.) of the termination point.

Dielectric

The dielectric is the insulation or nonconductive portion of a cable. Each conductor must be covered with a dielectric material to prevent the passage of current to other conductors or a conductor and other metal objects. Most cables use some form of plastic material, called polymers, to cover the cable conductors. These polymers are applied to the copper conductors and are both a proven and reliable method of insulating metal conductors.

Many UTP cables are insulated with polyvinyl chloride, known as PVC. PVC insulation is used for cables that are designed for inside building installations. PVC insulation does not meet the fire and performance requirements for high-speed networks. As a result, new materials such as fluorinated ethylene propylene, known as FEP, have been developed. FEP provides fire resistance required by the NEC for air plenums and the high-speed performance required by data grade twisted-pair cables to support high-speed networks.

Polyethylene, known as PE, is an insulation material used for cables designed for outdoor building installations. PE insulation provides better performance of copper conductors compared to PVC but can only be installed between buildings. PE is a petroleum-based material and cannot be installed inside buildings because of fire hazards that these cable jackets represent.

Cable Shield

The cable shield is an optional component in a communications cable (see Figure 2-4). Cable shields are used for either physical protection or electrical protection. An overall armor shield is used for direct buried cables for rodent protection. A braided or foil shield is used for electromagnetic protection for the signals traveling over the cable conductors.

A cable shield cable can be manufactured to cover any of the following cable components:

▼ The entire cable

■ Individual pairs in the cable

▲ A single conductor in the cable

A cable shield is designed to protect the signals traveling along the cable from electrical interference. Cable shields are effective when copper cables are installed in noisy electrical environments. The shield will prevent noise energy from corrupting the signals traveling across the cable conductors.

The cable shield is connected to ground on one side of the cable. Any noise energy coming into contact with the cable shield is run to ground. This protects the signals traveling on the cable conductors from this noise energy.

A second function of the cable shield is the keep electrical energy from the signals traveling across the cable conductors contained in the cable. This prevents these signals

Figure 2-4. Cable shields

from causing electromagnetic interference (EMI) to other systems or cables that are in close proximity.

Cable shields are made of the following materials:

▼ Foil

■ Wire strands

▲ Braided metal

Cable Jacket

The cable jacket isthe outer component of a cable. The jacket is a nonmetallic cable element that is used to hold the other cable components together and to protect the cable components from damage.

The type of jacket that is used for the cable will depend on where the cable is to be installed. Cables that are installed outside a building have different jacket requirements than cables installed inside a building. Cables that are installed outside a building are subjected to more abuse and must be constructed of different material than inside plant cables.

The NEC requires that cables used for communication system be suitable for the environment where they are to be installed. The NEC defines suitable as being tested as passing fire, smoke, and toxicity tests for specific building environments. Communication cables that are to be installed in an air plenum must be plenum rated. Communication cables that are to be installed in a building rise or vertical shaft must be riser rated.

Table 800-50 of the NEC requires that communications cables be tested and marked with the following labels shown in Table 2-1 for each type of communications cable.

Cable Marking	Type
CMP	Communications plenum cable
CMR	Communications rise cable
CM	Communications cable
CMX	Communications cable, limited use
CMUC	Undercarpet communications cable

Table 2-1. NEC Communications Cable Markings

CMP Communication Cables

The NEC requires that CMP communication cables be tested as suitable for use in air ducts, air plenums, and other spaces used for the distribution or return of environmental air. These cables must also exhibit adequate fire resistance and low smoke producing characteristics.

CMR Communication Cables

The NEC requires that CMR communication cables be tested as suitable for use in a vertical run in a building riser or shaft. These cables must also exhibit adequate fire resistance characteristics capable of inhibiting the spread of fire from floor to floor along the cable run.

CM Communication Cables

The NEC requires that CM communication cables be tested as suitable for general purpose communications use in all areas of a building except building riser or plenum spaces. These cables must also be listed as being resistant to the spread of fire.

CMX Limited Use Communication Cables

The NEC requires that CMX limited use communication cables be tested as suitable for use in dwellings and for use in raceways. These cables must also be listed as being flame retardant.

CMUC Under Carpet Communication Cables

The NEC requires that CMUC communication cables be tested as suitable for undercarpet use. These cables must also be listed as being flame retardant.

CONDUCTOR SIZES

Communications conductor sizes are usually referenced by the American Wire Gauge (AWG) sizes. There is no formal or legal standard for sizing copper conductors in the United States. Through usage and over time, the AWG conductor sizing specification has been accepted as the national standard. The AWG system is an extension of the original version published by the U.S. National Bureau of Standards.

AWG sizing is used to reference the size of conductors from 40 AWG up to 0000 (4/0) AWG. Conductors larger the 4/0 are usually sized in circular mills. The AWG sizing system is used extensively in the United States and is the general standard used for comparing the sizes of different conductors. Countries that do not use the AWG system typically reference wire size in millimeters.

The AWG system was established to represent the number of steps involved in the manufacturing of copper conductors. Copper conductors are extruded or drawn from larger wires to create smaller wires. The AWG sizing uses large numbers, such as 30, to represent smaller size conductors and smaller numbers, such as 0 or 0000, to represent larger size conductors. The AWG numbers represent the cross-sectional area for a given conductor. This is shown in Table 2-2.

TWISTED-PAIR CABLES

Many different types of cables use a twisted-pair construction. Twisted-pair cables are referred to as balanced cables in international cabling standards. Twisted-pair cables can be

AWG Size	Millimeters	Inches
0000 (4/0) AWG	12 mm	0.47 in.
19 AWG	0.91 mm	0.036 in.
22 AWG	0.64 mm	0.025 in.
24 AWG	0.51 mm	0.020 in.
26 AWG	0.40 mm	0.160 in.
30 AWG	0.25 mm	0.010 in.

Table 2-2.   AWG Conductor Sizing for Solid Conductors

either shielded or unshielded construction. The important characteristic of these cables is that the individual conductors are twisted together into pairs. The individual pairs typically have different twist rates in the cable to minimize crosstalk coupling between cable pairs.

NOTE: Note all UTP cables are twisted-pair construction. Older DIW cable is unshielded but does not use a twisted construction. Most modern multiconductor cables use a twisted-pair construction.

The following multiconductor cable types use twisted-pair construction:

▼ UTP cable

■ ScTP cable

▲ STP-A cable

Coaxial cable does not use twisted-pair construction because this is a single conductor type of media. Optical fiber cables do not use a twisted-pair construction. Optical fiber cable transmits light in the form of light pulses and is not susceptible to electrical noise and crosstalk.

Unshielded Twisted-Pair (UTP) Cable

A unshielded twisted-pair (UTP) cable is the most common type of media used for communications systems and in structured cabling systems (see Figure 2-5). UTP cable is used extensively due to its flexibility. UTP cable can be used for voice, low-speed data, high-speed data, audio and paging systems, and building automation and control systems. UTP cable can be used in both the horizontal and backbone cabling subsystems.

UTP cable is composed of pairs of wires twisted together surrounded by the cable jacket. UTP cables have no shield. The number of pairs in a UTP cable can range from 2 to

Figure 2-5.   UTP cable

1,800. For horizontal cables, the number of pairs recommended by industry standards is a four-pair cable. For backbone cables, the number of pairs will typically be some increment of 25, because multipair UTP cables are constructed in 25-pair binder groups.

The conductors of both horizontal and backbone UTP cables can either be 22 or 24 AWG, whereas 24 AWG size of UTP cable is the most common size. UTP cables used for both horizontal and backbone applications are typically solid conductor cables. UTP cables used in either work areas or telecommunications rooms are usually stranded conductor cables.

UTP cable, as the name implies, has no metallic shield around the cable pairs. This makes the cable small in diameter but unprotected against electrical interference. UTP cables typically have cable pairs that are tightly twisted together, which helps to improve its immunity to electrical noise and EMI.

UTP cable has a characteristic impedance rating of 100 ohms. This is why UTP cable is often referred to as 100-ohm UTP cable.

UTP Cable Categories

UTP cable has evolved over the years. Historically, UTP cables were only used for voice applications. Voice UTP cables only needed to carry analog signals. These signals are very robust and are not easily corrupted by electrical noise or EMI. As UTP cable was used for different systems, it became clear that better quality UTP cable would be required for supporting data systems that used digital signaling.

The evolution of UTP cable has created different categories or grades of UTP cable. The higher the category of UTP cable, the better the cable's performance characteristics. Higher category UTP cables are referred to as data grade UTP cables and low category UTP cables are referred to as voice grade UTP cables.

Industry cabling standards have standardized the category performance specifications for UTP cables. These are shown in Table 2-3.

Category	Description
Category 1	This is voice grade UTP cable rated up to 750 kHz
Category 2	This is voice grade UTP cable rated up to 1 MHz.
Category 3	This category of UTP cable is rated up to 16 MHz.
Category 4	This category of UTP cable is rated up to 20 MHz.
Category 5	This category of UTP cable is rated up to 100 MHz.
Category 5e	This category of UTP cable is rated up to 100 MHz.
Category 6	This category of UTP cable is rated up to 250 MHz.

Table 2-3. UTP Category Specifications

NOTE: Categories 1 and 2 are no longer recognized by industry cabling standards. Category 4 UTP cable is being phased out of industry cabling standards and is not recommended for new cable installations. Category 6 is a proposed standard by the TIA. It will become an official standard once the draft specification passes a vote by TIA members.

The *category designation* of a UTP cable indicates how well a cable will perform once it is installed in a building. A higher category rating indicates a better quality of UTP cable or component. A higher category also implies a more expensive cable.

UTP Horizontal Cable Color Code

Horizontal UTP cable is required to be a four-pair construction by industry cabling standards. Horizontal UTP cable has a characteristic impedance rating of 100 ohms +/- 15 percent. Horizontal cables typically have solid, 24 AWG conductors.

The four pairs of a horizontal cable have a different color code designation. The four colors used are

▼ Blue

■ Orange

■ Green

▲ Brown

Each pair has two conductors. One wire of the pair is assigned the pair color with a white stripe and the other wire of the pair is assigned the color white with the pair color stripe. The pair and color code designation for four-pair horizontal UTP cables are shown in Table 2-4.

Pair	Color Code	Abbreviation
Pair 1	White Blue	W-BL
	Blue	BL
Pair 2	White Orange	W-O
	Orange	O
Pair 3	White Green	W-G
	Green	G
Pair 4	White Brown	W-BR
	Brown	BR

Table 2-4. Horizontal UTP Cable Color Code

UTP Horizontal Connectors

Four-pair UTP horizontal cables are terminated with an eight-position modular connector in the work area (see Figure 2-6). Eight-position modular connectors are required to terminate all four pairs (eight conductors) or a four-pair horizontal cable. The modular connectors should use an insulation displacement contact (IDC) style connection method for terminating cable conductors.

Four-pair UTP horizontal cables are terminated with patch panels or cross-connect blocks in the telecommunications room (see Figure 2-7). If a patch panel is used, a four-pair UTP patch cord will connect the horizontal cable to the communication system equipment. If a cross-connect block is used, cross-connect wire must be used to connect the four-pair horizontal cable to a backbone cable.

Four-pair UTP horizontal cables must be terminated with a modular connector or other connecting hardware that is the same category rating as the cable. Terminating a category 5e UTP cable with a category 3 modular connector or patch panel will reduce the performance of the cable channel to category 3. In addition, all work area and equipment patch cords must be the same category rating as the horizontal cable or the performance of the channel will be reduced to the level of the work area or patch cords.

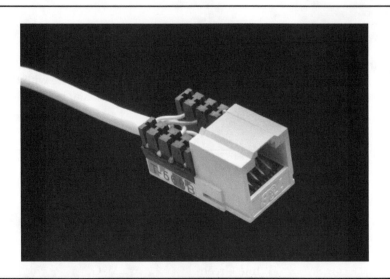

Figure 2-6. Modular connector

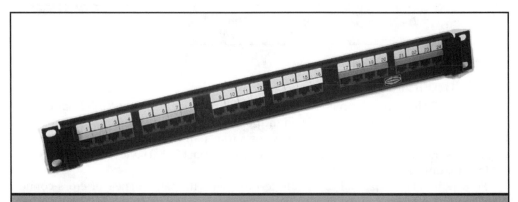

Figure 2-7. Patch panel

UTP Backbone Cable Color Code

UTP backbone cables are large, multipair cables. These cables are constructed of 25-pair binder groups. Each binder group is individually color coded and each pair within a 25-pair binder group is individually color coded. The color code for a 25-pair binder group is shown in Table 2-5.

Pair	Color Code
Pair 1	White / blue stripe Blue / white stripe
Pair 2	White / orange stripe Orange / white stripe
Pair 3	White / green stripe Green / white stripe
Pair 4	White / brown stripe Brown / white stripe
Pair 5	White / slate stripe Slate / white stripe
Pair 6	Red / blue stripe Blue / red stripe
Pair 7	Red / orange stripe Orange / red stripe
Pair 8	Red / green stripe Green / red stripe
Pair 9	Red / brown stripe Brown / red stripe
Pair 10	Red / slate stripe Slate / red stripe
Pair 11	Black / blue stripe Blue / black stripe
Pair 12	Black / orange stripe Orange / black stripe
Pair 13	Black / green stripe Green / black stripe
Pair 14	Black / brown stripe Brown / black stripe
Pair 15	Black / slate stripe Slate / black stripe

Table 2-5.   25-Pair Binder Group Color Coding

Pair 16	Yellow / blue stripe
	Blue / yellow stripe
Pair 17	Yellow / orange stripe
	Orange / yellow stripe
Pair 18	Yellow / green stripe
	Green / yellow stripe
Pair 19	Yellow / brown stripe
	Brown / yellow stripe
Pair 20	Yellow / slate stripe
	Slate / yellow stripe
Pair 21	Violet / blue stripe
	Blue / violet stripe
Pair 22	Violet / orange stripe
	Orange / violet stripe
Pair 23	Violet / green stripe
	Green / violet stripe
Pair 24	Violet / brown stripe
	Brown / violet stripe
Pair 25	Violet / slate stripe
	Slate / violet stripe

Table 2-5.   25-Pair Binder Group Color Coding (*continued*)

The 25-pair binder group is organized into five groups and there are five pairs in each group. The five color groups in a 25-pair binder are

▼ **White**   Pairs 1 to 5

■ **Red**   Pairs 6 to 10

■ **Black**   Pairs 11 to 15

■ **Yellow**   Pairs 16 to 20

▲ **Violet**   Pairs 21 to 25

Within each color group, the five pairs are designated with the group color code and the pair color code. The pair color code for each of the five pairs with a color coded group are

▼ **Blue**   The first pair of the color code group

■ **Orange**   The second pair of the color code group

■ **Green**   The third pair of the color code group

■ **Brown**   The fourth pair of the color code group

▲ **Slate**   The fifth pair of the color code group

Multipair UTP cables that have more than 25 pairs organize the 25-pair binder groups in color-coded groups using the same color-coding sequence. This is shown in Table 2-6.

Multipair UTP cables are organized so each pair in the cable is associated with a color-coded binder group. Each binder group is organized into color code groups and each pair is associated with a color code. This provides a mechanism to keep track of every cable pair in the cable.

Multipair UTP cables are classified as unshielded cables. However, multipair UTP cables actually have a shield surrounding the cable pairs (see Figure 2-8). The purpose of the cable shield in a multipair UTP cable is to both protect the cable pairs from EMI and other electrical noise and to provide a means to bond the cable shield. The cable shield must be bonded at any point where the cable pairs are accessed in the multipair cable to an approved ground in each telecommunications room. The NEC Section 800-40(a) states that the metallic cable shield must also be grounded at both ends to an approved building ground using a minimum of a 14 AWG insulated conductor. The ANSI/TIA/EIA-607 standard recommends bonding the metallic cable shield with a 6 AWG stranded insulated ground conductor to accommodate future code changes or other code requirements.

NOTE: The cable shield must be bonded using the correct hardware, such as a grounding clamp, that will make a proper connection and provide a connection point for the ground wire.

Bonding the cable shield will equalize any ground potential differences that can exist in a large commercial building due to electrical surges and foreign electrical voltages. Additional bonding connections are an effective method for protecting individuals from harm that can result from ground potential differences. The multiple bonding points will equalize potential differences between multiple ground points, divert foreign electrical currents and voltages, and partially cancel electrical transients.

Multipair UTP cables are typically terminated on a cross-connect block (see Figure 2-9). Cross-connect blocks provide a suitable means to terminate the large numbers of connectors associated with multipair UTP cables without taking up a large amount of space

Binder Group No.	Binder Group Color	Pair Numbers
Binder Group 1	White, blue	1 to 25
Binder Group 2	White, orange	26 to 50
Binder Group 3	White, green	51 to 75
Binder Group 4	White, brown	76 to 100
Binder Group 5	White, slate	101 to 125
Binder Group 6	Red, blue	126 to 150
Binder Group 7	Red, orange	151 to 175
Binder Group 8	Red, green	176 to 200
Binder Group 9	Red, brown	201 to 225
Binder Group 10	Red, slate	226 to 250
Binder Group 11	Black, blue	251 to 275
Binder Group 12	Black, orange	276 to 300
Binder Group 13	Black, green	301 to 325
Binder Group 14	Black, brown	326 to 350
Binder Group 15	Black, slate	351 to 375
Binder Group 16	Yellow, blue	376 to 300
Binder Group 17	Yellow, orange	401 to 425
Binder Group 18	Yellow, green	426 to 450
Binder Group 19	Yellow, brown	451 to 475
Binder Group 20	Yellow, slate	476 to 500
Binder Group 21	Violate, blue	501 to 525
Binder Group 22	Violate, orange	526 to 550
Binder Group 23	Violate, green	551 to 575
Binder Group 24	Violate, brown	576 to 600

Table 2-6.   Binder Group Color Coding

in a telecommunications room. Cross-connect jumper wire is used to connect the pairs of a multipair pair UTP cable to either

▼   Another multipair UTP cable

■   An equipment block wired to a communication system device

▲   A horizontal UTP cable

Figure 2-8. Multipair UTP cable shield

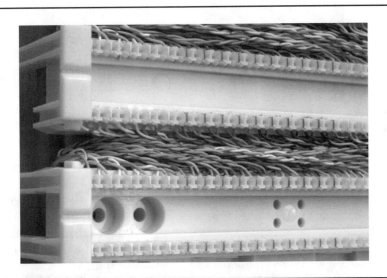

Figure 2-9. Multipair UTP cable termination

Screened Twisted-Pair (ScTP) Cable

Screened twisted-pair (ScTP) cable is similar to UTP cable, but this media has a foil shield surrounding the four cable pairs (see Figure 2-10). ScTP cables are four-pair cables. ScTP cable pairs are usually 24 AWG conductors. ScTP cables have a characteristic impedance rating of 100 ohms. Inside the cable jacket and running the length of the cable is a drain wire. This wire is used to ground the cable shield. The foil shield helps to protect the signals traveling over the cable pairs from noise and EMI.

Figure 2-10.   ScTP cable

ScTP Cable Color Code

ScTP cables have the same color code as UTP cables. This is shown in Table 2-7.

The specifications for ScTP cable are defined in the TIA/EIA IS-729, Technical Specifications for 100-Ohm Screened Twisted-Pair Cabling standard. The intent of the TIA/EIA IS-729 standard is to parallel the specifications established for 100 ohm UTP cable for cable performance and category ratings. The standard defines cable performance rating and shield grounding requirements. The standard also requires that ScTP cables be tested and meet the performance specifications established in TIA/EIA TSB-67.

ScTP cables are used in environments where extra shielding from EMI is desired. EMI noise or other electrical disturbances may be too strong to use unshielded cable in some installations. ScTP cable can be used in these electrically noisy environments to protect the integrity of the communication signals traveling over the cable conductors.

ScTP cables are also used in environments where communications systems or other electronic equipment are sensitive to electrical noise disturbing the reliable operation of the system equipment. ScTP cables would keep any energy from the transmitted signals

Pair	Color Code	Abbreviation
Pair 1	White Blue	W-BL
	Blue	BL
Pair 2	White Orange	W-O
	Orange	O
Pair 3	White Green	W-G
	Green	G
Pair 4	White Brown	W-BR
	Brown	BR

Table 2-7. ScTP Cable Color Code

traveling over the cable conductors contained within the cable. Any energy that would normally emanate from the cable conductors will hit the cable shield. Because the cable shield is grounded, any energy that would emanate from the cable is trapped by the foil shield and routed to ground.

ScTP cables require using both shielded modular connectors to terminate ScTP cable and shielded patch cords to user equipment (see Figure 2-11). ScTP shielded connectors provide a method to terminate the drain wire in the ScTP cable and create an electrically conductive path between the connector and the ScTP cable. This provides continuity of the cable shield and prevents electrical noise from entering the ScTP cable though the connector. Shielded patch cords would also provide shield continuity up to the communication equipment on both ends of the cable. Shielded connectors and patch cords with ScTP cable provides an end-to-end solution for protecting communication signals.

Shielded Twisted-Pair (STP) Cable

The shielded twisted-pair (STP) cable was created by IBM in 1984 (see Figure 2-12). IBM created a media that would be extremely reliable even in the most electrically noisy environments. IBM used STP cable for both terminal connections for data system connections and Token Ring LANs. STP cable can be used in both horizontal and backbone cabling subsystems for data applications only.

NOTE: STP cables do not support voice applications.

STP cables have a characteristic impedance of 150 ohms. STP cables are known as 150-ohm STP cable in the cabling industry. STP cable is composed of two pairs of wires twisted together. Each pair is surrounded by a foil shield and both shielded cable pairs are surrounded by braided cable shield. The entire cable is then covered by the cable jacket.

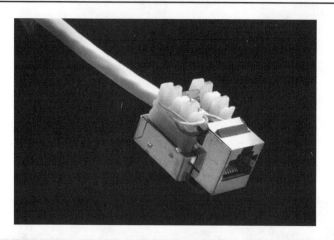

Figure 2-11.   ScTP modular connector

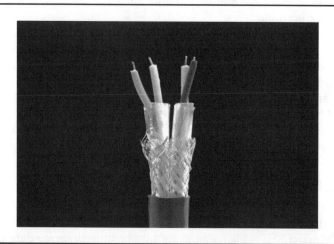

Figure 2-12.   STP cable

The conductors of both horizontal and backbone STP cables are 22 or 26 AWG, whereas 22 AWG size of STP cable is the only size supported by industry cabling standards for either horizontal or backbone cabling runs. Twenty-six AWG STP cables are only used for work area cords or equipment patch cords.

STP Cable Color Code

STP cables have a different color code than either UTP or ScTP cables as shown in Table 2-8.

Pair	Color code
Pair 1	Red
	Green
Pair 2	Black
	Orange (sometimes yellow)

Table 2-8. STP Cable Color Code

STP cables are extensively shielded cables. This makes the cable larger in size and more expensive than either UTP or ScTP cables. STP are classified as balanced cables that have the individual conductors twisted together into cable pairs. The double shielding of STP cables and the twisted-pair construction gives the cable superior immunity to electrical noise and EMI.

STP cables require shielded patch cords and special data connectors to terminate and use the cable. Shielded patch cords and connectors will provide continuity of the cable shield and prevent noise from entering the cable. STP cables require that the cable shield is grounded at one end of the cable (see Figure 2-13). STP cable shields are typically grounded by running a 6 AWG or larger ground wire from the telecommunications rack terminating the cables in the telecommunications room to an approved building ground.

STP Connectors

STP cable requires that a special type of connector be used to terminate the cable (see Figure 2-14). STP connectors are called by all of the following names:

▼ STP connector

■ Data connector

■ Universal data connector

▲ IBM data connector

STP connectors terminate the two cable pairs and provide a connection for the cable shield. STP cables use the same type of connector on both ends of the cable. STP data connectors are inserted into a patch panel in the telecommunications room and a STP face plate in the work area. STP patch cords are then used to connect the STP cable to the communication system equipment in the closet and work area.

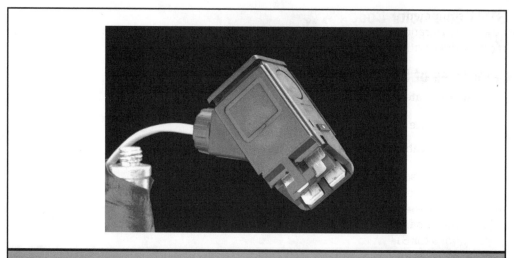

Figure 2-13.   STP connector

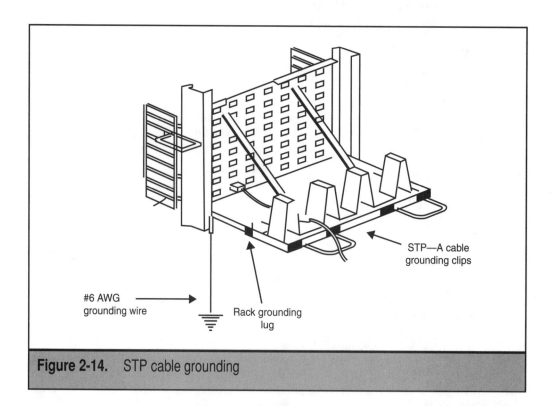

#6 AWG
grounding wire

Rack grounding
lug

STP—A cable
grounding clips

Figure 2-14.   STP cable grounding

STP equipment patch cords and work area line cords are 26 AWG cables. These cables are always a stranded conductor construction. This provides flexibility for routing or moving the cables without breaking the cable conductors.

Categories of STP Cable

There are two categories of STP cable:

▼ STP cable

▲ STP-A cable

STP cable describes the original specifications for STP cable defined by IBM in 1984. STP cable performance specifications are defined through 20 MHz. Because of the significant increase in LAN speed since 1984, the specifications for STP cable were enhanced in 1995. The enhanced form of STP cable is referred to as STP-A cable. The performance specifications for STP-A cable are defined through 300 MHz.

STP-A cables are a recognized media in the ANSI/TIA/EIA-568-A standard for both the horizontal and backbone subsystems.

STP-A cable is being removed from the ANSI/TIA/EIA-568-B.1 standard. STP-A cable will still be supported for existing installations but not recommended or supported for new installations.

HYBRID CABLE

Hybrid cables are defined as either a grouping of multiple cables covered by a single overall cable jacket or multiple cable jackets connected together to form a single cable unit (see Figure 2-15). Hybrid cables are used in cable installation projects where multiple cables must be pulled to the same destination location. Hybrid cables can reduce installation times and reduce installation costs.

For hybrid cables to be standards compliant they must meet the following requirements:

▼ The individual cables of the hybrid cable must be one of the recognized media types supported for the horizontal subsystem.

▲ Each cable type must meet the minimum transmission requirements and color code specifications for that cable type.

Hybrid cables can be constructed of cables that are the same type of cables that are different types. For example, a hybrid cable can consist of a UTP cable and an optical fiber cable or a UTP cable and a ScTP cable. Hybrid cables may also contain cables that have a different category performance rating. For example, a hybrid cable can contain a category 3 cable and a category 5e cable.

The ANSI/TIA/EIA-568-A-3 standard defines the specifications for hybrid cables. This standard provides an exact definition and clarification of a hybrid cable. For a hybrid cable to be standards compliant, it must be made up of cables that are recognized media in

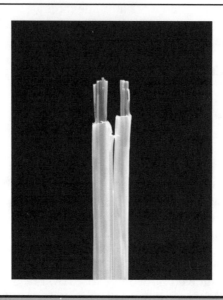

Figure 2-15. Hybrid cable example

the ANSI/TIA/EIA-568-A and ANSI/TIA/EIA-568-B.1 standards. It also requires that hybrid cables be rated for PS-NEXT loss specifications between the recognized cables inside the common sheath. The PS-NEXT loss specifications must be 3 dB better than the pair-to-pair NEXT measurements of the individual cables by themselves.

CAUTION: Hybrid cables are often selected as a media to be used in the horizontal subsystem because it will save time installing this type of media. Hybrid cables usually require more time to separate and terminate the different types of media in the telecommunications room. This extra time will negate the time saved pulling the cable.

COAXIAL CABLE

A coaxial (coax) cable is a copper cable like UTP, ScTP, and STP cables (see Figure 2-16). Coaxial cables have a center conductor that is either a copper or copper alloy construction surrounded by one or more cable shields. The difference between coaxial cables and other copper cables is that coaxial cables have only a single conductor. Other forms of

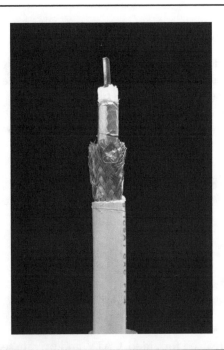

Figure 2-16.   Coaxial cable

copper cables have multiple conductors that are twisted together. Because coaxial cables only have a single conductor, they are oftentimes referred to as unbalanced types of media. The center conductor transmits positively charged signals and the shield transmits negatively charged signals. The center conductor is separated from the cable shield by a thick dielectric or insulation material.

The center conductor and cable shield form two concentric circles around the same axis or center. Coaxial cables are manufactured so the center conductor remains centered and a precise distance from the cable shield by the dielectric material between the two cable components. This cable construction enables high-frequency signals to be supported, which gives coaxial cable a high bandwidth rating. The shield surrounding a coaxial cable makes it very resistant to EMI.

Coaxial cables are used for different types of communications systems that require large bandwidth capacity. The applications that have historically used or continue to use coaxial cable are

▼ Computer networks

■ Data systems

■   CATV networks

▲   Private video networks

Early data systems and LANs use coaxial cable because UTP cable did not have enough bandwidth and optical fiber cables and electronics were extremely expensive. Today, both data system and LANs use UTP and optical fiber cable as the transmission media. Video networks are the primary applications continuing to use coaxial cable media. CATV and private video networks need to support high-frequency signals (as high as 750 MHz) over long distances.

Types of Coaxial Cables

There are many different types of coaxial cables sold in the market today. The most common types of coaxial cables used for communications systems include the following:

▼   RG-6/RG-59

■   RG-8/RG-58

▲   RG-62

RG-6/RG-59 Coaxial Cable

RG-6 and RG-59 cables are used for video, CATV, and private security video surveillance networks. Coaxial cables used for video networks have a

▼   Characteristic impedance of 75 ohms

■   Foil shield over the dielectric material and under the cable shield

■   Braided, metal cable shield

▲   Solid center conductor

RG-6 coaxial cable is the primary media installed in residential homes to support CATV. RG-59 can also be installed, but the center conductor is smaller in size and cannot support distances as long as RG-6 cable.

RG-8/RG-58 Coaxial Cable

The earliest versions of Ethernet LANs used coaxial cable as the transmission medium. Thicknet Ethernet LANs, called 10Base-5 Ethernet, used a thick, 50-ohm RG-8 coaxial cable for backbone LAN connections. Thinnet Ethernet LANs, called 10Base-2 Ethernet, used a thin, 50-ohm RG-58 A/U coaxial cable for station LAN connections.

Both RG-8 (Thicknet) and RG-58 (Thinnet) coaxial cables are no longer used for Ethernet LANs. UTP and optical fiber cables are less expensive and more reliable than coaxial cables.

RG-62 Coaxial Cable

For many years, IBM data terminals were connected to mainframe or minicomputer controllers using RG-62 coaxial cable. RG-62 coaxial cable has a characteristic impedance of 93 ohms. This media was an excellent media for data terminal connections. It supported long distance and was resistant to EMI noise.

RG-62 coaxial cable is not used for new data terminal installations. Either UTP or STP cables are used for these connections. RG-62 coaxial cable can still be found for old terminal installations.

Problems with Coaxial Cables

Coaxial cables are not used for most communication systems today for two reasons. First, there are so many different types of coaxial cables and selecting the wrong type will lead to signal incompatibilities and communication system problems. Second, coaxial cables have a different impedance rating and can only be used for a single system.

Coaxial cables have historically been an unreliable type of communications cable. Coaxial cable connectors that are installed incorrectly can cause a short in the cables and other signaling problems. Communications systems tend to work more reliably when other types of communications cables are used.

OPTICAL FIBER CABLE

Fiber optics is a simple method of transmitting information in the form of light pulses (see Figure 2-17). An *optical fiber* is a thin strand of glass or plastic that serves as the transmission medium for passing these light pulses.

Using light pulses to carry information serves the same purpose as copper cable carrying electrical signals for either telephone conversations or data communications. Any type of electrical signal that can be converted to light pulses can be transmitted in an optical fiber cable.

Optical Fiber Cable Components

Optical fiber cables have similar components in their construction to copper cables (see Figure 2-18). The main difference is that optical fiber cables use glass for transmitting light pulses whereas copper cables use some form of copper conductor to transmit electrical signals. Optical fiber cables transmit light pulses through the glass optical fiber. Optical fiber cables also have some form of protective buffer material covering the glass optical fibers and a cable sheath covering the entire cable configuration. Some optical fiber cables include a cable shield. Cable shields are an optional cable component and are only included in some types of optical fiber cables.

Figure 2-17.   Optical fiber cable

Optical Conductors

The conductor in an optical fiber cable is called an optical fiber. An optical fiber is the glass or plastic element that carries the transmitted light pulses. Optical fiber cables usually have between 2 and 288 optical fibers, sometimes called optical strands in a single cable.

NOTE: Optical fibers are never twisted together like copper conductors. Each optical strand can transmit signals without requiring two strands to be twisted together. Copper conductors are twisted together to make the cable more resistant to electrical noise. Optical fiber cable transmits signals as light pulses. These signals are immune from noise in this form.

The optical fiber is the glass element of an optical fiber cable. The optical fiber has two concentric layers of glass called the core and the cladding (see Figure 2-19). The inner layer of glass is called the core. The outer layer of glass is called the cladding. The core is the

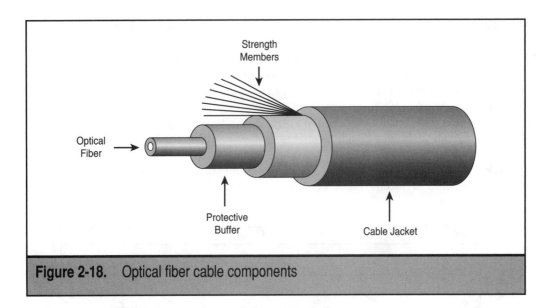

Figure 2-18.   Optical fiber cable components

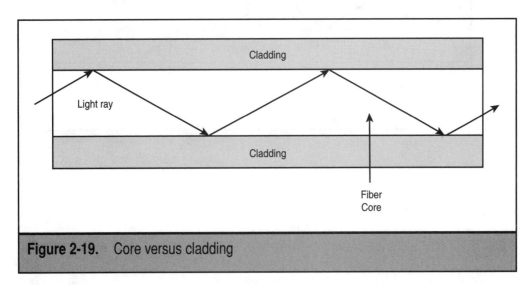

Figure 2-19.   Core versus cladding

light carrying part of the optical fiber cable. The cladding's job is to keep the light contained in the core.

The core and cladding of an optical fiber are both glass elements. The only difference between the core and cladding is that the two glass layers are manufactured to have a different refractive index. The core always has a higher refractive index than the cladding. This helps to keep light rays contained in the core because light tends to naturally bend towards the material with the higher refractive index rating.

Most optical fiber cables are described in terms of their core/cladding size. An optical fiber is represented as two numbers separated with a forward slash. For example, 50/125 or 62.5/125. The first number represents the size of the optical fiber core in microns. The second number represents the size of the combined optical fiber core and cladding in microns. Therefore, a 50/125 optical fiber has a core that is 50 microns in size and a cladding that is 125 microns in size.

Multimode optical fiber cables have a large core size (see Figure 2-20). Multimode optical fiber cables have an optical fiber that is so large it will enable multiple modes or rays of light to enter the core.

Singlemode optical fiber cables have a very small size core that only enables a single mode or ray of light into the cable's core (see Figure 2-21).

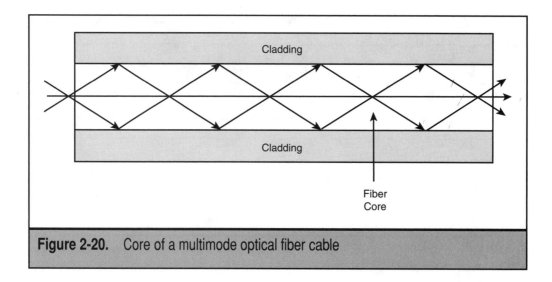

Figure 2-20.   Core of a multimode optical fiber cable

Numerical Aperture

The *numerical aperture* is a term that relates to the size of the core of an optical fiber (see Figure 2-22). The numerical aperture is the light gathering ability of an optical fiber cable. Light rays that are transmitted within the numerical aperture will be accepted into the core of the optical fiber. Light rays that are transmitted outside the acceptance cone will be lost as signal attenuation in the cladding.

The core size of an optical fiber cable defines the numerical aperture of the cable. The numerical aperture of an optical fiber core is based on a mathematical equation. This equation describes the maximum angle for transmitted light rays to be accepted into the core of the optical fiber. The numerical aperture defines a "cone of acceptance" for an optical fiber cable. The smaller the core size, the smaller the numerical aperture. The larger the core size, the larger the numerical aperture. This is shown in Table 2-9.

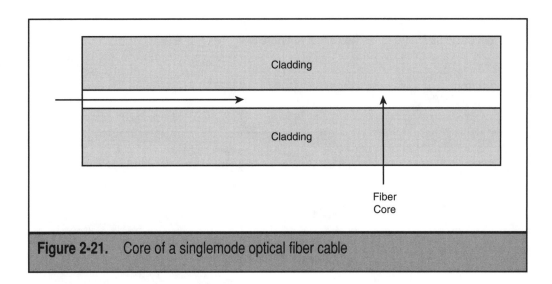

Figure 2-21.   Core of a singlemode optical fiber cable

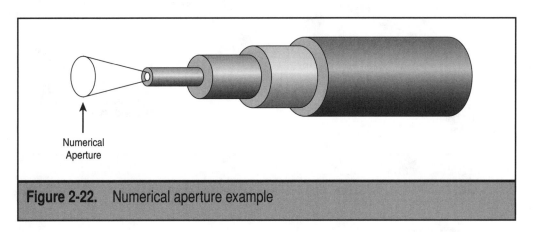

Figure 2-22.   Numerical aperture example

Optical fiber cables with a small numerical aperture require an optical transmitter with a very narrow optical light pattern, such as a laser optical transmitter. Lasers have a precise and directed light pattern. These transmitters can launch light rays into this small acceptance area for a singlemode optical fiber core. Optical fiber cables with a large numerical aperture can use an optical light source with a wide, undirected light pattern, such as a Light Emitting Diode (LED) optical transmitter (see Figure 2-23). LEDs have a wide, dispersed light pattern. A large numerical aperture will gather most of these light rays into the core of the optical fiber.

Fiber Cable Size	Numerical Aperture Size
50/125	0.20
62.5/125	0.275
100/140	0.290

Table 2-9.   Numerical Aperture for Multimode Optical Fiber Cables

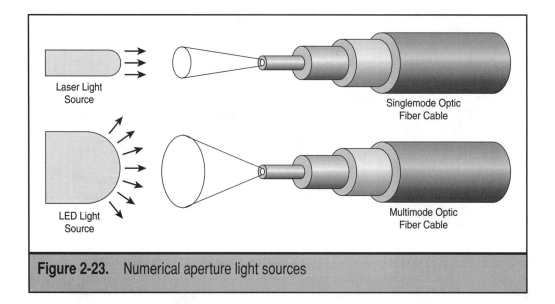

Figure 2-23.   Numerical aperture light sources

Primary Fiber Coating

A protective coating is placed over the glass optical fiber to provide mechanical protection for the glass optical fibers. This protective coating is called the *primary buffer*. The primary buffer is one or more layers of a polymer material. The primary buffer is a 250-micron polymer material that is applied to the glass optical fiber during the manufacturing process.

The primary buffer is designed to protect the optical fiber from shocks that might affect the optical or physical properties of the optical fiber. The primary buffer is also designed to protect the optical fiber from water damage to the glass optical fiber.

The fiber coating has no optical properties affecting the propagation of light within the optical fiber. The main function of the primary buffer coating is to provide mechanical protection for the optical fiber.

Protective Buffer Coating

Optical fiber cables are manufactured with additional buffering material to protect the glass optical fibers. A protective buffer is always added to an optical fiber cable in addition to the primary buffer.

There are two categories of protective buffering for an optical fiber cable:

▼ Tight buffer

▲ Loose buffer

Tight Buffer Cable   Tight buffer optical fiber cable has a 650-micron plastic buffer material applied directly over the 250-micron primary fiber coating (see Figure 2-24). Together, the two buffers create a 900-micron protective buffer.

This construction provides excellent crush and impact resistance. This type of construction also creates a cable that is small in size. It does not, however, protect the glass optical fiber as well from the stresses of temperature variations. In times of extreme heat or cold, the plastic buffer will either expand or contract more than the glass optical fiber. This may cause the glass optical fiber to crack or break.

Tight buffer optical fiber cable is used for indoor applications. Its small size makes the cable very flexible and enables a tight bend radii during installation. This makes the cable easy to install. Indoor environments also provide stable temperatures with minimal temperature variations. This is desirable for tight buffer optical fiber cable.

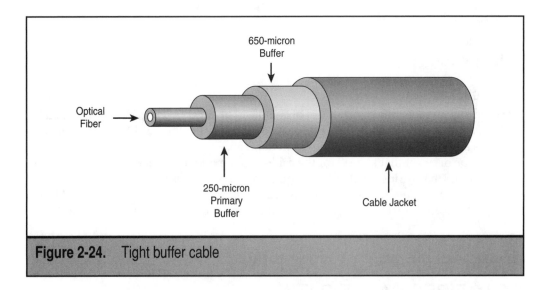

Figure 2-24.   Tight buffer cable

Loose Buffer Cable   Loose buffer optical fiber cable uses a plastic tube with a diameter several times the size of the optical fiber as a protective buffer. One or more optical fibers with a primary buffer lie within the large buffer tube. The optical fibers can move freely within the buffer tube. The large plastic tube isolates the optical fibers from the rest of the cable. This construction protects the optical fibers from any mechanical forces caused by the buffer expanding or contracting. The plastic buffer tube also becomes a load bearing element in the optical fiber cable.

The loose buffer construction provides better protection for the optical fibers in cases of extreme temperature variations. In times of extreme heat or cold, the plastic buffer is free to either expand or contract more than the glass optical fiber. This construction does not, however, provide protection against crush or impact forces.

Loose buffer optical fiber cable is used for outdoor applications. The cable's construction provides excellent protection for long pulls through outdoor conduits. This type of cable is also well suited for the wide temperature variations experienced outdoors. Most cable manufactures inject a water-protecting gel in the loose buffer tubes to protect the optical fiber from water damage.

Most loose buffer optical fiber cables cannot be used for indoor applications. The water protecting gel is typically a petroleum-based material. This material violates the fire protection regulations of local, state, and national fire codes.

Cable Strength Members

Optical fiber cables usually include one or more strength members to provide mechanical strength and rigidity to optical fiber cables. Strength member elements provide tensile strength for pulling the cable and provide additional protection for supporting the optical fibers.

Cable strength members can include all of the following elements:

▼ Aramid yarn

■ Steel

▲ Fiber glass rod

Cable Jacket

The cable jacket is the outer component of an optical fiber cable. The *jacket* is a nonmetallic cable element used to hold the other cable components together and to protect the optical fibers and other cable components from damage.

The type of jacket that is used for the cable will depend on where the cable is to be installed. Cables that are installed outside a building have different jacket requirements than cables installed inside a building. Cables that are installed outside a building are subjected to more abuse and must be constructed of different material than inside plant cables.

NATIONAL ELECTRICAL CODE (NEC) OPTICAL FIBER CABLE RATINGS

The NEC has a rating system for all cables installed in residential or commercial buildings. The NEC is concerned with safety and fire issues associated with installing cables in a building. The NEC requires that optical fiber cables used for communication systems be suitable for the environment where they are to be installed. The NEC defines suitable as being tested as passing fire, smoke, and toxicity tests for specific building environments. Optical fiber cables that are to be installed in an air plenum must be plenum rated. Optical fiber cables that are to be installed in a building riser or vertical shaft must be riser rated.

The NEC has identified three different intrabuilding areas inside a building. These areas relate to the spread of fire and smoke. Only cables that meet NEC fire and smoke requirements can be installed in the specified areas. NEC requires that cables be marked and specified for use in the following areas:

▼ **Plenum area**   A compartment or chamber that is part of or forms part of the air distribution system. A plenum area is also an area that contains the ducts of the air distribution system or which one or more air ducts are connected. Any room or building space where the primary function is air handling is considered to be a plenum space.

■ **Riser area**   Any opening or vertical shaft that cables can pass through from floor to floor.

▲ **General purpose area**   All other indoor areas that are not either a plenum or rise area.

The NEC divides optical fiber cables into three categories. Nonconductive optical fiber cables, conductive optics fiber cables, and hybrid optical fiber cables. Nonconductive optical fiber cables have no metal or electrically conductive elements in the cable. Conductive optical fiber cables contain metal or electrically conductive elements in the cable. The metal or electrically conductive elements are not designed to be current-carrying conductive elements. They have the capability of carrying electrical current, if exposed. A hybrid cable contains optical fibers and current carrying electrical conductors. Hybrid optical fiber cables are permitted to contain noncurrent carrying metallic elements such as strength member and vapor barriers. Hybrid optical fiber cables are classified as electrical cables and not communication cables.

Table 770-50 of the NEC requires that optical cables be tested and marked with the following labels shown in Table 2-10 for each type of optical fiber communications cable to be used in specific environments.

TYPES OF OPTICAL FIBER CABLE

Optical fiber cables are classified into two general categories based on the size of the optical fiber core. The two categories are called

▼ Singlemode optical fiber cable

▲ Multimode optical fiber cable

Cable Marking	Type
OFNP	Nonconductive optical fiber plenum cable
OFCP	Conductive optical fiber plenum cable
OFNR	Nonconductive optical fiber riser cable
OFCR	Conductive optical fiber riser cable
OFN	Nonconductive optical fiber cable
OFC	Conductive optical fiber cable

Table 2-10.   Optical Fiber Cable Markings

Singlemode Optical Fiber Cable

Singlemode optical fiber cable typically has a core ranging in size from eight to ten microns. This small core size only permits a single mode or ray of light to enter the core and travel through the cable. Singlemode optical fiber cables are used with laser fiber optic transmitters that operate at 1,310 or 1,550 nm.

Singlemode optical fiber cable is best suited for

▼ Long-distance applications

▲ Any application requiring extremely high bandwidth

Multimode Optical Fiber Cable

Multimode optical fiber cable has a very large size core. This large core permits many modes or rays of light to enter. Multimode optical fiber cables are used with LED fiber optic transmitters that operate at 850 or 1,300 nm. The large core of a multimode optical fiber cable is suited well for LED transmitters.

There are many different size multimode optical fiber cables. In the United States, the most common size multimode optical fiber cable is 62.5/125.

Multimode optical fiber cable is best suited for

▼ **Short distance applications**   2,000 m (6,560 ft.) or less

▲ **Low bandwidth applications**   Less than 200 Mb/s

Size Variations of Multimode Fiber Cable

Multimode optical fiber cable is available in many different core/cladding sizes (see Figure 2-25). Some of the different core/cladding sizes include

▼ 50/125 micron

■ 62.5/125 micron

▲ 100/140 micron

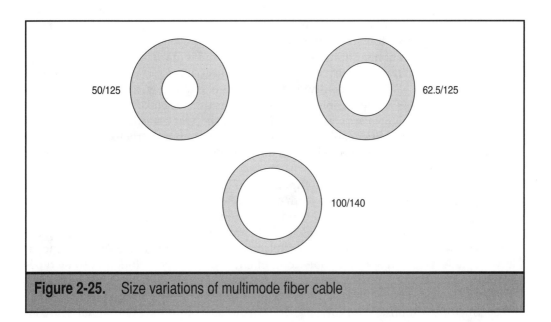

50/125

62.5/125

100/140

Figure 2-25. Size variations of multimode fiber cable

50/125 and 62.5/125 are the most common types of multimode optical fiber cable in use today. In the Untied States, 62.5/125 has been the most common type of multimode optical fiber cable used for communications system cabling. This media has been an allowed media type since the ANSI/TIA/EIA-568-A was originally published in 1991. During this time, 50/125 multimode optical fiber cable was not a recognized media type by the ANSI/TIA/EIA-568-A standard.

Both 50/125 and 62.5/125 micron multimode optical fiber cables are recognized media types in the ANSI/TIA/EIA-568-B.3 standard. This standard will supersede the ANSI/TIA/EIA-568-A cable standard as the recognized cabling standard in the United States.

100/140 micron multimode optical fiber cable is sometimes found in existing installations but is rarely every used for new installations. 100/140 multimode optical fiber cable is not a recognized media type in either the ANSI/TIA/EIA-568-A or the new ANSI/TIA/EIA-568-B.3 cabling standards. As a result, it is considered a nonstandard media type for new installations.

CHAPTER SUMMARY

Communications system signals are required to travel from some type of user device to a control module, device, or system. Communications signals must travel over some form of transmission medium. This transmission medium usually takes the form of some type of cable. The purpose of the transmission medium is to distribute communication system signals to user devices without interference or corruption of the system signals. The transmission medium should transmit signals reliably so the signal arrives at the receiving device of the communication system and can be interpreted without errors.

There are many different types of cable that have been used for communications systems over the years. Cable can be divided into two general categories of copper cables and optical fiber cables. Copper cables have conductors that are constructed of some form of copper metal. All signals are transmitted across the copper conductors in the form of electrical energy. Optical fiber cables have conductors that are constructed of either glass or plastic. All signals are transmitted across the glass or plastic conductors in the form of light energy or pulses.

All cables share the same basic components in their construction. All cables have a conductor for transmit signals, some form of insulation material over the conductor, and a cable sheath covering the insulated conductors and covering the entire cable configuration. Some cables include a cable shield. This protects the signals traveling along the cable from electrical interference and keeps electrical energy from emanating from the cable. Cable shields are an optional cable component and are only included in some types of cables.

The cable conductor is the most important component of any communications cable. The conductor is responsible for carrying the transmitted communication signal. The conductor of a copper cable is usually some form of copper metal material or copper metal composite material. Most copper cables that include multiple conductors twist the individual copper conductors together creating twisted pairs.

The dielectric is the insulation or nonconductive portion of a cable. Each conductor must be covered with a dielectric material to prevent the passage of current to other conductors or a conductor and other metal objects. Most cables use some form of plastic material, called polymers, to cover the cable conductors. These polymers are applied to the copper conductors and are both a proven and reliable method of insulating metal conductors.

The cable shield is an optional component in a communications cable. Cable shields are used for either physical protection or electrical protection. An overall armor shield is used for direct buried cables for rodent protection. A braided or foil shield is used for electromagnetic protection for the signals traveling over the cable conductors.

The cable jacket is the outer component of a cable. The jacket is a nonmetallic cable element used to hold the other cable components together and to protect the cable components from damage. The type of jacket that is used for the cable will depend on where the able is to be installed. The National Electrical Code (NEC) requires that cables used for communication systems be suitable for the environment where they are to be installed.

The NEC defines suitable as being tested as passing fire, smoke, and toxicity tests for specific building environments.

Communications conductor sizes are usually referenced by the American Wire Gauge (AWG) sizes. There is no formal or legal standard for sizing copper conductors in the United States. Through usage and over time, the AWG conductor sizing specification has been accepted as the national standard.

Many different types of cables use a twisted-pair construction. Twisted-pair cables can be either shielded or unshielded construction. The important characteristic of these cables is that the individual conductors are twisted together into pairs. The individual pairs typically have different twist rated in the cable to minimize crosstalk coupling between cable pairs. The following multiconductor cable types use twisted-pair construction: UTP cable, ScTP cable, and STP-A cable.

Unshielded twisted-pair (UTP) cable is the most common type of media used in communications systems and in structured cabling systems. UTP cable is used extensively due to its flexibility. UTP cable can be used for voice, low-speed data, high-speed data, audio and paging systems, and building automation and control systems. UTP cable can be used in both the horizontal and backbone cabling subsystems.

The evolution of UTP has created different categories or grades of UTP cable. The higher the category of UTP cable, the better the cable's performance characteristics. Higher category UTP cables are referred to as data grade UTP cables, and low category UTP cables are referred to as voice grade UTP cables. Industry cabling standards have standardized the category performance specifications for UTP cables.

Screened twisted-pair (ScTP) cable is similar to UTP cable, but this media has a foil shield surrounding the four-cable pairs. ScTP cables are four-pair cables. ScTP cable pairs are usually 24 AWG conductors. ScTP cables have a characteristic impedance rating of 100 ohms. Inside the cable jacket and running the length of the cable is a drain wire. This wire is used to ground the cable shield. The foil shield helps to protect the signals traveling over the cable pairs from noise and EMI.

Shielded twisted-pair cable (STP) was created to be extremely reliable even in the most electrically noisy environments. STP cable can be used in both horizontal and backbone cabling subsystems for data applications only. Current industry cabling standards do not recognize STP cable for new cabling installations.

A coaxial (coax) cable is a copper cable. Coaxial cables have a center conductor that is either a copper or copper alloy construction surrounded by one or more cable shields. The difference between coaxial cables and other copper cables is that coaxial cables have only a single conductor. Because coaxial cables only have a single conductor, they are oftentimes referred to as unbalanced types of media. The most common types of coaxial cables used for communications systems include RG6/RG59, RG-8/RG-58, and RG62.

An optical fiber is a thin strand of glass or plastic that serves as the transmission medium for passing these light pulses.

Using light pulses to carry information serves the same purpose as copper cable carrying electrical signals for either telephone conversations or data communications. Any type of electrical signal that can be converted to light pulses can be transmitted in an optical fiber cable. The conductor in an optical fiber cable is called an optical fiber. Optical fiber cables usually have between 2 and 288 optical fibers, sometime called optical strands, in a single cable.

The optical fiber is the glass element of an optical fiber cable. The optical fiber has two concentric layers of glass called the core and the cladding. The inner layer of glass is called the core. The outer layer of glass is called the cladding. The core is the light carrying part of the optical fiber cable. The cladding's job is to keep the light contained in the core.

Optical fiber cables are manufactured with additional buffering material to protect the glass optical fibers. A protective buffer is always added to an optical fiber cable in addition to the primary buffer. The two categories of protective buffering for an optical fiber cables are tight buffer and loose buffer.

Optical fiber cables usually include one or more strength members to provide mechanical strength and rigidity to optical fiber cables. Strength member elements provide tensile strength for pulling the cable and provide additional protection for supporting the optical fibers.

Optical fiber cables are classified into two general categories based on the size of the optical fiber core. The two categories are called singlemode optical fiber cable and multimode optical fiber cable. Singlemode optical fiber cable typically has a core ranging in size from eight to ten microns. This small core size only permits a single mode or ray of light to enter the core and travel through the cable. Multimode optical fiber cable has a very large size core. This large core permits many modes or rays of light to enter.

CHAPTER 3

Connectors and Connecting Hardware

There are many different types of hardware components used for communication cabling. Some hardware components are used to terminate the cables. These important cabling elements are called connecting hardware components. Other hardware components are used to organize, group, or support communication cables. These are called cable-supporting hardware components.

Connecting hardware is the name given to the cable components used to terminate communication cables. The term connecting hardware is a very broad term describing devices that terminate copper and fiber cable. The term means the connectors or other cabling devices required to connect two cables together. The term connecting hardware can be used to describe termination components in the telecommunications room (TR) as well as in the work area.

CONNECTOR DEFINITION

A *connector* is defined as a mechanical device that is used to terminate a communication cable and interconnect the cable to a piece of communication equipment or another communication cable (see Figure 3-1).

The term connector is used for both copper and optical fiber cables. In the case of copper cables, the connector is designed to make a physical electrical contact with the copper conductors of the cable. The copper connector will then be attached to a mating connector and create an electrical connection to the mated connector. In the case of opti-

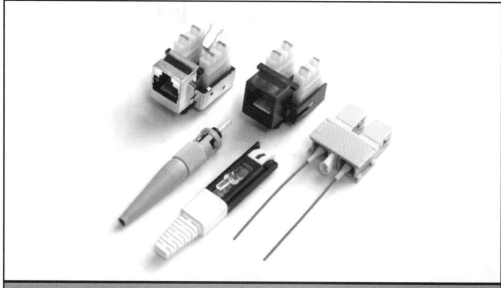

Figure 3-1.   Connector examples

cal fiber cables, the main function of the optical connector is to align the two optical fiber cables so light is able to pass between the two connectors.

Communication cable connectors are used to attach, connect, and decouple the cable from the following elements in a communication system:

▼ A transmitter

■ A receiver

▲ Another communication cable

All connectors have the same basic objectives. These objectives include the following:

▼ Provide physical alignment of the cable conductors or optical fibers

■ Provide a convenient method to connect and release the cable

■ Provide physical stability prevention slippage or separation

▲ Provide a low loss electrical or optical path

The primary job of a communication cable connector is to provide a stable and reliable connection path for communication signals. All connectors must be manufactured to fit connectors when attached to another connector and to provide proper alignment to make an electrical or optical circuit. Most connectors today are designed with a convenient quick release mechanism. This provides a convenient means to attach and release a connector. The connector must also be a low loss component in the communication link.

Communication connectors must be durable components in a communication link. Durability is defined as the connector's ability to withstand the abuse associated with basic use and the process of connecting and decoupling. The number of times a connector can be attached and released before showing any signs of failure is known as the connector's mean time between failure (MTBF).

The communication industry uses many different types of connectors to terminate different types of communication cables. The most common type of connectors for terminating communication cables are

▼ Unshielded twisted-pair (UTP) cable
   ■ Eight-position modular connector

■ Multipair UTP cable
   ■ Telco 50-pin connector

■ Shielded twisted-pair (ScTP) cable
   ■ Eight-position shielded modular connector

■ Shielded twisted-pair (STP) cable
   ■ Data connector

- Coaxial cable
  - N connector
  - BNC connector
  - F connector
- ▲ Optical fiber cable
  - ST connector
  - SC connector
  - Small form factor (SFF) connectors

UNSHIELDED TWISTED-PAIR (UTP) CONNECTORS

Unshielded twisted-pair (UTP) cables are terminated with eight-position modular outlet/connectors and modular plugs (see Figure 3-2). The modular outlet/connector is the type of connector used to terminate horizontal cables in the work area. These connectors are designated as female connectors. They are designed to connect to a male modular plug.

Modular outlets terminate the wires of a horizontal cable and provide a female jack space for attaching the male modular plug. The modular outlet has four to eight contact wires inside the female jack that connect to the terminated cable conductors. When viewed from the front, the contacts are numbered from one to eight, starting at the contact wire. The male modular plug will insert into the female jack and make a physical connection to these contacts.

Modular outlets/connectors are designed to terminate the wires of a horizontal UTP cable using insulation displacement contact (IDC) technology (see Figure 3-3). These con-

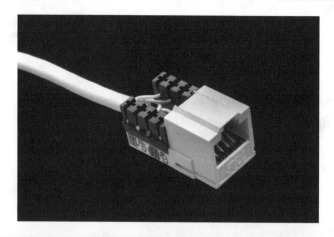

Figure 3-2.   UTP modular outlet/connector

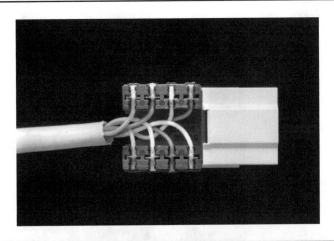

Figure 3-3.   UTP modular outlet/connector pair terminations example

nectors are designed with slots to terminate the individual cable conductors. The individual conductors of a UTP cable are inserted into these slots with a punch down tool or a special connector cap. The slots are designed to cut through the insulation on the wires and make a physical contact with the connector.

Modular outlets have evolved over the years. Early versions of these cable termination components used to have screws on the back of the outlet (see Figure 3-4). The individual wires of the cable had to be stripped and carefully wrapped around the screws, then the screws were tightened. These types of modular outlets can still be found in many homes today. The style of modulars outlet that uses screws is not recommended by either commercial cabling or residential cabling standards.

Modular plugs

Equipment patch cords and work area line cords are the cables that connect to a modular outlet/connector. These cables are terminated with a modular plug (see Figure 3-5). Modular plugs are male connectors. They are designed to attach to a female outlet/connector to make an electrical connection between the horizontal cable and the work area cable. The opposite end of the work area cable attaches to the user equipment.

Modular plugs have become the standard type of connector for telephones and for local area network (LAN) equipment such as hubs and network interface cards. Modular plugs are designed to attach to a modular outlet/connector. The insert into these connectors are held in place by the plastic tab at the top of the connector. The plastic tab is depressed to release the modular plug. This is a quick release feature of all modular plugs that is preferred by most customers.

Figure 3-4.   Modular outlet with screws

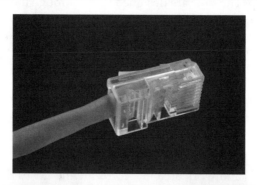

Figure 3-5.   Modular plug

Modular plugs are clear plastic connectors that attach to a modular line cord or patch cord. They are sometimes called ice cubes because they resemble a rectangular ice cube. The individual conductors of a line cord are inserted into the back of the connector and are crimped to make a physical connection. These connectors have four to eight slots with metal contacts in the slots. The crimped wires make physical contact with the metal contacts of the modular plug. The slots of the modular plug line up and make a physical connection with the metal contacts in the modular outlet. When the modular plug is snapped into the modular outlet/connection, the two connectors make a physical connection at these contact points.

Modular plugs are always a male connect that only attaches to the stranded conductors or a modular line or patch cord. The cable wires are inserted into the modular plug in a specific color-coded sequence and then crimped in place. Both ends of a modular cord must be configured the same so the wiring is straight through from end to end.

CAUTION: Modular plugs are not designed to attach directly to horizontal cables. These cables have solid conductor wires. Modular plugs are designed to attach to the stranded conductors used for work area line cords and equipment patch cords.

Modular Connector Configurations

Modular outlets have been used to terminate UTP cables for years. This is the reason there are so many different size and style modular connectors found in many commercial buildings today. Some modular connectors have four connectors, some have six conductors, and new modular connectors support eight conductors.

The telephone industry designated some modular jack configurations to be the standard jack types for specific applications. These modular jacks typically have an RJ in the jack name. The RJ stands for registered jack. Many people today commonly use the terms RJ11 to refer to either a four- or six-wire modular jack and an RJ45 to refer to an eight-position modular jacket. Industry cable standards do not use these designations because these jacks are registered and have specific wiring configurations. For example, an RJ45 modular connector has a resistor on pins 7 and 8. A standard eight-position modular outlet that is used to terminate a four-pair horizontal cable does not have a resistor across these two pins and therefore is not an RJ45 configuration. This modular outlet would simply be referred to as an eight-position modular outlet.

Some common modular connector configurations used in the communication industry are

▼ **4P4C** This is the abbreviation for a four-position, four-conductor modular connector. This type of modular connector is typically found on most residential phones.

■ **6P6C** This is the abbreviation for a six-position, six-conductor modular connector. This is the type of connector that is used for older data connections. Data terminals that connect to either a minicomputer or mainframe computer would use this type of connector.

▲ **8P8C** This is the abbreviation for an eight-position, eight-conductor modular connector. This is the type of modular outlet/connector that is specified in industry cabling standards to terminate four-pair horizontal cables.

Industry cabling standards require that only the eight-position modular connector, known as the 8P8C configuration, be used to terminate horizontal cables. The 8P8C connectors are required because these same standards require that only four-pair UTP cable is installed in the horizontal subsystem. The 8P8C type connector configuration is required to terminate all conductors of these cables.

Modular Outlet Configurations

Modular outlet/connectors are wired to create a modular outlet configuration. The modular outlet configuration defines how the cable conductors are terminated. There are different modular outlet configurations used today. The most common modular outlet configurations are

▼ T568A

■ T568B

▲ USOC

4P4C and 6P6C modular connectors always use a USOC configuration. This configuration organizes the wires on the horizontal cable into pairs starting on the middle pins of the modular connector. Pair 1 is always terminated on the middle pins of the modular connector and pair 2 is always terminated on the next two pins. If a 6P6C modular connector is used, the third pair is terminated on the outside pins 1 and 6. This is shown in Figure 3-6.

The USOC configuration has been used the longest for UTP cable. All modular outlets used for telephone service in residential homes are wired with a USOC configuration (see Figure 3-7).

8P8C modular connectors are typically wired with either a T568A or T568B configuration. These are the two modular outlet configurations supported by industry cabling standards. The USOC configuration is seldom used for eight-position modular outlets because this configuration is not supported by either the ANSI/TIA/EIA-568-A or the ANSI/TIA/EIA-568-B.1 structured cabling standards.

The T568A configuration is the primary modular outlet configuration for terminating four-pair horizontal UTP cables. The T568A modular configuration is recommended for new cabling installations by both the ANSI/TIA/EIA-568-A and ANSI/TIA/EIA-568-B.1 structured cabling standards.

The T568B configuration is an optional modular outlet configuration that is recognized by both the ANSI/TIA/EIA-568-A and ANSI/TIA/EIA-568-B.1 structured cabling standards (see Figure 3-8). The T568B modular outlet configuration is the recommended standard for the AVAYA Communications (formerly Lucent Technologies) Systimax structured cabling system. The T568B modular outlet configuration is also known as the AT&T 258A modular outlet configuration. This modular outlet configuration is recommended for existing installations that have existing modular outlets wired according to the T568B scheme. It is also used for new Systimax structured cabling installations. The T568B modular outlet configurations is shown in Figure 3-8.

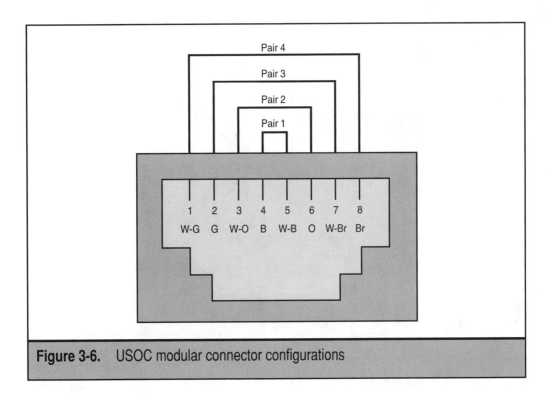

Figure 3-6. USOC modular connector configurations

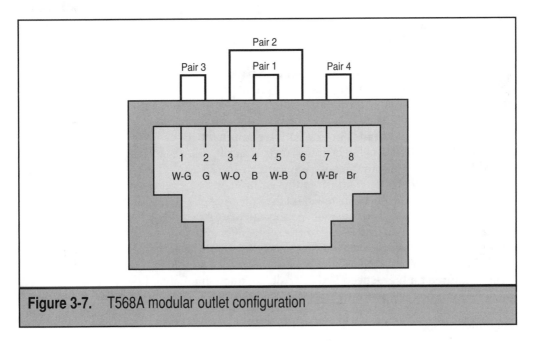

Figure 3-7. T568A modular outlet configuration

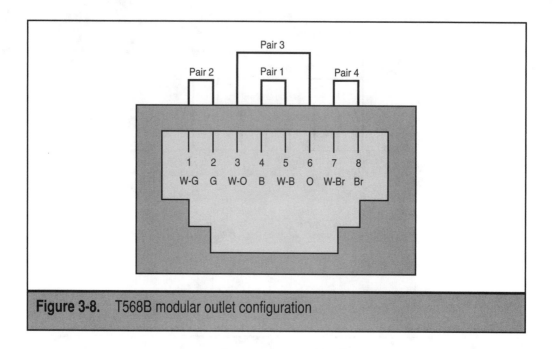

Figure 3-8. T568B modular outlet configuration

TELCO 50-PIN CONNECTORS

Multipair UTP cables are large pair count cables with pair counts ranging from 25 to 600 pairs. These large pair count cables are organized into 25-pair binder groups. Multipair UTP cables are usually terminated on punch down blocks.

Smaller 25-pair UTP backbone cables are used for connecting either telephone switches, data multiplexing, and LAN hubs to patch panels or punch down blocks. The 25-pair UTP cables are terminated with a Telco 50-pin connector (see Figure 3-9). The Telco 50-pin connector is capable of terminating all 25 pairs (50 conductors) in a modular connector. This is a convenient method for terminating 25-pair cables that must be regularly attached and removed from communication equipment.

Telco 50-pin connectors can be found on the back of older patch panels, selected punch down blocks, and on communication equipment. The 25-pair UTP cables terminated with a Telco 50-pin connector can attach to this equipment or be removed as needed. A male connector would typically be installed on the patch panel, punch down block, or the communication equipment, and a female connector would be installed on the 25-pair cable. The 25-pair cable is usually field-terminated using a butterfly tool.

Telco 50-pin connectors are not found very often for the equipment or cabling associated with high-speed LANs. These connectors do not provide the NEXT crosstalk protection required for high-speed LAN circuits to function reliably. Telco 50-pin connectors are often found on telephone equipment and low-speed data equipment and devices.

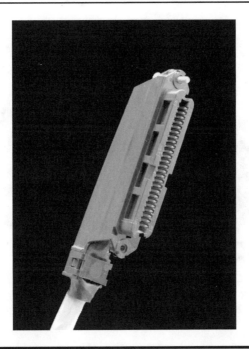

Figure 3-9.   Telco 50-pin connector

SCREENED TWISTED-PAIR (ScTP) CONNECTORS

Screened twisted-pair (ScTP) cables are terminated similar to UTP cables. ScTP cables are terminated with an eight-position modular shielded connector (see Figure 3-10). ScTP cables have an overall foil shield surrounding the cable pairs and a drain wire running the length of the cable. The foil shield provides electrical protection from electrical interference.

The modular connectors use to terminate ScTP cables are shielded connectors. The shield of the connector is bonded to the shield of the cable via the drain wire. This provides protection for the cable conductors along the entire length of the cable up to the modular connector. Any electrical noise would hit the foil cable shield and be run directly to ground.

ScTP modular connectors are similar to UTP modular connectors. Industry cabling standards recommend using only eight-position (8P8C) connectors to terminate four-pair ScTP horizontal cable. ScTP modular connectors also use IDC style terminations to attach the individual cable conductors to the connector.

ScTP modular connectors are available in both the T568A and T568B modular outlet configurations. The ScTP modular outlets have a color code to designate how the cable conductors are terminated to create either the T568A or T568B configuration.

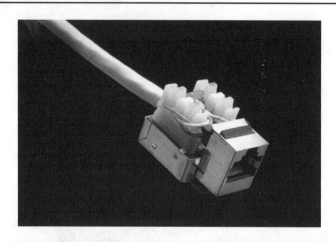

Figure 3-10.   ScTP modular connector

Modular Plug

ScTP modular connectors are female connectors. A male-shielded modular plug is used to connect to the modular connector. The modular plug for ScTP work areas and equipment patch cords is similar to a modular plug used for UTP cable. It is typically an eight-position plastic plug with a quick release tab on the top. The primary difference is that the plug has a metal shield around it. The metal shield of the modular plug makes physical contact to the metal shield surrounding the modular outlet. The shielded modular plugs, outlets, and cables create an electrically protected path for communication signals that are free from electrical interference.

SHIELDED TWISTED-PAIR (STP) CONNECTORS

Shielded twisted-pair (STP) cables are terminated with a special type of connector called a data connector (see Figure 3-11). The data connector was created specifically for STP cable. These connectors are designed with grounding bars built into the connector to create a physical bond connection to the foil shields surrounding each cable pair and the overall braided shield.

Data connectors are unique connectors because these connectors are designed to be self-mating connectors. A self-mating design was chosen for data connectors instead of using male and female data connectors. Data connectors are designed so a single connector can attach to the same type of connector, sometimes called a hermaphroditic connector. Turning a second connector 180 degrees will enable two connectors to connect together.

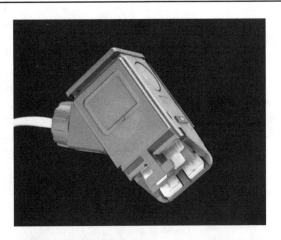

Figure 3-11. STP data connector

Data connectors were mostly found in Token Ring LAN environments. These LANs used STP cable as the transmission medium for the network. The default connector on most Token Ring equipment had data connector ports. These were designed to support 150-ohm STP cable. Token Ring LANs are being replaced by less expensive Ethernet LANs supporting UTP cable.

STP-A cable is a media that is recognized as an allowed media type for the horizontal subsystem by the ANSI/TIA/EIA-568-A standard. STP-A cable is being removed as a recognized media by the ANSI/TIA/EIA-568-B.1 standard. It will still be recognized for adding cables to an existing installation but will not be recommended for new cabling installations. As a result, the use of data connectors is expected to dwindle to the point where there may not be many of these connectors used in commercial buildings in the near future.

COAXIAL CABLE CONNECTORS

Coaxial cables are terminated with coaxial connectors. There are many different types of coaxial connectors used today in the communications industry. This is due to the large number of different size and type coaxial cables used for different types of communication systems. Some of the most common types of coaxial connectors are

▼ N connectors

■ BNC connectors

▲ F connectors

Coaxial connectors are specially designed connectors that work with coaxial cable. Coaxial connectors keep the center conductor electrically separated from the cable foil and braided shields. These connectors also provide a bonding connection to the foil and/or braided shield of the coaxial cable. When correctly terminated, the housing of the coaxial conductors make an electrical connection to the shield of the coaxial cable.

Coaxial cables are terminated with male connectors. Communication equipment with coaxial ports have female connectors. The male port terminating the coaxial cables can connect directly to the equipment ports. When two coaxial cables are required to connect together, a female to female coupler is used. The coupler enables two coaxial cables to attach to both ends and provides a physical connection.

N Connectors

An N style coaxial connector is the type of connector that is used with thick, 50-ohm coaxial cable, sometimes called RG-8, Thicknet cable (see Figure 3-12). The N connector is a large connector that is designed to support thick, 50-ohm coaxial cable used for early versions of Ethernet LANs.

The N style coaxial connector is a threaded connector. A coaxial cable is terminated with an N style coaxial connector. The threaded connector is either attached to an N style terminator or an N style barrel connector. A terminator is used to terminate the end of a coaxial cable. The barrel connector is used to extend the length of a coaxial cable. The N

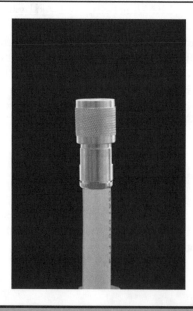

Figure 3-12.   N connector

connector is a male connector and both the N style terminator and barrel connectors are female connectors. The two connectors are screwed together to create a secure connection.

BNC Connectors

BNC connectors are the type of connector used with thin, 50-ohm coaxial cable, sometimes called RG58A/U Thinnet cable (see Figure 3-13). A BNC connector is a male connector. It attaches to the end of a RG58 coaxial cable. A female BNC connector is installed on communication equipment.

Figure 3-13.   BNC connector

The BNC connector is a bayonet style connector. This connector is designed to slide over the female connector and attach by turning the BNC connector. A half turn locks the connector into place. A half turn in the opposite direction will unlock the connector and enable it to be removed.

BNC connectors are used extensively on Thinnet Ethernet LANs (see Figure 3-14). The RG-58 coaxial cable is terminated with male BNC connectors. BNC T connectors are used to connect two RG-58 cables together. Thinnet Ethernet NICs have a female BNC connect installed on the back. This enables a BNC connector to attach to the Ethernet card with a simple half twist.

F Connectors

F connectors are the type of connector used with 75-ohm coaxial cable used for cable TV systems or CCTV systems (see Figure 3-15). The F connector is a male connector. These connectors are installed on the end of a 75-ohm, RG59 or RG-6 coaxial cable. Female F connectors are installed on communication equipment.

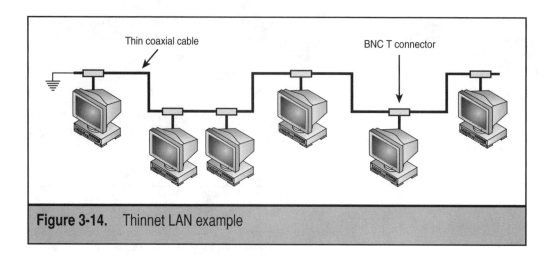

Thin coaxial cable

BNC T connector

Figure 3-14. Thinnet LAN example

Figure 3-15. F connector

CAUTION: There are different size F connectors to fit either RG-59 or RG-6 coaxial cable. RG-59 coaxial cable is smaller in diameter than RG-6 coaxial cable. As a result, RG-59 coaxial cable requires a smaller size F connector to correctly terminate the cable.

F connectors are threaded connectors. Male connectors are screwed onto a female F connector on a communication device or onto a female coupler. A couple enables two coaxial cables to be connected together. Couples are commonly installed in a wallplate. The coaxial horizontal cable is terminated with an F connector and attached to the back of the coupler, on the back side of the wallplate. A coaxial patch cable is terminated with an F connector and attached to the front of the couple, on the front of the wallplate. This is the usual configuration for a cable TV connection in a home.

OPTICAL FIBER CONNECTORS

Optical fiber connectors are used to terminate optical fiber cable just as copper connectors are used to terminate copper cable (see Figure 3-16). Optical fiber connectors are different than copper connectors because their primary function is to align the cores of two optical fiber cables to provide a low loss junction.

Optical fiber cables do not provide an electrical connection between two cables. The connection is an alignment function that will enable light rays to pass from one optical fiber to another optical fiber cable or a communication device. In fact, the alignment function performed by fiber connectors must be very precise. The core of a multimode optical fiber cable is either 50 or 62.5 microns. A misalignment of 10 micron is a misalignment of 16 to 20 percent of the core size. This type of misalignment will cause significant loss at the connection point.

Optical fiber connectors are always male connectors. A female connector is used on communication equipment. A coupler is the device that enables two cables connect together. The two connectors are inserted into the two ends of the optical fiber coupler (see Figure 3-17). The coupler aligns the two connectors to provide a low loss junction between the two connectors.

The ANSI/TIA/EIA-568-A standard recognizes two types of fiber connectors. ST and SC connectors are both supported in this version of the commercial building cabling standard.

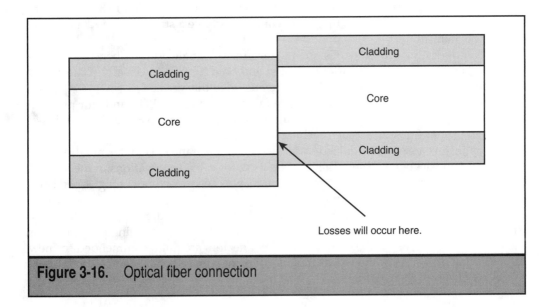

Figure 3-16.   Optical fiber connection

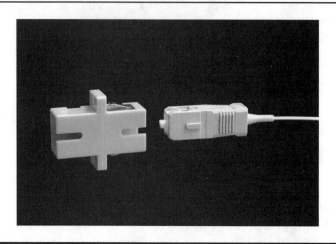

Figure 3-17.   Fiber connector and coupler

The revised version of the ANSI/TIA/EIA-568-A standard is called the ANSI/TIA/EIA-568-B standard. The ANSI/TIA/EIA-568-B.3 standard addresses optical fiber cable and connectors. This standard continues to recognize both ST and SC fiber connectors. It also recognizes SFF optical fiber connectors for premises cabling applications.

ST Connectors

ST fiber optic connectors were originally developed by AT&T (see Figure 3-18). The abbreviation ST stands for straight tip. These connectors have a straight tip and a bayonet locking mechanism.

ST fiber optic connectors are designed to terminate a single optical fiber. The connector is designed to attach to a glass optical fiber and hold it in place. Usually, some sort of epoxy adhesive secures the optical fiber to the inside of the ferrule.

ST fiber optic connectors are known as a PC type connector. PC stands for physical contact. This means that when two ST connectors are connected to a coupler, the tips of the two connector physically touch each other.

ST connectors are still recognized by industry cabling standards for terminating both horizontal and backbone cables. They can be used for cable terminations in the TR and the work area. In fact, it is very common to find ST ports on most types of high-speed networking devices.

The ANSI/TIA/EIA-568-A commercial building cabling standard supports the use of ST connectors for premises cabling applications. ST connectors are being phased out as the most common type of fiber connector. ST connectors are not recommended for new cabling installations. They are recognized as a type of connector that can be used for ex-

Figure 3-18. ST connector

isting installations that have ST connectors installed or that support equipment with ST connectors.

SC Connectors

SC fiber optic connectors are currently recommended by industry cabling standards for new cable installations. The 568SC optical fiber connect is the only type of connector recommended by the ANSI/TIA/EIA-568-A cabling standard (see Figure 3-19). A 568SC connector is a duplex connector. One SC connector supports one optical fiber and a second SC connector supports a second optical fiber cable. The primary benefit of a 568SC connector is that the configuration can be keyed to prevent transposing the optical fibers.

SC fiber optic connectors are similar to ST connectors (see Figure 3-20). SC connectors have a straight tip ferrule like ST connectors. They are also designed to support single optical fibers like ST connectors. However, SC connectors have a different attachment mechanism than ST connectors. SC connectors are classified as a tension type of fiber connector. The SC connector attaches to a fiber coupler and is held in place with tension. This enables the connector to slide on and off fiber couplers with gentle pressure and eliminates the need to push down and twist the connector to remove it, as is the case with ST connectors. It has been proven that ST connectors that are frequently removed and reattached show greater loss than those not frequency removed. This is due to scratching that can occur due to the pushing and turning and the movement of the connector during this process. SC connectors are free from this type of loss.

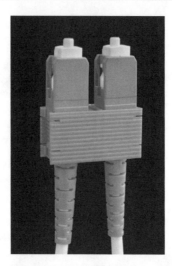

Figure 3-19.   568SC connector

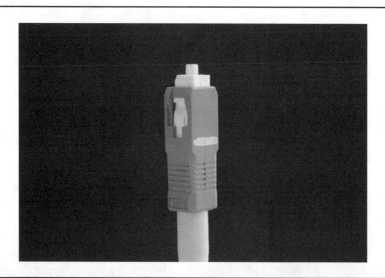

Figure 3-20.   SC connector

SC connectors can terminate both 50/125 μm and 62.5/125 multimode optical fiber cable and singlemode optical fiber cable. Industry cabling standards recommend that a beige color connector be used to terminate multimode optical fiber cable and a blue connector be used to terminate singlemode optical fiber cable.

Small Form Factor (SFF) Optical Fiber Connectors

Small form factor (SFF) fiber optic connectors are a new type of fiber connector that will eventually replace the existing ST and SC connectors. SFF is a term that describes fiber connectors that can terminate two or more optical fibers in a single connector. The entire connector takes up the same amount of space in a patch panel or a communication device as an eight-position modular connector.

SFF fiber connectors are preferred connectors because they terminate two optical fibers in a single connector. Most communications circuits require two optical fibers—one for transmitting signals and a second for receiving signals. SFF connectors reduce costs by requiring a single connector instead of two ST or SC connectors. A second cost saving is the labor required to terminate two fiber connectors. Another significant saving is in the space required to terminate SFF connectors. SFF connectors require half the space as a duplex SC connector on a patch panel or on communication equipment.

All SFF connectors will be supported in the ANSI/TIA/EIA-568-B.3 standard. The most common types of SFF connectors on the market today are

▼   MT-RJ SFF connectors

▲   Volition VF-45 connectors

MT-RJ Connectors

The MT-RJ fiber connector is a SFF connector co-developed by Tyco Electronics (formerly AMP) and Siecor (see Figure 3-21). The MT-RJ is similar to an eight-position modular plug. This type of fiber optic connector can terminate both 50/125 and 62.5/125 μm multimode optical fiber cables.

The MT-RJ was designed to be the same size as UTP modular outlets. This enables MT-RJ connectors to be installed in standard face plates in work area locations and patch panels in TRs. It attaches to an MT-RJ fiber coupler with a quick release tab like a UTP modular plug. The entire connector assembly fits into standard copper work area outlet and patch panels.

The MT-RJ fiber connector attaches to a fiber cable without using epoxy adhesives. The connector uses a mechanical splicing mechanism to hold the cleaved fiber in place. A key opens the fiber connector and enables the cleaved fiber to be inserted in the connector. The same key closes the connector securing the optical fiber in place.

Volition VF-45 Connectors

The Volition VF-45 fiber optic connector is another SFF fiber connector (see Figure 3-22). The volition connector was developed by 3M. The volition fiber connector is similar to

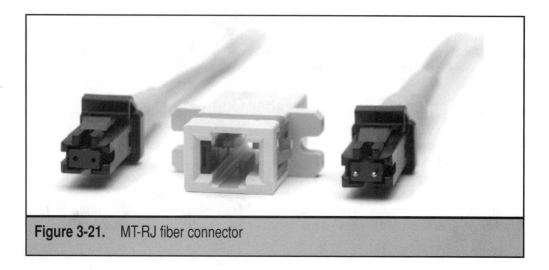

Figure 3-21. MT-RJ fiber connector

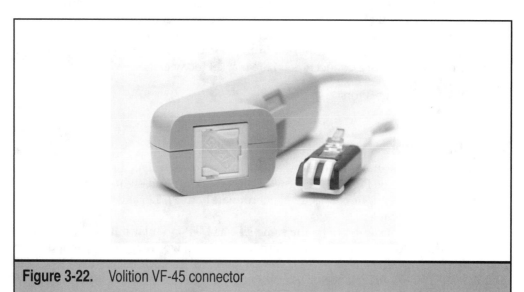

Figure 3-22. Volition VF-45 connector

an eight-position modular connector. This type of connector can terminate both 50/125 and 62.5/125 μm multimode and singlemode optical fiber cable types.

The Volition VF-45 fiber connector is designed with a plug and socket configuration. This configuration simulates the eight-position modular outlet/connector and modular plug. The Volition VF-45 fiber connector uses an epoxyless connection method to attach the optical fibers to the connector.

CONNECTING HARDWARE

Communications cables are terminated with connectors in the work area of a building. The opposite end of each communication cable is terminated on other types of connecting hardware in the TR.

The term *connecting hardware* is used extensively in the cabling industry. Connecting hardware is used to generically describe all cabling components that either terminate or support a communications cable. In fact, connectors are one of the primary types of connecting hardware.

Connecting hardware is necessary to terminate communications cables. This hardware provide a permanent termination for the cable pairs and provide flexibility. Connecting hardware enables the terminated communication cables to be used for different user applications and communication systems.

The most common connecting hardware components are

▼ Punch down blocks
   - 66 blocks
   - 110 blocks
   - BIX blocks
   - Krone blocks
■ Patch panels
   - Copper
   - Fiber
▲ Other types of cabling hardware
   - Communication racks
   - Wire management
   - D-rings
   - Cable ties

Punch Down Blocks

Punch down blocks, sometimes called connecting blocks, are connecting hardware devices commonly found in a TR (see Figure 3-23). They are used to terminate the conductors for either large multipair backbone cables or the conductors of multiple four-pair horizontal cables. Punch down blocks provide a stable and permanent location for communication cables.

Punch down blocks are mounted in TRs in commercial buildings. Backbone cable from other closets enter the closet through either conduits or backbone pathways and are terminated on punch down blocks. The backbone cable conductors can then be cross-connected using jumper wire to other punch down blocks.

Figure 3-23. Punch down block

Punch down blocks have slots that terminate cable conductors using IDC style terminations. One wire is terminated in each slot. Punch down blocks are usually designed to terminate cable conductors in 25-pair designations. Most punch down blocks are designed to support 50, 100, 250, 300, or 900 cable pairs per block. Different size and style punch down blocks can support different pair counts.

66 Blocks

66 blocks are the most common type of connecting blocks for terminating UTP cable used for telephone applications (see Figure 3-24). 66 block have been used for years by the telephone company to terminate UTP phone cables. 66 blocks can also be used for high-speed LAN environments using high quality category 5 or higher UTP cable.

66 blocks have 50 slots on the left side of the block and 50 slots on the right side of the block. Each side is capable of terminating 25 cable pairs. 66 blocks are mounted on either 89b or 89d brackets, or they can be directly attached to the plywood backboard with screws. These blocks can also be rack mounted for high-density cable installations.

66 blocks are vertical blocks. The cable conductors are terminated starting at the top left hand side of the block and working down the block. Once the bottom of the block is reached, the next set of cable conductors are terminated on the right side of the block from top to bottom. The blocks are usually mounted with four blocks mounted vertically to handle 100 cable pairs on each side of the block.

Figure 3-24. 66 blocks

66 block have metal clips on the front of the block. These clips are designed to provide an IDC terminate for communication cables. The cable conductors are inserted into each slot on the block and into the first metal clip on the side of the block being terminated. A punch down tool with a 66 blade is used to push the cable conductor into the clip. The clip is designed to cut through the wire insulation and make a physical connection with the wire. The punch down tool seats the wire into the clip so it will not move.

Once the cable conductors are terminated on the inside clip, a cross-connect jumper wire is punched down on the second clip on the same row. The first and second clips on the right and left side of the block are physically connected together. Once the jumper wire is punched down into the second metal clip, the cable conductor and the jumper wire are physically connected together.

110 Blocks

110 block was created by AT&T to support voice and data applications (see Figure 3-25). 110 blocks can either be wall mounted or rack mounted. If wall mounted, the 110-block legs are attached to the backboard with wood screws.

110 blocks are horizontal style blocks. They are comprised of 25-pair rows organized in a horizontal configuration. Cable conductors are terminated from the left top row across

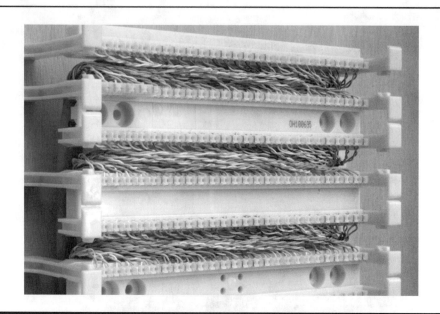

Figure 3-25.   110 block

the block to the right. The second 25-pair group of cable conductors are terminated on the next horizontal row from left to right.

110 blocks use IDC termination technology to make a physical connection to the cable pairs. Cable conductors are inserted into a slot in the block and seated using a punch down tool with a 110 blade attached. The punch down tool pushed the cable conductor into the conductor slot. The metal edges in the slot are designed to cut through the wire insulation and make a physical connection with the wire. The punch tool seats the wire into the slot so it not move.

Once the cable conductors are terminated on the 110 block, a C4 or C5 terminating clip is installed onto the 110 block over the terminated cable pairs. Jumper wires are punched down on top of the C clips. The C clips provide a pass-through connection between the cable conductors and the jumper wire.

BIX Blocks

BIX punch down blocks were created by Nortel (formerly Northern Telecom) to support voice and data applications. BIX blocks are a combination of a BIX mount and multiple BIX connectors that are used the terminate the cable conductors (see Figure 3-26). Once the cable wires are terminated in the BIX connectors, the connectors are attached to the BIX mount. BIX blocks can either be wall mounted or rack mounted. If wall mounted, the BIX mounts are attached to the backboard with wood screws.

Figure 3-26. BIX block

BIX blocks are horizontal style blocks similar to 110 blocks. They are comprised of 25-pair rows organized in a horizontal configuration. Cable conductors are terminated from the left top row across the block to the right. The second 25-pair group of cable conductors are terminated on the next horizontal row from left to right.

BIX blocks use IDC termination technology to make a physical connection to the cable pairs. Cable conductors are inserted into a slot in the block and seated using a BIX punch down tool. The punch down tool pushes the cable conductor into the conductor slot. The metal edges in the slot are designed to cut through the wire insulation and make a physical connection with the wire. The punch tool seats the wire into the slot so it not move.

Once the cable conductors are terminated on the BIX connectors, cross-connect jumper wire is punched down on the back side of the BIX connectors. The BIX connector provides a pass-through connections from the cable conductor to the jumper wires.

Krone Blocks

Krone blocks are similar to BIX blocks. These punch down blocks were created to support voice and high-speed data applications. Krone LSA blocks are manufactured with silver IDC contacts, which provide excellent electrical properties. Krone blocks are a combination of a mount and multiple Krone connector blocks that are used to terminate the cable conductors. Krone blocks are unique because they provide a disconnect capability.

A plug can be inserted into a wire pair to provide either a temporary or permanent disconnection of the wire connection. Krone blocks can either be wall mounted or rack mounted.

Krone blocks are horizontal style blocks are different than either 110 or BIX blocks. These blocks are comprised of either eight pair or ten pair rows organized in a horizontal configuration. Cable conductors are terminated from the left top row across the block to the right. The communication cables are terminated at a 45-degree angle and held in place by tension on the block.

Patch Panels

Patch panels are connecting hardware components that are used to terminate four-pair horizontal cables (see Figure 3-27). Patch panels have a terminating block on the back of the panel for terminating horizontal cable conductors. The front of the panel has eight-position modular ports. Patch panels are usually sold in either 12, 24, 48, or 96 port configurations.

Patch panels mount in a standard communications rack. Patch panels are usually mounted in the top of the rack and communications equipment is mounted in the lower part of the rack. Equipment patch cords with modular plugs on the ends are used to connect the patch panel ports to the equipment ports.

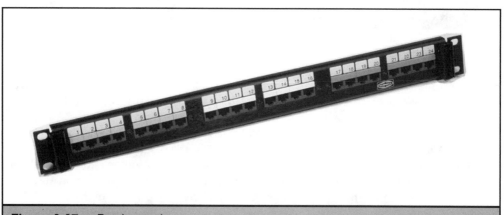

Figure 3-27. Patch panel

Other Types of Cabling Hardware

It is very common to use other types of cabling hardware to either support or to organize communications cables. These devices are usually found in telecommunications rooms where there are large numbers of cables in a small area. Some common cable hardware include

▼   Communication racks

■   Wire management panels

▲   Cable-supporting devices

Communication Racks

Communication racks are installed in TRs (see Figure 3-28). Communications racks are used to mount both cable termination equipment such as patch panels and punch down blocks. They are also used to mount communication equipment.

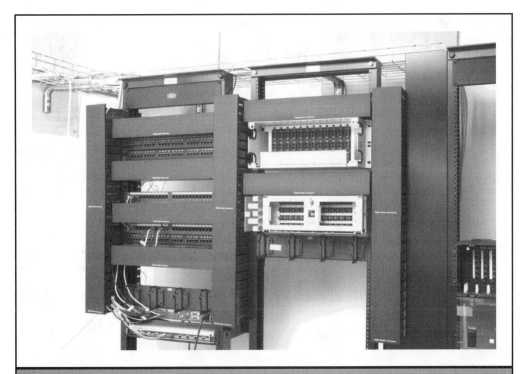

Figure 3-28.   Communication racks

Wire Management

Wire management panels are plastic or metal raceways installed on a communication rack (see Figure 3-29). They are used to provide a channel on the rack for routing patch cables

Figure 3-29.   Wire management panel

or horizontal cables either along or across the rack. The main purpose for installing wire management panels is to keep the communication racks organized.

Wire management panels are open raceway channels. Patch cables or horizontal cables are installed in these channels. Once all the cables are installed in the panels, the cover is placed on top of the panel. The major benefit of wire management panels is to hide the clutter and create an organized rack arrangement.

There are two primary types of wire management panels that are installed on communication racks:

▼   Horizontal wire management panels provide a cable pathway across the communication rack for patch cords that need to be routed across the communication rack.

▲   Vertical wire management panels provide a cable pathway along the length of the communication rack for cables that need to be routed vertically on the rack.

Both types of cable management panels can be installed on either the front or back sides of the communications rack.

Cable-Supporting Structures

There are other cable-supporting devices that are commonly used to organize cables and cable groups.

D-rings are metal or plastic rings that organize cables installed on the backboard in a TR (see Figure 3-30). D-rings are useful for organizing groups of cables that are to be terminated on punch down blocks installed on the backbone. D-rings are also commonly used to organize cross-connect jumper wires between punch down blocks.

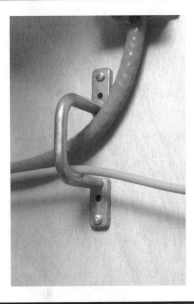

Figure 3-30.   D-ring

Cable ties are another common cabling device that is used to group and organize cables into manageable units (see Figure 3-31). Cable ties are plastic cable straps that are designed to loop over a cable and cinch tightly over a cable or group of cables. Cable ties are tightened by pulling the end of the cable tie.

Cable ties are useful for both grouping and organizing large numbers of cables. Cable ties can also be used to support a cable or separate a specific cable from a group of cables.

CAUTION: Never overtighten cables ties. Overtight cable ties can bind or kink the conductors of a communication cable. This can cause decreased performance of the cable in some cases.

Many cabling experts are recommending that Velcro cable ties be used to group cables together. Velcro cable ties are preferred because they can never be overtightened and cause cable performance degradation.

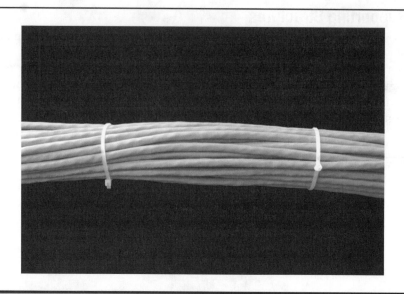

Figure 3-31.   Cable ties

CHAPTER SUMMARY

Connecting hardware is the name given to the cable components used to terminate communication cables. The term connecting hardware is a very broad term describing devices that terminate copper and fiber cable. The term means the connectors or other cabling devices required to connect two cables together. The term connecting hardware can be used to describe termination components in the telecommunications room (TR) as well as in the work area.

A connector is defined as a mechanical device that is used to terminate a communication cable and interconnect the cable to a piece of communication equipment or another communication cable. The term connector is used for both copper and optical fiber cables.

The primary job of a communication cable connector is to provide a stable and reliable connection path for communication signals. All connectors must be manufactured to fit connectors when attached to another connector and to provide proper alignment to make an electrical or optical circuit. The communication industry uses many different types of connectors to terminate different types of communication cables. The most common types of connectors for terminating communication cables are: eight-position modular connector, Telco 50-pin connector, eight-position shielded modular connector, Data connector, N connector, BNC connector, F connector, ST connector, SC connector, and small form factor (SFF) connectors.

Unshielded twisted-pair cables are terminated with eight-position modular outlet/connectors and modular plugs. The modular outlet/connector is the type of connector used to terminate horizontal cables in the work area. These connectors are designated as female connectors. They are designed to connect to a male modular plug.

Modular outlets/connectors are designed to terminate the wires of a horizontal UTP cable using insulation displacement contact (IDC) technology. These connectors are designed to with slots that terminate the individual cable conductors. The individual conductors of a UTP cable are inserted into these slots with a punch down tool or a special connector cap. The slots are designed to cut through the insulation on the wires and make physical contact with the connector.

Industry cabling standards require that only the eight-position modular connector, known as the 8P8C configuration, be used to terminate horizontal cables. The 8P8C connectors are required because these same standards require that only four-pair UTP cable is installed in the horizontal subsystem. The 8P8C type connector configuration is required to terminate all of the conductors of these cables.

The T568A configuration is the primary modular outlet configuration for terminating four-pair horizontal UTP cables. The T568A modular configuration is recommended for new cabling installations by both the ANSI/TIA/EIA-568-A and ANSI/TIA/EIA-568-B.1 structured cabling standards.

ScTP cables are terminated with an eight-position modular shielded connector. ScTP cables have an overall foil shield surrounding the cable pairs and a drain wire running the length of the cable. The modular connectors used to terminate ScTP cables are shielded connectors. The shield of the connector is bonded to the shield of the cable via the drain wire. This provides protection for the cable conductors along the entire length of the cable up to the modular connector. Any electrical noise would hit the foil cable shield and be run directly to ground.

Shielded twisted-pair (STP) cables are terminated with a special type of connector called a data connector. The data connector was created specifically for STP cable. These connectors are designed with grounding bars built into the connector to create a physical bond connection to the foil shields surrounding each cable pair and the overall braided shield.

Coaxial cables are terminated with coaxial connectors. There are many different types of coaxial connectors in use today in the communications industry. This is due to the large number of different sizes and types of coaxial cables used for different types of communication systems. Some of the most common types of coaxial connectors are: N connectors, BNC connectors, and F connectors.

Optical fiber connectors are used to terminate optical fiber cable just as copper connectors are used to terminate copper cable. Optical fiber connectors are different than copper connectors because their primary function is to align the cores of two optical fiber cables to provide a low loss junction.

The ANSI/TIA/EIA-568-A standard recognizes two types of fiber connectors. ST and SC connectors are both supported in this version of the commercial building cabling standard. The ANSI/TIA/EIA-568-B.3 standard addresses optical fiber cable and connectors. This standard continues to recognize both ST and SC fiber connectors. It also recognizes SFF optical fiber connectors for premises cabling applications.

Communications cables are terminated with connectors in the work area of a building. The opposite end of each communication cable is terminated on other types of connecting hardware in the TR. This hardware provides a permanent termination for the cable pairs and provide flexibility. The most common connecting hardware components are: punch down blocks and patch panels.

Punch down blocks are mounted in TRs in commercial buildings. Backbone cable from other closets enter the closet through either conduits or backbone pathways and are terminated on punch down blocks. The backbone cable conductors can then be cross-connected using jumper wire to other punch down blocks. Punch down blocks have slots that terminate cable conductors using IDC style terminations. One wire is terminated in each slot. Punch down blocks are usually designed to terminate cable conductors in 25-pair designation.

Patch panels are connecting hardware components that are used to terminate four-pair horizontal cables. Patch panels have a terminating block on the back of the panel for terminating horizontal cable conductors. The front of the panel has eight-position modular ports. Patch panels are usually sold in either 12, 24, 48, or 96 port configurations. Patch panels mount in a standard communications rack. Patch panels are usually mounted in the top of the rack and communications equipment is mounted in the lower part of the rack. Equipment patch cords with modular plugs on the ends are used to connect the patch panel ports to the equipment ports.

CHAPTER 4

Structured Cabling Systems

The communication cabling systems found in both commercial and residential buildings are planned and organized to support different communications systems and user applications. These cabling systems are also designed to support an average life cycle of ten years. Communication cabling systems are called structured cabling systems.

The concept of structured or organized cabling systems was to design a cabling system that would support a multiproduct and multivendor environment. This environment characterizes most commercial buildings. A planned and organized cabling system will cost less to install initially and cost less to maintain over the life of the system. Unplanned cabling systems tend to cost more to install and maintain over the life of the cabling system. A planned cabling system will be more reliable because it will be designed to support the user applications running in the building. It will tend to be less disruptive to the building occupant because the cabling system does not need to be continually upgraded. The process of upgrading a cabling system causes many disruptions due to the large amount of construction required to install and support communication cabling systems.

STRUCTURED CABLING SYSTEM DEFINITION

The term *structured cabling system* is a generic communication wiring scheme that is installed in a single building or cluster of buildings that is capable of supporting all forms of communication systems including: telephone systems, host computer systems, local area networks, video systems, and imaging systems (see Figure 4-1). As a result, structured cabling systems are sometimes referred to as either universal cabling systems or premises distribution systems.

A structured cabling system is a standards-based method of engineering and installing an entire communications cabling system. The communication cable system would include all forms of communication cabling, cable pathways, communication ground and bonding systems, supporting structures, and building spaces. In short, it describes all elements of a communication cabling system required to install, support, and maintain the system.

A structured cabling system is based on a hierarchy of independent cabling links or subsystems built in a physical star topology. Each subsystem is independent but designed to be interconnected to the other subsystems. This scheme enables each portion of a structured cabling system to be designed to meet the specific needs of the building and the users in the building. Each subsystem can also be upgraded and changed without affecting the other cabling subsystems. This scheme also provides specific guidelines for each subsystem with respect to what media types are supported and what distances can be supported. As a result, a structured cabling system provides the flexibility of application independence and supports multiple logical topologies.

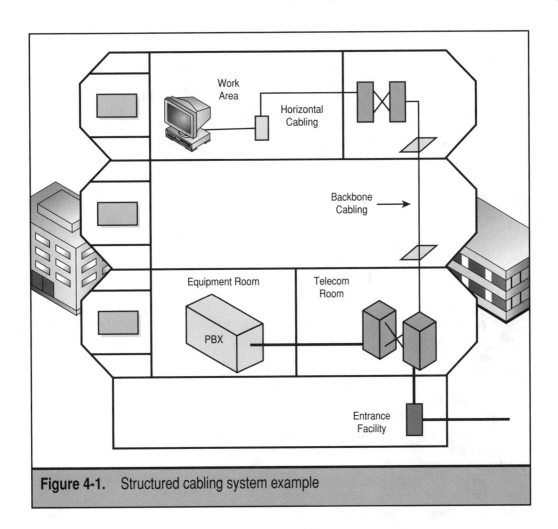

Figure 4-1.   Structured cabling system example

STRUCTURED CABLING SYSTEM HISTORY

The concept of structured cabling systems is relatively recent (see Figure 4-2). Before 1985, there was no standardization of structured cabling systems. Before 1985, the Bell Company handled all of the cabling needs for telephones. Voice networks used standard unshielded twisted-pair (UTP) cable as the transmission medium. Companies that had mainframe computers relied on the vendor of the mainframe computer to install and maintain the cabling required for that computer system.

Data networks, such as Ethernet, Token Ring, and Mainframe Computer Systems, used a variety of transmission media. This media could be: UTP cable, STP cable, or fiber optic cable. Different data systems called for different types of cable to be used. As a result, when data systems changed, so did the cable.

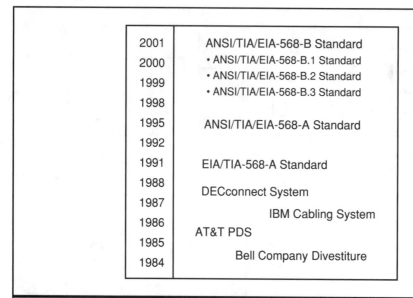

2001	ANSI/TIA/EIA-568-B Standard
2000	• ANSI/TIA/EIA-568-B.1 Standard
1999	• ANSI/TIA/EIA-568-B.2 Standard
	• ANSI/TIA/EIA-568-B.3 Standard
1998	
1995	ANSI/TIA/EIA-568-A Standard
1992	
1991	EIA/TIA-568-A Standard
1988	DECconnect System
1987	
	IBM Cabling System
1986	AT&T PDS
1985	
1984	Bell Company Divestiture

Figure 4-2.   Structured cabling systems history

Each type of communications system requires communications cabling for the system to share information and work correctly. Historically, each type of communications system required a different type of cable and required that the cable be installed in a different configuration. During the 1980s, vendors such as IBM, AT&T, and DEC developed their own structured cabling systems to address this problem.

The practice of using different cable types for each communication system created many problems for the groups responsible for designing, installing, and maintaining these systems. The communications industry needed a specification for a single type of cabling system that could support different communications systems and was vendor independent. Most companies had the problem of needing to maintain two different cabling systems: one for their voice system and one for their data system. The solution to this problem was to implement a single cabling system that was capable of supporting both voice and data systems.

In 1985, it was agreed that standards were required for both voice and data cabling systems. The Electronic Industries Association (EIA) was assigned the task of developing cabling standards for both commercial and residential buildings. In 1991, the Telecommunications Industry Association took over the development of all communication cabling standards. The result of this effort has been the development and standardization of the EIA/TIA-568 cabling standard.

The EIA/TIA-568 cabling standard was the first version of a structured cabling standard for commercial buildings. It was released and published in 1991. This standard was submitted to the American National Standards Institute, known as ANSI, to become a U.S. standard. It was then known as the ANSI/EIA/TIA-568 standard. In 1995, the ANSI/TIA/EIA-568 standard was updated; the revised version of the standard is known as the ANSI/TIA/EIA-568-A standard. In 2001, the ANSI/TIA/EIA-568-A is once again being updated to address technology changes that have taken place since 1995. The revised standard will be generically referred to as the ANSI/TIA/EIA-568-B standard.

The ANSI/TIA/EIA-568-B standard will actually consist of three different standards. Each of the three parts will define structured cabling systems.

▼   **ANSI/TIA/EIA-568-B.1**   Commercial building telecommunications cabling standard—generic requirements

■   **ANSI/TIA/EIA-568-B.2**   Commercial building telecommunications cabling standard—connecting hardware and components

▲   **ANSI/TIA/EIA-568-B.3**   Commercial building telecommunications cabling standard—optical fiber cabling

STRUCTURED CABLING SUBSYSTEMS

A structured cabling system is based on a concept of modular subsystems that are independent yet work together to create a complete building cabling system (see Figure 4-3). Each subsystem of a structured cabling system is designed and installed independently of the other cabling subsystems. Then all of the structured cabling systems are interconnected and work together as a single cabling system. This approach facilitates growth and flexibility as changes to one subsystem do not affect the others.

The subsystems of a structured cabling subsystem are

▼   Work area subsystem

■   Horizontal subsystem

■   Backbone subsystem

■   Telecommunications room (TR)

■   Equipment room (ER)

▲   Entrance facility (EF)

Work Area Subsystem

The *work area* is the space within a building where communication system users interact with communications equipment (see Figure 4-4). The work area is the building space designated for workers to sit during a typical business day. A work area may be a cubicle or an office. In either case, the work area usually consists of a desk, bookcases, computers, and communication devices such as phones or faxes.

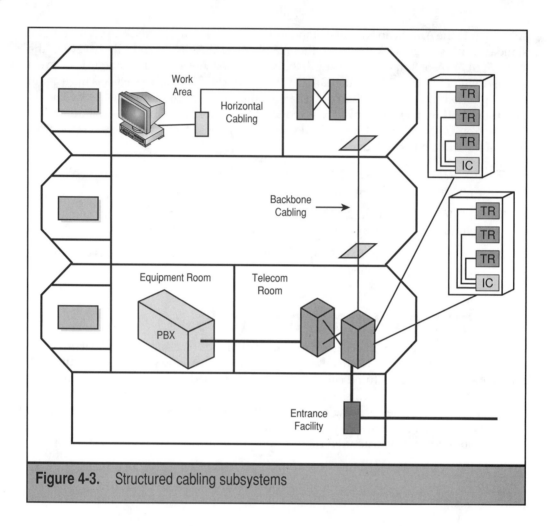

Figure 4-3. Structured cabling subsystems

The work area subsystem is the portion of the structured cabling system that connects directly to the communications equipment. It usually consists of a modular cord that connects to the telecommunications outlet. This cable provides a physical connection for the computers and communication devices residing in the work area to the horizontal cabling. The work area cabling subsystem may also include a variety of application specific hardware whose function is to enable the specialized equipment of send and receive signals over the communication cabling installed to the work area location.

Work Area Cabling

The *work area cabling* is defined as the cabling from the telecommunications outlet/connector to the station equipment. It includes a variety of hardware whose function is to connect a customer phone, PC, or other user device to the telecommunications outlet/connector.

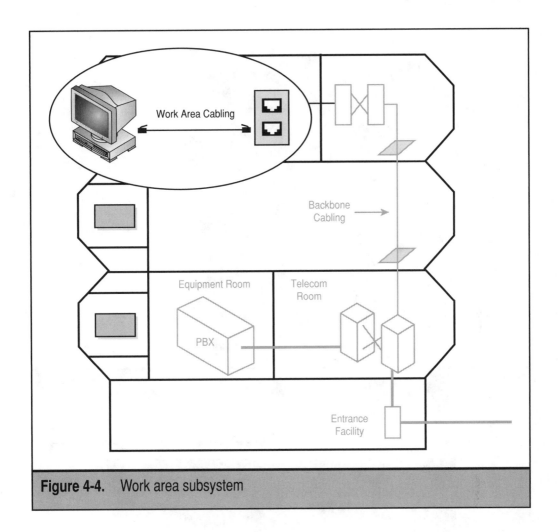

Figure 4-4. Work area subsystem

Work area cabling is nonpermanent cabling and is designed to be easy to change or replace. Modular plugs are used to terminate work area cable. These eight-position plugs are designed to fit into a telecommunications outlet that is used to terminate copper horizontal cables. The modular work area cords must be made with identical connectors on both ends (see Figure 4-5). This will keep the wiring continuity consistent from one end of the cable to the other.

Work area cables must always be made using stranded twisted-pair cable (see Figure 4-6). The stranded cable enables work area cables to be flexible, which is essential in the work area environment. Twisted-pair line cords will give the cable a round appearance. The twisted pairs will match the construction of copper horizontal cables that are also constructed using twisted-pair construction.

Flat and untwisted cable should never be used for work area cabling (see Figure 4-7). These cables do not support the differential signaling used by high-speed LAN

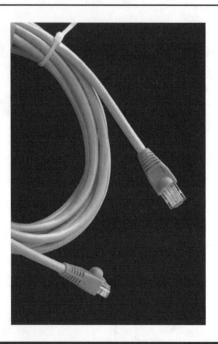

Figure 4-5.   Work area line cord

Figure 4-6.   Twisted-pair cable example

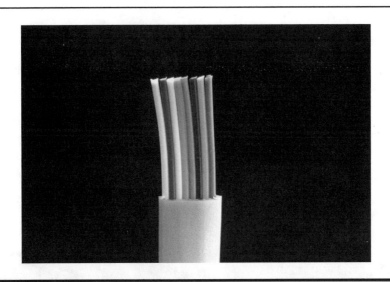

Figure 4-7.   Flat untwisted cable example

technologies. Flat, untwisted-pair cables were traditionally used for voice or low-speed data connections. High-speed LAN connections require twisted-pair cable construction. Twisted-pair line cords will cause less signal attenuation and signaling errors.

Work Area Cabling Distances

Work area cables are designed to be short, flexible cables. The maximum length for these cables is considered to be 5 m (16 ft.) (see Figure 4-8). However, the horizontal channel provides a provision of up to 10 m (33 ft.) for the combined length of the work area and closet patch cables or jumpers. The length of the work area cables can be increased if the length of the closet equipment or jumper cables are decreased.

Horizontal Cabling Subsystem

The ANSI/TIA/EIA-568-A and ANSI/TIA/EIA-568-B.1 standards define the *horizontal subsystem* as: "The horizontal subsystem is the portion of a structured cabling system that extends from the work area telecommunications outlet/connector to the horizontal cross-connect in the telecommunications closet."

The horizontal subsystem comes by its name based on the method of installing cables from the telecommunications closet to the telecommunications outlet (see Figure 4-9). Cables are installed horizontally in the cable pathways. These pathways run along the floor or in the ceiling of the building floors.

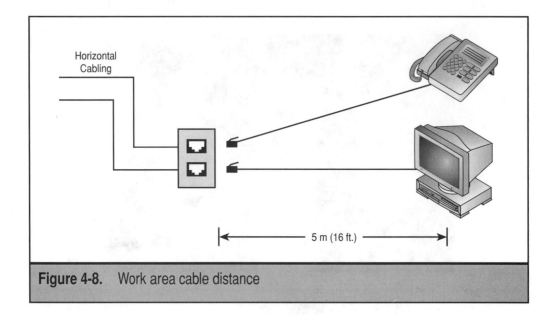

Figure 4-8.   Work area cable distance

The horizontal subsystem includes the following cabling components:

▼   Horizontal cable

■   Telecommunications outlet/connector

■   Horizontal cross-connect (HC) in the telecommunications closet

■   Equipment patch cords or jumper cables in the closet

▲   May also include an optional transition point (TP) or consolidation point connector

Some communication systems require that special adapters or other electrical components be installed for system devices to work correctly over the installed horizontal media. Industry cabling standards require that all application-specific devices must not be installed in the horizontal subsystem. If any special adapters or electronic devices are required, they must only be installed in the work area subsystem. These devices must always be external to the telecommunications outlet. This practice will guarantee that the special adapter will move with the communication device and keep the horizontal subsystem cabling the same throughout the building.

The horizontal subsystem must be designed to support a large number of applications. The following is a list of common user applications that the horizontal subsystem must support:

▼   Voice service

■   Premises switching equipment

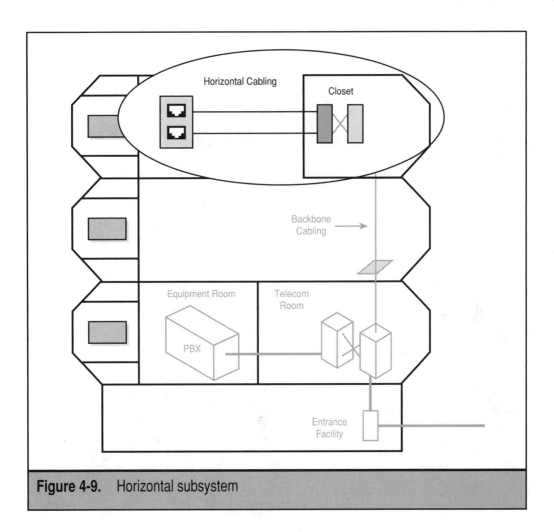

Figure 4-9. Horizontal subsystem

■ Data services

■ Local area networks

■ Video service

▲ Building signaling and automation systems

In addition to supporting existing communication services, the horizontal subsystem must be designed to accommodate future services and equipment moves, adds, and changes. Once installed, the horizontal cabling subsystem is less accessible than any other cabling subsystem. As a result, the horizontal subsystem cabling must be designed to reduce maintenance and cabling relocation costs.

Horizontal Cabling Topology

Industry cabling standards require that all cables installed in the horizontal cabling sub-system be installed in a physical star topology (see Figure 4-10). The horizontal cables connect each telecommunications outlet/connect in the work area locations to a HC located in a telecommunications closet. The telecommunications closet must be located on the same floor as the work areas that are being supported.

The horizontal cabling subsystem may contain an optional TP between the termination in the telecommunications closet and the telecommunications outlet/connector in the work area. The optional TP is necessary if flat, undercarpet cable is used in the work area. The round, horizontal cable is transitioned to flat undercarpet cable at this point in the horizontal cabling run. A second option is to use a consolidation point in the horizontal cabling run as a replacement to using a TP. The consolidation point is used in open office cabling environments.

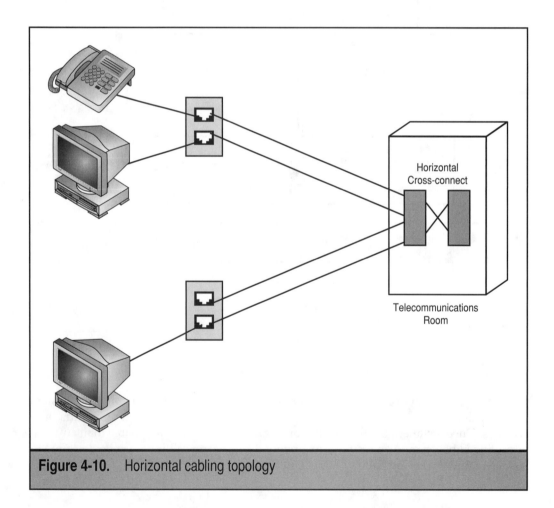

Figure 4-10.   Horizontal cabling topology

CAUTION: Each horizontal cabling run can support only one TP or consolidation point. Both cannot be used in the same horizontal cabling run.

The horizontal cabling must also be free of any splices or cable extensions. Each cabling run must be one continuous length of cable. Splice or cable extensions will add loss and cause signal reflections on the cabling run. Bridged taps or multiple appearance of the same cable pair are not allowed in horizontal cables. This practice will create impedance mismatches and cause signal reflections. In addition, using pairs from a horizontal cable to terminate multiple telecommunications outlets is also not allowed. A new horizontal cable must be installed to each telecommunications outlet.

Horizontal Cabling Distances

All cables installed in the horizontal cabling subsystem must be limited to a maximum of 90 m (295 ft.). This distance is measured from the termination of the cable on the HC in the telecommunications closet to the termination of the cable on the telecommunications outlet/connector (see Figure 4-11). This distance is independent of the media type installed in the horizontal subsystem.

Each horizontal cabling channel supports a 10 m (33 ft.) provision for patch cables or cross-connect jumpers in the closet and work area (see Figure 4-12). The work area line cords must be limited to a maximum of 5 m (16 ft.). The patch cords or cross-connect jumpers used in the closet must also be limited to a maximum of 5 m (16 ft.). The horizontal cabling channel includes the 90 m (295 ft.) of horizontal cable plus 10 m (33 ft.) of patch cords. Therefore, the maximum length of the horizontal cabling channel is 100 m (328 ft.).

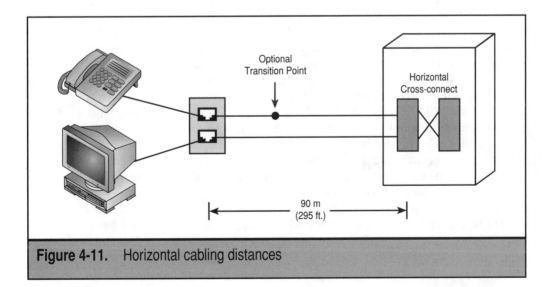

Figure 4-11. Horizontal cabling distances

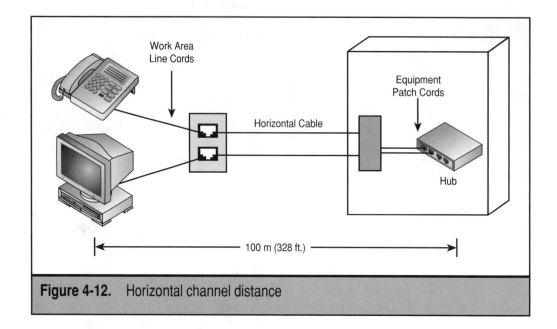

Figure 4-12. Horizontal channel distance

Horizontal Cabling Subsystem Recognized Cables

Industry cabling standards limit the types of cables that are allowed to be installed in the horizontal cabling subsystem. Each country has their own standard for structured cabling systems. Different structured cabling standards recognize different media types (see Figure 4-13). The standard for structured cabling systems used in the United States is the ANSI/TIA/EIA-568 standard. This standard was originally published in 1991. The standard was updated in 1995 and called the ANSI/TIA/EIA-568-A standard. The standard is scheduled to be updated in 2001 and called the ANSI/TIA/EIA-568-B standard.

The ANSI/TIA/EIA-568-B standard will be organized into three sections. The first section is the ANSI/TIA/EIA-568-B.1 standard. This document defines structured cabling standards, structured cabling subsystems, and cable specifications. The second section is the ANSI/TIA/EIA-568-B.2 standard. This document defines connecting hardware components and component performance. It also defines patch cord, equipment cords, and jumper cable performance specifications. The third section is the ANSI/TIA/EIA-568-B.3 standard. This document defines optical fiber cables and connecting hardware performance specifications. Together, all three documents are called the ANSI/TIA/EIA-568-B standard. This document will replace the ANSI/TIA/EIA-568-A standard as the recognized standard for structured cabling systems in the United States.

The recognized media types for the ANSI/TIA/EIA-568-B.1 standard are

▼ Four-pair, 100-ohm UTP or ScTP cable

■ Two or more strand 50/125 μm multimode optical fiber cable

▲ Two or more strand 62.5/125 μm multimode optical fiber cable

Figure 4-13.   Horizontal cable recognized media

 NOTE: The ANSI/TIA/EIA-568-A standard recognized 150-ohm STP-A cable as an allowed media type for the horizontal subsystem. The ANSI/TIA/EIA-568-B.1 standard recognizes this media for existing cabling installations but does not recommend this media for new installations.

Bundled and hybrid cables are recognized as acceptable for the horizontal subsystem provided that the media in the bundle or hybrid cables are one of the recognized media listed previously. In addition, hybrid cables must meet or exceed the transmission specifications for each media type and exceed the NEXT performance specifications by a minimum of 3 dB.

Backbone Cabling Subsystem

The *backbone cabling subsystem* is the cabling that provides the interconnection between telecommunications closets, ERs, and building EF spaces in a commercial building (see Figure 4-14). The backbone cabling subsystem also includes the cables between buildings in a campus environment.

The backbone cabling subsystem includes the following elements:

▼   Backbone cables

■   Intermediate and main cross-connections

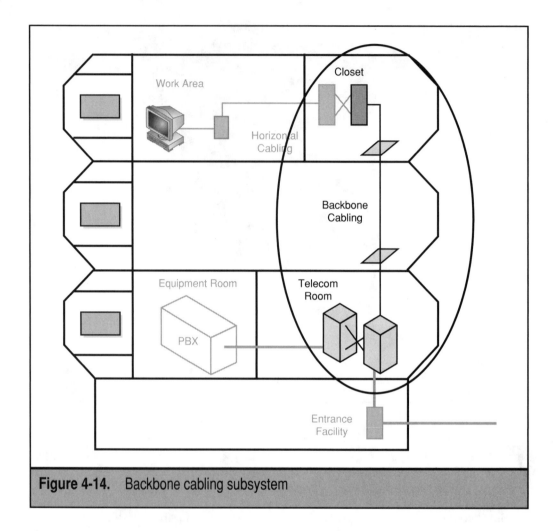

Figure 4-14. Backbone cabling subsystem

■ Punch blocks or other mechanical termination devices

▲ Patch cords or jumper cables used for backbone cross-connections

The backbone cabling subsystem is considered the most permanent cabling subsystem in the structured cabling system. The backbone cabling subsystem must be designed to support the current and future needs of the building it serves for three to ten years. This may include one or more planning periods for communication systems and cabling. The backbone cabling must accommodate growth and changes to the building communication systems without requiring the installation of new cables.

Backbone Cabling Subsystem Topology

Industry cabling standards require that all cables installed in the backbone cabling subsystem be installed in a hierarchical star topology (see Figure 4-15). A hierarchical star topology is created when each HC in a telecommunications closet is cabled either directly to a main cross-connect (MC) or to an intermediate cross-connect (IC) and then to an MC. The hierarchical star topology must be limited to a maximum of two hierarchical levels from the HC to the MC. This means that the path between any two HCs must pass through than three or fewer backbone cross-connects.

Backbone Cabling Subsystem Recognized Cables

Multiple types of media are recognized in the backbone cabling subsystem by industry cabling standards due to the wide range of applications that must be supported by this cabling subsystem (see Figure 4-16). The ANSI/TIA/EIA-568-B standard recognizes the following media types for use in the backbone cabling subsystem either individually or in combination:

▼ 100-ohm, twisted-pair cable

■ 50/125 µm multimode optical fiber cable

■ 62.5/125 µm multimode optical fiber cable

▲ Singlemode optical fiber cable

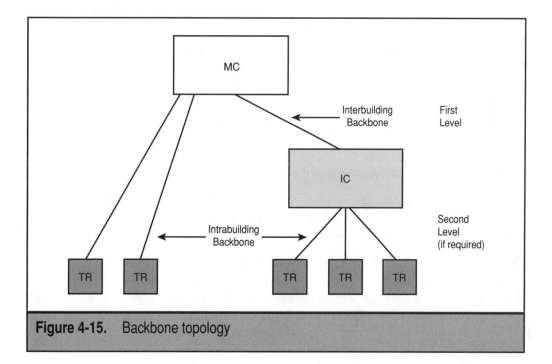

Figure 4-15.   Backbone topology

Figure 4-16. Backbone cabling recognized media

The exact media types selected for the backbone cabling subsystem will depend on the following considerations:

▼ The communication applications that must be supported

■ The required flexibility for the communications systems

■ The required useful life of the backbone media

■ The building or campus size

▲ The current and future size of the user population

For some backbone cabling projects, some or all of the previous information may not be known. In these situations, a worst case scenario can be used based on projected applications, required flexibility, useful life, and size of the user population.

Backbone Cabling Subsystem Distances

The maximum distances for the backbone cabling subsystem are depended on the media selected. The maximum distances for each media defined in the ANSI/TIA/EIA-568-B.1 standard are shown in Table 4-1.

The maximum backbone cabling system distances for each media from the HC to the IC can be adjusted based on the building size and maximum closet spacing distances.

Media Type	A HC-to MC-Distance	B HC-to-IC Distance	C IC-to-MC Distance
100-ohm, twisted-pair cable	800 m (2,624 ft.)	300 m (980 ft.)	500 m (1,640 ft.)
50/125 multimode fiber cable	2,000 m (6,560 ft.)	300 m (980 ft.)	1,700 m (5,575 ft.)
62.5/125 multi-mode fiber cable	2,000 m (6,560 ft.)	300 m (980 ft.)	1,700 m (5,575 ft.)
Singlemode optical fiber cable	3,000 m (9,840 ft.)	300 m (980 ft.)	2,700 m (8,855 ft.)

Table 4-1. Backbone Cabling Distances

When the maximum HC-to-IC distances that must be supported are less than the maximum distances shown in column B, the excess distance can be applied to the maximum distance from the IC to MC column C, if necessary. However, the total distance from the HC to the MC must never exceed the maximum distance in column A in Table 4-1.

Main Cross-Connect (MC) to Entrance Facility (EF) Distance   The distance from the MC in a building or campus and the EF must be included in the maximum distances for each media type. This distance is considered to be part of the backbone cabling subsystem. As a result, it is desirable to locate the MC as close as possible to the building entrance location. This will minimize this backbone cabling distance.

Telecommunications Rooms (TRs)

A *telecommunications room* (TR), also known as a telecommunications closet, is a space within a building that is used to terminate horizontal and backbone cables (see Figure 4-17). The primary function of this building space is to have a dedicated space to install cable termination hardware and communications equipment.

TRs are generally considered to be a floor serving building space. One TR is designed to serve up to 1,000 sq. m (10,000 sq. ft.) of usable floor space. Each commercial building must have at least one TR, and buildings with multiple floors must have one TR per floor. All horizontal cables that are installed to work area locations must be terminated in a TR located on the same floor.

The TR is also the location where horizontal cables are cross-connected to backbone cables. The cross-connections can be made using either flexible patch cables or jumper cables. This provides a means to extend both voice and data services from a centralized area to each work area location that needs the service. The cable termination hardware and cross-connect cables are collectively referred to as horizontal cross-connections.

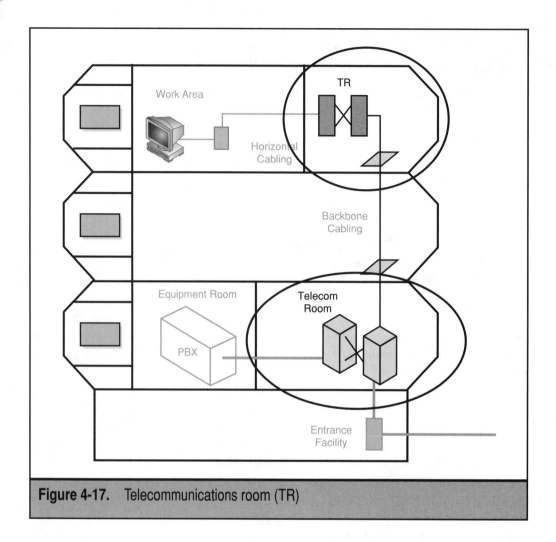

Figure 4-17.   Telecommunications room (TR)

The TR may also contain the IC or MC to support different portions of the backbone cabling subsystem. The TR can also be used for a backbone to backbone cross-connections. This provides a means to connect different TR together. Backbone to backbone cross-connections enable TRs to be tied together in a ring, bus, or tree configuration, if required by a communication system.

The TR is a designated and controlled area for housing communications equipment (see Figure 4-18). The TR may also need to support other building services to support the communication equipment, such as power, power conditioning/protection, heating, ventilating, air conditioning (HVAC), and grounding/bonding systems. This controlled area must be a dedicated space used for mounting and supporting all of the cables and cabling

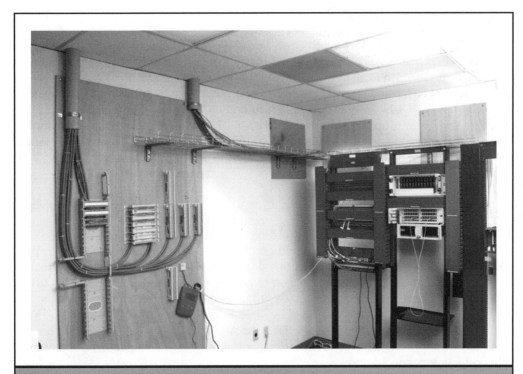

Figure 4-18. Telecommunications room (TR) example

structures necessary to provide connectivity to the communication equipment. Some of the cabling structures used in a TR include

▼ Communication racks

■ Ladder racks

■ Wire management panels (vertical and horizontal)

■ D-ring and other cable organization devices

▲ Slots and sleeves for routing cables through the TR

The TR may also contain a service provider demarcation point. This may include either passive cabling components or active equipment. These devices would normally be found in either the EF or the ER. In some cases, circumstances may require that the demarcation devices be installed in a TR.

TR LOCATION

The TR should always be located as close a possible to the center of the building or the work areas being served. This practice will limit the length of horizontal cables and limit the maximum length to 90 m (295 ft.) from the TR. Industry cabling standards also require that a TR be located on the same floor as the work area locations that it must serve.

TRs must always be accessible from a common hallway or other common area if the space is shared by multiple tenants in a multitenants in a commercial building. TRs should be vertically stacked in a multistory commercial building. This minimized cable distances when a cable must be run between two closets in the building.

TR SIZING

TRs are sized and provisioned according to the specifications defined in the ANSI/TIA/EIA-569-A standard for building pathways and spaces. he ANSI/TIA/EIA-569-A standard defines the size of TRs based on the usable square footage that must be served. The size specifications are based on providing telecommunications cabling to one individual work area per 10 sq. m (100 sq. ft.) of usable floor space. The actual size of a TR is based on the usable space defined in Table 4-2.

The size specifications defined for a TR is the ANSI/TIA/EIA-569-A standard should be capable of supporting the communication equipment, cable termination hardware, and other cable-supporting devices.

In an existing building or for a cabling retrofit project, the size of a TR may be smaller than the size recommended for new cable installations. If the size of the closet cannot be altered to meet the recommended size requirements, the minimum size of 1.2 m (4 ft.) deep by 1.8 m (6 ft.) wide, and 2.6 m (8.5 ft.) high must be provisioned for each 240 work area locations to be served.

If the usable floor space served is:	The interior dimensions of the TR must be:
500 sq. m (5,000 sq. ft.) or less	3.0 m by 2.4 m (10 by 8 ft.)
Larger than 500 sq. m and less than or equal to 800 sq. m (>5,000 to 8,000 sq. ft.)	3.0 m by 2.7 m (10 by 9 ft.)
Larger than 800 sq. m and less than or equal to 1,000 sq. m (>8,000 to 10,000 sq. ft.)	3.0 m by 3.4 m (10 by 11 ft.)

Table 4-2.   Telecommunications Room (TR) Sizing

Equipment Room (ER)

An *equipment room* (ER) is a special type of TR (see Figure 4-19). This is a special space in a building that is required to house and support common and/or special communications or data equipment. The function of an ER is to provide a controlled environment required by this complex and fragile equipment.

The ER is different than a TR. An ER is considered to serve an entire building or campus of buildings. A TR is considered to serve only a single floor or a portion of a single floor in a large commercial building. The ER must also support all the cables and cable

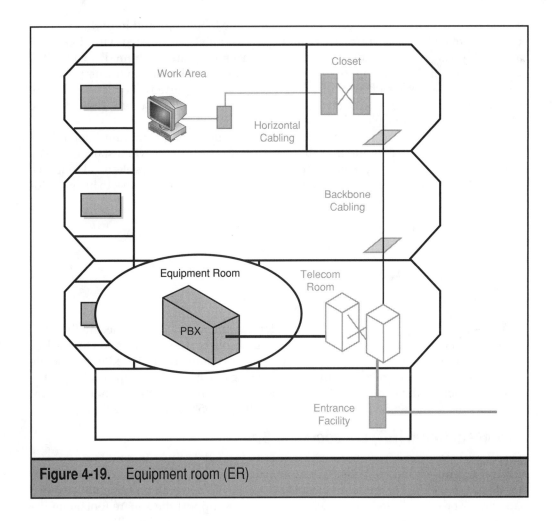

Figure 4-19.   Equipment room (ER)

pathways that are required to provided connectivity within the building and between buildings on a campus. ERs typically contain the following elements:

▼ Large communication and data equipment

■ Cable termination devices

■ Interbuilding and intrabuilding cable pathways

▲ Electrical protection devices required for the communication and data equipment

The ER in a building has special requirements due to the type and importance of the equipment that it must support. This building space must be designed with floors that can handle greater weight loads. It must also have a temperature and humidity controlled environment. This building space is usually large and complex due to the nature of the function that they serve and the equipment that must be supported. The ER is vital to the smooth operation for both voice and data systems for the building users. Therefore, the ER must be versatile, reliable, and professionally designed.

The ER must have the entire space dedicated to supporting communication equipment, communication cable, and the cable-supporting structures. Never install other non-communication types of equipment in the ER. Building services, such as electrical conduits, air ducts, or water pipes, must not pass through the ER. It is unacceptable to have the ER share space with or support the following functions:

▼ Electrical equipment or wiring

■ Mechanical equipment

■ Janitorial supplies

▲ Storage requirements

The ER must support all the communication cabling required to connect to the communication and data equipment. The ER will usually be the designed location for the MC or the IC in the backbone cabling hierarchy. This space must be designed to handle the large amount of cross-connections from the building or campus backbone cabling to the communication or data equipment ports. The ER must also support the horizontal cabling required for all work area locations within 90 m (295 ft.) of this building space.

Equipment Room (ER) Location and Size

The ER must be placed in a secure and centrally located position in a building or on a campus. A centrally located room will minimize the length of backbone cables to other closets and to the EF. The location selected must have access to all building and campus pathways. The site selected must be large enough to support the square footage of the building or all buildings on the campus and the user population. The ER must be located in close proximity to electrical service and protected from sources of electromagnetic interference.

The ER must never be located in a building space or environment that is subject to the following:

▼ Water or moisture invading the space

■ Excessive humidity

■ Excessive heat

▲ Any corrosive agents or gases that can harm equipment

The size of the ER is calculated based on the following factors:

▼ The size and amount of equipment that must be installed (current and future)

■ The size of the building or buildings that must be supported

▲ The growth requirements for the room

The ER must maintain strict temperature and humidity control to avoid damaging the communication and data devices. This requires having dedicated HVAC equipment or access to the main HVAC delivery system for the building in this room. It is also advisable to have a system that provides both dust and contamination control as well. This typical operating environment for the ER is shown in Table 4-3.

Entrance Facilities (EFs)

All of the communication cabling and all of the communication systems in a building must be connected to other cables. The EF is usually where the service providers, such as the telephone company, bring their cables into a building (see Figure 4-20). These cables provide services, such as dial tone, necessary for phone service in the building.

The EF is a specially designated space in a building usually located in the basement or on the first floor (ground level) where outside plant cables connect to the inside plant premises cabling. The EF usually contains the following cabling elements:

▼ Cables (copper and fiber optic)

■ Connecting hardware

Environmental Control	Operational Range
Temperature range	64 to 75 F° (18 to 24 C°)
Relative humidity	30 to 55%
Heat dissipation	750 to 5,000 BTUs per hour per cabinet

Table 4-3.   Telecommunications Room (TR) Environmental Requirements

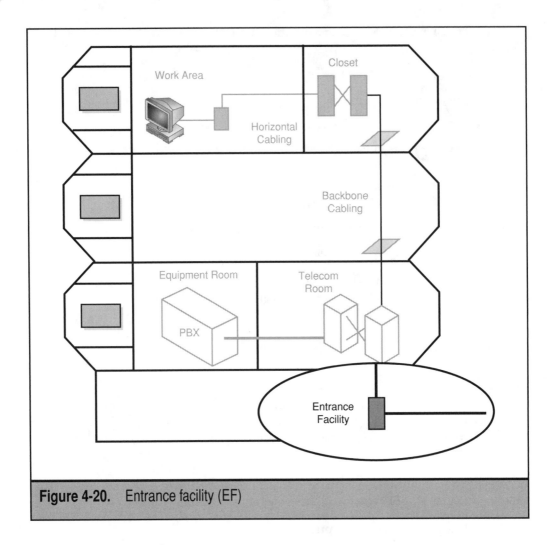

Figure 4-20.   Entrance facility (EF)

- ■ Protection devices
- ■ Grounding hardware
- ▲ Other devices necessary to connect to the outside plant cables

The EF is the building space where the demarcation point is installed. The demarcation point is a prescribed point where the regulated carrier or access providers (phone companies, cable TV companies, and so on) are required to end their service. The demarcation point is mandated by either federal or state regulations. These regulations require that a block be used to terminate the outside plant cables. The inside plant premises cabling is connected to the demarcation block by either a cross-connection or a splice.

There are three common types of entrances used for commercial buildings.

▼ **Underground entrance**   These use a conduit to provide a pathway for outside plant cables to a building.

■ **Buried entrance**   These use a trench or ditch to provide a pathway for outside plant cables to a building.

▲ **Aerial entrance**   These use overhead suspension of the cable to provide a pathway for outside plant cables to a building.

CHAPTER SUMMARY

The communication cabling systems found in both commercial and residential buildings are planned and organized to support different communications systems and user applications. These cabling systems are also designed to support an average life cycle of ten years. Communication cabling systems are called structured cabling systems. The concept of structured, or organized cabling systems, was to design a cabling system that would support a multiproduct and multivendor environment.

The term structured cabling system is a generic communication wiring scheme that is installed in a single building or cluster of buildings that is capable of supporting all forms of communication systems including: telephone systems, host computer systems, local area networks, video systems, and imaging systems. A structured cabling system is based on a hierarchy of independent cabling links or subsystems built in a physical star topology. Each subsystem is independent but designed to be interconnected to the other subsystems. This scheme enables each portion of a structured cabling system to be designed to meet the specific needs of the building and the users in the building. Each subsystem can also be upgraded and changed without affecting the other cabling subsystems. This scheme also provides specific guidelines for each subsystem with respect to what media types are supported and what distances can be supported The EIA/TIA-568 cabling standard was the first version of a structured cabling standard for commercial buildings.

A structured cabling system is based on a concept of modular subsystems that are independent yet work together to create a complete building cabling system. Each subsystem of a structured cabling system is designed and installed independently of the other cabling subsystems. Then all of the structured cabling systems are interconnected and work together as a single cabling system.

The subsystems of a structured cabling subsystem are the work area subsystem, horizontal subsystem, backbone subsystem, telecommunications room (TR), equipment room (ER), and entrance facility (EF). The work area cabling is defined as the cabling from the telecommunications outlet/connector to the station equipment. Work area cables are designed to be short, flexible cables. The maximum length for these cables is considered to be 5 m (16 ft.). The horizontal subsystem describes the cable installed from the work area to the TR. Industry cabling standards require that all cables installed in the horizontal cabling subsystem be installed in a physical star topology. All cables installed in the horizontal cabling subsystem must be limited to a maximum of 90 m (295 ft.).

The backbone cabling subsystem is the cabling that provides the interconnection between telecommunications closets, ERs, and building EF spaces in a commercial building. The backbone cabling subsystem also includes the cables between buildings in a campus environment. Industry cabling standards require that all cables installed in the backbone cabling subsystem be installed in a hierarchical star topology. The maximum distances for the backbone cabling subsystem are depended on the media selected.

A TR, also known as a telecommunications closet, is a space within a building that is used to terminate horizontal and backbone cables. The primary function of this building space is to have a dedicated space to install cable termination hardware and communications equipment. An ER is a special type of TR. This is a special space in a building that is required to house and support common and/or special communications or data equipment. The function of an ER is to provide a controlled environment required by this complex and fragile equipment.

The EF is usually where the service providers, such as the telephone company, bring their cables into a building. These cables provide services, such as dial tone, necessary for phone service in the building. The EF is a specially designated space in a building usually located in the basement or on the first floor (ground level) where outside plant cables connect to the inside plant premises cabling.

CHAPTER 5

Backbone Cabling

The term *backbone cabling* is used to describe the cabling that connects all of the building and campus telecommunications rooms (TRs) together. It also connects all closets to the building entrance facility. The backbone cable provides the transport medium allowing devices in different closets to communicate together.

BACKBONE CABLING DEFINITION

The term backbone has many different meanings. For local area and internetworks, a backbone can be an intermediate network connecting two or more networks together. For communications cabling, it means the cabling connecting the TRs, intermediate cross-connects (ICs), and main cross-connect (MC) together. Backbone communication cabling enables communications signals to travel to the TR; the backbone cabling will provide a path for these signals to travel to other closets in the building or campus of buildings.

BACKBONE CABLING SUBSYSTEM

The *backbone cabling subsystem* is defined by the ANSI/TIA/EIA-568-A and ANSI/TIA/EIA-568-B.1 standards as the portion of the structured cabling system that connects all TRs together in a single building or multiple buildings on a campus.

The backbone cabling subsystem can be made up of copper cables, optical fiber cables, or a combination of the two media types. The backbone cabling subsystem must accommodate many different technologies and user applications that are required to be transmitted between TRs and buildings on a campus. These include the following:

▼   Voice systems and applications

■   Data systems and applications

■   Video systems and applications

■   Local area network (LAN) systems and connections

■   Building automation and control systems and connections

▲   Other building signaling systems that may required in the building

There are many different terms used to describe the backbone cabling subsystem. These include the following:

▼   Backbone cabling

■   Vertical cabling

▲   Riser cabling

The terms vertical and riser cabling are sometimes used because backbone cables are usually installed vertically in a riser shaft to connect TRs together in multistory building. The backbone subsystem includes the backbone cables, backbone pathways that are used to support and distribute backbone cables, the terminating hardware in the TR, grounding and bonding devices, and the cross-connections and/or jumper cables to provide connections to other backbone or horizontal cables in the TR (see Figure 5-1).

The backbone cabling subsystem usually includes less cables than the horizontal cabling subsystem. The cables are usually large pair count UTP cables or multistrand optical fiber cables. Backbone cables are also more accessible once installed compared to horizontal cables. The backbone subsystem must be planned to support both current and future communication systems that will be supported in the building or campus of buildings. It is very important that the backbone cabling subsystem be planned to facilitate growth and accommodate new technologies.

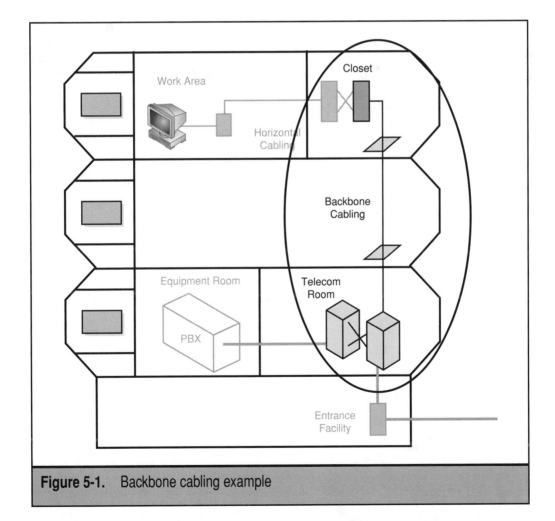

Figure 5-1.   Backbone cabling example

INTRABUILDING AND INTERBUILDING BACKBONE CABLES

The backbone cabling has historically been called riser cabling. This refers to a single multistory building. The riser is the cabling that would connect all of the TRs together. This cable was usually run in a vertical riser shaft from floor to floor. One of the problems with the term riser is that it only referred to the backbone cabling that was run vertically. It didn't address backbone cables that were installed horizontally, connecting multiple closets on the same floor. It also didn't address the cables that were run between buildings in a campus cable environment. Today, the term riser has been replaced with the following terms:

▼   Intrabuilding backbone cable

▲   Interbuilding backbone cable

The term *intrabuilding backbone cable* is used to refer to the backbone cables that connect closets together in a multistory building as well as closets on the same floor (see Figure 5-2). Intrabuilding means the backbone cables installed inside a building. This would include both copper and fiber cables installed either vertically and horizontally inside a building. The maximum distance for intrabuilding backbone cables is 300 m (984 ft.) between closets for all media types.

The term *interbuilding backbone cable* is used to refer to the backbone cables that connect buildings together in a campus environment (see Figure 5-3). Interbuilding means cables that are installed between buildings. This would include both copper and fiber cables installed between one of more building on a single campus. The maximum distance for interbuilding backbone cables are media dependent and will vary based on the type of cable installed as the interbuilding backbone media.

BACKBONE CABLING SYSTEM

The backbone cabling system consists of many elements besides the backbone media. It includes the following cables and cabling components:

▼   Backbone cable pathways

■   Backbone transmission media

■   Backbone support structures

▲   Telecommunications rooms (TRs, ICs, and MCs)

The backbone cable pathways include all of the elements that provide or create a route for the backbone cabling media. Backbone pathways include but are not limited to

▼   Vertical shafts

■   Conduits

■   Raceways

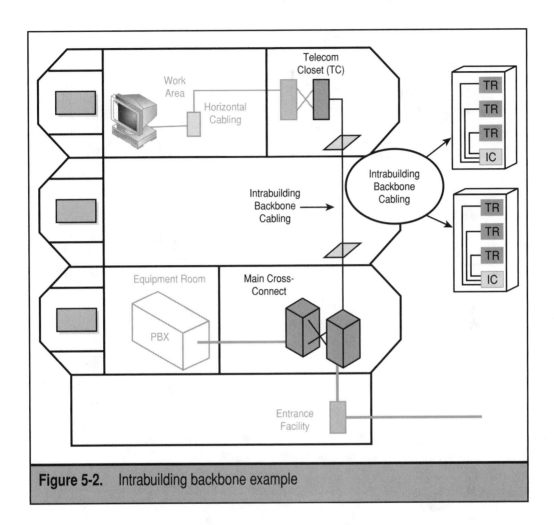

Figure 5-2. Intrabuilding backbone example

- ■ Cable trays
- ▲ Floor penetrations

Backbone transmission media includes the media that is used to transport communications signals between closets. The following are recognized media types for the backbone cabling subsystem for new installations:

- ▼ 100-ohm UTP cable
- ■ 50/125 μm multimode optical fiber cable
- ■ 62.5/125 μm multimode optical fiber cable
- ▲ Singlemode optical fiber cable

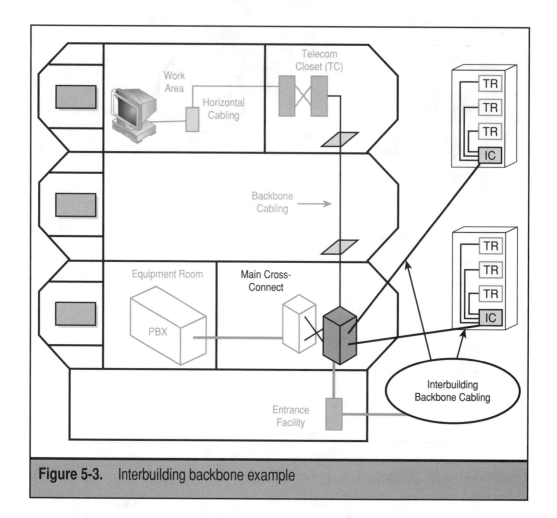

Figure 5-3. Interbuilding backbone example

NOTE: STP-A cables are an allowed backbone media in the ANSI/TIA/EIA-568-A standard. However, STP-A cable is removed as a recommended media for new cable installations in the ANSI/TIA/EIA-568-B.1 standard. It will still be enabled to add cables to an existing installation supporting STP-A cables.

The connecting hardware to terminate the backbone transmission media is also considered to be part of the backbone cabling. The connecting hardware includes any cabling device required to terminate, manage, and cross-connect backbone cable pairs. Backbone connecting hardware includes

▼ Punch down blocks

■ Patch panels

■   Interconnect devices

▲   Cross-connections

BACKBONE PATHWAYS

Backbone pathways are the cabling facilities that are designed to hold, protect, support, and provide access to the backbone cabling media installed between TRs.

Backbone pathways must be designed and installed to support backbone cables for all types of communications systems. Designing and installing the backbone pathway is extremely important because the pathway will always exist even if the backbone cables are changed. A well designed and installed backbone pathway will enable backbone cables to be changed easily with the least amount of disruption to communications systems and cost. Therefore, the backbone pathways must be designed to accommodate cabling growth and changes and minimize system disruptions or outages when the backbone pathways are accessed.

TYPES OF BACKBONE PATHWAYS

There are many different types of backbone pathways used in commercial buildings. Many commercial buildings support two or more different types of backbone distribution pathways due to building layout and construction considerations. The main types of backbone pathways used inside commercial buildings include

▼   **Sleeves**   Sections of conduit that connect vertically aligned closets in a multistory building. Sleeves usually extend from 1 to 4 in. above the floor of a TR and extend from 1 to 4 in., from the TR ceiling (see Figure 5-4). Normally, a trade size 4 conduit (4-in. diameter) is used for sleeves.

■   **Slots**   Square openings in the TR floor to enable cables to pass through the floor. Slots are used over sleeves when large numbers of cables must be installed between closets.

▲   **Conduits**   One or more metal conduits installed as a direct run or to a pull box between two TRs or a TR and an equipment room (ER) in the building (see Figure 5-5).

The main types of backbone pathways used between buildings in a campus are

▼   **Conduits**   One or more metal conduits installed as a direct run or to a pull box between a TR and the MC or IC and the MC between two buildings on a campus (see Figure 5-6). This type of pathway is also called an underground pathway.

■   **Tunnels**   An existing tunnel used for steam can also be used as a cable pathway between building on a campus.

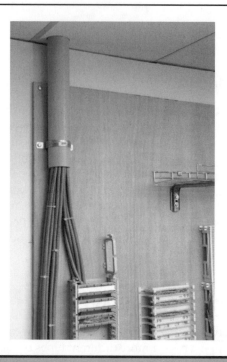

Figure 5-4.   Sleeve backbone pathway

- **Trenches**   This type of pathway would use trenches dug in the ground and would lay the backbone cables directly in the trench without conduits and would cover the trenches with dirt.

- **Aerial**   This type of pathway consists of stringing backbone cables from a building rooftop and poles to support the cable along the entire cable length between buildings.

SIZING BACKBONE PATHWAYS

Backbone pathways must be sized based on the number and size of the backbone cables that will be installed in the pathway. When sizing backbone pathways, the following conditions and variables must be take into account:

- The types of cables that currently need to be supported between TRs or from any TR and an ER

- The size of the cables to be installed

Figure 5-5.   Conduit backbone pathway

Figure 5-6.   Interbuilding backbone conduit

- The growth that must be considered for future cables being installed

- The cabling requirements (current and future) of other communications systems that must be installed

▲ The maximum fill of the pathway based on pathway length and configuration

Backbone pathways will vary in size based on the number and types of cables to be installed. As a general rule, the industry standards and best practices documents recommend a maximum fill ratio of 40 percent of the pathway's capacity. If some information about the number and types of cables to be installed are not known at the time of planning the backbone pathways, the 40 percent fill ratio can be used for planning purposes.

NOTE: Each type of backbone pathway has recommended maximum fill guidelines. Each pathway type has different construction requirements and support different fill levels. To find out the maximum fill levels for each type of pathway, consult the pathway manufacturer.

The number of sleeves or the size of the slots that are used for backbone cable pathways are based on the total usable floor area served by the TR. The minimum number of sleeves that should be installed in a TR is shown in Table 5-1.

The minimum size slots that should be installed in a TR are shown in Table 5-2.

Usable Floor Area Served in sq. m (sq. ft.)	Minimum Number of Sleeve to Install
0 to 5,000 sq. m (0 to 50,000 sq. ft.)	3
5,001 to 10,000 sq. m (50,001 to 100,000 sq. ft.)	4
10,001 to 30,000 sq. m (100,001 to 300,000 sq. ft.)	5 to 8
30,001 to 50,000 sq. m (300,001 to 500,000 sq. ft.)	9 to 12

Table 5-1.   Telecommunications Room Sleeve Numbers

FIRESTOPPING

Backbone cables installed in a sleeve or in a slot must be properly firestopped after the cables are in place. Firestopping is the process of creating a fire-rated barrier that will prevent both fire and smoke from spreading between floors in the event of a fire.

The purpose of firstopping is to reestablish the fire rating of a floor or wall before a penetration was created to enable communication cables to pass through the barrier. Firestopping is the process of installing specialty fire rated materials into penetrations to create a new barrier around the installed backbone cables.

Usable Floor Area Served in sq m (sq. ft.)	Minimum Size Slot in cm (in.)
0 to 25,000 sq. m (0 to 250,000 sq. ft.)	15 by 22.5 cm (6 by 9 in.)
25,001 to 50,000 sq. m (250,001 to 500,000 sq. ft.)	15 by 45 cm (6 by 18 in.)
50,001 to 100,000 sq. m (500,001 to 1,000,000 sq. ft.)	22.5 by 50 cm (9 by 20 in.)
100,001 to 140,000 sq. m (1,000,001 to 1,400,000 sq. ft.)	30 by 50 cm (12 by 20 in.)
140,001 to 200,000 sq. m (1,400,001 to 2,000,000 sq. ft.)	37.5 by 60 cm (15 by 24 in.)

Table 5-2. Telecommunications Room Slot Sizes

BONDING AND GROUNDING

Copper backbone cables and optical fiber backbone cables that have any metallic elements in the cable must be bonded and ground in each TR. Multipair UTP backbone cables have a metallic cable shield (see Figure 5-7). This shield must be bonded to the approved ground in the TR.

The telecommunications grounding busbar (TGB) is the approved ground located in each TR. The TGB is a dedicated ground device that is connected to the telecommunications main grounding busbar (TMGB) with a telecommunications bonding backbone (TBB) (see Figure 5-8). The metallic cable shield should be bonded to the TGB using a #6 AWG insulated conductor.

If the TR does not have a TGB installed, the metallic cable shield should be connected to one of the following approved ground locations:

▼ Power ground on the floor

■ Structural steel

▲ Equipment ground

Optical fiber cables that have metallic strength members should be bonded to the approved ground in the TR just like copper cables. If an optical fiber cable has no metallic cable elements, it does not need to be bonded to an approved ground.

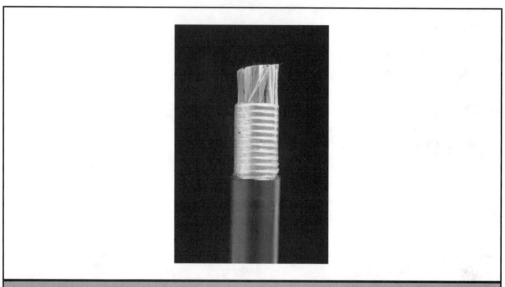

Figure 5-7.   Backbone shield example

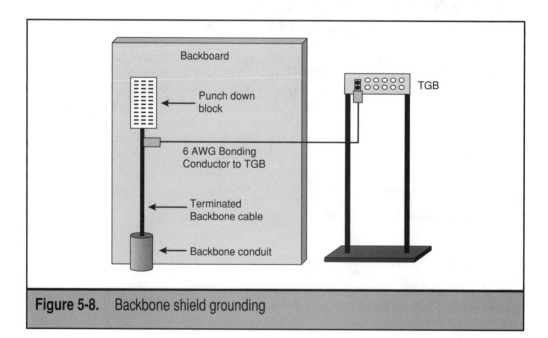

Figure 5-8.   Backbone shield grounding

BACKBONE CABLING TOPOLOGY

A structured cabling system is made up of individual cabling systems connected together. The backbone cabling subsystem is the cabling that ties all of the different cabling systems together to create an integrated cabling configuration.

Industry cabling standards requires that backbone cables be installed in a hierarchical star topology (see Figure 5-9). Each horizontal cross-connect (HC) in a TR is connected either directly to an MC or to an IC and then to the MC. TRs that are cabled directly to the MC use an intrabuilding backbone cable for this connection. TRs that are first connected to an IC use an intrabuilding backbone that uses this connection as well. The IC-to-MC connection uses a interbuilding backbone connection.

The ANSI/TIA/EIA-568-A and ANSI/TIA/EIA-568-B.1 cabling standards require that the hierarchical backbone topology have no more than two hierarchical levels of backbone cross-connects in the backbone cabling subsystem. There should be no more than one backbone cross-connect for a HC to reach the MC. This means that the path between any two HCs shall pass through three or fewer backbone cross-connects.

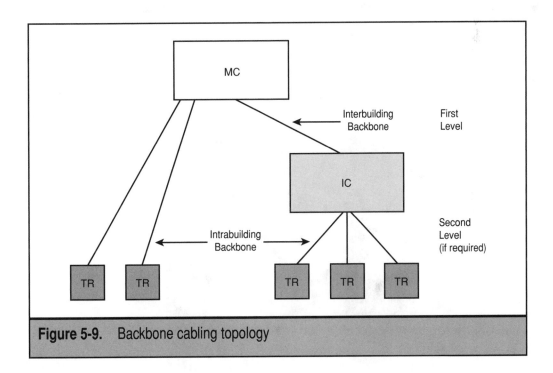

Figure 5-9.   Backbone cabling topology

Industry cabling standards require that backbone cable cross-connects shall only be located in the following building spaces:

▼ Floor TR

■ IC

▲ MC

The hierarchical star topology was selected because it offers the most flexibility for supporting different logical topologies and different communication systems. Both the ANSI/TIA/EIA-568-A and ANSI/TIA/EIA-568-B.1 cabling standards support installing additional cables between TRs and additional electronics to support: bus, ring, or tree topologies. These may be required by some types of specialized communication systems.

RECOGNIZED MEDIA TYPES

The four recognized media types for the backbone cabling subsystem are (see Figure 5-10)

▼ Four-pair, 100-ohm unshielded twisted-pair (UTP) cable

■ Two-strand 62.5/125 μm multimode optical fiber cable

Figure 5-10. Recognized backbone media

■   Two-strand 50/125 μm multimode optical fiber cable

▲   Singlemode optical fiber cable

The ANSI/TIA/EIA-568-A and ANSI/TIA/EIA-568-B.1 cabling standards support installing any recognized media type individually or any combination in the backbone cabling subsystem.

The actual media selected for the backbone subsystem will depend on the factors that will be specific to each building or campus of buildings. Consideration should be given to the following factors before media is selected for a new cable installation:

▼   Required flexibility for the current systems and applications

■   Required useful life of the backbone cabling subsystem

▲   Size of the building and user population

Multipair UTP backbone cables are used mostly for voice and low-speed data applications. If high-speed data applications are required to be supported over the backbone subsystem, it is recommended that a high-performance UTP cable be installed. Multimode optical fiber cables can be used to support voice, low-speed data, and high-speed data applications. Singlemode optical fiber cable is recommended for buildings where the users want to run gigabit networks and support distance in excess of 500 m (1,640 ft.), either within the building or between buildings.

Optical fiber cables used for the backbone subsystem should meet or exceed the performance specifications for both attenuation and bandwidth shown in Tables 5-3 and 5-4.

The minimum performance specifications for 50/125 μm and 62.5 μm multimode optical fiber cables are shown in Table 5-3.

The minimum performance specifications for singlemode optical fiber cable are shown in Table 5-4.

Cable Type	Maximum Attenuation (dB per km)		Minimum Bandwidth (MHz - km)	
	850 nm	1,300 nm	850 nm	1,300 nm
50/125 multimode optical fiber cable	3.5 dB	1.5 dB	500 MHz	500 MHz
62.5/125 multimode optical fiber cable	3.5 dB	1.5 dB	160 MHz	500 MHz

Table 5-3.   Multimode Cable Performance Specifications

Cable Type	Maximum Attenuation (dB per km)		Minimum Bandwidth (MHz - km)	
	1,310 nm	1,550 nm	1,310 nm	1,550 nm
Loose Tube Outside Plant Cable	0.5 dB	0.5 dB	Unlimited	Unlimited
Tight Buffer Inside Plant Cable	1.0 dB	1.0 dB	Unlimited	Unlimited

Table 5-4. Singlemode Cable Performance Specifications

BACKBONE CABLE DISTANCES

The maximum distances supported by backbone cables are media-dependent. The maximum distances defined by the ANSI/TIA/EIA-568-B standard for each allowed backbone media are shown in Tables 5-5, 5-6, 5-7, and 5-8.

The maximum distances for multipair UTP backbone cables are shown in Table 5-5. These distances are shown in Figure 5-11.

The 800 m (2,624 ft.) backbone cable distance supported for UTP cables are for voice or low-speed data applications only. Backbone UTP cable that are intended to be used for higher speed data applications must be limited to a maximum distance of 90 m (295 ft.) between any two TRs.

The maximum distances for 50/125 μm multimode optical fiber backbone cables are shown in Table 5-6. These distances are shown in Figure 5-12.

The maximum distances for 62.5/125 μm multimode optical fiber backbone cables are shown in Table 5-7. These distances are shown in Figure 5-13.

The maximum distances for singlemode optical fiber backbone cables are shown in Table 5-8. These distances are shown in Figure 5-14.

NOTE: The backbone cabling distances referenced in this chapter are based on the specifications published in the ANSI/TIA/EIA-568-B.1 structured cabling standard. These distance values differ slightly from the ANSI/TIA/EIA-568-A standard. The backbone cabling distances specified by the ANSI/TIA/EIA-568-A standard will be phased out and replaced with the specifications in the ANSI/TIA/EIA-568-B.1 standard.

Cable Slack

Each backbone cable run should have a provision for cable slack at both ends of the cable. Planning for cable slack in the cabling run will accommodate any minor cabling changes that may be necessary in the future. This may prevent having to install a new

Location	Distance
HC (FD) to MC (CD)	800 m (2,624 ft.)
HC (FD) to IC (BD)	300 m (984 ft.)
IC (BD) to MC (CD)	500 m (1,640 ft.)

Table 5-5. UTP Backbone Cable Distances

Location	Distance
HC (FD) to MC (CD)	2,000 m (6,560 ft.)
HC (FD) to IC (BD)	300 m (984 ft.)
IC (BD) to MC (CD)	1,700 m (5,575 ft.)

Table 5-6. 50/125 Multimode Backbone Cable Distances

Location	Distance
HC (FD) to MC (CD)	2,000 m (6,560 ft.)
HC (FD) to IC (BD)	300 m (984 ft.)
IC (BD) to MC (CD)	1,700 m (5,575 ft.)

Table 5-7. 62.5/125 Multimode Backbone Cable Distances

Location	Distance
HC (FD) to MC (CD)	3,000 m (9,840 ft.)
HC (FD) to IC (BD)	300 m (984 ft.)
IC (BD) to MC (CD)	2,700 m (8,855 ft.)

Table 5-8. Singlemode Backbone Cable Distances

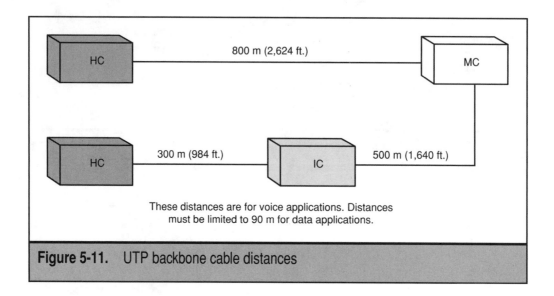

Figure 5-11. UTP backbone cable distances

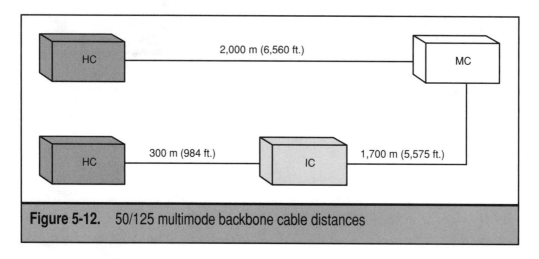

Figure 5-12. 50/125 multimode backbone cable distances

backbone cable if the termination hardware or communication racks must be moved in the TR. The slack on the backbone cable is commonly called a service loop. Service loops are usually stored above the TR. The exact amount of cabling for a backbone service loop will be different for each installation, but the general guidelines the cable slack in the work area and TR are 3 m (10 ft.) at each TR.

The amount of cable slack must be considered as part of the maximum allowable distance for the backbone cable. The maximum allowed length of each backbone cable must include all cable slack and must not exceed maximum distance for the recognized media type.

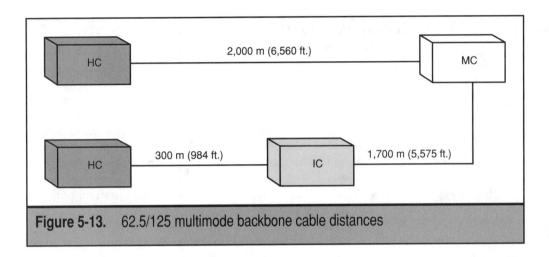

Figure 5-13. 62.5/125 multimode backbone cable distances

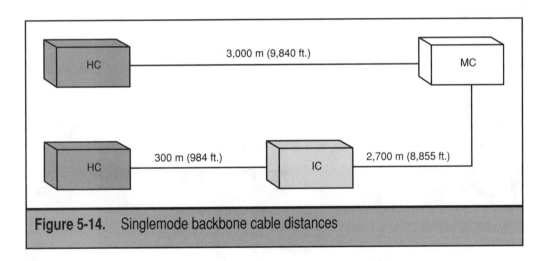

Figure 5-14. Singlemode backbone cable distances

WARNING: If a service loop is planned for a backbone cable, a method for storing the cable slack must also be considered for each installation. Avoid storing the service loop in bundled loops. This can cause interference between the cable pairs for copper cables. The cable loops should be free (un-bundled). Avoid loops that are too small (tight) and violate the minimum bend radius for optical fiber cables. Both practices will degrade the performance of both copper and fiber cables and may cause signaling problems in high-speed networks.

NATIONAL ELECTRICAL CODE (NEC) CABLE MARKINGS

The National Electrical Code (NEC) requires that cables used for communication systems be suitable for the environment where they are to be installed. The NEC defines suitable as being tested as passing fire, smoke, and toxicity tests for specific building environments. Communication cables that are to be installed in a building rise or vertical shaft must be riser rated.

Chapters 7 and 8 of the NEC require that the cables that are installed for the backbone subsystem for buildings in the United States meet or exceed these requirements. Chapter 7 addresses the cable rating for optical fiber cables. Chapter 8 addresses the cable ratings for copper communication cables.

Table 770-50 of the NEC requires that optical cables be tested and marked with the following labels shown in Table 5-9 for each type of optical fiber communications cable to be used in specific environments.

Table 800-50 of the NEC requires that communications cables be tested and marked with the following labels shown in Table 5-10 for each type of communications cable.

Cable Marking	Type
OFNP	Nonconductive optical fiber plenum cable
OFCP	Conductive optical fiber plenum cable
OFNR	Nonconductive optical fiber riser cable
OFCR	Conductive optical fiber riser cable
OFN	Nonconductive optical fiber cable
OFC	Conductive optical fiber cable

Table 5-9. NEC Optical Fiber Cable Markings

Cable Marking	Type
CMP	Communications plenum cable
CMR	Communications rise cable
CM	Communications cable
CMX	Communications cable, limited use
CMUC	Undercarpet communications cable

Table 5-10. NEC Communication Cable Markings

NEC ENTRANCE CABLE GUIDELINES

Interbuilding backbone cables are known as outside plant cables. This is because the cables are run outside from one building to another. Outside plant cables are usually constructed with a water proof gel material inside the cable jacket. This gel material is commonly called icky pick.

Outside plant cables are generally classified as unlisted cables. This is because the cable jackets are made of nonrated materials and do not have a NEC rating, which prevents them from being installed inside a building. In addition, the gel-filling compound is usually a petroleum-based product. This material will catch on fire and spread flames if exposed to a heat or open flames.

In the United States, the NEC permits outside plant cables to be run in a building in a horizontal configuration for a maximum distance of 15.2 m (50 ft). The cables are enabled to extend further than 15. 2 m (50 ft.) as long as the cable is enclosed in a rigid metal conduit that is properly grounded. These cables are never enabled to be run vertically in a building unless they are enclosed in a rigid metal conduit.

CENTRALIZED OPTICAL FIBER CABLING

A traditional structured cabling design typically involves each TR supporting communication equipment, such as LAN hubs. The communication equipment in each closet is then connected together using the backbone cabling subsystem.

An alternative to a communications cabling design in a commercial building is to implement centralized optical fiber cabling. This cabling approach would interconnect the horizontal optical fiber cables using a direct cable pull, interconnect connection, or a hard splice to an optical fiber backbone cable. This cabling configuration enables all communication system electronics to be placed in a centralized location in a commercial building.

A centralized optical fiber cabling configuration takes advantage of the low loss characteristics of optical fiber cable to support distances of up to 300 m (984 ft.). It also can provide a high level of security, flexibility, and manageability. Finally, this cabling approach can save money in communication system electronics.

Centralized optical fiber cabling is addressed in the TIA/EIA TSB-72. This standard defines three design options for implementing a centralized optical fiber cabling system. The allowed design options are a(n)

▼ Direct pull-through

■ Splice

▲ Interconnection

A centralized optical fiber cabling system does not permit the use of patch panels in the TR. A patch panel in the TR would add too much optical loss in the link. The three approaches described previously use low loss interconnections or splice mechanisms that contribute very little loss to the optical fiber link.

Direct Pull-Through

A direct pull-through is the first allowed option for centralized optical fiber cabling. This approach has optical fiber cables pulled from a centralized optical fiber cross-connect location, through the TR, and terminating the cable on a telecommunications outlet/connectors in each work area without any terminations, splices, or interconnections in the TR.

TSB-72 requires that the length of all direct pull-through cables be limited to a maximum distance of 90 m (295 ft.) from the centralized patch panel to the telecommunications outlet in the work area. TSB-72 also requires that direct pull-through cables consist of one continuous sheath. These cables cannot be made up of two cables spliced together. A direct pull-through example is shown Figure 5-15.

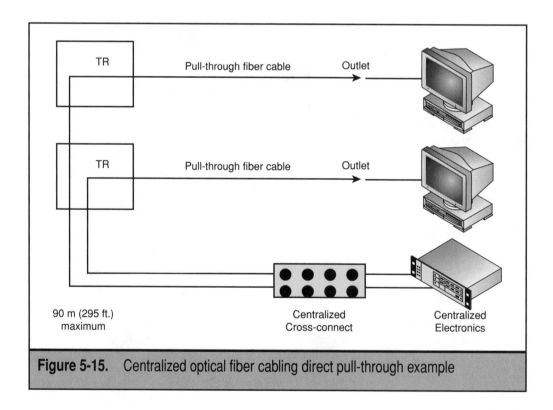

Figure 5-15. Centralized optical fiber cabling direct pull-through example

Splices

A splice in the TR is the second option for centralized optical fiber cabling (see Figure 5-16). This approach would enable a 90 m (295 ft.) horizontal cable to be installed from the TR to each work area location. A backbone cable would be installed from the centralized cross-connect to each TR. The horizontal optical fiber cables would be spliced to the optical fiber backbone cable. The splice can be either a mechanical or fusion splice.

TSB-72 requires that the length of all horizontal cables be limited to a maximum of 90 m (295 ft.) from the TR to each work area. This standard also requires that the combined length of the spliced backbone and horizontal cables be limited to a maximum of 300 m (984 ft.). This distance is measured from the termination at the centralized cross-connect to the termination at the work area outlet.

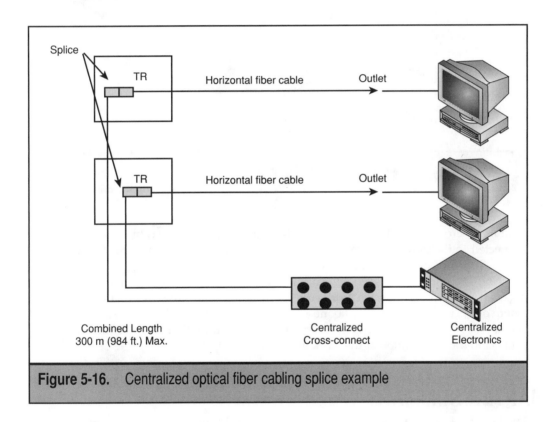

Figure 5-16. Centralized optical fiber cabling splice example

Interconnection

The use of an interconnect is the third option for centralized optical fiber cabling (see Figure 5-17). This approach would enable a 90 m (295 ft.) horizontal cable to be installed from the TR to each work area location. A backbone cable would be installed from the

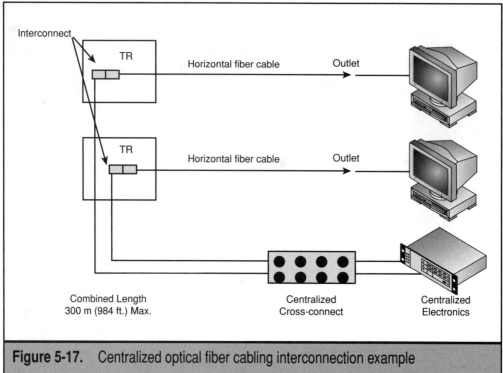

Figure 5-17.   Centralized optical fiber cabling interconnection example

centralized cross-connect to each TR. The horizontal optical fiber cables would be interconnected to the optical fiber backbone cable. The interconnection is the direct connection of two connectors without the use of patch cords.

TSB-72 requires that the length of all horizontal cables be limited to a maximum of 90 m (295 ft.) from the TR to each work area. This standard also requires that the combined length of the interconnected backbone and horizontal cables be limited to a maximum of 300 m (984 ft.). This distance is measured from the termination at the centralized cross-connect to the termination at the work area outlet.

CHAPTER SUMMARY

The term backbone cabling is used to describe the cabling that connects all of the building and campus TRs together. It also connects all closets to the building entrance facility. The backbone cable provides the transport medium allowing devices in different closets to communicate together. The backbone cabling subsystem can be made up of copper cables, optical fiber cables, or a combination of the two media types. The backbone cabling subsystem must accommodate many different technologies and user applications that are required to be transmitted between TRs and buildings on a campus.

The term intrabuilding backbone cable is used to refer to the backbone cables that connect closets together in a multistory building as well as closets on the same floor. Intrabuilding means the backbone cables installed inside a building. This would include both copper and fiber cables installed either vertically and horizontally inside a building. The maximum distance for intrabuilding backbone cables is 300 m (984 ft.) between closets for all media types.

The term interbuilding backbone cable is used to refer to the backbone cables that connect buildings together in a campus environment. Interbuilding means cables that are installed between buildings. This would be both copper and fiber cables installed between one or more buildings on a single campus. The maximum distance for interbuilding backbone cables is media-dependent and will vary based on the type of cable installed as the interbuilding backbone media.

The backbone cabling system consists of many elements besides the backbone media. The backbone cabling subsystem includes: backbone cable pathways, backbone transmission media, backbone support structures, and TRs (TRs, ICs, and MCs).

Backbone pathways are the cabling facilities that are designed to hold, protect, support, and provide access to the backbone cabling media installed between TRs. Backbone pathways must be designed and installed to support backbone cables for all types of communications systems.

Backbone pathways must be sized based on the number and size of the backbone cables that will be installed in the pathway. Backbone pathways will vary in size based on the number and types of cables to be installed. As a general rule, the industry standards and best practices documents recommend a maximum fill ratio of 40 percent of the pathway's capacity.

Backbone cables installed in a sleeve or in a slot must be properly firestopped after the cables are in place. Firestopping is the process of creating a fire-rated barrier that will prevent both fire and smoke from spreading between floors in the event of a fire.

Copper backbone cables and optical fiber backbone cables that have any metallic elements in the cable must be bonded and ground in each TR. The TGB is the approved ground located in each TR. The metallic cable shield should be bonded to the TGB using a #6 AWG insulated conductor.

The backbone cabling subsystem is the cabling that ties all of NEC the different cabling systems together to create an integrated cabling configuration. Industry cabling standards require that backbone cables be installed in a hierarchical star topology. The ANSI/TIA/EIA-568-A and ANSI/TIA/EIA-568-B.1 cabling standards require that the hierarchical backbone topology have no more than two hierarchical levels of backbone cross-connects in the backbone cabling subsystem. There should be no more than one backbone cross-connect for a HC to reach the MC.

The four recognized media types for the backbone cabling subsystem are four-pair, 100-Ohm UTP cable; two-strand 62.5/125 μm multimode optical fiber cable; two-strand 50/125 μm multimode optical fiber cable; and singlemode optical fiber cable. The

ANSI/TIA/EIA-568-A and ANSI/TIA/EIA-568-B.1 cabling standards support installing any recognized media type individually or any combination in the backbone cabling subsystem. The maximum distances supported by backbone cables is media-dependent.

The National Electrical Code (NEC) requires that cables used for communication systems be suitable for the environment where they are to be installed. Chapters 7 and 8 of the NEC require that the cables that are installed for the backbone subsystem for buildings in the United States meet or exceed these requirements. Chapter 7 addresses the cable rating for optical fiber cables. Chapter 8 addresses the cable ratings for copper communication cables.

An alternative to a communications cabling design in a commercial building is to implement centralized optical fiber cabling. This cabling approach would interconnect the horizontal optical fiber cables using a direct cable pull, interconnect connection, or a hard splice to an optical fiber backbone cable. This cabling configuration enables all communication system electronics to be place in a centralized location in a commercial building.

CHAPTER 6

Horizontal Cabling

HORIZONTAL SUBSYSTEM

The *horizontal subsystem* is defined by the ANSI/TIA/EIA-568-A and ANSI/TIA/EIA-568-B.1 standards as the portion of the structured cabling system that extends from the work area telecommunications outlet/connector to the horizontal cross-connect (HC) in the telecommunications room (TR). The horizontal subsystem must accommodate many different technologies and user applications required to the desk. These include the following:

▼ Voice systems and applications

■ Data systems and applications

■ Video systems and applications

■ Local area network (LAN) systems and connections

■ Building automation and control systems and connections

▲ Other building signaling systems that may required in the building

The term *horizontal cabling* is used to describe the part of the cabling subsystem that runs horizontally in floor pathways, ceiling pathways, or cable trays of a building (see Figure 6-1). The horizontal subsystem includes the horizontal cables, the telecommunications outlet/connector in the work area, the mechanical termination, and the horizontal cross-connections and/or jumper cables located in the TR.

The horizontal subsystem includes the largest amount of cable of any structured cabling subsystem. Once installed in the horizontal subsystem, the horizontal cables are less

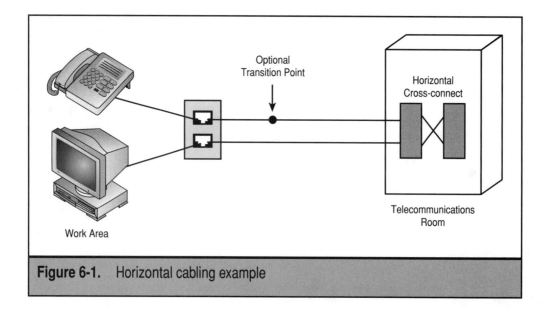

Figure 6-1.   Horizontal cabling example

accessible due to office personnel and furniture occupying the floor space served by the horizontal cabling. The horizontal subsystem must be planned to minimize the costs associated with maintenance and troubleshooting. The horizontal subsystem must be planned to facilitate growth and to accommodate device relocation. Finally, consideration must be given to installing a horizontal cabling system that will support future applications, which will minimize the possibility that the cabling will need to be changed in the future.

HORIZONTAL PATHWAYS

Horizontal pathways are the cabling facilities that are designed to hold, protect, support, and provide access to the horizontal cabling media installed between the TR and the work area.

Horizontal pathways must be designed and installed to support horizontal cables for all types of communications systems. Designing and installing the horizontal pathway is extremely important because the pathway will always exist even if the horizontal cables must be change. A well designed and installed horizontal pathway will enable horizontal cables to be changed easily with the least amount of cost. Therefore, the horizontal pathways must be designed to accommodate cabling growth and changes and minimize occupant disruptions when the horizontal pathways are accessed.

Types of Horizontal Pathways

There are many different types of horizontal pathways used in commercial buildings. Many commercial buildings support two or more different types of horizontal distribution pathways due to building layout and construction considerations. The main types of horizontal pathways used in commercial buildings include

- ▼ **Underfloor ducts**   A network of metal raceways embedded in the concrete floor or foundation.

- ■ **Cellular floors**   A network of metal raceways embedded in the floor of buildings using elevated steel construction.

- ■ **Conduits**   One or more metal conduits installed either under floors or above ceilings from the telecommunication closet to the work area locations.

- ■ **Access or raised floors**   A raised floor provides space under the floor panels for distributing communication cables. Access or raised floors are found in many computer rooms and equipment rooms (ERs).

- ■ **Ceiling distribution**   Utilizing the space between the building roof and the drop ceiling suspended above most building work areas. Cables installed in an open ceiling space must be supported to comply with local building codes.

- ▲ **Cable trays**   Prefabricated, metal, or plastic structures installed to distributed communication cables in large telecommunication closets, computer rooms, or ERs.

Underfloor Ducts

An *underfloor duct horizontal distribution system* is a network of metal raceways embedded in the concrete floor or foundation. *Ducts* are metal compartments that can support communication cables, electrical cables, and other low voltage cable types.

CAUTION: The NEC requires that duct compartments have a solid, metal partition that runs the length of the duct separating the communication and low voltage cables from the high voltage electrical power wiring.

Underfloor duct horizontal distribution systems are made up of

▼   Feeder ducts

▲   Distribution ducts

Feeder ducts are large ducts that start at the TR and extend to the distribution ducts. These ducts carry communication cables from the TR to the distribution ducts. Feeder ducts are typically open trenches or large capacity enclosed ducts. These ducts must be able to support the large quantities of cable that must be distributed from the TR to each work area on a floor.

If a horizontal duct distribution system must support both communication cable and high voltage electrical wires, a two-level distribution duct system can be installed. Lower level ducts support dedicated electrical and communications feeders from electrical service panels and TRs. Upper level ducts support electrical wires using standard size ducts and communication cables using large ducts.

Feed ducts must enter a TR through either an elbow or a slot. Open trench feeder ducts terminate using a slot 75 to 150 mm (3 to 6 in.) wide. Large capacity enclosed ducts terminate using an elbow at a plywood lined wall. The elbow must terminate a minimum of 100 mm (4 in.) above the finished floor of the closet.

Each distribution duct serves a specific floor area zone, called a cabling zone. The distribution ducts connect to the feeder ducts and extend to each cabling zone. Each distribution ducts must be linked to a TR through no more than one feeder duct. These ducts carry communication cables from the feeder duct to each building cabling zone.

The guidelines for sizing the capacity of both the feeder and distribution ducts are based on the usable floor space of the building floor. Ducts are sized for 650 sq. mm (1 sq. in.) of capacity for each 10 sq. m (100 sq. ft.) of usable floor space.

The maximum distance of the combined length of the feeder and distribution ducts must be carefully considered. The maximum length of all cables installed in the horizontal distribution ducts is 90 m (295 ft.) from the termination in the TR to the termination on the outlet in the work area.

Junction Boxes   *Junction boxes* are planned openings in an underfloor duct system. Junction boxes provide access to the inside of the duct for pulling cable. These openings also enable cable runs to change direction.

Junction boxes are always provided at the intersection point between feeder and distribution ducts. The minimum size of the opening for a junction box installed in a feeder duct is 125 mm (5 in.) in diameter. The maximum distance allowed between junction boxes installed in both feeder and distribution ducts is 18 m (60 ft.).

Cellular Floors

A *cellular floor horizontal distribution system* is a network of metal raceways embedded in the floor of buildings using elevated steel construction. These distribution systems support both communication cables and electrical power wires.

Cellular floor distribution system are made up of

▼   Feeder ducts or trench ducts

▲   Distribution cells

Feeder or trench ducts connect the TR to the distribution cells. Distribution cells provide a pathway to each cabling zone. Cellular floor modules typically include either two or three distribution cells. Communication cables are installed in one distribution cell to a cabling zone, and electrical wiring is installed in a separate cell.

Conduits

A *conduit horizontal distribution system* is one or more metal conduits installed either under floors or above ceilings from the telecommunication closet to the work area locations. Conduits terminate in outlet boxes that are installed in walls or in a floor location.

Conduits for horizontal distribution must use one of the following materials:

▼   Rigid metal conduit

■   Rigid nonmetallic conduit

■   Electrical metallic tubing

▲   Intermediate metal conduit

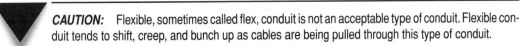

CAUTION: Flexible, sometimes called flex, conduit is not an acceptable type of conduit. Flexible conduit tends to shift, creep, and bunch up as cables are being pulled through this type of conduit.

Conduit runs must be limited to a maximum distance of 90 m (295 ft.) from the TR to the outlet box in the work area. This will limit the length of all horizontal cables installed in the conduits. Pull boxes must be installed in conduit runs that exceed 30 m (100 ft.). Industry standards recommend installing a pull box for each 30 m (100 ft.) of conduit.

Conduit runs must be installed in a direct route from the TR to each work area location. The industry standard limits each conduit run to a maximum of two, 90-degree bends in the entire conduit run or in a conduit section between two pull boxes. Each conduit may be bonded and grounded, on at least one end, according to national or more stringent local codes or standards.

Conduit Bend Radius   All conduit bends must be smooth and even over the entire length of the bend. The bend radius of a conduit is based on the size of the conduit. The bend radius of a conduit must be at least six times the internal diameter of the conduit. Conduit bend guidelines are shown in Table 6-1.

Conduit Internal Diameter	Conduit Bend Radius
50 mm (2 in.) or less	Six times the internal diameter of the conduit
More than 50 mm (2 in.)	Ten times the internal diameter of the conduit

Table 6-1.   Conduit Bend Radius

Conduit Terminations   Conduits that enter a TR must terminate in or near the corners of the closet. A preferred location for terminating conduits is as close as possible to the wall supporting the plywood backboard and cable termination devices. Any conduits that protrude through a floor or ceiling in a closet must be at least 25 to 75 mm (1 to 3 in.) beyond the floor or ceiling surface.

After conduits are installed, each conduit end must be reamed to smooth any rough edges that can cut or damage cable jackets. Verify that the entire length of the conduit is unobstructed, clean of any debris, and dry. Both ends of a terminated conduit must be labeled according to the specification of ANSI/TIA/EIA-606 standard.

All conduits must have a pull string installed for future cable pulls. The pull string must be any of the following materials:

▼   Standard rope cord

■   Plastic cord

▲   Nylon cord

The pull string installing in all conduits must have a minimum test rating of 200 lbs. The pull string will be attached to a cable to be installed in the conduit. A good installation practice is to attach a new pull string to any new cables to be installed. Using the old pull string to install the new cables will also install the new pull string.

Access or Raised Floors

An *access floor horizontal distribution system* provides space under the raised floor panels for distributing communication cables. Access floors are found in many computer rooms and ERs as a means of distributing communication cables.

An access floor consists of the following materials:

▼   Steel footings that connect to the subfloor and serve as the foundation of the access floor

- Pedestals that connect to the steel footings and raise the floor panels off the subfloor

- Stringers that provide lateral support for the access floor panels

▲ Modular floor panels that rest on the pedestals and stringers

CAUTION: Pedestals and stringers must be grounded and bonded according to national and local codes and standards.

The space under an access floor is often used for air distribution through the computer or ER. As a result, the space under an access floor is considered a plenum space. All cables and connecting hardware installed under an access floor must have a fire rating sufficient to support a plenum environment.

The industry cabling standards and guidelines recommend that communications cables and electrical wiring be installed in a raceway. The NEC requires that a solid metal partition separate the communication cables for the electrical wiring. If communication cables are installed under the access floor without a raceway, electrical wires should be installed in a rigid, metal conduit.

Ceiling Distribution

A *ceiling horizontal distribution system* utilizes the space between the building roof and the drop ceiling suspended above the building floor (see Figure 6-2). Communication cables

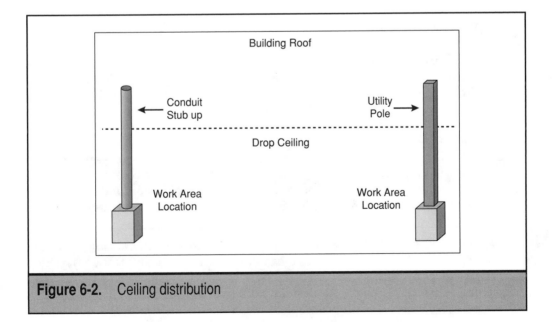

Figure 6-2. Ceiling distribution

are installed above drop ceiling tiles from the TR to each work area. Conduits, usually called stub up, are installed from wall mounted outlet locations and stubbed up into the ceiling space. A utility pole is stubbed up into the ceiling space for modular furniture work locations. The conduit stub ups and utility poles distribute cables to the work area locations.

Most local building codes classify the space above a drop ceiling and the building roof as a plenum space. All cables and connecting hardware installed above a drop ceiling must be plenum rated to comply with national and local building and fire codes.

> **WARNING:**   The NEC requires that all communication cables installed in the ceiling distribution space be identified along the cable route. Untagged cables will be considered abandoned. New NEC rules require that abandoned cables be removed from all building ceiling spaces to reduce the risk of fire dangers.

All communication cables installed in a ceiling distribution system must be properly supported. In addition, local building codes typically specify minimum spacing intervals for ceiling cable-supporting devices. This minimum spacing requirement is meant to limit the sag in cable runs and maintain a minimum height above the drop ceiling. Local building codes typically require a minimum of 150 mm (6 in.) of clearance above the ceiling tiles. Local building codes typically specify minimum cable supports at 1.2 to 1.5 m (4 to 5 ft.) intervals along the entire cable run. Cable-supporting devices can consist of the following cabling structures:

▼ Cable trays

▲ Open type cable supports

Cable Trays

A *cable tray horizontal distribution systems* are prefabricated, metal, or plastic structures installed to distribute communication cables in large telecommunication closets, computer rooms, or ERs (see Figure 6-3). These types of horizontal distribution systems are preferred over conduit systems in some environments because these cable-supporting structures provide greater accessibility to cables and a greater ability to move or change cables installed in them.

Cable trays are open, prefabricated support structures. Cable trays are structures that have a bottom to support communication cables, side rails to contain communications cables, and an open top. Cable trays can have a solid or ventilated bottom and side rails depending on the requirements for national and local building and fire codes.

> **CAUTION:**   Cable trays are not an appropriate pathway for distributing both communication cable and electrical wires. Cable trays should be dedicated for a single application. If a cable tray is shared for distributing both communication cables and electrical wires, the cables must be separated by a grounded metallic barrier running the entire length of the pathway.

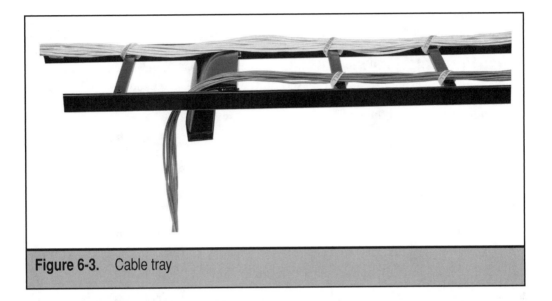

Figure 6-3.   Cable tray

The term cable tray is used to describe a large number of cable-supporting structures including the following:

▼   Ladder rack

■   Ventilated bottom trough

■   Solid bottom trough

▲   Spline

Cable trays are installed above drop ceilings for distribution from a TR to a computer room or ER. Cable trays are usually installed below drop ceilings inside of computer rooms or ERs. Cable trays attach to communication racks in computer rooms and ERs and provide a path for the cables to travel along the cable tray, down to communication rack, to be terminated on a connecting hardware component.

Cable trays are supported in a building using any of the following hardware components:

▼   L brackets

■   Trapeze supports

▲   Rod suspension brackets

The supporting hardware connects to the building structure and keeps the cable tray suspended. The load capacity of a cable tray is determined by the combined weight of the cable tray plus cables it must support and the length of the cable tray span. In the

United States, the specifications for supporting a cable tray are provided by the NEC, sections 318-9(b), 318-9(d), and 318-9(e).

Sizing Horizontal Pathways

Horizontal pathways must be sized based on the useable square footage that the pathway must serve on a building floor. Sizing horizontal pathways must also take into account the following conditions:

▼ The number of cables that must be installed to each work area

■ The size of the cable to be installed to each work area

■ The growth that must be considered for future cables being installed to the work area

■ The cabling requirements (current and future) of other communications systems that must be installed to the work area

▲ The maximum fill of the pathway based on pathway length and configuration

The usable square footage or usable office space is a measure of the building floor space that is available to building occupants for performing business duties and activities. The usable square footage of a floor includes open office area, common or shared areas of the building, and building hallways. Telecommunication closets, elevators, and other building service areas are not considered in the usable floor area calculations. The industry standard is to allocate one work area for every 10 sq. m (100 sq. ft.) of usable floor space.

Horizontal pathways will vary in size based on usable square footage and other variables associated with the number and types of cables to be installed. If some information about the number and types of cables to be installed are not known at the time of planning the horizontal pathways, industry standards recommend sizing horizontal pathways to support a minimum of three cables per work area.

Each type of horizontal pathway has recommended maximum fill guidelines. Each pathway type has different construction requirements and support different fill levels. To find out the maximum fill levels for each type of pathway, consult the pathway manufacturer.

Horizontal Cable Topology

The ANSI/TIA/EIA-568-A and ANSI/TIA/EIA-568-B.1 standards specify that all horizontal cabling must be installed in a physical star topology (see Figure 6-4). Each work area outlet/connector must be directly connected to the HC with a horizontal cable. Industry cabling standards prohibit daisy chaining work area outlet/connectors from a single horizontal cable. In addition, each horizontal cable must be terminated on a HC in a TR on the same floor as the work area terminating the opposite end of the cable.

Horizontal cables must be installed as one continuous cable run. No splices, cable extensions, or bridge taps are permitted. The only allowable exception is to support an optional transition point (TP). A TP is the point where round, horizontal cables are converted to flat, undercarpet cables.

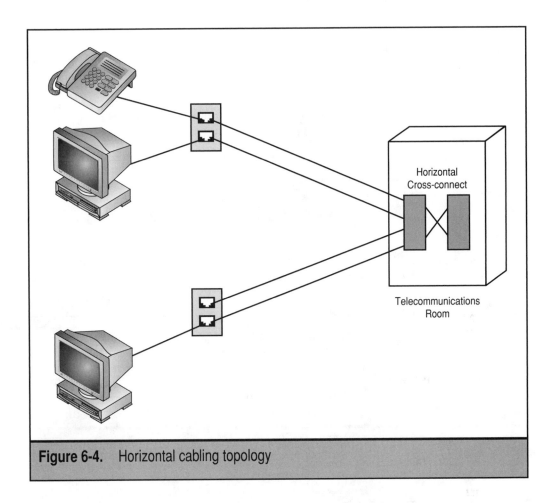

Figure 6-4. Horizontal cabling topology

RECOGNIZED MEDIA TYPES

Three types of media are recognized media types in the horizontal cabling subsystem. These media types are

▼ Four-pair, 100-ohm unshielded twisted-pair (UTP) cable

■ Two-strand 62.5/125 μm multimode optical fiber cable

▲ Two-strand 50/125 μm multimode optical fiber cable

The ANSI/TIA/EIA-568-A and ANSI/TIA/EIA-568-B.1 cabling standards support installing any recognized media type on any combination for the horizontal subsystem.

The recognized four-pair, 100-ohm media types for the horizontal subsystem are shown in Table 6-2.

Category	Description
Category 3	This category of UTP cable is rated up to 16 MHz.
Category 4	This category of UTP cable is rated up to 20 MHz.
Category 5	This category of UTP cable is rated up to 100 MHz.
Category 5e	This category of UTP cable is rated up to 100 MHz.
Category 6	This category of UTP cable is rated up to 250 MHz.

Table 6-2.   Recognized 100-Ohm UTP Cable Types

The recognized multimode optical fiber cables for the horizontal subsystem must meet the following performance specifications shown in Table 6-3.

Media Type	Maximum Attenuation		Minimum Bandwidth	
	850 nm	1,300 nm	850 nm	1,300 nm
50/125 μm multimode	3.5 dB	1.5 dB	500 MHz-km	500 MHz-km
62.5/125 μm multimode	3.5 dB	1.5 dB	160 MHz-km	500 MHz-km

Table 6-3.   Recognized Optical Fiber Cable Types

The ANSI/TIA/EIA-568-A standard supports STP-A cable as an allowed media type. The ANSI/TIA/EIA-568-B.1 standard does not recognize STP-A cable as an allowed media for new cabling installations. STP-A cable is recognized as a media that may be found at existing sites. The ANSI/TIA/EIA-568-B.1 standard supports the continued use of STP-A cable for these existing installations.

Hybrid Cables

Hybrid cables can be used as a media for the horizontal subsystem provided that the following conditions are satisfied:

▼   Cables types in the hybrid cable are a recognized media type for the horizontal subsystem.

■   Each cable type in the hybrid cable meets or exceeds the transmission specifications defined for that media type by industry cabling standards.

■   The color codes of the individual media conform to industry standards.

▲   The PS-NEXT crosstalk specifications exceed the pair-to-pair NEXT crosstalk specifications for each cable type. This requirement is defined in the ANSI/TIA/EIA-568-A-3 standard.

CABLING LINKS AND CHANNELS

Horizontal cabling runs are grouped into two major categories called

▼   Horizontal cabling links

▲   Horizontal cabling channels

The horizontal cabling link is the permanently installed horizontal cable from the TR to the outlet/connector used to terminate the cable in the work area (see Figure 6-5). A cabling link is also called the permanent link and the basic link. The cabling link includes the following components:

▼   Cable between the HC in the closet

■   Connecting hardware to terminate the horizontal cable in the TR

■   An optional TP or consolidation point (CP) connector

▲   An outlet/connector to terminate the cable in the work area

A cabling link does not include the patch cords in the TR or in the work area. The cabling link starts at the termination in the TR and ends at the termination at the outlet/connector in the work area.

The horizontal cabling channel includes all of the cabling components in the horizontal cabling subsystem. The cabling channel includes the following components:

▼   Cable between the HC in the closet

■   Connecting hardware to terminate the horizontal cable in the TR

■   An optional TP or CP connector

■   An outlet/connector to terminate the cable in the work area

■   Work area patch cords to connect user equipment to the horizontal cable

▲   Equipment patch cords to connect equipment in the TR to the horizontal cable or jumper wires to connect the horizontal cable to the backbone cable

The horizontal cabling channel contains the cabling link and also includes the equipment patch cords or jumper wires in the TR and the work area patch cords (see Figure 6-6). The channel is the most important of the two horizontal cabling links. Because the horizontal cabling channel included the patch cords on both ends, it will determine if the horizontal cable will support a given application.

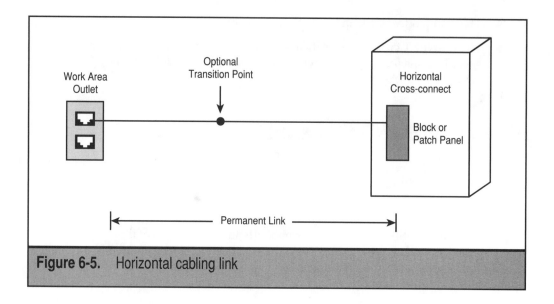

Figure 6-5. Horizontal cabling link

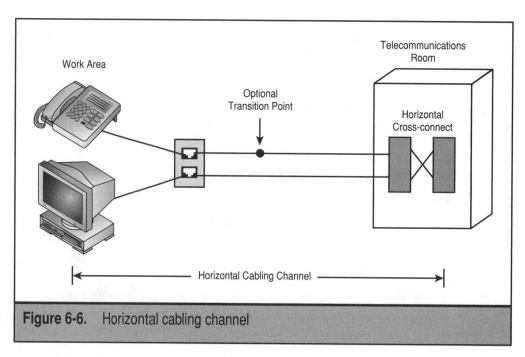

Figure 6-6. Horizontal cabling channel

CABLE LENGTH

The ANSI/TIA/EIA-568-A and ANSI/TIA/EIA-568-B.1 cabling standards limit the length of allowed recognized media types to a maximum of 90 m (295 ft.) from the termination on the HC in the TR to the outlet/connector in the work area (see Figure 6-7). This is called the permanent link. The permanent link is the cabling that is usually never changed or modified. It is terminated in the TR and in the work area and only changed when the cable is replaced.

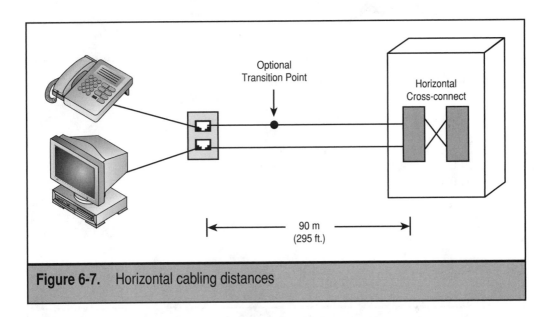

Optional
Transition Point

Horizontal
Cross-connect

90 m
(295 ft.)

Figure 6-7. Horizontal cabling distances

CAUTION: Many individuals incorrectly believe that multimode optical fiber cable runs can be longer that 90 m (295 ft.) and still be standards-compliant. Multimode optical fiber cable will support distances longer than 90 m (295 ft.) and will continue to work correctly, but distances that exceed 90 m (295 ft.) violate industry cabling standards.

Industry cabling standards make a 10 m (33 ft.) allowance for the combined length of equipment patch cables in the TR and work area patch cables. The recommended maximum distance for work area equipment patch cords is 5 m (16 ft.), and the recommended maximum distance for equipment patch cords in the TR is 5 m (16 ft.). This is shown in Table 6-4.

Industry cabling standards support any combination of lengths of these two types of patch cords as long as the combined length does not exceed 10 m (33 ft.). This is shown in Table 6-5.

Industry cabling standards support a maximum distance of 100 m (328 ft.) for the cabling channel. The cabling channel is the length of the permanent link plus the combined

Patch Cords	Recommended Maximum Distance
Work area patch cords	5 m (16 ft.)
Equipment cords in the TR	5 m (16 ft.)
Combined length	10 m (33 ft.)

Table 6-4.   Patch Cord Distances

Work Area Cords	Equipment Cords	Combined Length of Work Area and Equipment Cords
1 m (3 ft.)	9 m (30 ft.)	10 m (33 ft.)
2 m (6.5 ft.)	8 m (26 ft.)	10 m (33 ft.)
3 m (10 ft.)	7 m (23 ft.)	10 m (33 ft.)
4 m (13 ft.)	6 m (20 ft.)	10 m (33 ft.)
5 m (16 ft.)	5 m (16 ft.)	10 m (33 ft.)
6 m (20 ft.)	4 m (13 ft.)	10 m (33 ft.)
7 m (23 ft.)	3 m (10 ft.)	10 m (33 ft.)
8 m (26 ft.)	2 m (6.5 ft.)	10 m (33 ft.)
9 m (30 ft.)	1 m (3 ft.)	10 m (33 ft.)

Table 6-5.   Patch Cord Maximum Distances

length of the work area and equipment patch cords. This is the maximum distance supported by industry cabling standards for all recognized media types.

Cable Slack

Each cable run should have a provision for cable slack at both ends of the cable. Planning for cable slack in the cabling run will accommodate any minor cabling changes that may be necessary in the future. This may prevent having to install a new cable if the location of the outlet/connector must be moved. The exact amount of cabling slack will be different for each installation but the general guidelines the cable slack in the work area and TR are

▼   3 m (10 ft.) in the TR

▲   200 to 300 mm (8 to 12 in.) in the work area

The amount of cable slack must be considered as part of the maximum allowable distance for the horizontal cable link and channel. The maximum length, including all cable slack, must not exceed 90 m (295 ft.) for the horizontal cabling link.

WARNING: If cable slack is planned, a method for storing the cable slack must also be considered for each installation. Avoid storing the cabling slack for TRs in bundled loops. Avoid kinking the horizontal cables when storing cable slack in an outlet box in the work area. Both practices will degrade the performance of the cable and may cause signaling problems in high speed networks.

CABLE SELECTION

The ANSI/TIA/EIA-568-A and ANSI/TIA/EIA-568-B.1 cabling standards specify that there should be a minimum of two recognized cables installed to each work area location. Two cables must be installed because each work area supports at least one phone and one data device.

NOTE: Industry cabling standards support more than two cables installed to each work area. The standard specifies a minimum of two cables to prevent less than two cables being installed to each work area. If only one cable is installed, then only one service can be supported unless a second cable is installed.

The ANSI/TIA/EIA-568-A and ANSI/TIA/EIA-568-B.1 cabling standards recommend that two cables installed to each work area conform to the following configuration. The first cable should be a four-pair, 100-ohm UTP category 3 or higher cable, where category 5e is recommended. This cable will be used for voice applications. Voice applications will work sufficiently using a category 3 cable. A higher quality of UTP cable will also support voice applications and may also support future high-speed applications. The second cable will be used for data applications and must be a higher quality UTP cable or an optical fiber cable. A high quality cable is required to support the higher bandwidth requirements of most data applications.

The second cable can be any of the following cable types (see Figure 6-8):

▼   Four-pair, 100-ohm category 5e or higher UTP cable

■   Two-fiber 50/125 μm multimode optical fiber cable

▲   Two-fiber 62.5/125 μm multimode optical fiber cable

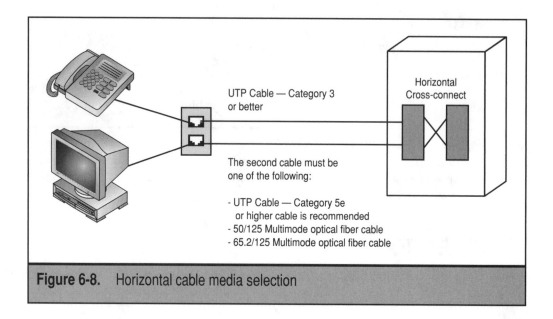

Figure 6-8.   Horizontal cable media selection

If a work area requires additional outlets for additional voice or data connections, industry standards require installing a recognized cable type for each outlet. This practice guarantees that each application has a dedicated horizontal cable and all four pairs of the horizontal cable are available for the application. Splitting cable pairs, which is the process of using a pair from a single cable for two or more connections, is prohibited by industry cabling standards. This practice is often done instead of installing a new horizontal cable. Splitting cable pairs can lead to compatibility issues with the two applications sharing the same cable. This practice may also limit upgrading to new technologies that require more than two pairs to operate. Many high-speed data applications, such as 1000Base-T gigabit Ethernet LANs, require four pair to operate over category 5e UTP cable. Horizontal cables that have split cable pairs cannot support this application.

WARNING: All cabling elements in a cabling link must be the same category rating. Mixing and matching horizontal cables, patch cords, modular connectors, and patch panels that have different category ratings will lower the rating of the cabling channels to the rating of the lowest rated component or cable. For example, if a category 3 modular outlet was used to terminate a category 6 UTP cable, the cabling link would be rated as category 3.

HORIZONTAL CONNECTING HARDWARE

Horizontal cables must be terminated in the TR and in the work area. The cabling components that are used to terminate copper and optical fiber cables are called connecting hardware. The connecting hardware for horizontal cables includes the following devices:

▼   Modular outlets/connectors

■   Patch panels and punch blocks

■   CP and TP connectors

▲   Optical fiber connectors

UTP Cable Connecting Hardware

Each four-pair UTP cable must be terminated with an eight-position modular outlet/connector in the work area (see Figure 6-9). The modular outlet/connector must use insulation displacement contact (IDC) technology to terminate the UTP cable pairs. The modular outlet/connector is mounted in a faceplate so the outlets are accessible for patch cord connections.

The opposite end of the cable must be terminated on either a patch panel or a punch block. These devices also use IDC technology to terminate the cable pairs. A patch panel is used to terminate a horizontal cable if the cable must connect to communication equipment installed in the TR (see Figure 6-10). Equipment patch cords are used to connect the pairs of the horizontal cable to the communication equipment port.

A punch block is used to terminate the horizontal cable if the cable is to be connected to communication equipment installed in the equipment or computer room through a backbone cable (see Figure 6-11). Jumper wires connect the pairs of the horizontal cable to pairs in a backbone cable. The opposite end of the backbone cable is connected to a port on the communication equipment.

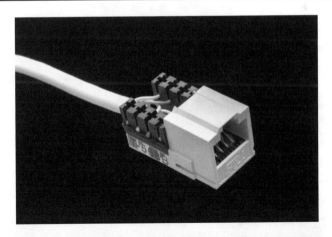

Figure 6-9.   Modular outlet example

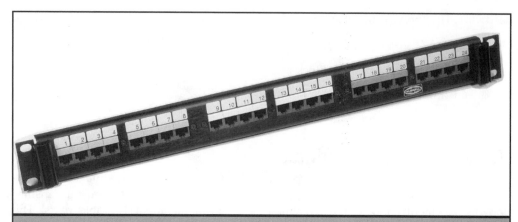

Figure 6-10.   Patch panel example

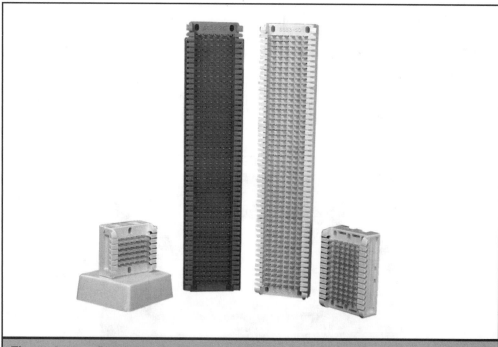

Figure 6-11.   Punch block example

Modular Jack Configurations

The ANSI/TIA/EIA-568-A and ANSI/TIA/EIA-568-B.1 cabling standards recognize two modular jack configurations. The two modular jack configurations are called the T568A and T568B. The two modular jack configurations are similar but terminate the UTP cable pairs in a slightly different order on the modular jack. The T568A modular jack configuration terminates the orange pair, known as pair 2, on pins 3 and 6 of the modular jack and the green pair, known as pair 3, on pins 1 and 2 of the modular jack. This is shown in Figure 6-12.

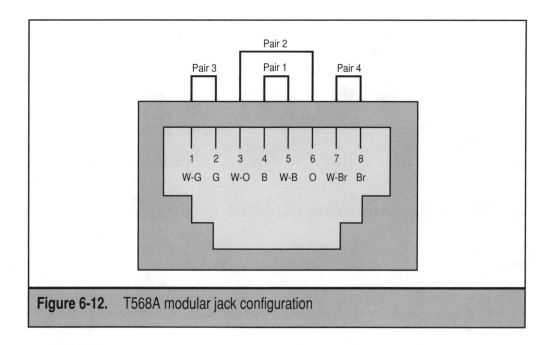

Figure 6-12.   T568A modular jack configuration

The T568B modular jack configuration terminates the orange pair (pair 2) on pins 1 and 2 of the modular jack and the green pair (pair 3) on pins 3 and 6. This is shown in Figure 6-13.

Every cabling component that has a modular port, such as modular outlet/connectors and patch panels, are manufactured to match either the T568A or T568B modular outlet configuration. Industry cabling standards specify that horizontal UTP cables must use a straight through wiring configuration. Using a T568A modular component on one end of an UTP link and T568B components on the opposite end of the same link will cross pairs 2 and 3 in the horizontal cable.

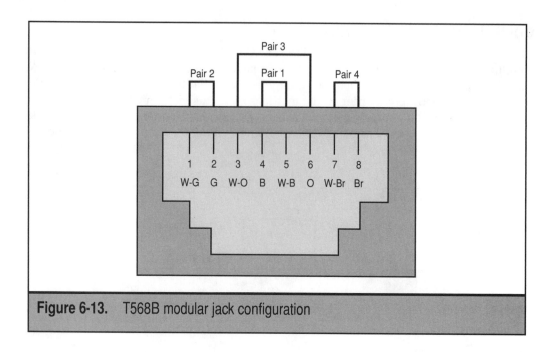

Figure 6-13. T568B modular jack configuration

Optical Fiber Cable Connecting Hardware

Optical fiber cables must be terminated with fiber optic connectors on both ends of the cable. In the work area, both strands of a horizontal optical fiber connect are terminated using a SC style fiber optic connector. A duplex SC fiber optic connector is also called a 568SC connector. The two SC fiber optic connectors are installed in a duplex fiber optic work area outlet. This is shown in Figure 6-14.

Both strands of a horizontal optical fiber cable are also terminated with a duplex SC fiber optic connector in the TR. The two SC fiber optic connectors are inserted into a patch panel either rack mounted or wall mounted in the closet. This is shown in Figure 6-15.

Horizontal optical fiber cables must have a cross-over in the horizontal cabling link from the termination in the work area to the termination in the TR. This is accomplished by connection cross-over schemes where position A on the back of the work area outlet and patch panel is connected to position B on the front of the work area outlet and patch panel. This is shown in Figure 6-16.

Figure 6-14.   Fiber optic work area outlet

Figure 6-15.   Fiber optic patch panel

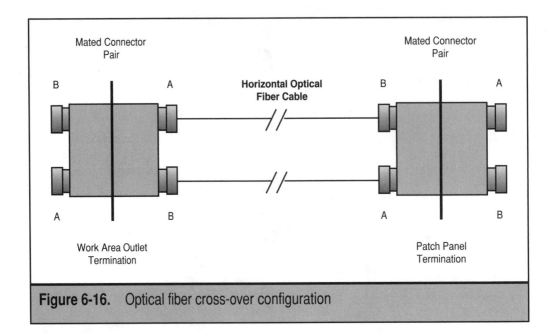

Mated Connector
Pair

B   A   **Horizontal Optical**   B   A
                                Fiber Cable

A   B   A   B

Work Area Outlet   Patch Panel
Termination   Termination

Mated Connector
Pair

Figure 6-16. Optical fiber cross-over configuration

CHAPTER SUMMARY

The horizontal subsystem is defined by the ANSI/TIA/EIA-568-A and ANSI/TIA/EIA-568-B.1 standards as the portion of the structured cabling system that extends from the work area telecommunications outlet/connector to the horizontal cross-connect (HC) in the telecommunications room (TR). The term horizontal cabling is used to describe the part of the cabling subsystem that runs horizontally in floor pathways, ceiling pathways or cable trays of a building. The horizontal subsystem includes the horizontal cables, the telecommunications outlet/connector in the work area, the mechanical termination, and the horizontal cross-connections and/or jumper cables located in the TR.

Horizontal pathways are the cabling facilities that are designed to hold, protect, support, and provide access to the horizontal cabling media installed between the TR and the work area. Horizontal pathways must be designed and installed to support horizontal cables for all types of communications systems. There are many different types of horizontal pathways used in commercial buildings. The main types of horizontal pathways used in commercial buildings include underfloor ducts, cellular floors, conduits, access or raised floors, ceiling distribution, and cable trays.

Horizontal pathways must be sized based on the useable square footage that the pathway must serve on a building floor. The usable square footage or usable office space is a measure of the building floor space that is available to building occupants for performing business duties and activities. The usable square footage of a floor includes open office area, common or shared areas of the building, and building hallways. Telecommunication closets, elevators, and other building service areas are not considered in the usable floor area calculations. The industry standard is to allocate one work area for every 10 sq. m (100 sq. ft.) of usable floor space.

The ANSI/TIA/EIA-568-A and ANSI/TIA/EIA-568-B.1 standards specify that all horizontal cabling must be installed in a physical star topology. Each work area outlet/connector must be directly connected to the HC with a horizontal cable. In addition, each horizontal cable must be terminated on a HC in a TR on the same floor as the work area terminating the opposite end of the cable.

The ANSI/TIA/EIA-568-A and ANSI/TIA/EIA-568-B.1 cabling standards limit the length of allowed recognized media types to a maximum of 90 m (295 ft.) from the termination on the HC in the TR to the outlet/connector in the work area. This is called the permanent link. Industry cabling standards make a 10 m (33 ft.) allowance for the combined length of equipment patch cables in the TR and work area patch cables. Industry cabling standards support a maximum distance of 100 m (328 ft.) for the cabling channel. The cabling channel is the length of the permanent link plus the combined length of the work area and equipment patch cords. This is the maximum distance supported by industry cabling standards for all recognized media types.

The ANSI/TIA/EIA-568-A and ANSI/TIA/EIA-568-B.1 cabling standards specify that there should be a minimum of two recognized cables installed to each work area location. Two cables must be installed because each work area supports at least one phone and one data device.

Each four-pair UTP cable must be terminated with an eight-position modular outlet/connector in the work area. The modular outlet/connector must use IDC technology to terminate the UTP cable pairs. The modular outlet/connector is mounted in a faceplate so the outlets are accessible for patch cord connections. The opposite end of the cable must be terminated on either a patch panel or a punch block. A punch block is used to terminate the horizontal cable if the cable is to be connected to communication equipment installed in the equipment or computer room through a backbone cable. Jumper wires connect the pairs of the horizontal cable to pairs in a backbone cable.

Optical fiber cables must be terminated with fiber optic connectors on both ends of the cable. In the work area, both strands of a horizontal optical fiber connect are terminated using a SC style fiber optic connector. Both strands of a horizontal optical fiber cable are also terminated with a duplex SC fiber optic connector in the TR. The two SC fiber optic connectors are inserted into a patch panel either rack mounted or wall mounted in the closet.

CHAPTER 7

Work Area Cabling

T he *work area* is the space within a building where employees, building occupants, or system users reside and interact with their communication equipment. This is also the area where the horizontal communication cables are terminated. This space usually includes the user communications equipment such as

- ▼ Computers
- ■ Phones
- ■ Modems
- ▲ Data terminals

The work area is also the portion of a structured cabling system that connects to the user's communication equipment. The specifications for work area cabling are unique to the needs of the cables that serve these building spaces. Work area cables and other cabling components must be designed to withstand the abuses that are common in work area spaces. These abuses include but are not limited to the following:

- ▼ Kinking the cables due to tight spaces
- ■ Crushing the cables due to rolling furniture and people stepping on or walking over the cables
- ■ Pulling forces on the cables from users
- ▲ Pinching the cables from heavy furniture being moved

The work area subsystem includes the following cables and cabling components:

- ▼ Modular line cords
- ■ Cabling components
- ▲ Special adapters

NOTE: Modular connectors/outlets are found in the work area, but these devices are considered to be part of the horizontal subsystem. They are part of the horizontal subsystem because they are used to permanently terminate the horizontal cable in the work area.

WORK AREA LOCATIONS

Work area locations can be placed in any usable square footage in a building or on a building floor. Careful consideration must be given when planning work area locations in a building. In general, work area locations should be selected to provide a safe and comfortable working space for the intended occupant.

Each employee or occupant of a building is normally assigned one work area location for performing his or her work duties. This location is typically an office or cubicle. Industry planning guidelines recommend allocating a minimum of 10 sq. m (100 sq. ft.) of useable floor space per work area location. Industry cabling standards also require that a minimum of two approved media types be installed to each work area location.

Each planned work area location must be within 90 m (295 ft.) from a telecommunications room (TR). This is the maximum distance allowed for all recognized media types. In addition, each work area must have a power outlet located in or near it. This will support power to all communication equipment required in this building space.

WORK AREA OUTLET LOCATIONS

Industry cabling standards require that each work area location be provided with a minimum of one work area outlet location. A work area outlet location is usually a faceplate supporting two or more modular outlets/connectors. Each outlet of connection must terminate one approved type of horizontal media. Therefore, each work area location must be supported by a minimum of two modular outlets/connectors and two approved horizontal cables.

Work area outlets can be placed in different locations for each work area. The exact location is usually a function of the horizontal pathway connecting the work area to the TR. Work area outlet locations can be installed in any of the following areas:

▼   On the wall

■   On the floor

■   On a power pole

▲   On the modular furniture

Work area outlets are usually mounted on the wall when above ceiling or conduit distribution systems are used for horizontal cable distribution. Work area outlets are usually mounted on the floor when underfloor ducts, cellular floor, or access floor systems are used for horizontal cable distribution. Work area outlets are usually mounted on power poles when above ceiling or cable tray distribution systems are used for horizontal cable distribution. Work area outlets are usually mounted on modular furniture when there are no walls or floors available.

WORK AREA LINE CORDS

User equipment includes the types of devices found in a user work space that need a physical connection to the horizontal cables. User equipment would include voice devices, such as analog or digital telephone sets, modems installed in your computer, or data devices, such as a desktop or laptop computer, with a network interface card.

Work area line cords, sometimes called modular line cords or just line cords, are the cables used in the work area subsystem (see Figure 7-1). These cords are used to connect communication devices to the horizontal cabling. Modular line cords have a plastic modular plug on each end of the cord. Both the voice and data industries have standardized on an eight position modular plug. The eight position modular plug is a quick connect and release style of interface connector. The plug on one end of the work area cord is inserted into the communication device, such as telephone or LAN card in a PC, and the plug on the opposite end of the cord is inserted in the telecommunications outlet/connector. This plug makes physical contact with the terminated horizontal cable.

NOTE: The telecommunications (voice and data) industries have standardized the eight-position modular connector. The telephone industry is converting from using an RJ12C modular connector, commonly called a RJ11 connector. These are the type of modular connectors that you will typically plug your phone into in your home. The ANSI/TIA/EIA-570-A standard, which is the residential cabling standard, specifies that all new residential cabling should be terminated with an eight-position modular connector.

Figure 7-1. Modular cord example

WORK AREA MEDIA

Work area line cords should always be made using a stranded type of media. Stranded media is preferred for work area environments because stranded media is more flexible than solid conductor media. This means that the media can take the twisting and bending of the media as it is typical of in the work area without the cable conductors breaking. In addition, stranded media can support more acute bends without causing signal degradation and losses.

Work area line cords must also be constructed where the cable pairs are twisted together, called twisted-pair construction. Twisted-pair construction is specified and required for work area cords by industry cabling standards. Twisted-pair construction is capable of transmitting voice signals and required for transmitting high-speed data signals. All recognized copper horizontal cables are required to use twisted-pair construction to support balanced differential signaling. The twisted-pair construction of the work area cords will match the twisted-pair construction of the horizontal cables.

Work area line cords for voice systems oftentimes use a flat style line cord (see Figure 7-2). The cable pairs in this type of line cord are not twisted together, but instead, the cable pairs lay flat inside the cable. Flat line cords can be used for telephones because of the type of signaling used by phone systems. Phone signaling does not require the cable pairs to be twisted together. However, new digital phones may require twisted-pair work area cables.

Twisted-pair cords are always required by high-speed LAN equipment. This equipment uses a balanced signaling. The cable pairs must be twisted together to support this signaling scheme. Flat and untwisted work area cables will attenuate the balanced signals. This will result in reduced cabling distances being supported or the cabling link not working at all for these applications.

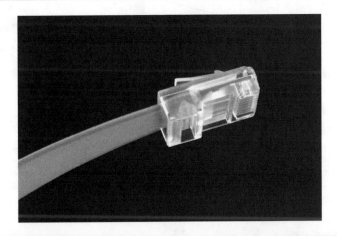

Figure 7-2. Flat line cord example

The cabling industry has standardized on using twisted-pair construction for both voice and high-speed LAN work area cords. These cords are not required but will work for voice systems. These cords will also work for high-speed data systems.

WORK AREA CABLING DISTANCES

Industry cabling standards provide a maximum provision of 10 m (33 ft.) for the combined length of work area and TR equipment cords (see Figure 7-3). Industry cabling standards recommend a maximum of 5 m (16 ft.) for work area cables. This leaves a provision for a maximum of 5 m (16 ft.) cords in the TR.

The ANSI/TIA/EIA-568-A and ANSI/TIA/EIA-568-B.1 standards enable the length of the work area cables to be increased if less than 5 m (16 ft.) equipment cords are required in the TR. For example, if 3 m (10 ft.) equipment cords are required in the TR, the length of the work area cords can be increased to 7 m (23 ft.).

The 5 m (16 ft.) recommended length for work area cables is used for planning purposes. During the planning phase of the project, the exact length of the TR equipment cables may not be known. The 5 m (16 ft.) distance provides a standard distance guideline that can be adjusted once more information about the cabling installation is known.

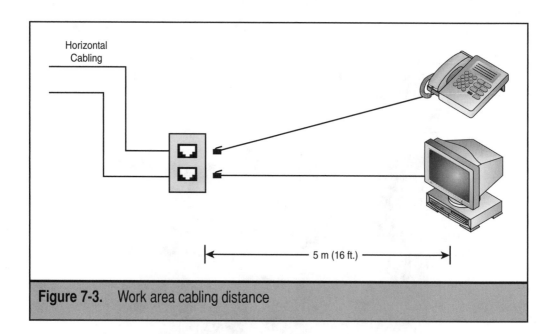

Figure 7-3. Work area cabling distance

WORK AREA CABLE QUALITY

It is recommended that the quality of media used in the work area should be the same or better than the quality of media used for the horizontal cabling. This means that a cabling system that uses category 5e cable in the horizontal subsystem must use category 5e or higher line cords in the work area.

Work area cords that have a lower performance rating than the installed horizontal media should never be used. Using a lower performance work area cord will lower the rating of the entire cable channel. The work area cord will exhibit higher attenuation and lower NEXT than the horizontal cable. The length of the work area cord is short so the additional attenuation from the lower quality cord will usually add a few dB of additional loss to the channel. The extra dBs of loss may not matter if the channel length is short and there is additional margin in the channel. However, lower quality cords can be a problem if the channel length is long and there is no additional margin. The extra dBs may be enough to cause the channel to fail certification tests. This problem may be magnified when high-frequency signals are transmitted over the channel. The losses caused by the lower performance work area cord will add larger losses to the channel at these higher frequencies.

The NEXT rating for lower performance work area cords is a greater problem for the cable channel. The NEXT rating for the entire cabling channel is based on the lowest rated component in the channel. Using a category 3 work area cord for a category 5e channel will cause the channel to fail a certification test.

CAUTION: We have seen many installations where the customer spends money to install a high quality category 5e or category 6 cable horizontal cable and then decides to used category 3 rated work area cords. Many customers or installation contractors make this decision because the category 3 cords are less expensive than high performance category 5e or category 6 cords. Most of these users and contractors incorrectly believe that the short work area cord will not have a significant impact on the performance of the cable channel.

In reality, the work area cord may be the most important cable in the horizontal cable channel. The maximum attenuation allowed for the channel is a fixed amount. The work area cord should minimize the amount of attenuation that it contributes to the entire channel. The NEXT test measures the signal coupling on the near end or the first 20 m (66 ft.) of the channel. This distance includes the entire length of the work area cord and only the first 15 m (49.2 ft) of the horizontal media. This is the reason why the work area cords should be the same quality or higher than the horizontal media.

CABLING COMPONENTS AND SPECIAL ADAPTERS

Application-specific components are sometimes required in a work area to support different media types, to match cable impedance, or to support legacy computer equipment. Any cabling components or special adapters that are required for equipment installed in the work area must be part of the work area subsystem (see Figure 7-4). Industry cabling

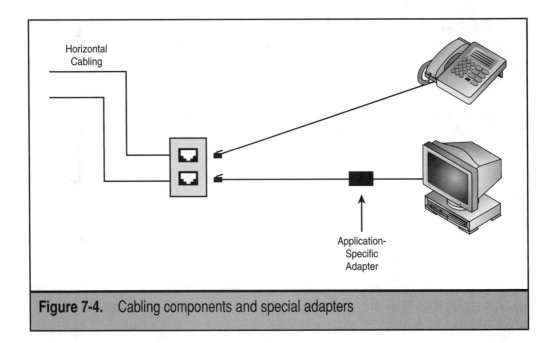

Horizontal Cabling

Application-Specific Adapter

Figure 7-4. Cabling components and special adapters

standards require that application-specific cabling components and special adapters required in the work area must remain external to the outlet/connector. This will enable the application-specific adapter to move with the user equipment. Moving the adapter will enable the equipment to use any other horizontal cable in the building without having to modify the cable. The requirement of keeping special cabling components and special adapters external to the outlet/connector guarantees that the horizontal cabling will remain generic. If the first device is moved, the next device attaches to the horizontal cable without it needing to be changed or modified in any way.

There are many different types of cabling devices that would qualify and fall into the category of being a special cabling component or special adapter (see Figure 7-5). Special cabling components and special adapters would include the following devices:

▼ Passive adapters that are used when the horizontal cable type is different from that required by the equipment

■ Active adapters that are used when the user devices are using different signaling schemes and need to communicate together

■ Adapters enabling pair transpositions for compatibility purposes

■ "Y" adapters that permit two services to run on a single cable

▲ Termination resistors

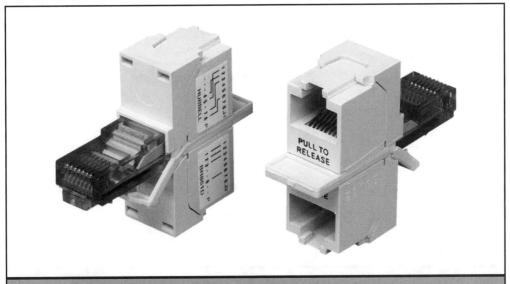

Figure 7-5. Cabling components and special adapters

TELECOMMUNICATIONS OUTLET

The telecommunications outlet/connector is an interface between the horizontal cabling and the work area cabling (see Figure 7-6). As stated earlier, the telecommunications outlet is not part of the work area cabling subsystem. It is actually part of the horizontal cabling subsystem. The telecommunications outlet is the interface for the work area cabling to connect with the horizontal cabling. An 8-pin modular jack provides a standard interface point between these two cabling subsystems. The eight-position modular connector (commonly called a RJ45 connector) is capable of interfacing with various discrete voice, data, and LAN devices and complies with the ANSI/TIA/EIA-568-A and the ANSI/TIA/EIA-568-B.1 standard.

A minimum of two telecommunications outlets/connectors (ports) should be provided for each work area location in a building. More than two telecommunications outlets/connectors can be installed in each work area location. Industry standards require a minimum of two outlets/connectors (ports) because most work area locations typically have cabling requirements for at least one voice and one data device.

In the ANSI/TIA/EIA cabling standards, the telecommunications outlet is referred to as the telecommunications outlet/connector. It is called this because many telecommunications outlets are designed with a separate modular connector, which snaps into a faceplate (see Figure 7-7). The horizontal cable terminates on the back of the connector. A modular line cord will make a connection to the horizontal cable on the front of the outlet/connector.

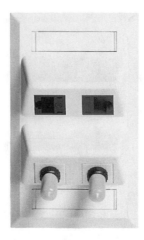

Figure 7-6. Telecommunications outlet

Figure 7-7. Modular outlet/connector inserted into a faceplate

TELECOMMUNICATIONS OUTLET CONFIGURATIONS

Eight-position modular outlets (ISO 8877) are recommended to terminate UTP and ScTP horizontal cables used for voice and data applications (see Figure 7-8). The eight-position modular outlet (commonly called a RJ45 connector) is the standard outlet for terminating copper horizontal cables in both residential and commercial buildings. The eight-position modular outlet will enable all four pairs of a UTP or ScTP horizontal cable to be terminated on the modular outlet.

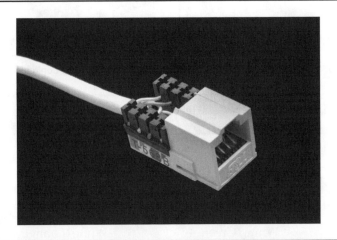

Figure 7-8. Eight-position modular outlet

NOTE: Modular outlets are also available in four- and six-position configurations. These configurations are commonly called RJ11 connectors and may be found in commercial and residential buildings. These connectors are not recommended or supported by industry cabling standards because they cannot terminate all four pairs of a horizontal UTP cable.

All eight-position modular outlets should be wired according to the T568A or T568B configurations (see Figure 7-9). These configurations are specified in the ANSI/TIA/EIA-568-A and ANSI/TIA/EIA-568-B.1 cabling standards. This is shown in Figure 7-9.

The T568A and T568B modular outlet configurations are very similar. Both outlet configurations terminate the blue pair on pins 4 and 5 and the brown pair on pins 7 and 8. The difference between the two modular outlet configurations is where the orange and green pairs are terminated. The T568A modular outlet has the orange pair terminated on pins 3 and 6 and the green pair terminated on pins 1 and 2. The T568B modular outlet configuration has the orange pair termination on pins 1 and 2 and the green pair terminated on pins 3 and 6. The four pairs of a horizontal cable should be terminated on a telecommunications outlet according to Table 7-1.

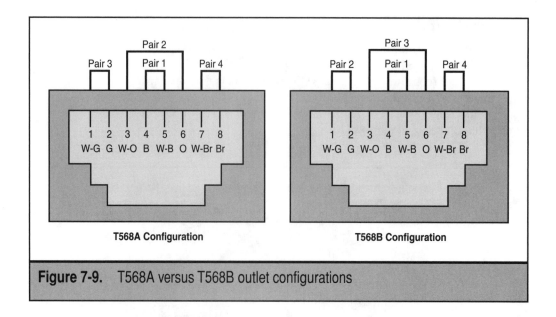

Figure 7-9.   T568A versus T568B outlet configurations

Pin Number	T568A Termination Configuration	T568B Termination Configuration
Pin 1	White/Green	White/Orange
Pin 2	Green/White	Orange/White
Pin 3	White/Orange	White/Green
Pin 4	White/Blue	White/Blue
Pin 5	Blue/White	Blue/White
Pin 6	Orange/White	Green/White
Pin 7	White/Brown	White/Brown
Pin 8	Brown/White	Brown/White

Table 7-1.   Modular Outlet Termination Positions

The T568A configuration is the recommended outlet termination scheme for new installations. In addition, this is the only modular outlet configuration supported by the U.S. Federal government. The T568B modular outlet configuration is defined as an optional termination scheme. This configuration is also supported by industry standards for existing installations.

NOTE: The T568B configuration is a Lucent Technology (formerly AT&T) standard and popular with many installation contractors. Many connector and patch panel manufacturers also use the T568B modular outlet configuration as their company standard. If you order a connector or patch panel, the cable termination component conforms to the T568B outlet configuration.

OPEN OFFICE CABLING

Recent developments in open office designs have introduced some changes to standard horizontal and work area cabling practices. Office environments that have modular cubicles taking up and entire building floor are called open office environments. The term open office was created to describe these office environments that have no walls dividing the usable floor space. Instead, low-walled modular furniture is installed in these building spaces to create employee work areas.

Open office environments are characterized by frequent moving and rearranging of the modular furniture. The constant furniture rearrangements are usually required to adapt to ever changing requirements of the employees and their need to create small work groups. These work spaces can also change as the user population changes or work group configurations need to change over time.

Open office cabling strategies are designed to adapt to the frequent moves and changes to the modular furniture. Standard cabling practices that conform to the ANSI/TIA/EIA-568-A and ANSI/TIA/EIA-568-B.1 cabling standards would require that a new horizontal cable be pulled for each cubicle location each time the furniture is moved or reconfigured. Open office cabling incorporates an interconnect in the horizontal cabling. This optional element in the horizontal subsystem enables the open office space and modular furniture to be reconfigured as needed without requiring that new horizontal cables be installed. The interconnect will only require that the cabling from the interconnect to the modular be reinstalled to adapt to the new modular furniture configuration. This means that the horizontal cabling from the closet to the interconnect can remain undisturbed.

The open office cabling specifications were originally published in the TIA/EIA TSB-75 standard. The specifications in this standard will be incorporated into the new ANSI/TIA/EIA-568-B.1 standard. Both standards specify that the following cabling components can be used for open office cabling systems:

▼ Multi-user telecommunications outlet assembly (MUTOA)

▲ Consolidation point (CP)

MULTI-USER TELECOMMUNICATIONS OUTLET ASSEMBLY (MUTOA)

The *multi-user telecommunications outlet assembly* (MUTOA) is a multiple port telecommunications outlet (see Figure 7-10). This cabling component is useful in open office environments where office furniture is moved or rearranged frequently. The MUTOA enables multiple horizontal cables to be terminated in a common location on the floor. Work area cords are then run from the MUTOA to each individual work area location. The use of the MUTOA enables the horizontal cables to remain intact and undisturbed when the modular furniture is moved or rearranged. The work area cords are the only cables that need to be changed.

The MUTOA is a multiport telecommunications outlet that serves an entire furniture cluster (a group of cubicles). Horizontal cables are terminated on the MUTOA, and work area cords connect the communication equipment to the MUTOA ports. The MUTOA replaces the need to install a telecommunications outlet in each work area location. This device serves this function for each piece of communication equipment required in each work area.

The MUTOA must be installed at a location on a building floor so that the furniture cluster served by the MUTOA has access to this device. In addition, each furniture cluster must be served by at least one MUTOA. The location selected for each MUTOA must be a fully accessible and permanent location on the building floor. Examples of acceptable locations would include permanent building walls and columns. Areas that would be classified as unacceptable locations include movable walls or partitions, on movable modular furniture panels or in any obstructed location. Never install MUTOA devices in

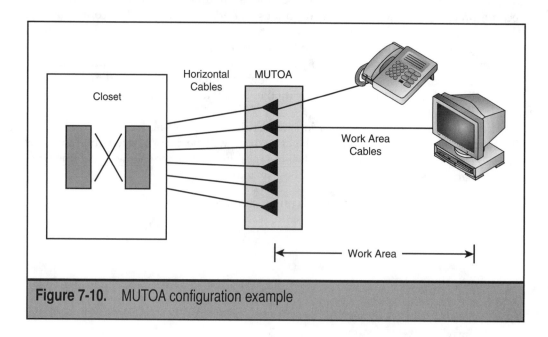

Figure 7-10.   MUTOA configuration example

the ceiling. The furniture may be rearranged in the future making this an obstructed location. The MUTOA can be installed on a furniture panel provided that the panel is permanently secured to the building.

The MUTOA must be limited to serving a maximum of 12 work area locations. If each work area is required to be supported by four horizontal cables, the MUTOA must have a minimum of 48 ports. If the MUTOA device selected for an installation does not have 48 ports, then the MUTOA must serve a smaller number of work locations, and more than one MUTOA must be installed to server the furniture cluster.

The MUTOA must be installed in a permanent and centralized location. This will require that the length of the work area cords be increased from the recommended 5 m (16 ft.) to a 22 m (71 ft.) distance to support the additional distance to the MUTOA. The TIA/EIA TSB-75 and ANSI/TIA/EIA-568-B.1 standards created for following distance chart that defines the maximum length of work area cords based on the length of the horizontal cables to the MUTOA.

Table 7-2 illustrates that the maximum length of the channel is reduced when the length of the work area cords are increased. This is because work area cords are stranded and these cables exhibit 20 percent more attenuation than solid conductor cables. The maximum length of work area cords must be limited to 22 m (71 ft.).

The work area cords that connect to the MUTOA must be uniquely labeled according to the specifications defined in the ANSI/TIA/EIA-606 standard. In addition, each port on the MUTOA must be labeled to include the length of the work area cord attached to that port.

Horizontal Cable Length	Work Area Cord Length	Combined Length of WA and Closet Cords	Maximum Channel Length
90 m (295 ft.)	5 m (16 ft.)	10 m (33 ft.)	100 m (328 ft.)
85 m (297 ft.)	9 m (30 ft.)	14 m (46 ft.)	99 m (325 ft.)
80 m (262 ft.)	13 m (44 ft.)	18 m (60 ft.)	98 m (321 ft.)
75 m (246 ft.)	17 m (57 ft.)	22 m (71 ft.)	97 m (318 ft.)
70 m (230 ft.)	22 m (71 ft.)	27 m (89 ft.)	97 m (318 ft.)

Table 7-2. MUTOA Work Area Cord Maximum Length

CONSOLIDATION POINT (CP)

The *consolidation point* (CP) is an interconnection point contained within the horizontal cable run (see Figure 7-11). The CP is an interconnect device that is installed replacing the optional transition point (TP) allowed in each horizontal cabling run. Industry cabling standards require that no more than one CP be installed in the same horizontal cabling channel or link. In addition, because the CP is used in lieu of the TP, only one CP or TP is enabled to be used in the same horizontal cabling channel or link.

The CP hardware is defined as an interconnect and not a cross-connection style termination. An interconnect does not enable any administration of the cabling pairs at this termination point like a cross-connection. Solid conduct horizontal cable extends from the CP and must be terminated with a telecommunications outlet in each work area location. The CP configuration uses a telecommunications outlet in each work area location and uses standard 5 m (16 ft.) work area cords.

The CP is different from the MUTOA in a couple of ways. First, the CP is part of the horizontal cabling subsystem. The cables that extend from the CP and terminate on a TP in the work area are also part of the horizontal subsystem. The MUTOA is the equivalent of a telecommunications outlet and is also part of the horizontal subsystem. The work area cords that connect the MUTOA to the communication equipment are part of the work area subsystem. When modular furniture in an open office environment is rearranged, the horizontal cable from the CP to the telecommunications outlets will be replaced. The modular cords will be the only cables replaced in a MUTOA configuration.

The CP must be installed at a location on a building floor so it is accessible to the furniture cluster it must serve. In addition, each furniture cluster must be served by at least

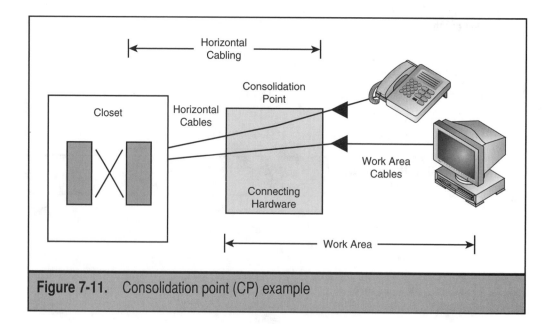

Figure 7-11.   Consolidation point (CP) example

one CP. The location selected for each CP must be a fully accessible and permanent location on the building floor. Examples of acceptable locations would include permanent building walls and columns. Areas that would be classified as unacceptable locations include movable walls or partitions, on movable modular furniture panels or in any obstructed location. Never install CP interconnect devices in ceiling spaces. The furniture may be rearranged in the future making this an obstructed location. The CP can be installed on a furniture panel provided that the panel is permanently secured to the building. Industry cabling standards recommend installing the CP a minimum of 15 m (49.2 ft) from the TR. Finally, never use a CP for a direct connection to active communication equipment.

The CP must be limited to serving a maximum of 12 work area locations. If each work area is required to be supported by four horizontal cables, the CP must have a minimum of 48 ports for cable interconnections. The CP must be designed to accommodate growth for each furniture cluster. CPs must be labeled according to the specifications in the ANSI/TIA/EIA-606 standard. Any cable change not associated with a reconfiguration of the modular furniture must be performed at the cross-connect in the TR.

UNDERCARPET CABLING SYSTEMS

Undercarpet cabling systems are another cabling variation that may be found in the work area. An undercarpet cabling system is sometimes required in work area locations where there are no means for distributing horizontal cables to a work area. These cabling systems use a flat style cable to run under the carpet to each work area location.

Undercapet cables are installed under carpets to prevent workers or other building occupants from tripping over the exposed horizontal cables. Standard round twisted-pair cable is run from the TR as close as practice to each work area. Then the round horizontal cable is transitioned to a flat cable and run under the carpet to each work area location. The optional TP is the location where the two cable types connect together in the horizontal cabling run.

The TP is similar to the CP. The TP must be at a centralized and permanent location on the building floor. A junction box, sometimes called a transition box, is normally installed in a permanent building location such as a permanent wall or column. The box must have access to the floor surface and access to the horizontal distribution system. The box must be sized based on the number of undercarpet cables that must be supported. Table 7-3 provides minimum box size recommendations.

UNDERCARPET CABLE TYPES

Undercarpet cable is generically defined as low profile or flat cable. This type of cable can be directly on the building concrete slab and covered with carpet or carpet squares.

Number of Flat Undercarpet Cables	Minimum Box Size		
4 Pair Cables	Height	Width	Depth
3	75 mm (3 in.)	125 mm (5 in.)	38 mm (1.5 in.)
4	75 mm (3 in.)	200 mm (8 in.)	38 mm (1.5 in.)
6	75 mm (3 in.)	250 mm (10 in.)	38 mm (1.5 in.)
8	75 mm (3 in.)	300 mm (12 in.)	38 mm (1.5 in.)

Table 7-3. Minimum Box Size Recommendations

Undercarpet cable is available for the following media types:

▼ UTP cable

■ ScTP cable

■ STP-A cable

■ Coaxial cable

▲ Optical fiber cable

Twisted-pair undercarpet cables must always be made using twisted-pair construction. The individual cable pairs are twisted together supporting balanced signaling scheme but the entire cable configuration is flat and is to be installed under carpets without creating unsightly bumps or causing a tripping hazard.

USING UNDERCARPET CABLE

Undercarpet cables should be used as part of the horizontal cabling when an adequate distribution method for the horizontal cables is not provided to each work area location. It is recommended that undercarpet cable be installed in a zone configuration (see Figure 7-12). This will limit the distance of the flat undercarpet cables. This will also keep the TP as the center of the undercarpet cabling zone.

It is recommend that undercarpet cabling zones be limited to a maximum of a 9 m by 9 m (30 by 30 ft.) area. Undercarpet cable runs should be kept to a maximum length of 10 m (33 ft.) or less. Each undercarpet cable zone should include a small number of work area locations. This will limit outages or disruptions if the cabling must be repaired or rearranged.

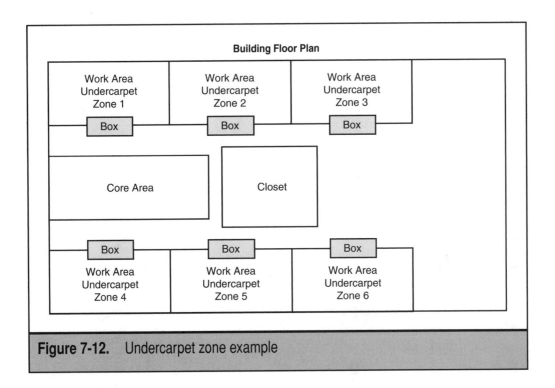

Figure 7-12.   Undercarpet zone example

Undercarpet cabling should be the last choice for a horizontal distribution system due to its high cost and limited flexibility. If undercarpet cabling is used, verify that work area locations have been finalized and all construction has been completed before installing the undercarpet cables. If undercarpet power cables are to be installed, verify that sufficient separation exists between the power and communication cables according the local, state, and national electrical codes. Power cables must never cross over undercarpet communications cable. The power cables must maintain a minimum separation of 150 mm (6 in.) at all times.

CHAPTER SUMMARY

The work area is the space within a building where employees, building occupants, or system users reside and interact with their communication equipment. This is also the area where the horizontal communication cables are terminated. The work area is also the portion of a structured cabling system that connects to the user's communication equipment.

Work area locations can be placed in any usable square footage in a building or on a building floor. Each employee or occupant of a building is normally assigned one work area location for performing their work duties. This location is typically an office or cubicle.

Industry planning guidelines recommend allocating a minimum of 10 sq. m (100 sq. ft.) of useable floor space per work area location. Industry cabling standards also require that a minimum of two approved media types be installed to each work area location.

Industry cabling standards require that each work area location be provided with a minimum of one work area outlet location. A work area outlet location is usually a faceplate supporting two or more modular outlet/connectors. Each outlet of connection must terminate one approved type of horizontal media. Therefore, each work area location must be supported by a minimum of two modular outlet/connections and two approved horizontal cables.

User equipment includes the types of devices found in a user work space that need a physical connection to the horizontal cables. Work area line cords, sometimes called modular line cords or just line cords, are the cables used in the work area subsystem. These cords are used to connect communication devices to the horizontal cabling. Work area line cords should always be made using a stranded type of media. Stranded media is preferred for work area environments because stranded media is more flexible than solid conductor media. This means that the media can take the twisting and bending of the media as it is typical of in the work area without the cable conductors breaking. Work area line cords must also be constructed where the cable pairs are twisted together.

Industry cabling standards provide a maximum provision of 10 m (33 ft.) for the combined length of work area and TR equipment cords. Industry cabling standards recommend a maximum of 5 m (16 ft.) for work area cables. This leaves a provision for a maximum of 5 m (16 ft.) cords in the TR.

It is recommended that the quality of media used in the work area should be the same or better than the quality of media used for the horizontal cabling. Work area cords that have a lower performance rating than the installed horizontal media should never be used. The work area cord will exhibit higher attenuation and lower NEXT than the horizontal cable.

Application-specific components are sometimes required in a work area to support different media types, to match cable impedance, or to support legacy computer equipment. Any cabling components or special adapters that are required for equipment installed in the work area must be part of the work area subsystem. Industry cabling standards require that application-specific cabling components and special adapters required in the work area must remain external to the outlet/connector.

The telecommunications outlet/connector is an interface between the horizontal cabling and the work area cabling. The telecommunications outlet is the interface for the work area cabling to connect with the horizontal cabling. An 8-pin modular jack provides a standard interface point between these two cabling subsystems. A minimum of two telecommunications outlets/connectors (ports) should be provided for each work area location in a building. More than two telecommunications outlets/connectors can be installed in each work area location. Industry standards require a minimum of two outlets/connectors (ports) because most work area locations typically have cabling requirements for at least one voice and one data device.

Eight-position modular outlets (ISO 8877) are recommended to terminate UTP and ScTP horizontal cables used for voice and data applications. All eight position modular outlets should be wired according to the T568A or T568B configurations. These configurations are specified in the ANSI/TIA/EIA-568-A and ANSI/TIA/EIA-568-B.1 cabling standards. The T568A configuration is the recommended outlet termination scheme for new installations. The T568B modular outlet configuration is defined as an optional termination scheme. This configuration is also supported by industry standards for existing installations.

Open office environments are characterized by frequent moving and rearranging of the modular furniture. Open office cabling strategies are designed to adapt to the frequent moves and changes to the modular furniture. Open office cabling incorporates an interconnect in the horizontal cabling. This optional element in the horizontal subsystem enables the open office space and modular furniture to be reconfigured as needed without requiring that new horizontal cables be installed.

The multi-user telecommunications outlet assembly (MUTOA) is a multiple port telecommunications outlet. The MUTOA enables multiple horizontal cables to be terminated in a common location on the floor. Work area cords are then run from the MUTOA to each individual work area location. The consolidation point (CP) is an interconnection point contained within the horizontal cable run. Industry cabling standards require that no more than one CP be installed in the same horizontal cabling channel or link.

Undercarpet cabling systems are another cabling variation that may be found in the work area. These cabling systems use a flat style cable to run under the carpet to each work area location. Undercarpet cable is generically defined as low profile or flat cable. This type of cable can be directly on the building concrete slab and covered with carpet or carpet squares.

CHAPTER 8

Structured Cabling Standards and Organizations

The design and installation of communication cabling requires knowledge of numerous codes and standards. There are required codes that mandate how an installation is to be completed and what materials must be used. There are standards that address system performance and describe the recommended practices to guarantee system operation.

This chapter will describe the important codes and standards that pertain to the design and installation of communications cabling systems.

CONSTRUCTION CODES

Codes and standards are very important for communications cabling and the entire construction industry. The purpose of a code is to ensure safety and a minimum level of quality. When adopted by an agency having authority, a code has the force of law behind it and possible regulatory powers associated with it. This enables codes to be enforced by law.

Codes pertain to the following aspects of the construction industry:

▼   Building codes

■   Electrical codes

▲   Fire codes

Codes address minimum safety performance specifications and do not address system performance specifications. This is the function of a standard.

National Electrical Code (NEC)

The most important code that impacts the installation of communication cabling systems is the National Electrical Code (NEC). The NEC was developed by the National Fire Protection Association (NFPA).

The NEC is used by the following individuals or organizations:

▼   Insurance companies and/or lawyers to establish liability in the event of a fire or injury

■   Fire inspectors or building inspectors for building code enforcement

▲   Installation contractors to promote a safe and compliant installation

The NEC specifies minimum provisions for the installation of electrical and communication cables to provide safety and to guarantee a quality installation. The major intent is to protect people and property from harm due to electrical hazards, construction defects or injury from fire or smoke. The NEC is updated every three years.

Most federal government agencies, state government agencies, and local municipalities use the NEC, in whole or in part, as their legal electrical code. It is very common for a state or local municipality to adopt the basic framework of the NEC and add more stringent requirements.

The articles and chapters that are relevant for the installation of communication cable are

▼ **Article 250**   Defines electrical grounding requirements.

■ **Article 725**   Defines how electrical circuits are classified. The classifications are: Class 1, Class 2, and Class 3 remote control, signaling, and power limited systems. It also defines what types of circuits can be co-installed within a single raceway or conduit.

■ **Article 760**   Defines the system and cabling requirements for fire alarm systems.

■ **Article 770**   Addresses the installation of optical fiber cables and raceways. It addresses the markings for optical fiber cable and the environments for the installation for each cable type.

■ **Article 800**   Contains the requirements for communication systems. It addresses cable markings for communication cables. It also addresses the physical separation required for communication cables and grounding and bonding requirements.

■ **Article 810**   Contains the requirements for radio and television equipment.

▲ **Article 820**   Contains the requirements for community antenna television cabling and equipment.

STANDARDS

Standards are different than codes. The purpose of a standard is to ensure some minimum level of performance for a component or an entire system.

The Telecommunications Industry Association (TIA) defines a *standard* as

"A document that establishes engineering and technical requirements for processes, procedures, practices and methods that have been decreed by authority or adoption by consensus."

Standards play an important part in providing uniformity in structured cabling systems design. These standards become the foundation upon which structured cabling systems and new technologies are based.

Standards have proven to be extremely critical for the telecommunications cabling industry. Standards have enabled cabling systems to be designed and installed without knowing what communication systems or applications were to be utilized, yet knowing that all desired applications would work, provided the standards were followed. In addition, standards enable a communication cabling system to grow and change as technology changes. This reduces disruption to existing services and reduces the costs of moves, adds, and changes.

TELECOMMUNICATIONS
CABLING STANDARDS PRODUCERS

Many organizations exist today that are involved with the development and formalization for standards. Most manufacturers work with standards organizations to verify that their products are standards compliant. These organization that are responsible for developing and publishing standards in North America include the following:

▼ American National Standards Institute (ANSI)

■ Electronic Industries Alliance (EIA)

■ Telecommunications Industry Association (TIA)

■ Canadian Standards Association (CSA)

▲ Institute of Electrical and Electronic Engineers (IEEE)

There are also similar organizations that develop standards internationally. They are typically responsible for developing standards for a particular country or group of countries. The international standards organizations include the following:

▼ **International Organization for Standardization/International Electrotechnical Commission (ISO/IEC)**   This is the top organization for creating and publishing international standards. It publishes the International Standard 11801:2000-Generic Cabling for Customer Premises.

▲ **European Standards Group (CENELEC)**   This is the European Committee for Electrotechnical Standardization. This organization is responsible for issuing standards representing contributions from 19 European countries.

There are other organizations that are solely concerned with developing safety standards. These organizations include the following:

▼ Underwriters Laboratories (UL)

■ Electrical Testing Laboratories (ETL)

■ Federal Communications Commission (FCC)

■ National Electrical Code (NEC)

■ Canadian Electrical Code (CEC)

▲ Canadian Standards Association (CSA)

American National Standards Institute (ANSI)

ANSI is the primary organization with the responsibility of creating standards for the United States. ANSI was created in 1918 and has been developing and publishing U.S.

standards ever since. ANSI is responsible for the coordination, formalization, and adoption of national standards for the United States.

ANSI is also responsible for representing the United States at international standards meetings and conferences. International standards meetings are the place where international standards are proposed, voted on, and formalized.

ANSI doesn't write or create all standards. Sometimes organizations, such as the IEEE, develop a standard, which is forwarded to ANSI. ANSI will review the standard and vote on the document to become a formal U.S. standard. Once a document is approved to become a U.S. standard, it is designated with ANSI in the title. Examples include the ANSI/TIA/EIA-568-A and ANSI/TIA/EIA-568-B cabling standards.

Electronic Industries Alliance (EIA)

The EIA is a trade organization for electronic devices and system manufacturers. The EIA has the responsibility for setting standards that will be used by member groups.

The EIA has long been involved in the establishment of standards relating to communications systems and the signaling methods used for these systems. The best known example is the development of the EIA-232 (formerly known as the RS-232) interface. It defines a standard interface and signaling scheme that every device manufacturer can use in their communication equipment.

Telecommunications Industry Association (TIA)

The TIA is the most important standards organization for communication cabling systems and standards. It was formed in 1988. The TIA represents the telecommunications sector of the EIA. It is responsible for the development, updating, and publishing of standards related to communication cabling. The TIA has developed and published the following standards related to communications cabling:

- ▼ **ANSI/TIA/EIA-568-A**   Commercial building telecommunications cabling standard (to be updated and released as the ANSI/TIA/EIA-568-B standard)

- ■ **ANSI/TIA/EIA-569-A**   Commercial building standard for pathways and spaces

- ■ **ANSI/TIA/EIA-570-A**   Residential and light commercial telecommunications wiring standard

- ■ **ANSI/TIA/EIA-606**   Administration standard for telecommunications infrastructure of commercial buildings

- ■ **ANSI/TIA/EIA-607**   Commercial building grounding and bonding requirements for telecommunications

- ▲ **ANSI/TIA/EIA-758**   Customer-owned outside plant

TIA cabling standards are created by a committee with members representing both manufacturers and end users. The committee responsible for communication cabling standards is TR-42. The formal name for this committee is the User Premises Telecommunications Infrastructure. The TR-42 committee has been divided into multiple subcommittees to address the different aspects of communication cabling. These include the following:

▼ **TR-42.1**   Commercial building telecommunications cabling

■ **TR-42.2**   Residential telecommunications infrastructure

■ **TR-42.3**   Commercial building telecommunications pathways and spaces

■ **TR-42.4**   Outside plant telecommunications infrastructure

■ **TR-42.5**   Telecommunications infrastructure terms and symbols

■ **TR-42.6**   Telecommunications infrastructure and equipment administration

■ **TR-42.7**   Telecommunications copper cabling systems

■ **TR-42.8**   Telecommunications optical fiber cabling systems

▲ **TR-42.9**   Industrial telecommunications infrastructure

Canadian Standards Association (CSA)

The CSA is a nonprofit, independent organization operating a listing service for electrical and electronic materials and equipment designated for use in Canada. The CSA has the responsibility for developing and publishing the Canadian equivalents of the ANSI/TIA/EIA cabling standards.

The CSA has published an equivalent Canadian version for each of the TIA cabling standards. These standards are identical to their U.S. counterparts except that the Canadian Electrical Code (CEC) is referenced in these standards instead of the U.S. NEC. These standards are

▼ **CSA T529**   Commercial building telecommunications cabling standard

■ **CSA T530**   Commercial building standard for pathways and spaces

■ **CSA T525**   Residential and light commercial telecommunications wiring standard

■ **CSA T528**   Administration standard for telecommunications infrastructure of commercial buildings

▲ **CSA T527**   Commercial building grounding and bonding requirements for telecommunications

Institute of Electrical and Electronic Engineers (IEEE)

The Institute of Electrical and Electronic Engineers (IEEE) is an organization that develops standards for local area networks (LANs). The LAN standards and specifications developed usually address the physical layer electronics and cabling requirements.

The IEEE stated Project 802 in the early 1980s to create LAN standards that would be compatible with the OSI model. The LANs defined and developed by the IEEE correlate to the two lowest layers of the OSI model. All of the IEEE developed LAN standards are part of project 802. These include the following standards:

▼ **IEEE 802.1**   Higher layer LAN protocols

■ **IEEE 802.2**   Logical Link Control (LLC)

■ **IEEE 802.3**   Carrier Sense Multiple Access with Collision Detection (CSMA/CD)

■ **IEEE 802.4**   Token Bus

■ **IEEE 802.5**   Token Ring

■ **IEEE 802.6**   Metropolitan Area Networks (MANs)

■ **IEEE 802.7**   Broadband technologies

■ **IEEE 802.8**   Optical fiber technology

■ **IEEE 802.9**   Integrated services

■ **IEEE 802.10**   LAN security

■ **IEEE 802.11**   Wireless LANs

■ **IEEE 802.12**   Demand priority

■ **IEEE 802.14**   Cable modems

■ **IEEE 802.15**   Wireless Personal Area Network

■ **IEEE 802.16**   Broadband wireless access

▲ **IEEE 802.17**   Resilient Packet Ring

The IEEE creates standards and submits all of them to ANSI. ANSI will vote on the standards, and they will become U.S. standards. ANSI will in turn submit U.S. standards to the ISO where they will be voted on to become international standards.

TIA/EIA TELECOMMUNICATIONS CABLING STANDARDS

In the United States, communication cabling standards are created and published by the TIA. The important TIA cabling standards are

▼ **ANSI/TIA/EIA-568-A**   Commercial building telecommunications cabling standard (to be updated and released as the ANSI/TIA/EIA-568-B standard)

■ **ANSI/TIA/EIA-569-A**   Commercial building standard for pathways and spaces

- **ANSI/TIA/EIA-570-A**   Residential and light commercial telecommunications wiring standard

- **ANSI/TIA/EIA-606**   Administration standard for telecommunications infrastructure of commercial buildings

- **ANSI/TIA/EIA-607**   Commercial building grounding and bonding requirements for telecommunications

All of the TIA cabling standards are reviewed in this chapter. For greater understanding of any of the following standards, it is recommended that you purchase a copy of the standard from the TIA.

ANSI/TIA/EIA-568 Standard

The ANSI/TIA/EIA-568-A standard is defined as the commercial building telecommunications standard. This standard provides guidelines and recommendations for the design, selection of materials, and installation for communication cabling systems.

The ANSI/TIA/EIA-568-A standard is the second edition of the commercial building telecommunications cabling standard. The original standard was released in 1991. It was known as the EIA/TIA-568 standard. In 1995, the standard was updated and republished as the ANSI/TIA/EIA-568-A standard. In 1999, the process of updating the standard began again, and a revised version of the commercial building telecommunications cabling standard is being republished in 2001 and will be known as the ANSI/TIA/EIA-568-B standard. The ANSI/TIA/EIA-568-B standard will actually be three individual standards:

- ANSI/TIA/EIA-568-B.1

- ANSI/TIA/EIA-568-B.2

- ANSI/TIA/EIA-568-B.3

Each section of the ANSI/TIA/EIA-568-B standard will address a different aspect of a telecommunications cabling. This standard will be described later in this chapter.

ANSI/TIA/EIA-568 Standard Overview

The ANSI/TIA/EIA-568 standard was originally published in 1991. This standard was written to specify a generic telecommunications cabling system for commercial buildings. The intent was to promote cabling systems that would support both a multivendor and multiproduct environment. The primary objective of the standard was to enable the planning and installation of a structured cabling system that would be designed and installed.

The ANSI/TIA/EIA-568 standard specifies minimum requirements for telecommunications cabling. The standard makes recommendations in the areas of

- Cabling topologies

- Maximum cabling distances

■ Performance of cables and connecting hardware

▲ Configuration of telecommunications outlet/connectors

The ANSI/TIA/EIA-568 standard is intended to support a variety of building types and user applications. This standard can be used for all buildings that meet the criteria:

▼ A geographic distance of up to 3,000 m (9,840 ft.) between cable termination points

■ Office space up to 1,000,000 sq. m (10,000,000 sq. ft.)

▲ A user population of up to 50,000 individuals

The ANSI/TIA/EIA-568 standard is intended to support the following user applications and have a useful life in excess of ten years. The user applications include

▼ Voice systems

■ Data systems

■ Video systems

■ Imaging systems

■ Security and control systems

▲ Building energy and management systems

The ANSI/TIA/EIA-568 standard was updated in 1995. The reviewed version of the standard is called the ANSI/TIA/EIA-568-A standard. The release of the ANSI/TIA/EIA-568-A standard phased out original ANSI/TIA/EIA-568 standard.

NOTE: The ANSI/TIA/EIA-568-A standard will be referenced throughout the remainder of this chapter. A description of the ANSI/TIA/EIA-568-B standard will follow. The section describing the ANSI/TIA/EIA-568-B standard will primarily focus on the differences between the two standards.

ANSI/TIA/EIA-568-A STANDARD

The ANSI/TIA/EIA-568-A standard is organized by cabling subsystems (see Figure 8-1). The communication subsystem is defined by the following:

▼ Work area cabling

■ Horizontal cabling

■ Backbone cabling

■ Telecommunications rooms (TRs)

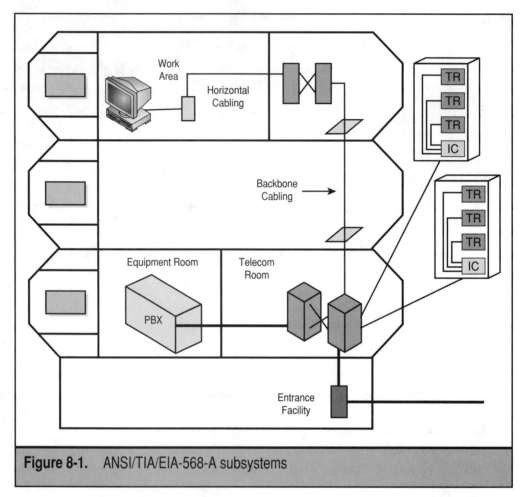

Figure 8-1. ANSI/TIA/EIA-568-A subsystems

■ Equipment rooms (ERs)

■ Entrance facility (EF)

▲ Administration

Work Area Cabling

The ANSI/TIA/EIA-568-A standard uses the term work area cabling to describe the cabling that extends from the telecommunications outlet/connector to the user equipment installed in the work area (see Figure 8-2).

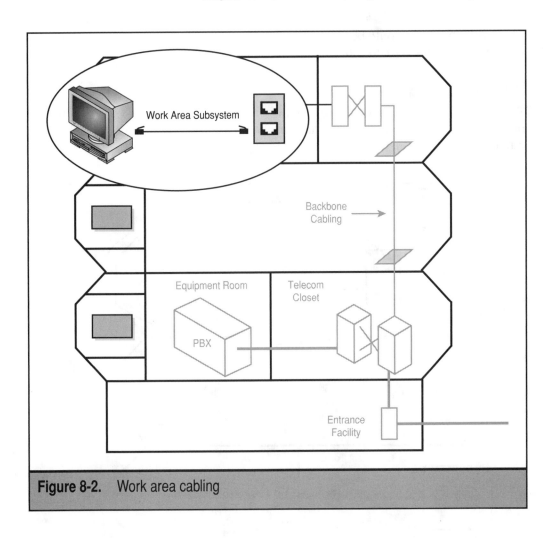

Figure 8-2. Work area cabling

The ANSI/TIA/EIA-568-A standard defines the work area cabling as having the following characteristics:

▼ Generally considered to be nonpermanent cables and easily changed.

■ Maximum work area cable length is 3 m (10 ft.).

■ Work area should always be made of stranded media to provide flexibility.

■ Work area cords must have identical connectors on both ends.

▲ Any cabling adapter or impedance matching device should remain external to the telecommunications outlet/connector used to terminate the horizontal cable.

Work area cables should be the same or higher quality that the horizontal media that is terminated on the telecommunications outlet/connector.

Horizontal Cabling

The ANSI/TIA/EIA-568-A standard uses the term horizontal cabling to describe the portion of a structured cabling system that runs horizontally along the floor or ceiling of a building from the TR to the work area (see Figure 8-3).

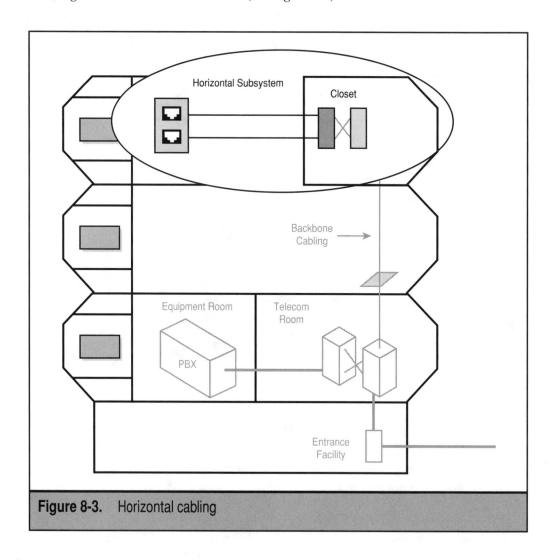

Figure 8-3.   Horizontal cabling

The ANSI/TIA/EIA-568-A standard defines the horizontal subsystem as having the following characteristics:

▼ Contains the greatest quantity of cables.

■ The cables, once installed, are not easily accessible.

■ All installed cables should accommodate a variety of user applications to the desk.

▲ The cabling should be designed to minimize disruptions if the cabling must be changed.

Horizontal Cabling Topology

The recommendations for the horizontal cabling topology include the following (see Figure 8-4):

▼ Horizontal cables must always be installed in a physical star topology.

■ Each work area telecommunications outlet/connector must connect to a horizontal cross-connect (HC) located on the same floor.

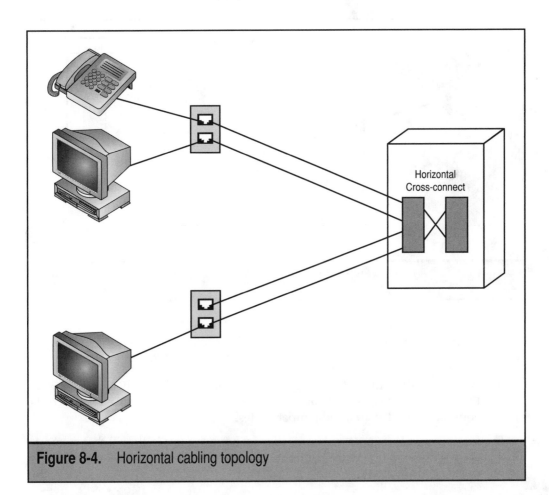

Figure 8-4. Horizontal cabling topology

■ Application specific electronics, such as BALUNS or media filters, must not be part of the horizontal cabling. These devices must be external to the telecommunications outlet/connector.

■ Each horizontal cabling run shall have no more than one transition point (TP). This is the interconnection point between round horizontal cable and flat undercarpet cable.

▲ Bridge taps (multiple appearances of the same cable pair) and splices are not enabled in the horizontal cabling.

Horizontal Cabling Distances

The ANSI/TIA/EIA-568-A standard specifies that regardless of media installed for the horizontal cabling, the maximum distance for all horizontal cables is limited to 90 m (295 ft.) (see Figure 8-5). This distance is measured for termination at the HC in the TR to the termination of the outlet/connector in the work area.

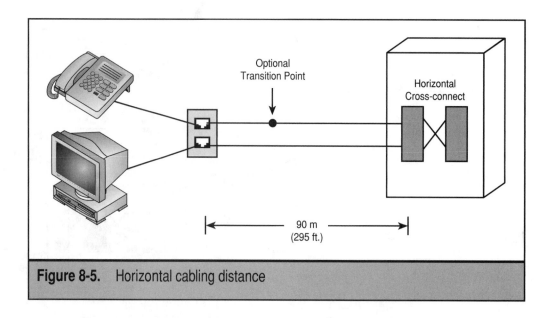

Figure 8-5. Horizontal cabling distance

The ANSI/TIA/EIA-568-A standard also makes the following distance provisions for regarding work area line cords and equipment patch or jumper cables.

▼ An allowance of 10 m (33 ft.) is provisioned for each cabling channel. This 10 m (33 ft.) provision is the maximum combined length for the work area line cords, equipment patch cords, and jumper cables.

■ Equipment patch cords and cross-connect jumper wires in the TR that connect the horizontal cables to the communication system equipment should not exceed 6 m (20 ft.).

▲ Work area line cords used to connect user equipment to the horizontal cable in the work area should not exceed 3 m (10 ft.).

Recognized Media

The ANSI/TIA/EIA-568-A standard recognizes three types of cables for the horizontal subsystem (see Figure 8-6):

▼ Four-pair, 100-ohm UTP cable

■ Two-pair, 150-ohm STP-A cable

▲ Two-strand 62.5/125 multimode optical fiber cable

The original version of the TIA/EIA-568 standard supported 50-ohm coaxial cable as an allowed media type of the horizontal subsystem. The ANSI/TIA/EIA-568-A standard eliminated this media as recognized for new cabling installation. It is still supported for sites that have 50-ohm coaxial cable installed.

The ANSI/TIA/EIA-568-A standard also recognizes the use of hybrid cables in the horizontal subsystem. These are cables consisting of more than one recognized media type

Figure 8-6. Horizontal recognized media

under a common cable jacket. These cables are enabled as long as all media in the hybrid cable are one of the supported media for new cabling installation and hybrid cables meet the power sum NEXT requirements for backbone cables.

Backbone Cabling

The ANSI/TIA/EIA-568-A standard uses the term *backbone cabling* to describe the portion of a structured cabling system that runs between TRs, EFs, and ERs in a single building or a group of buildings on a campus.

Backbone Cabling Topology

The recommendations for the backbone cabling topology include the following (see Figure 8-7):

▼ Backbone cabling shall follow a hierarchical star topology.

■ Each HC in a TR must be connected to either the main cross-connect (MC) or to an intermediate cross-connect (IC) and then to the MC.

■ There shall be no more than two hierarchical levels in the backbone cabling.

■ The path between any two HCs in any two TRs shall pass through three or fewer backbone cross-connects.

■ A maximum of one backbone cross-connect shall be passed through to reach the MC.

▲ Bridge taps are not permitted as part of the backbone cabling.

Recognized Media

The ANSI/TIA/EIA-568-A standard recognizes four types of cables for the backbone subsystem (see Figure 8-8):

▼ 100-ohm UTP backbone cable

■ 150-ohm STP-A cable

■ 62.5/125 multimode optical fiber cable

▲ Singlemode optical fiber cable

The original version of the TIA/EIA-568 standard supported 50-ohm coaxial cable as an allowed media type of the horizontal subsystem. The ANSI/TIA/EIA-568-A standard eliminated this media as recognized for new cabling installation. It is still supported for sites that have 50-ohm coaxial cable installed.

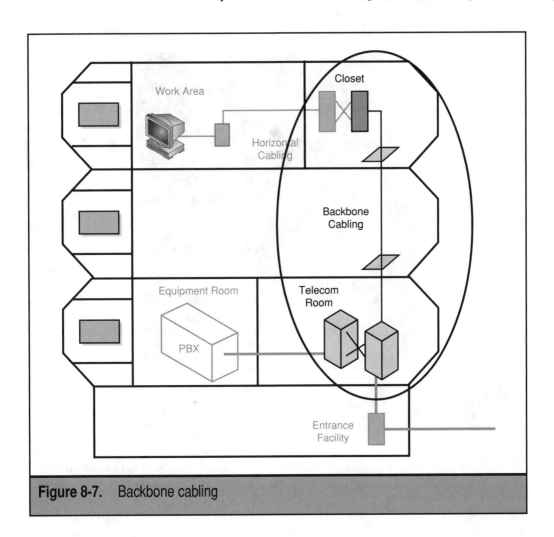

Figure 8-7.   Backbone cabling

Backbone Cabling Distances

The maximum distances supported by any of the recognized backbone media is different for each media type and where the media is installed. The maximum distance for each type of backbone media is listed in the following.

100-ohm UTP cable supports a maximum distance of 800 m (2,624 ft.). This is illustrated as follows:

▼   HC (FD) to MC (CD) = 800 m (2,624 ft.)

■   HC (FD) to IC (BD) = 300 m (984 ft.)

▲   IC (BD) to MC (CD) = 500 m (1,640 ft.)

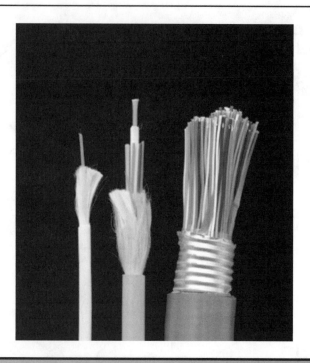

Figure 8-8. Backbone recognized media

These cabling distances are meant to support voice or low-speed data applications. If the 100-ohm UTP backbone cable is to support high-speed LAN or data applications, the maximum distance must be limited to 90 m (295 ft.).

150-ohm STP-A cable supports a maximum distance of 90 m (295 ft.) between any two termination points. This is illustrated as follows:

▼ HC (FD) to MC (CD) = 90 m (295 ft.)

■ HC (FD) to IC (BD) = 90 m (295 ft.)

▲ IC (BD) to MC (CD) = 90 m (295 ft.)

NOTE: 150-ohm STP-A cable is limited to 90 m (295 ft.) distances because this media is only used for high-speed data applications.

62.5/125 multimode optical fiber cable supports a maximum distance 2,000 m (6,560 ft.). This is illustrated as follows:

▼ HC (FD) to MC (CD) = 2,000 m (6,560 ft.)

■ HC (FD) to IC (BD) = 500 m (1,640 ft.)

▲ IC (BD) to MC (CD) = 1,500 m (4,920 ft.)

Singlemode optical fiber cable supports a maximum distance of 3,000 m (9,840 ft.). This is illustrated as follows:

▼ HC (FD) to MC (CD) = 3,000 m (9,840 ft.)

■ HC (FD) to IC (BD) = 500 m (1,640 ft.)

▲ IC (BD) to MC (CD) = 2,500 m (8,200 ft.)

NOTE: The ANSI/TIA/EIA-568-A standard recognizes that the maximum distance supported by singlemode optical fiber cable greatly exceeds the 3,000 m (9,840 ft.) distance limit referenced in the standard. It states that distances in excess of the maximum 3,000 m (9,840 ft.) distance limit are outside the scope of the ANSI/TIA/EIA-568-A standard.

TIA/EIA TSBs

The ANSI/TIA/EIA-568-A cabling standard is an evolving document. It attempts to keep up with technology changes that are occurring constantly. However, the standard is only revised and published every four to five years. To prevent the standard from becoming obsolete, the TIA publishes Technician or Telecommunications Systems Bulletins (TSBs) and addendums. These TSBs and addendums provide modifications and updates to the standard to address changes in technology. When the ANSI/TIA/EIA-568-A standard is updated and republished, all TSBs and addendums will be incorporated into the new version of the ANSI/TIA/EIA-568-A standard.

The TSBs that were added to the ANSI/TIA/EIA-568-A standard are

▼ **TIA/EIA TSB67** Transmission performance specifications for field testing of unshielded twisted-pair and screened twisted-pair cabling systems

■ **TIA/EIA TSB72** Centralized optical fiber

■ **TIA/EIA TSB75** Additional horizontal cabling practices for open offices

■ **TIA/EIA TSB95** Additional transmission performance guidelines for four-pair, 100-ohm category 5 cabling

The addendums that were added to the ANSI/TIA/EIA-568-A standard are

▼ **ANSI/TIA/EIA-568-A-1** Propagation delay and delay skew specifications for 100-ohm, four-pair cable

■ **ANSI/TIA/EIA-568-A-2** Corrections and additions to TIA/EIA-568-A

- **ANSI/TIA/EIA-568-A-3**   Addendum No. 3 to TIA/EIA-568-A

- **ANSI/TIA/EIA-568-A-4**   Production modular cord Near End Crosstalk (NEXT), loss test methods and requirements for unshielded twisted-pair cabling

▲ **ANSI/TIA/EIA-568-A-5**   Transmission performance specifications for four-pair, 100-ohm category 5e cabling

ANSI/TIA/EIA-568-B STANDARD

The ANSI/TIA/EIA-568-A standard is currently being revised and updated. The new version of the commercial building telecommunications cabling standard will be known as the ANSI/TIA/EIA-568-B standard.

The ANSI/TIA/EIA-568-B standard will actually consist of three different standards. Each of the three parts will define structured cabling systems.

▼ **ANSI/TIA/EIA-568-B.1**   Commercial building telecommunications cabling standard—generic requirements

- **ANSI/TIA/EIA-568-B.2**   Commercial building telecommunications cabling standard—connecting hardware and components

▲ **ANSI/TIA/EIA-568-B.3**   Commercial building telecommunications cabling standard—optical fiber cabling

The new standards will not actually be totally new. They will contain most of the information contained in the ANSI/TIA/EIA-568-A standard. They will also contain all of the TSBs and addendums that were published since the ANSI/TIA/EIA-568-A standard came out in 1995.

The ANSI/TIA/EIA-568-B standard will have some major differences compared to the ANSI/TIA/EIA-568-A standard. A few of the most significant differences are

▼ Category 5e will be the minimum quality of UTP cable that will be recommended for commercial buildings.

- Category 4 UTP cable will be eliminated as a recognized horizontal and backbone media.

- STP-A cable will be eliminated as a recognized horizontal and backbone media for new cabling installations.

- 50/125 μm multimode optical fiber cable will be added as a recognized horizontal and backbone media for new cabling installations.

- Small form factor (SFF) optical fiber connectors are an allowed connector type to terminate singlemode and multimode optical fiber cables in the TR, ER, and EF.

- The maximum distance of work area cables will be increased to 5 m (16 ft.).

- The maximum distance for equipment patch cords or jumper wires in the TR will be reduced to 5 m (16 ft.).

- The provision for work area and TR equipment patch cords or jumper wires will remain the same at 10 m (33 ft.).

▲ Backbone distances will be slightly changed. The overall maximum cable distances will remain the same, but the maximum distance from the HC (FD) to IC (BD) will be reduced to a maximum of 300 m (984 ft.). This change enables the IC (BD) to MC (CD) cable distances to be increased by 200 m (656 ft.).

The ANSI/TIA/EIA-568-B.1 standard makes the following distance recommendations for the recognized backbone media types.

The maximum distances for multipair UTP backbone cables are shown in Table 8-1. The maximum distances for 50/125 μm multimode optical fiber backbone cables are shown in Table 8-2.

The maximum distances for 62.5/125 μm multimode optical fiber backbone cables are shown in Table 8-3. The maximum distances for singlemode optical fiber backbone cables are shown in Table 8-4.

Location	Distance
HC (FD) to MC (CD)	800 m (2,624 ft.)
HC (FD) to IC (BD)	300 m (984 ft.)
IC (BD) to MC (CD)	500 m (1,640 ft.)

Table 8-1. UTP Backbone Cabling Distances

Location	Distance
HC (FD) to MC (CD)	2,000 m (6,560 ft.)
HC (FD) to IC (BD)	300 m (984 ft.)
IC (BD) to MC (CD)	1,700 m (5,575 ft.)

Table 8-2. 50/125 Backbone Cabling Distances

Location	Distance
HC (FD) to MC (CD)	2,000 m (6,560 ft.)
HC (FD) to IC (BD)	300 m (984 ft.)
IC (BD) to MC (CD)	1,700 m (5,575 ft.)

Table 8-3. 62.5/125 Backbone Cabling Distances

Location	Distance
HC (FD) to MC (CD)	3,000 m (9,840 ft.)
HC (FD) to IC (BD)	300 m (984 ft.)
IC (BD) to MC (CD)	2,700 m (8,855 ft.)

Table 8-4. Singlemode Backbone Cabling Distances

ANSI/TIA/EIA-569-A STANDARD

The ANSI/TIA/EIA-569-A standard is the commercial building standard for telecommunications pathways and spaces. This is the second version of this standard to be published by the TIA.

The primary focus of the ANSI/TIA/EIA-569-A standard is to provide design specifications and guidance for all building facilities relating to telecommunications systems and components. The standard provides design and sizing recommendations for building infrastructure to support structured cabling systems.

The ANSI/TIA/EIA-569-A standard identifies six different methods for distributing horizontal cabling from the telecommunications closet (TC) to the work area. These methods are

▼ Underfloor ducts

■ Access floors

■ Conduits

■ Cable trays and wireways

■ Ceiling pathways

▲ Perimeter raceways

These pathways must be designed to handle all recognized types of horizontal media including: unshielded twisted-pair cable, shielded twisted-pair cable, and multimode optical fiber cable.

The ANSI/TIA/EIA-569-A standard identifies four different methods for distributing interbuilding backbone cables to multiple buildings on a campus. These methods are

▼ **Underground backbone pathways** Includes the use of conduits, ducts, or troughs.

■ **Direct buried backbone pathways** Describes the direct burial of cables, without the use of conduits, by trenching, auguring, or boring.

■ **Aerial backbone pathways** Covers running cables above ground. This includes: using poles, supporting cables, separating cables from sources of power, protecting cables, and attaching cables to a building.

▲ **Tunnel backbone pathways** Discusses the provisions for running conduit, trays, wireways, or support strands in a tunnel.

The ANSI/TIA/EIA-569-A standard makes recommendations for the TC location and sizing in a commercial building. All size recommendations are based on the useable floor space that the closet will be serving. The standard makes the following recommendations:

▼ A minimum of one TC per floor.

■ Additional TCs are recommended when the
   ■ Usable floor area to be served is greater than 1,000 sq. m (10,000 sq. ft.).
   ■ Length of the horizontal distribution cable required to reach the work area is greater than 90 m (295 ft.).

■ Locate the TC as close to the building's center, called the building's core, as possible.

▲ When there are multiple TCs per floor, it is recommended to interconnect these with at least one 4-in. conduit.

The ANSI/TIA/EIA-569-A standard makes recommendations on the size of the TC based on the usable floor space served by the closet. The actual size of a TR is based on the usable space defined in Table 8-5.

The size specifications defined for a TR in the ANSI/TIA/EIA-569-A standard should be capable of supporting the communication equipment, cable termination hardware, and other cable-supporting devices.

In an existing building or for a cabling retrofit project, the size of a TR may be smaller than the size recommended for new cable installations. If the size of the closet cannot be altered to meet the recommended size requirements, the minimum size of 1.2 m (4 ft.) deep by 1.8 m (6 ft.) wide and 2.6 m (8.5 ft.) high must be provisioned for each 240 work area locations to be served.

If the usable floor space served is:	The interior dimensions of the TR must be:
500 sq. m (5,000 sq. ft.) or less	3.0 m by 2.4 m (10 by 8 ft.)
Larger than 500 sq. m and less than or equal to 800 sq. m (>5,000 to 8,000 sq. ft.)	3.0 m by 2.7 m (10 by 9 ft.)
Larger than 800 sq. m and less than or equal to 1,000 sq. m (>8,000 to 10,000 sq. ft.)	3.0 m by 3.4 m (10 by 11 ft.)

Table 8-5. Telecommunications Room (TR) Sizing Recommendations

ANSI/TIA/EIA-569-A Addendums

The ANSI/TIA/EIA-569-A standard is similar to the ANSI/TIA/EIA-568-A standard. The standard is always evolving to address changes in technology. The addendums that have been added to the ANSI/TIA/EIA-569-A standard are listed in the following:

▼ **ANSI/TIA/EIA-569-A-1**   Addendum 1—Surface raceways

■ **ANSI/TIA/EIA-569-A-2**   Addendum 2—Furniture pathways and spaces

■ **ANSI/TIA/EIA-569-A-3**   Addendum 3—Access floors

▲ **ANSI/TIA/EIA-569-A-4**   Addendum 4—Poke-thru fittings

ANSI/TIA/EIA-570-A STANDARD

The ANSI/TIA/EIA-570-A standard is the residential and light commercial building telecommunications cabling standard. This is the second version of this standard to be published by the TIA.

The ANSI/TIA/EIA-570-A standard is a premises cabling standard for residential and light commercial buildings. It is intended for buildings that have requirements of between one to four voice circuits. It is also intended to support various types of customer voice and data equipment.

The standard addresses the recent shift of responsibility for the residential cabling from the Local Exchange Carrier (service provider) to the owner of the building. This standard also recognizes residential and light commercial buildings as environments that may have voice and data requirements similar to those found in commercial buildings.

ANSI/TIA/EIA-606 STANDARD

The ANSI/TIA/EIA-606 standard is the administration standard for the telecommunications infrastructure of commercial buildings. It was published in 1993 and there have been no updates to this standard.

The ANSI/TIA/EIA-606 standard provides a uniform administration scheme for all structured cabling system elements that are independent of user applications.

The ANSI/TIA/EIA-606 standard is based on three administration concepts:

▼ Unique identifiers

■ Records

▲ Linkages

Each component of a structured cabling system and the supporting hardware are assigned a unique label linking the component to its record. Records contain information about or related to a specific cabling or infrastructure component. Linkages are logical connections between identifiers and records. They also link one record to another, if a linkage is required.

The ANSI/TIA/EIA-606 standard identifies five major areas of administration. These areas are

▼ Telecommunications spaces

■ Telecommunications pathways

■ Transmission media

■ Termination hardware

▲ Bonding and grounding

NOTE: End-user and application-specific devices are not included in this standard.

The ANSI/TIA/EIA-606 standard identifies color codes that should be assigned to each subsystem or infrastructure element of a structured cabling system. Color coding can simplify structured cabling system administration. The following color code recommendations for these structured cabling system elements are shown in Table 8-6.

ANSI/TIA/EIA-607 STANDARD

The ANSI/TIA/EIA-607 standard is the commercial building grounding and bonding requirements for telecommunications. This standard was published in 1994 and there have

Color	Element
Orange	Demarcation point—central office termination.
Green	Termination of network connections on the customer side of the demarcation point.
Purple	Termination of cables originating from common equipment such as PBXs, LANs, or mainframe/minicomputers.
White	First level backbone media termination in the building containing the main cross-connect.
Gray	Second level backbone media termination in the building containing the main cross-connect.
Blue	Termination of horizontal cables. Required only in the TR end of horizontal cable, not at the outlet.
Brown	Interbuilding backbone cable termination.
Yellow	Termination of auxiliary circuits, alarms, security, and other miscellaneous circuits.
Red	Termination of key telephone systems.

Table 8-6. 606 Standard Color Code Designations

been no updates to this standard. The ANSI/TIA/EIA-607 standard identifies the issues of bonding and grounding as it relates to structured cabling systems.

IMPORTANT: The recommendations made in the ANSI/TIA/EIA-607 standard *do not* supersede the bonding and grounding requirements of national and local electrical codes. This document makes bonding and grounding recommendations for the purpose of meeting structured cabling performance requirements.

The ANSI/TIA/EIA-607 standard identifies various terms throughout the documents (see Figure 8-9). It is important to have an understanding of these terms to fully understand the recommendations described in this document.

▼ **Bonding**   A permanent joining of metallic parts for the purpose of forming an electrically conductive path so as to ensure electrical continuity and capacity to safely conduct any current that is foreign to the communication system.

■ **Bonding conductor**   A conductor used to interconnect the telecommunications bonding infrastructure to the telecommunications equipment power ground of the building.

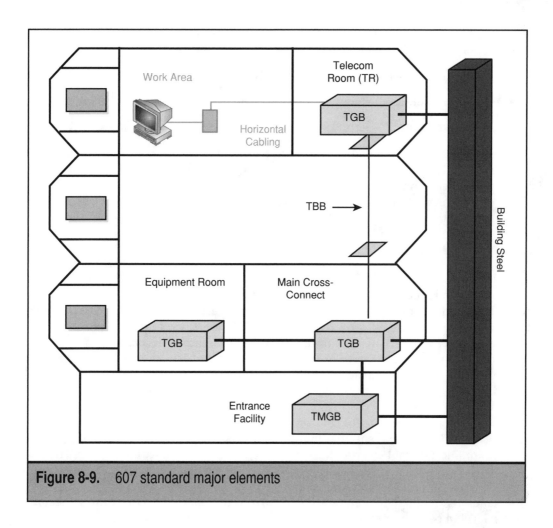

Figure 8-9.   607 standard major elements

- ■ **Ground**   An intentional or accidental conducting connection between any electrical circuit and earth.

- ■ **Effective ground**   An intentional connection between any electrical circuit and earth of sufficiently low impedance to prevent the buildup of voltages that could potentially result in unnecessary hazard to connected equipment or persons.

- ■ **Telecommunications bonding backbone (TBB)**   A copper conductor used to connect the telecommunications main grounding busbar to the telecommunications grounding busbar.

- ▲ **Telecommunications main grounding busbar (TMGB)**   Refers to a busbar bonded to the telecommunications equipment power ground by the bonding conductor.

The ANSI/TIA/EIA-607 standard identifies three major elements to provide grounding and bonding for a structured cabling system. These elements are

▼ Telecommunications bonding backbone (TBB)

■ Telecommunications main grounding busbar (TMGB)

▲ Telecommunications grounding busbar (TGB)

The TMGB serves as a dedicated building grounding electrode for a structured cabling system. The TGB is located in each TC. It serves as a common central point of connection for telecommunications equipment located in the closet. The TBB is intended to reduce or equalize differences between telecommunications systems bonded to it.

CHAPTER SUMMARY

The design and installation of communication cabling requires knowledge of numerous codes and standards. There are required codes that mandate how an installation is to be completed and what materials must be used. There are also standards that address system performance and describe the recommended practices to guarantee system operation.

Codes and standards are very important for communications cabling and the entire construction industry. The purpose of a code is to ensure safety and a minimum level of quality. When adopted by an agency having authority, a code has the force of law behind it and possible regulatory powers associated with it. This enables codes to be enforced by law.

The most important code that impacts the installation of communication cabling systems is the NEC. The NEC specifies minimum provisions for the installation of electrical and communication cables to provide safety and guarantee a quality installation. The major intent is to protect people and property from harm due to electrical hazards, construction defects, or injury from fire or smoke.

Standards are different than codes. The purpose of a standard is to ensure some minimum level of performance for a component or an entire system. Standards play an important part in providing uniformity in structured cabling systems design. These standards become the foundation upon which structured cabling systems and new technologies are based.

Many organizations exist today that are involved with the development and formalization of standards. Most manufacturers work with standards organizations to verify that their products are standards compliant. The major standards organizations that are responsible for developing and publishing standards in North America include: American National Standards Institute (ANSI), Electronic Industries Alliance (EIA), Telecommunications Industry Association (TIA), Canadian Standards Association (CSA), and the Institute of Electrical and Electronic Engineers (IEEE). The major organizations that develop standards internationally are: International Organization for Standardization/International Electrotechnical Commission (ISO/IEC) and the European Standards Group (CENELEC).

The TIA is the most important standards organization for communication cabling system and standards. The TIA represent the telecommunications sector of the EIA. The TIA is responsible for the development, updating, and publishing of standards related to communication cabling.

The Institute of Electrical and Electronic Engineers (IEEE) is an organization that develops standards for local area networks. The local area network (LAN) standards and specifications developed usually address the physical layer electronics and cabling requirements.

The ANSI/TIA/EIA-568-A standard is defined as the commercial building telecommunications standard. This standard provides guidelines and recommendations for the design, selection of materials, and installation for communication cabling systems. The ANSI/TIA/EIA-568-A standard is organized by cabling subsystems. The ANSI/TIA/EIA-568-A standard defines the following communication subsystems: work area cabling, horizontal cabling, backbone cabling, telecommunications rooms (TRs), equipment rooms (ERs), entrance facility (EF), and system administration.

The ANSI/TIA/EIA-569-A standard is the commercial building standard for telecommunications pathways and spaces. This standard provides design and sizing recommendations for building infrastructure to support structured cabling systems. The ANSI/TIA/EIA-569-A standard also makes recommendations for the telecommunications closet (TC) location and sizing in a commercial building.

The ANSI/TIA/EIA-570-A standard is the residential and light commercial building telecommunications cabling standard. This is the second version of this standard to be published by the TIA. The ANSI/TIA/EIA-570-A standard is a premises cabling standard for residential and light commercial buildings. It is intended for buildings that have requirements of between one to four voice circuits. It is also intended to support various types of customer voice and data equipment.

The ANSI/TIA/EIA-606 standard is the administration standard for the telecommunications infrastructure of commercial buildings. The ANSI/TIA/EIA-606 standard provides a uniform administration scheme for all structured cabling system elements that are independent of user applications. The ANSI/TIA/EIA-606 standard also identifies color codes that should be assigned to each subsystem or infrastructure element of a structured cabling system.

The ANSI/TIA/EIA-607 standard is the commercial building grounding and bonding requirements for telecommunications. The ANSI/TIA/EIA-607 standard identifies the issues of bonding and grounding as it relates to structured cabling systems.

CHAPTER 9

Transmission Fundamentals

Communication cables have different characteristics and performance specifications. This is the main reason that there are so many different types of cables sold today. For a communication cable to work for a specific communication system, the cable must be correctly matched to work with the system.

Communication systems that have correctly matched cables will perform correctly and provide proper system performance and long term system reliability. Communication systems that have cables that are incorrectly matched will cause system reliability problems. On one extreme, the system may not work at all. In most cases, the system works with reduced system performance. For example, using the incorrect type of cable for a high-speed LAN may cause the network to not function at all. The incorrect type of cable may cause the high-speed network to operate at either reduced speeds or the errors caused by the cable may cause the LAN to have reduced throughput.

In order to correctly match a network media with a communication system, it is important to understand the different signaling methods used communication systems. It is also important to understand the different characteristics of communications cables and their effects on transmitted signals. This chapter describes important transmission fundamentals of communications systems and communication cables.

TYPES OF SIGNALS

Communication systems use communication cables to send signals between the different system components. All communication systems send communication signals across communication cables. The communication signals are sent between the main switch or control unit and systems devices. The communications signals represent information that must be shared between the different system components. Communication system signals can take one of two forms:

▼   Analog signals

▲   Digital signals

Analog Signals

Analog signals are waveforms that are constantly varying from a positive to negative direction using zero as a reference point (see Figure 9-1). These signals can be modulated to carry information over communication cables.

Many different types of communication systems have used or continue to use analog signals to transmit information. Radio signals are transmitted in an analog format. Voice information has traditionally been transmitted as analog signals. Today, most voice information is transmitted in a digital format.

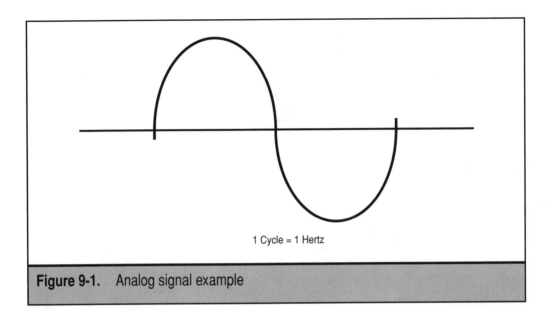

1 Cycle = 1 Hertz

Figure 9-1.   Analog signal example

Analog signals are measured using two parameters:

▼   Amplitude

▲   Frequency

Amplitude is the height of the analog signal (see Figure 9-2). The amplitude represents the power of the signal. The higher the amplitude, the more powerful the signal. Conversely, the smaller the signal amplitude, the weaker the signal. Frequency refers to the number of cycles of the analog signal. The higher the frequency, the more information can be carried by the analog signal.

To transmit information, analog signals can be used as carrier signals. The carrier signal can be modulated to carry information. The carrier signal is modulated and follows variations to the input signal. The changes can be demodulated at the opposite end of the link. Analog signals can be modulated using the following techniques:

▼   **Amplitude modulation**   This technique modulates the height of the carrier signal.

■   **Frequency modulation**   This technique modulates the width of the carrier signal.

▲   **Phase shift modulation**   This technique modulates the phase of the carrier signal.

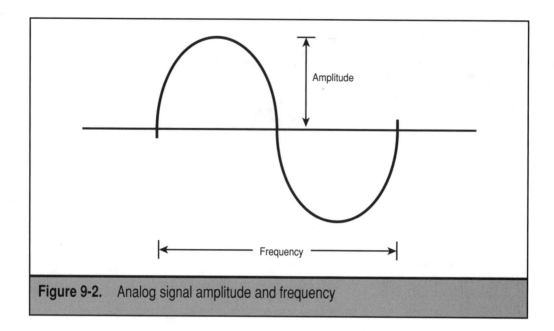

Figure 9-2.   Analog signal amplitude and frequency

Digital Signals

Digital signals are transmitted signals that are represented as discrete pulses (see Figure 9-3). Digital signals look like square waves instead of the rounded wave forms of analog signals. Square digital signals represent either a 1 or a 0.

Most communication systems use digital signals to transmit information. Computers and other electronic devices communicate by sending streams of 1's and 0's. This information is sent across a communication cable in a digital format. If analog information, such as the human voice, is to be sent using digital signaling, the analog signals must first be converted to digital signals using a process called sampling. An example of a digital signal is shown in Figure 9-3.

Digital signals are preferred for sending communication information. These signals can be transmitted with less chance of becoming corrupt and causing system errors when traveling over a communication cable. Most electronic devices and communication networks use digital signaling. Electronic devices, such as computer systems, use digital signals for processing information. This is also the signaling method used when electronic devices communicate together over a network. Digital signals are encoded and transmitted over a communication cable.

Digital signals are the preferred signaling method for communication networks. Digital signals provide more reliable and clearer signals compared to analog signals. Analog signals do not have any predefined shape or height. If noise or other energy sources alter or change the shape of the analog signals, the communication equipment has no way to eliminate the noise. This results in static and poor signal quality on the communication sys-

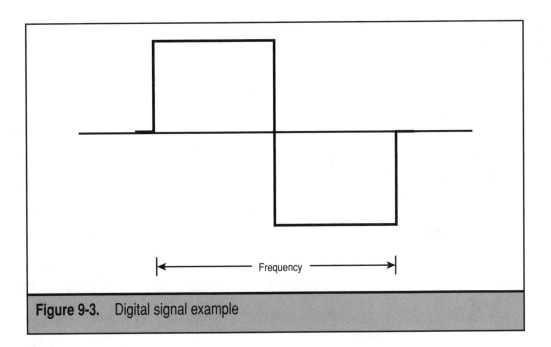

Figure 9-3.   Digital signal example

tem. Digital signals have a predefined shape and height. If noise or other energy sources alter or change the shape of the signal, the communications equipment can repeat the signal and strip the noise out of the signal stream. This results in clear signals and excellent signal quality on the communication system.

RESISTANCE

Resistance is a property of a copper communication cable's conductors. Resistance is a term that indicates the amount of opposition of a given conductor to the flow of electricity. Resistance in a communication conductor results in heat being generated.

Resistance is expressed in a measurement called ohms. One ohm of resistance enables one ampere of current to flow through a conductor when one volt of electricity is supplied.

AMPERAGE

Electrical current flow is measured in amperage, also called amps. *Amperage* is a term that is used to define the strength of an electrical current measured in amperes.

All electrical circuits have electrical current flowing through them. The amperage rating of a communication cabling describes the maximum current the cable can safely carry without exceeding the cable's insulation limitations.

VOLTAGE

The term *voltage* is used to describe a unit of electromotive force or difference in potential between two points in a circuit. A unit of electromotive force is called a volt. One volt can move one amperage of current from a point of lower potential to a point of higher potential.

OHMS LAW

The relationship of voltage, amperage, or resistance in any circuit can be determined by using the formula for Ohm's Law. If two of these values are known, the third can be determined. The formula for Ohm's Law can be expressed using any of the following equations:

▼ $V = I \cdot R$

■ $R = V / I$

▲ $I = V / R$

where,

V = Voltage
I = Current flow (amperes)
R = Resistance

If the amperage of a circuit is 3 amps and the resistance of a circuit is 4 ohms, then the voltage can be calculated as follows:

$V = I \cdot R$
$V = 3 \cdot 4$
$V = 12$ volts

If the voltage of a circuit is 110 volts and the current of a circuit is 15 amps, then the resistance can be calculated as follows:

$R = V / I$
$R = 110 / 15$
$R = 7.33$ ohms

If the voltage of a circuit is 25 volts and the resistance of a circuit is 10 ohms, then the amperage can be calculated as follows:

$I = V / R$
$I = 25 / 10$
$I = 2.5$ amps

FREQUENCY

The term *frequency* is used to express the number of cycles per second of a transmitted signal (see Figure 9-4). Frequency is used when referring to different types of signals including: alternating current, radio signals, and analog signals. Frequency is also a term used to define the bandwidth of a communications channel.

Frequency refers to the number of positive and negative cycles that occur in a defined time interval (such as per second). Frequency is often stated as hertz. One hertz is equal to one positive-to-negative cycle.

Higher frequencies are associated with higher transmission capacity. A carrier signal that has a high frequency can transmit more information than a low frequency. A communication cable that has a high-frequency rating can carry more information than a cable with a low-frequency rating. Therefore, higher frequencies are able to transmit more information.

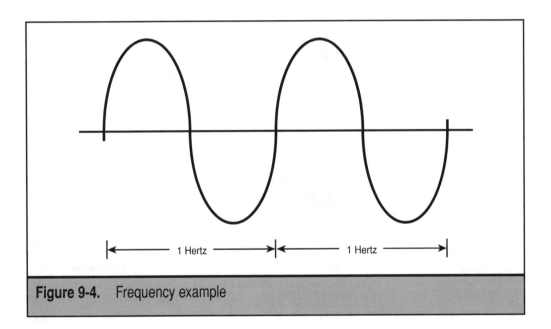

Figure 9-4. Frequency example

MEASURING FREQUENCY

Signal frequencies are usually referenced by the number of cycles per second. The communication industry will usually reference signals in either thousands, millions, or billions of cycles per second. One thousand cycles is known as a kilohertz (kHz), one million cycles is known as a megahertz (MHz), and one billion cycles is known as a gigahertz (GHz). These frequency measurements are shown in Table 9-1.

Unit	Abbreviation	Value
Kilohertz	kHz	1,000 hertz
Megahertz	MHz	1,000,000 hertz
Gigahertz	GHz	1,000,000,000 hertz

Table 9-1. Frequency Measurements

BANDWIDTH

The *bandwidth* of a communications cable is defined as the information carrying capacity of the media. The bandwidth of a communication cable is specified in MHz.

The MHz rating of a cable is the range of frequencies supported by the cable.

The MHz range for most copper communication cables is specified from 1 MHz to the highest frequency range support by the media, such as 100 MHz. This is shown in Table 9-2.

Category Rating	Bandwidth MHz Range Supported
Category 3 Cable	1 to 16 MHz
Category 4 Cable	1 to 20 MHz
Category 5 Cable	1 to 100 MHz
Category 5e Cable	1 to 100 MHz
Category 6 Cable	1 to 250 MHz
Category 7 Cable	1 to 600 MHz

Table 9-2. Copper Communication Cable Bandwidth Ratings

The megahertz range for optical fiber cables is also specified in MHz. The bandwidth rating for optical fiber cables differs depending on the type of optical fiber cable. Singlemode optical fiber cables are generally rated as having unlimited bandwidth. Multimode optical fiber cables have very definite bandwidth limitations (see Figure 9-5). The bandwidth of a multimode optical fiber cable will vary based on the size of the optical core and the wavelength of the optical transmitter. The smaller the core, the greater the cable's bandwidth rating. The longer the transmitter wavelength, the more bandwidth a multimode optical fiber cable will provide.

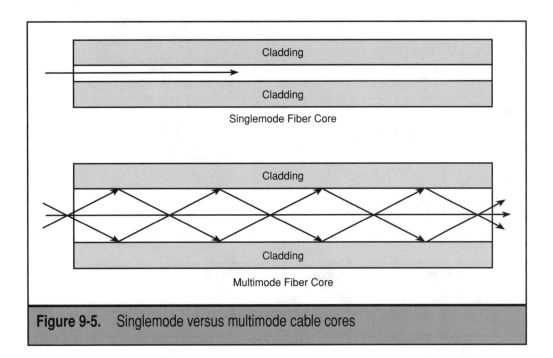

Figure 9-5. Singlemode versus multimode cable cores

Multimode optical fiber cables have a larger core (light carrying element of the cable) than singlemode optical fiber cables. The name singlemode means that the core is so small that only a single mode or ray can enter the core. A multimode optical fiber cable enables many thousands of light rays into the core. The thousands of light rays combine to create the output pulse at the end of the cable. Each light ray in a multimode optical fiber cable will travel a slightly different path through the core. This results in some rays arriving at the opposite end of the cable faster than others. This phenomenon results in the output pulse being wider or spreading out due to traveling through the core of the cable, compared to the original input light pulses. The spreading out of the light pulses is called modal dispersion.

Modal dispersion limits the bandwidth of a multimode optical fiber cable (see Figure 9-6). The larger the optical fiber cable's core, the greater the effect of modal dispersion on light pulses transmitted through the cable. The smaller the optical fiber cable's core, the less the effect of modal dispersion on light pulses transmitted through the cable.

Distance is another factor that relates to the bandwidth of a multimode optical fiber cable. The longer the length of the cable, the greater the effect of modal dispersion. Some light pulses will travel longer distances than others. This will result in modal dispersion having a greater effect on the output pulses. The bandwidth of optical fiber cable is rated based on a 1,000 m (3,280 ft.) or 1 kilometer (km) of distance.

The bandwidth of different optical fiber cables and different wavelengths is shown in Table 9-3.

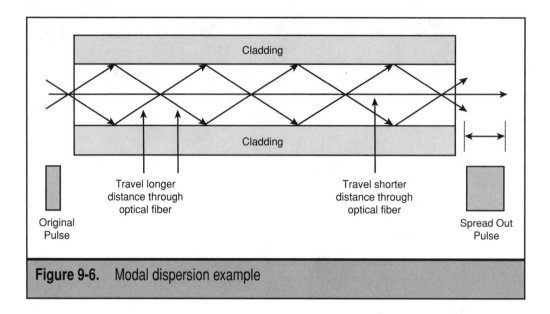

Figure 9-6. Modal dispersion example

Optical Fiber Cable Type	Bandwidth Rating in MHz	
	850 nm	1,300 nm
50/125 μm multimode optical fiber cable	500 MHz	500 MHz
62.5/125 μm multimode optical fiber cable	160 MHz	500 MHz
Singlemode optical fiber cable	———	Unlimited

Table 9-3. Optical Fiber Cable Bandwidth Ratings

NOTE: 850 and 1,300 nm are wavelengths for multimode optical fiber cables. 850 nm is not a wavelength used for singlemode optical fiber cables. 1,300 and 1,550 nm are common wavelengths for singlemode optical fiber cables.

MEGAHERTZ (MHz) VERSUS MEGABITS (Mb/s)

A common source of confusion in the communication cable industry is the difference between megahertz (MHz) and megabits (Mb/s). Both terms relate to bandwidth. *Mb/s* is a term used to describe the information carrying capacity of a data network. Data systems or local area networks (LANs) are described in the number of bits per second that can be transmitted by the network. *MHz* is a term to describe the information carrying capacity of a communication cable or a communication channel.

DECIBELS (DBs)

The term *deciBel* (dB) is a standard measurement unit for signal strength. It was created by Alexander Graham Bell. This is the reason why the Bel is always capitalized in the word deciBel.

A deciBel is used to identify the power or strength of a signal. It can also be used to measure the ratio or difference between two signals, such as the difference between an input signal and an output signal.

A deciBel is most often used to describe the level of sound for building environments or the level of sound systems. The higher the dB level, the louder the sound level. Typical environments and their dB sound rating are shown in Table 9-4.

The human ear is a very sensitive instrument. A 1 dB change in sound is the minimum that can be detected by the human ear. Humans are used to having noise surrounding them at all times. A quiet noise level is about 55 dBs; a noisy environment is about 70 dBs; and an environment that can damage your hearing is 90 dBs or higher.

Environment	dB Rating
Quiet office environment	55 dBs
Department store	65 dBs
Restaurant	70 dBs
Supermarket	75 dBs
Print shop	80 dBs
Manufacturing floor	85 dBs
Machine shop floor	90 dBs
Airport runway	100 dBs

Table 9-4.   dB Sound Rating Table

A dB measurement is a logarithmic measurement. This means that the dB measurement scale is not linear. A plus 3 dB change doubles the power rating of a noise and a minus 3 dB change halves the noise level. The formula computing deciBels is

dB ≐ 10 log (P1 / P2)

where,

P1 = Device output power
P2 = Device input power

A dB scale (see Table 9-5) will illustrate the difference in signal power between different dB ratings.

Decibels	Power Rating
0 dB	1.0
3 dB	2.0
6 dB	4.0
9 dB	7.9
12 dB	15.8
15 dB	31.6
18 dB	63.1
21 dB	125.9
24 dB	251.2
27 dB	500
30 dB	1000

Table 9-5. dB Power Ratings

The dB power rating table provides referenced information regarding actual sound noise levels in different environments. For example, there is a 15 dB difference between a restaurant and a quiet office environment. This means that the restaurant is 36.1 times louder than a quiet office environment. An airport runway is over 1,000 times louder than a quiet office environment.

A deciBel is a common unit of measurement in communications cables. Most cable test measurement devices will provide test results in dB. In the case of testing communication cables, dBs are used to indicate the difference in voltage signal levels traveling through a cable. DeciBels are used for

▼ Attenuation

■ NEXT

- PS NEXT
- ELFEXT
- PS ELFEXT
- ▲ ACR

ATTENUATION

Attenuation is defined as the reduction of a transmitted signal due to resistance encountered by the signal as it is traveling down a cable (see Figure 9-7). Attenuation causes signals to shrink as they travel along a cable.

In all communication systems (voice system, low-speed data system, or LAN), there needs to be enough of the original signal remaining at the opposite end of the cable so the receiver can determine what the signal was when it was originally sent by the transmitter.

Attenuation is a type of insertion loss. When considering the total insertion loss of a communication link, all cabling components in the cabling link will contribute to the total attenuation value of the link. The total insertion loss for a link is the sum of all of the

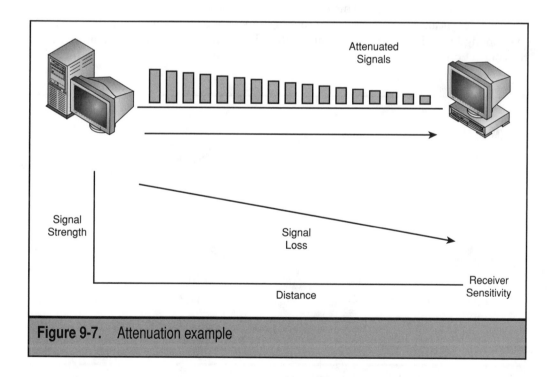

Figure 9-7. Attenuation example

cables and cabling components. All of the following cabling components in a cabling link add attenuation.

▼ Communication cable

■ Modular outlets / connectors

■ Patch panels

■ Horizontal cross-connect (HC)

■ Transition point (TP) connections

▲ Consolidation point (CP) connections

Communication cable is the main contributing factor to the attenuation of a link. The longer the link, the more attenuation the link will exhibit. Connecting hardware components also add attenuation to a link. The attenuation added by these cabling components is very small compared to the cable.

Attenuation is measured in dB. The dB rating is specified per unit length of cable (usually 100 m). Measurements are taken at specified swept/stepped frequency levels. The higher the attenuation dB value, the greater the attenuation (signal loss) and the weaker the received signal. For copper cables, the higher the transmitted frequency, the more attenuation a cable will exhibit. This is shown in Table 9-6.

A communication signal will lose some of its power and shrink at each connection point in a cabling link. This is due to the transmitted signal having to transition or jump across the connection point between the cable and the termination component (see Figure 9-8).

Frequency (MHz)	Category 3 (dB)	Category 5e (dB)
1.0	2.6	2.0
4.0	5.6	4.1
8.0	8.5	5.8
10.0	9.7	6.5
16.0	13.1	8.2
20.0	——	9.3
25.0	——	10.4
31.25	——	11.7
62.5	——	17.0
100.0	——	22.0

Table 9-6.   Horizontal Cable Attenuation

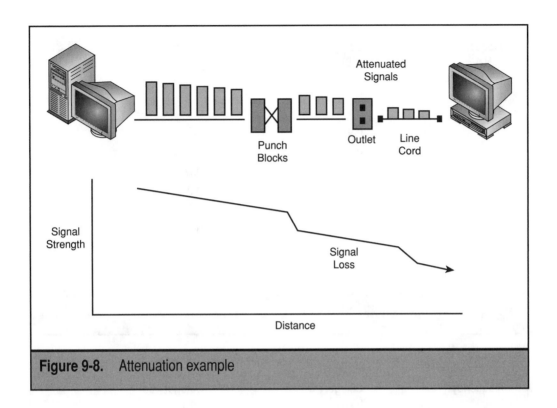

Figure 9-8. Attenuation example

Each cabling component will add a small amount of loss in the cabling link. A category 3 component adds more loss into the cabling link than a category 5e component. The cabling components are similar to communication cables. They induce small losses at lower frequencies and greater losses at higher frequencies. These losses are exhibited in Table 9-7.

NOTE: The values listed in the component attenuation table include the losses associated with terminating the cable pairs on the component. These loss values are correct if the proper termination techniques are used. If the proper termination techniques are not used, additional losses may be imposed on the link.

The permanent link includes 90 m (295 ft.) of horizontal cable and two terminations. One termination is in the closet and the other termination is in the work area. The permanent link may also contain an optional TP or CP connection. The permanent link includes losses associated with the cable and the cable connections. Therefore, the attenuation values for the permanent link will be higher that those for just communications cable. These values are shown Table 9-8.

The channel includes 90 m (295 ft.) of horizontal cable, up to four component terminations, and up to 10 m (33 ft.) of patch cords used in the work area and telecommunications room (TR). The channel includes two additional terminations and 10 m (33 ft.) of

Frequency (MHz)	Category 3 (dB)	Category 5e (dB)
1.0	0.4	0.1
4.0	0.4	0.1
8.0	0.4	0.1
10.0	0.4	0.1
16.0	0.4	0.2
20.0	——	0.2
25.0	——	0.2
31.25	——	0.2
62.5	——	0.3
100.0	——	0.4

Table 9-7.   Component Attenuation

Frequency (MHz)	Category 3 (dB)	Category 5e (dB)
1.0	3.5	2.1
4.0	6.2	3.9
8.0	8.9	5.5
10.0	9.9	6.2
16.0	13.0	7.9
20.0	——	8.9
25.0	——	10.0
31.25	——	11.2
62.5	——	16.2
100.0	——	21.0

Table 9-8.   Permanent Link Attenuation

stranded patch cords compared to the permanent link. Therefore, the attenuation values for the channel are higher than the attenuation values for the permanent link. These values are shown in Table 9-9.

Frequency (MHz)	Category 3 (dB)	Category 5e (dB)
1.0	4.2	2.5
4.0	7.3	4.5
8.0	10.2	6.3
10.0	11.5	7.1
16.0	14.9	9.1
20.0	——	10.3
25.0	——	11.4
31.25	——	12.9
62.5	——	18.6
100.0	——	24.0

Table 9-9.   Channel Link Attenuation

The attenuation values in Table 9-9 illustrate that a category 5e channel will exhibit lower attenuation values at lower frequencies and higher attenuation values at higher frequencies. This is shown in Figure 9-9.

NEXT

Near end crosstalk (NEXT) is a measure of the amount of energy that will pass to other pairs within the same cable when a signal is transmitted over a single pair from the same end of the cable (see Figure 9-10). NEXT is also called pair-to-pair NEXT because all pair combinations are measured. The term *near end* means that the measurement is being taken from the same end of the cable as the transmitted signal. The energy that leaks out from the transmitting cable pair is considered to be noise within that cable because it will interfere with other signals being received over any nontransmitting cable pair.

NEXT is one of the most important parameters for a UTP cable. A UTP cable should have a high NEXT rating. This means that very little energy should be transferred to other cable pairs when a signal is transmitted over another cable pair within the same cable.

This energy that is transferred from the transmitting cable pair to other pairs in a cable is the most significant source of noise in a high-speed network. If enough energy is transferred to a cable pair that is receiving a LAN signal, the receiver may not be able to

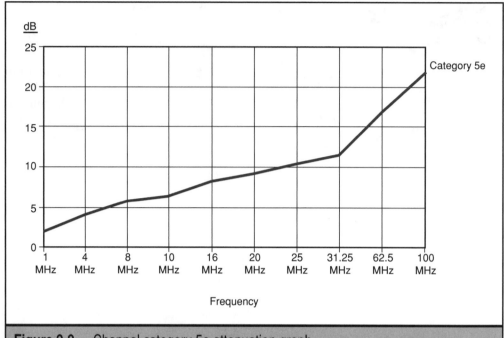

Figure 9-9.   Channel category 5e attenuation graph

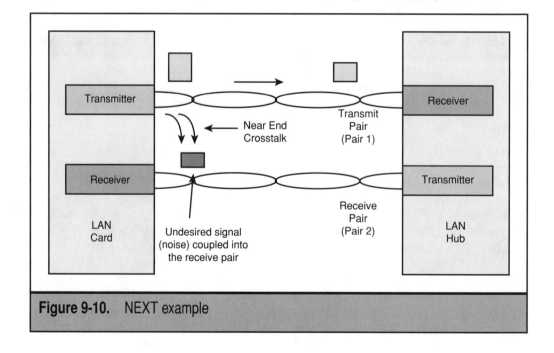

Figure 9-10.   NEXT example

distinguish between the wanted signal being received and the unwanted energy (noise) from another cable pair.

NEXT is measured in dB. The dB rating is specified for each component individually. Measurements are taken at specified swept/stepped frequency levels. The higher the NEXT dB value the better. A high NEXT dB value means that very little of the signal from the transmitting cable pair can be measured on the nontransmitting pairs of the cable. A low NEXT dB value means that more of the signal from the transmitting cable pair can be measured on the nontransmitting pairs of the cable. For copper cables, the higher the transmitted frequency, the lower NEXT dB values communication cables exhibit.

The formula for measuring NEXT for the cable is

$$NEXT\ (f) \geq NEXT\ (0.772) - 15\log\ (f\ /\ 0.772)$$

This equation produces the values shown in the following table. The NEXT loss values for a given cable will decrease as the frequency increases. The minimum NEXT loss for any pair combination measured at room temperature must be greater than the values shown in Table 9-10 for any given frequency.

The permanent link includes 90 m (295 ft.) of horizontal cable and two terminations. One termination is in the closet and the other termination is in the work area. The worst case pair-to-pair NEXT loss values are not cumulative like attenuation insertion loss measurements. The additional terminations in the link will result in lower dB loss values due to the cable pair terminations on the cabling components.

Frequency (MHz)	Category 3 (dB)	Category 5e (dB)
1.0	41	62
4.0	32	53
8.0	27	48
10.0	26	47
16.0	23	44
20.0	——	42
25.0	——	41
31.25	——	39
62.5	——	35
100.0	——	32

Table 9-10.   NEXT Loss Cable Values

The formula for measuring NEXT for the permanent link is

$$\text{NEXT}(f) = -20\log\left(10^{-\text{NEXT cable}/20} + 2 \cdot 10^{-\text{NEXT connector}/20}\right)$$

This equation produces the values shown in Table 9-11.

This equation produces the values for the permanent link NEXT loss from a frequency of 1 to 100 MHz. The measured values for the permanent link must exceed the values shown in Table 9-11.

Frequency (MHz)	Category 3 (dB)	Category 5e (dB)
1.0	40.1	>60
4.0	30.7	54.8
8.0	25.9	50.0
10.0	24.3	48.5
16.0	21.0	45.2
20.0	——	43.7
25.0	——	42.1
31.25	——	40.5
62.5	——	35.7
100.0	——	32.3

Table 9-11.   Permanent Link NEXT Loss Values

The channel includes 90 m (295 ft.) of horizontal cable, up to four component terminations, and up to 10 m (33 ft.) of patch cords used in the work area and TR. The channel includes two additional terminations and 10 m (33 ft.) of stranded patch cords compared to the permanent link. The additional terminations in the link will result in lower dB loss values due to the cable pair terminations on the cabling components. The measured values for the channel must exceed the values shown in Table 9-12.

The NEXT values in the previous table illustrates that a category 5e channel will exhibit higher NEXT values at lower frequencies and lower NEXT values at higher frequencies. This is shown in Figure 9-11.

Frequency (MHz)	Category 3 (dB)	Category 5e (dB)
1.0	39.1	>60
4.0	29.3	53.5
8.0	24.3	48.6
10.0	22.7	47.0
16.0	19.3	43.6
20.0	——	42.0
25.0	——	40.3
31.25	——	38.7
62.5	——	33.6
100.0	——	30.1

Table 9-12. Channel NEXT Loss Values

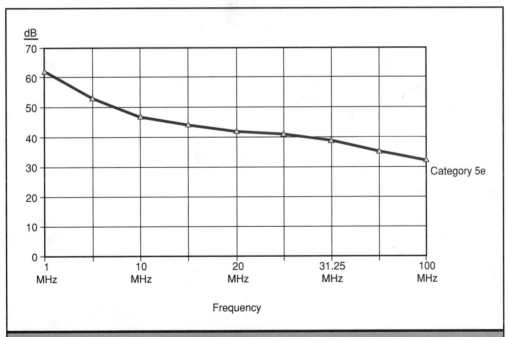

Figure 9-11. Channel category 5e NEXT graph

POWER SUM NEXT

Power sum near end crosstalk (PS NEXT) is a measure of the total crosstalk energy that can be measured on a nonactive cable pair when more than one pair is active or being used simultaneously (see Figure 9-12). Power sum is a formula that totals the crosstalk energy being contributed by each active pair on a nonactive pair measured on the same end of the cable as the transmitted signals.

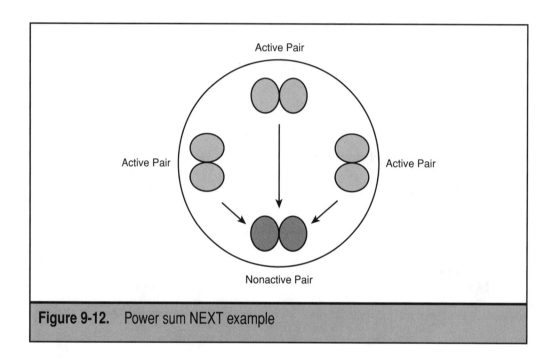

Figure 9-12. Power sum NEXT example

NEXT measurements only looked at energy coupled into passive (receiving) cable pairs when a single pair was active (transmitting). PS NEXT measures energy coupled into a single cable pair when multiple cable pairs are active. This measurement takes into account the combined crosstalk on a single receive pair from multiple near end disturbers operating at the same time.

PS NEXT is a new measurement for UTP cabling systems. The measurement was never specified for category 3, category 4, and category 5 cables. PS NEXT is specified for category 5e and higher UTP cables. This measurement is important for applications that use multiple pairs for sending signals. Many high-speed LAN technologies, such as 100Base-T4 and 1000Base-T, use this signaling technique.

The formula for calculating PS NEXT on a four-pair UTP cable is

$$PSNEXT = -10\log(10^{-x1/10} + 10^{-x2/10} + 10^{-x3/10})\ dB$$

where x1, x2, and x3 are the pair to pair crosstalk measurements in dB between a receive pair and three active transmitting pairs.

The PS NEXT measurements for a category 5e or higher cable are lower than the worst case pair-to-pair NEXT measurements for the same cable. This is due to multiple active pairs in the cable that transfer more measurable energy into a receiving (nontransmitting) cable pair. The previous equation for PS NEXT will produce a distribution chart for a frequency range from 1 to 100 MHz. The measured values for the permanent link must exceed the values shown in Table 9-13.

Frequency (MHz)	Category 5e (dB)
1.0	>57
4.0	51.8
8.0	47.0
10.0	45.5
16.0	42.2
20.0	40.7
25.0	39.1
31.25	37.5
62.5	32.7
100.0	29.3

Table 9-13.   PS NEXT for a Category 5e Permanent Link

The channel includes 90 m (295 ft.) of horizontal cable, up to four component terminations, and up to 10 m (33 ft.) of patch cords used in the work area and TR. The channel includes two additional terminations and 10 m (33 ft.) of stranded patch cords compared to the permanent link. The additional terminations in the link will result in lower dB loss values due to the cable pair terminations on the cabling components. The measured values for the channel must exceed the values shown in Table 9-14.

FEXT AND ELFEXT

Far end crosstalk (FEXT) is defined as the crosstalk coupling caused by a transmitter at the near end of a cable link into another cable pair measured at the far end of the link (see Figure 9-13). FEXT is similar to NEXT, except the crosstalk between the cable pairs is measured at the far end of the cable instead of the near end of the cable.

Frequency (MHz)	Category 5e (dB)
1.0	>57
4.0	50.5
8.0	45.6
10.0	44.0
16.0	40.6
20.0	39.0
25.0	37.3
31.25	35.7
62.5	30.6
100.0	27.1

Table 9-14.   PS NEXT for a Category 5e Channel

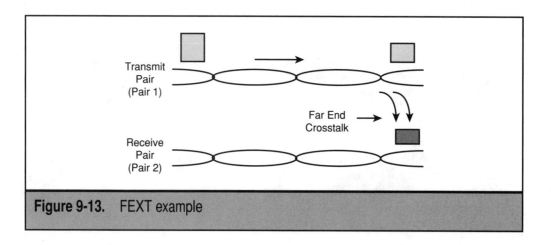

Figure 9-13.   FEXT example

FEXT is not a very useful measurement because it is length dependent. Equal Level Far End Crosstalk (ELFEXT) is a more meaningful measurement for UTP cables. ELFEXT is a normalized signal measure. It takes out attenuation length effects from the crosstalk measurement. ELFEXT is a measure of FEXT for any length UTP cable.

ELFEXT is a new transmission parameter for UTP cable. This parameter was never measured for category 3, category 4, or category 5 cables. ELFEXT is specified for category 5e and higher UTP cables. This measurement is important for applications that use multiple pairs simultaneously for full-duplex transmission. Many high-speed LAN technologies, such as 100Base-T4 and 1000Base-T, use this signaling technique.

Industry cabling standards require that ELFEXT be measured for all cable pair combinations for components and cabling. The formula for calculating ELFEXT for a four-pair UTP on the permanent link is

$$\text{pair-to-pair ELFEXT} \geq -20\log(10^{-\text{pair-to-pair ELFEXT cable}\ /\ 20} + 3 \cdot 10^{-\text{pair-to-pair FEXT connector}\ /\ 20})\ dB$$

The ELFEXT equation will produce a distribution chart for a frequency range from 1 to 100 MHz. The measured values for the permanent link must exceed the values shown in Table 9-15.

Frequency (MHz)	Category 5e (dB)
1.0	58.6
4.0	46.6
8.0	40.6
10.0	38.6
16.0	34.5
20.0	32.6
25.0	30.7
31.25	28.7
62.5	22.7
100.0	18.6

Table 9-15. ELFEXT for a Category 5e Permanent Link

The formula for calculating ELFEXT for a four-pair UTP on the channel is

$$\text{pair-to-pair ELFEXT} \geq -20\log(10^{-\text{pair-to-pair ELFEXT cable}\ /\ 20} + 4 \cdot 10^{-\text{pair-to-pair FEXT connector}\ /\ 20})\ dB$$

The channel includes 90 m (295 ft.) of horizontal cable, up to four component terminations and up to 10 m (33 ft.) of patch cords used in the work area and TR. The channel includes two additional terminations and 10 m (33 ft.) of stranded patch cords compared to the permanent link. The additional terminations in the link will result in lower dB loss values due to the cable pair terminations on the cabling components. The measured values for the channel must exceed the values shown in Table 9-16.

Frequency (MHz)	Category 5e (dB)
1.0	>57
4.0	50.5
8.0	45.6
10.0	44.0
16.0	40.6
20.0	39.0
25.0	37.3
31.25	35.7
62.5	30.6
100.0	27.1

Table 9-16.   ELFEXT for a Category 5e Channel

PS ELFEXT

Power sum equal level far end crosstalk (PS ELFEXT) is a measure of the total crosstalk energy that can be measured on a nonactive cable pair when more than one pair is active or being used simultaneously (see Figure 9-14). Power sum is a formula that totals the crosstalk energy being contributed by each active pair on a nonactive pair measured at the far end of the cable.

ELFEXT measurements only looked at energy coupled into passive (receiving) cable pairs when a single pair was active (transmitting). This is the reason that ELFEXT is often called pair-to-pair ELFEXT. PS ELFEXT measures energy coupled into a single cable pair when multiple cable pairs are active just like PS NEXT. This measurement takes into account the combined crosstalk on a single receive pair from multiple far end disturbers operating at the same time.

PS ELFEXT is a new measurement for UTP cabling systems. The measurement was never specified for category 3, category 4, and category 5 cables. PS ELFEXT is specified for category 5e and higher UTP cables. This measurement is important for applications that use multiple pairs for sending signals. Many high-speed LAN technologies, such as 100Base-T4 and 1000Base-T, use this signaling technique.

The formula for calculating PS ELFEXT on a four-pair UTP cable for the permanent link is

$$\mathrm{PSNEXT}_{\text{permanent link}} \geq -20\log(10^{-\text{PS ELFEXT cable}/20} + 3 \cdot 10^{-\text{PS FEXT connectors}/20})\ \mathrm{dB}$$

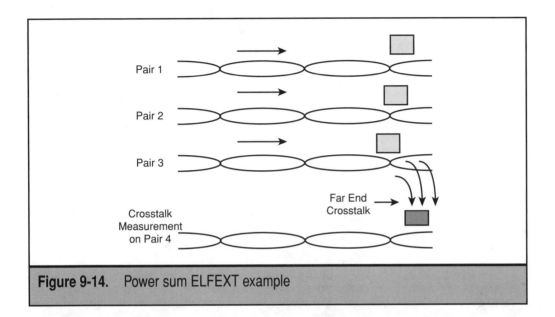

Figure 9-14.   Power sum ELFEXT example

The PS ELFEXT equation will produce a distribution chart for a frequency range from 1 to 100 MHz. The measured values for the permanent link must exceed the values shown in Table 9-17.

The PS ELFEXT measurements for a category 5e or higher cable are lower than the worst case pair-to-pair ELFEXT measurements for the same cable. This is due to multiple active pairs in the cable transfer more measurable energy into a receiving (nontransmitting) cable pair.

The formula for calculating PS ELFEXT on a four-pair UTP cable for the channel is

$$PSNEXT_{channel} \geq -20\log(10^{-PS\ ELFEXT\ cable/20} + 4 \cdot 10^{-PS\ FEXT\ connectors\ /20})\ dB$$

The PS ELFEXT equation will produce a distribution chart for a frequency range from 1 to 100 MHz. The measured values for the channel must exceed the values shown in Table 9-18.

ATTENUATION-TO-CROSSTALK RATIO (ACR)

Attenuation-to-Crosstalk Ratio (ACR) provides an indication of whether a signal can be received properly, although unwanted energy from a transmitting pair may be interfering with the received signal (see Figure 9-15).

ACR is the most important parameter in determining the stability of a cabling run and indicating its ability to handle high-speed data signals reliably. As the name implies, ACR is based on the actual attenuation and NEXT of a cable. The ACR is a measure of whether the coupled energy from the NEXT components of the cable will be stronger than the at-

Frequency (MHz)	Category 5e (dB)
1.0	55.6
4.0	43.6
8.0	37.5
10.0	35.6
16.0	31.5
20.0	29.6
25.0	27.7
31.25	25.7
62.5	19.7
100.0	15.6

Table 9-17.   PS ELFEXT for a Category 5e Permanent Link

Frequency (MHz)	Category 5e (dB)
1.0	54.4
4.0	42.4
8.0	36.3
10.0	34.4
16.0	30.3
20.0	28.4
25.0	26.4
31.25	24.5
62.5	18.5
100.0	14.4

Table 9-18.   PS ELFEXT for a Category 5e Channel

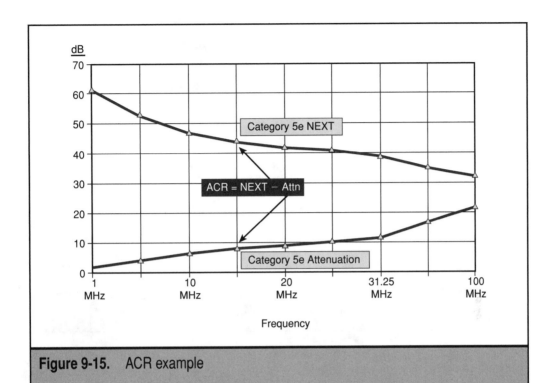

Figure 9-15.   ACR example

tenuated signal. If the NEXT energy is stronger, the receiver may receive the NEXT energy instead of the actual signal traveling down the cable. This will cause errors on the network.

The formula for determining the ACR of a cable is

$$ACR = NEXT - Attenuation$$

If the NEXT rating of a cable is 34 dB at a given frequency and the attenuation of the cable is 10 dB at a given frequency, the ACR is calculated as follows:

$$ACR = 34 - 10$$
$$ACR = 14 \text{ dB.}$$

The ACR of a cable will shrink as the frequency of the transmitted signal increases. This is because the attenuation of the cable increases and the NEXT rating decreases. The ACR equation will produce a distribution chart for a frequency range from 1 to 100 MHz. The measured values for a category 3 and a category 5e channel must exceed the values shown in Table 9-19.

NOTE: ACR is also commonly referred to as *Signal-to-Noise Ratio* (SNR). SNR is the relationship between the level of the received signal in a communication system or or network compared to the level of noise. ACR relates to communication cables, not the entire communication system or network.

Frequency (MHz)	Category 3 (dB)	Category 5e (dB)
1.0	34.9	57.5
4.0	22.0	49.0
8.0	14.1	42.3
10.0	10.5	39.9
16.0	4.4	34.5
20.0	——	31.7
25.0	——	28.9
31.25	——	25.8
62.5	——	15.0
100.0	——	6.1

Table 9-19.   ACR for a Category 3 and Category 5e Channel

PROPAGATION DELAY

Propagation delay is defined as the amount of time needed for a transmitted signal to travel over a single pair of a communication cable (see Figure 9-16). Because propagation delay measures that actual signal travel time, the propagation delay of a cable will increase as the length of the cable increases.

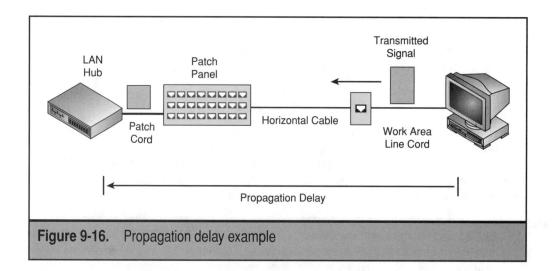

Figure 9-16.   Propagation delay example

The propagation delay will be slightly different for each pair of a communication cable. This is due to the fact that all four pairs have a different twist rate. This means that some cable pairs in a cable are twisted more than other pairs in the same cable. Increasing the twist rate of cable pairs reduces the NEXT within the cable but increases the length of the cable pairs that are tightly twisted. The cable pairs with more twists are longer and this results in these cable pairs having a larger amount of propagation delay.

Propagation delay is typically measured in nanoseconds (ns) for 100 m of cable. The propagation delay of a cable can also be referenced as the minimum of propagation. This is a measure of how fast the signal travels through a cable. This is normally listed as a percentage. This number represents the speed of the signal traveling over the cable pairs compared to the speed of light. These numbers are shown in Table 9-20.

Frequency (MHz)	Maximum Propagation Delay (ns per 100 m [328 ft.])	Maximum Velocity of Propagation (% Speed of Light)
1.0	570 ns	58.5 %
10.0	545 ns	61.1 %
100.0	538 ns	62.0 %

Table 9-20. Propagation Delay for a Category 5e Channel

DELAY SKEW

Delay skew is defined as the difference in the propagation delay between the fastest and slowest pairs of the same UTP cable (see Figure 9-17).

Delay skew is becoming an important specification for UTP cable because new, high-speed LAN technologies are using multiple cable pairs to transmit data signals. As a result, it is important to have the multiple data signals arrive at the opposite end of the cable at approximately the same time. This is critical for a received signal to be properly decoded. Cables that exceed the maximum delay skew parameter will result in the receiving equipment mixed up and corrupt.

Industry standards specify that delay skew for a UTP cable shall not exceed 45 ns for all frequencies between 2 and 12.5 MHz for a 100 m horizontal cable run.

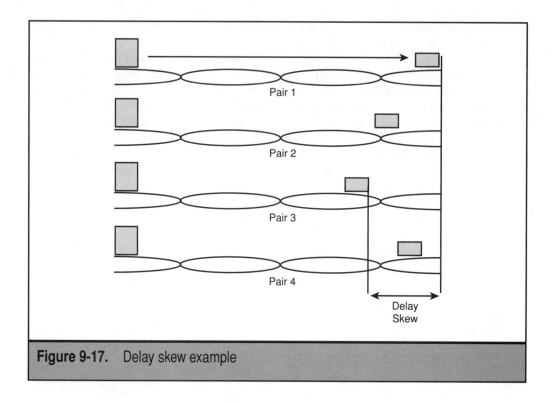

Figure 9-17. Delay skew example

CHARACTERISTIC IMPEDANCE

Characteristic impedance is defined as the total opposition to the flow of electrons imposed by a communications cable and is measured in ohms. All copper communication cables have a defined characteristic impedance rating. The characteristic impedance rating for a communication cable is a function of the diameter of the cable conductors and dielectric constant of the insulation material covering the cable conductors.

A communication cable's characteristic impedance is a combination of the following three variables:

▼ Cable capacitance

■ Cable inductance

▲ Cable resistance

The characteristic impedance of a cable must be a uniform rating across the entire length of the cable. A cable's impedance rating is also independent of the cable's length. This means that 10 m of a communication cable must have the same impedance rating as 100 m of the cable.

Every communication cable must have a consistent and uniform characteristic impedance rating. In addition, all cables and components in a cabling link must have a uniform characteristic impedance rating. Any impedance discontinuity in a cabling link will result in signal reflections on the cabling link. Cable reflections will cause signal loss and may result in signal corruption or collisions to other signals traveling across the cable link.

Communication cables have the following characteristic impedance ratings:

▼ UTP cables have a characteristic impedance rating of 100 ohms $+/-$ 15 percent.

■ ScTP cables have a characteristic impedance rating of 100 ohms $+/-$ 15 percent.

▲ STP-A cables have a characteristic impedance rating of 150 ohms $+/-$ 10 percent.

The different categories of UTP and ScTP cables have a defined characteristic impedance in the frequency range of 1 MHz to their specified frequency range of 16 MHz, 20 MHz, 100 MHz, or 250 MHz. The maximum frequency range is based on the category rating of the cable. STP-A cables have a defined characteristic impedance in the frequency range of 1 to 300 MHz.

Coaxial cables have a different impedance rating than twisted-pair cables. In fact, there are many different types of coaxial cables, and each type has a different characteristic impedance rating. The characteristic impedance ratings for different types of coaxial cables include the following:

▼ RG-58 cables have a characteristic impedance rating of 50 ohms $+/-$ 1 percent.

■ RG-59 cables have a characteristic impedance rating of 75 ohms $+/-$ 1 percent.

▲ RG-62 cables have a characteristic impedance rating of 93 ohms $+/-$ 1 percent.

Communication cable connecting hardware also has a specific and defined characteristic impedance rating. UTP and ScTP connecting hardware and modular connectors have a characteristic impedance rating of 100 ohms $+/-$ 15 percent. STP-A connectors and other cabling components have a characteristic impedance rating of 150 ohms $+/-$ 10 percent. The same is true for coaxial cable connectors and other connecting hardware components.

IMPEDANCE MATCHING

Electronic components, such as LAN NICs and hubs, are designed to transmit signals over cables that match a specified impedance rating. Because different communication cables have different impedance ratings, it is important to use the correct type of communication cables to connect specific types of equipment together. The characteristic impedance of the equipment must be matched to the characteristic impedance rating of the communication cables. Mismatching the incorrect types of communications cables and communication equipment result in signal reflections.

Impedance mismatches will cause signal reflections in a cable or LAN circuit. Signal reflects will cause interference and corruption to the transmitted information signal. For example, signal reflections on an Ethernet LAN will cause collisions between data frames. The corrupted data frames must be retransmitted on the LAN causing reduced network throughput and higher traffic levels.

Impedance matching must always be considered when different types of cables are connected to various types of electronic components. UTP, STP-A, and coaxial cables each have a different impedance rating. Using UTP cable to connect LAN equipment that was designed for either STP-A or coaxial cable will cause an impedance mismatch. If a cable must be connected to an electronic device that has a different impedance rating, an impedance matching component must be used to eliminate signal reflections, such as a BALUN or media filter.

RETURN LOSS

Return loss is a measure of the reflected energy caused by impedance mismatches in the cabling system (see Figure 9-18). Impedance mismatches occur on a communication cable link when the termination impedance (component impedance) does not exactly match the characteristic impedance of the cable. The resulting impedance discontinuity creates a bias in the link. Electrical energy will hit the bias, and extra energy is necessary to overcome the bias in the link. This results in signal loss to the transmitted signal traveling over the bias and a small amount of energy being reflected back to the transmitter. Therefore, impedance mismatches cause both signal loss and reflected noise on the link.

The amount of reflected energy is a direct function of the degree of impedance mismatch between the communication cable and cable termination components in the link. Ideally, the communication cable and the cable termination components will be closely

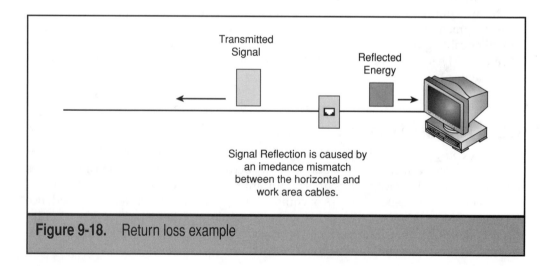

Figure 9-18.   Return loss example

matched and very little signal reflections will result. Even small differences between the communication cable and connecting hardware components can result in large differences. For example, UTP communications cables and connecting hardware can have a characteristic impedance rating of 100 ohms $+/-$ 15 percent. This permits cable and connectors with an impedance rating from 85 to 115 ohms. This can result in a compliant cable having an impedance rating of 110 ohms and a compliant connector having an impedance rating of 90 ohms. There is a 20-ohm characteristic impedance difference between the compliant cable and the connector. This will result in significant signal reflections between the two components.

In reality, the impedance of two connected components are likely to be more closely matched. A cable with a 97-ohm rating could be connected to a cable with a 102-ohm rating. Both cables are very close to the optimum 100-ohm specification, yet there is a 5 ohm difference between these two cables when connected together. Again, this impedance mismatch will cause signal reflections on the cable link.

Return loss is a new measurement for UTP cabling systems. This measurement was never specified for category 3, category 4, or category 5 cables. Return loss measurements are taken for a category 5e or higher UTP link from one to the highest measured frequency for the category of cable. This measurement is important for applications that send and receive over the same cable pair, such as Gigabit Ethernet over UTP cable, called 1000Base-T.

The noise caused from impedance mismatches in the cabling system is a significant contributor to the overall noise budget for a communication system or a network. In order to reduce return loss, cable and connecting hardware must be closely matched.

The formula for calculating return loss for the permanent link is

▼   **1 to 20 MHz**   19 dB

▲   **20 to 100 MHz** $19 - 10 \cdot \log (f / 20)$ dB

The return loss equation will produce a distribution chart for a frequency range from 20 to 100 MHz. The measured values for the permanent link must exceed the values shown in Table 9-21.

Frequency (MHz)	Category 5e (dB)
1 to 20.0	19.0
25.0	18.0
31.25	17.0
62.5	14.0
100.0	12.0

Table 9-21.   Return Loss for a Category 5e Permanent Link

The formula for calculating return loss for the channel is

▼ **1 to 20 MHz**   17 dB

▲ **20 to 100 MHz** $17 - 10 \cdot \log (f / 20)$ dB

The return loss equation will produce a distribution chart for a frequency range from 20 to 100 MHz. The measured values for the channel must exceed the values shown in Table 9-22.

Frequency (MHz)	Category 5e (dB)
1 to 20.0	19.0
25.0	18.0
31.25	17.0
62.5	14.0
100.0	12.0

Table 9-22.   Return Loss for a Category 5e Channel

The maximum return loss for a channel tested at 100 MHz is 10 dB. This will guarantee that return loss will not cause signaling errors in excess of the BER specifications for a communication system or a network.

CAPACITANCE

Capacitance is defined as the ability of a material or cable to store an electrical charge (see Figure 9-19). All copper communication cables have a capacitance. Capacitance is due to either the two wires of a pair not being twisted together (parallel to each other) or capacitance can exist between the cable's conductors and the cable's shield.

Mutual capacitance is the capacitance between the two conductors of a cable pair. This is the typical type of capacitance that exists in a UTP cable. The amount of mutual capacitance that a cable will exhibit is a function of the number of twists in the cable pair and the insulation material applied to the cable conductors.

Capacitance in a communications cable creates resistance for transmitted digital signals and will cause the signals to be skewed (delayed). Transmitted signals that have been altered by the effects of capacitance in a cable will have rounded edges. This signal will

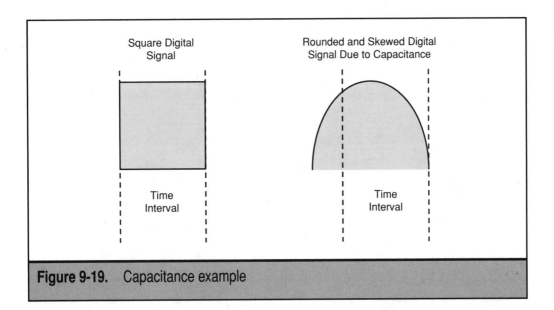

Figure 9-19. Capacitance example

also be pushed into the next signal's time slot. These signal characteristics may cause the receiver to have problems correctly receiving and decoding the signals.

The transmission property of capacitance is measured in Farads. Capacitance in communication cable is very small and is measured in pico-Farads (pF). Twisted-pair communication cables typically exhibit between 14 to 20 pF per foot. Lower quality UTP cables are characterized by the cable pairs being loosely twisted together, resulting in the cable pairs running parallel to one anther for long distances. These cables will exhibit larger amounts of mutual capacitance of about 20 pF/ft. Category 5/5e and category 6 UTP cables have cable pairs that are tightly twisted together. There, cables will usually exhibit a lower amount of mutual capacitance of 14 pF/ft.

INDUCTANCE

Inductance is the property of an electrical circuit where radiating magnetic fields will induce electron flows (current of a measured voltage level) in an adjacent circuit or cable (see Figure 9-20). Inductance is caused by electric motors or other industrial equipment that produce magnetic fields. The measurement for inductance is a Henry.

UTP cables are susceptible to inductance because the cable pairs are unshielded. UTP cables must be moved far enough away from the sources of the magnetic fields so inductance does not interfere with the signals being sent over the UTP cable.

Inductive reactance is the term used to define the extent that inductance affects the transmission of signals over a UTP cable.

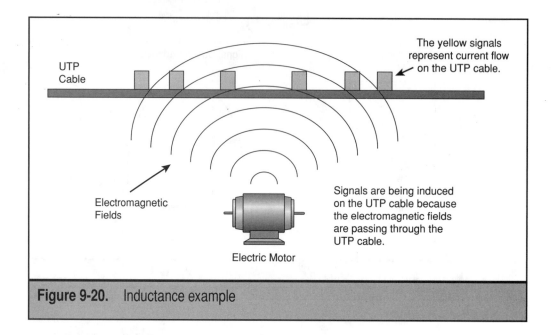

The yellow signals represent current flow on the UTP cable.

UTP Cable

Electromagnetic Fields

Signals are being induced on the UTP cable because the electromagnetic fields are passing through the UTP cable.

Electric Motor

Figure 9-20. Inductance example

BALANCED AND UNBALANCED CABLES

Communication cables are defined as either being a balanced or an unbalanced type of cable. Coaxial cables are defined as being unbalanced cables. This means that the electrical characteristics with respect to ground of the center conductor and the cable shield are not equal. Twisted-pair cables are defined as being balanced cables (see Figure 9-21). This means that both conductors of a cable pair have the same voltage reference to ground. UTP, STP-A, and ScTP cables are all defined as being balanced cables.

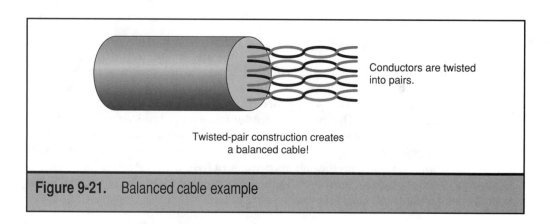

Conductors are twisted into pairs.

Twisted-pair construction creates a balanced cable!

Figure 9-21. Balanced cable example

Balanced cables are preferred for transmitting communication signals. Balanced cables can support differential signaling (see Figure 9-22). Differential signaling is the type of signaling used on LANs. In differential signaling, the positive portion of the signal is transmitted on one wire of the cable pair, and the negative portion of the signal is transmitted on the second wire of the same cable pair.

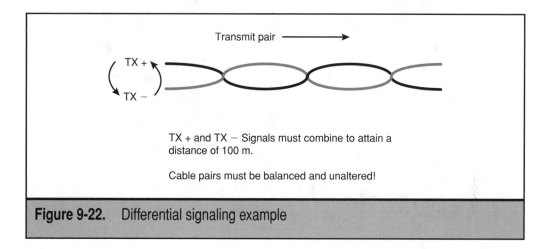

Transmit pair

TX +

TX −

TX + and TX − Signals must combine to attain a distance of 100 m.

Cable pairs must be balanced and unaltered!

Figure 9-22. Differential signaling example

Differential signaling is more robust and reliable for signaling over UTP cables. Any noise imposed on the UTP cable will show up on both the positive and negative portions of the transmitted signal. This provides a means for the signal to be cancelled out and eliminated at the receiver. Differential signaling also provides a means for electromagnetic energy from the cable to be self canceling. This means that the signals will not interfere with other electronic devices operating in the area of the communication cable.

BALUNS

A *BALUN* is a component that can compensate for impedance differences between UTP and coaxial cables (see Figure 9-23). The term BALUN is an acronym for the primary function performed by the BALUN. This device enables balanced twisted-pair cables to be connected to unbalanced coaxial cables. Therefore, it performs a BALanced-to-UNbalanced signal conversion function between the two cable types. A BALUN also compensates for the different characteristic impedance rating between the two types of cables.

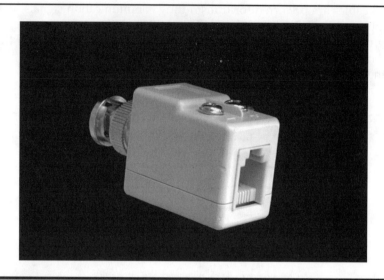

Figure 9-23. BALUN example

MEDIA FILTER

A *media filter* is another cabling component that performs an impedance matching function. Media filters are different from BALUNS. Media filters are used between two balanced cables that have different characteristic impedance ratings. A media filter will filter out noise or other electrical energy from entering or radiating from the cable. It also provides an important impedance matching function between two otherwise incompatible cable types.

Media filters are often used between 100-ohm UTP cables and 150-ohm STP-A cables. They eliminate unwanted frequencies that may cause interference and may be harmful to other systems in the area.

Media filters were first used to provide a means to connect Token Ring LAN equipment together using UTP cable. The original Token Ring equipment was designed to support 150-ohm STP-A cables. Using 100-ohm UTP cables to connect this equipment together would cause signal reflections and excessive signal loss over the UTP cables.

ELECTROMAGNETIC INTERFERENCE

Noise is called *electromagnetic interference* (EMI). The potential for EMI is great inside a large commercial building where multiple electrical and electronic systems share the same space (see Figure 9-24). Many of these systems generate signals or operate signals that are in frequency or over slightly overlay. The systems that operate in the same frequency range

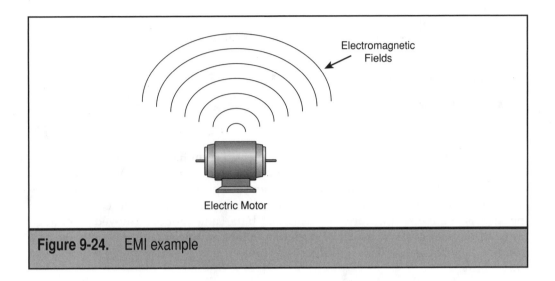

Electromagnetic
Fields

Electric Motor

Figure 9-24.   EMI example

or overlap with other equipment operating in a similar frequency range will interfere with each other.

There are many different sources of EMI. Some a man made sources and others are naturals sources. Examples of man-made sources of EMI include

▼   Electric power cables and devices

■   Communication devices and systems

■   Large equipment with large motors

▲   Heaters and fluorescent lights

Examples of natural sources of EMI include

▼   Static electricity

■   Lightning discharges

▲   Magnetic disturbances

Large, industrial motors and equipment produce strong electromagnetic fields. These fields can cause electrical induction to occur on a copper communication cable. In addition, anything that generates either an electrical spark or radiates other types of electrical energy is considered a source of noise. The electromagnetic fields will cause signals to be induced into a UTP cable, and these signals may interfere with the transmitted voice or data signals traveling over the same cable. The stronger the electromagnetic fields created by the device, the farther away the cable must be routed to protect it against the effects of the noise.

Copper communication cables are very susceptible to noise interfering with signals traveling over a cable. EMI can enter a communication cable by any of the following methods:

▼   Induction

■   Conduction

▲   Coupling

Copper communication cables must be protected from EMI by either using proper installation techniques or by using a technique to shield the cable and block the unwanted signals from entering. If EMI is a problem in a particular area of a building, copper communication cables must be installed far enough away from sources of noise so the effect is minimal on the transmitted signals. If the cable cannot be moved far enough away, the copper cables must be protected by either a cable shield or be encased in a grounded metal conduit. This will shield the cable and protect it from the affects of the EMI energy.

Optical fiber communication cables are not susceptible to EMI noise. Optical fiber cables transmit communication signals in the form of light pulses. These signals are not affected by electrical noise energy. If noise is a severe problem and a reasonable solution cannot be found, replacing copper communication cables with optical fiber cables is an option.

ELECTROMAGNETIC COMPATIBILITY

Electromagnetic compatibility is defined as the ability of a device or a system of devices to function correctly without causing electrical signals that interfere or disturb other devices or systems working in the same space or environment.

A device is considered to be electromagnetically compatible with other devices when all devices can coexist and function correctly without introducing unwanted electromagnetic interference.

Electromagnetic compatibility has two components:

▼   Emission

▲   Immunity

In order for communication systems and electronic devices to be considered electromagnetically compatible, these devices must be checked and verified that they can operate in the same environment without causing EMI to other systems. The systems must be checked to verify that they do not produce emissions that interfere with other systems. Next, each system must be checked to verify that it is immune to the EMI and other noise being produced by other devices.

SIGNALING

Signaling is the term that is used to describe the process of transmitting signals over a communication cable. Either analog or digital signals can be used for communication signaling.

Signaling is a very broad term. It can be used to describe how signals are transmitted over a communication cable. It can also be used to describe how the communication channel is being used to transmit information.

BROADBAND VERSUS BASEBAND SIGNALING

The terms *broadband* and *baseband* have been used to describe the different types of signaling used for communication systems and networks. Broadband refers to a form of analog signaling and multiple signals that are transmitted at the same time. Cable TV networks use broadband signaling. Multiple signals are simultaneously sent across a coaxial cable TV network. Each signal is sent at a different frequency so the signals do not interfere with each other. A second type of signaling is called baseband signaling. Baseband signaling is used for LANs and other communication networks. In baseband signaling, only a single signal can be transmitted across a communication cable at any given time. This permits only one network user or communication device to transmit at any time. If more than one signal is sent on a baseband network, a collision will result.

TYPES OF TRANSMISSION LINES

Another definition of signaling is to describe how communication lines or circuits are used to transmit communication signals. There are three defined forms or types of transmission lines used for communication systems. These are

▼ Simplex lines or channels

■ Half-duplex lines or channels

▲ Full-duplex lines or channels

Simplex lines are only capable of transmitting signals in one direction (see Figure 9-25).

Half-duplex lines are capable of transmitting signals in both directions, but in only one direction at a time (see Figure 9-26).

Full-duplex lines are capable of transmitting signals in both directions simultaneously (see Figure 9-27).

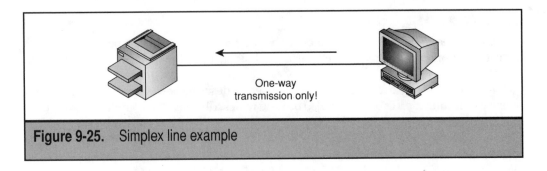

Figure 9-25.   Simplex line example

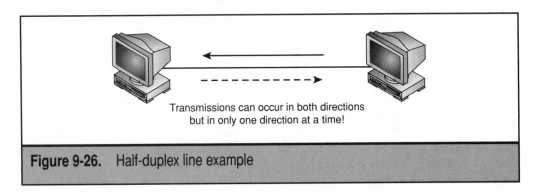

Figure 9-26.   Half-duplex line example

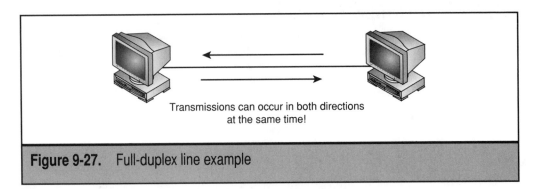

Figure 9-27.   Full-duplex line example

ASYNCHRONOUS TRANSMISSION

Asynchronous transmission is a type of transmission scheme where individual signals are transmitted over a communication channel without a regular time relationship in the signal characters or the bits that represent them.

Asynchronous transmission lines use start and stop bits to indicate the beginning and end of a group of eight transmitted bits.

SYNCHRONOUS TRANSMISSION

Synchronous transmission is a type of transmission scheme where individual signals are transmitted over a communication channel with a specified and regular time relationship between the signal characters or the bits that represent them.

Synchronous transmission uses a clocking mechanism to synchronize the sending and receiving devices on the communications channel.

CHAPTER SUMMARY

Communication systems that have correctly matched cables will perform correctly and provide proper system performance and long-term system reliability. Communication systems that have incorrectly matched cables will cause system reliability problems. In order to correctly match a network media with a communication system, it is important to understand the different signaling methods used in communication systems.

Communication systems use communication cables to send signals between the different system components. All communication systems send communication signals across communication cables. Communication system signals can take one of either analog signals or digital signals. Analog signals are waveforms that are constantly varying from a positive to negative direction using zero as a reference point. These signals can be modulated to carry information over communication cables. Digital signals are transmitted signals that are represented as discrete pulses. Digital signals look like square waves instead of the rounded wave forms of analog signals. Square digital signals represent either a 1 or 0. Most communication systems use digital signals to transmit information.

The relationship of voltage, amperage, or resistance in any circuit can be determined by using the formula for Ohm's Law. If two of these values are known, the third can be determined.

The bandwidth of a communications cable is defined as the information carrying capacity of the media. The bandwidth of a communication cable is specified in MHz. The MHz rating of a cable is the range of frequencies supported by the cable. Megabits per second (Mb/s) is a term used to describe the information carrying capacity of a data network. Data systems or local area networks (LANs) are described in the number of bits per second that can be transmitted by the network. Megahertz (MHz) is a term to describe the information carrying capacity of a communication cable or a communication channel.

A deciBel (dB) is used to identify the power or strength of a signal. It can also be used to measure the ratio or difference between two signals, such as the difference between an input signal and an output signal.

Attenuation is defined as the reduction of a transmitted signal due to resistance encountered by the signal as it is traveling down a cable. Attenuation causes signals to shrink as they travel along a cable. Attenuation is measured in dB. The dB rating is specified per unit length of cable (usually 100 m). Measurements are taken at specified swept/stepped frequency levels. The higher the attenuation dB value, the greater the attenuation (signal loss) and the weaker the received signal.

Near end crosstalk (NEXT) is a measure of the amount of energy that will pass to other pairs within the same cable when a signal is transmitted over a single pair from the same end of the cable. NEXT is measured in dB. The dB rating is specified for each component individually. Measurements are taken at specified swept/stepped frequency levels. The higher the NEXT dB value the better. Power sum near end crosstalk (PS NEXT) is a measure of the total crosstalk energy that can be measured on a nonactive cable pair when more than one pair is active or being used simultaneously.

Far end crosstalk (FEXT) is defined as the crosstalk coupling caused by a transmitter at the near end of a cable link into another cable pair measured at the far end of the link. ELFEXT is a measure of FEXT for any length UTP cable. Power sum equal level far end crosstalk (PS ELFEXT) is a measure of the total crosstalk energy that can be measured on a nonactive cable pair when more than one pair is active or being used simultaneously.

Propagation delay is defined as the amount of time needed for a transmitted signal to travel over a single pair of a communication cable. Propagation delay is typically measured in nanoseconds (ns) for 100 m of cable. This is a measure of how fast the signal travels through a cable. Delay skew is defined as the difference in the propagation delay between the fastest and slowest pairs of the same UTP cable.

Characteristic impedance is defined as the total opposition to the flow of electrons imposed by a communications cable and is measured in ohms. The characteristic impedance of a cable must be a uniform rating across the entire length of the cable. A cable's impedance rating is also independent of the cable's length. Communication cables have different characteristic impedance ratings. The characteristic impedance of the equipment must be matched to the characteristic impedance rating of the communication cables. Mismatching the incorrect types of communications cables and communication equipment result in signal reflections.

Return loss is a measure of the reflected energy caused by impedance mismatches in the cabling system. Impedance mismatches occur on a communication cable link when the termination impedance (component impedance) does not exactly match the characteristic impedance of the cable. The amount of reflected energy is a direct function of the degree of impedance mismatch between the communication cable and the cable termination components in the link. Ideally, the communication cable and the cable termination components will be closely matched and very little signal reflections will result.

Capacitance is defined as the ability of a material or cable to store an electrical charge. Capacitance is due to either the two wires of a pair not twisted together (parallel to each other) or capacitance can exist between the cable's conductors and the cable's shield. Mutual capacitance is the capacitance between the two conductors of a cable pair. The transmission property of capacitance is measured in Farads.

Communication cables are defined as either being a balanced or an unbalanced type of cable. Coaxial cables are defined as being unbalanced cables. Twisted-pair cables are defined as being balanced cables. UTP, STP-A, and ScTP cables are all defined as being balanced cables.

Noise is called electromagnetic interference (EMI). Many of these systems generate signals or operate using signals that are in the same frequency range. The systems that operate in the same frequency range or overlap with other equipment operating in a similar frequency range will interfere with each other. There are many different sources of EMI. Some are man-made sources and others are naturals sources.

Electromagnetic compatibility is defined as the ability of a device or a system of devices to function correctly without causing electrical signals that interfere or disturb other devices or systems working in the same space or environment. A device is considered to be electromagnetically compatible with other devices when all devices can coexist and function correctly without introducing unwanted electromagnetic interference.

Signaling is the term that is used to describe the process of transmitting signals over a communication cable. Signaling is a very broad term. It can be used to describe how signals are transmitted over a communication cable. It can also be used to describe how the communication channel is being used to transmit information.

PART II

Installing and Testing

CHAPTER 10

Plans and Specifications

All construction and communication projects are planned. The first phase of a project is the planning stage. Planning must always be done before construction begins on a project. The planning stage will enable project drawings and specifications to be developed. The project construction will follow the instruction and specification defined in the project drawings. This chapter will describe the planning and design process for the construction industry and define the specifications for communication cabling systems.

PLANS AND DRAWINGS

Plans and designs are produced by the architect. An *architect* is the lead design professional for a construction project. The architect is hired by the building owner and is responsible for managing all phases of a construction project and project designs.

A *plan* is a graphical or pictorial representation of the project. A plan usually includes the overall view of the project.

Drawings are the detailed drawing for smaller portions of a project. Drawings are commonly referred to as Architectural, Mechanical, and Electrical (AME) drawings.

▼ **Architectural drawings**   These drawings describe and define the structure of a building. Included in these drawings are the details for the construction of walls, floors, and ceiling.

■ **Mechanical drawings**   These drawings describe and define the installation of building services such as plumbing, heating, ventilation, and air conditioning.

▲ **Electrical drawings**   These drawings describe and define the installation of electrical systems such as power, motors, lighting, alarms, and related electrical systems. These drawings also describe communication and other low voltage systems.

DESIGN AND CONSTRUCTION PROCESS

The process for creating a plan and then a design for a project starts with a customer identifying the desire to start a construction project. The customer can be a home owner or a commercial building owner. The owner hires an architect to perform the duties of a lead design professional and to establish the project scope and budget. The architect is then responsible for assembling a team of design engineers and specialized consultants who work together to create a schematic design and develop an estimate for completing the project.

The second step in the process is for the project schematic and budget to be presented back to the customer for review. During this meeting, the project schematic is modified and the budget checked. If the project schematic is correct and the project can be built within budget, the design team will begin developing detailed designs for each phase of the project.

For communications cabling projects, a Professional Engineer (PE), Electrical Engineer (EE), or a Registered Communications Distribution Designer (RCDD) will develop the detailed designs.

Each member of the design team prepares the construction documents for each phase of the project. Then the project is put out to bid the form of a request for quote (RFQ). Bids are received from qualified contractors and a contract(s) is awarded to the successful bidder(s). Only after the complete planning and design process is completed will the construction begin. The entire process is represented in Figure 10-1.

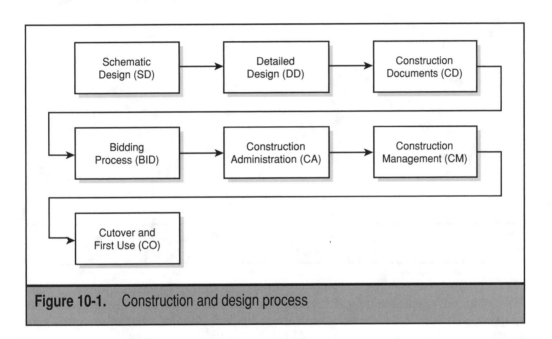

Figure 10-1. Construction and design process

BLUEPRINTS

One of the primary requirements for an architect is to create project blueprints (see Figure 10-2). Blueprints are detailed drawings that describe in a picture form the specifications for a building or project.

A *blueprint* is defined as:

"An architectural plan or a set of technical drawings that provide details about a construction project."

The name blueprint come from the color of the paper for blueprint plans. When blueprints are reproduced, the text and graphics are shown as dark blue on the paper. The paper itself is also blue in color.

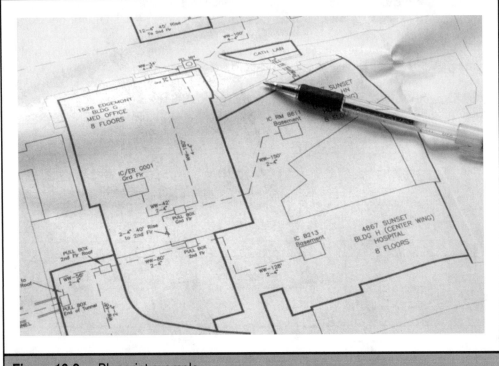

Figure 10-2.   Blueprint example

A blueprint is a plan that provides a pictorial of a project. Blueprint drawings use text, graphics, symbols, and abbreviations to show the details for an electrical, plumbing, or communication cabling project. A set of blueprint drawings will include

▼   Project view drawings

■   Detail drawings

▲   Logical drawings of how things connect together

Together these drawings show in pictures how a communications system will be built once the installation is complete.

Specifications are written documents that go along with the blueprints. These documents provide a detailed, written description of a communication cabling project.

Blueprint Legend

The *blueprint legend* defines how to accurately read a blueprint (see Figure 10-3). The blueprint legend includes the following information:

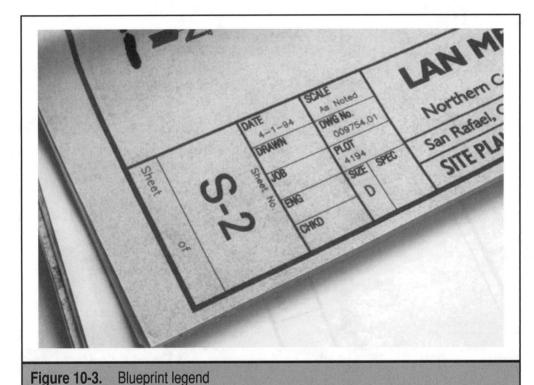

Figure 10-3.   Blueprint legend

▼ **Customer name and address**   Lists the customer name and location of the building.

■ **Scale**   Indicates the actual size of the lines on the drawing. For example, a $1/4$-in. line on the blueprint might equal 1 ft.

■ **Size**   Indicates the size of the blueprint drawing. Typical blueprint sizes are D and E drawings.

▲ **Symbols**   Indicate the meaning of symbols used in the drawings.

The symbols and abbreviations use on blueprints to represent communication cabling components are shown in Figure 10-4.

BLUEPRINT CHECKLIST

Before starting a communication cabling project, take time to review the project blueprints. Verify that you understand how to read the blueprints and the symbols used to designate

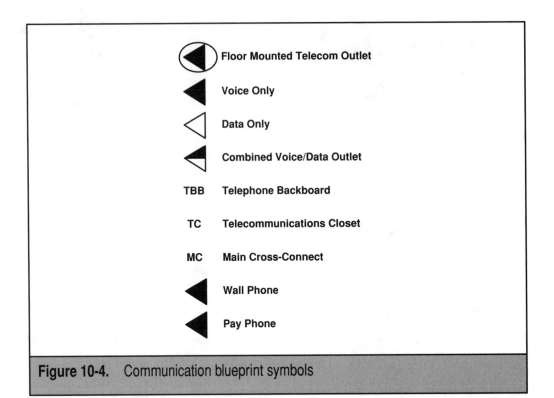

Figure 10-4.   Communication blueprint symbols

telecommunications cabling pathways and cable drops. Review the cable drop lengths and verify that they do not exceed industry standards. A cabling project can be designed incorrectly, and the cable installers represent the last chance to correct any problems with the project design before to project is installed and making changes will be significantly more expensive.

The following checklist is the recommended sequence for examining the blueprints in detail prior to starting a communication cabling project:

1. Confirm the scale used for the blueprint drawings.

2. Verify that the correct telecommunications cabling symbols are in the legend. Some projects may have blueprints drawn by different architectural firms. Therefore, the symbols used on the blueprints may be different.

3. Verify that voice/data drawings, backbone diagrams, or closet diagrams have been provided by the architect.

4. Identify the locations for the main cross-connect (MC) and telecommunications closets (TCs) on the drawings.

5. Verify (by the blueprints or walking the job site) that the location of the MC and the TCs are within the 90 m (295 ft.) maximum distance limit for horizontal cabling specified by the ANSI/TIA/EIA-568-A cabling standard.

6. Verify that the closet size is large enough for the cable, cabling equipment, and other electronic equipment planned for each closet space.

7. Confirm rack configurations for each telecommunications room (TR) and equipment room (ER).

8. Verify the specifications described on the blueprints for all cable support systems.

9. Confirm the specifications for wall penetrations defined by the blueprints.

10. Confirm the backbone requirements (cables and pathways) for each closet. Verify that adequate pathway space and termination space is available in each closet.

11. Examine horizontal cable routes and pathways to all workstation locations.

12. Verify grounding requirements for each closet and confirm that they are ANSI/TIA/EIA-607 compliant.

As Built Drawings

It is very common that during the construction or installation of a project that the plan needs to be changed due to unforeseen circumstances. For example, a wall cannot be moved because it is a load bearing wall, or a conduit must be installed in a different location because an air conditioning vent is already installed in a given location.

The plan or blueprint shows how the project is supposed to be installed. The as built drawings will show how the project was actually installed. These drawings are usually completed by the installation contractor. The as built drawings should be placed with the original project blueprints. This will provide accurate information for the individuals either planning or working on a new project.

CSI MASTERFORMAT

The blueprints created by virtually every private architect follows the MasterFormat™. This is a specified format that has been defined by the Construction Specifications Institute (CSI). The MasterFormat™ is a master list of numbers and titles for organizing information about construction requirements, products, and activities into a standard sequence.

The MasterFormat™ was introduced in 1963, and the current edition is the 1995 edition. CSI section format consists of three parts:

Part 1   General—administrative
Part 2   Products—materials
Part 3   Execution—installation
Front end   Intro, bid forms, conditions, and so on

Division 1   General requirements
Division 2   Site construction
Division 3   Concrete
Division 4   Masonry
Division 5   Metals
Division 6   Woods and plastics
Division 7   Thermal and moisture protection
Division 8   Doors and windows
Division 9   Finishes
Division 10   Specialties
Division 11   Equipment
Division 12   Furnishings
Division 13   Special construction
Division 14   Conveying systems
Division 15   Mechanical
Division 16   Electrical

Current Model and History

The CSI MasterFormat™ does not have a division designated for communication cabling. Currently, the construction specifications and designs for communication cabling are placed at the end of Division 16—Electrical requirements.

The reasons that communication cabling or other low voltage technologies are not part of the current CSI MasterFormat™ goes back to the FCC break up of AT&T in 1984. The design specifications and engineering documents that served as the telephone company installation and design standard were incorporated into building blueprints by architects. Once the bell system was broken up, the building owner became responsible for the communication cabling inside of the building. The building owner had the right to do the cabling any way and following any standard.

The problem with communication cabling and other low voltage communication cabling being placed in Division 16 was that very little consideration was given to these systems. Many times the communication cabling was left out of the planning process all together.

DIVISION 16

Division 16 is the section of the CSI MasterFormat™ that addresses electrical requirements of a building. Communication systems use electricity and are therefore classified under this division.

The organization for division 16 includes the following topics:

▼   16100 General provisions

■   16200 Basic materials and methods

■ 16300 Electrical service system

■ 16400 Electrical distribution system

■ 16500 Electrical motor and power equipment

■ 16600 Lighting fixtures, lamps, and controls

■ 16700 Communications

▲ 16800 Sound and video

The communications section 16700 is broken down into the following subsections:

▼ 16710 Communication circuits

■ 16720 Telephone and intercommunication equipment

■ 16740 Communication and data processing equipment

■ 16770 Cable transmission and reception equipment

■ 16780 Broadcast transmission and reception equipment

▲ 16790 Microwave transmission and reception equipment

The sound and video section 16800 is broken down into the following subsections:

▼ 16810 Sound and video circuits

■ 16820 Sound reinforcement

■ 16830 Broadcast studio audio equipment

■ 16840 Broadcast studio video equipment

■ 16850 Television equipment

▲ 16880 Multimedia equipment

Communication cabling and supporting structures are usually only included in about two pages of most blueprints. Cabling infrastructure components, such as conduits or pull boxes, are specified. The communication cabling typically needs to be planned and designed by the owner or by the company that will be moving into a building. The communication cabling is usually installed after the building is completed in most cases. This results in higher installation costs.

Communication cabling is considered by many to be the fourth utility in a commercial or residential building. The CSI has been evaluating adding communication cabling in a new division. It is currently proposed that a Division 17 be added to the CSI MasterFormat™ when this document is updated in 2002. Division 17 will be designated for telecommunications. This means all communication systems, cabling, and supporting structures will be defined in this division.

DIVISION 17

Division 17 is a comprehensive model that will be used to plan, build, and manage technology infrastructures in a manner that is consistent with the established design and construction industry.

The proposed model for Division 17 will provide a structure to organize and define a comprehensive set of performance specifications for all low voltage communication systems and their associated cabling requirements. The Division 17 organizational model specifically addresses the following:

▼ Inside and outside cable plants

▲ LAN and WAN requirements for

- Data systems
- Voice systems
- Video/audio systems
- Security systems
- Intrabuilding communication systems

The proposed Division 17 model will include the following sections:

▼ Front-end requirements

■ 17000 General requirements

■ 17100 Cable plant

■ 17200 LAN

■ 17300 Voice

■ 17400 Audio/video

■ 17500 WAN

■ 17600 Architectural, electrical, and mechanical systems

■ 17700 Intrabuilding communication systems

■ 17800 Building automation and control

▲ 17900 Security, access, and surveillance

This is a comprehensive model that encompasses all types of communications and building automation systems that are currently being installed in commercial buildings. Each section currently defined will be broken down into subsections that provide greater detail and associated drawing.

The section for cable plant section 17100 will be broken down into the following subsections:

▼   17110 Communication equipment rooms

■   17120 Main equipment rooms (ERs) and service entrances

■   17130 Interior pathways

■   17140 Exterior pathways

■   17150 Backbone requirements

■   17160 Horizontal requirements

■   17170 Testing, identification, and administration

■   17180 Cutover and training

▲   17190 Support and warranty

Each of these subsections can be further broken down to define the level of detail necessary for any project. An example of further breaking down the subsection of communication ERs Section 17110 would include details on the following components found in this building space:

▼   Equipment racks/cabinets/shelves

■   Cable management—vertical and horizontal

■   Patch panels

■   Fiber patch panels

■   Backboards

■   Termination blocks

■   Aluminum ladder rack

■   Tie wraps

■   D-rings and T posts

▲   Grounding bars

The performance specifications would follow the format defined in the CSI MasterFormat™ specifications for

Part 1   General—administrative
Part 2   Products—materials
Part 3   Execution—installation

This will result in a definition for minimum quality requirements, how a product shall be manufactured, and how a product shall be installed. An example of the format is as follows:

SECTION 17110

Communication Equipment Rooms and Spaces

Part 1   General

1.1 Work Included

A. Provide all labor, materials, tools, and equipment required to complete the installation of all work specified in the project RFQ and in the contract documents.

Part 2   Products

2.1 Equipment Cabinets and Floor Mounted Racks

A. All supplied cabinets and communication racks shall meet the following physical specifications:

     1.   Plexiglass doors and solid metal sides

     2.   All racks shall have a 19 in. width

     3.   All cabinets and racks must be 7 ft. (84 in.) tall

Part 3   Execution

3.1 Cabinets

A. All cabinets must be secured to the floor to prevent free movement.
B. Cabinets must provide both vertical and horizontal wire management panels.

3.2 Free Standing Communication Racks

A. All free standing communication racks shall be anchored to the floor.
B. All communication racks must provide both vertical and horizontal wire management panels.

T SERIES DRAWINGS

Division 17 also defines a format for creating drawings to plan and communicate the technology requirements with clients and other design professionals. The T drawings defined in Division 17 will provide the format for a design professional to clearly communicate quantity and location of the specific products. Table 10-1 shows the T drawings currently proposed for Division 17.

T Drawing Number	Description	Included in the Drawings
T0	Campus or site plan	Exterior pathways and Inter-building backbones.
T1	Layout of complete building per floor	Serving zone boundaries and backbone systems.
T2	Serving zones drawing(s)	Drop locations and cable IDs.
T3	Communication equipment room(s)	Plan views—tech and AMEP and elevations—racks and walls.
T4	Typical drawings	Faceplate labeling, firestopping, ADA, safety, and other cabling requirements.
T5	Schedules for cutovers	These are not drawings but schedules and lists of items to be completed.

Table 10-1.   Division 17 T Drawings

Drawing Cover

The drawings must include a cover sheet that describes the customer and the location of the project.

The T drawings will be taken from standard architectural building blueprints. The telecommunications cabling and supporting structures will be added for each portion of the building or campus.

T0 Drawings

T0 drawings show physical and logical connections from the perspective of an entire campus, such as actual building locations, exterior pathways, and interbuilding backbone cabling on plan view drawings and major system nodes and related connections on the logical system drawings.

T1 Drawings

T1 drawings are the layout of complete building per floor. The drawing indicates location of serving zones, communication equipment rooms, access points, pathways, and other systems that need to be viewed from the complete building perspective.

The T1 drawings will include separate drawings for the plan views and the logical views. A plan view and logical view must be created for the cable pathways and building spaces. A plan view and logical view must be created for each type of media used in the new cable installation project.

The plan view for the cable pathways shows the location of all spaces on the building floor plans. The logical view will show all of the building spaces and how they are connected together. The plan view will show the cable termination locations on the building floor plans. The logical view will show how each of the building spaces are connected together on the floor.

T2 Drawings

The building is divided up by its serving zones. T2 drawings indicate drop locations, communication equipment rooms, access points, and detail callouts for communication equipment rooms and other congested areas.

The T2 drawings will have logical drawings for the pathways and the media to be installed. The logical pathway view will show the logical pathways for each building zone. The logical cable view will show the logical cable runs for each building zone.

T3 Drawings

T3 drawings are a detailed look at the communication equipment room. The drawing indicates technology layout (communications racks, ladder racks, and so on), mechanical/electrical layout, rack elevation, and backboard elevation. They may also be an enlargement of a congested area of T1 or T2.

The T3 drawings can also contain logical T3 drawings showing pathway views.

T4 Drawings

T4 drawings are detailed drawings of symbols and typical cabling elements such as faceplate labeling, faceplate types, installation procedures, detail racking, and raceways.

NOTE: Additional drawings can be used in conjunction with the drawings listed previously.

T4 drawings can also include symbols that are to be used for installation projects.

T5 Drawings

T5 drawings are the installation schedules for cutovers. These are not drawings but schedules and lists of items to be completed. These are usually completed by the project supervisor.

CHAPTER SUMMARY

The first phase of a project is the planning stage. Planning must always be done before construction begins on a project. The planning stage will enable project drawings and specifications to be developed. A plan is a graphical or pictorial representation of the project. A plan usually includes the overall view of the project.

Drawings are the detailed drawing for smaller portions of a project. Drawings are commonly referred to as Architectural, Mechanical, and Electrical (AME) drawings.

Plans and designs are produced by the architect. An architect is the lead design professional for a construction project. The architect is hired by the building owner and is responsible for managing all phases of a construction project and project designs.

For communications cabling projects, a Professional Engineer (PE), an Electrical Engineer (EE), or a Registered Communications Distribution Designer (RCDD) will develop the detailed designs. Each member of the design team prepares the construction documents for each phase of the project. Then the project is put out to bid the form of a request for quote (RFQ).

One of the primary requirements for an architect is to create project blueprints. Blueprints are detailed drawings that describe in a picture form the specifications for a building or project. A blueprint is a plan that provides a pictorial of a project. Blueprint drawings use text, graphics, symbols, and abbreviations to show the details for an electrical, plumbing, or communication cabling project. Specifications are written documents that go along with the blueprints. These documents provide a detailed written description of a communication cabling project.

It is very common that during the construction or installation of a project that the plan needs to be changed due to unforeseen circumstances. The plan or blueprint shows how the project is supposed to be installed. The as built drawings will show how the project was actually installed. These drawings are usually completed by the installation contractor.

The blueprints created by virtually every private architect follow the MasterFormat™. This is specified format that has been defined by the Construction Specifications Institute (CSI). CSI section format consists of three Parts: Part 1—General defining administrative information; Part 2—Products defining the materials required for the project; and Part 3—Execution defining how the project will be installed.

The CSI MasterFormat™ does not have a division designated for communication cabling. Currently, the construction specifications and designs for communication cabling are placed at the end of Division 16—Electrical requirements.

Division 17 is a comprehensive model that will be used to plan, build, and manage technology infrastructures in a manner that is consistent with the established design and construction industry. The proposed model for Division 17 will provide a structure to organize and define a comprehensive set of performance specifications for all low voltage communication systems and their associated cabling requirements.

Division 17 also defines a format for creating drawings to plan and communicate the technology requirements with clients and other design professionals. The T drawings defined in Division 17 will provide the format for a design professional to clearly communicate quantity and location of the specific products. Division 17 proposes six levels of drawings: T0 for campus or site plan; T1 for the layout of a complete building or floor; T2 for the cabling zones for each floor; T3 for the design of communication equipment rooms; T4 for typical drawings such as faceplate labeling; and T5 for schedules and cutovers.

CHAPTER 11

Installation Safety, Hazardous Environments, and Protective Equipment

Every company is responsible for providing both safety training and a safe working environment for their employees. All companies must establish safety procedures and provide employee training on following established safety procedures while on the job. Safety training must be given on a regular basis and not because an injury occurred.

Although every company is responsible for providing both safety training and a safe working environment, safety is ultimately the responsibility of every worker on a job site. Each worker on a job site must follow the established job site and company safety procedures. Not following established safety procedures may cause injuries to others as well as to yourself.

This chapter will describe common safety practices, hazardous environments, and protective equipment that can be used to prevent construction injuries.

OSHA

In 1970, Congress passed the Occupational Safety and Health Act (OSHA). OSHA attempts to ensure a safe and sound environment for every working person.

OSHA has the responsibility for performing job site field inspections and enforcement. OSHA also has the authority, granted by the Department of Labor, to levy fines and/or shut down job sites if hazards are found or the site does not comply with OSHA regulations.

The two OSHA requirements related to the telecommunications industry are

▼ **OSHA regulations**   1910, occupational safety and health standards

▲ **OSHA regulations**   1926, safety and health regulation for construction

COMPANY SAFETY PLAN

Every company should have a safety plan. This plan should describe company safety procedures to avoid construction-related injuries. The main objective of a company safety plan is to enable work to be completed correctly without any injuries to company employees.

Employee injuries are very expensive to a company. If the injury is severe, the employee will be off of work. This will result in lost productivity and delays in the project completion date. The employee may need to draw workers' compensation insurance. This will result in the company paying higher insurance premiums on all employees. In addition, the injury may result in a lawsuit costing the company time and money on the impending legal matters.

The best way for a company to avoid employee injuries is to create a company safety plan. This plan should be written and a copy must be given to all employees. Formal training on the plan must be given to all employees before they start working on a job site.

A company safety plan should include the following items:

▼   Accident prevention

■   Job site communication

■   Barricades and warning devices

■   Designated work areas

■   Fire safety

■   Good housekeeping

■   Avoiding horseplay

■   Covering floor openings

■   Avoiding unsafe actions

■   Avoiding unsafe conditions

■   First aid

■   Personal safety

■   Attitude

■   Proper clothing

■   Eye safety

■   Proper footwear

■   Head protection

■   Avoid back injuries

▲   Lifting fundamentals

CONSTRUCTION ACCIDENTS

Construction-related accidents affect thousands of workers each year. The cause of most accidents usually fall into two basic categories. The first is unsafe actions and the second is unsafe conditions.

Common unsafe actions include the following:

▼   Unauthorized use or operation of heavy equipment/power tools

■   Failure to secure climbing devices

■   Working at an unsafe speed or using unsafe methods

■   Failure to warn others or failure to heed a warning from a sign or co-workers

- Disabling safety mechanisms on power equipment
- Using broken or defective equipment
- Using power tools or other equipment improperly
- Standing in an unsafe location or not providing enough clearance from a hazard
- Touching or servicing moving equipment parts
- Standing on moving equipment
- Horseplay, distracting, or startling others
- ▲ Failure to wear protective equipment at all or correctly

Unsafe conditions include the following:

- ▼ Poor housekeeping
- Lack of adequate warning systems
- Fire or explosion hazards
- Unsafe climbing devices
- Unexpected movements of equipment or climbing devices
- Congestion hazards
- Inadequate illumination
- Hazardous or defective tools
- ▲ Electrical hazards

Accident Prevention

The best way to treat accidents is to prevent them all together. Every worker must make accident prevention his or her top priority every day on the job. This job should never be left to others to perform. A few simple things that can be done to prevent accidents on a job site include

- ▼ Report unsafe working conditions to project supervisor immediately.
- Avoid horseplay and discourage other workers from playing practical jokes.
- Follow all warning signs and adhere to your company's established safety procedures.
- Use safe and proven procedures for performing job tasks.
- Follow the job plan. Never take shortcuts that can lead to injury.

- ■ Make suggestions for improving safety conditions.

- ■ Keep all work areas neat or orderly.

- ▲ Dress properly for the job.

Accident prevention starts with the employees. The first step is learning accident prevention procedures. The next step is incorporating these procedures into everyday job activities.

Good Housekeeping

Good housekeeping is the process of putting away all tools and keeping your work area clean. This is one of the easiest and simplest things that makes a big difference between having a safe and unsafe work environment.

Keeping your work area clean saves project installation time and keeps the job site safe for all workers. Trash such as newspapers, food wrappers, and excess material scraps should be thrown away before they have a chance of causing an injury. If a housekeeping issue is identified that cannot be cleaned up immediately, it should be reported to the project supervisor.

Project materials and tools that are no longer needed should be stored properly. This will avoid theft or damage to unused materials. Resist the temptation of throwing everything in one big pile. All tools and materials should be stored in their correct place. This will save time later when one of these tools is needed at a later time.

Avoiding Horseplay

Horseplay and practical jokes are very common on most job sites. Most horseplay or practical jokes occur during lulls in the project work and while workers are relaxing. These may be funny when everything goes right. What happens when something goes wrong?

Horseplay and practical jokes can cause unforeseen injuries on a job work site. Horseplay or practical jokes that go wrong and cause injuries can lead to injuries and possible lawsuits. Injuries that result from either horseplay or practical jokes are not covered by workers' compensation insurance. If you were the joker, you may be liable for paying for lost wages and civil damages. In addition, you will most likely lose your job.

There is nothing wrong with laughing on the job site. Each worker must be prepared to step in and stop horseplay that is getting out of hand. Practical jokes should be avoided all together.

First Aid

It is recommended that every cable installer or other employees working on a job site take a course in first aid and cardiopulmonary resuscitation (CPR).

Every cable installer must be trained to administer proper first aid for job-related injuries and CPR for any persons who have stopped breathing or their heart has stopped.

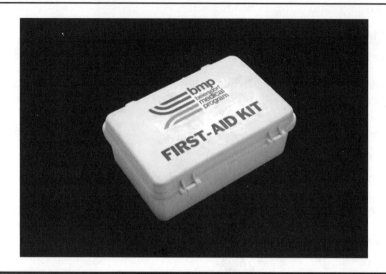

Figure 11-1. First aid kit

First aid kits should always be on site and accessible to all employees (see Figure 11-1). It is also highly recommended that first aid kits with a portable eye washing station be present at every job site. First aid kits should be periodically checked to verify that supplies are adequately stocked and they've not passed their expiration date.

JOB SITE COMMUNICATION

Proper and timely communications are mandatory while working on a job site. Supervisors must be in constant communication with the members of their installation team.

Cable installers must be in constant contact with their supervisor and other team members working in their area of the building. Timely and proper communication can get the job completed faster with less chance of injuries. Any warning signs and hazards should always be reported to both the job supervisor and other team members.

TOOLS AND EQUIPMENT

Tool and equipment safety must always be considered when working on a job. Tools and other installation equipment should only be used for their intended purposes. For example, never hammer a nail with a flashlight or use a sharp knife to tighten a screw on a wall plate. These activities may cause an injury or damage the tool.

Tools should be regularly inspected to ensure that they are in safe working condition. Always pay close attention to the tool handles to make sure they are not broken or damaged. These can give way, causing a job injury.

Broken or unsafe tools should be flagged and taken out of use so no one will suffer an injury from the damaged tool.

POWER TOOL SAFETY

Power tools are simple devices that just about everyone can operate safely. However, power tools should never be taken lightly. Power tool safety should always be your top priority when using these devices on a job site.

Power tools are devices that present multiple dangers including:

- ▼ Electrical hazards
- ■ Fast-moving parts
- ▲ Sharp edges

The biggest danger associated with power tools is faulty or damaged equipment. The power tool may break while it is being used and cause a serious injury. As a result, power tools and other power equipment must be inspected regularly. Never use a power device unless you have personally inspected it and verified that it is safe to use.

Always follow the manufacturer's instructions when working with dangerous mechanical equipment such as cable tuggers or ramset guns. Always read the tool's instructions and if necessary, receive the proper training before attempting to use the tool alone.

The most potentially lethal danger associated with using power tools is electrical shocks or possible electrocution. Power cords must be inspected to verify that the ground prong has not been cut off or damaged. This will prevent the tool from being properly grounded. Never use a power tool's cord for lifting or carrying. The power cord for most tools is not designed to support the tool's weight and will damage the cord.

SCAFFOLDING AND LADDER SAFETY

Scaffolds and ladders are involved in virtually every type of construction project. For communication cabling projects, scaffolds and ladders are both used during the project construction. Scaffolds are usually used to install cable trays and other large cable-supporting structures. Ladders are smaller devices usually used when pulling communication cables.

Each year, many injuries occur due to falls from scaffolds and ladders. Most of these injuries can be avoided by paying close attention to how these lifting devices are set up, using good housekeeping, and always using correct safety precautions.

Scaffolds must be set up correctly. Follow these safety guidelines when setting up scaffolding on a job site.

▼ Pole scaffolds should be anchored lengthwise and height-wise. This will prevent the scaffold structure from falling when individuals are working on it. The distance between anchor points depends on factors such as their location and materials. Consult your company's safety manuals and OSHA regulations for exact anchoring specifications.

■ Free-standing tower scaffolds must be guyed if their height is more than three times the scaffold's width at the base.

■ Always follow the scaffold manufacturer's instructions for assembling and locking scaffold components.

■ If working outside of a building, foundation sills should be placed under the scaffold legs.

▲ Never use improvised scaffolds or piling boxes on an existing scaffold instead of raising the scaffolding height. This can lead to personal injury.

Scaffolding heights can reach 15 to 20 ft. during a construction project. Falls from these heights can result in serious injuries or possibly death. To avoid the possibility of a scaffolding-related injury, the following precautions should be taken:

▼ Inspect scaffolds every day before working on them. Inspect connection points, the foundation, guard rails, tie-ins, and bracing to verify that they are secure.

■ Avoid piling extra reels of cable on a scaffold and remove all materials and tools at the end of each working day. Falling tools or materials can cause injuries to those below the scaffold.

■ Never overload scaffolds. Learn the weight limit of the scaffold you are working on and adhere to this limitation.

■ Always check scaffold guying or securing ropes. Look for damage, weaknesses, or missing components.

▲ OSHA has rules regarding the correct use of scaffolds on a construction site. These rules were rewritten and published in 1996. The OSHA scaffolding rules include the following:

    ■ Makeshift devices or ladders should never be used to raise workers to the height of a scaffold.

    ■ The maximum distance between a building wall and the scaffold is 14 in. If this distance is exceeded, a guard rail must be installed.

    ■ Planking on scaffolds must be at least 18 in. and planks should never be painted.

    ■ Scaffolding parts should never be interchanged.

Portable Ladders

Every cable installer must know how to use a portable ladder safely. Installing cables above a drop ceiling requires the following:

▼ Choosing the correct ladder

▲ Placing it securely on a flat surface

You should always choose the correct type and size ladder for the job. Never use a metal ladder if there is a chance of either you or the ladder touching electrical cables or devices. Ladders that are made of wood or fiberglass will solve this problem. Avoid using ladders that are too small. This may promote climbing on the top step and may cause falls.

Ladders must always be placed on a flat, solid surface. If a flat and solid surface cannot be found, the ladder must be held in place by another workers or secured to prevent ladder movement. Verify that the support arms are fully intended and locked in place. Finally, verify that the ladder is set at the correct angle and distance from the work location (see Figure 11-2).

The correct distance for an extension ladder is based on the length of the ladder. The base of the ladder should be placed away from the wall at a distance that is equal to 25 percent of the ladder's height. This means that the base of a 20 ft. ladder would be placed 4 ft. from the wall.

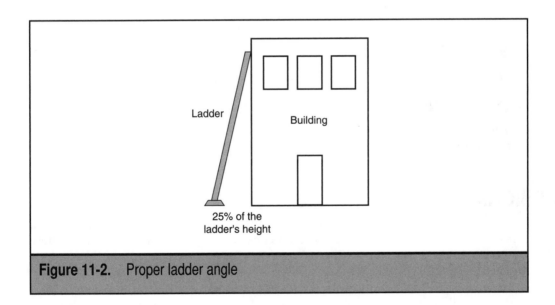

Ladder

Building

25% of the
ladder's height

Figure 11-2.   Proper ladder angle

Always inspect a ladder carefully before using it. Ladders should be inspected before each use to make sure that

▼   Steps and side rails are tight.

■   Rubber, anti-skid feet are in correct working order.

■   Side rails are not bent or damaged.

■   Rings and steps are clean and free from liquids or other material that may cause a slip.

▲   Ladder is dry to prevent potential shock hazards.

A proper ladder inspection should become part of your personal safety routine each time you use a ladder. If a ladder is damaged, never use it.

Always set up your ladder so it will be out of high traffic areas of a building. Always use orange codes to designate a work area around the ladder. Never place a ladder in front of a door that opens toward the ladder unless you have verified that the door is locked or foot traffic is blocked so the door will not be used while the ladder is being used.

Always follow these safety steps when using a ladder:

▼   Never exceed the ladder's safety weight rating or weight limit.

■   Always climb up or down facing the ladder.

■   Never stand on the top step or top shelf of the ladder.

■   Never leave tools or equipment on the ladder.

■   Never drop or throw tools while standing on the ladder.

■   Never lean out over the ladder's side rails. Move the ladder instead.

▲   Always climb off the ladder to move it.

Always use the correct tools for the job. If the job requires a ladder, always use the correct type of ladder and not a makeshift climbing device.

DESIGNATING WORK AREAS

Work areas are dangerous places for those that are not trained. A cabling installation work area should always be designated using safety cones and bright yellow caution tape. Safety cones and yellow caution tape will restrict access to a work area and alert others that the area is unsafe.

When designating the work area, leave sufficient space in the designated work space to perform all necessary job tasks. In addition, try not to block access to doorways or hallways.

Finally, never leave open floor panels, ceiling panels, or dangerous equipment unattended. Open panels should always be closed when work ceases and dangerous equipment put away.

COMPRESSED AIR

Compressed air is another common item found on many construction job sites. It is used to operate equipment, such as nail guns, and is a valuable work-saving device. Compressed air is a useful but dangerous construction tool. This tool can represent a significant hazard if used incorrectly.

Horseplay is the biggest problem associated with compressed air. Inexperienced workers believe that compressed air is harmless. They may not realize that air driven at a high enough velocity can cause many types of injuries. In fact, compressed air can be deadly if used incorrectly.

The pressure from an air hose can many injuries including

▼ Popping the eyes out of their sockets with 12 psi of air pressure

■ Rupturing eardrums from up to 4 in. inches away with 40 psi of air pressure

▲ Forcing air under the skin with 80 psi and possibly causing a brain aneurysm

FLAMMABLE LIQUIDS

The job of installing communication cable can sometimes involve the use of different chemicals to lubricate and clean cables. These seemingly benign lubricants and cleaners can be harmful it not treated carefully.

Flammable liquids are any fluid or compound that gives off flammable vapors. These vapors cannot be seen and sometimes cannot be smelled. It these vapors are in high enough concentrations, any spark can ignite them causing a fire.

A few common example of flammable liquids would include

▼ Solvents

■ Cleaning fluids

▲ Fuels

The safest way to handle these flammable liquids or compounds is to keep the lids of their containers tightly sealed. When using these fluids, always work in a well ventilated space.

CAUTION: Empty containers should always be disposed of correctly. These containers may contain vapors in heavy concentrations. Even a spark from static electricity can cause them to ignite.

HAZARDOUS ENVIRONMENTS

Installing telecommunications cables can be a dangerous activity due to the environments and spaces where the cables are terminated. Some work locations present hazards and must be identified.

Electrical Hazards

Electrical hazards are probably the most common type of hazard for communication cable installers. This is due to the close proximity between telecommunications (voice and data) cabling and electrical cabling. Both telecommunications cabling and electrical cabling are installed behind walls, under floors, and above ceilings in commercial buildings. In some buildings, telecommunications cabling and electrical cabling are terminated in the same spaces.

Electrical circuits should always be treated as if they are active, even if you know the power has been turned off. These circuits may become active at any time. When working around electrical circuits, always maintain proper clearances and wear the necessary personal protective equipment for electrical hazards.

Never work on or near electrical circuits or equipment while standing in water. If standing water exists, take extra precautions to verify that no electrical power circuits are near your work environment.

Lightning Hazards

Lightning hazards can exist for telecommunications cable installers working indoors. New construction and renovation projects may have incomplete lightning protection systems. Lightning strikes can travel across a copper cable and into inside plant copper cables.

Always use caution when working on premises cables that are connected to outside plant cables. Primary protectors must be used to terminate outside plant cables and protect against electrical surges caused by electrical faults or lightning strikes.

Catwalk Hazards

Cable installers may need to use catwalks to install cable in large buildings. Catwalks are large metal walkways constructed above ceilings in very large commercial buildings. They provide a working space above ceiling and can be useful when pulling cables in commercial buildings.

When required to work on a catwalk, always stay inside the catwalk railings and never leave the catwalk for any reason. Never venture off the catwalk onto beams or other structures. Avoid dropping tools or materials from the catwalk. This activity can injure any individual working below or passing beneath the catwalk.

Crawl Space Hazards

Cable installers may need to work in crawl spaces of some commercial buildings. Crawl spaces are the confined spaces either above or below a work area. These building spaces can present hazards to your head. As a result, protective head gear should always be worn when working in confined crawl spaces.

Before entering a crawl space, identify any hazards that exist. Hazards can exist from sharp or protruding objects. When walking through a crawl space, only walk or crawl in designated areas. Avoid leaving designated areas. In some cases, you may need to wear breathing protection while working in the crawl space.

Chemical and Product Hazards

Always be aware of any chemical or product hazards that exist on a job site. Material Safety Data (MSD) sheets are required by OSHA to be onsite for all hazardous products that are being used or stored on the job. The MSD sheets identify dangers presented by dangerous chemicals or products. They also provide vital, safe-handling information and procedures for all hazardous products.

Gas Hazards

Gas is a hazard whenever present on a job site. Gases are especially hazardous in confined spaces, such as cable vaults or manhole environments. Most gas vapor is heavier than air and will accumulate in these low building spaces.

Before entering a confined space, verify that the space is completely free from gas hazards. A gas detection kit can determine if any gas is present. Gas must be blown out before it is safe to enter.

Never dispose of cigarettes or matches in basements, vaults, or manholes. If any explosive vapors exist in these spaces, an explosion may result.

Optical Fiber Hazards

Optical fiber fragments are small and sharp pieces of glass. Fiber fragments are created when terminating optical fiber cables. These small pieces of glass can easily penetrate fingers or eyes. Once in your skin, they can be very difficult or maybe even impossible to remove.

The best way to deal with the dangers associated with fiber fragments is to acknowledge the potential danger and develop safety procedures for disposing of them. Basic safety procedures working with optical fibers include the following:

▼ Always wear eye protection.

■ Always wear protective gloves.

■ Try to work on a flat, dark surface. A dark surface provides a contrast to the clear fiber fragments.

■ Only work in environments that have little or no air flow, which can blow fiber fragments.

■ Smooth, flat floors are preferable work areas over carpeted areas because they can be swept clean.

▲ Always wash your hands before touching your eyes or face. Small glass fragments can stick to the oils on your hands.

Battery Hazards

Some telecommunications spaces house batteries. Working in and around batteries can be dangerous unless the proper safety precautions are taken.

Working around storage batteries requires that

▼ All cable technicians have proper training for handling battery electrolytes.

■ All cable technicians wear eye and full face protection.

■ All cable technicians wear acid resistant gloves and aprons.

▲ All cable technicians must receive proper emergency training for handling spills and performing proper cleanup procedures.

Never make contact with batteries or battery cables with metal objects. Batteries can have large current levels and contact with metal objects can cause serious harm.

Asbestos Hazards

Some cable installation environments present asbestos hazards to cable installers. Asbestos is a substance that was used extensively for building insulation before being banned in 1978. Breathing asbestos fibers has been linked to cancer of the

▼ Lungs

■ Stomach

■ Colon

▲ Esophagus

The danger with asbestos is when asbestos fibers are released into the air. This can occur during a cable installation project. This is caused by disturbing asbestos by sawing, drilling, or just rubbing against asbestos material. Working in an asbestos environment requires full breathing protection, protective suits, and specialized training.

PROTECTIVE EQUIPMENT

Protective equipment is the safety gear typically worn on a job site to protect each worker from job-related injuries. When used correctly, protective equipment will greatly reduce the risk of injury from common construction area hazards.

The exact protective equipment that a cable installer should wear will depend on the following:

▼ Job safety requirements defined by local, state, and national laws or specifications

■ Installation environment

▲ Specific hazards of a given task or the equipment required for the task

Protective equipment should be part of every cable installer's tool kit. It is highly recommended that each cable installer own their protective equipment so it will be comfortable and fit correctly. Finally, never having to share equipment means that all workers on a job are protected from job-related dangers.

All cable installers should be trained on the proper use and adjustment of their protective equipment. You should learn the following:

▼ When protective equipment is required.

■ How to put on, adjust, and take off protective equipment. Each cable installer should also know how protective equipment should look and feel once put on correctly.

■ Exactly what hazards each piece of protective equipment is designed to protect you against.

▲ The correct maintenance for each piece of protective equipment.

Remember, wearing protective equipment incorrectly or equipment that is the wrong size may be the same as not wearing any protective equipment at all.

Headgear/Hard Hat

Cable installers should always wear helmets or hard hats when working in areas that:

▼ Have the potential of falling or flying objects

■ Have the potential for electrical shock

▲ Present a danger of bumping or cutting your head

All helmets or hard hats should be adjusted so they fit correctly. Headgear that is too large may slip and block your vision or fall off your head. Headgear should always be inspected before wearing it in a hazardous environment.

Eye Protection

Cable installers should always wear eye protection when working on a job site. Eye protection would include

▼ Safety glasses (see Figure 11-3)

■ Goggles

▲ A face shield

Eye protection will protect your eyes from a variety of work related dangers including

▼ Working with any tools that drill or bore into concrete

■ Working with or near batteries or battery electrolytes

■ Using power-fastening tools or other tools that can cause hard or sharp materials to become airborne

■ Working with optical fiber fragments

▲ Any other situation where you are working at or above eye level with installation or termination tools

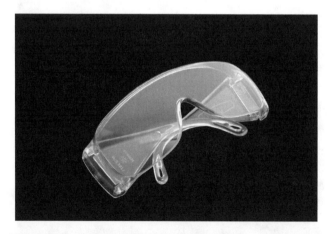

Figure 11-3.   Safety glasses

Breathing Protection

Breathing protection may be required on job sites where harmful dust, smoke, gases, chemical vapors, or other pollutants present a breathing hazard. If a breathing hazard exists on a job site, never work without using proper breathing protective equipment.

There are different types of breathing protective devices used in specific work environments. These include the following:

▼ **Filter mask**   This would be used for moderately hazardous environments due to dust.

▲ **Gas mask or respirator**   These devices would be required in more serious environments.

CAUTION: The effects of breathing some hazardous dust or gases may not show up until hours, weeks, or years after the actual exposure.

Lifting Belt

Lifting belts provide lower back support when lifting heavy objects. Lifting belts should always be worn when lifting heavy tools or equipment. Many job sites require all workers to wear a lifting belt.

Each worker should also learn and use proper lifting techniques when lifting heavy tools and equipment. Proper lifting techniques include lifting with your legs and not your back. This is the best way to avoid lifting injuries.

Protective Footwear

Correct footwear should always be worn on a job site. Protective footwear will protect your feet from injuries due to falling objects and puncture wounds from sharp objects. Protective footwear will also provide proper support on the job.

The recommended protective footwear for cable installers are leather boots. It is also highly recommended that your boots have a steel toe or steel shanks.

Gloves

Protective gloves should always be worn when performing tasks that have the potential for hand injuries (see Figure 11-4). Working with sharp tools or sharp materials represent hand hazards. Gloves also protect hands from chemical spills and extreme temperatures.

Detection Badges

Some work environments require cable installers to wear detection badges to monitor exposure levels to hazardous substances. Before working in such an area, you should be

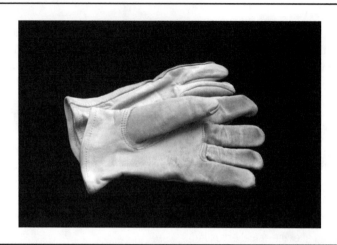

Figure 11-4. Gloves

trained on the dangers of these areas. You should also be trained on correctly using and monitoring detection badge readings.

Never exceed specified time limits in a hazardous environment even if your detection badge indicates that it is safe to do so.

Hearing Protection

Hearing protection may be required in high noise areas of a job site or when working with specific equipment on a job site (see Figure 11-5).

Hearing protection should always be worn when ambient noise levels exceed comfortable listening levels. Proper hearing protection includes the use of ear plugs or headsets. Never use makeshift ear plugs from paper or cotton. These do not provide adequate hearing protection.

Clothing

Clothing is a very important piece of protective equipment. Incorrect or ill-fitting clothing causes many accidents each year.

Work clothing should be reasonably snug while enabling a cable installer free movement when performing job tasks. Loose fitting or baggy clothing is very dangerous and should never be worn. This type of clothing can be caught on tools or in exposed machinery parts.

Avoid wearing jewelry and metal bracelets while working on telecommunications circuits or near electrical circuits.

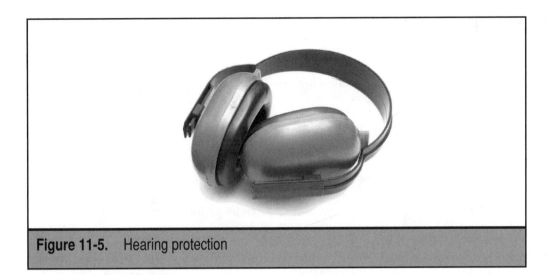

Figure 11-5.   Hearing protection

WHAT TO DO IF AN ACCIDENT OCCURS?

If an accident occurs on a job site, the very first thing to do is to evaluate the injured individual or individuals. If the accident is major, call for help immediately. If the injury is minor, fully examine each individual and determine if additional medical attention is needed by anyone.

Always remain calm when an injury occurs. Staying calm will keep the situation in control and avoid creating more confusion. This will also prevent the injured individual(s) from becoming stressed and possibly making their condition worse.

The following procedures should be followed:

▼   Have someone call 911.

■   Never move an injured individual or individuals unless they are in grave danger by remaining where they fell.

■   Never leave the injured individual(s) alone, if possible.

■   Provide calm, reassuring discussion with the injured individual(s).

▲   Administer proper first aid immediately.

Once all individuals have been attended to, the cause of the accident must be investigated and the cause discovered. All accidents must be reported to the office and the appropriate authorities. A complete written report must be filed describing the accident and cause(s) in detail.

CHAPTER SUMMARY

Every company is responsible for providing safety training and providing a safe working environment for their employees. All companies must establish safety procedures and provide employee training on following established safety procedures while on the job. Safety training must be given on a regular basis and not because an injury occurred.

OSHA has the responsibility for performing job site field inspections and enforcement. OSHA also has the authority, granted by the Department of Labor, to levy fines and/or shut down job sites if hazards are found or the site does not comply with OSHA regulations.

Every company should have a safety plan. This plan should describe company safety procedures to avoid construction-related injuries. The main objective of a company safety plan is to enable work to be completed correctly without any injuries to company employees.

The best way to treat accidents is to prevent them all together. Every worker must make accident prevention his or her top priority every day on the job. This job should never be left to others to perform. Accident prevention starts with the employees. The first step is learning accident prevention procedures. The next step is incorporating these procedures into everyday job activities.

It is recommended that every cable installer or other employees working on a job site take a course in first aid and cardiopulmonary resuscitation (CPR). Every cable installer must be trained to administer proper first aid for job-related injuries and CPR for any persons who have stopped breathing or their heart has stopped. First aid kits should always be on site and accessible to all employees.

Scaffolds and ladders are involved in virtually every type of construction project. For communication cabling projects, scaffolds and ladders are both used during the project construction. Scaffolds are usually used to install cable trays and other large cable-supporting structures. Ladders are smaller devices usually used when pulling communication cables. Each year, many injuries occur due to falls from scaffolds and ladders.

A cabling installation work area should always be designated using safety cones and bright yellow caution tape. Safety cones and yellow caution tape will restrict access to a work area and alert others that the area is unsafe.

Electrical hazards are probably the most common type of hazard for communication cable installers. This is due to the close proximity between telecommunications (voice and data) cabling and electrical cabling. Both telecommunications cabling and electrical cabling are installed behind walls, under floors, and above ceilings in commercial buildings. In some buildings, telecommunications cabling and electrical cabling are terminated in the same spaces.

Protective equipment is the safety gear typically worn on a job site to protect each worker from job-related injuries. When used correctly, protective equipment will greatly reduce the risk of injury from common construction area hazards. Protective equipment should be part of every cable installer's tool kit.

If an accident occurs on a job site, the very first thing to do is to evaluate the injured individual or individuals. If the accident is major, call for help immediately. If the injury is minor, fully examine each individual and determine if additional medical attention is needed by anyone. Always remain calm when an injury occurs. All accidents must be reported to the office and to the appropriate authorities. A complete written report must be filed describing the accident and cause(s) in detail.

CHAPTER 12

Grounding and Bonding

Grounding and bonding systems are very important for telecommunications systems. These systems guarantee that telecommunications systems run as designed without errors associated with improper grounding of equipment. Studies indicate that 90 percent of all on-site problems are due to nonexistent or improper grounding and bonding practices.

Telecommunications grounding and bonding is additional grounding and bonding installed specifically for telecommunications. This is not a replacement for grounding and bonding specified by the NEC but typically is additional to address telecommunications system performance. This chapter will describe grounding and bonding systems required by communication cabling systems.

NATIONAL ELECTRICAL CODE

The National Electrical Code (NEC) is published by the National Fire Protection Association. The NEC is a code document that defines the requirements for installation of electrical conductors and electrical equipment within public and private buildings. The purpose of the NEC is practical safeguarding and protection for both individuals and property from hazards from the use of and exposure to electricity.

The NEC was originally developed as a unified effort by insurance, electrical, and architectural companies. Each type of company has a common interest in promoting electrical safety in commercial and residential buildings. Today this document serves as the basis for most electrical and communication cabling related codes that must be followed during a cable installation.

The NEC is a comprehensive set of codes related to both electrical and communication cabling. Communication cabling is covered in Chapter 8 of the NEC and is titled "Communications Systems." Article 800 covers the installation of communication cables for the following types of low-voltage communication systems:

▼ Telephone systems

■ Telegraph systems

■ Burglar alarm systems

▲ Other central station systems

ELECTRICAL EXPOSURE

Communication cables have exposure to electrical currents. The NEC Article 800-2 defines a communication cable as "exposed" when

"The cable or circuit is in such a position that, in case of failure of supports or insulation, contact with another cable or circuit may result."

All communication cables are considered exposed to electrical current because of where these cables are installed in a building or in a campus configuration. Communication cables are installed in very close proximity to electrical conductors on walls and above ceilings. The degree of exposure is also determined by where the cable is installed. Exposure can be defined in the following two areas:

▼ Outside building exposure

▲ Inside building exposure

Outside Building Exposure

All copper communication cables, or any dielectric cables that have a conductive element, are conductors or electrical energy. When these types of cables are run between buildings, they are electrically exposed to lightning. These cables would carry a lightning strike along the cable and into any cables that are connected to these cables.

The NEC requires that all copper communication cables, or other cables with conductive elements, be protected on both ends at the building entrances. A listed primary protector must be used for over voltage protection against transient voltages that may be inadvertently coupled into the cable. These voltages will travel along the cable is seek the least resistant path to ground. The primary protector will block these transient voltages from entering the building cabling usually by blowing a fuse and creating an open in the cable path.

The NEC requires that if a single conductor is exposed, than all cable pairs must be protected on both ends of the cable. This would mean that if a single cable pair in a 600-pair cable is exposed, all of the 600 pairs must be terminated on a primary protector at the building entrance.

The NEC has provisions that specify the requirements for communication cables that terminate on a primary protector. Article 800-12(c) states:

"When a primary protector is installed inside the building, the communications wires and cables shall enter the building either through a noncombustible, nonabsorbent insulating bushing or through a metal raceway. Raceways and bushing shall slope upward from the outside or, where this cannot be done, drip loops shall be formed in the communications wires and cables immediately before they enter the building. Raceways shall be equipped with an approved service head. More than one communication cable shall be permitted to enter through a single raceway or bushing. Conduits or other metal raceways located ahead of the primary protector shall be grounded."

The NEC requires that communication cables must be separated from electrical light or power conductors. The NEC Article 800-11(a) states:

"Underground communications wires and cables in a raceway, handhole, or manhole containing electrical light, power, Class 1, or nonpower-limited fire alarm conductors shall be in a section separated from such conductors by means of brick, concrete or tile partitions or by means of a suitable barrier."

The NEC requires that communication cables not in a raceway must be sufficiently separated from electrical light and power conductors. The NEC Article 800-12(b) states:

"Communications wires and cables in accordance with Section 800-12(a) shall be separated at least 4 in. (102 mm) from electric light or power conductors not in a raceway or cable, or be permanently separated from conductors of the other system by a continuous and firmly fixed nonconductor in addition to the insulation of the wires, such as a porcelain tubes or flexible tubing."

The NEC requires that communication cables installed in a building have sufficient separation from the lightning conductors that make up the lightning protection system of a building. The NEC Article 800-13 states:

"Where practicable, a separation of at least 6 ft. (1.83 m) shall be maintained between communications wires and cables on buildings and lightning conductors."

Not all cables that run between buildings are considered exposed. The NEC defines three exceptions for declaring an interbuilding backbone cable as exposed. The NEC states:

"Interbuilding circuits are considered to have a lightning exposure unless one or more of the following conditions exists:

1. Circuits in large metropolitan areas where large buildings are close together and sufficiently high to intercept lightning.

2. Interbuilding cable runs of 42.7 m (140 ft.) of less, directly buried or in underground conduit, where a continuous metallic cable shield or a continuous metallic conduit containing the cable is bonded to each building grounding electrode system.

3. Areas having an average of five or fewer thunderstorm days per year and earth resistivity of less than 100 ohm-meters. Such areas are found along the Pacific coast."

Inside Building Exposure

The risk of electrical exposure is significantly less inside a building compared to the risk outside a building. Buildings have extensive grounding and bonding systems that must be installed for electrical protection. In addition, buildings also have lightning protection systems that will protect against lighting strikes being coupled into inside building cables.

Communication cables are exposed to electrical hazards inside a building. Copper communication cables are installed in the same vicinity as electrical power conductors. There is the possibility of accidental contact with power conductors, which would cause power fault induction.

The NEC requires that communication cables only be installed in conduits or cable pathways with other communication or low voltage, called power limited, cables. The NEC Article 800-52(a) states:

"Communications cables shall be permitted in the same raceway or enclosure with cables of any of the following:

1. Class 2 and Class 3 remote control, signaling and power limited circuits in compliance with Article 725.

2. Power limited fire alarm systems in compliance with Article 760.

3. Nonconductive and conductive optical fiber cables in compliance with Article 770.

4. Community antenna television and radio distribution systems in compliance with Article 820.

5. Low power network powered broadband communications circuits in compliance with Article 830."

The NEC also states that communication cables cannot be run in the same pathways as electrical power and class 1 circuits. The NEC Article 800-52(b) states:

"Class 1 circuits shall not be run in the same cable with communications circuits."

A second important provision of the NEC prohibits installing communication cables in raceways, compartments, and boxes with electric light and power circuits. The NEC Article 800-52(c).1 states:

"Communications conductors shall not be placed in any raceway, compartment, outlet box, junction box, or similar fitting with conductors of electric light, power, Class 1, nonpower-limited fire alarm or medium power network-powered broadband communications circuits."

The NEC does provide a means to run communication cables in the cable raceway as electrical lighting and power circuits. The NEC requires a barrier to exist between the communication cables and the electrical lighting and power conductors. This is stated in the exceptions that follow Article 800-52(c).1. Exception number 1 states:

"Where all of the conductors of electric light, power, Class 1, nonpower-limited fire alarm, and medium power network-powered broadband communications circuits are separated from all of the conductors of communication circuits by a barrier."

A second exception permits electric lighting and power conductors to be placed in the same outlet or junction box. This exception permits the coexistence of electric lighting and power conductors and communication cables in outlets or junction boxes if the power conductors supply to the communications equipment. It also requires that a minimum separation is maintained between the types of conductors. Exception number 2 states:

"Power conductors in outlet boxes, junction boxes, or similar fitting or compartments where such conductors are introduced solely for power supply to communications equipment. The power circuit conductors shall be routed within the enclosure to maintain a minimum of 0.25 in. (6.35 mm) separation from the communication circuit conductors."

Separation from Power Circuits

The NEC also requires that communication cables have a minimum of a 2.0 in. (50.8 mm) separation from electric light and power conductors that are not enclosed in a conduit or raceway. The NEC Article 800-52(c).2 states:

"Communications wire and cables shall be separated at least 2.0 in. (50.8 mm) from conductors of any electric light, power, Class 1, nonpower-limited fire alarm, or medium power network-powered broadband communications circuits."

The NEC have two defined exceptions to the mandatory 2 in. (50.8 mm) separation of electric light and power conductors from communication conductors. The first exception specifies situations where either the electric lighting or power conductors or the communication conductors are enclosed in a raceway. Exception number 1 states:

"Where either (1) all of the conductors of the electric light, power, Class 1, nonpower-limited fire alarm, and medium power network-powered broadband communications circuits are in a raceway or in metal sheathed, metal-clad, nonmetallic-sheathed, Type AC or Type UF cables, or (2) all of the conductors or communications circuits are encased in a raceway."

The second exception addresses the situation where the electric lighting and power conductors are permanently separated from the communication conductors. Exception number 2 states:

"Where the communications wires and cables are permanently separated from the conductors of electric light, power, Class 1, nonpower-limited fire alarm, and medium power network-powered broadband communication circuits by a continuous and firmly fixed nonconductor, such as porcelain tubes or flexible tubing, in addition to the insulation on the wire."

The NEC also requires that communication cable be properly supported in raceways or other cable-supporting devices designed specifically for the purpose of supporting communication cables. The NEC prohibits supporting communication cables, by means of strapping or lashing, to raceways supporting electric lighting or power conductors. This practice exposes the communication cable to electrical transient surges that would be run to the ground through the raceway. The NEC Article 800-52(e) states:

"Communications cables or wires shall not be strapped, tapped, or attached by any means to the exterior of any conduit or raceway as a means of support."

RESULTS FROM ELECTRICAL EXPOSURE

The communication cabling designer and cable installers must make the safeguarding of personnel, property, and communication system equipment from foreign electrical voltages and currents a primary responsibility. Foreign electrical currents or voltages are electrical activity that are not normally carried in or expected in communication cabling system or cable-supporting structures.

Results for electrical exposure to foreign electrical voltages or currents could be

▼ Death by electrocution

■ Cardiac arrest

■ Seizures

■ Electrical burns

▲ Long- and short-term numbness in hands and arms

The resulting effects from electrical currents or voltages differ for individuals and situations where the electrical contact occurs. The actual injuries that may result from electrical contact are primarily determined by the magnitude of the electrical current and duration of shock. There have been documented cases where only a few hundred milliamperes of electrical current can be fatal.

PREVENTING ELECTRICAL EXPOSURE HAZARDS

The NEC is the primary document that defines both electrical exposure and the remedies for safeguarding against these hazards. The NEC requires that electrical systems and all metallic supporting structures be grounded and bonded to limit hazardous voltages or currents. Grounding and bonding practices prevent the following in communication cables:

▼ Electrical voltage or current power faults

■ Lightning faults

■ Electrical induction voltage or current faults

▲ Ground potential faults

The NEC Article 250 defines electrical bonding and grounding. This article defines the general requirements grounding and bonding and the specific requirements for

▼ Electrical systems, circuits, and equipment required, permitted, or not permitted to be grounded

■ Electrical circuit conductors to be grounded on building electrical grounding systems

■ The recommended location of grounding connections

■ The required types and sizes of grounding and bonding conductors and grounding electrodes

■ The required methods for grounding and bonding

▲ The various conditions where guards, isolation, or insulation may be substituted for grounding

Communication cabling and supporting structures are not specifically covered in Article 250. The requirements for communication cabling and supporting structures are defined in the NEC Article 800-40. The specific grounding and bonding requirements defined in Article 800-40 must conform to the requirements defined in Article 250.

GROUNDING DEFINITION

The NEC article 100 defines a *ground* as:

"A conducting connection, whether intentional or unintentional, between electrical circuits or equipment and the earth, or some conducting body that serves in place of the earth."

Electrical systems and communication cabling systems that are required to be grounded must be connected to the earth. The grounding mechanism must provide a reliable means to safely conduct the voltages imposed by lightning, line surges, or unintentional contact with high voltage lines or equipment to ground.

BONDING DEFINITION

The NEC article 100 and 250-70 defines *bonding* as:

"The permanent joining of the metallic conducting parts of equipment and conductor enclosures to assure an electrically conductive path between them that will ensure electrical continuity and have sufficient capacity to safely conduct any foreign current likely to be imposed to ground."

Bonding is required because electrically conductive materials such as structural steel, metal cable trays, and metallic supporting structures may become energized in the event of making contact with: lightning, line surges, or unintentional contact with high voltage lines. The practice of creating effective bonding is to create a reliable path for such fault currents to the electrical system ground. Effective bonding practices help to equalize potential caused by either lightning and electrical system faults that would otherwise damage equipment and harm individuals.

The NEC requires that metal raceways, cable trays, racks, enclosures, or metal cable armoring must be effectively bonded to ensure the capacity to conduct any fault current to ground. The NEC Article 250-96 states:

"Metal raceways, cable trays, cable armor, cable sheath, enclosures, frames, fittings, and other metal noncurrent carrying parts that are able to serve as grounding conductors, with or without the use of supplementary equipment grounding conductors, shall be effectively bonded where necessary to ensure electrical continuity and the capacity to conduct safely any fault currents likely to be imposed on them. Any nonconductive paint, enamel, or similar coating shall be removed at threads, contact points, and contact surfaces or be connected by means of fittings designed so as to make such removal unnecessary."

GROUNDING AND BONDING OF COMMUNICATION SYSTEMS

The grounding and bonding requirements defined by the NEC describe a fault current path that shall be permanent and electrically continuous. It must also be capable of safely conducting the maximum current or voltage likely to be imposed on it. Finally, it must have sufficiently low impedance to guarantee that the fault moves to ground along the intended path.

The other NEC articles for grounding and bonding for communication systems are shown in Table 12-1.

Description	NEC Article-Section
Audio signaling processing, amplification, and reproduction equipment	Article 640-7
Information technology equipment	Article 645-15
Circuits and equipment operating at less than 50 volts	Article 720
Class 1, Class 2, and Class 3 remote controlled, signaling, and power-limited circuits	Article 725-6
Fire alarm systems	Article 760-6
Communications circuits	Article 800
Radio and television equipment	Article 810
Community antenna television	Article 820-33
Radio distribution systems	Articles 820-40 and 820-41

Table 12-1.   NEC Communication Systems Grounding and Bonding Articles

GROUNDING ELECTRODE SYSTEM

The NEC defines the ground source for a building to be a grounding electrode system. The grounding electrode system is made up of the components to create and provide a low resistance conductor path to the earth. This system consists of the

▼   Grounding electrode

▲   Grounding electrode conductor

Grounding Electrode

The grounding electrode is defined as any component that serves as a low resistance conductor path to route hazardous electrical currents or voltages to the earth. The NEC requires that the grounding electrode shall be as near as practicable to the grounding conductor and must be one of the following elements:

▼   A functionally grounded structural metal frame or member of the building

■   A grounded metal water pipe within 1.5 m (5 ft.) from the entry point into the building

■   Concrete encased electrodes

- Ground rings

▲ Any made electrodes

Whichever of these elements that exist in a building must be bonded together to form the grounding electrode system.

Metal Water Pipe

The NEC enables a metal water pipe to be used as a grounding electrode provided that it meets the following requirements:

▼ It is in direct contact with the earth for 3 m (10 ft.) or more.

- It is electrically continuous or made electrically continuous by bonding around insulated joints or pipe sections to the points of the grounding electrode.

▲ The water pipe shall be used in conjunction with a supplemental made electrode.

Metal Frame of the Building

The NEC permits the use of a building metal frame or building structural steel where it is effectively grounded. The ground connection point must be tested and verified to be effectively grounded with a meggar.

Concrete Encased Electrode

The NEC permits a concrete encased electrode to be used as a grounding electrode. The concrete encased electrode must meet the following requirements:

▼ The electrode must be encased by at least 2 in. (50 mm) of concrete.

- The electrode must be located at or near the bottom of a concrete foundation that is in direct contact with the earth.

▲ Concrete must contain at least 20 ft. (6 m) of bare or zinc galvanized electrically conductive coated steel reinforcing bars or rods at least 0.5 in. (13 mm) or 20 ft. of copper conductors not smaller than #4 AWG.

Ground Ring

The NEC permits a ground ring to be used as a grounding electrode. A ground ring is a conductive conductor encircling the building structure and in direct contact with the earth. The ground ring must meet the following requirements:

▼ The ground conductor must be buried below the ground surface of no less than 2.5 ft. (76 cm).

- The ground conductor must be at least 20 ft. (6 m) long.

▲ The ground conductor must be a minimum of a #2 AWG conductor.

Made or Other Electrodes

The NEC mandates that if none of the other elements are available to serve as a grounding electrode, a made electrode must be used. The following elements are permitted as made electrodes:

▼ Other local metal underground systems or structures

■ Rod or pipe electrodes

▲ Plate electrodes

Any type of made electrode must provide a low resistance path to ground of 25 ohms or less. Any element that does not provide a ground path of 25 ohms or less must be augmented by an additional electrode. If an additional electrode is required, it must be separated by at least 6 ft. from the other electrode.

Metal Underground Systems or Structures

Metal underground systems or structures would include underground piping or underground tanks.

Rod or Pipe Electrodes

Rod or pipe electrodes shall be at least 8 ft. (2.5 m) in length. The rod or pipes used for grounding electrodes must meet the following requirements:

▼ Pipes or conduit must be at least $3/4$ in. trade size and galvanized or otherwise coated to protect against corrosion.

■ Rods of iron or steel must be at least $5/8$ in. in diameter.

▲ Rods or pipes must be in direct contact with the earth for at least 8 ft. and be driven into the soil at least 8 ft., and the upper end shall be flush with the ground surface.

Plate Electrodes

Plate electrodes consist of metal plates that are in direct contact with the soil. The requirements for plate electrodes include the following:

▼ The plate must be at least 2 sq. ft. of surface in contact with the soil.

■ Plates of either iron or steel must be at least $1/4$ in. thick.

▲ Plates must be installed at least 2.5 ft. below the ground surface.

Unacceptable Grounding Electrodes

The NEC defines unacceptable elements for grounding electrodes. The following elements are not considered acceptable as a grounding electrode:

▼ Aluminum electrodes because of the lower conductive properties of this metal

■ Metal underground gas piping systems because of the hazardous nature of these pipes

▲ Interior water piper located more than 1.5 m (5 ft.) from the entry point into the building because of the use of PVC piping inside of buildings

Grounding Electrode Conductor

The grounding electrode conductor is the wiring used to make a low resistance connection from any available grounding electrode in the grounding electrode system to the equipment grounding system or equipment grounding conductor. The grounding conductor must be a continuous or unspliced wire unless the splice is one of the following:

▼ Irreversible compression type connectors listed for the purpose

▲ Exothermic welding process

The NEC enables the grounding electrode conductor to be either bare or insulated wire. The grounding electrode conductor is usually composed of the following materials:

▼ Tin-plated copper

■ Copper

▲ Copper alloy

The NEC prohibits the use of insulated, bare, or copper clad aluminum where there is direct contact with the earth as a grounding conductor. These materials are highly corrosive when in contact with the earth and have lower conductivity properties.

Grounding Electrode Conductor Sizing

The NEC requires that the grounding electrode conductor be sized according to Article 250, Table 250-66. Table 250-66 requires the minimum size for the grounding electrode conductor to be a #6 AWG wire. In some cases, the minimum size conductor specified by the NEC must be larger.

Grounding Electrode Conductor Connections

The NEC defines the permitted methods for connecting the grounding electrode conductor to the grounding electrode. The connection of the grounding electrode conductor must be made using a method that will guarantee a permanent and effective grounding path.

The recognized methods to anchor and connect the grounding electrode conductor to the grounding electrode include the following:

▼ Exothermic welding

■ UL listed lugs

■   UL listed pressure connectors

▲   UL listed clamps

All allowed lugs, connectors, and clamps must be listed for direct burial applications in soil. All lugs, connectors, and clamps must be used to terminate one grounding conductor only unless the device is listed for multiple conductors.

The resistance of the grounding electrode system should be no more than 25 ohms when measured with an earth megger. It is recommended that the resistance of the grounding electrode system be measured on an annual basis.

Grounding Electrode Conductor Routing

The NEC requires that the grounding conductor must be run in such a way that it is free from exposure to physical damage. The grounding conductor is permitted to be run inside the building or along the building surface without requiring mechanical protection provided it is securely fastened to the building. If the possibility exists where the grounding conductor may be exposed to physical damage, the conductor must be mechanically protected. The conductors must be installed in one of the following:

▼   Rigid metal conduit

■   Intermediate metal conduit

■   Rigid nonmetallic conduit

■   Electrical metallic tubing

▲   Cable armor

NOTE: If the grounding conductor is run in a metallic conduit, both ends of the conduit must be bonded.

When installing a grounding electrode conductor, the following guidelines should be followed:

▼   Grounding electrode conductors should be as short as possible.

■   Grounding electrode conductors should be as straight as possible.

■   Avoid right-angle bends in the conductor.

■   No splices should exist in the conductor.

■   All connections should be free from corrosion.

■   The grounding electrode conductors should be at least a #6 AWG conductor, as specified by the NEC.

▲   All connections should be inspected once a year for tightness and completeness.

NOTE: The only exception for the provision for no splices is the connection to the busbar.

TELECOMMUNICATIONS GROUNDING AND BONDING

The grounding requirements for communication cabling and supporting structures are defined in Article 800 of the NEC. Communications grounding and bonding is always defined as "additional" grounding and bonding to specifically support communication systems and equipment. Communications grounding and bonding requirements never replace the need for electrical grounding and bonding but always supplement these requirements.

Communications grounding and bonding is installed for the following reasons:

▼   To minimize hazards associated with electrical currents and voltages that may be induced onto communications systems or communication system cabling

■   To provide extra protection for the electrical grounding and bonding system

▲   To lower the system ground reference impedance and verify that a low resistance path exists to ground

NEC ARTICLES 800-33 AND 800-40

The NEC Articles 800-33 and 800-40 cover grounding requirements for communication cables and primary protectors. These NEC articles address the proper grounding and protection of communication cables entering a building. The NEC requirements in Article 800 differ slightly from those found in Article 250 for electrical grounding and bonding system. Article 800 requirements are less stringent than those in Article 250. The differences are primarily due to the lower voltages associated with communication systems compared to electrical systems.

The NEC Article 800-33 defines cable grounding for cables entering buildings. This article states:

"The metallic sheath of communications cables entering buildings shall be grounded as close as practical to the point of entrance."

The NEC Article 800-40 defines grounding methods for communications cabling and primary protectors. This article also defines the communication grounding conductor as having the following characteristics:

▼   Insulated and shall be listed as suitable for the purpose.

■   Copper or other corrosive resistant material, stranded, or solid.

■   The conductor must be a minimum of a #14 AWG conductor.

- The conductor must be run to the grounding electrode in as straight a line as practicable.

▲ The conductor must be protected from physical damage. If run in a metal raceway, both ends must be bonded to the grounding conductor.

TELECOMMUNICATIONS GROUNDING LOCATIONS

The best choice for the telecommunications ground is to attach directly to the grounding electrode system. If a direct connection to the grounding electrode system is not available, connect to closest electrical service ground. In buildings where a connection to the grounding electrode system or the electrical service ground is not available, it is recommended to connect to one of the following:

▼ Grounding electrode (new or existing)

▲ A new ground rod driven into the earth

Installing a new ground rod is considered a last resort for a telecommunications ground. The NEC Section 800-40(b) specifies a minimum of a 13 mm (^{1}/$_2$ in.) diameter and 1.5 m (5 ft.) long ground rod driven completely into the ground.

COMMUNICATIONS BONDING LOCATIONS

The usual locations for communications bonding are

▼ Communications entrance facility (EF) for sites with exposed cable

- Equipment room (ER)

▲ Communications equipment closet

Communications bonding conductors must always be copper wire. These conductors should also be insulated wires to minimize the possibility of unintentional grounding. When installing communication bonding conductors, avoid bending or changing direction in the conductor. Try to keep the conductor as straight as possible.

The NEC Section 800-40(a) requires that communication bonding conductors be a minimum of 14 AWG, solid or stranded, insulated wire. Because other NEC grounding articles and sections specify a minimum of a #6 AWG wire, it is recommended that the minimum size bonding conductor should be a #6 AWG stranded conductor wire. This size wire will meet code requirements and enable for future changes, if necessary.

TELECOMMUNICATIONS GROUNDING AND BONDING STANDARD

The ANSI/TIA/EIA-607 standard is the commercial building grounding and bonding requirements for telecommunications. This standard was written specifically to address the grounding and bonding requirements for telecommunications cabling systems and their supporting structures inside of a building. This standard also addresses the fact that grounding and bonding systems are important for the reliable operation of communication system equipment. The telecommunications grounding and bonding system must be capable of supporting a multivendor and multiproduct environment.

The ANSI/TIA/EIA-607 standard defines a uniform telecommunications grounding and bonding system for commercial buildings. This standard ensures that communication systems can be deployed in all commercial buildings as a standard and uniform practice. This standard defines the minimum requirements for telecommunications grounding and bonding to support and promote the proper operation for the communications equipment being used in commercial buildings today.

The ANSI/TIA/EIA-607 standard defines a telecommunications grounding and bonding system and the interconnections to the building electrical grounding system. The recommendations made in this standard do not supersede the bonding and grounding requirements of national and local electrical code. This document makes bonding and grounding recommendations for the purpose of meeting communication system performance requirements.

The ANSI/TIA/EIA-607 standard does not provide specifications for the following items and issues:

▼ Grounding, bonding, and communications equipment to its associated communications cabling

■ Amounts of surge current immunity or voltage levels the communication cable's insulation will withstand before melting

■ Methods and practices for testing, verifying, and maintaining the bonding and grounding system

■ The actions or methods to use for the problems of electromagnetic interference (EMI) and radio frequency interference (RFI)

■ Minimum primary and secondary protector requirements

■ User safety practices

■ Grounding and bonding practices of local communication service providers

■ The installation and maintenance of service provider's primary protection, which are mandated by FCC rules

▲ Requirements for the electrical service entrance

TELECOMMUNICATIONS GROUNDING AND BONDING SYSTEM

The telecommunications grounding and bonding system starts with a physical connection to the building grounding electrode system and extends to every telecommunications room (TR) in the building (see Figure 12-1). A telecommunications grounding and bonding system defined by the ANSI/TIA/EIA-607 standards includes the following elements:

▼ Bonding conductor for telecommunications

■ Telecommunications main grounding busbar (TMGB)

■ Telecommunications bonding backbone (TBB)

■ Telecommunications grounding busbar (TGB)

▲ Telecommunications bonding backbone interconnecting bonding conductor (TBBIBC)

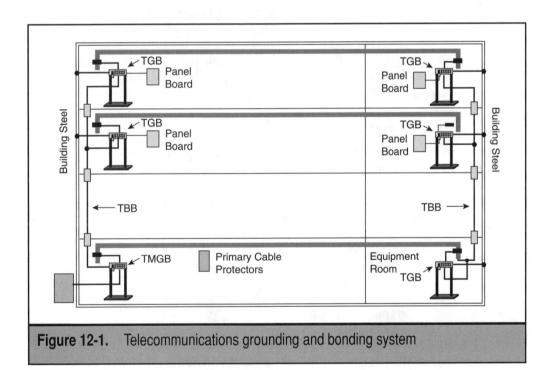

Figure 12-1. Telecommunications grounding and bonding system

The basic grounding and bonding elements are located in the following building spaces of a commercial building:

▼ Equipment room (ER)

■ Entrance facility (EF)

▲ Telecommunications room (TR)

The standard also address the cable pathways between the building spaces and the cable terminations in each space.

BONDING CONDUCTOR FOR TELECOMMUNICATIONS

The ANSI/TIA/EIA-607 standard requires that all communications bonding conductors be listed for the intended purpose and approved by a nationally recognized testing laboratory such as UL or ETL. Bonding conductors must always be insulated wires. The standard also requires that bonding conductors be made of copper metal. Other metal types are not supported for use as a bonding conductor by the ANSI/TIA/EIA-607 standard. In addition, the minimum size of all bonding conductors must be at least a #6 AWG wire.

The ANSI/TIA/EIA-607 standard prohibits placing bonding conductors in a metallic conduit made of iron. This standard requires that if the bonding conductor must be placed in an iron conduit longer than 1 m (3 ft.) in length, then bonding conductor must be bonded at each end of the conduit. The wires used for bonding the bonding conductor must be at least a #6 AWG wire.

Color Coding and Labels

The ANSI/TIA/EIA-607 standard requires that all bonding conductors be labeled (see Figure 12-2). The label must be placed on the conductors as close as possible to the termination position on each end of the conductor. The labels used on the conductor must always be nonmetallic material. The exact size and configuration of the label is not defined by the standard. In addition, the labeling scheme to be used must conform to the ANSI/TIA/EIA-606 or ANSI/TIA/EIA-606-A standard.

The ANSI/TIA/EIA-607 standard requires that each bonding conductor have a label, in addition to the identification label with the following or similar information printed on it:

"Warning—If this connector or cable is loose or must be removed, please call the building telecommunications manager."

The ANSI/TIA/EIA-607 standard requires that every bonding conductor be designated as a bonding conductor by having a green colored insulation.

The bonding conductor will connect TMGB to the building grounding system. The connection will create a low resistance bond between the TMGB and the building grounding system. The bonding conductor must be a minimum of a #6 AWG wire but must be

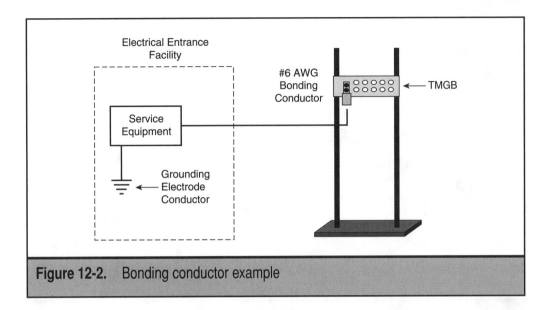

Figure 12-2. Bonding conductor example

at least as large as the TBB. If an installation uses a larger gauge wire for the TBB, the bonding conductor size must be increased as well.

TELECOMMUNICATIONS MAIN GROUNDING BUSBAR (TMGB)

The ANSI/TIA/EIA-607 standard defines a single component as the center of the telecommunications grounding and bonding system called the TMGB (see Figure 12-3). The TMGB is a dedicated grounding and bonding element that connects to the building grounding system. It serves as a dedicated extension of the building grounding system for telecommunications equipment, cabling, and cable-supporting structures.

The ANSI/TIA/EIA-607 standard requires that only one TMGB should be installed in each commercial building. Telecommunications grounding busbars (TGBs) must be installed in each TR. The TGBs in each TR must be connected to the TMGB using the TBB.

The TMGB must be installed in a location that is accessible to all personnel requiring access to this component, such as electricians and cable installers. The TMGB must be installed in a central location in the building. Each TBB conductor will connect to the TMGB and be run to each TR. A centralized location for the TMGB will minimize the length of these conductors.

The preferred location for the TMGB would be in the EF. The building space usually provides a convenient connection to the building grounding system. Other locations in a

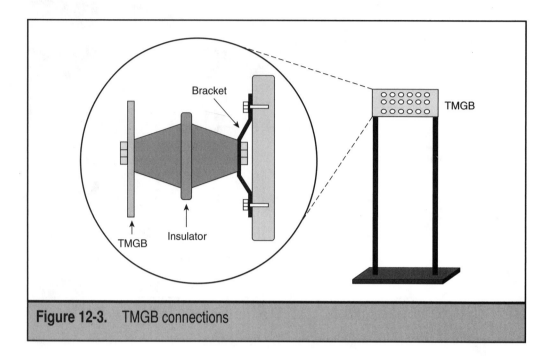

Figure 12-3.   TMGB connections

commercial building, such as the ER, can also be used. The exact location is not defined by the ANSI/TIA/EIA-607 standard. The selected location should serve to minimize the length of the TBB conductors.

The TMGB would serve as the dedicated ground source of all communications equipment that is installed in the same space. The TGBs would serve as the dedicated ground source for all communication equipment installed in a TR.

Telecommunications Main Grounding Busbar (TMGB) Description

The ANSI/TIA/EIA-607 standard requires that the TMGB meet the specific configuration guidelines defined in Section 5.4.5. The standard requires that the TMGB shall

- ▼ Be a predrilled copper busbar.

- ■ Have predrilled holes for TBB connections. The holes must conform to the NEMA bolt hole sizing and spacing requirements.

- ■ Be a minimum of 6 mm (0.25 in.) thick.

- ▲ Be a minimum of 100 mm (4.0 in.) wide.

The ANSI/TIA/EIA-607 standard states that the length of the TMGB can be variable. The length selected should match the type of communications rack where the TMGB will be installed. Communication racks are usually 19 or 23 in. wide. Figure 12-4 illustrates a typical TMGB.

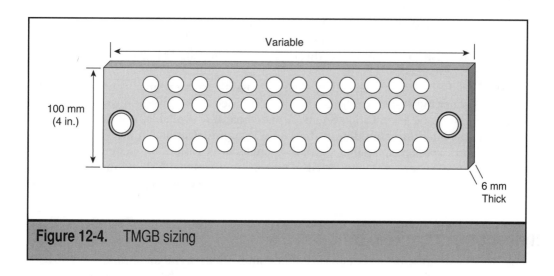

Figure 12-4. TMGB sizing

Installation of the TMGB

The TMGB should be mounted on a permanent location in a commercial building. If installed on a communications rack, the TMGB must be insulated from the rack (see Figure 12-5). The exact location on a communication rack (top or bottom) will depend on the routing of the TBB conductors. If the access for the TBB conductors to enter

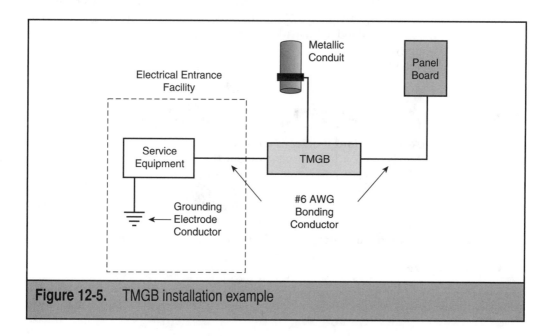

Figure 12-5. TMGB installation example

the building space that supports the TMGB is through underground trenches or an access floor system, then the TMGB should be installed near the bottom of the rack. If the access is through a conduit or an overhead cable tray, then the TMGB should be installed near the top of the rack.

The TMGB should be installed as close as possible to the nearest connection to the building grounding system or the connection provided to the grounding system for the telecommunications grounding system. A panelboard, if available, is a dedicated connection to the building grounding system for telecommunications. If the TMGB is located in the same space as the panelboard, the panelboards's alternating equipment bus or enclosure must be bonded to the TMGB. The NEC requires that TMGB must be installed to adhere to the clearances required by applicable electrical codes for grounding and bonding connections.

Connections to the TMGB

The TMGB will support connections to either a single TBB conductor or multiple TBB conductors. The connection of either the bonding conductor or the TBB conductors to the TMGB must use one of the following approved connection methods:

▼   Two-hole compression connector

■   Exothermic weld

▲   Any other equivalent connection method is enabled

The TMBG will serve as the grounding source for all communications equipment installed in the same space. The devices can be connected to the TMGB using a single hole lug connector, but the ANSI/TIA/EIA-607 standard recommends using a two-hole lug.

The ANSI/TIA/EIA-607 standard also requires that all metallic raceways that are used by or support communications cable and are installed in the same building space as the TMGB must be bonded to the TMGB.

TELECOMMUNICATIONS BONDING BACKBONE (TBB)

The ANSI/TIA/EIA-607 standard requires that each TGB installed in a TR be connected to the TMGB. The TBB is the conductor that provides this connection (see Figure 12-6).

The fundamental function of TBB is to either reduce or equalize potential differences between the different parts of the communication cabling system and cable-supporting structure devices. The TBB will provide the connection from each TGB through the building backbone pathways to the TGMB to provide this function.

The TBB configuration will differ from building to building due to factors such as

▼   Building size

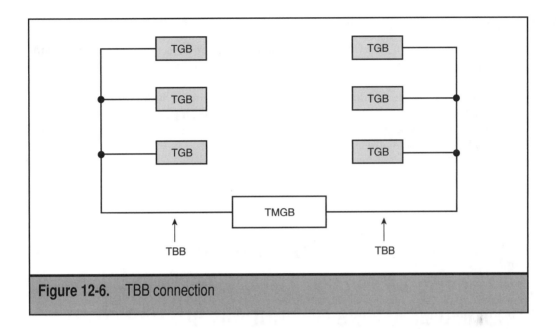

Figure 12-6.   TBB connection

- Building construction and pathway issues
- ▲ Size of the communication cabling and supporting structures

The ANSI/TIA/EIA-607 standard requires that the design of the TBB must support the following:

- ▼ Be consistent and compatible with the intrabuilding backbone cable subsystem
- If necessary, support multiple TBBs through the intrabuilding backbone pathways
- ▲ Be installed and routed to minimize TBB conductor lengths

CAUTION: The ANSI/TIA/EIA-607 standard prohibits using either a metal water pipe or a metallic cable shield as a TBB for new installations.

TBB Conductor Size

The ANSI/TIA/EIA-607 standard requires that the TBB always be an insulated copper conductor. The standard does not permit other types of conductors to be used. The TBB must be a minimum of a #6 AWG conductor. The ANSI/TIA/EIA-607 provides the ability to specify conductor sizes up to 3/0 for the TBB.

TBB Installation Considerations

The ANSI/TIA/EIA-607 standard requires that the TBB conductors be installed in a manner that protects them from damage. The conductors should be routed to minimize conductor turns and length.

The TBB conductors should ideally be installed as a single conductor from each TGB to the TMGB. Each TBB should be installed without splices, if possible. If splices are necessary, they should be kept to a minimum and located in designed building spaces. Splice connections should be made using either

▼ Irreversible compression type connectors

■ Exothermic welding

▲ Any other approved method is acceptable

All splice points must be appropriately supported and protected from mechanical damage.

TELECOMMUNICATIONS GROUNDING BUSBAR (TGB)

The telecommunications grounding busbar (TGB) is the single grounding point for all communications equipment, cabling, and cable-supporting structure devices in a TR. The TGB must be installed inside of each TR. Each TGB must be connected to the TMGB using the TBB.

The ANSI/TIA/EIA-607 standard enables multiple TGBs to be installed in each TR. The exact number and the location of each TGB is not specified in the ANSI/TIA/EIA-607 standard. Each TGB should be installed to provide the greatest flexibility and accessibility in the TR for telecommunications grounding and bonding.

Telecommunications Grounding Busbar (TGB) Description

The ANSI/TIA/EIA-607 standard requires that the TGB meet the specific configuration guidelines defined in Section 5.5.1. The standard requires that the TGB

▼ Be a predrilled copper busbar.

■ Have predrilled holes for TBB connections. The holes must conform to the NEMA bolt hole sizing and spacing requirements.

■ Be a minimum of 6 mm (0.25 in.) thick.

▲ Be a minimum of 50 mm (2.0 in.) wide.

The ANSI/TIA/EIA-607 standard states that the length of the TGB can be variable.

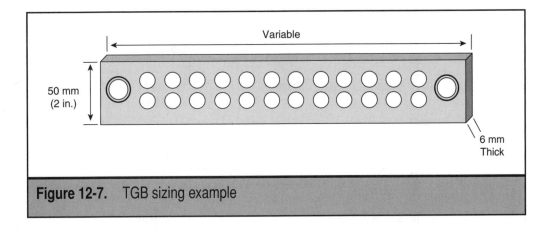

Figure 12-7. TGB sizing example

The length selected should match the type of communications rack where the TGB will be installed. Communication racks installed in TRs are usually 19 or 23 in. wide. Figure 12-7 illustrates a typical TGB.

Installation of the TGB

The TGB should be mounted on a permanent location in a TR. If installed on a communications rack, the TGB must be insulated from the rack. The exact location on a communication rack (top or bottom) will depend on the routing of the TBB conductors into the TR from the backbone pathway. If the access for the TBB conductors is through underground trenches or an access floor system, then the TGB should be installed near the bottom of the rack. If the access is through a conduit or an overhead cable tray, then the TGB should be installed near the top of the rack.

The TGB should be installed as close as possible to the nearest connection to the building grounding system or the connection provided to the grounding system for the telecommunications grounding system. A panelboard, if available, is a dedicated connection to the building grounding system for telecommunications. If the TGB is located in the same space as the panelboard, the panelboards's alternating equipment bus or enclosure must be bonded to the TGB. The NEC requires that TGB must be installed to adhere to the clearances required by applicable electrical codes for grounding and bonding connections.

The TGB in each TR must be bonded to the structural steel with a listed bonding conductor (see Figure 12-8). When the building steel is readily accessible to the TR, the bonding conductors must be at least a #6 AWG conductor. The ANSI/TIA/EIA-607 standard permits the connection to either vertical or horizontal structural steel members.

NOTE: The ANSI/TIA/EIA-607 standard does not require the steel bars of a reinforced concrete building to be bonded to either the TGB or TBB.

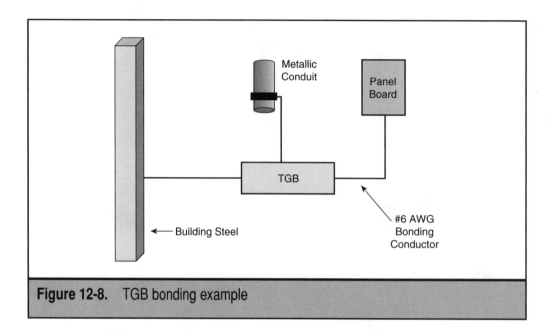

Figure 12-8.   TGB bonding example

The ANSI/TIA/EIA-607 standard requires that all bonding conductors be continuous conductors. The conductor must be run in as straight a line as practicable. The standard also recommends that the TBB be routed in the shortest possible path possible.

The TGB will support connections to either a single TBB conductor or multiple TBB conductors. The ANSI/TIA/EIA-607 standard specifies that the connections of the TBB to the TGB must use a two-hole compression connector. Other connection methods are prohibited by the standard.

TELECOMMUNICATIONS BONDING BACKBONE INTERCONNECTING BONDING CONDUCTOR (TBBIBC)

The ANSI/TIA/EIA-607 standard requires that when two or more TBBs are installed vertically in the intrabuilding backbone pathway, the TBBs must be bonded together. The telecommunications bonding backbone interconnecting bonding conductor (TBBIBC) is the component used for this function (see Figure 12-9). The ANSI/TIA/EIA-607 standard requires that the TBBIBC be installed at the top floor and a minimum of every third floor. The minimum size of the TBBIBC must be no smaller than the TBB conductor size.

The TBBIBC would also be used to bond two or more TGBs installed in the same TR together. The TBBIBC is also used to bond the TGBs installed in different TRs that reside on the same floor of the building. This connection would follow the same requirements as bonding multiple TBBs at the top floor and a minimum of every third floor.

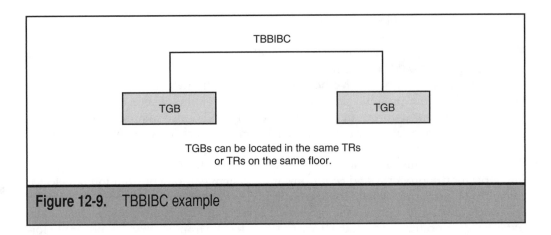

Figure 12-9.   TBBIBC example

CHAPTER SUMMARY

Telecommunications grounding and bonding is additional grounding and bonding installed specifically for telecommunications. This is not a replacement for grounding and bonding specified by the National Electrical Code (NEC) but typically is additional to address telecommunications system performance.

The NEC is published by the National Fire Protection Association. The NEC is a code document that defines the requirements for installation of electrical conductors and electrical equipment within public and private buildings. The purpose of the NEC is practical safeguarding and protection for both individuals and property from hazards from the use of and exposure to electricity.

The NEC is a comprehensive set of codes related to both electrical and communication cabling. Communication cabling is covered in Chapter 8 of the NEC and is titled "Communications Systems." Article 800 covers the installation of communication cables for telephone systems, telegraph systems, burglar alarm systems, and other central station systems.

All communication cables are considered exposed to electrical current because of where these cables are installed in a building or in a campus configuration. Communication cables are installed in very close proximity to electrical conductors on walls and above ceilings. The degree of exposure is also determined by where the cable is installed. Exposure can be defined as outside building exposure and inside building exposure.

All copper communication cables or any dielectric cables that have a conductive element are conductors or electrical energy. When these types of cables are run between buildings, they are electrically exposed to lightning. The NEC requires that all copper communication cables or other cables with conductive elements be protected on both ends at the building entrances. A listed primary protector must be used for over voltage protection against transient voltages that may be inadvertently coupled into the cable.

Communication cables are exposed to electrical hazards inside a building. Copper communication cables are installed in the same vicinity as electrical power conductors. There is the possibility of accidental contact with power conductors, which would cause power fault induction. The NEC requires that communication cables only be installed in conduits or cable pathways with other communication or low voltage, called power limited, cables. The NEC prohibits the practice of running communication cables in the same pathways as electrical power and class 1 circuits. The NEC also requires that communication cables have a minimum of a 2.0 in. (50.8 mm) separation from electric light and power conductors that are not enclosed in a conduit or raceway.

The communication cabling designer and cable installers must make the safeguarding of personnel, property, and communication system equipment from foreign electrical voltages and current a primary responsibility. Foreign electrical currents, or voltages, are electrical activities that are not normally carried in or expected in communication cabling system or cable-supporting structures. The results from electrical exposure to foreign electrical voltages or currents could be death by electrocution, cardiac arrest, seizures, electrical burns, and long- and short-term numbness in hands and arms.

The NEC is the primary document that defines both electrical exposure and the remedies for safeguarding against these hazards. The NEC requires that electrical systems and all metallic supporting structures be grounded and bonded to limit hazardous voltages or currents. The NEC Article 250 defines electrical bonding and grounding.

The grounding and bonding requirements defined by the NEC describe a fault current path that shall be permanent and electrically continuous. It must also be capable of safely conducting the maximum current or voltage likely to be imposed on it. Finally, it must have sufficiently low impedance to guarantee that the fault moves to ground along the intended path.

The NEC defines the ground source for a building to be a grounding electrode system. The grounding electrode is defined as any component that serves as a low resistance conductor path to route hazardous electrical current or voltages to the earth. The grounding conductor and must be one of the following elements: a functionally grounded structural metal frame or member of the building, a grounded metal water pipe within 1.5 m (5 ft.) from the entry point into the building, concrete encased electrodes, ground rings, or any made electrodes.

The grounding electrode conductor is the wiring used to make a low resistance connection from any available grounding electrode in the grounding electrode system to the equipment grounding system or equipment grounding conductor. The grounding conductor must be a continuous or unspliced wire. The NEC enables the grounding electrode conductor to be either bare or insulated wire. The NEC requires that the grounding electrode conductor to be a #6 AWG wire.

The grounding requirements for communication cabling and supporting structures are defined in Article 800 of the NEC. Communications grounding and bonding is always defined as "additional" grounding and bonding to specifically support communication systems and equipment. Communications grounding and bonding requirements never replace the need for electrical grounding and bonding but always supplement these requirements.

The ANSI/TIA/EIA-607 standard is the commercial building grounding and bonding requirements for telecommunications. This standard was written specifically to address the grounding and bonding requirements for telecommunications cabling systems and their supporting structures inside a building. This standard also addresses the fact that grounding and bonding systems are important for the reliable operation of communication system equipment. The telecommunications grounding and bonding system must be capable of supporting a multivendor and multiproduct environment.

The ANSI/TIA/EIA-607 standard requires that all communications bonding conductors be listed for the intended purpose and approved by a nationally recognized testing laboratory such as UL or ETL. Bonding conductors must always be insulated wires. The standard also requires that bonding conductors be made of copper metal. In addition, the minimum size of all bonding conductors must be at least a #6 AWG wire.

The ANSI/TIA/EIA-607 standard defines a single component as the center of the telecommunications grounding and bonding system called the telecommunications main grounding busbar (TMGB). The TMGB is a dedicated grounding and bonding element that connects to the building grounding system.

The ANSI/TIA/EIA-607 standard requires that each telecommunications grounding busbar (TGB) installed in a telecommunications room (TR) to be connected to the TMGB. The fundamental function of TBB is to either reduce or equalize potential differences between the different parts of the communication cabling system and cable-supporting structure devices. The TBB will provide the connection from each TGB through the building backbone pathways to the TGMB to provide this function.

The TGB is the single grounding point for all communications equipment, cabling, and cable-supporting structure devices in a telecommunications room. The TGB must be installed inside of each telecommunications room. Each TGB must be connected to the TMGB using the TBB.

The ANSI/TIA/EIA-607 standard requires that when two or more TBBs are installed vertically in the intrabuilding backbone pathway, the TBBs must be bonded together. The telecommunications bonding backbone interconnecting bonding conductor (TBBIBC) is the component used for this function.

CHAPTER 13

Building Telecommunications Rooms

The *telecommunications room* (TR) is the space where both horizontal and backbone cables are terminated. The TR is very seldom ready for these cables to be installed in them. Most of the time the TR is a space in the building that must be prepared and readied to support communication cables. Most cable installations require that punch down blocks be mounted and communication racks be installed in the TR. In addition, supporting structures, such as ladder racks and D-rings, must be installed to properly route and support the communication cables in the TR. This chapter will describe how to properly prepare the TR to support communication cables.

TELECOMMUNICATIONS ROOMS (TRs)

A TR, sometimes called either a telecommunications closet or a horizontal closet, is a building space that is designated for the termination of horizontal and backbone cables. The TR is the recognized connection point between the backbone and horizontal cable pathways. This space is also the place where any required termination hardware is mounted.

The TR is a designated space for housing the following:

▼ Telecommunications cables

■ Telecommunications equipment

▲ Cross-connections

Industry cabling standards require that every building must be served by at least one TR or equipment room (ER). Industry standards also require that there be at least one TR per floor. There is no limit as to the maximum number of telecommunication rooms that can be supported per building. The useable floor space determines the maximum number of closets for a building.

Telecommunications closets are designated building spaces that are used to support the following cabling components and equipment:

▼ Horizontal cable to backbone cable cross-connections

■ Entrance facilities

■ Telecommunications equipment

■ Local area network (LAN) equipment

▲ Computer equipment

All horizontal cables installed to each work area must be directly cabled back to the TR. In addition, all horizontal cables must be terminated in a TR that resides on the same floor as the work area being served.

TELECOMMUNICATIONS ROOM (TR) DESIGN

TRs must be designed and sized correctly to support communication cables and communication equipment. This is usually the job of a professional engineer or an RCDD™. The design should address the proper layout of the TR during construction. The design should cover construction specifications in the following areas:

▼ Slots or sleeves

■ Cable ladder racks

■ Backboards

■ Communication racks

■ Wire management

■ Grounding and bonding

▲ Communication equipment

The cable installers are the individuals that are responsible for interpreting the TR designs and performing the actual construction activities. In a new construction project, most of the TRs supporting structures may already be installed so only the communications cables need to be installed to complete the project. In a retrofit project most of the TRs cable-supporting structures may need to be installed before the communication cables can be installed and terminated.

Slots and Sleeves

Slots or sleeves are typically used to run either backbone or horizontal communication cables into or through a TR.

▼ A *slot* is a rectangular opening in the TR floor.

▲ A *sleeve* is a round conduit installed in a core hole through the floor or ceiling of a TR.

New cable installation projects will usually have either a slot or multiple sleeves installed in each TR. Slots and sleeves provide a pathway for backbone communication cables that must be run into or through the TR. Industry standards recommend installing a minimum of two, trade size 4 conduits between vertically aligned TRs.

Existing buildings where a cabling retrofit project may be taking place will not usually have available capacity in existing cable slots or sleeves. In many cases, new core holes must be drilled to install sleeves, which will provide a backbone pathway between TRs for new backbone communication cables. This activity may become part of the required work for a retrofit cable installation project.

CAUTION: Always consult a structural engineer before drilling core holes in a TR. Drilling core holes may weaken the building's structure and present a significant hazard to building occupants.

When performing core drilling in a TR, all core holes should be placed on the left side of the room (see Figure 13-1). This will promote an orderly growth of the TR backboards from left to right. The core holes should be placed in a location to ease cable installation activities in the TR.

A core drilling machine is used to drill core holes in a TR floor. The core drill will provide a hole that can support a trade size 4 sleeve installed in it. All sleeves must have the appropriate bushing installed to securely mount it in the core hole. The sleeve must protrude a minimum of 1 in. and a maximum of 3 in. above the TR floor or from the TR ceiling. This prevents water or other fluids that are spilled on the floor from entering the sleeve. In addition, all sleeves must be properly firestopped once installed.

IMPORTANT: Sleeves must always be firestopped once installed. The sleeve will nullify the fire rating of the TR floor once installed. The fire stop will reestablish the fire rating to the original rating when the TR was first constructed. When it is time to install backbone cables in the sleeves, the fire stop material must be removed and reinstalled with the cables in place.

When conduits enter a TR from the ceiling, they must be terminated to end at the top of the plywood backboard. When the conduits enter the TR from the floor, they must be terminated at the bottom of the plywood backboard.

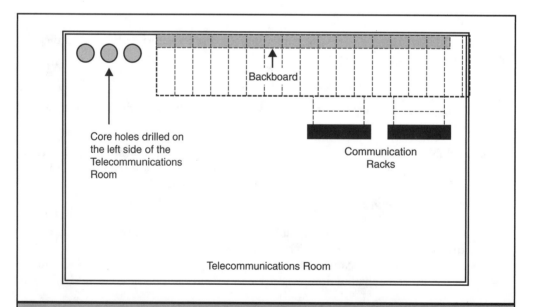

Figure 13-1. Core drill placement

CABLE-SUPPORTING STRUCTURES

Cable-supporting structures are those devices that hold and support telecommunication cables that are run in cable pathways. These devices include

▼ Cable trays

■ Wire basket raceways

■ Underfloor ducts or trenches

■ Conduits

▲ Other supporting hardware devices such as J hooks, caddy clamps, or bridle rings

The cable-supporting structures must be installed before the communication cables can be installed into the TR. Horizontal pathways may exist in the building or may need to be added. If the horizontal pathways do not exist or are insufficient to support the new communication cables, additional pathways must be added. Once installed, the horizontal pathways will permit the communication cables to run into the TR to be terminated.

Horizontal pathways usually end at the TR. In most cases, it is the responsibility of the cable installation contractor to add additional cable supporting structures for routing the communication cables into the TR. The cable-supporting structures that must be addressed when building the TR are the

▼ Cable trays or other hardware that provide the pathway for cables entering the TR

▲ Ladder racks that support communication cables inside the TR

In some projects, the horizontal pathway may not extend all the way to the TR or into the TR. If the horizontal pathway does not extend into the TR, additional supporting hardware is required to support the communication cables. Ladder racks are installed in the TR to support and route the communications cables inside of the TR.

Before installing any supporting structures in a TR, the proper sequence of steps must be performed. This will guarantee that the supporting structures will be installed correctly and not need to be replaced or redone at a later date. The following are the steps for installing the cable supporting structure:

1. Obtain building blueprints or job design drawings.

2. Identify if existing support structures exist to the TR and within the TR.

3. If support structures exist, verify the load capacity of the existing cable supporting structure.

4. Verify the ability of the existing support structure to support the total cable weight of the existing cables with the weight of the new cables.

5. Verify that sufficient cable support installation access is available before starting the installation.

6. Verify that the cable support structure will separate or provide a separation between high- and low-voltage cables. The NEC requires a solid and continuous barrier if both power cables and communications cables are run in the same pathway.

7. Verify that cable-support materials and tools are available before starting the installation.

8. When installing the cable-support structures, avoid areas that have high EMI or RFI.

9. Drill holes in all designated locations to install cable-supporting hardware, such as threaded rods, and other required hardware.

10. Install cable-supporting hardware, where necessary, along the cable path.

11. Attach cable trays or ladder racks on the installed supporting hardware.

12. Ground the cable-supporting structure to the nearest TGB or TMGB.

13. Label the cable-supporting structure per the ANSI/TIA/EIA-606 standard.

14. Document the newly installed cable-supporting structure on building blueprints or job drawings.

BACKBOARDS

Sheets of plywood are installed in TRs to provide a location for mounting cable termination and organization hardware. Plywood is a common material installed in TRs because it provides a uniform surface and cable termination hardware can be installed with common wood screws.

Plywood sheets that are 8 ft. high and 4 ft. wide are installed on the walls of the TR. The plywood backboard is installed with the 8-ft. long dimension running from the ceiling to the floor. The bottom of the plywood backboard will normally be installed 4 to 6 in. above the TR floor.

The quality of a sheet of plywood is defined by finished grades ranging from A to D. Grade A plywood sheets have a smooth surface without any knotholes. Grade D plywood sheets have a rough surface and usually contain large knotholes. The different qualities of plywood are listed in Table 13-1.

Plywood manufacturers produce plywood sheets with different grades on each side. One side may be Grade A and the other side may be Grade C. This would result in a plywood sheet that is Grade A/C.

Industry cabling standards recommend using plywood sheets that are Grade A/C for TR backboards. The plywood should also be void of knotholes through the plywood sheets. The Grade A side of the plywood backboard should be installed so it is exposed in the TR. The Grade C side of the plywood backboard should be installed against the TR wall.

The plywood sheets used for the TR backboards should be $3/4$ inch thick. One-inch thick plywood can also be used but is unnecessary in most casts. The $3/4$-in. thick plywood

Plywood Grade	Description
Grade A	Grade A plywood is the highest grade of plywood and it is free of surface flaws.
Grade B	Grade B plywood may contain surface flaws such a knotholes. The knotholes are cut out and replaced with smooth wood.
Grade C	Grade C plywood contains some surface flaws and occasional small knotholes.
Grade D	Grade D plywood has a rough surface and typically contains large knotholes.

Table 13-1. Plywood Grades

sheets provide sufficient strength for mounting cable termination hardware and communication equipment without the fear of the mounting screws pulling out of the wood. Industry standards recommend against using plywood sheets that are less than $3/4$ in. thick. Wood screws are likely to penetrate through the back side of the plywood backboard. Heavy communications equipment is likely to pull the wood screws out of the backboard.

Industry standards require that the plywood sheets used for TR backboards must be painted with two coats of light colored, fire resistant paint. The paint color should match the color required in the project specification. Never use fire retardant plywood as the TR backboard. This type of wood is treated with a type of saline solution that prevents paint from adhering to the plywood surface. Paint will crack and flake off the plywood surface over time. In addition, the saline finish causes metal mounting hardware to corrode over time. This is similar to the effects of installing hardware in a location close to the sea with a high salt content in the air.

Industry standards require that at least one wall of the closet have a $3/4$-in. plywood backboard securely mounted to the wall if the TR has a communication rack installed in it. Plywood backboards should be installed on two walls of the TR if it has no communications racks, or to accommodate future growth requirements. Plywood backboards can be installed on as many walls of the TR as required by the project specification or the TR design.

Installing Backboards

The plywood sheets must be securely and permanently mounted to the TR walls. The plywood backboards may be required to support heavy communication equipment. Therefore, the plywood backboard must be mounted to support the weight of all mounted equipment and not pull off of the wall. Always verify the load rating of the wall before installing the backboard to the TR wall.

Plywood backboards must be attached to the wall studs if possible. Long wood screws can be used to secure the plywood backboard to the TR wall studs. If the plywood backboard must attach to the wall where no studs are located, toggle bolts can be used to attach the plywood backboard to the drywall. Toggle bolts are designed to expand and provide sufficient support into the drywall material. Never use wood screws directly into drywall without inserting onto a wall stud. Wood screws do not provide sufficient gripping power into the drywall material and will pull out when weight is applied to the plywood backboard.

The attachment hardware must be both long enough and strong enough to securely mount the plywood backboard to the TR walls. Wood screws should be at least 2 in. (50 mm) long to appropriately attach to the plywood backboard to the wall studs. Never use wood screws that are shorter than 1 $1/4$ in. long. Toggle bolts should be at least 3 in. (75 mm) long to enable the wing nuts to open completely behind the drywall. In addition, the toggle bolts must be at least $1/4$ in. in diameter to provide sufficient strength.

Wood screws or toggle bolts must be placed around the entire perimeter to securely mount the plywood backboard to the TR walls. The mounting hardware should be installed 2 in. (50 mm) from the corners of the plywood backboard. Other screws of toggle bolts are then placed 2 in. (50 mm) from the edge of the plywood backboard every 22 in. (550 mm). This spacing interval will place three attachment points across the top and bottom of the plywood backboard and five attachment points on each side. This is shown in Figure 13-2.

It is recommended that the mounting hardware heads be recessed when installed. Recessing the wood screw or toggle bolt heads will provide more surface space on the plywood backboard for mounting cable termination hardware and communication equipment. Mount hardware that is not recessed may limit the flexibility of the backboard and prevent future growth.

Installing Multiple Backboards

Some cable installation projects may require more than one plywood backboard to be installed in a TR. Some TRs have large walls and require more that one backboard to be installed on the same wall. Some TRs require that plywood backboards be installed on adjacent walls.

Plywood backboards that are installed side by side on the same wall of the TR should be mounted without any spaces between the backboards (see Figure 13-3). This will create an uninterrupted work space for mounting cable termination hardware and communication equipment. Plywood backboards that must be installed on adjacent walls should be installed plumb with no space between the two backboards. The first backboard must be installed so it butts up to the side wall of the TR. The second plywood backboard should be butted up to the first backboard and attached to the side wall of the TR. The two plywood backboards should meet squarely in the corner creating a 90-degree angle (see Figure 13-4).

Occasionally a cable installation project requires installing plywood backboards on each wall of the TR. These projects require mounting multiple plywood backboards in

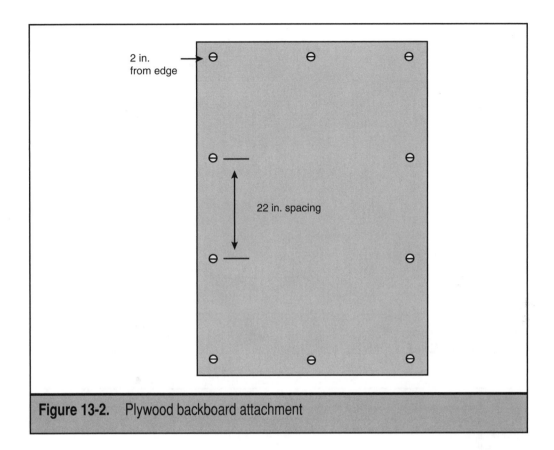

2 in.
from edge

22 in. spacing

Figure 13-2.   Plywood backboard attachment

the TR and securing them permanently to the TR walls. Multiple backboards will enhance the usable wall space in the TR for mounting cable termination hardware and communications equipment. Multiple backboards also provide space for the securing and mounting other cable supporting hardware for either pass through backbone cables. Finally this configuration will promote the orderly expansion and growth for more communication cables and communication equipment.

INSTALLING LADDER RACKS

Ladder racks are a type of cable tray that are commonly installed in a TR. Ladder racks are typically constructed of either a solid bar or tubular steel stock. Sections of ladder racks are usually sold in 8- to 10-ft. long sections. The width of each ladder rack section varies from 6 in. to 36 in. The depth of each section ranges from $1/2$ to $1^1/2$ in. Each section is constructed of two side rails with rungs spaced every 12 inches. A ladder rack is a type of open bottom cable tray, which is lighter than a solid bottom type of cable tray.

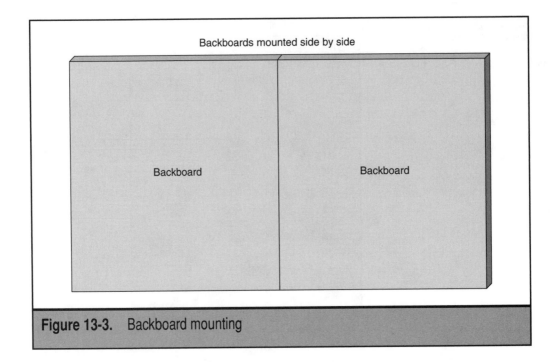

Backboards mounted side by side

Backboard

Backboard

Figure 13-3. Backboard mounting

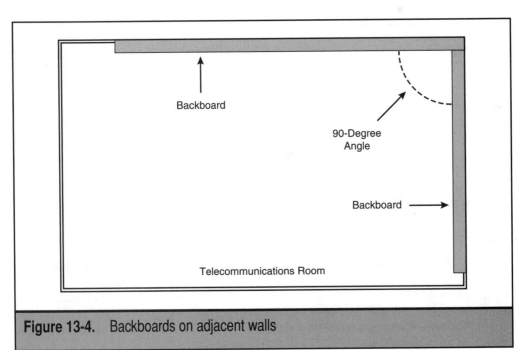

Backboard

90-Degree
Angle

Backboard

Telecommunications Room

Figure 13-4. Backboards on adjacent walls

Ladder racks are common fixtures in most TRs. These devices are used to support and route communication cables around the parameter of the TR. Ladder racks also provide a secondary function of securing and supporting the top of the communication racks installed in the TR. The ladder rack provides a pathway for communication cables to reach the communication racks in the TR.

Ladder racks are usually supported from below with wall brackets or from above the ceiling with threaded rods. Wall brackets are the first choice for supporting ladder rack sections in a TR. Wall bracket hardware can be installed in less time and therefore is less expensive. The number of brackets that must be installed will depend on the required load capacity for the ladder rack. Ceiling supports may be required in TRs with large load capacity requirements or when wall brackets cannot be installed.

The ANSI/TIA/EIA-569-A standard requires that support brackets be placed no further than 24 in. from the end of the ladder rack section (see Figure 13-5). The ANSI/TIA/EIA-569-A standard also requires that a bracket be placed at the joint between two ladder rack sections. This standard also mandates that supports be placed at 5-ft. intervals between mandatory bracket locations.

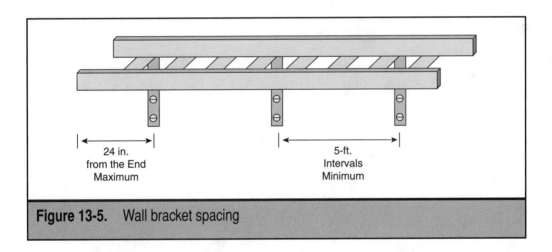

Figure 13-5. Wall bracket spacing

Wall brackets must be properly secured and anchored to the TR walls. Wood screws 1 1/4 in. in length can be used to secure the brackets to TR wall studs. Toggle bolts 2 in. long and 1/4 in. in diameter can be used to secure the wall brackets to drywall. Wall brackets that are not properly secured will not be able to support the weight of the ladder rack when heavy copper cables are installed in the TR.

Attaching Communication Racks to Ladder Racks

Communication racks are usually installed below the ladder racks and attached to the bottom of the ladder racks. If a communication rack is installed so it is not under a section of ladder rack, a short piece of ladder rack is usually run to the communication racks from the parameter ladder rack. Drop outs are usually installed in the ladder rack sections above each communication rack. The drop outs are curved pieces of metal that provide a smooth transition for communication cables dropping down to the communication rack to be terminated.

Communication cables are installed in the ladder rack. The cables can be secured to the ladder rack section with cable ties to keep the cables organized. The cables are run on the ladder rack to the required termination point in the TR. The cables are fed through the drop outs and run to the required termination position on the rack.

Industry cabling standards recommend installing ladder racks on the same walls of the TR that support plywood backboards. It is highly recommended that ladder racks be installed on all walls of the TR. This will provide a pathway to all areas of the TR and support future communication racks installed in the TR (see Figure 13-6).

The ladder racks sections must be a minimum of 12 in. wide to properly support communication cables (see Figure 13-7). Ladder rack sections that are wider and probably unnecessary for most TRs. Ladder racks that are less than 12 in. wide may not provide enough space for supporting cables or adding new cables in the future.

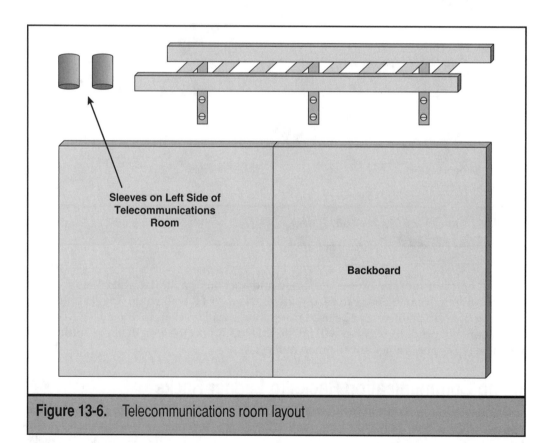

Sleeves on Left Side of
Telecommunications
Room

Backboard

Figure 13-6.   Telecommunications room layout

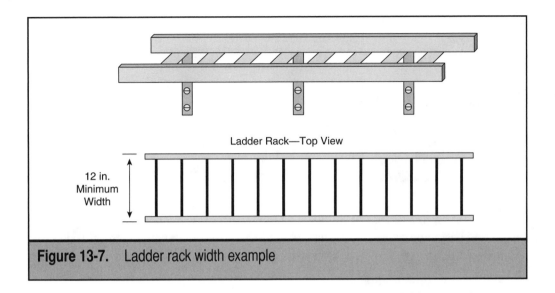

Ladder Rack—Top View

12 in.
Minimum
Width

Figure 13-7. Ladder rack width example

MOUNTING CABLE TERMINATION HARDWARE

Cable termination hardware is mounted in the TR once all of the plywood backboards and ladder rack sections are installed. Most TRs install punch down blocks on the plywood backboards. A very large installation may have the punch down blocks installed on communication racks in the TR. Horizontal voice cables are usually terminated on punch down blocks. Multipair copper backbone cables are also terminated on punch down blocks. The multipair backbone cables are run to other TRs or directly to the ER and connected to common communication equipment such as a PBX voice switch. The punch down blocks provide a convenient method for cross-connecting the horizontal cables to the backbone cable pairs.

Horizontal communication cables used for high-speed data applications are usually terminated on patch panels. Patch panels are installed on communication racks along with the high-speed data equipment. Horizontal data cables terminate on the back of the patch panel. A patch cord is used to connect the horizontal cable to the data equipment.

Before mounting any cable termination hardware on the TR backboards, plan for a clear space of 5 to 6 in. at the top and bottom of the backboard for cable routing along the backboard. In addition, plan for 6 in. from the edge of the backboard for routing cables vertically.

Terminating space should be planned and allocated on the TR backboards for mounting cable termination hardware. The guidelines shown in Table 13-2 should be used for planning and calculating cable terminating space.

Media Type	Space Allocation
Twisted-pair cable terminations	4 sq. in. (2,600 sq. mm) for each four-pair cable to be terminated or cross-connected
Optical fiber cable terminations	2 sq. in. (1,300 sq. mm) for each optical fiber pair to be terminated or cross-connected

Table 13-2.   Termination Space Allocation Guidelines

Punch down blocks should be planned to terminate horizontal cables on one set of blocks and backbone cables on another set of blocks. The blocks can be configured in two of the following ways:

▼ Vertical configuration

▲ Horizontal configuration

A vertical configuration is where the punch down blocks for terminating the horizontal cables are mounted either above or below the punch down blocks for terminating the backbone cables. Cross-connections between the two types of blocks are made vertically. A horizontal configuration is where the punch down blocks for terminating the horizontal cables are mounted next to the punch down blocks for terminating the backbone cables. Cross-connections between the two types of blocks are made horizontally.

A vertical configuration is usually preferred over a horizontal configuration. A vertical configuration enables the growth of both types of blocks to occur to the right on the TR backboard. A horizontal configuration enables the growth to occur down. If growth is required to the right, a space must be planned before the backbone blocks are mounted.

Punch down blocks should always be installed starting at the left side of the TR backboard. Additional blocks are added down and to the right. Punch down blocks should never be mounted in the middle of the backboard. Mounting punch down on the left side of the backboard maximizes backboard space and more easily accommodates future growth (see Figure 13-8).

Maximum Cross-Connect Wire Distances

Industry cabling standards define a maximum allocation for ERs and TR equipment patch cables and cross-connect jumper wires. The ANSI/TIA/EIA-568-A and ANSI/TIA/EIA-568-B.1 standards specify a 10 m (33 ft.) allocation for the combined length for work area and closet cable lengths.

The maximum space between punch down block termination horizontal cables and backbone cables in a TR is 5 m (16 ft.). This distance can be increased if the length of the work area cables is less than 5 m (16 ft.).

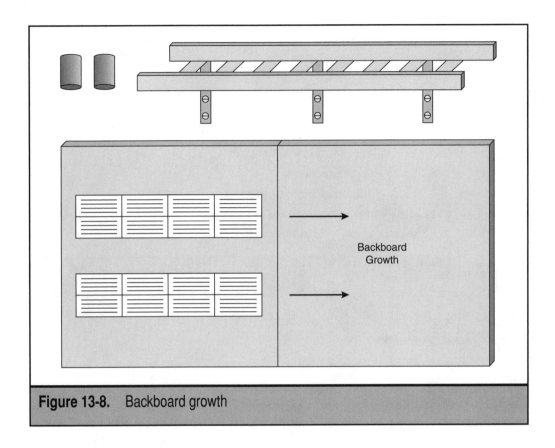

Figure 13-8.   Backboard growth

IC (BD) and MC (CD) TRs are used to terminate backbone cables. The maximum length of the cross-connect jumper wires is allowed to be longer in these building spaces. Industry cabling standards recommend that the maximum cross-connect wire lengths between backbone termination blocks in these TRs are 20 m (66 ft.).

Termination Block Field Color Codes

The ANSI/TIA/EIA-606 standard requires that punch down blocks be color coded to identify the type of communication cable terminated on the block. Color-coded termination blocks facilitate cable plant administration and documentation. The recommended termination block color code designations are shown in Table 13-3.

The ANSI/TIA/EIA-606 standard does not specify or mandate how the punch down blocks must be color coded. The acceptable methods for color coding punch down block terminations include the following:

▼   Colored backboards

■   Colored blocks

Color	Description
Orange	Demarcation point for central office terminations
Green	Network connections to the demarcation point
Purple	Common equipment connections
White	First level backbone connections
Gray	Second level backbone connections
Blue	Horizontal connections
Brown	Interbuilding backbone connections
Yellow	Miscellaneous connections
Red	Reserved for the future

Table 13-3.   Punch Down Block Color Coding

- ■ Colored block covers
- ▲ Colored block labels

Backboard Cable Routing

Communication cables that are run along a backboard must be properly supported. The following cabling hardware used for supporting cables on a backboard include

- ▼ D-rings
- ▲ Mushrooms

D-rings are metal or plastic hardware components that are used to support and organize communication cables installed on a backboard (see Figure 13-9). These devices are shaped to resemble the letter D. Each end has a hole where a screw is used to mount the ring to the plywood backboard.

D-rings can support a single cable or small groups of cables. Multiple D-rings installed vertically or horizontally create a pathway on the backboard for routing multiple cables between termination points (see Figure 13-10). D-rings can also be used to route cross-connect wires between groups of blocks mounted on the backboard.

A mushroom is a plastic peg that is attached to the plywood backboard (see Figure 13-11). Mushrooms are often installed between punch down blocks. One mushroom is usually mounted above each row of punch down blocks. A cross-connect wire is routed over the mushrooms to another punch down block. The mushrooms help to keep the cross-connect wire organized.

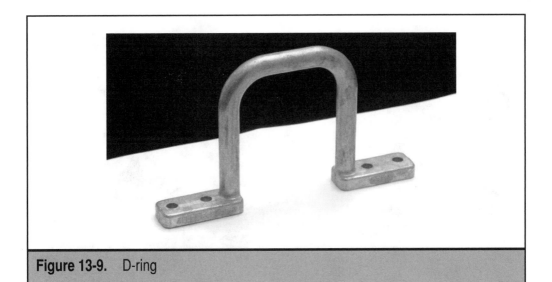

Figure 13-9. D-ring

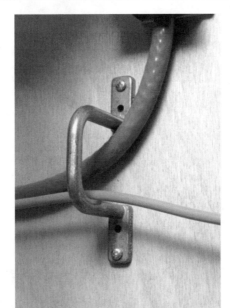

Figure 13-10. D-ring on a backboard

Figure 13-11. Mushroom on a backboard

Termination Block Clearances

Punch down blocks must be mounted in a TR so there is a clear space in front of the blocks (see Figure 13-12). Proper clearances are required by the NEC from electrical equipment and equipment power wiring. Industry standards recommend allocating a minimum of 1 m (3 ft.) of clear working space in front of all punch down block fields. This will provide adequate working space for adding new cables or performing cable maintenance.

COMMUNICATION RACKS AND CABINETS

Communication racks and cabinets are installed in TRs to mount patch panels and communication equipment. Communication racks and cabinets provide a designated place to mount cable termination devices and communication equipment. Both communication racks and cabinets keep the cable termination hardware, equipment, and the associated cables organized.

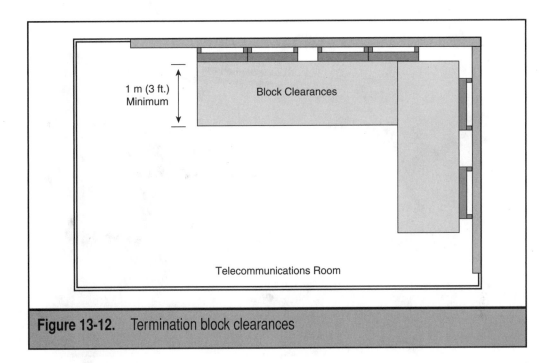

Figure 13-12. Termination block clearances

TRs that do not have communication racks or cabinets installed in them are usually very disorganized. All cable termination hardware must be mounted on the plywood backboards. Communication equipment must also be installed either on the plywood backboard or in communications racks. TRs without communication racks have no organized method for growth. New equipment often is mounted on the floor or other temporary locations. These TRs have no organized method to handle cross-connect wires and equipment patch cords.

Communication racks are sometimes called equipment racks or relay frames (see Figure 13-13). These devices are metal frames that have two vertical support members and a horizontal support base and top. Communication racks usually are ordered in 19-inch widths and 7-ft. heights. Common widths for communication racks used in the communication industry are 19 and 23 in. The vertical supports have threaded holes along the entire length of the column. Patch panels, wire management channels, and communication equipment are attached to the vertical supports with screws or bolts.

Communication Rack Clearances

The ANSI/TIA/EIA-568-A and ANSI/TIA/EIA-568-B.1 standards require that communication racks be accessible from the front and the rear. Communication racks must have clear space allocated in front, behind, and alongside. The clear space will enable cable installation personnel enough space to install new cables or perform maintenance work.

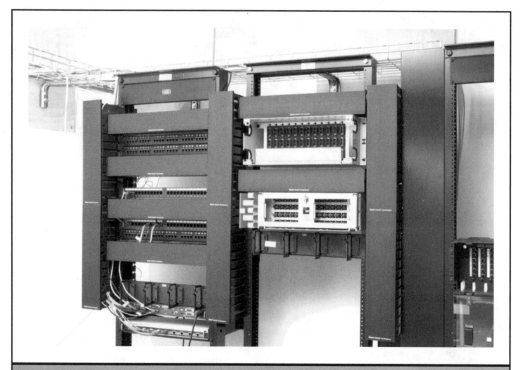

Figure 13-13.   Communication Rack

Multiple communication racks should be arranged in a row in the TR. Each rack usually has a bolt hole on the side that enables the racks to be joined together. When multiple racks are connected together, industry standards require access on the side of the racks for front to rear access.

Communication racks must support the following clearances in the TR (see Figure 13-14):

▼   Thirty-six inches in front of the communication rack(s)

■   Thirty inches behind the communication rack(s)

▲   Thirty inches on the side of the communication rack(s) for front to rear access

Always install communication racks and adhere to industry clearance requirements. When installing communication racks, always follow a logical layout for growth and future requirements in the closet. This would include installing the first communication racks against a wall of the TR and adding new racks to the first as growth requirements dictate.

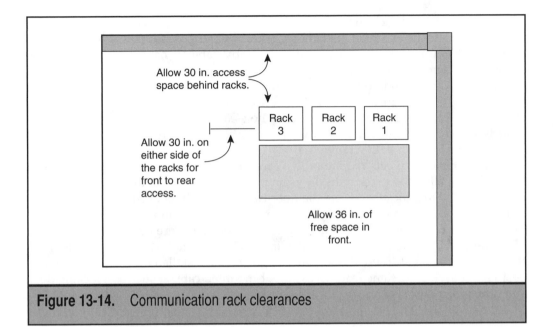

Figure 13-14.   Communication rack clearances

Securing Communication Racks

Communication racks must be securely mounted and supported in a TR. Properly supporting communication racks will keep cabling personnel safe and protect the cables from damage that may result if the racks fall over in the TR.

Communication racks should be placed approximately 30 in. from the wall of the TR. If the communication rack is not positioned under any sections of a ladder rack, a section of the ladder rack should be run to the communication rack. This will provide a pathway for communication cables that must be terminated on the racks. It will also provide support for the communication rack. Some cable project designs require that communication racks also be supported at the base. Bolts can be used to secure the base of the rack into the TR floor.

In some areas of the country, the communication racks must be secured to meet seismic support requirements. Seismic support is required communication rack bracing that will secure the rack and prevent it from moving or falling over during an earthquake.

Cabinets

Cabinets are enclosures for mounting communication equipment in a TR. Cabinets serve the same basic function as communication racks. In fact, a cabinet is a communication rack surrounded by a metal enclosure. Cabinets may be used in a TR to secure communication equipment.

Cabinets are metal enclosures with solid walls, a top, a bottom, and usually a locking door. Cabinets can be ordered with fans, electric power strips, and shelves to support expensive and secure communication equipment. Most cabinets have a Plexiglas door on the front and a metal door in back.

Cabinets have a standard communication frame installed in the cabinet for mounting communication hardware and shelves. Cable access to the communication frame is usually through knockouts or other prepunched holes in the cabinet enclosure. Cables are routed to cabinets across ladder racks. Communication cables are usually terminated on patch panels mounted on the frame.

Floor-mounted cabinets require more space than communication racks. Additional space must be allocated to open the doors on the front and back of the cabinets. If a cabinet is installed in a location where the door cannot be fully opened, this may prevent communication equipment from being either installed or removed from the cabinet. Moving a cabinet is very difficult once communication cables are installed.

Wall-mounted cabinets can be installed in TRs that may not have enough space for a floor-mounted cabinet. These devices are designed to be installed on the plywood backboard and provide the same features as a floor-mounted cabinet such as a locking door and ventilation fans.

MOUNTING PATCH PANELS

Patch panels are mounted on either communication racks or in cabinets (see Figure 13-15). Patch panels are available in either: 12, 24, 48, or 96 port configurations. Patch panels attach to communication racks using standard screws or bolts. Horizontal communication cables terminate the punch down slots on the back of the patch panel.

The most important consideration when terminating horizontal cables is to route the cable properly. Do not violate the minimum bend radius when routing the cable to the termination position on the patch panel. Cables that violate the minimum bend radius will exhibit lower performance and may result in more transmitted bit errors. Most patch panel manufacturers provide a support bar that will help maintain the proper bend radius for cables terminating on the patch panel.

Never mount more than two patch panels in a row on the communications rack. A horizontal wire management panel should always be installed after two patch panels (see Figure 13-16). The wire management panel will provide a device to route and store patch cords connecting to each patch panel port. The wire management panels will keep the front of the communication rack organized.

WIRE MANAGEMENT

Communication racks should always be installed with proper wire management panels. Wire management panels provide a pathway for routing communication cables along the rack to their designated termination position. They are also used for providing a cable

Figure 13-15. Patch panel on a communication rack

path for patch cords to connect to patch panels and equipment ports. They provide a means to organize patch cord routing and store excess patch cord slack.

Wire management panels provide organization for communication racks. Without wire management panels, communication racks become very disorganized and sloppy looking. The two types of wire management panels used on communication racks are

▼ Vertical wire management panels

▲ Horizontal wire management panels

Vertical wire management panels provide a pathway for cables running vertically on the communication rack. These wire management panels are usually used to organize horizontal cables that drop down from the ladder rack. The vertical wire management panels enable specific cables to exit the wire management panels at their designated termination position on the rack.

Each communication rack should have at least one vertical wire management panel. It is highly recommended that each rack have two vertical wire management panels. The vertical wire management panels provide a location to house cable slack while maintaining a neat and orderly appearance for horizontal cables terminating on the rack.

Figure 13-16.   Horizontal wire management

Horizontal wire management panels provide a pathway for cables running horizontally on the communication rack. These wire management panels are usually used to organize patch cables that are connected to a patch panel port and must be run to an equipment port. The horizontal wire management panels enable the patch cords to be routed along the front of the communication rack to the vertical wire management panels and down to the desired connection port of the required communication device.

Every communication rack should have at least one horizontal wire management panel. It is highly recommended that each rack have a horizontal wire management panel between two patch panels and between communication devices. The horizontal wire management panels provide a location to house cable slack while maintaining a neat and orderly appearance for all patch cords used on the rack.

CABLE SLACK

When running communication cables to a TR, it is also recommended that some cable slack should be left in the cable run. Cable slack is usefully for the following conditions:

▼   Reconfiguration of the TR

■   Moving cables away from sources of noise

■   Moving cables into other horizontal cable pathways

▲   For future cable system reconfigurations

Industry standards recommend leaving between 1 and 3 ft. of slack at both ends of installed horizontal cables. For backbone cables, it is recommended that you leave a service loop of between 5 and 10 ft. This will accommodate moving termination hardware or communication racks in the closet.

Cable slack should be stored in a secure location that will prevent the cable from becoming damaged. If the horizontal pathways enter the TR through the ceiling, the cable slack should be store above the TR. If the horizontal pathways enter the TR through the floor, the cable slack should be stored below or inside the TR.

Cable slack must be stored correctly to prevent signaling problems in the cable. It is also important to store cable slack on loose loops. Never tightly bundle cable loops together. This can cause noise problems within the cable.

INSTALLING GROUNDING AND BONDING INFRASTRUCTURE

The ANSI/TIA/EIA-607 standard defines the grounding and bonding requirements for a telecommunications cabling system. The telecommunications grounding and bonding system starts with a physical connection to the building grounding electrode system and extends to every TR in the building (see Figure 13-17). A telecommunications grounding and bonding system defined by the ANSI/TIA/EIA-607 standards includes the following elements:

▼   Bonding conductor for telecommunications

■   Telecommunications main grounding busbar (TMGB)

■   Telecommunications bonding backbone (TBB)

■   Telecommunications grounding busbar (TGB)

▲   Telecommunications bonding backbone interconnecting bonding conductor (TBBIBC)

The ANSI/TIA/EIA-607 standard defines a single component as the center of the telecommunications grounding and bonding system called the TMGB. The TMGB is a dedicated grounding and bonding element that connects to the building grounding system. It serves as a dedicated extension of the building grounding system for telecommunications equipment, cabling, and cable supporting structures.

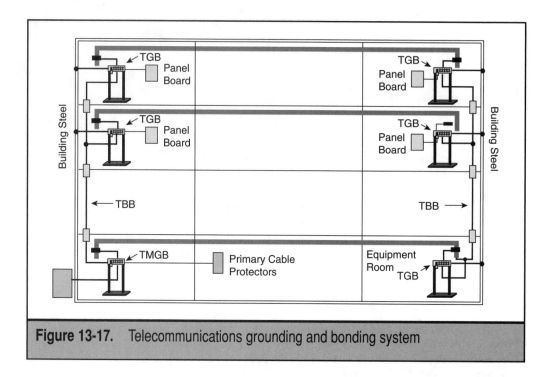

Figure 13-17.   Telecommunications grounding and bonding system

The ANSI/TIA/EIA-607 standard requires that each TGB installed in a TR be connected to the TMGB. The TBB is the conductor that provides this connection.

The ANSI/TIA/EIA-607 standard requires that a TGB be installed in each TR. The TGB is the single grounding point for all communications equipment, cabling, and cable supporting structure devices in a TR. Each TGB must be connected to the TMGB using the TBB.

The ANSI/TIA/EIA-607 standard enables multiple TGBs to be installed in each TR. The exact number and the location of each TGB is not specified in the ANSI/TIA/EIA-607 standard. Each TGB should be installed to provide the greatest flexibility and accessibility in the TR for telecommunications grounding and bonding.

Installation of the TGB

The TGB should be mounted on a permanent location in a TR (see Figure 13-18). If installed on a communications rack, the TGB must be insulated from the rack. The exact location on a communication rack (top or bottom) will depend on the routing of the TBB conductors into the TR from the backbone pathway. If the access for the TBB conductors is through underground trenches or an access floor system, then the TGB should be installed near the bottom of the rack. If the access is through a conduit or an overhead cable tray, then the TGB should be installed near the top of the rack.

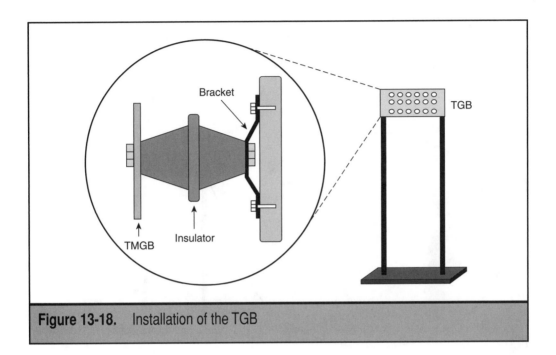

Figure 13-18. Installation of the TGB

The TGB should be installed as close as possible to the nearest connection to the building grounding system or the connection provided to the grounding system for the telecommunications grounding system. A panelboard, if available, is a dedicated connection to the building grounding system for telecommunications. If the TGB is located in the same space as the panelboard, the panelboard's alternating equipment bus or enclosure must be bonded to the TGB. The NEC requires that TGB be installed to adhere to the clearances required by applicable electrical codes for grounding and bonding connections.

The TGB in each TR must be bonded to the structural steel with a listed bonding conductor. When the building steel is readily accessible to the TR, the bonding conductors must be at least a #6 AWG conductor. The ANSI/TIA/EIA-607 standard permits the connection to either vertical or horizontal structural steel members.

Connecting to the TGB

The ANSI/TIA/EIA-607 standard requires that all ladder racks and communication racks be connected to the TGB in each TR (see Figure 13-19). All bonding conductors used to establish a connection to the TGB must be listed and approved for the specific purpose. All bonding conductors must be a minimum of a #6 AWG conductor with green insulation. Connections to the TGB must be made using a two-hole compression lug.

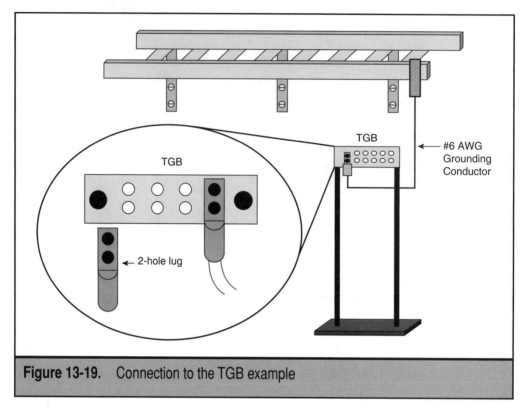

Figure 13-19.   Connection to the TGB example

INSTALLING COMMUNICATION EQUIPMENT

Communication equipment is installed in the TR once the cable-supporting hardware and communication racks or cabinets have been installed. Communication equipment is typically installed in the TR with the following methods:

▼ Wall mounting

■ Rack mounting

▲ Cabinet mounting

Small communication devices are usually wall mounted in a TR. These devices are usually limited to one or two. These devices mount to the TR backboard using either wood screws or a manufacturer-supplied bracket.

Larger types of communication equipment or larger numbers of communication devices are usually installed in a communication rack. The communication rack will enable the communication equipment to be mounted in an organized manner in the TR.

Communication equipment that is very sensitive or should not be touched is usually mounted in a communications cabinet. The communications cabinet will enable the door to be locked so only authorized personnel will have access to this equipment. The Plexiglas door on the cabinet will enable the status lights of the communication equipment to be monitored at all times.

Communication equipment must be installed to conform to the equipment manufacturer's specifications. Installing either passive or active communication equipment in a TR requires verifying TR temperature and humidity levels. The recommended temperature and humidity levels for TRs with communication equipment are shown in Table 13-4.

Equipment Type	Recommended Temperature Range	Recommended Humidity Range
Passive equipment	10 to 35 C° 50 to 95 F°	Humidity levels below 85% relative humidity
Active equipment	18 to 24 C° 64 to 75 F°	Humidity levels in the range of 30 to 55% relative humidity

Table 13-4.   Telecommunications Room (TR) Temperature and Humidity Levels

Equipment Clearances

The NEC require that all communication equipment maintain minimum clearances from communication racks or other objects in a TR. The NEC requires 1 m (3 ft.) of clear space both in front and behind communication equipment. The clear space will enable a safe margin from the electrical equipment and provide appropriate personnel enough space to perform maintenance work.

CHAPTER SUMMARY

The telecommunications room (TR) is the space where both horizontal and backbone cables are terminated. A TR is a building space that is designated for the termination of horizontal and backbone cables. The TR is the recognized connection point between the backbone and horizontal cable pathways. This space is also the place where any required termination hardware is mounted.

Slot or sleeves are typically used to run either backbone or horizontal communication cables into or through a TR. A slot is a rectangular opening in the TR floor. A sleeve is a round conduit installed in a core hole through the floor or ceiling of a TR.

Cable-supporting structures are those devices that hold and support telecommunication cables that are run in cable pathways. These devices include cable trays, wire basket raceways, underfloor ducts or trenches, conduits, and other supporting hardware devices such as J hooks, caddy clamps, or bridle rings. The cable-supporting structures must be installed before the communication cables can be installed into the TR.

Sheets of plywood are installed in TRs to provide a location for mounting cable termination and organization hardware. Plywood is a common material installed in TRs because it provides a uniform surface, and cable termination hardware can be installed with common wood screws. Plywood sheets that are 8 ft. high and 4 ft. wide are installed on the walls of the TR.

Industry cabling standards recommend using plywood sheets that are Grade A/C for TR backboards. The plywood sheets used for the TR backboard should be $3/4$-inch thick.

The plywood sheets must be securely and permanently mounted to the TR walls. The plywood backboards may be required to support heavy communication equipment. Plywood backboards must be attached to the wall studs if possible. Long wood screws can be used to secure the plywood backboard to the TR wall studs. If the plywood backboard must attach to the wall where no studs are located, toggle bolts can be used to attach the plywood backboard to the drywall.

Some cable installation projects may require more than one plywood backboard to be installed in a TR. Plywood backboards that are installed side by side on the same wall of the TR should be mounted without any spaces between the backboards. This will create an uninterrupted work space for mounting cable termination hardware and communication equipment. Plywood backboards that must be installed on adjacent walls should be installed plumb with no space between the two backboards. The two plywood backboards should meet squarely in the corner creating a 90-degree angle.

Ladder racks are a type of cable tray that are commonly installed in a TR. These devices are used to support and route communication cables around the parameter of the TR. The ladder rack provides a pathway for communication cables to reach the communication racks in the TR.

Ladder racks are usually supported from below with wall brackets or from above the ceiling with threaded rods. Wall brackets are the first choice for supporting ladder rack sections in a TR. Ceiling supports may be required in TRs with large load capacity requirements or when wall brackets cannot be installed. The ANSI/TIA/EIA-569-A standard requires that support brackets must be placed no further than 24 in. from the end of the ladder rack section. The ANSI/TIA/EIA-569-A standard also requires that a bracket be placed at the joint between two ladder rack sections. This standard also mandates that support be placed at 5-ft. intervals between mandatory bracket locations.

Communication racks are usually installed below the ladder racks and attached to the bottom of the ladder racks. If a communication rack is installed so it is not under a section of ladder rack, a short piece of ladder rack is usually run to the communication racks from the parameter ladder rack. Drop outs are usually installed in the ladder rack sections above each communication rack. The cables are fed through the drop outs and run to the required termination position on the rack.

Cable termination hardware is mounted in the TR once all of the plywood backboards and ladder rack sections are installed. Before mounting any cable termination hardware on the TR backboards, plan for a clear space of 5 to 6 in. at the top and bottom of the backboard for cable routing along the backboard. In addition, plan for 6 in. from the edge of the backboard for routing cables vertically. Twisted-pair cable terminations will require allocating approximately 4 sq. in. (2,600 sq. mm) for each four-pair cable to be terminated or cross-connected. Optical fiber cable terminations will require allocating approximately 2 sq. in. (1,300 sq. mm) for each optical fiber pair to be terminated or cross-connected.

Communication cables that are run along a backboard must be properly supported. D-rings and mushroom cabling hardware are used for supporting cables on a backboard. D-rings are metal or plastic hardware components that are used to support and organize communication cables installed on a backboard. A mushroom is a plastic peg that is attached to the plywood backboard. Mushrooms often are installed between punch down blocks for routing cross-connect wire.

Punch down blocks must be mounted in a TR so there is clear space in front of the blocks. Industry standards recommend allocating a minimum of 1 m (3 ft.) of clear working space in front of all punch down block fields. This will provide adequate working space for adding new cables or performing cable maintenance.

The ANSI/TIA/EIA-568-A and ANSI/TIA/EIA-568-B.1 standards require that communication racks be accessible from the front and the rear. Communication racks must have a clear space allocated in front, behind, and alongside. Communication racks must support 36 in. in front of the communication rack(s), 30 in. behind the communication rack(s), and 30 in. on the side of the communication rack(s) for front to rear access.

Communication racks must be securely mounted and supported in a TR. Properly supporting communication racks will keep cabling personnel safe and protect the cables from damage that may result if the racks fall over in the TR. Communication racks should be placed approximately 30 in. from the wall of the TR. Some cable project designs require that communication racks also be supported at the base. Bolts can be used to secure the base of the rack into the TR floor.

Patch panels are mounted on either communication racks or in cabinets. Patch panels attach to communication racks using standard screws or bolts. Never mount more than two patch panels in a row on the communications rack. A horizontal wire management panel should always be installed after two patch panels. The wire management panel will provide a device to route and store patch cords connecting to each patch panel port. The wire management panels will keep the front of the communication rack organized.

The ANSI/TIA/EIA-607 standard defines the grounding and bonding requirements for a telecommunications cabling system. The ANSI/TIA/EIA-607 standard defines a single component as the center of the telecommunications grounding and bonding system called the telecommunications main grounding busbar (TMGB). The TMGB is a dedicated grounding and bonding element that connects to the building grounding system. The ANSI/TIA/EIA-607 standard requires that a telecommunications grounding busbar (TGB) be installed in each TR. The TGB is the single grounding point for all communications equipment, cabling, and cable supporting structure devices in a TR. Each TGB must be connected to the TMGB using the telecommunications bonding backbone (TBB).

The TGB in each TR must be bonded to the structural steel with a listed bonding conductor. When the building steel is readily accessible to the TR, the bonding conductors must be at least a #6 AWG conductor. The ANSI/TIA/EIA-607 standard permits the connection to either vertical or horizontal structural steel members.

The ANSI/TIA/EIA-607 standard requires that all ladder racks and communication racks be connected to the TGB in each TR. All bonding conductors and bonding connectors used to establish a connection to the TGB must be listed and approved for the specific purpose. All bonding conductors must be a minimum of a #6 AWG conductor with green insulation. Connections to the TGB must be made using a two-hole compression lug.

CHAPTER 14

Cable-Supporting Structures

*C**able-supporting structures* are the hardware elements required to support communication cables. In the early 1980s when data cabling was being installed to support data terminals and new local area networks (LANs), communication cables were often installed on drop ceilings without any supporting structures. The weight of the copper communication cables has caused ceilings to collapse and pose a severe fire hazard in commercial buildings.

Cable-supporting structures are installed solely for the purpose of supporting communication cables. They prevent cables from lying on drop ceiling tiles and from resting on electrical wires and conduits. Cable-supporting hardware also serves the function of keeping communication cables organized.

There are many different types of cable-supporting hardware. Each type is used for different situations and for different types of cables. This chapter will describe the most common types of cable-supporting hardware and define when it should be installed in a building.

CABLE-SUPPORTING STRUCTURES

Cable-supporting structures are additional hardware for supporting communication cables. These are usually in addition to the cable pathways that are usually installed when a building is constructed. Cable-supporting structures are often required to augment existing cable pathways because they become full of cables. Another common reason for installing cable-supporting structures is because cable pathways are nonexistent.

Cable-supporting hardware is most commonly installed in the horizontal subsystem. The reason is that the exact configuration of each building floor is usually unknown when a building is under construction. Horizontal pathways that are planned to run under the floor must be installed during the building construction. Horizontal pathways installed above the ceiling may be undersized or not installed at all during the building construction. As a result, it is very common for a cable project to also require the installation of cable-supporting structures to support above ceiling horizontal cables.

There are many different types of cable-supporting structures. Some of the most common include the following:

▼ Cable trays

■ Wire basket raceways

■ Conduits

■ J hooks or cable hangers

■ Surface mount raceways

▲ Ladder racks

Cable Trays

Cable trays are the most common type of cable-supporting structures installed in commercial buildings (see Figure 14-1). Cable trays are pathways that are installed either above a ceiling or below a raised floor in a commercial building. They provide support and protection from horizontal and backbone cables between the telecommunications room (TR) and the work area.

Cable trays are manufactured in many different configurations. Cable trays are made of both steel and aluminum. Some types of cable trays are constructed of solid bar stock and are designed for heavy load environments. Other types of cable trays are constructed of tube stock and used for medium- or light-load environments.

NOTE: If a cable tray is constructed of a nonmetallic material and installed in a plenum-rated building space, the cable tray must be plenum rated.

The most common types of cable trays include the following:

▼ Ladder type

■ Ventilated trough

■ Solid trough

▲ Spine type

Figure 14-1.   Cable tray

Ladder type cable trays, sometimes called ladder racks, get their name because this type of cable tray resembles a ladder when viewed from the top or bottom (see Figure 14-2). Ladder type cable trays are typically constructed of either solid bar or tubular steel stock. Standard sections of ladder racks are usually sold in 8-to-10 ft. long sections. The width of each ladder rack section varies from 6 to 36 in. The depth of each section ranges from $1/2$ to $1\,1/2$ in. Each section is constructed of two side rails with rungs spaced every 12 in. Ladder rack is a type of open bottom cable tray, which is lighter than a solid bottom type of cable tray.

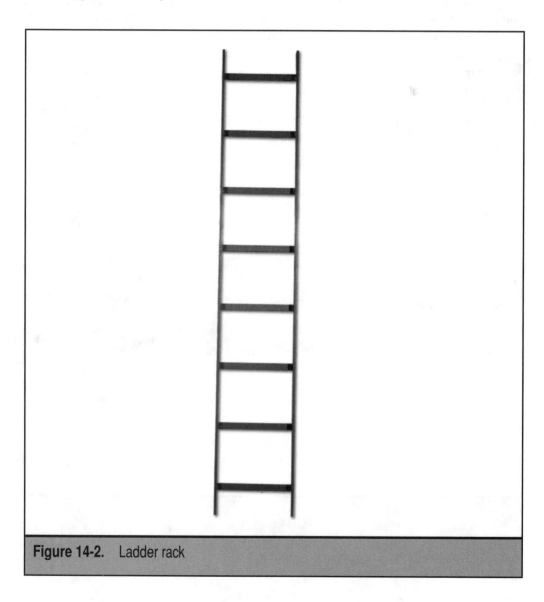

Figure 14-2. Ladder rack

Ventilated trough cable trays are constructed of two side rails with flat rungs spaced every 4 to 6 in. apart. These types of cable trays provide greater support for communication cables installed in them. This type of cable tray is heavier than the ladder rack type cable tray, but it can support greater cable loads without damaging communication cables. Standard sections of ventilated trough cable trays are usually sold in 8-to-10 ft. long sections. The width of each section varies from 6 to 36 in. The depth of each section ranges from $1/2$ to $1\ 1/2$ in.

Solid bottom cable trays are constructed of two side rails with a solid, continuous bottom. These types of cable trays provide the greatest support for communication cables installed in them. This type of cable tray is heavier than either ladder type cable trays and ventilated trough cable trays, but it can support greater cable loads without damaging communication cables. Standard sections of solid bottom cable trays are usually sold in 8-to-10 ft. long sections. The width of each section varies from 6 to 36 in. The depth of each section ranges from $1/2$ to $1\ 1/2$ in.

A spine type cable tray is an open tray with a center, rigid spine. Metal fingers type cable supports curve out or protrude out at right angles from the spine. These types of cable trays provide very little support for communication cables installed in them. They are design for environments where light horizontal cables will be installed. This type of cable tray is very light and easy to install. Standard sections of spine cable trays are usually sold in 8-to-10 ft. long sections. The width of the cable support fingers for each section varies from 6 to 12 in. wide. The depth of each section ranges from 2 to 6 in.

Cable Tray Design

The design of TRs and general office layout practices are based on the assumption of one work area per 10 sq. m (100 sq. ft.) of usable office space. Horizontal cable pathways are designed to support a minimum of three horizontal cables per work area. Each horizontal cable pathway must be sized to provide 650 sq. mm (1 sq. in.) of cross-sectional area for each work area to accommodate the three horizontal cables. If the number of work areas or number of cables is more than the minimum planning numbers, the size of the horizontal pathway must be adjusted to accommodate the larger number of cables.

All horizontal cable trays must be designed to accommodate all planned horizontal cables. In addition, the cable tray must be designed to support future growth of new cables added to the building. Under no circumstances should the overall fill ratio of the cable tray exceed 50 percent of the cable trays maximum capacity.

Installing Cable Trays

Cable trays must be adequately supported when installed in a commercial building. These structures will support the weight of all copper and optical fiber cables run along the cable pathway. Cable trays must be engineered and constructed to support the maximum weight of all anticipated cables that will be run in the cable trays.

Cable trays must be installed so the completed cable pathway permits the communication cables to be installed according to industry cabling specifications. Cable trays should never be installed so the installed communication cables exceed the minimum bend radius for that cable type. The cable tray must be supported so the entire structure and the anticipated loads are correctly and safely secured.

Cable tray supports should be located where practicable and accessible. Cable tray supports should always be placed at the connection point between two cable tray sections. Additional cable tray supports must be placed at quarter section intervals. Cable trays supports must always be placed within 24 in. from the cable tray ends.

Cable trays are supported using the following support devices:

▼ Trapeze

■ Individual rod suspension

▲ Support brackets

NOTE: Cable trays that are installed below raised floors can be supported by spacers.

Trapeze cable tray supports are designed to support a cable tray section from below (see Figure 14-3). A metal support member is installed below the cable tray. The horizontal support member is secured to the ceiling with two threaded rod supports. The threaded rods are secured to the building structure with clamps or other type of fasteners. Trapeze cable tray supports provide the best and most secure support for cable tray sections because two threaded rods are used for each horizontal support.

Individual rod suspension cable tray supports are designed to secure cables tray sections along the entire length of the cable tray (see Figure 14-4). A single threaded rod is connected to the building structure and attached to the cable tray with clamps, brackets,

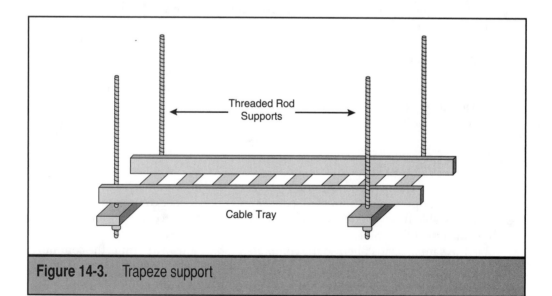

Figure 14-3. Trapeze support

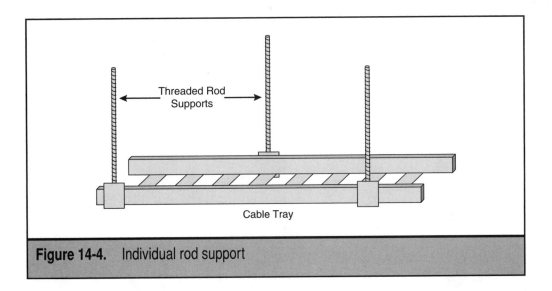

Threaded Rod
Supports

Cable Tray

Figure 14-4.   Individual rod support

or bolts. Multiple rods are attached to the cable tray at required support points and intervals to correctly support the cable tray. The individual rod suspension system is less expensive than a trapeze support system. This type of support system saves time and labor costs because only one suspension rod is installed at each support point along the cable tray path.

Support bracket cable tray supports provide support to a cable tray from below (see Figure 14-5). Support brackets must be properly secured and anchored to the building structure. Wood screws 1 1/4 in. in length can be used to secure the brackets to wood studs or other wood structures above the ceiling. Toggle bolts 2 in. long and 1/4 in. in diameter can also be used to secure the wall brackets to drywall building structures. Wall brackets that are not properly secured will not be able to support the weight of the ladder rack when heavy copper cables are installed in the TR.

Space Above Cable Trays

Cable trays should always be installed with sufficient space above the cable tray structure. This practice of allocating free space above the cable tray structure will permit cable to be added or taken out of the cable tray easily. Never install the cable tray so other building services will restrict access to the cable tray structure.

The ANSI/TIA/EIA-569-A standard specifies that all cable trays have a minimum of 300 mm (12 in.) of access headroom above the cable tray structure (see Figure 14-6). This free space must be maintained and cannot be used by additional cable trays or other building services such as air conditioning ducts. Cable trays that do not have sufficient clearance will be more difficult to pull cables in, and this factor will increase labor costs.

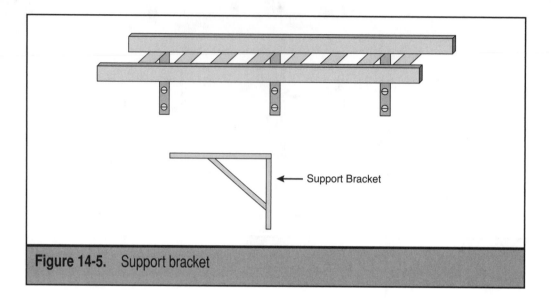

Figure 14-5.   Support bracket

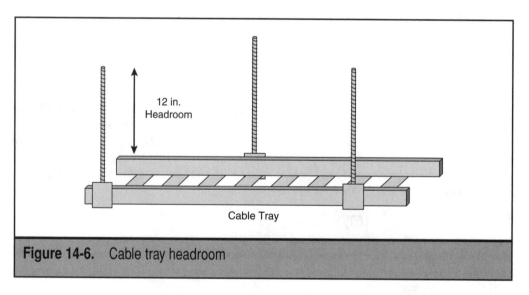

Figure 14-6.   Cable tray headroom

Checking the Inside of Cable Trays

The inside of cable trays must be free from sharp edges or protrusions. These can cut the cable jackets and damage the communication cable conductors during cable installation. Cable trays should always be inspected after the installation is complete for elements that can cause cable damage.

Cable tray supporting hardware, such as threaded rods or bolts, can have rough surfaces and can cause damage to the communication cables as they are being installed. Protect all rough, sharp, or abrasive surfaces with some type of smooth surface material.

CAUTION: Avoid overfilling cable trays. Communication cables that exceed the capacity of the cable tray are more likely to become damaged due to sharp, rough, or abrasive metal parts of the cable tray or the cable tray supports.

Firestopping Cable Trays

Cable trays that penetrate fire barriers must be properly firestopped. A fire-rated barrier is an opening in any wall, floor, or fire wall installed either above a ceiling or below a raised floor. Cable trays that penetrate any such fire-rated barrier must be sufficiently firestopped. The firestop methods used must conform to national, state, and local firestop requirements.

Grounding Cable Trays

Industry cabling standards and national codes require that metal cable trays be properly grounded (see Figure 14-7). Each section of a cable tray must be connected to an approved

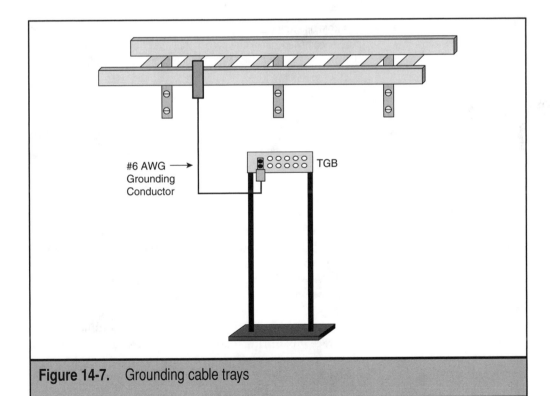

Figure 14-7. Grounding cable trays

ground. The NEC Article 645-15 requires that all noncurrent carrying metal parts of the information technology system be grounded in accordance with Article 250. The NEC Article 645-15 states:

"All exposed noncurrent carrying metal parts of an information technology system shall be grounded in accordance with Article 250 or shall be double insulated."

Cable Tray Accessories

Drop outs are common accessories used on cable trays at points where cables enter or exit the support structure. The drop outs are curved pieces of metal that provide a smooth transition for communication cables dropping down from a cable tray section. These devices provide a smooth transition and are used to prevent communication cables from violating the minimum bend radius. Drop outs are typically installed at the beginning and end of the cable tray. Drop outs may also be added along the cable tray paths and points where cables will be added. Drop outs are always installed when a cable tray connects to a communication rack.

Elbows, reducers, crossovers, and tees are components that are used to adapt the cable tray structure to accommodate direction changes, size changes, and height changes. The specific accessory components must be purchased from the same manufacturer of the cable tray. This practice will guarantee that the accessory components will fit and work correctly with the cable tray structure.

WARNING: Using accessories from different cable tray manufacturers may be hazardous and may weaken the cable tray structure. Noncompliant cable tray accessories may not fit correctly and these components may separate or fall off when the load of communication cables are added.

Wire Basket Raceways

Wire basket raceways, sometimes called rod stock raceways, are the newest type of cable-supporting structures (see Figure 14-8). These types of raceways are constructed of thin metal rods that are connected together to form a cable tray or raceway. The thin metal rods are typically constructed of high strength steel. The steel rods are approximately $5/16$ of an inch in diameter. Horizontal steel rods attached to one or more vertical rods construct a wire basket raceway.

Wire basket raceway is a generic term to describe many different types of cable trays or raceway products constructed of thin metal rods. These raceway products are popular because they are less expensive than traditional cable tray structures. These products are also lighter and easier to install. Wire basket raceway products can either be hand bent or bent with a simple tool to make the shape of the raceway conform to the unique contours of each commercial building.

Wire basket raceways have an open top configuration enabling communication cables simply to be dropped into the raceway during installation. Wire basket raceways are now being used for horizontal cable-supporting structures in many retrofit cabling projects where existing cable tray capacity has been exceeded or is nonexistent.

Figure 14-8.   Wire basket raceway

Wire basket raceways also provide excellent support for communication cables. Most wire basket raceway products have horizontal supports every 4 to 6 in. This supports copper communication cables without permitting any cable sag along the length of the raceway. This characteristic is very important to support and maintain the high performance of category 5e and category 6 cables.

Wire basket raceway products are very light and strong. These types of supporting structures are easy to support above a ceiling. Metal brackets or beam clamps are usually used to support raceway sections. These structures can be easily cut with standard cutting tools to fit the raceway into virtually any building space required.

There are many manufactures of this type of cable raceways. Some of the manufacturers include

▼   B-line

■   Cablofil

■   GS metals

▲   Snake tray

Each manufacturer produces products that would be classified as wire basket raceway. Each company has a unique design associated with their products that prevents them from being copied by other manufacturers.

Installation of Wire Basket Raceway

Wire basket type raceways are installed using the same basic methods as standard solid bars or steel tube cable trays. The primary difference is that this type of cable pathway is lighter and does not require the amount of supporting hardware compared to standard cable tray structures. In addition, the support intervals are less stringent than for heavier cable tray structures.

Wire basket raceways are supported using the following types of hardware:

▼ Support brackets

■ Support clips, hangers, or beam clamps

NOTE: Threaded rods can be used to support wire basket raceways. These devices may provide an attachment point to the building structure if a standard bracket or clamp cannot reach the building support. Threaded rods are not necessary for their strength because wire basket raceway is a light material.

Wire basket raceway products are usually supported with support brackets mounted to the building structure (see Figure 14-9). Wood screws, metal screws, concrete fasteners, or masonry fasteners can be used to install support brackets to the building. The support brackets are then attached to the wire basket raceway sections with connector clips.

Wire basket raceway can also be supported using either support clips, hangers, or beam clamps. Support clips, hangers, or beam clamps can be attached to any portion of the building structure, such as structural beams, to support the wire basket raceway.

The ANSI/TIA/EIA-569-A standard requires wire basket raceway products to be supported.

Space Above Wire Basket Raceways

Wire basket raceways should always be installed with sufficient space above the cable tray structure. This practice of allocating free space above the cable tray structure will permit cables to be added or taken out of the cable trays easily. Never install the cable tray so other building services will restrict access to the cable tray structure.

The ANSI/TIA/EIA-569-A standard specifies that all wire basket raceways must have a minimum of 300 mm (12 in.) of access headroom above the raceway structure. This free space must be maintained and cannot be used by additional raceways, cable trays, or other building services such as air conditioning ducts. Raceways that do not have sufficient clearance will be more difficult to pull cables in, and this factor will increase labor costs.

Figure 14-9.   Wire basket raceway support

Checking the Inside of Wire Basket Raceways

The inside surface of wire basket raceways must be free from sharp edges or protrusions. These can cut the cable jackets and damage the communication cable conductors during cable installation. Wire basket raceways should always be inspected after the installation is complete for elements that can cause cable damage. Carefully inspect wire rods that were cut during the installation of the raceway. Sharp edges should be filed smooth or covered with tape or another type of smooth surface.

CAUTION: Avoid overfilling wire basket raceways. Communication cables that exceed the capacity of the wire basket raceway are more likely to become damaged due to sharp, rough, or abrasive metal parts of the wire basket raceway or the wire basket raceway supports.

Firestopping Wire Basket Raceways

Wire basket raceways that penetrate fire barriers must be properly firestopped. A fire-rated barrier is an opening in any wall, floor, or fire wall installed either above a ceiling or below a raised floor. Wire basket raceways that penetrate any such fire-rated barrier must be sufficiently firestopped. The firestop methods used must conform to national, state, and local firestop requirements.

Grounding Wire Basket Raceways

Industry cabling standards and national codes require that metal wire basket raceways be properly grounded. Each section of a cable tray must be connected to an approved ground. The NEC Article 645-15 requires that all noncurrent carrying metal parts of the information technology system be grounded in accordance with Article 250. The NEC Article 645-15 states:

"All exposed noncurrent carrying metal parts of an information technology system shall be grounded in accordance with Article 250 or shall be double insulated."

Wire Basket Raceways Accessories

The accessories for a wire basket raceway are the same as those for a cable tray support structure. Typical raceway accessories include the following:

▼ Elbows

■ Reducers

■ Crossovers

■ Tees

▲ Drop outs

Elbows, reducers, crossovers, and tees are components that are used to adapt the wire basket raceway structure to accommodate direction changes, size changes, and height changes. The specific accessory components must be purchased from the same manufacturer of the wire basket raceway. This practice will guarantee that the accessory components will fit and work correctly with the raceway structure.

Drop outs are common accessories used on wire basket raceways at points where cables enter or exit the support structure. The drop outs are curved pieces of metal that provide a smooth transition for communication cables dropping down from a raceway section. These devices are used to prevent communication cables from violating the minimum bend radius. Drop outs are typically installed at the beginning and end of the wire basket raceway. Drop outs may also be added along the raceway paths and points where cables will be added. Drop outs are always installed when a cable tray connects to a communication rack.

WARNING: Using accessories from different wire basket raceway manufacturers may be hazardous and may weaken the raceway structure. Noncompliant wire basket raceway accessories may not fit correctly, and these components may separate or fall off when the load of communication cables is added.

Conduits

Conduits are used for both horizontal and backbone cable pathways in commercial buildings (see Figure 14-10). Conduits are commonly installed for cable pathways between buildings or between closets for backbone cables. Conduits are also used for horizontal pathways between two points in a building.

The major types of conduits that are installed in commercial buildings include the following:

▼ Electrical Metallic Tubing (EMT)

■ Intermediate Metallic Conduit (IMC)

▲ Galvanized Rigid Conduit (GRC)

A Polyvinyl chloride (PVC) conduit is a nonmetallic conduit and should not be used in commercial buildings. PVC conduits will emit toxic smoke and gases when exposed to heat or flames. The only allowed application for PVC conduit is under concrete slabs of a building when building codes permit this type of conduit to be installed.

Figure 14-10. Conduit

Electrical Metallic Tubing (EMT)

Electrical Metallic Tubing (EMT) is a conduit with thin walls. EMT is a type of conduit that is used extensively as a cable-supporting structure for both electrical wiring and communication cables.

Standard EMT sections are 3 m (10 ft.) in length. EMT is available in sizes ranging from $1/2$ to 4 in. (trade size 4). The ends of EMT are not threaded. Couplings are used to connect two sections of EMT together.

The major advantages of EMT over other types of conduits are that EMT is a less expensive type of conduit. The thin walls of EMT also mean that this type of conduit weighs less and is easier to install than other types of conduits. EMT is used to provide physical protection for a cable or wire inside of a building where severe destructive forces are not expected.

Intermediate Metallic Conduit (IMC)

Intermediate Metallic Conduit (IMC) is a heavier conduit than EMT. The walls of IMC conduit are thicker than EMT, making this type of conduit stronger. IMC is also a type of conduit that is used extensively as a cable-supporting structure for both electrical wiring and communication cables.

Standard IMC sections are 3 m (10 ft.) in length. IMC is available in sizes ranging from $1/2$ to 6 in. (trade size 6). The ends of EMT are factory threaded. Screw-on couplings are used to connect two sections of IMC together.

The major advantages of IMC over other types of conduits are that IMC is thicker and therefore stronger than EMT conduits. This type of conduit will provide greater protection against mechanical damage than EMT. In addition, the threaded ends mean that couplings are tighter and attached more securely.

The disadvantages of IMC are that this conduit is thicker and heavier than EMT. This means that this type of conduit costs more to install than EMT. Another disadvantage is that screw-on couplings are more expensive.

Galvanized Rigid Conduit (GRC)

Galvanized Rigid Conduit (GRC) is a heavier conduit than IMC. The walls of GRC are thicker than IMC, making this type of conduit the strongest. GRC is also a type of conduit that is used extensively as a cable-supporting structure for both electrical wiring and communication cables.

Standard GRC sections are 3 m (10 ft.) in length. GRC is available in sizes ranging from $1/2$ to 6 in. (trade size 6). The ends of GRC are factory threaded just like IMC. Straight tapped screw-on couplings are used to connect two sections of GRC together.

The major advantages of GRC over other types of conduit are that GRC is thicker and therefore stronger than both IMC and EMT conduits. This type of conduit will provide greater protection against mechanical damage than either IMC or EMT. In addition, the threaded ends mean that couplings are tighter and attached securely.

The disadvantages of GRC are that this conduit is thicker and heavier than IMC. This means that this type of conduit costs as must as 30 percent more to install than IMC for communication cable pathways. Another disadvantage is that screw-on couplings are more expensive than the couplings used for EMT conduits.

Unacceptable Conduit

Industry cabling standards recommend against installing flexible metallic conduits, sometimes called flex conduits or just flex, for horizontal pathways and supporting structures. Flexible conduits tend to shift and move substantially when communication cables are being installed. In addition, a flexible conduit is difficult to fish through in order to install a pull string or another cable.

A flexible conduit is usually installed in commercial buildings without being properly secured to the building structure. This causes the conduit sections to move, making this type of conduit difficult to locate if it moves behind or inside a wall. Flexible conduits also tend to have sharp edges that can cut or damage the cable jackets and may damage the cable conductors.

Conduit Runs

Conduits should be installed in a commercial building to run in the most direct route possible between termination points. The entire conduit run should contain a maximum of two 90-degree bends. The maximum length of the entire conduit run must be 90 m (295 ft.) or less between termination points. All conduits installed in a commercial building must be bonded to ground. Conduits that run between two TRs should be bonded in each TR. Conduits that run from a work area to a TR should be bonded in the TR only.

The ANSI/TIA/EIA-569-A standard recommends installing a pull box for the following conduit runs:

▼   Conduit length is greater than 30 m (100 ft.)

■   Conduit run has more than two 90-degree bends

▲   Conduit run has a reverse U bend

Conduit Supports

Conduit runs that are installed above a drop ceiling must be properly supported with conduit hangers or other supporting devices. Conduit support hardware is required to keep conduits secure and prevent conduit movements when communication cables are installed. Conduit support hardware will keep conduits above ceiling tiles and prevent the conduit from sagging. The supporting hardware used to support conduits include the following devices:

▼   Pipe hangers

■   Trapeze

▲   One-piece conduit hanger

A conduit pipe hanger is a pear shaped bracket that is attached to the end of a threaded rod. The threaded rod is secured to the building structure using the appropriate anchoring components. Concrete anchors can secure the threaded rod to a concrete structure, and beam clamps can secure the threaded rod to building support beams. The opposite end of the threaded rod is attached to the pipe hanger with a nut and locking washers.

Conduit pipe hangers should be installed at the end of the conduit in the ceiling space. Additional pipe hangers should be placed at conduit joints. Pipe hangers should be installed between supported joint locations at 1.2 m (4.0 ft.) intervals along the entire conduit length.

A trapeze can also be used to support conduit runs. Trapeze conduit supports are designed to support a conduit using a metal support member that is attached to the building structure. The horizontal support member is secured to the ceiling with two threaded rod supports. The threaded rods are secured to the building structure with clamps or other types of fasteners. Trapeze conduit supports are usually used to support multiple conduit runs.

A one-piece conduit hanger is another device that can be used to support a conduit above a ceiling. The one-piece conduit hanger includes a bolt as part of the hanger hardware. The one-piece conduit hanger is attached to the building structure using a clamp or specialized hanger bracket. The one-piece conduit hanger is used when the conduit is close to the building support members.

The NEC Article 330-11(a) prohibits using support wires that do not provide secure support as the sole supporting mechanisms for conduits. It also forbids using ceiling support wires to support conduits above the ceiling. NEC Article 330-11(a) states:

"Raceways, cable assemblies, boxes, cabinets, and fittings shall be securely fastened in place. Support wires that do not provide secure support shall not be permitted as the sole support. Support wires and associated fittings that provide secure support and that are installed in addition to the ceiling grid support wires, shall be permitted as the sole support. Where independent support wires are used, they shall be secured at both ends. Cable and raceways shall not be supported by ceiling grids."

Conduit Bends

Conduit runs that must be installed around obstacles or corners must be bent. Conduit sections can be bent using specialized tools and equipment. Hand conduit benders can be used to bend conduits: 16 mm (0.5 in.) trade size, 21 mm (0.75 in.) trade size, and 27 mm (1.0 in.) trade size. Bending either 35 mm (1.25 in.) trade size and 41 mm (1.5 in.) trade size conduits is difficult with a hand bender. These larger conduits are better being bent with a conduit bending machine.

Conduits bends must never exceed the minimum bend radius defined by industry cabling standards. Conduit bends should always be long, sweeping bends that never violate the minimum bend radius specifications. The conduit minimum bend radius specifications are shown in Table 14-1.

Conduit Internal Diameter	Minimum Bend Radius
50 mm (2.0 in.) or less	6 times the internal conduit diameter
More than 50 mm (2.0 in.)	10 times the internal conduit diameter

Table 14-1. Conduit Bend Radius Specifications

Conduit Elbows

Conduit elbows are factory manufactured conduit bend sections. Conduit elbows are pre-bent conduit sections. These components are available in standard conduit bend angles including: 11.25 degree, 15 degree, 22.5 degree, 30 degree, 45 degree, and 90 degree. In addition, custom elbows with different angles can be ordered from most distributors.

Conduit elbows are available for all conduit trade sizes. Conduit elbows are usually manufactured with standard leg lengths of both sides of the elbow. Custom conduit elbow leg lengths can be ordered. In addition, elbows with long sweeping bends can also be custom ordered from most distributors.

Conduit Fill Ratio

The ANSI/TIA/EIA-569-A standard provides guidelines for maximum fill for conduits supporting communication cables. The maximum fill for a conduit is based on the internal conduit size and the outside diameter of the cables to be installed in the conduit. The ANSI/TIA/EIA-569-A standards permit the following conduit fill percentages:

▼ One cable = 53 percent of the conduit's internal diameter

■ Two cables = 31 percent of the conduit's internal diameter

▲ Three or more cables = 40 percent of the conduit's internal diameter

The total capacity of a conduit is reduced by 15 percent for each 90-degree bend in the conduit run. Two 90-degree conduit bends would reduce the conduit capacity by 30 percent.

Conduit Terminations

Conduits that are terminated in TRs may require additional supports to prevent the conduits from moving. Conduits that enter a TR from overhead must be attached to the top of the plywood backboard using channel stock hardware and conduit brackets. Conduits that enter the TR from below the floor typically do not require additional supports. The design for the TR will usually indicate the type of conduit supports that must be installed and the exact location for mounting the supports in the TR.

Conduit brackets should be constructed of a metallic material. These devices should provide electrical continuity between the conduit, channel stock, and conduit brackets. This will provide a bonding connection between the conduit-supporting hardware and the conduits. The conduits should be bonded to either the TMGB or the TGB with a #6 AWG bonding conductor. A grounding bushing should be used to attach the bonding conductor to one of the conduits attached to the channel stock support.

Backbone conduits that terminate in the TR should be terminated in a bushing. The bushing should extend into the TR 25 to 75 mm (1 to 3 in.) above the finished floor or below the finished ceiling.

Backbone conduits that support large pair count copper backbone cables must be secured in the TR. Industry standards require that these conduits be secured in a manner that prevents the conduits from moving while communication cables are being installed or after communication cables are installed. Cross brace hardware should be installed in the TR to secure the conduits and prevent movements.

The ends of all conduits must be reamed to prevent sharp edges and rough metal burrs from damaging communication cable jackets or the cable conductors. A chase nipple should be installed on the end of the conduit to reduce damage to the cable sheath. A *chase nipple* is a plastic ring or other type of insert placed into the conduit coupling or connector. The plastic ring prevents the cable jackets from making contact with the sharp threads of the conduit end or conduit fitting.

After a conduit is installed, the conduit must be left

▼   Reamed and fitted with the correct conduit bushings

■   Labeled for identification

■   Capped to prevent debris from blocking the conduit

▲   With a pull string installed

CABLE-SUPPORTING HARDWARE

The communication cabling industry is full of innovation. As a result, new products are constantly being developed to support communication cables. Many of the products are small support devices.

Small support cable-supporting devices are usually installed to support either a single communication cable or a small group of cables. They are normally installed in buildings that have no horizontal pathways or where the horizontal pathways are full.

The ANSI/TIA/EIA-569-A standard requires that all communication cables installed in an open ceiling environment must be supported. The standard states:

"Where zone conduit or cable tray is not available in a suspended ceiling space and where telecommunications cables are allowed to be placed in the ceiling, adequate open top cable supports, located on 1,220 to 1,525 mm (48 to 60 in.) centers, shall be provided. Where larger quantities of cables (50 to 75 cables) are bunched together in the ceiling at a congested area, such as close to the TR, special supports shall be designed and installed to carry the additional weight."

The cabling industry includes many cable-support products that are manufactured to provide support for communication cables. The most common types of cable-supporting devices include the following:

▼   J hooks

■   Bridle rings

■   Cable clip

▲   Cable straps

J Hook Support Devices

J hook is a generic term for a cable-supporting hardware that is shaped like the letter J. A J hook is a prefabricated cable-supporting device that is attached to a building wall or support beam. Actual hook or flat pieces of metal that are shaped like the letter J are referred to as J hooks. The design of a J hook permits communication cables to be installed in the J hook hardware easily. The J hook devices are placed at 1.2 to 1.5 m (4 to 5 ft.) intervals along the cable run or at required support points.

J hook devices that are flat on the bottom are recommended for supporting copper communication cables. Some J hook devices are manufactured out of round metallic rods. These devices should not be used to support copper communication cables. Round rod supports will bend and cause the cables on the bottom of the group being supported by the J hook to become bent. This may cause signaling problems on the copper communication cables.

Bridle Rings

Bridle rings are cable-supporting devices that have an open ring at the end of the support device. Bridle rings are screwed into wood support beams or attached to building steel beams with a clip. Bridle rings are convenient for supporting a single cable or a small group of five to ten cables.

Cable Clips

Cable clips are a common type of cable-supporting component that is sold by many different types of manufacturers. Cable clips are small, curved metal clips that are designed to attach to building beams or to suspension wires by snapping onto these support structures. These clips are usually designed to support a single communication cable.

Cable Straps

Cable straps are a relatively new type of cable-supporting device. Cable straps are wide straps made of plastic. These cable-supporting devices wrap around a group of cables to support them. The both ends of the cable strap then must be attached to a J hook, bracket, or some other type of cable-supporting device.

The benefit of using a cable strap is that this device can be completely removed from the communication cables. If a single cable needs to be removed or added to the cable bundle, the strap can be removed and then reattached to the cable group. Cable straps reduce the time and labor associated with cable maintenance.

CHAPTER SUMMARY

Cable-supporting structures are the hardware elements required to support communication cables. Cable-supporting structures are installed solely for the purpose of supporting communication cables. They prevent cables from lying on drop ceiling tiles and from resting on electrical wires and conduits. Cable-supporting hardware also serves the function of keeping communication cables organized.

Cable-supporting hardware is most commonly installed in the horizontal subsystem. The reason is that the exact configuration of each building floor is usually unknown when a building is under construction. There are many different types of cable-supporting structures. Some of the most common include cable trays, wire basket raceways, conduits, J hooks, or cable hangers, surface mount raceways, and ladder racks.

Cable trays are the most common type of cable-supporting structures installed in commercial buildings. Cable trays are pathways that are installed either above a ceiling or below a raised floor in a commercial building. The most common types of cable trays include ladder type, ventilated trough, solid trough, and spine type.

Each horizontal cable pathway must be sized to provide 650 sq. mm (1 sq. in.) of cross-sectional area for each work area to accommodate the three horizontal cables. All horizontal cable trays must be designed to accommodate all planned horizontal cables. In addition, the cable tray must be designed to support future growth of new cables added to the building. Under no circumstances should the overall fill ratio of the cable tray exceed 50 percent of the cable tray's maximum capacity.

Cable trays must be installed so the completed cable pathway permits the communication cables to be installed according to industry cabling specifications. Cable tray supports should always be placed at the connection point between two cable tray sections. Additional cable tray supports must be placed at quarter section intervals. Cable tray supports must always be placed within 24 in. from the cable tray ends. Cable trays are supported using trapeze, individual rod suspension, and support brackets.

Cable trays should always be installed with sufficient space above the cable tray structure. This practice of allocating free space above the cable tray structure will permit cables to be added or taken out of the cable tray easily. Never install the cable tray so other building services will restrict access to the cable tray structure. The ANSI/TIA/EIA-569-A standard specifies that all cable trays must have a minimum of 300 mm (12 in.) of access headroom above the cable tray structure. This free space must be maintained and cannot be used by additional cable trays or other building services such as air conditioning ducts.

The inside of cable trays must be free from sharp edges or protrusions. Cable trays should always be inspected after the installation is complete for elements that can cause cable damage. Protect all rough, sharp, or abrasive surfaces with some type of smooth surface material.

Cable trays that penetrate fire barriers must be properly firestopped. A fire-rated barrier is an opening in any wall, floor, or fire wall installed either above a ceiling or below a raised floor. The firestop methods used must conform to national, state, and local firestop requirements.

Industry cabling standards and national codes require that metal cable trays be properly grounded. Each section of a cable tray must be connected to an approved ground. The NEC Article 645-15 requires that all noncurrent carrying metal parts of the information technology system be grounded in accordance with Article 250 of the NEC.

Drop outs are common accessories used on cable trays at points where cables enter or exit the support structure. These devices provide a smooth transition and are used to prevent communication cables from violating the minimum bend radius. Drop outs are typically installed at the beginning and end of the cable tray. Drop outs are always installed when a cable tray connects to a communication rack.

Elbows, reducers, crossovers, and tees are the components that are used to adapt the cable tray structure to accommodate direction changes, size changes, and height changes. The specific accessory components must be purchased from the same manufacturer of the cable tray.

Wire basket raceways, sometimes called rod stock raceways, are the newest type of cable-supporting structures. These types of raceways are constructed of thin metal rods that are connected together to form a cable tray or raceway. The thin metal rods are typically constructed of high strength steel. Wire basket raceway is a generic term to describe many different types of cable tray or raceway products constructed of thin metal rods. These raceway products are popular because they are less expensive than traditional cable tray structures. These products are also lighter and easier to install. Wire basket raceways that penetrate fire barriers must be properly firestopped.

Conduits are used for both horizontal and backbone cable pathways in commercial buildings. Conduits are commonly installed for cable pathways between buildings or between closets for backbone cables. Conduits are also used for horizontal pathways between two points in a building. The major types of conduits that are installed in commercial buildings are electrical metallic tubing (EMT), intermediate metallic conduit (IMC), and galvanized rigid conduit (GRC). PVC conduit is a nonmetallic conduit and should not be used in commercial buildings. PVC conduits will emit toxic smoke and gases when exposed to heat or flames. The only allowed application for PVC conduits is under concrete slabs of a building with building codes permitting this type of conduit to be installed.

Industry cabling standards recommend against installing flexible metallic conduits, sometimes called flex conduits or just flex, for horizontal pathways and supporting structures. Flexible conduits tend to shift and move substantially when communication cables are being installed. In addition, a flexible conduit is difficult to fish through in order to install a pull string or another cable.

Conduit bends must never exceed the minimum bend radius defined by industry cabling standards. Conduit bends should always be long, sweeping bends that never violate the minimum bend radius specifications. The conduit minimum bend radius specifications are 6 times the internal conduit diameter for conduits that are 50 mm (2 in.) or less and 10 times the internal conduit diameter for conduits that are greater than 50 mm (2 in.).

The ANSI/TIA/EIA-569-A standard provides guidelines for maximum fill for conduits supporting communication cables. The maximum fill for a conduit is based on the internal conduit size and the outside diameter of the cables to be installed in the conduit. The ANSI/TIA/EIA-569-A standards permit a 53 percent fill of the conduits internal diameter when one cable is installed, 31 percent fill of the conduits internal diameter for two cables, and a 40 percent fill of the conduits internal diameter for three or more cables. The total capacity of a conduit is reduced by 15 percent for each 90-degree bend in the conduit run.

Small support cable-supporting devices are usually installed to support either a single communication cable or a small group of cables. They are normally installed in buildings that have no horizontal pathways or where the horizontal pathways are full. The most common types of cable-supporting devices are J hooks, bridle rings, cable clips, and cable straps.

CHAPTER 15

Firestopping

Firestopping is a critical part of cable installation projects. Proper firestopping procedures and practices are critical for saving lives in the event of a fire. Flames and toxic smoke can cause significant damage to property in a very short amount of time. Once a fire has started in a building, it can spread in a short amount of time to other parts of the building through holes in the walls and floors.

The process of installing communication cables often requires that holes are cut into walls and floors. *Firestopping* is the practice of closing all holes created during the cable installation project.

This chapter will describe the process of installing qualified firestop systems in buildings.

FIRE PROTECTION

Fire protection is the primary concern for commercial buildings. The NEC is a document written and updated by the National Fire Protection Association (NFPA).

A comprehensive fire protection program must include

▼   Fire prevention activities and practices

■   Fire detection systems

■   Fire containment systems and devices

▲   Fire suppression systems

FIRESTOPPING

Fire prevention and safety are an essential part of a cable installer's job. Cable installation projects usually require creating holes in walls and fire-rated barriers for cable pathways. The holes in fire-rated barriers must always be resealed to reestablish the original fire rating of the barrier. The most common way that smoke and fire spread is through holes that are not resealed.

Firestopping is the process of installing qualified firestop materials in all penetrations created during the installation of communication cables. A firestop system will reestablish the original fire rating of the penetrated barrier. The cable installer is the person responsible for using both approved firestopping methods and approved materials. In addition, the cable installer must firestop any hole created by the removal of cable or cable-supporting structures during the installation project.

Firestopping holes and penetrations in commercial buildings is necessary for the following reasons:

▼   Firestopping is a practice that saves lives every year.

■   Firestopping systems will protect a commercial building from the spread of flames and smoke.

■ Firestopped holes and penetrations will provide building occupants with more time to escape a building in the event of a fire.

▲ Proper firestopping practices will limit liabilities from fire damage and fire-related injuries.

Most individuals that die in building fires die from toxic smoke and gases. Flames are not usually the cause of most fire-related deaths in buildings. Firestop systems must be installed to prevent toxic smoke and gases from traveling through building penetrations.

Performing Firestopping in a Building

Firestopping must be performed in a building when a penetration is created during the installation of the following items for a cable installation project (see Figure 15-1):

▼ Communication cables

■ Cable trays

■ Conduits

Figure 15-1.   Firestopping example

■ Wire ways

▲ Innerducts

Firestopping must be performed any time communication cables are installed for

▼ New construction projects

■ Renovation projects

▲ Retrofit projects

The codes that address the proper installation of firestop systems are different for each country. The specific code requirements are also different depending on what state or city the building is located. Each country usually has its own national codes. Each state may have different or more stringent codes than the national codes. Finally, each local municipality may have different and more stringent codes than either national or state codes.

The cable installer is responsible for learning the exact codes that apply to the country, state, and city for the building is located. Local building inspectors are responsible for checking buildings for proper firestops. All buildings that are not in compliance will not be issued a certificate of occupancy. This means that no one is allowed to work in the building until the problem is corrected. Building inspectors can also issue a corrective order and shut a building down if the problem is not corrected in the specified time limit.

PENETRATIONS

Firestop systems are designed to fill penetrations in building floors and walls. There are two classifications of penetrations:

▼ Through penetrations

▲ Membrane penetrations

A *through penetration* is a hole that passes completely through a fire-rated barrier. A through penetration can be a hole cut into a concrete floor to install a conduit or a hole cut through a fire-rated wall. Through penetrations are usually required to install conduits or cables that must pass through a solid fire barrier.

A *membrane penetration* is a partial penetration in a wall or a single surface fire barrier penetration. A hole in one side of a wall to install a telecommunications outlet would constitute a membrane penetration.

Firestopping codes and standards require that both through and membrane penetrations in any fire-rated floor, wall, or fire barrier be sealed with a qualified firestop product. The firestop product must be tested by an independent third-party lab to meet the qualified requirement. In addition, all firestop products must be installed exactly as described in the manufacturer's instructions. Fire and building codes prohibit the substitution of any part of the firestop assembly. The cable installer can be held legally and financially liable for using nonqualified or unlisted firestop products in a commercial building.

FIRESTOPPING SYSTEMS

Firestop systems are made up of a combination of products to reestablish the original rating of a penetrated fire barrier. Firestop systems may be made of a single material or a combination of materials that provide a balance of

▼   Heat resistance

■   Adequate sealing at extreme temperatures

■   Durability to stay in place and stay intact during a fire

▲   Structural integrity to survive the erosive effects of a high-powered hose stream

The exact firestop material that must be used for a cable installation project will be mandated by the following:

▼   Local building and fire codes

■   Installation efficiency

■   Long-term maintenance

▲   Future changes to the cabling system

Mechanical versus Nonmechanical Firestop Systems

Firestop systems are divided into two categories:

▼   Mechanical firestop systems

▲   Nonmechanical firestop systems

Mechanical firestop systems consist of fire system components that are designed to fit into standard openings in fire barriers.

Nonmechanical firestop systems consist of fire system components that are designed to fit into nonstandard openings in fire barriers. The choice of exactly what type of firestop system to use for an installation will depend on the penetrations that must be firestopped for the cable installation project.

FIRESTOP PRODUCTS

Firestop products have unique properties that make these materials desirable in the event of a fire. The materials used for a firestop system will have one of the following characteristics:

▼   Endothermic

■   Intumescent

▲   Ablative

Endothermic firestop products are designed to absorb heat. These products are used when the firestop is used with a fire-rated barrier and flammable materials are located on the opposite side of the barrier.

Intumescent firestop products are designed to swell or become enlarged due to the influence of heat. These firestop products are used if a cable or conduit burns away during a fire and leaves a hole in the firestop. An intumescent firestop will block the hole created by the cable or conduit melting away.

Ablative firestop products are designed to develop a hard char, which helps this type of product resist erosion from the volatile effects of flames and super-heated gases. Ablative firestops are usefully where cables are continually added to a building. These firestop systems will remain pliable until heat is present. The hard char will prevent fire, smoke, and gases from passing through the firestop.

FIRESTOPPING STANDARDS

Firestop materials used in a firestop system must be tested to pass the following standards:

▼   ASTM E814

▲   UL 1479

The firestop products used in a firestop system must be tested and approved for the intended purpose. The testing and approval comes from a certified and independent laboratory. These laboratories perform tests that conform to the American Society of Testing Material (ASTM) standards. A few of the laboratories that are certified to perform firestop testing include

▼   Factory Mutual Systems (FM)

■   Omega Point Laboratory (OPL)

■   Underwriters Laboratories (UL)

▲   Inchcape Warnock Hersey

FIRESTOPPING TESTING

All firestop systems must be completely and thoroughly tested using the same testing methods and test criteria. Through penetration firestop systems are tested under positive pressure. The testings are made for specific time and temperature intervals. This process enables each firestop system to be assessed under the same controlled conditions to evaluate its performance.

The steps for conducting a test of a firestopping system include the following:

1. Install the firestop system into a test fire barrier.
2. Allow sufficient time for the product to dry and setup properly.
3. Expose the firestop system to control fire exposures. These exposures are conducted as specific temperatures and for a specific time duration.
4. After the time duration, the firestop is subjected to a direct hose stream.

All firestop systems must be subjected to the following fire exposures for time and temperature:

▼ One hour at 977 C° (1,700 F°)

■ Two hours at 1,010 C° (1,850 F°)

■ Three hours at 1,052 C° (1,935 F°)

▲ Four hours at 1,093 C° (2,000 F°)

FIRESTOP RATING CLASSIFICATIONS

The two firestop rating classifications of F and T for through penetration firestop systems used in the United States are defined in the ASTM E814 standard. A third fire rating classification of L for through penetration firestop systems used in the United States is defined in the UL 1479 standard.

The three ratings for through penetration firestop systems used in the United States include the following:

▼ F rating

■ T rating

▲ L rating

The F rating is a required rating for all through penetration firestop systems. The F rating evaluates if the firestop system can withstand the direct fire exposure for the testing period without permitting flames to pass through the firestop barrier. This rating also evaluates if a fire occurs on the opposite side of the barrier from heat transmission through the firestop. Finally, this rating evaluates if an opening occurs in the firestop due to the hose stream. This rating looks for the projection of water beyond the exposed side of the firestop.

The T rating is a required rating for all through penetration firestop systems. The T rating evaluates if the firestop system can limit the temperature rise of the firestop system during the testing period. This rating requires that the temperature on any unexposed surface increase no more than 180 C° (325 F°) above the ambient test temperature.

The L rating is an optional part of the UL 1479 standard and not included in the ASTM E814 standard. This rating measures the firestop system's ability to effectively stop smoke and gases from passing through the barrier. The L rating tests are conducted at 204 C° (400 F°).

MECHANICAL FIRESTOP SYSTEMS

Mechanical firestop systems consist of premanufactured products and devices that are preshaped and sized to fit into or around standard penetrations. Mechanical firestop systems are manufactured to fit around standard sizes of

▼ Conduits

■ Cables

■ Core holes

▲ Other penetrations commonly found in commercial buildings

Mechanical firestop systems are designed to fit and expand into standard building openings. The mechanical firestop is secured and held into place by tension. Cables and conduits are secured with elastomeric materials to provide a tight seal.

NONMECHANICAL FIRESTOP SYSTEMS

Nonmechanical firestop systems are designed to fit and expand into nonstandard building openings. These firestop systems are required when a penetration is irregularly shaped or is an irregular size. Nonmechanical firestop material would include the following:

▼ Firestop putties

■ Firestop caulks

■ Firestop silicone foam

▲ Other pliable firestop materials

Nonmechanical firestop materials are soft and pliable. They can easily be shaped to cover large and irregularly shaped openings in a fire barrier. These materials tend to either harden or swell under the influence of heat.

Firestop Putties

Firestop putties are one of the most common types of nonmechanical firestop material. Firestop putty has a long life and is very easy to install. Firestop putties typically provide intumescent properties that will cause these products to swell around the installed communication cables. Many firestop putties sold today also provide endothermic properties. The ability to absorb heat gives these materials the required T rating.

Firetop putties tends to remain permanently soft and pliable until exposed to heat. They allow reentry into a firestopped cable pathway for adding new cables or removing old cables. Firestop putties are usually installed in conjunction with ceramic fiber or rock wool fill materials. These characteristics make firestop putties useful for firestopping communication cables and supporting structures.

Firestop Caulks

Firestop caulks are another very common type of nonmechanical firestop material used for firestopping communication cables and supporting structures. Firestop caulks are preferred for very large openings that must be firestopped. This firestop material is dispensed from large pails or smaller caulking tubes.

Firestop caulks are available in the following compositions:

- Latex compositions
- Water-based compositions
- Solvent-based compositions

Caulks have the advantages of being a self leveling material and a material that tends to stick to various surfaces easily. These characteristics make this type of firestop material easy to install.

Firestop Silicone Foam

Firestop silicone foam is another type of firestop material that is capable of easily sealing large openings in fire-rated barriers. Firestop silicone foam expands when exposed to heat to create a cellular structure that blocks fire, flames, and smoke.

CAUTION: Silicone foams must only be used in openings that are structurally sound. The openings must be capable of withstanding the expansive forces of the silicone foam.

FIRESTOPPING THROUGH PENETRATIONS

Firestopping a through penetration requires firestopping both sides of the penetrated fire barrier. The firestop material, such as a putty or caulk, is installed on one side of the barrier. A certified fill material is placed inside the penetration to fill the space between the two sides of the barrier. The opposite side of the fire-rated barrier is sealed.

Steps for Firestopping a Conduit Through Penetration

The steps for installing a firestop putty seal in a conduit are as follows:

1. Tear off a small portion of putty. The amount must be sufficient to completely cover the conduit opening.

2. Use the putty to build a bottom layer in the conduit opening.

3. Fill in the conduit opening with some type of fire retardant ceramic fiber or other fill material. Place enough fiber material in the conduit opening to fill the space, stopping before reaching the upper rim.

4. Use more putty to build a lid on the top of the conduit opening (follow the manufacturer's instructions for lid thickness).

CAUTION: Always follow the manufacturer's instructions for the bottom thickness.

FIRESTOPPING MEMBRANE PENETRATIONS

Membrane penetrations are usually easier to seal than through penetrations. The penetration on one side of the wall must be firestopped. This usually involves placing either firestop putty or caulk over the penetration. In addition, membrane penetrations are usually small in size.

Steps for Firestopping an Outlet Box Membrane Penetration

The firestopping steps for sealing an outlet box are as follows:

1. Take the firestop putty and create a flat pad approximately 13 mm ($^{1}/_{2}$ in.) thick, approximately 100 mm (4 in.) wide and approximately 150 mm (6 in.) long. Place the first firestop putty pad so the edges are touching the wall stud and covering half of the outlet box. The putty pad should be pressed on the edges to seal the outlet box.

2. Take a second firestop putty pad and place it so the pad touches the wall stud and covers the other side of the outlet box. The two putty pads should overlap in the middle of the outlet box.

NOTE: If the two putty pads do not overlap, a third putty pad should be placed so it covers the outlet box and overlaps the other two pads.

3. Once all the firestop putty pads are in place, press the seams of the firestop putty pads together. This will join the pads and create an effective firestop barrier.

CHAPTER SUMMARY

Firestopping is a critical part of cable installation projects. Proper firestopping procedures and practices are critical for saving lives in the event of a fire. Flames and toxic smoke can cause significant damage to property in a very short amount of time. Fire protection is the primary concern for the commercial buildings.

Cable installation projects usually require creating holes in walls and fire-rated barriers for cable pathways. The holes in fire-rated barriers must always be resealed to reestablish the original fire rating of the barrier. Firestopping is the process of installing qualified firestop materials in all penetrations created during the installation of communication cables. A firestop system will reestablish the original fire rating of the penetrated barrier.

The cable installer is the person responsible for using both approved firestopping methods and approved materials. In addition, the cable installer must firestop any hole created by the removal of cables or cable-supporting structures during the installation project. Firestop systems must be installed to prevent toxic smoke and gases from traveling through building penetrations.

Firestopping must be performed in a building when a penetration is created during the installation of communication cables, cable trays, conduits, wire ways, and innerducts. Firestopping must be performed any time communication cables are installed for new construction projects, renovation projects, and retrofit projects.

The codes that address the proper installation of firestop systems are different for each country. The specific code requirements are also different depending on where in the state or city the building is located. The cable installer is responsible for learning the exact codes that apply to the country, state, and city where the building is located. Local building inspectors are responsible for checking buildings for proper firestops.

Firestop systems are designed to fill penetrations in building floors and walls. A through penetration is a hole that passes completely through a fire-rated barrier. A membrane penetration is a partial penetration in a wall or a single surface fire barrier penetration. Firestopping codes and standards require that both through and membrane penetrations in any fire-rated floor, wall, or fire barrier be sealed with a qualified firestopping product.

Firestop systems are made up of a combination of products to reestablish the original rating of a penetrated fire barrier. Firestop systems may be made of a single material or a combination of materials that provide a balance of heat resistance, adequate sealing at extreme temperatures, durability to stay in place and stay intact during a fire, and structural integrity to survive the erosive effects of a high powered hose stream.

Firestop systems are divided into mechanical firestop systems and nonmechanical firestop systems. Mechanical firestop systems consist of fire system components that are designed to fit into standard openings in fire barriers. Nonmechanical firestop systems consist of fire system components that are designed to fit into nonstandard openings in fire barriers.

Firestop materials used in a firestop system must be tested to pass the ASTM E814 and UL 1479 standards. The firestop products used in a firestop system must be tested and approved for the intended purpose. The testing and approval comes from a certified and independent laboratory. All firestop systems must be completely and thoroughly tested using the same testing methods and test criteria.

The two firestop rating classifications of F and T for through penetration firestop systems used in the United States are defined in the ASTM E814 standard. A third fire rating classification of L for through penetration firestop systems used in the United States is defined in the UL 1479 standard.

Mechanical firestop systems consist of premanufactured products and devices that are preshaped and sized to fit into or around standard penetrations. Mechanical firestop systems are manufactured to fit around standard size conduits, cables, core holes, and other penetrations commonly found in commercial buildings. Cables and conduits are secured with elastomeric materials to provide a tight seal.

Nonmechanical firestop systems are designed to fit and expand into nonstandard building openings. These firestop systems are required when a penetration is irregularly shaped or is an irregular size. Nonmechanical firestop material would include firestop putties, firestop caulks, firestop silicone foam, and pliable firestop materials. These materials tend to either harden or swell under the influence of heat.

Firestopping a through penetration requires firestopping both sides of the penetrated fire barrier. The firestop material, such as putty or caulk, is installed on one side of the barrier. A certified fill material is placed inside the penetration to fill the space between the two sides of the barrier. The opposite side of the fire-rated barrier is sealed.

Membrane penetrations are usually easier to seal than through penetrations. The penetration on one side of the wall must be firestopped. This usually involves placing either firestop putty or a caulk over the penetration. In addition, membrane penetrations are usually small in size.

CHAPTER 16

Precabling Preparation

E very communications cable installation project starts with precabling preparation. This process actually involves many different tasks. These can be divided into two general categories:

▼ Planning the cable installation project

▲ Performing the necessary construction to start the actual cable installation

There are many tasks involved in planning a telecommunications cabling installation. The precable preparation are the front end tasks that must be completed before the communication cables are installed. The planning is a very important phase of every cable installation project. This step must be completed before any of the construction tasks are started. All of the precabling preparation tasks will be completed before the cable installation begins. This section will describe the tasks involved in the precabling preparation for a cable installation project.

PRECABLING PREPARATION

Every communication cable installation project should start with a thorough and complete analysis of the impending project. The precabling preparation is a series of activities that are designed to either gather critical information about the building or the cable installation project itself. The information gathered during the planning stage of the cable installation project is required for the installation phase of the project to go smoothly.

Precabling preparation involves the following tasks:

▼ Site survey

■ Develop a job plan

■ Investigate telecommunications rooms (TRs)

■ Build TRs

■ Investigate existing horizontal and backbone cable pathways

■ Install cable-supporting structures

■ Installing pull ropes in backbone cable pathways

■ Install pull strings in horizontal cable pathways

■ Designate the exact cable drop locations

▲ Prepare work areas

PERFORMING A SITE SURVEY

The site survey is the first task for a cabling installation project. The site survey is critical for determining exactly what is necessary for a cabling project. The site survey will enable a complete job plan to be developed for the project.

The site survey includes the following tasks:

▼ Obtain project drawings and building blueprints.

■ Job walk through.

■ Safety check.

■ Identify project contacts.

■ Determine the tools, equipment, and materials necessary to complete the job.

■ Determine pulling routes and identify any problems for installing cable.

▲ Identify special considerations for the project.

The findings of the site survey should be documented and discussed with the project installation team.

Obtain Project Drawings and Building Blueprints

Every cable installation project must be completely and accurately documented. The documentation for a cable installation project is usually developed by the project consultant or the customer. The project documentation is usually developed before the project goes out to bid. The project drawing should include detailed information for each of the following areas:

▼ Cable drop locations

■ Location of cable pathways

■ Grounding and bonding locations

■ TR layouts

▲ Project labeling requirements

The project design can be formal drawings integrated with the building architectural design or informal drawings. The project drawings can be formal blueprints drawn to scale or nonscaled drawings. The purpose of the project drawings is to identify the exact location for each cable drop for the installation project. The primary requirement for project drawings is that they are detailed drawings. They must provide the cable installation team with the exact information necessary to correctly perform and complete the cable installation project.

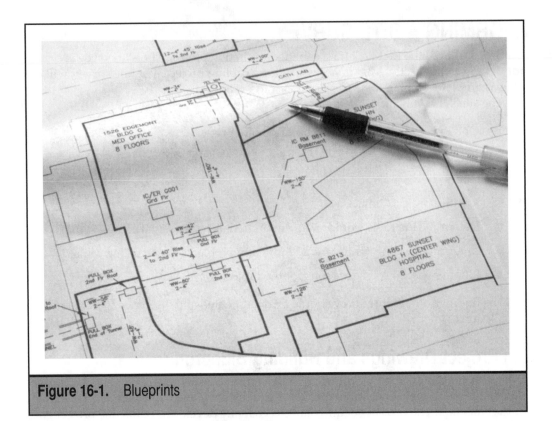

Figure 16-1. Blueprints

The project documentation is usually drawn on standard building blueprints (see Figure 16-1). The building blueprints show the exact architectural layout of the building where the cable installation project will take place. The correlation of the project drawings with the building blueprints will give the cable installation team the exact drop locations and clearance information when performing the cable installation project.

Job Walk Through

A walk through of the building must be performed before every cable installation project. The job walk through should be conducted with the project drawings and building blueprints. The purpose of the job walk through is to investigate every TR and every drop location. The accuracy of the project drawings should be confirmed during the job walk through. The job walk through should provide an opportunity to confirm the exact cable drop locations, mark up building blueprints, and make installation-specific notes that will be used later in the project.

Safety Check

A safety check must be performed prior to the start of the cable installation project. The safety check must identify possible safety hazards present on the job site. The safety check is normally conducted during the job walk through. Notes must be taken regarding possible safety hazards that may be encountered during the installation project. Each cable installer working on the job site must be made aware of all safety hazards identified during the safety check.

Identify Project Contacts

All cable installation projects have important customer contacts that must be identified before the project begins. The project contacts are those individuals that must be consulted before important construction decisions are made. Project status reports will be presented to the project contacts. At the end of the project, all necessary project sign-offs will usually be performed by these individuals. Project contacts usually include the following types of individuals:

▼   Information technology manager

■   Facilities manager

▲   Security manager

Determine Project Tools, Equipment, and Materials

The site survey should also include creating a detailed list for all of the tools, equipment, and materials that will be required to complete the cable installation project. Long conduit runs will usually require mechanical pulling equipment to install backbone cables. Inadequate cable-supporting structures will require installing new or additional cable-supporting structures and securing these components to the building structure. All of the construction hardware, mechanical tools, hand tools, and other miscellaneous material should be identified and purchased for the project.

Determine Pulling Routes and Identify Any Problems for Installing Cable

During the job walk through, the cable pulling routes from the TR to each work area location should be investigated. The horizontal and backbone cable pathways must be checked carefully. Access to all cable pathways must also be determined. This investigation will identify if any special equipment, such as lifts, are required to install the communication cable above ceilings. It may also identify that additional workers, such as carpet repair personnel, are required to either cut the carpet in order to open access floor trenches or to repair the carpet after the floor trenches are closed.

Identify Special Considerations for the Project

Every cable installation project has special considerations that are unique to the building where the cable installation project is being installed. The building should be surveyed and project contacts must be consulted to obtain information about any special consideration that must be performed during the cable installation project such as

▼ Firestopping

■ Customer labeling preferences

■ Building security requirements

■ Access to the building

▲ Whether the installation will impact other tenants in the building

DEVELOPING A JOB PLAN

A job plan describes the exact details on exactly how the cable installation is to be completed (see Figure 16-2). The job plan can take the form of

▼ A simple check list

▲ A more formal GANTT or PERT chart

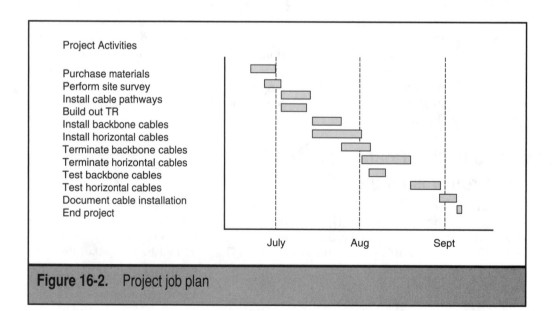

Figure 16-2. Project job plan

A simple check list would include all the activities that must be completed and the order that each should be completed. A more formal job plan would include developing both GANTT and PERT charts. These charts would identify the project task by date, identify the anticipated duration for each task, and identify the critical path for the entire project.

A job plan describes all aspects of the cable installation job including

▼ Staffing requirements

■ Site requirements

▲ Scheduling requirements

Developing a Job Plan—Requirements

There are no formal or specific format requirements for a written job plan. These will vary depending on the needs of the job supervisor. Some of the common items that are written into most job plans include

▼ Construction materials list

■ Cable material list

■ Cable terminating equipment list

■ Construction and termination tool list

■ Project task list and task descriptions, usually divided by day, week, and month

■ Overall project schedule and task contingencies

▲ Specific job requirements including
   ■ Cable labeling scheme
   ■ Cable termination and splicing methods to be used
   ■ Labor estimates
   ■ Miscellaneous duties

TELECOMMUNICATIONS ROOMS (TRs)

A *telecommunications room* (TR), sometimes called either a telecommunications closet or a horizontal closet, is a building space that is designated for the termination of horizontal and backbone cables (see Figure 16-3). The TR is the recognized connection point between the backbone and horizontal cable pathways. This space is also the place where any required termination hardware is mounted.

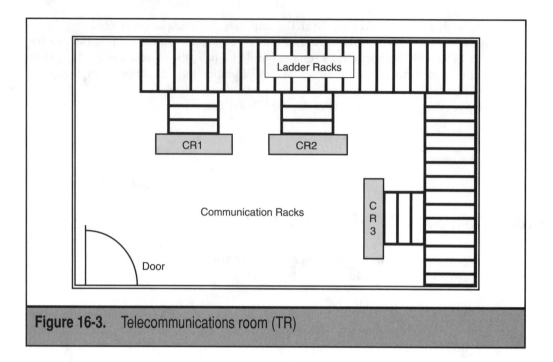

Figure 16-3. Telecommunications room (TR)

The TR is a designated space for housing the following:

▼ Telecommunications cables

■ Telecommunications equipment

▲ Cross-connections

Industry cabling standards require that every building must be served by at least one TR or equipment room (ER). Industry standards also require that there be at least one TR per floor. There is no limit as to the maximum number of TRs that can be supported per building. The useable floor space determines the maximum number of closets for a building.

Telecommunications closets are designated building spaces that are used to support the following cabling components and equipment:

▼ Horizontal cable to backbone cable cross-connections

■ Entrance facilities (EFs)

■ Telecommunications equipment

■ Local area network (LAN) equipment

▲ Computer equipment

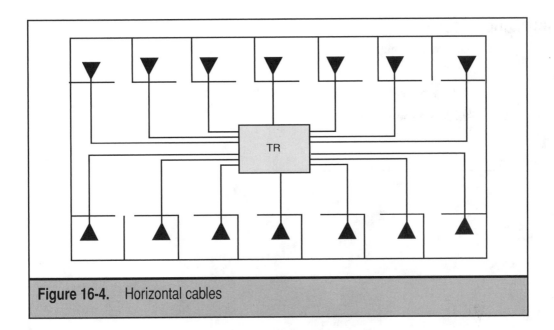

Figure 16-4. Horizontal cables

All horizontal cables installed to each work area must be directly cabled back to the TR (see Figure 16-4). In addition, all horizontal cables must be terminated in a TR that resides on the same floor as the work area being served.

INVESTIGATE BUILDING TELECOMMUNICATIONS ROOMS (TRs)

Every TR must be investigated during the site survey. The detailed project drawings for each TR must be used to confirm the design of the room.

The following items must be investigated:

▼ Slots or sleeves in the TR

■ TR cable-supporting structures

■ Backboards

■ Communication racks and cabinets

■ Wire management

■ Grounding and bonding

▲ Location for installing communication equipment

Slots and Sleeves

Slot or sleeves are typically used to run either backbone or horizontal communication cables into or through a TR.

▼ A *slot* is a rectangular opening in the TR floor.

▲ A *sleeve* is a round conduit installed in a core hole through the floor or ceiling of a TR (see Figure 16-5).

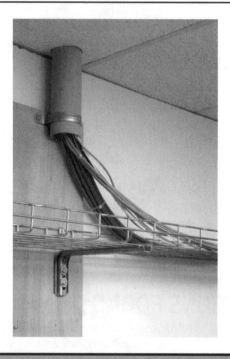

Figure 16-5. Sleeve

New cable installation projects will usually have either a slot or multiple sleeves installed in each TR. Slots and sleeves provide a pathway for backbone communication cables that must be run into or through the TR. Industry standards recommend installing a minimum of two, trade size 4 conduits between vertically aligned TRs.

Telecommunications Room (TR) Cable-Supporting Structures

The TR cable-supporting structures must be installed before the communication cables can be installed into the TR. Horizontal pathways may exist in the building or may need to be added. If the horizontal pathways do not exist or are insufficient to support the new communication cables, additional pathways must be added. Once installed, the horizontal pathways will permit the communication cables to run into the TR to be terminated.

Horizontal pathways usually end at the TR. In most cases, it is the responsibility of the cable installation contractor to add additional cable-supporting structures for routing the communication cables into the TR. The cable-supporting structures that must be addressed when building the TR are

▼   The cable trays or other hardware that provide the pathway for cables entering the TR

▲   Ladder racks that support communication cables inside of the TR

Backboards

Sheets of plywood are installed in TRs to provide a location for mounting cable termination and organization hardware. Plywood is a common material installed in TRs because it provides a uniform surface, and cable termination hardware can be installed with common wood screws.

Plywood sheets that are 8 ft. high and 4 ft. wide are installed on the walls of the TR. The plywood backboard is installed with the 8-ft. long dimension running from the ceiling to the floor (see Figure 16-6). The bottom of the plywood backboard will normally be installed 4 to 6 in. above the TR floor.

The backboards are critical to every cable installation project. Each backboard must be individually analyzed and investigated for the following information:

▼   Is there adequate space for mounting cable termination hardware on existing backboards?

■   Do new backboards need to be installed in the TR?

■   Is there sufficient clearances for the cable termination hardware?

■   Is there sufficient space on each backboard for routing and supporting all communication cables?

▲   What are the maximum cross-connect distances on the backboards? Do they conform to the maximum distances specified by industry cabling standards?

Communication Racks and Cabinets

Communication racks and cabinets are installed in TRs to mount patch panels and communication equipment (see Figure 16-7). Communication racks and cabinets provide a designated place to mount cable termination devices and communication equipment. Both communication racks and cabinets keep the cable termination hardware, equipment, and the associated cables organized.

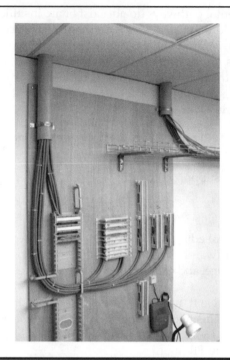

Figure 16-6. Telecommunications room (TR) backboard

TRs that do not have communication racks or cabinets installed in them are usually very disorganized. All cable termination hardware must be mounted on the plywood backboards. Communication equipment must also be installed either on the plywood backboard or on the communication racks located in the TR. TRs without communication racks have no organized method for growth. New equipment oftentimes is mounted on the floor or other temporary locations. These TRs have no organized method to handle cross-connect wires and equipment patch cords.

The communication racks and the cabinets installed in each TR must be investigated. Each rack or cabinet in the TR must be investigated for the following:

▼ Do the existing racks and cabinets have enough space for the installation of all cable hardware components required for this cabling project?

■ Is there enough space to install new racks or cabinets?

■ Is there sufficient clearances for all communication racks and cabinets?

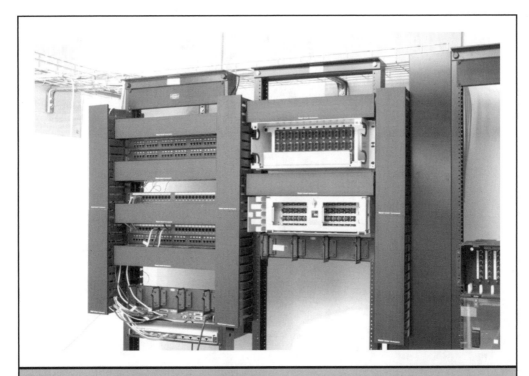

Figure 16-7.   Communication rack

- Is there adequate support for each communication rack?

- ▲ Does the communication installation project require any additional support for communication racks?

Wire Management

Communication racks should always be installed with proper wire management panels (see Figure 16-8). Wire management panels provide a pathway for routing communication cables along the rack to their designated termination position. They are also used to provide a cable path for patch cords to connect to patch panels and equipment ports. They provide a means to organize patch cord routing and store excess patch cord slack.

Wire management panels provide organization for communication racks. Without wire management panels, communication racks become very disorganized and sloppy looking. The two types of wire management panels used on communication racks are

- ▼ Vertical wire management panels (see Figure 16-9)

- ▲ Horizontal wire management panels (see Figure 16-10)

Figure 16-8.   Wire management panels

Each communication rack must be investigated to determine if each has adequate wire management panels. The investigation should include the following:

▼   Do all communication racks have vertical wire management panels?

■   Do all communication racks have horizontal wire management panels?

▲   Do the communication racks have a sufficient number of horizontal wire management panels?

Telecommunications Grounding and Bonding

The ANSI/TIA/EIA-607 standard defines the grounding and bonding requirements for a telecommunications cabling system. The telecommunications grounding and bonding system starts with a physical connection to the building grounding electrode system and extends to every TR in the building. A telecommunications grounding and bonding system defined by the ANSI/TIA/EIA-607 standards include the following elements:

Figure 16-9.   Vertical wire management panel

▼   Bonding conductor for telecommunications

■   Telecommunications main grounding busbar (TMGB)

■   Telecommunications bonding backbone (TBB)

■   Telecommunications grounding busbar (TGB)

▲   Telecommunications bonding backbone interconnecting bonding conductor (TBBIBC)

The site survey should carefully analyze the telecommunications grounding and bonding system. The grounding and bonding system must be connected to an approved building grounding source. Each TR must contain a TGB. Each TGB must be connected to the TMGB using an approved TBB.

If the site survey identifies that the telecommunications grounding and bonding system is incomplete or not installed correctly, the system must be corrected.

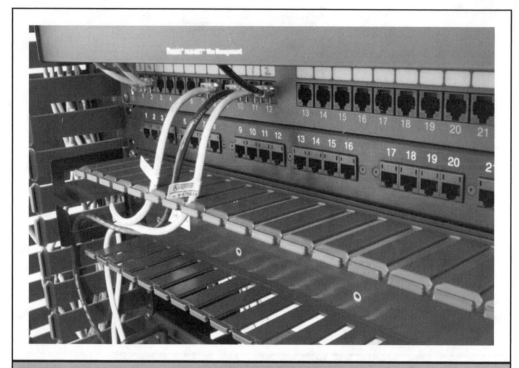

Figure 16-10. Horizontal wire management panel

Installation of Communication Equipment

Communication equipment is installed in the TR once the cable-supporting hardware and communication racks or cabinets have been installed. Communication equipment is typically installed in the TR using the following methods:

▼ Wall mounting

■ Rack mounting

▲ Cabinet mounting

Each TR must be investigated to determine if all planned communication equipment can be supported. The investigation should include the following:

▼ Can the existing installation racks or cabinets support the new communication equipment?

■ Will the new communication racks and cabinets be capable of supporting the new communication equipment?

- ■ Does the TR have sufficient power for the new equipment?

- ▲ Does the TR have the correct temperature and humidity levels required by the new communication equipment?

BUILDING TELECOMMUNICATIONS ROOMS (TRs)

The site survey of each TR will identify if each room is properly constructed for the cable installation project. The problems identified during the investigation of each TR must be corrected before the cable installation phase of the project begins.

Any problems in the TR will be corrected during the construction phase of the cable installation project. All construction work, such as adding new communication racks or cable-supporting structures, will enable the new communication cables to be installed according to the specifications in the job drawings.

INVESTIGATE HORIZONTAL AND BACKBONE PATHWAYS

The next step when conducting the precabling preparation is to survey both the horizontal and backbone cable pathways. Each pathway must be carefully surveyed to determine if the new communication cables can be supported in the existing pathways. If the existing cable pathways are inadequate or nonexistent, new pathways must be installed before the cable installation phase of the project can begin.

The pathway investigation should include

- ▼ Horizontal cable pathways

- ▲ Backbone cable pathways

Survey Horizontal Cable Paths

The first step when starting to pull horizontal cables is to survey the cable paths or cable runs. This activity involves starting at the place where each cabling run will start and inspecting the cable pathway to each work area. Most horizontal cables are pulled from the TR to each work area location.

The TR itself should be the first stop during the survey process. The closet should be built out before the horizontal cables are pulled. The location of the communication racks and the backboard should be identified in each closet (see Figure 16-11). These are the places where horizontal cables are terminated in the TR. Category 3 voice cables are usually terminated or block mounted on the backboard, and category 5e or higher UTP cables are terminated on patch panels mounted on communication racks.

The next step in the survey process is to identify where the horizontal cables will exit the TR. Most TRs are supported by horizontal pathways. These pathways may enter the TR underground or above the ceiling. The horizontal cables should be pulled to run the cables in the horizontal pathways to each work area location. The survey of the TR should

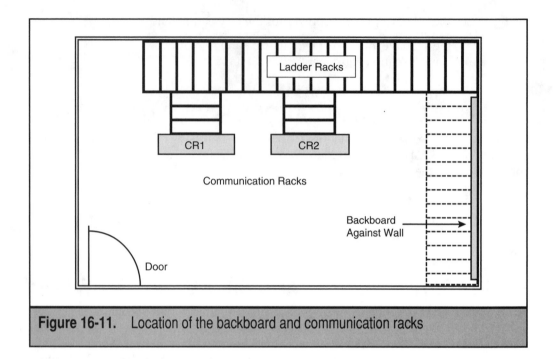

Figure 16-11. Location of the backboard and communication racks

also verify that cable-supporting hardware, such as ladder racks, are installed to support the horizontal cables from the punch down blocks and communications racks to the horizontal pathways (see Figure 16-12).

The next step is to investigate each horizontal pathway from the TR to the work area locations. If the horizontal pathway is an underfloor trench, the trench must be opened. If the horizontal pathway is a cable tray installed above the ceiling, use a ladder and open the ceiling tiles to see the cable tray. In either case, the horizontal pathway should be analyzed, and a determination must be made if the pathway can support the new horizontal cables that must be installed. If your survey identifies that the horizontal pathways are full or not capable of supporting the new horizontal cables, an alternate pathway must be used or a new pathway must be installed before the horizontal cables are pulled.

Survey Backbone Cable Paths

The first step when starting to pull backbone cables is to survey the cable paths between TRs. This activity involves starting at either the main cross-connect (MC) or intermediate cross-connect (IC) in each building and investigating the backbone cable paths to each TR and ER.

Each backbone pathway must be surveyed before any cables are installed. The survey should look for the following:

Figure 16-12.   Telecommunications room (TR) ladder racks

- ▼ Conduit between TRs
- ■ Conduit capacity
- ■ Conduit utilization
- ■ Innerduct in all cable pathways that will be supporting optical fiber backbone cables
- ■ Conduit fill ratio
- ■ How backbone cables will enter and exit conduits
- ■ Supporting structures between TRs
- ▲ Cable pulling points

If your survey identifies that the backbone pathways are full or not capable of supporting the new backbone cables, an alternate pathway must be used or a new pathway must be installed before the backbone cables are pulled.

INSTALLING CABLE PATHWAYS AND SUPPORTING STRUCTURE

The site survey of the backbone and horizontal cable pathways will identify if any cable pathways or other supporting structures must be installed. The cable pathways and required supporting structures must be installed before the communication cable phase of the project begins. The cable pathway and additional supporting structures must be installed during the construction phase of the cable installation project.

Steps for Installing Cable-Supporting Structures

The steps for installing the cable-supporting structures include the following:

1. Obtain building blueprints or job design drawings.

2. Verify the load capacity of the existing cable-supporting structure (if any).

3. Verify the ability of the existing support structure to support the total cable weight of the existing cables with the weight of the new cables.

4. Verify that sufficient cable support installation access is available before starting the installation.

5. Verify that the cable support structure will separate or provide a separation between high-voltage and low-voltage cables. The NEC requires a solid metal, continuous barrier if both power cables and communications cables are run in the same pathway.

6. Verify that cable support material and tools are available before starting the installation.

7. When installing the cable support structures, avoid areas that have high EMI or RFI.

8. Drill holes in all designated locations to install cable-supporting hardware such as threaded rods and other required hardware.

9. Install cable-supporting hardware, where necessary along the cable path.

10. Attach cable trays or ladder racks on the installed supporting hardware.

11. Ground the cable-supporting structure to the nearest TGB or TMGB.

12. Label the cable-supporting structure per the ANSI/TIA/EIA-606 standard.

13. Document the newly installed cable-supporting structure on building blueprints or job drawings.

INSTALLING PULL ROPES AND PULL STRINGS

Pull ropes and strings must be installed in the following cable pathways before communication cables can be installed. Pull ropes or pull strings must be installed in the following cable pathways:

▼ Backbone pathways

▲ Horizontal pathways

Install Pull Ropes in Backbone Pathways

The first step in pulling backbone cable is to install a pull rope in every backbone pathway. Lighter pull strings are installed in horizontal pathways. Heavier pull ropes are usually installed in backbone cable pathways. The heavier pull rope is used to pull the large backbone cables through the backbone cable pathways such as conduits. Horizontal backbone cables may be installed in cable trays. These pathways may not require a pull rope because these cable pathways are open and the backbone cables can also be installed in these support structures by hand.

Select the correct type of pull rope to install in backbone pathways. Use a plastic or nylon line with a minimum test rating of 200 lbs. of pulling tension. Avoid installing ropes that will deteriorate or break when exposed to heat caused by pulling friction. Avoid using ropes that have a tendency to twist as pulling tension is applied.

Pull ropes are usually installed with a fishtape. A *fishtape* is a flexible, metal or fiberglass device that can be inserted into a conduit (see Figure 16-13). These tools are manufactured in 50-, 100-, 150-, and 200-ft. lengths. The flexible nature of this tool enables it to work its way through conduits that have cables installed in them. The fishtape is inserted in one end of a conduit and pushed through the entire conduit length. The pull rope is attached to the end of the fishtape with tape. The fishtape is then reeled back to install the pull rope in the conduit.

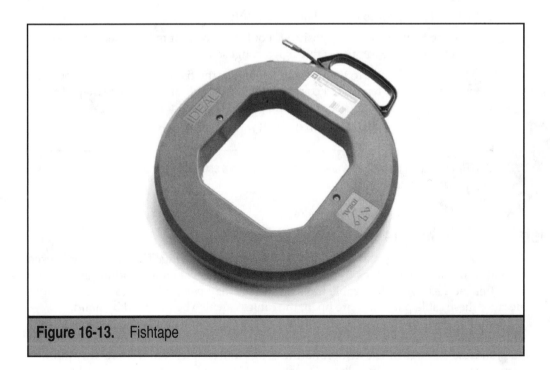

Figure 16-13.   Fishtape

Long conduits usually have pull boxes along the conduit run. Industry standards recommend that a pull box should be installed after each 30 m (100 ft.) section of conduit. Each conduit section between pull boxes should have a pull rope installed in it. Avoid installing pull rope through a pull box. These cable pulls will be difficult as the conduit sections become crowded with cables.

Each pull rope must be secured at each end once it is installed in the backbone conduits. The pull rope can be tied to the conduit bushing or secured to another apparatus in the TR or the pull box. Once a pull rope is installed in a conduit, it can be used to pull backbone cables.

The activity of installing pull ropes can be difficult and take a long time if the backbone conduits already have cables installed in them. A good practice is to attach a new pull rope, called a trailer rope, to any backbone cables that are installed using the pull rope. The new pull rope will be installed when the backbone cables are pulled through the conduit.

The steps for installing a pull rope in a conduit are as follows:

1. Estimate the length of the conduit. This can be done by measuring the distance on building blueprints or following the conduit and walking off the distance.

2. Select a fishtape that will be long enough to reach the opposite end of the conduit.

3. Insert a fishtape into one end of the conduit.

4. Push the fishtape to the opposite end of the conduit. It may be necessary to twist the fishtape to push it through a congested conduit.

5. Attach the pull rope to the hook on the end of the fishtape with tape. Taper the tape to create a streamlined configuration. This will prevent the fishtape from getting caught on cables as it is being pulled through the conduit.

6. Reel the fishtape in and secure the pull rope on both ends of the conduit.

CAUTION: Never insert a fishtape in a conduit that has electrical wires running in it. This is an electrical hazard and could lead to electrocution.

Installing Pull Strings in Horizontal Pathways

Each horizontal pathway should be equipped with a pull string. The pull string is used to pull communication cables through the cable pathways such as conduits and under-floor trenches. Above ceiling cable trays or J hooks may use pull strings to install cable. Because these cable pathways are open, the cables can also be installed by hand.

Pull strings are usually installed with a fishtape. A fishtape is a flexible, metal or fiber-glass device that can be inserted into a conduit. These tools are manufactured in 50-, 100-, 150-, and 200-ft. lengths. The flexible nature of this tool enables it to work its way through conduits that have cables installed in them. This fishtape is inserted in one end of a conduit and pushed through the entire conduit length. The pull string is attached to the end of the fishtape with tape. The fishtape is then reeled back, installing the pull string in the conduit.

Long conduits usually have pull boxes along the conduit run. Industry standards recommend that a pull box should be installed after each 30 m (100 ft.) section of conduit. Each conduit section between pull boxes should have a pull string installed in it. Avoid installing pull strings through a pull box. These cable pulls will be difficult as the conduit sections become crowded with cables.

Each pull string must be secured at each end once they are installed. The pull string can be tied to the outlet box in the work area. The opposite end can be tied to anything convenient in the TR. Once a pull string is installed in a conduit, it can be used to pull horizontal cables.

The process of installing a pull string can be difficult and take a long time if the conduit already has cables installed in it. A good practice is to attach a new pull string, called a trailer string, to any cables that are installed using the pull string. The new pull string will be installed when the cables are pulled through the conduit.

The steps for installing a pull string in a conduit are as follows:

1. Estimate the length of the conduit. This can be done by measuring the distance on building blueprints or following the conduit and walking off the distance.

2. Select a fishtape that will be long enough to reach the opposite end of the conduit.

3. Insert a fishtape into one end of the conduit.

4. Push the fishtape to the opposite end of the conduit. It may be necessary to twist the fishtape to push it through a congested conduit.

5. Attach the pull string to the hook on the end of the fishtape with tape. Taper the tape to create a streamlined configuration. This will prevent the fishtape from getting caught on cables as it is being pulled through the conduit.

6. Reel the fishtape in and secure the pull string on both ends of the conduit.

CAUTION: Never insert a fishtape in a conduit that has electrical wires running in it. This is an electrical hazard and could lead to electrocution.

DESIGNATE CABLE DROP LOCATIONS

The exact drop locations for each horizontal cable must be identified during the site survey. The exact drop location means making a decision on exactly what wall of an office and exactly where the faceplate will be installed. These decisions must be made before the communication cables are installed. Once the exact location for each cable drop is known, then the work area can be prepared.

PREPARE WORK AREAS

Installing communication cables to the work area of a building requires that the work area is properly prepared for installing new communication cables. Preparing the work area usually involves moving furniture to gain access to the ceiling space and to gain access to the work space walls.

Preparing work areas involves the following steps:

1. Moving furniture

2. Disassembling furniture or cubicles

3. Preparing station locations

4. Installing the telecommunications outlet mounting hardware

5. Installing any required conduit stub ups

6. Installing any required utility poles

Moving Furniture

One of the primary tasks that is required to prepare the work area involves moving furniture. Furniture may need to be moved to enable a portable step ladder to be set up or to gain access to the horizontal pathway. Always create enough work space to properly set up a ladder where the communication cables are installed above the drop ceiling in the building.

Never move heavy office furniture alone. When lifting or moving office furniture, work with a partner. Large pieces of furniture can be heavy and awkward. Heavy pieces of office furniture should only be moved with dollies or other moving devices. Every individual that will be lifting or moving office furniture must use the proper lifting technique and wear a lifting belt. The correct lifting technique requires keeping your back straight and lifting with your legs. This technique will prevent serious back injuries from occurring while on the job.

Disassembling Furniture or Cubicles

Many times office furniture must be disassembled in order to be moved. Large desks, office cubicles, and bookcases may have to be taken apart to clear a work area before a communication cable can be pulled. Sometimes a large desk or bookcase must be moved to position a ladder correctly for accessing the ceiling space. Some office cubicles must be disassembled in order to gain access to the cable raceways on the furniture panels.

Always take your time when disassembling office furniture. All screws and other furniture parts must be kept in a secure location. A time saving technique is to label all furniture pieces. This will save time when the furniture must be reassembled.

Station Locations

There are three types of station locations typically found in commercial buildings. These include the following:

▼ Wall mounted locations

■ Floor mounted locations

▲ Cubicle locations

A *wall mounted station location* is where the telecommunications outlet will be installed in the wall of the work area. Offices and other building work spaces located next to building walls are examples of a wall mounted work location. These work area locations require that the communication cable be installed inside of the wall and the telecommunications outlet be installed in the wall.

A *floor mounted station location* is where the telecommunications outlet will be installed on the floor of the work area in the wall. Floor mounted station locations are found in buildings that use underground trenches to distribute communication cables to the work area locations. These work area locations require mounting the telecommunications outlet on a floor monument secured to the floor of the building.

A *cubicle station location* is where the telecommunications outlet will be installed in a modular furniture cubicle. Open office spaces that have metal modular furniture for employee work spaces are an example of a cubicle work location. These locations require that the communication cables are run under the floor through trenches or over the ceiling. All communication cables that run over the drop ceiling must come down a utility pole into the cubicle work location.

Preparing a Wall Mounted Station Location

When preparing wall mounted station locations, all of the following factors should be considered:

▼ Always separate communications outlets from electrical outlets.

■ Install the communication outlets near the equipment that they serve.

■ Verify that users will have access to the outlets.

▲ Install outlets at the same height as electrical outlets.

The faceplate that supports the telecommunications outlet must be mounted to the wall in these work locations. The faceplates must be mounted in such a way that they will be permanently secured to the wall. The telecommunications outlets for a wall mounted station location are mounted to the wall using one of the following methods:

▼ Conduit stub up from outlet box

■ Home run conduit from outlet box to the TR

- ■ Mud ring/dry wall adapter
- ▲ Surface mounted outlet box

Steps for Preparing a Wall Mounted Station Location   The steps for preparing a wall mounted station location for pulling a cable are as follows:

1. Determine the type of outlet and the location of the outlet from the job blueprints. Verify that the height is the same as all electrical outlets in the room.
2. Determine the outlet mounting method to be used for the installation.
3. Identify the proper tools and materials that will be needed to complete the installation.
4. Determine if an outlet box, mud ring, or drywall adapter must be installed to mount the outlet faceplate.
5. If necessary, install a stub up conduit into the ceiling space.
6. Install outlet box, mud ring, or drywall adapter, if necessary.
7. Install a pull string from the ceiling space to the outlet box, mud ring, or drywall adapter.
8. Perform all necessary housekeeping to clean up the work area. Always vacuum drywall dust if the installation required cutting into the drywall.

Preparing a Floor Mounted Station Location

Floor mounted station locations are created when one of the following horizontal distribution systems are used for routing communication cables to the work area location:

- ▼ Cellular/underground raceways
- ■ Raised floors
- ■ Poke thru
- ▲ Under carpet

The faceplate that supports the telecommunications outlet must be mounted to the floor or a floor structure in these work locations. The faceplates must be mounted in such a way that they will be permanently secured. The telecommunications outlets for a floor mounted station location are usually mounted to the floor monument that is attached to the building floor.

Steps for Preparing a Floor Mounted Station Location   The steps for preparing a floor mounted station location for pulling a cable are as follows:

1. Investigate the floor design and distribution method that is used in the building.
2. Determine the location of all outlets from the project blueprints.

3. Determine how horizontal cables are routed to each outlet location.

4. Identify the proper tools and materials that will be needed to complete the installation.

5. Install the mounting hardware for the outlet box. This is usually attached to the cable pathway.

6. If necessary, prepare or make any necessary adjustments or attachments to the cable pathway for the mounting hardware.

7. If necessary, install conduits or other required couplings.

8. Attach the outlet box or floor monument hardware.

9. Install a pull string through the horizontal pathway to the outlet box or floor monument.

10. Perform all necessary housekeeping to clean up the work area.

Preparing a Utility Pole or Modular Furniture Station Location

Work area outlets installed on utility poles are very common in open office environments that use modular furniture. Modular furniture is usually installed in small groups or clusters. These modular furniture clusters can be easily served by a single utility pole.

The faceplate that supports the telecommunications outlet must be mounted to the utility pole or modular furniture in these work locations. The faceplates must be mounted in such a way that they will be permanently secured. The telecommunications outlets for a modular furniture station location are usually mounted using one of the following methods:

▼   Velcro

■   Two-sided adhesive tape

■   Magnetic strips

▲   Screws

Steps for Preparing a Utility Pole or Modular Furniture Station Location   The steps for preparing a utility pole/modular furniture station location for pulling a cable are as follows:

1. Determine the type of outlet and the location of the outlet from the job blueprints. Verify that the height of all outlets are uniform for the installation.

2. Determine the outlet mounting method to be used for the installation.

3. Identify the proper tools and materials that will be needed to complete the installation.

4. If necessary, prepare or make any necessary adjustments or attachments to the cable pathway for mounting the utility pole.

5. Verify the location of all utility poles from the job blueprints.

6. Install all utility poles in their designated location and install all necessary supporting hardware.

7. Install outlet boxes or mounting hardware to the utility pole or modular furniture.

8. Install a pull string through the horizontal pathway, utility pole to the outlet box.

9. Perform all necessary housekeeping to clean up the work area.

CHAPTER SUMMARY

Every communications cable installation project starts with precabling preparation. The precabling preparation is a series of activities that are designed to either gather critical information about the building or the cable installation project itself. Precabling preparation involves the site survey, developing a job plan, investigating the telecommunications room (TR), building TRs, investigating existing horizontal and backbone cable pathways, installing cable-supporting structures, installing pull ropes in backbone cable pathways, installing pull strings in horizontal cable pathways, designating the exact cable drop locations, and preparing work areas.

The site survey is the first task for a cabling installation project. The site survey includes obtaining the project drawings and building blueprints; performing the job walk through; performing a safety check; identifying project contacts; determining the tools; equipment, and materials necessary to complete the job; determining cable pulling routes; identifying problems for installing cable; and identifying special considerations for the project. The findings of the site survey should be documented and discussed with the project installation team.

The documentation for a cable installation project is usually developed by the project consultant or the customer. The purpose of the project drawings is to identify the exact location for each cable drop for the installation project. The primary requirement for project drawings is that they are detailed drawings. They must provide the cable installation team with the exact information necessary to correctly perform and complete the cable installation project. The project documentation is usually developed before the project goes out to bid. The project drawing should include detailed information for cable drop locations, the location of cable pathways, grounding and bonding locations, TR layouts, and project labeling requirements. The project documentation is usually drawn on standard building blueprints.

The job walk through should be conducted with the project drawings and building blueprints. The purpose of the job walk through is to investigate every TR and every drop location. The job walk through should provide an opportunity to confirm the exact cable drop locations, mark up building blueprints, and make installation-specific notes that will be used later in the project. The accuracy of the project drawings should be confirmed during the job walk through.

A safety check must be performed prior to the start of the cable installation project. The safety check must identify possible safety hazards present on the job site. The safety check is normally conducted during the job walk through. Each cable installer working on the job site must be made aware of all identified safety hazards identified during the safety check.

Every cable installation project has special considerations that are unique to the building where the cable installation project is being installed. The building should be surveyed and project contacts must be consulted to obtain information about any special consideration that must be performed during the cable installation project such as: firestopping, customer labeling preferences, building security requirements, access to the building, and whether the installation will impact other tenants in the building.

A job plan describes the exact details on exactly how the cable installation is to be completed. The job plan can take the form of a simple check list or a more formal GANTT or PERT chart. A simple check list would include all the activities that must be completed and the order that each should be completed. A more formal job plan would include developing both GANTT and PERT charts.

A job plan describes all aspects of the cable installation job including: staffing requirements, site requirements, and scheduling requirements. There are no formal or specific format requirements for a written job plan. Some of the common items that are written into most job plans include: construction materials list, cable material list, cable terminating equipment list, construction and termination tool list, project task list and task descriptions, overall project schedule, and task contingencies and job specific requirements.

A telecommunications room (TR) is a building space that is designated for the termination of horizontal and backbone cables. The TR is the recognized connection point between the backbone and horizontal cable pathways. The TR is a designated space for housing telecommunications cables, telecommunications equipment, and cross-connections. Industry cabling standards require that every building must be served by at least one TR or equipment room (ER). Industry standards also require that there be at least one TR per floor. There is no limit as to the maximum number of TRs that can be supported per building.

Every TR must be investigated during the site survey. Sheets of plywood are installed in TRs to provide a location for mounting cable termination and organization hardware. Plywood is a common material installed in TRs because it provides a uniform surface, and cable termination hardware can be installed with common wood screws.

Communication racks and cabinets are installed in TRs to mount patch panels and communication equipment. Communication racks and cabinets provide a designated place to mount cable termination devices and communication equipment. Communication racks should always be installed with proper wire management panels. Wire management panels provide a pathway for routing communication cables along the rack to their designated termination position. They provide a means to organize patch cord routing and store excess patch cord slack.

The ANSI/TIA/EIA-607 standard defines the grounding and bonding requirements for a telecommunications cabling system. The telecommunications grounding and bonding system starts with a physical connection to the building grounding electrode system and extends to every TR in the building. A telecommunications grounding and bonding system defined by the ANSI/TIA/EIA-607 standards includes a bonding conductor for telecommunications, a telecommunications main grounding busbar (TMGB), a telecommunications bonding backbone (TBB), a telecommunications grounding busbar (TGB), and a telecommunications bonding backbone interconnecting bonding conductor (TBBIBC).

The site survey should carefully analyze the telecommunications grounding and bonding system. The grounding and bonding system must be connected to an approved building grounding source. Each TR must contain a TGB. Each TGB must be connected to the TMGB using an approved TBB.

The next step when conducting the precabling preparation is to survey both the horizontal and backbone cable pathways. Each pathway must be carefully surveyed to determine if the new communication cables can be supported in the existing pathways. If the existing cable pathways are inadequate or nonexistent, new pathways must be installed before the cable installation phase of the project can begin. If your survey identifies that the horizontal or backbone pathways are full or not capable of supporting the new cables, an alternate pathway must be used or a new pathway must be installed before the cables are pulled.

Pull ropes and strings must be installed in the following cable pathways before communication cables can be installed. Pull ropes or pull strings must be installed in all backbone and horizontal pathways. Pull ropes are usually installed with a fishtape. The fishtape is inserted in one end of a conduit and pushed through the entire conduit length. The pull rope is attached to the end of the fishtape with tape. The fishtape is then reeled back to install the pull rope in the conduit.

The exact drop locations for each horizontal cable must be identified during the site survey. The exact drop location means making a decision on exactly what wall of an office and exactly where the faceplate will be installed. These decisions must be made before the communication cables are installed. Once the exact location for each cable drop is known, the work area can be prepared.

Preparing the work area usually involves moving furniture to gain access to the ceiling space and to the work space walls. Preparing work areas involves moving furniture, disassembling furniture or cubicles, preparing station locations, installing the telecommunications outlet mounting hardware, installing any required conduit stub ups, and installing any required utility poles.

CHAPTER 17

Pulling Backbone Cables

Multipair copper and optical fiber cables are installed for the backbone subsystem. Backbone communication cables are installed between telecommunications rooms (TRs) for voice, low-speed data systems, and high-speed data systems.

Pulling backbone cables requires careful planning due to the heavy weight of copper cables and the long cable lengths associated with backbone cables. Backbone cables are usually shipped on large and heavy cable reels. These reels must be set up properly for the installation to be completed correctly and safely.

Backbone cables must be installed in many different types of cable pathways including: conduits, maintenance holes, building entrance conduits, and aerial pathways. These pathways can be congested and difficult to install new backbone cables in them. Heavy backbone cables or backbone cables that must be installed through long conduit sections may require mechanical pulling equipment be used to complete the installation.

This chapter will describe the correct procedures for installing copper and optical fiber backbone cables.

ALLOWED MEDIA TYPES

The ANSI/TIA/EIA-568-B.1 standard released in 2001 supports the following media type in the backbone subsystem for new cable installations (see Figure 17-1):

▼   100-ohm UTP cable

■   62.5/125 μm multimode optical fiber cable

■   50/125 μm multimode optical fiber cable

▲   Singlemode optical fiber cable

The 100-ohm UTP copper backbone cables are multipair cables. These cables are primarily used for voice and low-speed data applications. If 100-ohm UTP cable is required for high-speed data applications, a four-pair category 5e or category 6 UTP cable should be installed between TRs.

Optical fiber cables are the primary type of media installed for the backbone subsystem to support high-speed applications. Optical fiber cable is also primarily used for long distance applications. Copper backbone cables have a maximum distance that can be supported. This is based on the resistance of the cable and the distance that the communication signals must travel.

Industry surveys indicate that most voice applications are supported over multipair copper backbone cables, and over 85 percent of all high-speed data applications are supported over optical fiber cable.

Historically other types of copper media, such as thick coaxial cable and STP-A cables, have been installed for the backbone subsystem. This practice has been phased out over the last ten years because coaxial cable is not supported by the ANSI/TIA/EIA-568-A standards for new installations and STP-A cable was eliminated as a recognized media type from the ANSI/TIA/EIA-568-B.1 standard as well. ScTP copper cables are support-

Figure 17-1.   Allowed backbone media types

ed in both the ANSI/TIA/EIA-568-A and ANSI/TIA/EIA-568-B.1 standards, but this media type is not used as a backbone media. As a result, multipair UTP copper cables and optical fiber cables are the primary media types installed for the backbone subsystem.

PULLING BACKBONE CABLES

The steps required for pulling multipair copper backbone cables are similar to the steps for pulling optical fiber backbone cables. However, multipair copper backbone cables are much heavier than multistrand optical fiber cables. This means that the actual steps and equipment for pulling the two types of media will be slightly different.

The basic steps involved in pulling both copper and optical fiber backbone cables include the following:

1. Survey backbone cable paths.

2. Set up and designate backbone cable work areas.

3. Install pull ropes in backbone pathways.

4. Set up cable reels.

5. Label each cable and the cable reel.

6. Attach cables to the pull rope.

7. Pull backbone cables.

Survey Backbone Cable Paths

The first step when starting to pull backbone cables is to survey the cable paths between TRs. This activity involves starting at either the main cross-connect (MC) or intermediate cross-connect (IC) in each building and investigating the backbone cable paths to each TR and the equipment room (ER).

Each backbone pathway must be surveyed before any cables are installed. The survey should look for the following:

▼ Conduits between TRs

■ Conduit capacity

■ Conduit utilization

■ Innerducts in all cable pathways that will be supporting optical fiber backbone cables

■ Conduit fill ratio

■ How backbone cables will enter and exit conduits

■ Supporting structures between TRs

▲ Cable pulling points

Conduits Between Telecommunications Rooms (TRs)

Backbone cables are usually installed in conduit pathways that enter and exit TRs (see Figure 17-2). These conduits may or may not continue all the way to the next TR. Some conduits end at the TR wall and other run to another TR or ER.

Each backbone conduit must be investigated to identify the length and path for each. Conduits that end at a TR wall must be used in conjunction with other types of pathways. Conduits that are continuous must be investigated to primarily identify if any bends are in the conduit run that may make installing backbone cables difficult.

Conduits must be clearly identified and labeled according to the specifications defined in the ANSI/TIA/EIA-606 standard. Each conduit must have a unique identification. The numbering scheme should include both the originating and terminating points for the conduit. If during the conduit path investigation individual conduit runs are discovered to be unlabeled, take the time to label each correctly. This will save time during the actual cable installation.

Figure 17-2. Conduits in the telecommunications room

Conduit Available Capacity

All backbone conduits should be carefully investigated, and the available capacity for each should be documented. Conduits that have other backbone cables installed in them may not be able to support the new backbone cables that are planned for a new cable installation project. If a conduit run does not have enough capacity to install a new backbone cable, a new conduit must be installed before the backbone cable can be pulled.

Conduit Utilization

Conduits that support backbone cables should be dedicated to supporting a single media type. This would mean that one backbone conduit should be used to support copper backbone cables, and a second conduit should be used to support optical fiber backbone cables.

Copper and optical fiber backbone cables should never be installed in the same conduit. Copper backbone cables are very heavy. Pulling these cables into a conduit that has an optical fiber backbone cable installed in it may damage the optical fiber cable. The weight of the copper cable may damage the optical fibers or tear out the optical fiber backbone cable completely.

Innerduct

Innerducts should be installed in all conduits that will support optical fiber backbone cables. The proper size and number of innerducts must be selected based on the conduit trade size and the number of backbone cables that must be supported. A trade size 4 conduit can accommodate three, 1.25-in. innerducts.

Fill Ratio

The ANSI/TIA/EIA-569-A standard provides guidelines for the maximum fill for conduits supporting backbone communication cables. The maximum fill for a conduit is based on the internal conduit size and the outside diameter of the cables to be installed in the conduit. The ANSI/TIA/EIA-569-A standards permit the following conduit fill percentages:

▼ One cable = 53 percent of the conduits internal diameter.

■ Two cables = 31 percent of the conduits internal diameter.

▲ Three or more cables = 40 percent of the conduits internal diameter.

The total capacity of a conduit is reduced by 15 percent for each 90-degree bend in the conduit run. Two, 90-degree conduit bends would reduce the conduit capacity by 30 percent.

Backbone Cables Entering and Exiting Conduits

Copper and optical fiber backbone cables are thick cables. These cables require a larger bend radius than smaller, horizontal cables. The placement of conduits in a TR will have an impact on the routing of backbone cables in the TR.

Backbone conduit pathways must be terminated in the TR so that all backbone cables that enter or exit the conduit will not violate the cable's minimum bend radius. In some cases, large backbone cables are so still and inflexible that it may be impossible to route them into or out of a conduit without wrapping the cable completely around the TR first.

Supporting Structures Between Telecommunications Rooms (TRs)

Horizontal backbone cables are backbone cables that are installed between two TRs that are located on the same floor of a building. Industry cabling standards recommend installing a 75 mm (3 in.) trade size conduit between TRs. If this conduit is full or does not exist, the horizontal backbone cables must be installed in horizontal pathways between the two rooms.

Horizontal pathways, such as cable trays, must be carefully examined to determine if these structures can support the additional weight of a backbone cable. The capacity of the horizontal pathway should also evaluated. Industry standards recommend that under no circumstances should the overall fill ratio of the cable tray exceed 50 percent of the pathway's maximum capacity.

Cable Pulling Points

When performing the survey of the backbone pathways, cable pulling points must be identified. Cable pulling points are the locations in the backbone cable pathway where cable installers must be placed to pull the cable. These are generally places where the backbone cable will either get hung up or possibly damaged during the cable pull. Cable installers should be positioned at all designed cable pulling points in the backbone cable pathways.

Common cable pulling points include the following locations:

▼ At pull boxes

■ At the end of conduits

▲ At sharp corners or sharp bends along the backbone cable pathway

Devices, such as cable pulleys, sometimes called bullwheels, can be placed at sharp corners. This can prevent the cable from violating the minimum bend radius if the backbone cable gets pressed against the corner during the cable pull. The cable pulley will guide the cable around the sharp corner without altering the cable pairs or damaging optical fiber strands inside of the cable.

Cable Team

Pulling backbone cables usually requires two or more individuals on the cable team. Horizontal cables can be pulled by a single person, but the job moves much faster when two individuals work together as a team. When horizontal cables are pulled, the cable is usually pulled along using a pull string or pushed along using a long pole.

The first cable installer will attach the cable to a pull string or a cable pole and hand the cables to the second individual. Depending on the type of horizontal pathway, the second person may be positioned on a ladder or near the entrance to a floor duct. The first individual can feed cable slack off of the cable reels, and the second individual starts the cable pull.

Set Up and Designate Backbone Pulling Work Areas

Once the survey of the backbone cable pathways is complete, the cable pulling setup must be completed. The cable pulling setup involves organizing all of the tools and materials necessary to complete the backbone cable pulls. The setup is one of the most important tasks to complete so the installation proceeds smoothly and is completed quickly. This is especially true for the installation of backbone cables. Installations where the proper setup has not been completed before the cable pulls are started are usually marred by delays associated with finding necessary tools or obtaining the correct materials.

Part of the setup process is activity of designating and securing the work area. This is a simple activity but one that is an important safety consideration. When working inside a building, the work area should be designated and secured. Orange cones and yellow caution tape are typically used for this function. The use of orange cones and yellow caution tape will alert employees and others about possible dangers by entering this area. It will also serve to restrict access to anyone other than authorized members of the cabling crew.

Installing backbone cables is a more dangerous activity than installing horizontal cables. Backbone cables are larger and heavier cables. These cables are shipped on cable reels that are large and extremely heavy. Finally, installing backbone cables may require using mechanical pulling equipment. All of these conditions combine to make the work area for pulling backbone cables very dangerous.

Install Pull Ropes in Backbone Pathways

The first step in pulling backbone cable is to install a pull rope in every backbone pathway. Lighter pull strings are installed in horizontal pathways. Heavier pull ropes are usually installed in backbone cable pathways. The heavier pull rope is used to pull the large backbone cables through the backbone cable pathways such as conduits. Horizontal backbone cables may be installed in cable trays. These pathways may not require a pull rope because these cable pathways are open and the backbone cables can also be installed in these support structures by hand.

Select the correct type of pull rope to install in backbone pathways. Use a plastic or nylon line with a minimum test rating of 200 lbs. of pulling tension. Avoid installing ropes that will deteriorate or break when exposed to heat caused by pulling friction. Avoid using ropes that have a tendency to twist as pulling tension is applied.

Pull ropes are usually installed with a fishtape. A *fishtape* is a flexible, metal or fiberglass device that can be inserted into a conduit. These tools are manufactured in 50, 100, 150, and 200 ft. lengths. The flexible nature of this tool enables it to work its way through conduits that have cables installed in them. This fishtape is inserted in one end of a conduit and pushed through the entire conduit length. The pull rope is attached to the end of the fishtape with tape. The fishtape is then reeled back to install the pull rope in the conduit.

Long conduits usually have pull boxes along the conduit run. Industry standards recommend that a pull box should be installed after each 30 m (100 ft.) section of conduit. Each conduit section between pull boxes should have a pull rope installed in it. Avoid installing pull rope through a pull box. These cable pulls will be difficult as the conduit sections become crowded with cables.

Each pull rope must be secured at each end once they are installed in the backbone conduits. The pull rope can be tied to the conduit bushing or secured to another apparatus in the TR or the pull box. Once a pull rope is installed in a conduit, it can be used to pull backbone cables.

The activity of installing a pull rope can be difficult and take a long time if the backbone conduits already have cables installed in them. A good practice is to attach a new pull rope, called a trailer rope, to any backbone cables that are installed using the pull rope. The new pull rope will be installed when the backbone cables are pulled through the conduit.

The steps for installing a pull rope in a conduit are as follows:

1. Estimate the length of the conduit. This can be done by measuring the distance on building blueprints or following the conduit and walking off the distance.

2. Select a fishtape that will be long enough to reach the opposite end of the conduit.

3. Insert a fishtape into one end of the conduit.

4. Push the fishtape to the opposite end of the conduit. It may be necessary to twist the fishtape to push it through a congested conduit.

5. Attach the pull rope to the hook on the end of the fishtape with tape. Taper the tape to create a streamlined configuration. This will prevent the fishtape from getting caught on cables as it is being pulled through the conduit.

6. Reel the fishtape in and secure the pull rope on both ends of the conduit.

CAUTION: Never insert a fishtape in a conduit that has electrical wires running in it. This is an electrical hazard and could lead to electrocution.

Set Up Cable Reels

Backbone cables are large cables that are usually shipped on large cable reels. The cable reels for backbone cables are usually made of wood. Backbone cables are usually shipped on reels sold in lengths ranging from 305 m (1,000 ft.) to 5,000 m (16,400 ft.). Backbone cable reels can be over 5 ft. tall. Together, the backbone cables and the wooden cable reel can weight hundreds of pounds.

CAUTION: Never try to move or lift a backbone cable reel alone. Backbone cable reels should only be moved or lifted when a sufficient number of cable team members are available to help.

Backbone cable reels should be shipped to the job site on a truck with a hydraulic lifting gate. A lifting gate will enable the large cable reel to be lowered and rolled off the truck. Never ship large backbone cable reels on a truck with a hydraulic lifting gate. The large backbone cable reels may be dropped and cause serious injury to one of the cable installation team members.

Most backbone cables are installed using a top down installation approach. This approach will require moving the backbone cable reel to the top floor of the building and installing the backbone cable from the top floors to lower floors. This cable installation method uses gravity to help install the backbone cable through the backbone cable pathway.

Backbone cable reels should be lifted to high building floors using a freight elevator. Large backbone cables should never be carried up stairs unless a freight elevator is unavailable in the building and there is a sufficient number of workers to lift the backbone cable reel without the possibility of injuries.

Before starting the backbone cable pull, the backbone cable reel must be set up so the cable can easily feed into the backbone cable pathway. The cable reel must be positioned so the cable will pay off the reel easily without getting tangled or kinked.

Large backbone cable reels must be placed on a cable jackstand. *Cable jackstands* are adjustable devices that support different sizes and weight cable reels. A metal rod is inserted through the cable reel, and the reel is lifted on the cable jacks so the reel spins freely.

CAUTION: Always verify that the metal rod that is used to support the cable reel is sufficient to support the weight of the cable reel. A metal rod that is too small may break, causing an injury.

When multiple, smaller backbone cables must be pulled at the same time, the backbone cable reels can be placed on a cable tree. *A cable tree* is a device that enables multiple cable reels to be installed so they can all spin freely. This device enables multiple cables to be pulled at the same time with the cables becoming hung up on the cable reels. Most cable trees are mounted on wheels so this device can be easily moved without requiring that the cable reels be taken off.

Select a location for the cable tree or cable jackstand that provides enough work space. The ideal location for the cable tree or cable jackstand is near the feed point for the horizontal pathway. If the TR is too small, the cable tree and jackstand may need to be set up in the hallway outside the TR.

Label Each Cable and the Cable Reel

Once the backbone cable reels are set up for the cable pull, each backbone cable must be uniquely labeled. A cable label must be attached to each backbone cable and the corresponding label attached to the backbone cable reel.

Cable labels should be placed approximately 6 to 12 in. from the end of the cable. This will prevent the label from being covered by tape when the cable is attached to a pull rope. In addition, the cable label is likely to remain on the cable when the cable jacket is stripped off to terminate the cable. The backbone cable must be cut from the cable reel once it is pulled through the backbone pathway. The cable label is attached to the other cable end. A new article in the 2002 National Electrical Code requires that all communication cables be labeled on each end. Unlabeled cables are considered abandoned cables and must be removed from commercial buildings.

Most cable installers will leave excess cable on both ends of the backbone cable run. The excess cable slack is called a service loop. Industry standards recommend leaving a 3 m (10 ft.) to 10 m (33 ft.) service loop in a backbone cable run. The service loop will permit the backbone cable to be moved or the cable terminations in the TR to be reconfigured.

Attach Cables to Pull Ropes

The last step before horizontal cables are pulled is to attach pull ropes to the cables. Pull ropes are attached to backbone cables by one of the following methods:

▼ Pulling eye

■ Pulling grip

▲ Directly tying the pull rope to the backbone cable

A pull rope can be attached to a backbone cable using a pulling eye. A pulling eye forms the backbone cable conductors into a loop. The conductors are taped together and to the cable jacket. A pulling eye distributes the pulling force evenly across all of the backbone cable pairs and the cable jacket.

A pull rope can be attached to the backbone cable using a meshed pulling grip. A *pulling grip* is a flexible, meshed gripping device that is slid over the backbone cable jacket. The meshed grip is tied to the pulling rope and secured with tape. The opposite end of the pulling grip is attached to the backbone cable jacket. The pulling grip will clamp down on the cable jacket when pressure is applied to the pull rope.

A pull rope can be tied directly onto a large backbone cable using a series of half hitch knots or a rolling hitch knot. The pull rope is tied onto the backbone cable and then secured in place with tape. The hitch knots stay tight when pressure is applied to the pull rope.

It is recommended to use a pulling swivel when pulling backbone cables with a pull rope. A *pulling swivel* is a device that turns as the rope is being pulled. A pulling swivel will prevent the pull rope and backbone cable from being twisted while it is being installed in the backbone cable pathway. Twisted backbone cables can suffer reduced performance due to the cable pairs being under tensions. Twisting a backbone cable may cause individual cable pairs to break.

The backbone cables must be arranged so the taped configuration is streamlined. This will prevent the backbone cable from becoming hung up on any cables or other obstructions as it is pulled through the cable pathway.

Pulling Backbone Cables

Backbone cables are pulled between TRs in a commercial building. The ANSI/TIA/EIA-568-A and ANSI/TIA/EIA-568-B.1 standards require that all intrabuilding backbone cables be installed in a physical star topology. This means that backbone cables will be installed from the MC to each TR or from the IC to each TR in the building.

The ANSI/TIA/EIA-568-A and ANSI/TIA/EIA-568-B.1 standards also permit backbone cables installed between TRs in the same floor or same building. These cables must be installed in addition to the backbone cables that connect each TR to either the MC or IC.

Backbone cables will be installed in one of the following configurations in a building:

▼ Top down

■ Bottom up

▲ Horizontally

Pulling Backbone Cables from the Top Down

TRs in multistory commercial buildings tend to be lined up vertically from floor to floor. These TRs have backbone conduits that link each TR to the room above and the room below. The pathway from the bottom TR to the top TR is through each TR.

Backbone cables are usually installed between vertically aligned closets in a multi-story commercial building. Backbone cables tend to be large pair count cables and are usually extremely heavy. In most cases, the best way to install these cables is to lower the cables from the top floor down to the bottom floor.

Some information that must be known before the backbone cable pull can begin include

▼ Determination must be made on how to manage and support the cable's weight as the cable is being installed.

▲ Based on the cable's size and weight, determine if cable pulleys and a cable brake will be necessary to control the cable's decent.

Steps for Pulling Backbone Cables from the Top Down   The steps for installing backbone cables in a vertical shaft or through multiple TRs vertically aligned from top to bottom are as follows:

1. Investigate and visually verify the vertical cable path. Confirm that adequate space exists for installing and supporting the backbone cable in each closet.

2. Move the cable reel to the top floor of the vertical shaft and as close as possible to the vertical shaft opening.

3. Using orange cones and yellow caution tape, designate a cable pulling work area. Inside the work area, place the cable reel on a jackstand.

4. If necessary, attach a cable reel brake to the cable reel.

5. If necessary, attach the cable pulleys at the top of the vertical shaft to support the cable's weight.

6. Attach a pull rope to the backbone cable.

7. The project supervisor must determine the communication method to be used during the cable installation and confirm that all workers are capable of communicating with their co-workers.

8. Start the cable pull by lowering the pull rope. Feed the pull rope through the backbone cable pathway.

9. Install the backbone cable through the backbone pathway and support the cable in each closet until the cable is installed.

10. Label both cable ends, and if not already done, label the backbone cable pathway.

11. Document the cable installation on building blueprints.

Pulling Backbone Cables from the Bottom Up

Backbone cables can also be installed from the first floor of a multistory building to a higher floor through the backbone pathway. In some cases, it may not be possible to bring the cable reel to an upper floor and install the backbone cable from the top down. This can happen if the cable reel is too large for an elevator or the building hallways are too narrow. In these cases, the backbone cable must be installed from the bottom floor to the highest floor.

Pulling a backbone cable from the bottom up through a vertical riser requires

▼ A mechanical pulling device

▲ A strong pulling rope

The pulling rope used for all backbone cable pulls from bottom to top must be of sufficient tensile strength to lift the cable up the vertical pathway. Always confirm the pulling strength of the cable being used for these cable pulls. Pull ropes that are not strong enough will break and may cause injury to one of the cable installation team members.

Steps for Pulling Backbone Cable from the Bottom Up   The steps for installing a backbone cable in a vertical shaft from the bottom up are as follows:

1. Investigate and visually verify the vertical cable path. Confirm that adequate space exists for installing and supporting the backbone cable in each closet.

2. Move the cable reel as close as possible to the bottom of the vertical shaft opening.

3. Using orange cones and yellow caution tape, designate a cable pulling work area. Inside the work area, place the cable reel on a jackstand.

4. Based on the size and weight of the backbone cable to be installed and height of the vertical shaft, determine the appropriate size and strength of the pull rope.

5. Before starting the cable pull, confirm that the strength of the pull rope is sufficient to support the cable's weight while it is being installed. Pull ropes that break may cause workers to be injured.

6. If necessary, attach a cable pulley at the top of the vertical shaft to support the cable's weight.

7. Install the pull rope over the cable pulley.

8. Attach the pull rope to the backbone cable using a method that will not damage the backbone cable.

9. The project supervisor must determine the communication method to be used during the cable installation and confirm that all workers are capable of communicating with their co-workers.

10. Attach a mechanical cable tugger to the pull rope.

11. Lubricate the backbone cable jacket. This will reduce friction while the cable is being installed.

12. Start the mechanical cable tugger slowly and notify the cable installation team when the cable pulling starts.

13. Continue the cable installation until the cable is completely installed.

14. Route through the backbone cable pathway and secure the backbone cable in each closet as necessary.

15. Label both cable ends and if not already done, label the backbone cable pathway.

16. Document the cable installation on building blueprints.

Pulling Backbone Cable Horizontally

Backbone cables can be installed horizontally to connect TRs located on the same floor of a building. These cables are called horizontal backbone cables. Horizontal backbone cables are pulled and supported the same way as horizontal cables. Horizontal backbone cables are larger and heavier than horizontal cables and may need additional labor and larger supporting structures compared to horizontal cables.

Horizontal backbone cables may need to be installed using mechanical pulling equipment if the backbone cables are installed through a conduit with other cables installed in it. The friction created by the cable jackets rubbing together requires a large amount of pulling force to install the backbone cables. Cable lubricant should be used to reduce the friction caused by the cable jackets rubbing together. This will require less pulling force and enable the backbone cables to be installed easier.

Steps for Pulling Backbone Cable Horizontally   The steps for installing a backbone cable horizontally are as follows:

1. Attach a pull rope to the backbone cable. If the cable is very large and heavy, mechanical pulling equipment may be required.

2. If necessary, install cable pulleys along the horizontal backbone cable path. Cable pulleys should be installed at each turn in the pathway and at distances not to exceed 30 m (100 ft.).

3. The project supervisor must determine the communication method to be used during the cable installation and confirm that all workers are capable of communicating with their co-workers.

4. Using the pull rope, pull the backbone cable along the horizontal cable pathway until it is completely installed.

5. Route and secure cable in any intermediate or pass through closets, as necessary.

6. Label both cable ends and if not already done, label the horizontal backbone cable pathway.

7. Document the cable installation on building blueprints.

PULLING BACKBONE CABLE

The process of pulling backbone cables requires that the cables are handled and installed correctly without damaging the cable or the cable conductors. This means that the following issues must be considered during the backbone cabling installation:

▼ Handling backbone cables

■ Maximum pulling force

■ Maximum backbone cable distances

■ Avoiding sources of noise

■ Vertical cable support

▲ Grounding and bonding

Handling Backbone Cables

The first issue to address during the cable installation process is correctly handling the backbone cables. Both copper UTP and optical fiber backbone cables are susceptible to degradation and possible damage if the cables are abused during the cable installation.

Most communications systems, such as DSL and digital telephony, use a balanced signaling scheme. The signaling scheme requires that the backbone and horizontal cable pairs be twisted together. A balanced transmission scheme requires that the twisted cable pairs be symmetrical or twisted evenly throughout the entire cable run. This symmetry guarantees that when "balanced" signals are transmitted down the pair, the resulting electromagnetic fields are self-canceling. If one of the pairs of a UTP cable was slightly unbalanced, the cable may emit unwanted electromagnetic radiation and may be susceptible to unwanted noise. When the cable's geometry is disturbed, the cable pairs may become unbalanced, resulting in the cable generating unwanted signals or in it picking up unwanted noise signals.

Backbone cables must be handled carefully during the cable installation. The primary objective is not to alter or disturb the cable pairs individually or alter how the cable pairs are arranged inside the cable jacket. Changing the cable configuration will reduce the cable's performance specifications. This means that the cable will have higher attenuation and lower NEXT after the cables are installed due to the cable pair alterations.

Handling backbone cables correctly means taking the time and care to guarantee that the cable is not abused during the installation. Avoid kinking and crushing the cable during the cable pulling. Once the cable's configuration has been altered by either kinking or crushing, the cable's performance properties cannot be restored.

Maximum Pulling Force

A related issue to handling backbone cables correctly is knowing the maximum pulling force that can be applied to backbone cables when they are being pulled. *Pulling force* is defined as the force that is applied to a communication cable as it is being installed.

Excessive pulling force applied to cables during the installation process can damage the cable conductors. Pulling the cable too hard will change the configuration of the individual cable pairs or how the cable pairs lay inside the cable jacket. In extreme cases, too much pulling force will either stretch or possibly even break the cable conductors.

Excessive pulling force can also have an adverse effect on the cable's jacket and insulation. The cable jacket can become stretched or ripped off the cable exposing the cable pairs. Excessive pulling force can also stretch or crack the insulation surrounding the individual conductors in the cable. This can result in shorts occurring between the individual cable conductors.

The maximum pulling force for a backbone cable will usually be specified by the cable's manufacturer. The specifications for the cable will define the maximum pulling force that can be applied to the cable before the cable's performance begins to deteriorate. Industry standards also recommend avoiding jerking communication cables that become stuck during the cable pull. Jerking the cable may place more pulling force on a cable than is allowed by the cable's specifications.

Avoid the temptation of pulling as hard as possible to complete the cable pull. A good technique is to use a large amount of lubricant instead of a large amount of pulling force. The lubricant will reduce friction between the cable jackets and ease the cable through the conduit. Avoid installing cables in congested or full conduits. If multiple copper cables are installed in a conduit, industry standards recommend a maximum fill ratio of 40 percent of the conduit capacity.

Maximum Backbone Cable Distance

When pulling backbone cables, it is very important not to exceed the maximum cable distances supported by industry cabling standards. Cables that exceed the maximum cable distances will exhibit high attenuation. The transmitted signals will shrink due to the long cable length. The transmitted signals must be strong enough for the receiving equipment to decode them correctly. Excessive attenuation on horizontal cables may lead to excessive bit errors on a high-speed network.

The maximum length for a horizontal cable defined in the ANSI/TIA/EIA-568-A and ANSI/TIA/EIA-568-B.1 standards are shown in Tables 17-1 to 17-4. The maximum distance for UTP backbone cables used for voice applications are shown in Table 17-1.

Location	Maximum Distance
MC (CD) to HC (FD)	800 m (2,624 ft.)
MC (CD) to IC (BD)	500 m (1,640 ft.)
IC (BD) to HC (FD)	300 m (984 ft.)

Table 17-1.   Maximum UTP Backbone Cable Distances

NOTE: UTP backbone cables used for high-speed data applications are limited to a maximum of 90 m (295 ft.) between any two TR locations.

The maximum distance for 50/125 multimode optical fiber backbone cables are shown in Table 17-2.

Location	Maximum Distance
MC (CD) to HC (FD)	2,000 m (6,560 ft.)
MC (CD) to IC (BD)	1,700 m (5,575 ft.)
IC (BD) to HC (FD)	300 m (984 ft.)

Table 17-2. Maximum 50/125 Optical Fiber Backbone Cable Distances

The maximum distance for 62.5/125 multimode optical fiber backbone cables are shown in Table 17-3.

Location	Maximum Distance
MC (CD) to HC (FD)	2,000 m (6,560 ft.)
MC (CD) to IC (BD)	1,700 m (5,575 ft.)
IC (BD) to HC (FD)	300 m (984 ft.)

Table 17-3. Maximum 62.5/125 Optical Fiber Backbone Cable Distances

The maximum distance for singlemode optical fiber backbone cables are shown in Table 17-4.

Avoiding Sources of Noise

Multipair UTP backbone cables are classified as unshielded, twisted-pair cables. These cables actually have a metal shield inside of the cable jacket surrounding all of the cable pairs. Backbone cables should be installed to avoid sources of noise in a commercial building.

Location	Maximum Distance
MC (CD) to HC (FD)	3,000 m (9,840 ft.)
MC (CD) to IC (BD)	2,700 m (8,855 ft.)
IC (BD) to HC (FD)	300 m (984 ft.)

Table 17-4.   Maximum Singlemode Optical Fiber Backbone Cable Distances

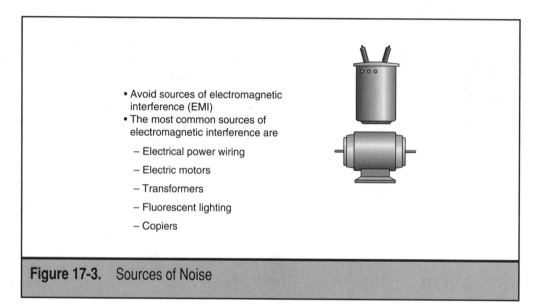

- Avoid sources of electromagnetic interference (EMI)
- The most common sources of electromagnetic interference are
  - Electrical power wiring
  - Electric motors
  - Transformers
  - Fluorescent lighting
  - Copiers

Figure 17-3.   Sources of Noise

The most common sources of noise in a commercial building are

▼   Electrical power wiring

■   Large motors and generators usually associated with large industrial equipment

■   Transformers

■   Fluorescent lights

▲   Photocopiers

The backbone cable should be routed away from sources of electrical noise. Backbone cable pathways must be bonded to an approved building ground. The cable shield must be bonded in each TR where the cable is terminated. The bonding connection will route any coupled noise energy to ground and prevent ground potential differences on the cable.

Cables installed above the ceiling must be suspended so the cables have a minimum 12-in. clearance above florescent lights and florescent light ballasts. It is the cable installer's responsibility to be aware of potential sources of noise and to avoid installing copper communication cables near noise sources.

Some commercial buildings are very noisy environments. These environments may cause signaling problems in copper communications cables. If noise is a problem on a copper communications cable, one of the following options can be implemented:

▼ Separate the cable from the source of the noise.

■ Enclose the unshielded communication cable in a metallic conduit.

▲ Replace the unshielded cable with either a shielded cable or an optical fiber cable.

The least expensive way to protect an unshielded cable from electrical noise is to simply move it away from the source of the noise. Noise energy must be coupled into a copper cable for the noise to affect or corrupt the signals traveling over the cable. The coupling process occurs when the sources of the noise and the cable are in close proximity to each other. The greater the distance, the less coupling will occur.

Metallic conduits provide excellent protection for unshielded copper cables. The metallic conduits must be bonded to an approved building ground. Any noise energy that hits the metallic conduit will be run to ground. None of the electrical noise energy will disrupt the signals traveling across the unshielded communication cable.

If the unshielded cable cannot be moved or enclosed in a metallic conduit, the cable can be replaced with a cable this is not as susceptible to the electrical noise. Optical fiber cables can be used instead of copper cables in these environments. These cables transmit signals in the form of light pulses instead of electrical pulses. Electrical noise energy will not disturb these light signals.

Vertical Cable Support

Backbone cables must be properly supported when installed in vertical pathways. The term maximum vertical rise defines the cable's support requirements. The *maximum vertical rise* is the distance over which the cable is vertically self-supporting. This distance is a function of the weight of the cable and its maximum tensile rating.

The use of cable supports in the vertical pathway is recommended

▼ At the top of each vertical rise

▲ Every time the vertical rise rating of the cable is exceeded

Properly supporting a backbone cable will guarantee that the cable will not become damaged due to its own cable weight. Cables that are not properly supported will have diminished performance and possible broken cable pairs inside of the cable jacket.

Grounding and Bonding Backbone Cables

Multipair UTP backbone cables have an overall cable shield under the cable jacket and surrounding the cable pairs. The cable shield provides physical protection to the cable pairs and serves as a coupled bonding conductor. The shield in copper backbone cables must be bonded to an approved ground location in each TR. The shield must be bonded using a #6 AWG conductor to either the TMGB or the TGB.

The steps for bonding the backbone cable shield are as follows:

1. Strip the cable jacket and the cable shield off the cable conductors on the backbone cable.

2. Slit the cable jacket without cutting the cable shield.

3. Place the bonding clip under the cable jacket and over the cable shield.

4. Wrap electrical tape around the bonding clip, securing it in place.

5. Attach the outside of the bonding clip over the inside clip and secure it with a nut.

6. Attach the bonding conductor to the bonding clip.

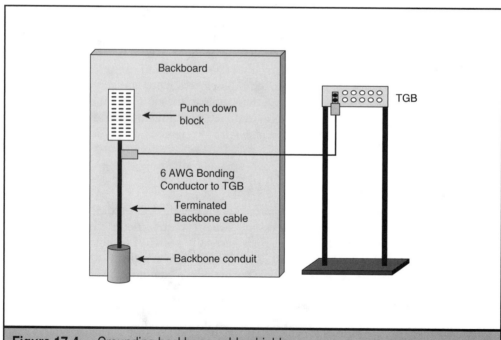

Figure 17-4. Grounding backbone cable shields

INSTALLING OPTICAL FIBER BACKBONE CABLES

The process of installing optical fiber backbone cables is similar to installing copper backbone cables. There are some differences due to the different types of media and the different weights of optical fiber backbone cables. The remaining pages of this chapter will address how to install optical fiber backbone cables.

Testing the Optical Fiber Cable Before Pulling

It is extremely important to test optical fiber cable for continuity before the installation begins. This simple practice will identify any cable that has been damaged before it is installed. Optical fiber cable should be tested for continuity while on the reel. This requires having access to both ends of the cable. The cable should be ordered with access to both ends from the cable manufacturer.

The fiber cable can be tested for continuity by shining a flashlight into one end of the cable. A power meter or OTDR can also be used, but the bare optical fibers must be terminated with a fiber optic connector on both ends to use either of these devices to perform the continuity test.

Considerations for Pulling Fiber Optic Cable

Although optical fiber cables are installed like copper cable, there are a few important differences that should be taken into consideration:

▼ Optical fiber cable is glass and therefore breakable. Care must be taken not to bend or flex a fiber cable beyond its minimum bend radius.

▲ The tensile rating of fiber is less than the rating for copper cables. Care must be taken not to exceed the maximum tensile rating when pulling the cable.

If during the installation of the cable you exceed the minimum bend radius or maximum tensile rating, the fibers within the cable will break or shatter, and the cable will be useless. It is important to adhere to the following specifications during the cable installation:

▼ Minimum bend radius

▲ Maximum tensile rating

Minimum Bend Radius

When installing optical fiber cable, it is important not to violate the minimum bend radius allowed for the cable. The minimum bend radius of an optical fiber cable is 20 times the outside diameter of the cable when the cable is being installed. Larger size and fiber count fiber optic cables will require a larger minimum bend radius than smaller cables.

NOTE: The minimum bend radius of an optical fiber cable is ten times the outside diameter of the cable when the cable is terminated.

Maximum Tensile Rating

All optical fiber cables have a maximum tensile rating, sometimes called maximum tensile load. This rating is specified by the manufacturer of the fiber cable. The *maximum tensile load* is the maximum amount of stress that can be placed on the cable while it is being pulled before the cable becomes damaged.

Never exceed the cable's maximum tensile rating during installation. When a winch or pulling machine is used during installation, it is recommended that a dynamometer (sometimes called a tensiometer) be used to monitor the tension of the cable. After the cable is installed, verify that no residual tension remains on the cable.

Attaching the Fiber Optic Cable to the Pull Rope

The first step in successfully pulling an optical fiber cable is to correctly attach the pull rope to the cable. Optical fiber cable is fragile and can be damaged during the cable pulling stage if the pull rope is not attached to the cable correctly. The pull rope must be attached to the cable so stress is not placed on the glass optical fibers.

Optical fiber cables should be pulled using the strength members of the cable or the strength members and the cable jacket. The strength members facilitate the cable installation and distribute the pulling load. This reduces the stress on the glass optical fibers. The exact method for attaching the pull rope to the optical fiber cable will differ depending on the size and the construction of the cable.

Attaching the Pull Rope to an Optical Fiber Backbone Cable

Larger size optical fiber cables are typically used for interbuilding or intrabuilding backbone applications. These cables are typically constructed with 12 to 144 or more optical fibers, aramid yarn strength members, additional strength members, and the cable jacket. Cables with greater than 12 optical fibers will typically have the fibers packaged into groups of 6 or 12 fibers, and a fiberglass rod will separate the groups in the middle of the cable.

For larger optical fiber cables, the pull rope is attached to both the cable jacket and the cable strength members. A meshed pulling grip is attached to the cable jacket. Both the meshed pulling grip and the strength members are attached to the pulling swivel using the following steps:

1. Strip back the cable jacket about 12 to 24 in. removing the fiber, antibend rod, and any armor shielding leaving only the aramid yarn strength members.

2. If using a meshed pulling grip, wrap friction tape over 3 to 6 in. of the cable jacket and slide the pulling grip over the cable jacket.

3. Separate the aramid yarn into two strand groups.

4. Pass each strand in opposite directions through the pulling swivel.

5. Attach both the pulling grip and the aramid yard strength members to the pulling swivel.

6. Wrap tape around the pulling grip and aramid yarn up to the pulling swivel starting at the cable jacket.

Meshed Pulling Grips

Meshed pulling grips have been used for a long time to pull cables. Meshed pulling grips are mainly used with power pulling equipment. They help to reduce the chances of snagging or kinking cables.

Pulling grips used for optical fiber cables are slightly different than those used for copper cables. The pulling grips for optical fiber cable are designed for the cable's lighter weight and looser construction. Pulling grips are designed to fit over the cable's jacket. Some manufacturers are designing smaller pulling grips that attach directly to the strength members of an optical fiber cable. The proper pulling grip must be selected to match the cable's diameter so it fits securely. If the wrong grip is selected, the cable can snap or the grip can break loose causing the cable to be repulled.

Lubricants

The use of lubricants is highly recommended during optical fiber cable pulls. Lubricants will reduce friction between the cable jacket and the innerduct or other cables installed in the innerduct. Lubricants should be used regardless of the length or duration of the cable pull.

Innerducts should be lubricated before optical fiber cable is installed. The lubricant can be distributed in the innerduct by pulling a swab in front of the cable. It may also be injected with a pump or a gravity device. Additional amounts of lubricant may be necessary before bends and known off-sets in the conduit. It is also recommended to lubricate the pull rope. This will reduce friction and pull rope tension.

Most optical fiber cable manufacturers recommend using a water-based pulling lubricant. Never use detergent-based lubricants such as dish washing detergent or liquid hand soap. Most detergents become sticky when they dry. Detergents have a tendency to dry out the cable jacket causing it to crack over time. Take the time to check the lubricant manufacturer's specifications to verify that the lubricant you are using is approved for use with PE or PVC cable sheaths.

Installing Innerducts in a Conduit

Innerducts should be installed in all cable pathways that support optical fiber cable. If an innerduct is either full or nonexistent, a new innerduct must be installed.

An innerduct is installed just like cable. It is installed with a pull rope. The innerduct can either be pulled by hand or by power pulling equipment. If the conduit is straight or has less than two 90-degree bends, it may be possible to push the innerduct through the conduit.

The steps for installing an innerduct in a conduit are as follows:

1. If the innerduct was purchased with a pull string, cut off the first 2 to 3 ft. of the innerduct without cutting the pull string.

2. Cut a 1-in. notch into the innerduct with a knife.

3. Insert the pull rope into the notch and wrap the pull string around the innerduct and tie it into a knot.

4. Wrap tape around the pull string to prevent it from becoming cut or damaged during the installation.

These steps should be performed while the innerduct is still on the roll:

5. Attach the pull rope in the conduit to the innerduct and pull the innerduct through the conduit.

6. Once the innerduct is installed, leave 10 ft. of extra innerduct from the conduit entrance before cutting it from the reel.

7. Cut the innerduct back to the conduit entrance without cutting the pull string.

8. Unwrap the tape at the far end of the innerduct and untie the pull string.

Unreeling Fiber Optic Cable

There are times when the optical fiber cable spool cannot be set up for the cable pull. The work space may be too small for placing the able reel on jackstands. If optical fiber cable reels cannot be set up to spin freely during the cable pull, the optical fiber cable must be taken off the cable reel.

CAUTION: Unreeling optical fiber cable is not recommended and should only be done in situations where the cable reel cannot be set up to spin freely.

If the cable must be unreeled during the installation, use the figure-eight configuration to prevent the cable from kinking or twisting. Avoid coiling the optical fiber cable in a continuous direction for all lengths that exceed 30 m (100 ft.). The preferred size of the figure-eight is about 4.5 m (15 ft.) in length with each loop about 1.5 to 2.5 m (5 to 8 ft.) in diameter. This configuration will accommodate both loose buffered and tight buffered cable. The figure-eights for tight buffered cables can be smaller in size.

General Procedures for Pulling Optical Fiber Cable

The steps for pulling optical fiber cable may differ slightly depending on the environment and the type of cable being installed. Although the exact procedures will slightly differ for each environment, most of the general procedures are the same.

The general procedures for pulling optical fiber cable are as follows:

1. Before pulling the cable, test the cable to eliminate any possibility that the cable is damaged.

2. Set up the cable spools so the cable pays off the top of the spools.

3. Reel the cable off the spool to avoid twisting or placing excess strain on the cable.

4. Set the cable spools so they are in a straight line with the cable run.

5. When multiple cables need to be installed, they should be placed in the innerduct at the same time.

6. When applying tension to the cable, always use the cable's strength members and never the optical fibers.

7. Do not pull on the outer jacket. This may temporarily elongate it. When the cable jacket returns to its normal state, the fiber and buffer may be compressed during the retraction of the cable's jacket. This may cause macrobend attenuation in the cable.

8. Pull uniformly on the cable keeping the pulling force below the maximum tensile rating for the cable.

9. Avoid jerking or applying excessive pulling force on the cable even for short periods of time.

10. When pulling multiple cables, pull cables that are the same size and weight together and do not violate the maximum pulling tension for the lowest rated cable in the group.

11. Never violate the minimum bend radius for the cable. This is usually 20 times the cable's diameter when the cable is being installed.

12. Never use power pulling equipment for inside plant optical fiber cables such as horizontal or intrabuilding backbone cables. These cables should always be pulled by hand.

13. When using power pulling equipment, always use tension monitoring equipment and break away swivels.

14. Always use innerducts to protect the fiber cable from damage by sharp corners or protrusions in the cable pathway.

15. Do not pull optical fiber cables with copper cables.

16. Do not deform the optical fiber cable's jacket by using cable ties or straps to secure the cable.

CHAPTER SUMMARY

Multipair copper and optical fiber cables are installed for the backbone subsystem. Backbone communication cables are installed between telelcommuncations rooms (TRs) for voice, low-speed data systems, and high-speed data systems. The ANSI/TIA/EIA-568-B.1 standard supports 100-ohm UTP cable, 62.5/125 μm multimode optical fiber cable, 50/125 μm multimode optical fiber cable, and singlemode optical fiber cable types in the backbone subsystem for new cable installations.

The basic steps involved in pulling both copper and optical fiber backbone cables include survey backbone cable paths, setting up and designating backbone cable work areas, installing pull ropes in backbone pathways, setting up cable reels, labeling each cable and the cable reel, attaching cables to pull rope, and pulling backbone cables.

Each backbone pathway must be surveyed before any cables are installed. The survey should look at the conduit between TRs, conduit capacity, conduit utilization, conduit fill ratio, how the backbone cables will enter and exit conduits, supporting structures between TRs, and cable pulling points.

Once the survey of the backbone cable pathways is complete, the cable pulling setup must be completed. The cable pulling setup involves organizing all of the tools and materials necessary to complete the backbone cable pulls. Part of the setup process is the activity of designating and securing the work area. Orange cones and yellow caution tape are typically used for this function. The next step involves installing a pull rope in every backbone pathway. A plastic or nylon line with a minimum test rating of 200 lbs. of pulling tension should be selected for a pull rope. Pull ropes are usually installed with a fishtape. A good practice is to attach a new pull rope, called a trailer rope, to any backbone cables that are installed using the pull rope. The new pull rope will be installed when the backbone cables are pulled through the conduit.

Backbone cables are usually shipped on large cable reels. Before starting the backbone cable pull, the backbone cable reel must be set up so the cable can easily feed into the backbone cable pathway. Large backbone cable reels must be placed on a cable jackstand. The cable reel must be positioned so the cable will pay off the reel easily without getting tangled or kinked.

Once the backbone cable reels are set up for the cable pull, each backbone cable must be uniquely labeled. A cable label must be attached to each backbone cable and the corresponding label attached to the backbone cable reel. Cable labels should be placed approximately 6 to 12 in. from the end of the cable. This will prevent the label from being covered by tape when the cable is attached to a pull rope. Industry standards recommend leaving a 3 m (10 ft.) to 10 m (33 ft.) service loop in a backbone cable run. The service loop will permit the backbone cable to be moved or the cable terminations in the TR to be reconfigured.

The last step before horizontal cables are pulled is to attach pull ropes to the cables. Pull ropes are attached to backbone cables by one of the following methods: pulling eye, pulling grip, and directly tying the pull rope to the backbone cable. It is recommended to use a pulling swivel when pulling backbone cables with a pull rope. A pulling swivel will prevent the pull rope and backbone cable from being twisted while it is being installed in the backbone cable pathway.

Backbone cables are pulled between TRs in a commercial building. The ANSI/TIA/EIA-568-A and ANSI/TIA/EIA-568-B.1 standards require that all intrabuilding backbone cables be installed in a physical star topology. Backbone cables will be installed in one of the following configurations in a building: top down, bottom up, or horizontally. Most backbone cables are installed top down because most TRs in multistory commercial buildings tend to be lined up vertically from floor to floor. These TRs have backbone conduits that link each TR to the room above and the room below. This permits the backbone cable to be lowered through the TRs. Backbone cables can also be installed from the first floor of a multistory building to a higher floor through the backbone pathway. Pulling a backbone cable from the bottom up through a vertical riser requires a mechanical pulling device and a strong pulling rope.

Backbone cables can be installed horizontally to connect TRs located on the same floor of a building. Horizontal backbone cables may need to be installed using mechanical pulling equipment if the backbone cables are installed through a conduit with other cables installed in it. The friction created by the cable jackets rubbing together requires a large amount of pulling force to install the backbone cables. Cable lubricants should be used to reduce the friction caused by the cable jackets rubbing together. This will require less pulling force and enable the backbone cables to be installed easier.

The process of pulling backbone cables requires that the cables are handled and installed correctly without damaging the cable or the cable conductors. This means that the following issues must be considered during the backbone cabling installation: proper handling of the backbone cables, maximum pulling force, maximum backbone cable distances, avoiding sources of noise, vertical cable supports, and grounding and bonding of the backbone cable shield.

Backbone cables must be handled carefully during the cable installation. The primary objective is not to alter or disturb the cable pairs individually or alter how the cable pairs are arranged inside the cable jacket. A related issue to handling backbone cables correctly is knowing the maximum pulling force that can be applied to backbone cables when they are being pulled. The maximum pulling force for a backbone cable will usually be specified by the cable's manufacturer. If multiple copper cables are installed in a conduit, industry standards recommend a maximum fill ratio of 40 percent of the conduit capacity.

When pulling backbone cables, it is very important not to exceed the maximum cable distances supported by industry cabling standards. Cables that exceed the maximum cable distances will exhibit high attenuation. Excessive attenuation on horizontal cables may lead to excessive bit errors on a high-speed network.

Backbone cables should be installed to avoid sources of noise in a commercial building. The most common sources of noise in a commercial building are: electrical power wiring, large motors and generators usually associated with large industrial equipment, transformers, fluorescent lights, and photocopiers. Cables installed above the ceiling must be suspended to the cable and have a minimum of 12 in. of clearance above florescent lights and florescent light ballasts.

Backbone cables must be properly supported when installed in vertical pathways. The maximum vertical rise is the distance over which the cable is vertically self-supporting.

This distance is a function of the weight of the cable and its maximum tensile rating. The use of cable supports in the vertical pathway is recommended at the top of each vertical rise and every time the vertical rise rating of the cable is exceeded. Properly supporting a backbone cable will guarantee that the cable will not become damaged due to its own cable weight.

Multipair UTP backbone cables have an overall cable shield under the cable jacket and surrounding the cable pairs. The shield in copper backbone cables must be bonded to an approved ground location in each TR. The shield must be bonded using a #6 AWG conductor to either to TMGB or the TGB.

It is extremely important to test optical fiber cable for continuity before the installation begins. Optical fiber cable should be tested for continuity while on the reel. The fiber cable can be tested for continuity by shining a flashlight into one end of the cable. A power meter or OTDR can also be used but the bare optical fibers must be terminated with a fiber optic connector on both ends to use either of these devices to perform the continuity test.

When installing optical fiber cable, it is important not to violate the minimum bend radius allowed for the cable. The minimum bend radius of an optical fiber cable is 20 times the outside diameter of the cable when the cable is being installed. Larger size and fiber count fiber optic cables will require a larger minimum bend radius than smaller cables.

The maximum tensile load is the maximum amount of stress that can be placed on the cable while it is being pulled before the cable becomes damaged. Never exceed the cable's maximum tensile rating during installation. When a winch or pulling machine is used during installation, it is recommended that a dynamometer (sometimes called a tensiometer) be used to monitor the tension of the cable. After the cable is installed, verify that no residual tension remains on the cable.

The first step in successfully pulling an optical fiber cable is to correctly attach the pull rope to the cable. The pull rope must be attached to the cable so stress is not placed on the glass optical fibers. Optical fiber cables should be pulled using the strength members of the cable or the strength members and the cable jacket. The strength members facilitate the cable installation and distribute the pulling load. For larger optical fiber cables, the pull rope is attached to both the cable jacket and the cable strength members. A meshed pulling grip is attached to the cable jacket.

The use of lubricants is highly recommended during optical fiber cable pulls. Lubricants will reduce friction between the cable jacket and the innerduct or other cables installed in the innerduct. Lubricants should be used regardless of the length or duration of the cable pull. The lubricant can be distributed in the innerduct by pulling a swab in front of the cable. It may also be injected with a pump or a gravity device.

Innerducts should be installed in all cable pathways that support optical fiber cable. An innerduct is installed just like cable. It is installed with a pull rope. The innerduct can either be pulled by hand or by power pulling equipment. If the conduit is straight or has less than two 90-degree bends, it may be possible to push the innerduct through the conduit.

There are times when the optical fiber cable spool cannot be set up for the cable pull. If optical fiber cable reels cannot be set up to spin freely during the cable pull, the optical fiber cable must be taken off the cable reel using a figure-eight configuration to prevent the cable from kinking or twisting. Avoid coiling the optical fiber cable in a continuous direction for all lengths that exceed 30 m (100 ft.). The preferred size of the figure-eight is about 4.5 m (15 ft.) in length with each loop about 1.5 to 2.5 m (5 to 8 ft.) in diameter. This configuration will accommodate both loose buffered and tight buffered cable.

CHAPTER 18

Pulling Copper Horizontal Cable

Copper cables can be used for both horizontal and backbone media types. Large multipair UTP cables are used for backbone applications. Smaller, four-pair cables are installed for horizontal applications.

Horizontal cables are installed from the telecommunications room (TR) to the work area. These cables can be installed in a cable pathway that can run either below the floor or above the ceiling. Horizontal cables can also be installed above the ceiling of a building in the open space between the ceiling and the roof. This chapter will describe how to install copper horizontal cables.

ALLOWED MEDIA TYPES

The ANSI/TIA/EIA-568-B.1 standard released in 2001 supports the following media types in the horizontal subsystem for new cable installations (see Figure 18-1):

▼ 100-ohm UTP cable

■ 62.5/125 µm multimode optical fiber cable

▲ 50/125 µm multimode optical fiber cable

Figure 18-1.   Recognized horizontal media

One-hundred ohm UTP copper cables are the primary type of media installed for the horizontal subsystem (see Figure 18-2). These types of cables are preferred because most applications can be supported over UTP cable. Voice systems were the first to work over UTP cable. High-speed local area networks (LANs) were modified to operate over data grade UTP cables. This is the reason that the ANSI/TIA/EIA-568-B.1 standard recommends that a minimum of two cables be installed to each work area. One cable should be a category 3 UTP cable for voice applications and the other should be a data grade category 5e or high cable.

Industry surveys indicate that over 75 percent of all installed horizontal cables are category 5 or higher quality cable. Data grade category 5, category 5e, and category 6 UTP cables are required to support high-speed LAN applications. These cables offer excellent performance and low cost, but they must be installed correctly.

Historically other types of copper media, such as coaxial cable and STP-A cables, have been installed for the horizontal subsystem. This practice has been phased out over the last ten years because coaxial cable is not supported by the ANSI/TIA/EIA-568-A standards for new installations, and STP-A cable was eliminated as a recognized media type from the ANSI/TIA/EIA-568-B.1 standard as well. ScTP copper cables are supported in both the ANSI/TIA/EIA-568-A and ANSI/TIA/EIA-568-B.1 standards, but this media

Figure 18-2.   Horizontal UTP cable

type is not used as much as UTP cable. As a result, UTP cables are the primary type of copper cable installed for the horizontal subsystem.

PULLING HORIZONTAL CABLES

Pulling horizontal cables is a series of steps that are performed to install horizontal copper cable successfully:

1. Survey horizontal cable paths.

2. Set up and designate the work area.

3. Install pull strings.

4. Set up cable reels or boxes.

5. Label each cable and the cable reel or box.

6. Attach cables to pull strings.

7. Pull cables.

Survey Horizontal Cable Paths

The first step when starting to pull horizontal cables is to survey the cable paths or cable runs. This activity involves starting at the place where the cabling runs will start and inspecting the path to each work area. Most horizontal cables are pulled from the TR to each work area location.

The TR itself should be the first stop during the survey process (see Figure 18-3). The closet should be built out before the horizontal cables are pulled. The location of the communication racks and the backboard should be identified in each closet. These are the places where horizontal cables are terminated in the TR. Category 3 voice cables are usually terminated on punch down blocks mounted on the backboard, and category 5e or higher UTP cables are terminated on patch panels mounted on communication racks.

The next step in the survey process is to identify where the horizontal cables will exit the TR. Most TRs are supported by horizontal pathways. These pathways may enter the TR underground or above the ceiling. The horizontal cables should be pulled to run the cables in the horizontal pathways to each work area location. The survey of the TR should also verify that cable-supporting hardware, such as ladder racks, are installed to support the horizontal cables from the punch down blocks and communications racks to the horizontal pathways (see Figure 18-4).

The next step is to investigate each horizontal pathway from the TR to the work area locations. If the pathway is an underfloor trench, the trench must be opened. If the pathway is a cable tray installed above the ceiling, use a ladder and open the ceiling tiles to see the cable tray. In either case, the horizontal should be analyzed and a determination

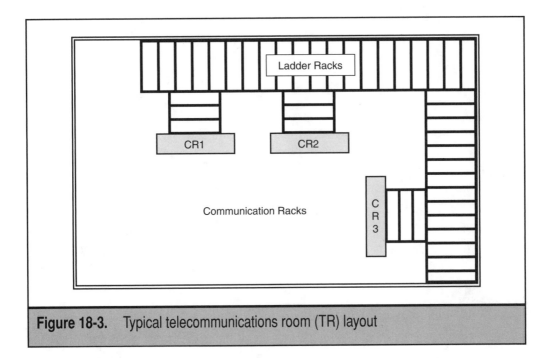

Figure 18-3. Typical telecommunications room (TR) layout

must be made whether the pathway can support the new horizontal cables that must be installed. If your survey identifies that the horizontal pathways are full or not capable of supporting the new horizontal cables, an alternate pathway must be used or a new pathway must be installed before the horizontal cables are pulled.

Set Up and Designate the Work Area

Once the survey of the horizontal cable runs is complete, the cable pulling setup must be completed. The cable pulling setup involves organizing all of the tools and materials necessary to complete the horizontal cable pulls. The setup is one of the most important tasks to complete so the installation proceeds smoothly and is completed quickly. Installations where the proper setup has not been completed before the cable pulls are started are usually marred by delays associated with finding necessary tools or obtaining the correct materials.

Part of the setup process is the activity of designating and securing the work area. This is a simple activity but one that is an important safety consideration. When working inside a building, the work area should be designated and secured. Orange cones and yellow caution tape are typically used for this function. The use of orange cones and yellow caution tape will alert employees and others about possible dangers by entering this area. It will also serve to restrict access to anyone other than authorized members of the cabling crew.

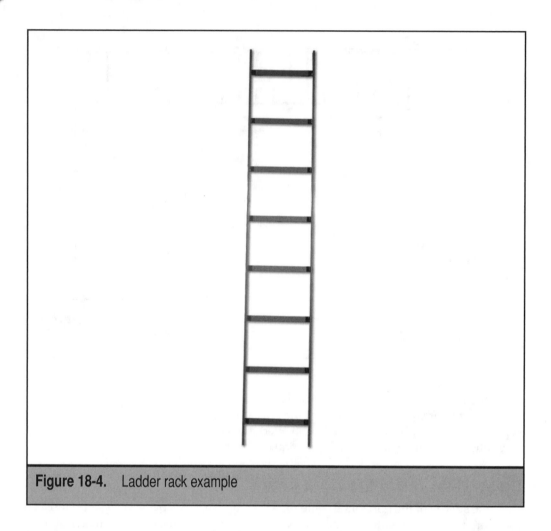

Figure 18-4.   Ladder rack example

Installing Pull Strings

Each horizontal pathway should be equipped with a pull string. The pull string is used to pull communication cables through the cable pathways such as conduits and under-floor trenches. Above ceiling cable trays or J hooks may use pull strings to install cable. Because these cable pathways are open, the cables can also be installed by hand.

Pull strings are usually installed with a fishtape. A *fishtape* is a flexible, metal or fiber-glass device that can be inserted into a conduit. These tools are manufactured in 50-, 100-, 150-, and 200-ft. lengths. The flexible nature of this tool enables it to work its way through conduits that have cables installed in them. The fishtape is inserted in one end of a conduit and pushed through the entire conduit length. The pull string is attached to the end of the fishtape with tape. The fishtape is then reeled back, installing the pull string in the conduit.

Long conduits usually have pull boxes along the conduit run. Industry standards recommend that a pull box should be installed after each 30 m (100 ft) section of conduit. Each conduit section between pull boxes should have a pull string installed in it. Avoid installing pull strings through a pull box. These cable pulls will be difficult as the conduit sections become crowded with cables.

Each pull string must be secured at each end once they are installed. The pull string can be tied to the outlet box in the work area. The opposite end can be tied to anything convenient in the TR. Once a pull string is installed in a conduit it can be used to pull horizontal cables.

The process of installing a pull string can be difficult and take a long time if the conduit already has cables installed in it. A good practice is to attach a new pull string, called a trailer string, to any cables that are installed using the pull sting. The new pull string will be installed when the cables are pulled through the conduit.

The steps for installing a pull string in a conduit are as follows:

1. Estimate the length of the conduit. This can be done by measuring the distance on building blueprints or following the conduit and walking off the distance.

2. Select a fishtape that will be long enough to reach the opposite end of the conduit.

3. Insert a fishtape into one end of the conduit.

4. Push the fishtape until it reaches the opposite end of the conduit. It may be necessary to twist the fishtape to push it through a congested conduit.

5   Attach the pull string to the hook on the end of the fishtape with tape. Taper the tape to create a streamlined configuration. This will prevent the fishtape from getting caught on cables as it is being pulled through the conduit.

6. Reel the fishtape in and secure the pull string on both ends of the conduit.

CAUTION: Never insert a fishtape into a conduit that has electrical wires running in it. This is an electrical hazard and could lead to electrocution.

Set Up Cable Reels or Boxes

Industry cabling standards specify that four-pair UTP cables should be installed for the horizontal subsystem. Larger cables are not supported for horizontal cable runs. Four-pair UTP cables are typically sold in 305 m (1,000 ft.) increments. The cable is usually shipped on cable reels. Some cable manufacturers ship their cable in easy payout boxes.

Before starting the cable pull, the cable reels or boxes must be set up so the cable can easily feed into the horizontal cable pathway. The cable reels or boxes must be positioned so the cable will pay off easily without getting tangled or kinked.

When multiple horizontal cables must be pulled at the same time, the cable reels can be placed on a cable tree. A cable tree is a device that enables multiple cable reels to be installed so they can all spin freely. They enable multiple cables to be pulled at the same time without the cables becoming hung up on the cable reels. Most cable trees are mounted on wheels so this device can be easily moved without requiring that the cable reels be taken off.

Cable reels that hold 1,500 ft. or 5,000 ft. cable length are usually too large and heavy to fit on a cable tree. Large cable reels must be placed on a cable jackstand. Cable jackstands are adjustable devices that support different sizes and weights of cable reels. A metal rod is inserted through the cable reel, and the reel is lifted on the cable jacks so that the reel spins freely.

CAUTION: Always verify that the metal rod that is used to support the cable reel is sufficient to support the weight of the cable reel. A metal rod that is too small may break, causing an injury.

Select a location for the cable tree or cable jackstand that provides enough work space. The ideal location for the cable tree or cable jackstand is near the feed point for the horizontal pathway. If the TR is too small, the cable tree and jackstand may need to be set up in the hallway outside of the TR.

Label Each Cable End

Once the cable reels or boxes are set up for the cable pull, each cable must be uniquely labeled. A cable label must be attached to each horizontal cable and the corresponding label attached to the cable reel or box.

Cable labels should be placed approximately 3 to 6 in. from the end of the cable. This will prevent the label from being covered by tape when the cable is attached to a pull string. In addition, the cable label is likely to remain on the cable even if the cable jacket is stripped off the cable end to terminate the cable. Once the cable is pulled through the horizontal pathway, cut the cable from the reel or box and label the cable end.

Most cable installers will leave excess cable on both ends of the cable run. This excess cable is cut off when the cable is terminated in the TR and in the work area. Always move or attach a new cable label to the cable as the old label is cut off with the excess cable slack. Although the termination device is labeled, the cable should always remain labeled behind the wall. A new article in the 2002 National Electrical Code requires that all communication cables be labeled on each end. Unlabeled cables are considered abandoned cables and must be removed from commercial buildings.

Attaching Pull Strings to Cables

The last step before horizontal cables are pulled is to attach pull strings to the cables. All of the horizontal cables that are to be pulled together will be formed into a grouped and attached to the same pull string. The lead edge of each cable, above the cable label, will be taped to the pull string.

The cables must be arranged so the taped configuration is streamlined. Each cable should be staggered to create a point. This will prevent the cable group from becoming hung up on any cables or other obstructions in the cable pathway.

Pulling Cable

Pulling horizontal copper cables is the activity of running the cables from the TR through the horizontal pathways to each work area location. During the pulling process, it is important that the cables are installed correctly. This means that the following issues must be considered during the cabling installation activity:

▼   Proper handling of the cable

■   Maximum pulling force

■   Not exceeding maximum cable distances

■   Avoiding sources of noise

■   Minimum bend radius

■   Supporting the cable

■   Cable slack

▲   Bundling cables

Handling UTP Cable

The first issue to address during the cable installation process is correctly handling the horizontal copper cables. UTP cables are designed with the cable pairs twisted together and a cable jacket keeping the cable together. UTP cables are manufactured with the cable pairs twisted into pairs. The twisted cable pairs create a balanced media configuration.

Communications systems, such as high-speed LANs, use a balanced signaling scheme. The signaling scheme requires that the horizontal cable pairs be twisted together. A balanced transmission scheme requires that the twisted cable pairs be symmetrical or twisted evenly throughout the entire cable run. This symmetry guarantees that when balanced signals are transmitted down the pair, the resulting electromagnetic fields are self-canceling. If one of the pairs of a UTP cable was slightly unbalanced, the cable may emit unwanted electromagnetic radiation and may be susceptible to unwanted noise. When the cable's geometry is disturbed, the cable pairs may become unbalanced, resulting in the cable generating unwanted signals or in it picking up unwanted noise signals.

Horizontal UTP cables must be handled carefully during the cable installation. The primary objective is not to alter or disturb the cable pairs individually or alter how the cable pairs are arranged inside the cable jacket. Changing the cable configuration will reduce the cable's performance specifications. This means that the cable will have higher attenuation and lower NEXT after the cables are installed due to the cable pair alterations.

Handling horizontal cables correctly means taking the time and care to guarantee that the cables are not abused during the installation. Avoid kinking and crushing the cable during the cable pulling. Once the cable's configuration has been altered by either kinking or crushing, the cable's performance properties cannot be restored by simply straightening the kinks out of the cable. The degree of diminished cable performance will most likely be discovered during the cable certification process.

Maximum Pulling Force

A related issue to handling UTP cables correctly is knowing the maximum pulling force that can be applied to copper UTP cables when they are being pulled. *Pulling force* is defined as the force that is applied to a communication cable as it is being installed.

Excessive pulling force applied to cables during the installation process can damage the cable conductors. Pulling the cable too hard will change the configuration of the individual cable pairs or how the cable pairs lay inside the cable jacket. In extreme cases, too much pulling force will either stretch or possibly even break the cable conductors.

Excessive pulling force can also have an adverse effect on the cable's jacket and insulation. The cable jacket can become stretched or ripped off of the cable exposing the cable pairs. Excessive pulling force can also stretch or crack the insulation surrounding the individual conductors in the cable. This can result in shorts occurring between the individual cable conductors.

The industry cabling standards specify that a maximum of 25 lbs. (110 N) of pulling force should be used when installing copper cables. This recommendation is made to avoid the pitfalls of placing too much force on copper cables. This practice will prevent stretching or damaging the cable conductors. Industry standards also recommend avoiding jerking communication cables that become stuck during the cable pull. Jerking the cable may place more than 25 lbs. of pulling force on a cable.

There are times, when pulling a copper cable through a conduit, that the cables become stuck, and more than 25 lbs. of pulling force must be applied. Avoid the temptation of pulling as hard as possible to complete the cable pull. A good technique is to use a large amount of lubricant instead of a large amount of pulling force. The lubricant will reduce friction between the cable jackets and ease the cable through the conduit. Avoid installing cables in congested or full conduits. If multiple copper cables are installed in a conduit, industry standards recommend a maximum fill ratio of 40 percent of the conduit capacity.

Maximum Horizontal Cable Distance

When pulling copper horizontal cables, it is very important not to exceed the maximum cable distances supported by industry cabling standards. Cables that exceed the maximum cable distances will exhibit high attenuation. The transmitted signals will shrink due to the long cable length. The transmitted signals must be strong enough for the receiving equipment to decode them correctly. Excessive attenuation on horizontal cables may lead to excessive bit errors on a high-speed network.

The maximum length for a horizontal cable defined in the ANSI/TIA/EIA-568-A and ANSI/TIA/EIA-568-B.1 standards is 90 m (295 ft.) (see Figure 18-5). This distance is defined from the termination of the cable in the horizontal closet, usually at a punch down block or patch panel, to the termination of the cable in the work area. The 90 m (295 ft.)

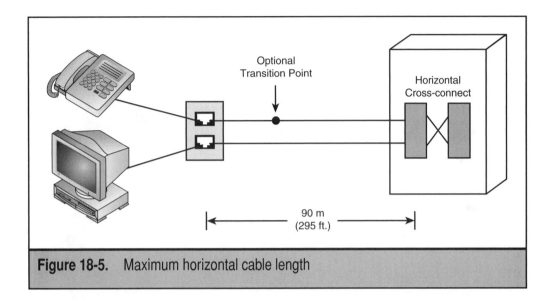

Figure 18-5. Maximum horizontal cable length

distance would also include routing the horizontal cable around any obstructions from the closet to the work area location. This is the industry-accepted distance for all types of recognized horizontal cables.

The ANSI/TIA/EIA-568-A and ANSI/TIA/EIA-568-B.1 standards also define the maximum distance for the channel (see Figure 18-6). The maximum distance for a communications channel is 100 m (328 ft.). The overall channel includes up to 90 m (295 ft.) of horizontal cable, an outlet/connector, an optional transition connection, and two connections at the cross-connect in the closet. The total length of the equipment cords, cross-connect wire/patch cords, and line cords is 10 m (33 ft.).

Avoiding Sources of Noise

Unshielded twisted-pair cables, as the name implies, have no shields contained in the cable. These cables have four cable pairs surrounded by the cable jacket. Electrical energy, commonly called noise, can be easily coupled onto these cables. Noise can corrupt communication signals and make them unusable by the receiving communication equipment.

A commercial building is full of devices that generate electrical noise. The most common sources of noise in a commercial building (see Figure 18-7) are

▼ Electrical power wiring

■ Large motors and generators usually associated with large industrial equipment

■ Transformers

■ Fluorescent lights

▲ Photocopiers

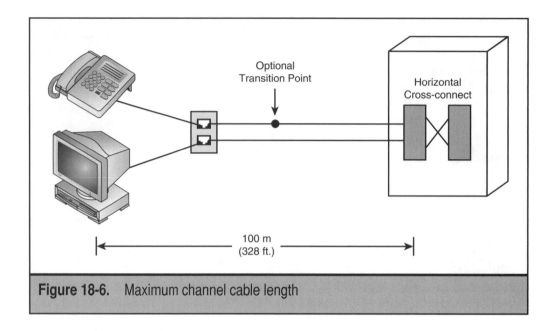

Figure 18-6.   Maximum channel cable length

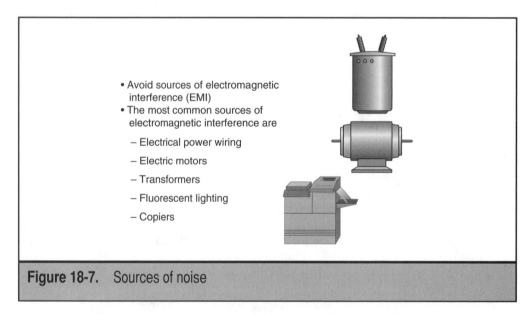

- Avoid sources of electromagnetic interference (EMI)
- The most common sources of electromagnetic interference are
  - Electrical power wiring
  - Electric motors
  - Transformers
  - Fluorescent lighting
  - Copiers

Figure 18-7.   Sources of noise

The cable installer must route UTP cables away from source of electrical noise when pulling horizontal cables. Cable pathways must be bonded to an approved building ground. Cables installed above the ceiling must be suspended above the ceiling tiles and have a minimum of 12 in. of clearance above florescent lights and florescent light ballasts.

It is the cable installer's responsibility to be aware of potential sources of noise and to avoid installing copper communication cables near noise sources.

Some commercial buildings are very noisy environments. These environments may cause signaling problems in unshielded communications cables. If noise is a problem on a copper communications cable, one of the following options can be implemented:

▼ Separate the cable from the source of the noise.

■ Enclose the unshielded communication cable in a metallic conduit.

▲ Replace the unshielded cable with either a shielded cable or an optical fiber cable.

The least expensive way to protect an unshielded cable from electrical noise is to simply move it away from the source of the noise. Noise energy must be coupled into an unshielded cable for the noise to affect or corrupt the signals traveling over the cable (see Figure 18-8). The coupling process occurs when the source of the noise and the cable are in close proximity to each other. The greater the distance the less coupling will occur.

Communication cables can easily be moved away from electrical noise if the source of the noise can be determined. Many times unshielded communication cables are affected by noise, but the source of the noise cannot be determined.

A second issue associated with moving a communication cable is where to move it. If the cable is installed in the horizontal pathway, there might be no other pathway to move the cable from the TR to the specific work area location. Installing a new pathway may be too expensive or take too much time.

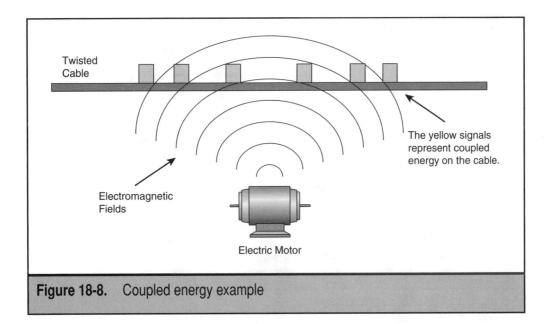

Twisted Cable

The yellow signals represent coupled energy on the cable.

Electromagnetic Fields

Electric Motor

Figure 18-8. Coupled energy example

Metallic conduits provide excellent protection for unshielded copper cables. The metallic conduits must be bonded to an approved building ground. Any noise energy that hits the metallic conduit will be run to ground. None of the electrical noise energy will disrupt the signals traveling across the unshielded communication cable.

The problem with metallic conduits is that they are expensive and difficult to install in an existing building. Metallic conduits are typically installed above a drop ceiling in an existing building. These cable pathways must be properly installed, supported, and grounded. The labor to perform these tasks is also very expensive.

If the unshielded cable cannot be moved or enclosed in a metallic conduit, the cable can be replaced with a cable that is not as susceptible to the electrical noise. ScTP cables have an overall foil shield that is bonded to ground. Noise energy will hit the cable shield, and the energy will be routed to ground. Optical fiber cables can also be used. These cables transmit signals in the form of light pulses instead of electrical pulses. Electrical noise energy will not disturb these light signals.

Minimum Bend Radius

Horizontal copper cables can be easily bent during the cable pull. All copper cables have a minimum bend radius that should not be violated when the cable is being pulled. The minimum bend radius is the smallest bend that may be put into a cable before the geometry of the cable changes. A change in the cable geometry will result in a degradation of the cable's performance rating.

The minimum bend radius of a four-pair UTP cable during installation is four times the outside diameter of the cable while the cable is being pulled (see Figure 18-9). A four-pair UTP horizontal cable has an outside diameter of approximately 6.25 mm ($^1/_4$ in.). A

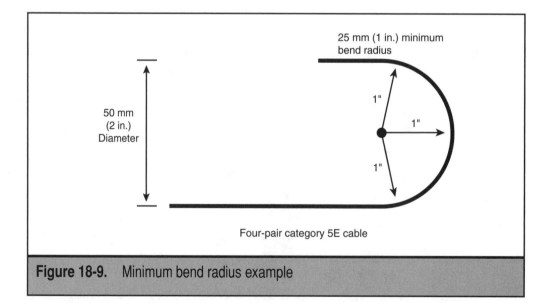

Figure 18-9.   Minimum bend radius example

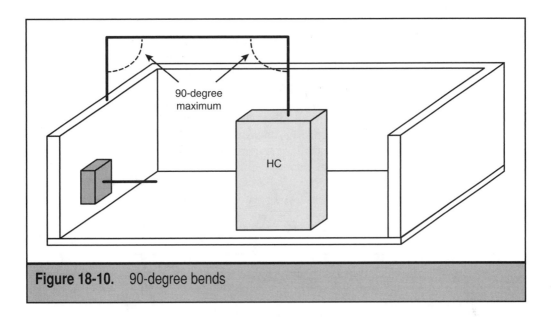

Figure 18-10.   90-degree bends

minimum bend radius of four times the outside diameter would result in a bend radius of no more than 25 mm (1 in.) when the cable is being pulled.

A second issue associated with the cable's minimum bend radius is that it is must not exceed a 90-degree bend on any UTP cable (see Figure 18-10). The 90-degree bend is a precaution for copper communications cables. If the cable does not have any 90-degree bends then the minimum bend radius cannot be violated on the cable. It is also recommended that the number of 90-degree bends should be kept to a minimum in the cable run.

Avoid temporarily hanging cables over a rigid hook or nail while the cable is being pulled. This practice can cause the cable to kink or violate the minimum bend radius. It may also cause increased attenuation in the cable pairs.

If a UTP cable is installed in a conduit, industry guidelines state that horizontal conduits should have no more than two 90-degree bends (180 degrees total) in the entire conduit run. The conduit must have a pull box installed in any conduit section with bends totaling 180 degrees. The section of conduit extending from the pull box is bound by the same requirements.

Suspending Cable

Horizontal cables that are not installed in a cable tray or some other type of cable pathway above the ceiling must be properly supported. Cable supports prevent the cable from resting on the ceiling tiles. Many location municipalities have codes that define the supporting of communication cables and minimum sag requirements. Buildings that do not have the communication cables properly supported will not receive a certificate of occupancy. The building tenants must correct the problem or have their contractor correct the problem before they are allowed to move into the building.

When horizontal cables are installed above drop ceilings, they must be properly secured with a cable tray or another type of suspension apparatus such as J hooks. The suspension equipment used must be designed for cables so it does not pinch, crush, or kink the cables at the bottom. No matter what type of cable suspension apparatus is used, it should be designed to hold the cables permanently.

Local codes will dictate the suspension requirements when installing communication cables. Local codes are written to prevent cables from resting on ceiling tiles and causing a fire hazard. In addition to safety concerns, correctly supporting a communication cable will avoid undue stress on the cable due to its own weight.

If the local code regarding cable suspension intervals is not known, a good rule of thumb is to suspend a cable every 1.2 to 1.5 m (4 to 5 ft.) (see Figure 18-11). This suspension interval is close enough so that cable sag can be avoided between the suspension points.

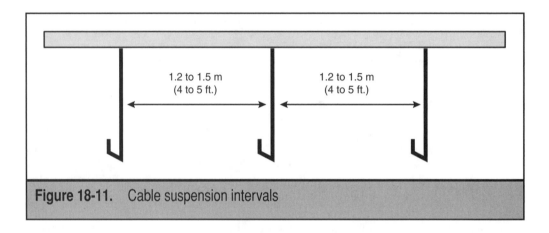

Figure 18-11.   Cable suspension intervals

Cable Team   Pulling horizontal cable usually requires two or more individuals on the cable team. Horizontal cables can be pulled by a single person, but the job moves much faster when two individuals work together as a team. When horizontal cables are pulled, the cable is usually pulled along using a pull string or pushed along using a long pole. The first cable installer will attach the cable to a pull string or a cable pole and hand the cables to the second individual. Depending on the type of horizontal pathway, the second person may be positioned on a ladder or near the entrance to a floor duct. The first individual can feed cable slack off of the cable reels and the second individual can start the cable pull.

Cable Pull Points   Cable pulling points are the locations in the horizontal cable run where cable installers are placed to pull the cable. These are generally places where the horizontal cable will either get hung up or possibly damaged during the cable pull. Cable installers should be positioned at all designed cable pulling points in the horizontal cable run. Common cable pulling points include the following locations:

▼   Pull boxes

■   The end of conduits

▲   Sharp corners or sharp bends along the horizontal cable pathway

Devices, such as cable pulleys, sometimes called bullwheels, can be placed at sharp corners. This can prevent the cable from violating the minimum bend radius if the cable gets pressed against the corner during the cable pull. The cable pulley will guide the cable around the sharp corner without altering the cable pairs inside the cable.

Opening Ceiling Tiles   Horizontal cables that are installed over a drop ceiling must be installed in the cavity between the ceiling tiles and the roof. This space usually contains building structures such as air handling ducts and the wires that hold up the ceiling. A typical drop ceiling is made of metal "T" bars that are held up by support wires. The ceiling tiles fit in the space created by the metal "T" bars. The ceiling tiles must be pushed straight up and then pushed either forward or backward over the "T" bars. This will open a working space in the ceiling for pulling cables. A good rule of thumb is to open a ceiling tile about every 3 m (10 ft.) along the cable path from the TR to the work area. Ladders are placed below each ceiling opening. Using an 8-ft. ladder, a cable installer can work above the drop ceiling to pull communication cables.

Communication cables must be placed in cable pathways installed above the drop ceiling. If no cable pathway exists, cable-supporting devices, such as J hooks or caddy clamps, can be installed to support the horizontal cables. J hooks are screwed into wood beams or attached to concrete. J hooks are open metal hooks shaped like the letter J. Horizontal cables are then placed in the J hooks to support the cables.

Caddy clamps attach to steal beams. Caddy clamps are an example of specialized cable supports that have been created to support horizontal cables installed above a drop ceiling.

Local codes and most general contractors prohibit installing cable-supporting devices on the metal "T" bars or the support wires that support the drop ceiling. The weight of the horizontal cables can cause the ceiling to buckle. Most local building codes permit a cable-supporting device to be attached to a support wire that is not used to support the drop ceiling.

Once all horizontal cables are installed above the drop ceiling and the cables are properly labeled and supported, the ceiling tiles must be replaced. The ceiling tiles must be placed squarely over the opening in the "T" bar frame and dropped into place. Ceiling tiles that are not square will not set down on the "T" bar frame correctly.

Air Plenum   The space above a drop ceiling is considered to be a plenum space according to most local building codes. An *air plenum* is defined as a space related to the air handling system in a building. These building spaces require that plenum-rated cables be installed to conform to fire codes. Building inspectors can mandate that all nonplenum-rated cable be removed if it is found to occupy a building plenum space. Table 800-50 of the NEC requires that communications cables be tested and marked with the following labels shown in Table 18-1 for each type of communications cable.

Cable Marking	Type
CMP	Communications plenum cable
CMR	Communications rise cable
CM	Communications cable
CMX	Communications cable, limited use
CMUC	Undercarpet communications cable

Table 18-1. NEC Cable Markings

The NEC requires that CMP communication cables shall be tested as suitable for use in air ducts, air plenums, and other spaces used for the distribution or return of environmental air. These cables must also exhibit adequate fire resistance and low smoke producing characteristics.

Ladder Setup   Every cable installer that is pulling horizontal cable above a ceiling will be working on portable ladders. It is very important to always consider safety when working with ladders. Installing cables above a drop ceiling requires the following:

▼   Choosing the correct size ladder

▲   Setting up the ladder on a flat surface

You should always choose the correct type and size ladder for the job. Never use a ladder that is too small. This will promote climbing and standing on the top rungs of the ladder. Any slip during a cable pull could result in a fall to the floor.

Avoid using metal ladders in areas of the building where there is a chance of electrical shock or making contact with electrical cables or devices. Ladders that are made of wood or fiberglass are a better choice. These materials will not conduct electrical currents if accidental contact is made with an electrical wire or device.

Ladders must always be placed on a flat, solid surface such as the building floor. If a flat and solid surface cannot be found, the ladder must be held in place by another worker or secured to prevent ladder movement. Before climbing on the ladder, verify that the support arms are fully intended and locked in place. This will prevent the ladder from collapsing when someone climbs on it.

Ladder Inspection   Always inspect a ladder carefully before using it. Ladders should be inspected before each use for the following:

▼   Steps and side rails are tight.

■   Rubber, anti-skid feet are in correct working order.

- ■ Side rails are not bent or damaged.

- ■ Rings and steps are clean and free from liquids or other material that may cause a slip.

- ▲ Ladder is dry to prevent potential shock hazards.

A proper ladder inspection should become part of your personal safety routine each time you use a ladder. The most important rule concerning ladder safety is that if a ladder is damaged, never use it.

Ladder Placement   Always set up and position your ladder so it will be out of high traffic areas of a building. Always use orange codes to designate a work area around the ladder. Never place a ladder in front of a door that opens toward the ladder unless you have verified that the door is locked or foot traffic is blocked so the door will not be used while the ladder is being used. Always follow these safety steps when using a ladder:

- ▼ Never exceed the ladder's safety weight rating or weight limit.

- ■ Always climb up or down facing the ladder.

- ■ Never stand on the top step or top shelf of the ladder.

- ■ Never leave tools or equipment on the ladder.

- ■ Never drop or throw tools while standing on the ladder.

- ■ Never lean out over the ladder's side rails. Move the ladder instead.

- ▲ Always climb off the ladder to move it.

Always use the correct tools for the job. If the job requires a ladder, always use the correct type of ladder and not a makeshift climbing device.

Opening Cable Trenches   Some commercial buildings use underground trenches to distribute horizontal cables from the TR to each work area location. These trenches are usually located under carpets or under tile floors. The trench is usually covered with a large metal plate that is flush with the floor height. Carpet squares or tile is glued to the lid to hide its presence in the building floor. The carpet squares or tile must be removed from the trench covers to have access to these horizontal pathways. The trench covers are usually made of steel and are very heavy. Care must be used when removing these heavy metal covers. Two people are normally required to safely open the cable trench and remove the cover. The cable trench covers are removed at 15 m (50 ft.) intervals along the horizontal pathway. A pull string is used to pull horizontal cables between the opening in the trench. If a pull string does not exist, a fishtape can be used to install a pull string.

Horizontal cables are installed in the underground trench. When pulling cables through the trench, care must be taken not to cut the cable jackets on sharp metal edges in the trench. Do not exceed 25 lbs. (110 N) of pulling force when pulling the cables. If either the pull string or the cables get stuck, open another trench cover to free the cables.

This practice will guarantee that the copper cables do not become damaged during the installation.

> **CAUTION:** Horizontal copper cables must never be installed in the same pathway as high-voltage power cables. If power cables are installed in a trench, the NEC requires that a solid metal partition be placed between the power cables and the communications cables. The solid metal partition must run the entire length of the trench to conform to NEC specifications.

Once all horizontal cables are installed in the trench, the trench covers must be replaced. This is done by aligning the edges of the cover with the trench lip and placing the cover squarely over the trench. Once the cover is aligned it is then lowered into place. Screws are used to secure the trench cover and adjust the lid height to be flush with the floor. The carpet squares or tiles are reattached to the covers once all of the covers have been replaced.

Cable Slack

Copper communication cables should always be installed with slack in the cable run. The cable slack will enable the cable to be moved away from the sources of noise along the cable path. It also permits the TR to be reconfigured and the cable to be moved while requiring that new cables be installed.

A general rule of thumb for cable slack is to allocate the following:

▼ 12 to 16 in. in the work area

▲ 3 m (10 ft.) in the TR

Never install a copper cable where it is tight and therefore under stress. All copper communication cables that are installed without any slack in the cable run will stretch. Over time, the cable's performance will decline. If the performance decline is too severe, the cable will have to be replaced.

Bundling Communication Cables

The horizontal subsystem includes the largest number of cables in any other cabling subsystem. The job of pulling horizontal cables also requires that the cables remain organized. This is typically done by bundling groups of horizontal cables together. The cables are usually grouped based on where they are to be terminated in the TR.

Cable ties are typically used by cable installers for bundling horizontal cables into groups (see Figure 18-12). When using cable ties to bundle or secure cables, do not apply the cable ties too tightly. A rule of thumb when using cable ties to group cable together is that all cable ties should be finger tight only. Cable ties should never be tightened with pliers. Overly tight cable ties can pinch cables on the outside of a cable bundle. The pinching will cause the cable pairs to become deformed, and this may decrease the cable's performance.

To avoid the problem of overcinching cable ties, many cabling professionals are recommending that cable ties be replaced by either Velcro straps, nail on cable clamps, or

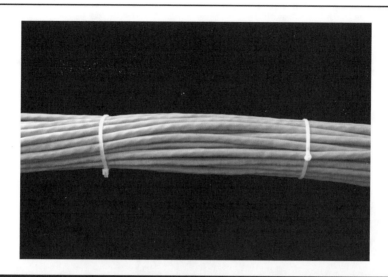

Figure 18-12.   Cable tie example

D-rings (see Figure 18-13). These devices can be used to properly position and support cables while keeping the cable jackets from becoming compressed or damaged.

PULLING HORIZONTAL UTP CABLE IN A CONDUIT

The steps for pulling horizontal UTP cable in a conduit are as follows:

1. Estimate the length of the cable run.

   The cable can be pulled with a pull string. If the pull string does not exist, use a fishtape to install the pull string.

2. Based on the cable length estimate, verify that the fishtape is long enough.

3. Before starting the cable installation, designate the work area using orange cones and yellow caution tape.

4. Run the fishtape through conduit. If the conduit has cables installed in it or has bends, use a flexible tip on the end of the fishtape.

5. Once the fishtape has been fished through the conduit, attach a pull string to the end of the fishtape and secure it in place with tape. Be careful to taper the tape so the fishtape with the pull string attached can be easily pulled back through the conduit.

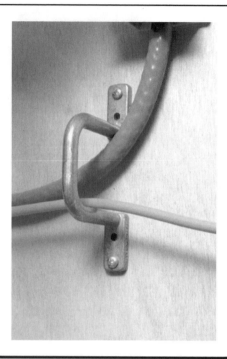

Figure 18-13.   D-ring example

6. Once the pull string is in place, disconnect the pull string from the fishtape. If not already done, roll up the fishtape and put it away.

7. Set up cable reels on a cable tree or set up cable payout boxes so the horizontal cables will feed out without getting hung up or kinked.

8. Label each cable and the corresponding cable reel or box and attach the cables to be pulled to the pull string.

9. Attach a new pull string to the cable group so as the first is being used; a new pull string will be in place for the next cable pull.

10. Pull horizontal cables using the pull string and never exceed 25 lbs. of pulling force.

11. While pulling cable, never exceed the cable's minimum bend radius of four times the cable diameter (about 1 in.).

12. Before cutting the cable, leave a minimum of 12 in. of cable slack in the work area (maybe more) and a minimum of 3 m (10 ft.) of cable slack in the closet.

The exact lengths are determined by the building layout and how close the cables are to the final termination location.

13. Label each cable using a label that meets the job specifications.

14. Document the cable runs on building blueprints.

PULLING UTP HORIZONTAL CABLE IN AN OPEN CEILING

The steps for pulling horizontal UTP cable in an open ceiling are as follows:

1. Estimate the length of the cable run.

2. Before starting the cable installation, designate the work area using orange cones and yellow caution tape.

3. Install a pull string in the open ceiling along the cable path.

4. Set up cable reels on a cable tree or set up cable payout boxes so the horizontal cables will feed out without getting hung up or kinked.

5. Label each cable and the corresponding cable reel or box and attach the cables to be pulled to the pull string.

6. Attach a new pull string to the cable group so as the first is being used; a new pull string will be in place for the next cable pull.

7. Pull horizontal cables using the pull string and never exceed 25 lbs. of pulling force.

8. While pulling cable, never exceed the cable's minimum bend radius of four times the cable diameter (about 1 in.).

9. When pulling the cable along the cable path, be careful not to damage the cable from sharp objects in the ceiling space.

10. Once the cables are installed along the cable path, lift the cables into the cable-supporting structure with a gopher pole or by hand.

11. Before cutting the cable, leave a minimum of 12 in. of cable slack in the work area (maybe more) and a minimum of 3 m (10 ft.) of cable slack in the closet. The exact lengths are determined by the building layout and how close the cables are to the final termination location.

12. Label each cable using a label that meets the job specifications.

13. Document the cable runs on building blueprints.

CHAPTER SUMMARY

Horizontal cables are installed from the telecommunications room (TR) to the work area. Smaller, four-pair cables are installed for horizontal applications. These cables can be installed in a cable pathway that can run either below the floor or above the ceiling. Horizontal cables can also be installed above the ceiling of a building in the open space between the ceiling and the roof.

The ANSI/TIA/EIA-568-B.1 standard supports the following media type in the horizontal subsystem for new cable installations: 100-ohm UTP cable, 62.5/125 μm multimode optical fiber cable and 50/125 μm multimode optical fiber cable. One-hundred-ohm UTP copper cables are the primary type of media installed for the horizontal subsystem. These types of cables are preferred because most applications can be supported over UTP cable.

Installing horizontal cables requires performing a series of steps to install horizontal copper cable successfully. These steps include: surveying horizontal cable paths, setting up and designating the work area, installing pull strings, setting up cable reels or boxes, labeling each cable and the cable reel or box, and attaching cables to the pull string and pulling cables.

Surveying the horizontal cable pathways involves surveying the cable paths or cable runs from each work area to the TR. The TR itself should be the first stop during the survey process. The closet should be built out before the horizontal cables are pulled. The next step is to investigate each horizontal pathway from the TR to the work area locations. If the pathway is an underfloor trench, the trench must be opened. If the pathway is a cable tray installed above the ceiling, use a ladder and open the ceiling tiles to see the cable tray. If your survey identifies that the horizontal pathways are full or not capable of supporting the new horizontal cables, an alternate pathway must be used or a new pathway must be installed before the horizontal cables are pulled.

The cable pulling setup involves organizing all of the tools and materials necessary to complete the horizontal cable pulls. Part of the setup process is the activity of designating and securing the work area. Orange cones and yellow caution tape are typically used for this function.

Each horizontal pathway should be equipped with a pull string. The pull string is used to pull communication cables through the cable pathways such as conduits and underfloor trenches. Pull strings are usually installed with a fishtape. The pull string is attached to the end of the fishtape with tape. The fishtape is then reeled back, installing the pull string in the conduit.

Before starting the cable pull, the cable reels or boxes must be set up so the cable can easily feed into the horizontal cable pathway. The cable reels or boxes must be positioned so the cable will pay off easily without getting tangled or kinked.

When multiple horizontal cables must be pulled at the same time, the cable reels can be placed on a cable tree. Large cable reels must be placed on a cable jackstand. Cable jackstands are adjustable devices that support different sizes and weights of cable reels. Select a location for the cable tree or cable jackstand that provides enough work space. The ideal location for the cable tree or cable jackstand is near the feed point for the horizontal pathway.

Once the cable reels or boxes are set up for the cable pull, each cable must be uniquely labeled. A cable label must be attached to each horizontal cable and the corresponding label attached to the cable reel or box. Cable labels should be place approximately 3 to 6 in. from the end of the cable. This will prevent the label from being covered by tape when the cable is attached to a pull string.

The last step before horizontal cables are pulled is to attach pull strings to the cables. All of the horizontal cables that are to be pulled together will be formed into a group and attached to the same pull string. The lead edge of each cable, above the cable label, will be taped to the pull string. The cables must be arranged so the taped configuration is streamlined. This will prevent the cable group from becoming hung up on any cables or other obstructions in the cable pathway.

Pulling horizontal copper cables is the activity of running the cables from the TR through the horizontal pathways to each work area location. Horizontal UTP cables must be handled carefully during the cable installation. The industry cabling standards specify that a maximum of 25 lbs. (110 N) of pulling force be used when installing copper cables. The maximum length for a horizontal cable defined in the ANSI/TIA/EIA-568-A and ANSI/TIA/EIA-568-B.1 standards is 90 m (295 ft.). The ANSI/TIA/EIA-568-A and ANSI/TIA/EIA-568-B.1 standards also define the maximum distance for the channel as 100 m (328 ft.). The total length of the equipment cords, cross-connect wire/patch cords, and line cords is 10 m (33 ft.). UTP horizontal cables must be routed away from sources of electrical noise. Avoid violating the minimum bend radius of four times the outside diameter of the cable while the cable is being pulled.

Horizontal cables that are not installed in a cable tray or some other type of cable pathway above the ceiling must be properly supported. Cable supports prevent the cable from resting on the ceiling tiles. When horizontal cables are installed above drop ceilings, they must be properly secured with a cable tray or another type of suspension apparatus such as J hooks. The suspension equipment used must be designed for cables so it does not pinch, crush, or kink the cables at the bottom. No matter what type of cable suspension apparatus is used, it should be designed to hold the cables permanently.

Local codes will dictate the suspension requirements when installing communication cables. Local codes are written to prevent cables from resting on ceiling tiles and causing a fire hazard. If the local code regarding cable suspension intervals is not known, a good rule of thumb is to suspend a cable every 1.2 to 1.5 m (4 to 5 ft.).

Cable pulling points are the locations in the horizontal cable run where cable installers are placed to pull the cable. These are generally places where the horizontal cable will either get hung up or possibly damaged during the cable pull. Common cable pulling points are at pull boxes, at the end of conduits, and at sharp corners or sharp bends along the horizontal cable pathway.

Horizontal cables that are installed over a drop ceiling must be installed in the cavity between the ceiling tiles and the roof. Communication cables must be placed in cable pathways installed above the drop ceiling. If no cable pathway exists, cable-supporting devices, such as J hooks or caddy clamps, can be installed to support the horizontal cables. J hook are screwed into wood beams or attached to concrete.

The space above a drop ceiling is considered to be a plenum space according to most local building codes. An air plenum is defined as a space related to the air handling system in a building. These building spaces require that plenum-rated cables be installed to conform to fire codes.

Every cable installer that is pulling horizontal cable above a ceiling will be working on portable ladders. Installing cables above a drop ceiling requires choosing the correct size ladder and setting up the ladder on a flat surface. Avoid using metal ladders in areas of the building where there is a chance of electrical shock or making contact with electrical cables or devices. Ladders must always be placed on a flat, solid surface such as the building floor. Always inspect a ladder carefully before using it. A proper ladder inspection should become part of your personal safety routine each time you use a ladder.

Always set up and position your ladder so it will be out of high traffic areas of a building. Always use orange codes to designate a work area around the ladder. Never place a ladder in front of a door that opens toward the ladder unless you have verified that the door is locked or foot traffic is blocked so the door will not be used while the ladder is being used.

Horizontal cables are usually grouped based on where they are to be terminated in the TR. Cable ties are typically used by cable installers for bundling horizontal cables into groups. When using cable ties to bundle or secure cables, do not apply the cable ties too tightly. Overly tight cable ties can pinch cables on the outside of a cable bundle. The pinching will cause the cable pairs to become deformed, and this may decrease the cable's performance.

CHAPTER 19

Copper Terminations and Splices

Installing copper cables in a building is the first step to being able to use these cables for a communication system. Cable termination is the next step in the cable installation process. The new copper cables must be terminated so they can be utilized in a communication system for transmitting signals between system devices.

Cable termination involves the following activities:

▼ Group the communication cables by termination position in the telecommunications room (TR).

■ Organize the communication cables into properly dressed cable bundles.

■ Label the communication cables.

▲ Perform the actual termination of the cable conductors on the terminating hardware components.

Punch down blocks and patch panels are the components used to terminate the communication cable conductors in the TR. Modular outlets/connectors are the components used to terminate the communication cable conductors in the work area. Work area and equipment patch cords are used to make a connection to the communication devices.

Copper communication cables must be terminated with a connecting hardware component in order to be used by a communication system. Connecting hardware components provide the means to attach and detach the communication cable from communication devices. If the cable is not terminated properly, signaling problems will occur over the cable.

This chapter will describe the proper procedures for terminating copper communication cables. It will describe the procedures for terminating copper cables on punch down blocks, patch panels, and modular connectors/outlets. This chapter will also describe the steps for splicing copper communication cables together.

TERMINATING COPPER CABLES

The proper termination of copper communication cables is critical for the proper transmission of communication signals.

Terminating copper communication cables requires that the cable pairs be connected properly to the connecting hardware components. The optimum termination occurs when a low resistance connection is established with the wires of the communication cable and the connecting hardware. The termination of the wire must create a gas-tight connection against the metal contact points in the connecting hardware. A gas-tight connection increases the reliability of the termination by preventing environmental factors, such as humidity and gases, from causing corrosion. Corrosion would increase the contact resistance and degrade the signals traveling across the contact point in the link.

COMMUNICATION CABLE CONNECTIONS

Connecting hardware components are the devices that are designed to terminate the conductors of a communication cable. Different methods have been developed to terminate the individual conductors of a communication cable and have the conductors securely in place. Two of the most common methods used to terminate the conductors of a communication cable are

▼ Screw down terminals

▲ Insulation Displacement Contact (IDC)

Screw Down Terminals

Connecting hardware components have evolved over the years. Early versions of these cable termination components used screws to terminate the individual wires of a communication cable (see Figure 19-1). The individual wires of the cable had to be stripped and carefully wrapped around the screws before the screws were tightened. Wire wrap blocks and screw down type modular outlets require that the cable pairs be separated in order to terminate them on these cabling components. The individual conductors could touch other wires and cause a short condition if the cable installation technician was not careful.

Screw type modular outlets can still be found in many homes today. Screw down type modular outlets are not recommended by either commercial cabling or residential cabling

Figure 19-1. Screw down termination

standards for terminating communication cables. These connecting hardware devices induce more signal loss by separating cable pairs and are generally less reliable.

Insulation Displacement Contact

The recommended method for terminating copper communication cables is using an IDC method (see Figure 19-2). This termination method cuts through the insulation surrounding a wire and creates a connection with the metal contacts of the connecting hardware. The physical contact occurs between the outer surface of the communication cable wire and the metal contacts in the connecting hardware. This creates electrical continuity between the wire and the connecting hardware component.

An IDC connection is achieved by pushing a wire into a wire termination slot on a connecting hardware component. A punch down tool is used to push the wire into the termination slot and cut off the excess wire. The metal contacts will cut into the insulation material as the wire is inserted into the termination slot. This will result in a gas-tight connection between the wire and the connection hardware component.

IDC connecting hardware devices have become the standard for cable termination hardware. These devices do not require that the individual cable conductors be stripped before being terminated. IDC connections save a significant amount of time compared to screw down connections.

IDC connections are more reliable and induce less loss into a communication link. The wire insulation is only removed at the contact point of the wire. This prevents shorts between the wires of a communication cable. IDC connections also enable the two wires of

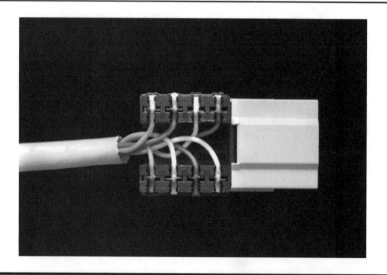

Figure 19-2.   IDC connection

a cable pair to remain twisted up to the point of termination of the connecting hardware component. This will reduce signal loss of the link.

CONNECTING HARDWARE COMPONENTS

Communication cables are terminated on connecting hardware components. Connecting hardware is the name given to the cable components used to terminate communication cables. The term *connecting hardware* is a very broad term describing devices that terminate copper and fiber cable. The term means the connectors or other cabling devices required to connect two cables together. The term connecting hardware can be used to describe termination components in the TR as well as in the work area.

Connecting hardware components would include the following components:

▼ Punch down blocks

■ Patch panels

■ Modular outlets/connectors

▲ Modular plugs

Punch Down Blocks

Punch down blocks, sometimes called connecting blocks, are connecting hardware devices commonly found in a TR. They are used to terminate the conductors for either large multipair backbone cables or the conductors of multiple four-pair horizontal cables. Punch down blocks provide a stable and permanent location for communication cables.

Punch down blocks are mounted in the TRs of commercial buildings. Backbone cable from other closets enter the closet through either conduits or backbone pathways and are terminated on punch down blocks. The backbone cable conductors can then be cross-connected using jumper wire to other punch down blocks.

Punch down blocks have slots that terminate cable conductors using IDC style terminations. One wire is terminated in each slot. Punch down blocks are usually designed to terminate cable conductors in 25-pair designations. Most punch down block are designed to support 50, 100, 250, 300, or 900 cable pairs per block. Different sizes and styles of punch down blocks can support different pair counts.

66 Blocks

66 blocks are the most common type of connecting blocks for terminating UTP cable used for telephone applications. 66 block have been used for years by the telephone company to terminate UTP phone cables. 66 blocks can also be used for high-speed LAN environments using high quality category 5 or higher UTP cable.

66 blocks have 50 slots on the left side of the block and 50 slots on the right side of the block. Each side is capable of terminating 25 cable pairs. 66 blocks are mounted on either 89b or 89d brackets, or they can be directly attached to the plywood backboard with screws. These blocks can also be rack mounted for high-density cable installations.

66 blocks have metal clips on the front of the block. These clips are designed to provide an IDC terminatation for communication cables. The cable conductors are inserted into each slot on the block and into the first metal clip on the side of the block being terminated. A punch down tool with a 66 blade is used to push the cable conductor into the clip. The clip is designed to cut through the wire insulation and make a physical connection with the wire. The punch down tool seats the wire into the clip so it will not move.

110 Blocks

110 blocks were created by AT&T to support voice and data applications. 110 blocks can either be wall mounted or rack mounted. If wall mounted, the 110 block legs are attached to the backboard with wood screws.

110 blocks are horizontal style blocks. They are comprised of 25-pair rows organized in a horizontal configuration. Cable conductors are terminated from the left top row across the block to the right. The second 25-pair group of cable conductors is terminated on the next horizontal row from left to right.

110 blocks use IDC termination technology to make a physical connection for all of the cable pairs of either a backbone or horizontal cable. Cable conductors are inserted into a slot in the block and seated using a punch down tool with a 110 blade attached. The punch down tool pushes the cable conductor into the conductor slot. The metal edges in the slot are designed to cut through the wire insulation and make a physical connection with the wire. The punch tool seats the wire into the slot so it does not move.

BIX Blocks

BIX punch down blocks were created by Nortel (formerly Northern Telecom) to support voice and data applications. *BIX blocks* are a combination of a BIX mount and multiple BIX connectors that are used to terminate the cable conductors. Once the cable wires are terminated in the BIX connectors, the connectors are attached to the BIX mount. BIX blocks can either be wall mounted or rack mounted. If wall mounted, the BIX mounts are attached to the backboard with wood screws.

BIX blocks are horizontal style blocks similar to 110 blocks. They are comprised of 25-pair rows organized in a horizontal configuration. Cable conductors are terminated from the left top row across the block to the right. The second 25-pair group of cable conductors is terminated on the next horizontal row from left to right.

BIX blocks use IDC termination technology to make a physical connection to the cable pairs. Cable conductors are inserted into a slot in the block and are seated using a BIX punch down tool. The punch down tool pushes the cable conductor into the conductor slot. The metal edges in the slot are designed to cut through the wire insulation and make a physical connection with the wire. The punch tool seats the wire into the slot so it does not move.

Krone Blocks

Krone blocks are similar to BIX blocks. These punch down blocks were created to support voice and high-speed data applications. Krone LSA blocks are manufactured with silver IDC contacts, which provide excellent electrical properties. Krone blocks are a combination of a mount and multiple Krone connector blocks that are used to terminate the cable conductors. Krone blocks are unique because they provide a disconnect capability. A plug can be inserted into a wire pair to provide either a temporary or permanent disconnection of the wire connection. Krone blocks can either be wall mounted or rack mounted.

Patch Panels

Patch panels are connecting hardware components that are used to terminate four-pair horizontal cables. Patch panels have a terminating block on the back of the panel for terminating horizontal cable conductors. The front of the panel has eight-position modular ports. Patch panels are usually sold in either 12, 24, 48, or 96 port configurations.

Patch panels use IDC termination technology to make a physical connection to the cable pairs. Cable conductors are inserted into a slot in the block located on the back of the patch panel and seated using a punch down tool. The punch down tool pushes the cable conductor into the conductor slot. The metal edges in the slot are designed to cut through the wire insulation and make a physical connection with the wire. The punch tool seats the wire into the slot so it does not move.

Modular Connectors/Outlets

Unshielded, twisted-pair cables are terminated with eight-position modular outlets/connectors and modular plugs. The modular outlet/connector is the type of connector used to terminate horizontal cables in the work area (see Figure 19-3). These connectors are designated as female connectors. They are designed to connect to a male modular plug.

Modular outlets/connectors are designed to terminate the wires of horizontal UTP cables using IDC technology. These connectors are designed to with slots. The individual conductors of a UTP cable are inserted into these slots with a punch down tool or a special connector cap. The slots are designed to cut through the insulation on the wires and make a physical contact with the connector.

Modular Plugs

Equipment patch cords and work area line cords are the cables that connect to a modular outlet/connector. These cables are terminated with a modular plug. Modular plugs are male connectors. They are designed to attach to a female outlet/connector to make an electrical connection between the horizontal cable and the work area cable. The opposite end of the work area cable attaches to the user equipment.

Modular plugs are clear, plastic connectors that attach to a modular line cord or patch cord. The individual conductors of a line cord are inserted into the back of the connector and crimped to make an IDC physical connection. These connectors have four to eight slots with metal contacts in the slots. The crimped wires make physical contact with the metal contacts of the modular plug. The slots of the modular plug line up and make a physical connection with the metal contacts in the modular outlet. When the modular plug

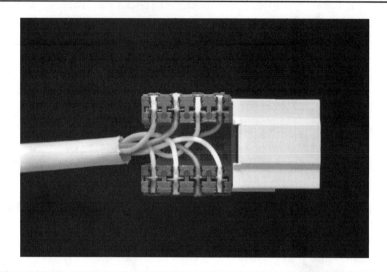

Figure 19-3. Modular outlet termination

is snapped into the modular outlet/connection, the two connectors make a physical connection at these contact points (see Figure 19-4).

Modular plugs are always a male connect that only attaches to the stranded conductors or a modular line or patch cord. The cable wires are inserted into the modular plug in a specific color-coded sequence and then crimped in place. Both ends of a modular cord must be configured the same so the wiring is straight through from end to end.

CABLE TERMINATION TOOLS

The tools to terminate copper cables are very simple. Copper cables only require a few tools to complete the cable termination in the TR and in the work area. The tools for performing a copper cable termination include the following:

▼ Cable jacket stripper or ringing tool

■ Punch down tool

▲ Crimp tool

Cable Jacket Stripper

A standard wire stripper or ringing tool is used to strip the copper cable jacket (see Figure 19-5). An 18 or 20 AWG wire stripper can be used to remove the cable jacket. This

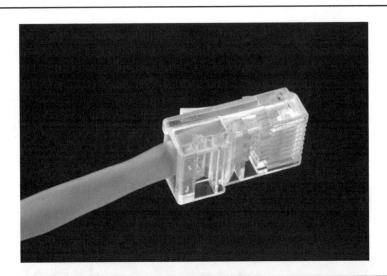

Figure 19-4.   Modular plug termination

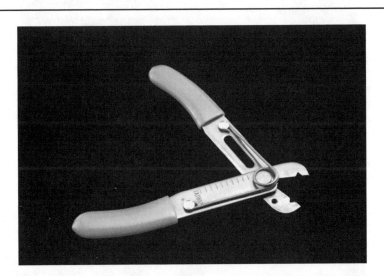

Figure 19-5.   Cable jacket stripper

tool will cut the cable's jacket without damaging the copper conductors. There are many types of strippers that will work for this job. The stripper that you use should be sharp and easy to handle.

A ringing tool can also be used to cut the cable's jacket (see Figure 19-6). A *ringing tool* is a specialized stripping tool with a cutter blade. A ringing tool has different size slots for stripping different size cables. The tool is slid over the copper cable and rotated in a circle to cut the cable jacket. The ringing tool will remove the cable jacket without damaging the optical fibers or cable strength members.

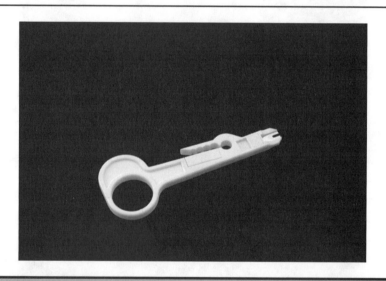

Figure 19-6.   Ringing tool

CAUTION: Lineman's scissors can also be used to remove the cable jacket. Always used extreme caution if using scissors to remove the cable jacket. This tool is very sharp and can easily cut into the cable conductors and nick the insulation on the wires. Lineman's scissors should not be the first choice as a cable stripping tool.

Rip Cord

Many copper cables are manufactured with a pull string inside of the cable jacket. The pull string can be used to remove the cable jacket. This technique is very safe and will not damage the cable conductors.

The steps for using the rip cord for removing the cable jacket are as follows (see Figure 19-7):

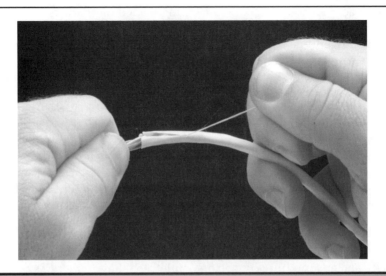

Figure 19-7.   Stripping a cable with a rip cord

1. Measure the amount of the cable jacket to be removed.
2. Mark the point of the cable jacket to be removed with a marker.
3. Remove enough of the cable jacket to access the rip cord.
4. Grab the rip cord with your fingers or a pair of pliers.
5. Pull the rip cord against the cable jacket until it reaches the designated cable jacket removal point.
6. Carefully remove the cable jacket using either scissors or a straight edge cutter.

Punch Down Tool

A punch down tool is the tool used to terminate solid conductor cables into IDC style connecting hardware components. The punch down tool is specially designed to perform IDC terminations.

The punch down tool is a simple termination tool that has a handle and a blade. The blade is designed to fit a specific type of termination slot. Each type of punch down block has a different termination slot configuration and requires a specific type of blade. Most punch down tools are designed to have replaceable blades. This enables the same punch down tool to be used with different types of punch down blocks and modular connectors.

Punch down blocks can also be classified as to how they terminate the wires on a connecting hardware device. The two categories of punch down tools are

▼ High-impact punch down tools

▲ Low-impact punch down tools

A high-impact punch down tool has a spring-loaded mechanism built into the tool. Pushing on the tool compresses the spring. When enough pressure is placed on the tool, the spring releases, adding extra force to the termination. The high-impact punch down tool pushes the wire into the termination slot on the connecting hardware component. A high-impact punch down tool provides consistent terminations that are tight and seated correctly in the connecting hardware termination slot. Communication cables should be terminated using a high-impact type punch down tool on: 66 blocks, 110 blocks, and most modular connectors/outlets.

A low-impact punch down tool does not have a spring-loaded mechanism built into the tool. These punch down tools are meant to push the wire into the termination slot of the connecting hardware device without extra force of a spring mechanism. Low-impact punch down tools are preferred by some punch down block manufacturers because these devices do not compress the cable inductors in the termination slot and add extra signal attenuation. A low-impact punch down tool also provides consistent terminations that are tight and seated correctly in the connecting hardware termination slot. Communication cables should be terminated using a low-impact type punch down tool on: BIX blocks, Krone blocks, and any modular connectors/outlets that have either BIX or Krone termination slots.

STEPS TERMINATING COPPER COMMUNICATION CABLES

After the communication cables have been pulled and the TRs built, the communication cables must be organized and terminated. The first step for performing cable terminations is performing the pretermination cabling activities. These activities are required to organize the communication cables and place them in the proper position for termination.

The steps involved in terminating copper communication cables are as follows:

1. Perform the pretermination cable activities.
2. Terminate multipair backbone cables in the TR.
3. Terminate the horizontal cable in the TR.
4. Terminate the horizontal cable in the work area.

PRETERMINATION ACTIVITIES

Pretermination functions involve a few steps that prepare each cable for the actual termination procedure. Pretermination functions are very important when termination cables in a TR. The first activity involves organizing the cables by destination. Cables need to be placed in close proximity to the point of termination.

The next pretermination activity is the forming and dressing of the communication cables. Forming and dressing the cables involve correctly aligning and positioning the cables in a neat and orderly mode for termination. This will also guarantee that the cables will be long enough to reach the designated termination position.

Pretermination Activity Steps

The pretermination steps for terminating communication cables are as follows:

1. Organize the horizontal cables by their termination position. This will keep all the cables that are terminated in the location the same length.

2. Form and dress the individual groups of horizontal cables. Cable ties are usually used for this function.

NOTE: Do not overtighten cable ties that are used to group cables together.

3. Determine cable length and cable slack requirements based on the closet configuration. Always leave enough cable slack to route the cables to their designated termination position.

4. Always use proper cable management hardware to route the cables to their designated termination position and to store cable slack.

TERMINATE MULTIPAIR UTP CABLES

The 100-ohm UTP copper backbone cables are multipair cables. These cables are primarily used for voice and low-speed data applications. Backbone cables are pulled between TRs in a commercial building. The ANSI/TIA/EIA-568-A and ANSI/TIA/EIA-568-B.1 standards require that all intrabuilding backbone cables be installed in a physical star topology. This means that backbone cables will be installed from the main cross-connect (MC) to each TR or from the intermediate cross-connect (IC) to each TR in the building.

The ANSI/TIA/EIA-568-A and ANSI/TIA/EIA-568-B.1 standards also permit backbone cables installed between TRs in the same floor or same building. These cables must be installed in addition to the backbone cables that connect each TR to either the MC or IC.

Once the multipair backbone cables are pulled to each TR, the cables must be properly terminated (see Figure 19-8). Terminating multipair UTP backbone cables requires that the cable jacket be removed and the cable shield be properly bonded to an approved telecommunications ground in the TR such as the TGB. The cable jacket must be removed to expose the cable pairs. Provide enough slack to terminate each cable pair in the proper termination position. A #6 AWG bonding conductor must be used to make the bonding connection to the TGB.

Once the cable jacket is removed and the cable shield is bonded, the cable pairs must be terminated. The first step to terminate the cable pairs in the multipair UTP cable is to separate the 25 binder groups. Identify each binder group with tape of cable ties. Feed each of the 25-pair binder groups into the correct slots on a punch down block. The cable

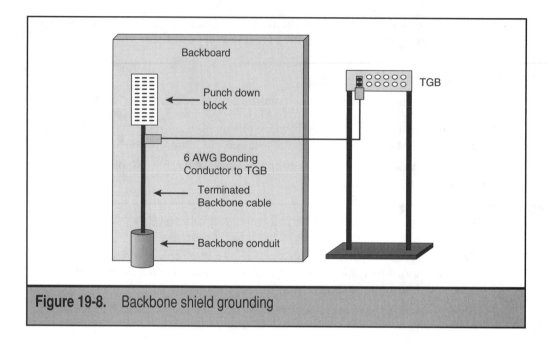

Figure 19-8. Backbone shield grounding

pairs must be terminated in the correct sequence on the punch down block using the correct type of punch down tool.

Steps for Terminating Multipair UTP Cable

The steps for terminating multipair UTP cable are as follows:

1. Decide on the method and the amount of the cable's jacket that must be removed to correctly terminate the multipair UTP cable. Whenever removing the cable's jacket, always be careful not to nick the cable conductors. This can cause shorts or may cause wires to break.

2. Remove the cable jacket per ANSI/TIA/EIA industry standards and/or manufacturer specifications, if they differ, with a cable knife or a ringing tool. Be careful not to cut or damage the cable conductors.

3. Bond the cable's shield to the TGB in the TR using a #6 AWG bonding conductor.

4. Separate each binder group by unwrapping the cable strands; tie off and identify each binder group (see Figure 19-9).

5. Fan out each cable pair from the different binder groups and organize the cable pairs by major color-coded groups.

6. Place each cable pair into the proper slot on the punch down block maintaining twists up to $1/2$ in. (13 mm) from the termination point. Before terminating the

Figure 19-9. Separate each binder group.

cable pairs, visually verify that each cable pair is placed in the proper termination position.

7. Terminate each cable pair using the proper type of termination tool (see Figure 19-10). When terminating cable pairs, always use caution not to nick or cut any wires.

8. When all cable pairs are terminated in the multipair UTP cable, install the proper strain relief devices to support the cable.

TERMINATING HORIZONTAL TWISTED-PAIR CABLES

The ANSI/TIA/EIA-568-A and ANSI/TIA/EIA-568-B.1 standards specify that all horizontal cabling must be installed in a physical star topology. Each work area outlet/connector must be directly connected to the horizontal cross-connect (HC) with a horizontal cable. Industry cabling standards prohibit daisy chaining work area outlets/connectors

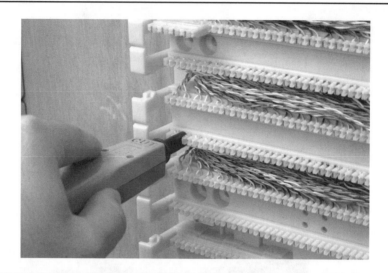

Figure 19-10. Terminate cable pairs using a punch down tool.

from a single horizontal cable. In addition, each horizontal cable must be terminated on a HC in a TR on the same floor as the work area terminating the opposite end of the cable.

The steps for terminating twisted-pair cables are as follows:

1. Remove the cable jacket.
2. Minimize cable pair untwisting.
3. Avoid separating cable pairs.
4. Do not violate the cable's minimum bend radius.

Cable Jacket Removal

Research has proven that removing a large amount of the cable jackets can degrade the performance of a category 5e cable. Twisted-pair cables are manufactured so that the individual pairs are arranged to lay in a specific configuration. The cable jacket keeps all the pairs of the cable in this specific configuration. When the cable jacket is removed, the pairs may shift positions. The new position of the cable pairs may result in the cable having reduce performance specifications.

Industry cabling standards do not specify exactly how much of the cable jacket to remove to perform the cable termination. The ANSI/TIA/EIA-568-A and ANSI/TIA/EIA-568-B.1 standards specify that to remove only as much of the cable jacket as necessary to properly terminate the cable pairs.

The last consideration when removing the cable jacket on a twisted-pair cable is to be careful not to nick or cut any of the wires. If a wire is nicked, the cable pair may experience more attenuation. In addition, the wire will be very weak and may break when moved. This could cause maintenance problems in the future.

Untwisting Cable Pairs

One of the worst things that a technician can do is untwist the two wires that make up a cable pair. Many technicians untwist cable pairs and fan out the individual conductors to more easily terminate the conductors on an outlet or patch panel. When the conductors of a cable pair are untwisted, the cable will suffer from increased attenuation and reduced NEXT.

The ANSI/TIA/EIA-568-A and ANSI/TIA/EIA-568-B standards recommend that all cable pairs should remain twisted up to the point of termination in the TR and in the work area. The cable pair termination should have no more than 13 mm ($^1/_2$ in.) of untwisted wire. All categories of twisted-pair cable must use the maximum of 13 mm ($^1/_2$ in.) untwisting specification at all terminations in the communication cabling system.

NOTE: The ANSI/TIA/EIA-568-A standard specifies that category 4 cables should have no more than 25 mm (1 in.) of untwisted wire at any termination point. Category 4 cables have been phased out of the ANSI/TIA/EIA-568-B standard as an allowed media type for commercial buildings.

Cable Pair Separation

The two wires of a cable pair must always remain together when performing cable terminations. Avoid terminations where the two wires of a cable pair separate. This condition will cause excessive loss on the cable run. Balanced signals cannot properly combine on a cable pair where the wires have been separated. This causes unwanted signal attenuation on the cable pair.

The most common cause for two wires of a cable pair separating is that too much of the cable jacket has been removed. This exposes a large amount of the cable pair. Moving or pushing a cable pair upward can cause the two wires of the pair to separate. This situation can be avoided by visually inspecting the cable pairs after they are terminated.

Minimum Bend Radius

Horizontal copper cables can be easily bent during the cable termination. All copper cables have a minimum bend radius that should not be violated when the cable is being terminated. The minimum bend radius is the smallest bend that may be put into a cable before the geometry of the cable changes. A change in the cable geometry will result in a degradation of the cable's performance rating.

The minimum bend radius of a four-pair UTP cable during installation is four times the outside diameter of the cable while the cable is being pulled. A four-pair UTP horizontal cable has an outside diameter of approximately 6.25 mm ($^1/_4$ in.). A minimum bend radius of four times the outside diameter would result in a bend radius of no more than 25 mm (1 in.) when the cable is being pulled.

TERMINATING CABLES IN THE TELECOMMUNICATIONS ROOM (TR)

Horizontal cables must be terminated in the TR. The same general termination techniques should be used when terminating the cables on a punch down block or patch panel.

A few key techniques that should always be used when terminating twisted-pair cables in a TR are as follows:

1. Do not violate the minimum bend radius of four times the outside diameter of the cable (1 in.).
2. The maximum untwisting of the cable pairs should be no more than 13 mm ($^1/_2$ in.) at any termination point.
3. Remove only as much of the cable jacket as necessary to terminate the cable pairs.
4. The individual wires of each cable pair should always be kept together.

TERMINATING TWISTED-PAIR CABLES ON A 66 BLOCK

Perform the following steps to terminate a twisted-pair cable on a 66 block:

1. Mount the block's bracket (usually an 89B bracket) on the plywood backboard or cross-connect frame (see Figure 19-11).
2. Route the twisted-pair cables through the bracket and distribute six cables through the left side and six cables through the right side.
3. Snap the 66 block onto the bracket (see Figure 19-12).
4. Cut each of the cables to length, leaving a little slack in each cable for future terminations.
5. Strip each twisted-pair cable, removing only as much of the cable jacket as necessary to terminate the cable pairs.
6. Insert each cable pair through alternating fanning slots in the 66 block.
7. Once the cable pairs are inside the block's fanning strip, separate the two wires of each cable pair and pull the wires so that the last twist in the cable pair is no more than 13 mm ($^1/_2$ in.) from the termination clips.

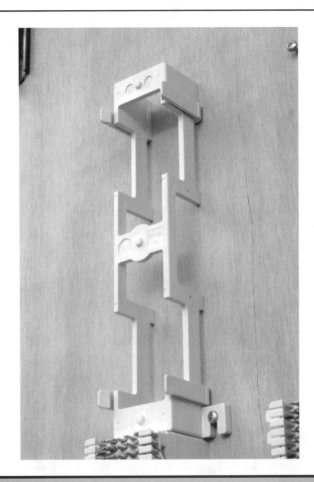

Figure 19-11.   Mount the bracket on the backboard.

8. Once you have verified that there is no more than 13 mm ($^1/_2$ in.) of untwisted wire, terminate the wires of the cable pair on the first clip next to the fanning strip with a punch down tool.

9. Repeat the procedure for all cable pairs.

10. Label the 66 block when all cables are terminated.

Labeling can be done on the fanning strip, on a designation strip that fits over the fanning strip, or on a cover that fits over the face of the 66 block. Printed labels are preferred. If hand writing labels, use a permanent marker and write clearly.

Figure 19-12. Snap the 66 block onto the bracket.

TERMINATING TWISTED-PAIR CABLES ON A 110 BLOCK

The procedures for terminating twisted-pair cables on a 110 block are similar to the procedures for terminating twisted-pair cables on a 66 block. Perform the following steps to terminate a twisted-pair cable on a 110 block.

1. Mount the block on the plywood backboard or cross-connect frame (see Figure 19-13).

2. Route the twisted-pair cables under the block and distribute six cables through the left side into the slot on the 110 wire base and six cables through the right side into the slot on the 110 wire base.

3. Cut each of the cables to length, leaving a little slack in each cable for future terminations.

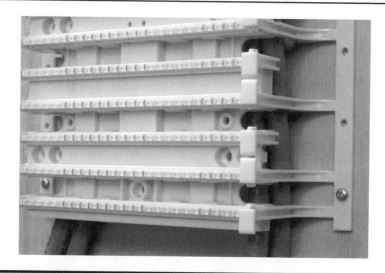

Figure 19-13.   Mount the 110 block on the backboard.

4. Strip each twisted-pair cable, removing only as much cable jacket as necessary to terminate the cable pairs.

5. Lace each cable pair in the retention slots on the 110 block starting with the blue pair in the first position. Separate the two wires of each cable pair and pull the wires so that the last twist in the cable pair is no more than 13 mm ($^1/_2$ in.) from the retaining slot.

6. Once you have verified that there is no more than 13 mm ($^1/_2$ in.) of untwisted wire, terminate all of the wires of the twisted-pair cable on the retaining slot and cut off the excess wire with a punch down tool.

7. Repeat the procedure for all twisted-pair cables.

8. Once all cables are terminated, place a 110 clip over the appropriate position of the 110 wire base (see Figure 19-14). Using a five-pair punch down tool, terminate the 110 clip onto the 110 wire base.

TERMINATING TWISTED-PAIR CABLES ON A PATCH PANEL

Patch panels are connecting hardware components that are used to terminate four-pair horizontal cables. Patch panels have a terminating block on the back of the panel for

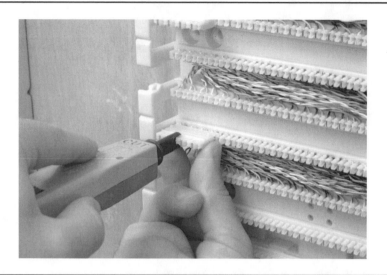

Figure 19-14.   Install a 110 clip on the 110 block.

terminating horizontal cable conductors. The front of the panel has eight-position modular ports. Patch panels are usually sold in either 12, 24, 48, or 96 port configurations.

Patch panels mount in a standard communications rack. Patch panels are usually mounted in the top of the rack, and communications equipment is mounted in the lower part of the rack. Equipment patch cords with modular plugs on the ends are used to connect the patch panel ports to the equipment ports.

Steps for Terminating Twisted-Pair Cables on a Patch Panel

Perform the following steps to terminate a twisted-pair cable on a 110 block:

1. Mount the patch panel on a communication rack (see Figure 19-15).

2. Route the twisted-pair cables down the wire management panel on the communication rack and through the wire slot.

3. Cut each of the cables to length, leaving a little slack in each cable for future terminations.

4. Strip each twisted-pair cable, removing only as much cable jacket as necessary to terminate the cable pairs.

5. Lace each cable pair in the retention slots on the block mounted on the back of the patch panel starting with the blue pair in the first position.

Figure 19-15. Mount the patch panel on the communication rack.

6. Separate the two wires of each cable pair and insert the wires in the retaining slots so that the last twist in the cable pair is no more than 13 mm ($^1/_2$ in.) from the retaining slot.

7. Once you have verified that there is no more than 13 mm ($^1/_2$ in.) of untwisted wire, terminate all of the wires of the twisted-pair cable on the retaining slot and cut off the excess wire with a punch down tool.

8. Repeat the procedure for all twisted-pair cables.

TERMINATING TWISTED-PAIR CABLES ON A MODULAR OUTLET

The ANSI/TIA/EIA-568-A and ANSI/TIA/EIA-568-B standards require that each horizontal cable be terminated with a modular outlet/connector in the work area. The modular outlet has four to eight contact wires inside the female jack that connect to the terminated cable conductors. When viewed from the front, the contacts are numbered from 1 to 8 starting at the contact wire. The male modular plug will insert into the female jack and make a physical connection to these contacts.

Modular outlets/connectors are designed to terminate the wires of a horizontal UTP cable using IDC technology. These connectors are designed to with slots that are used to terminate the individual cable conductors. The individual conductors of a UTP cable are inserted into these slots with a punch down tool or a special connector cap. The slots are designed to cut through the insulation on the wires and make a physical contact with the connector. Screw down type connectors/outlets should never be used to terminate twisted-pair cables.

There are the many different types of modular outlets/connectors sold today. IDC style modular outlets/connectors can be divided into two basic categories:

▼   Punch down tool style

▲   Stuffer cap style

Punch Down Style Modular Connector

The punch down style modular outlet/connector requires a punch down tool to terminate the individual wires of each cable pair onto the outlet (see Figure 19-16). This style of modular outlet requires that the technician place the individual wires in the proper termination positions before punching the wires down. Each termination slot of the modular outlets are color coded. The color-coded slots will identify the proper location for each wire of a twisted-pair cable.

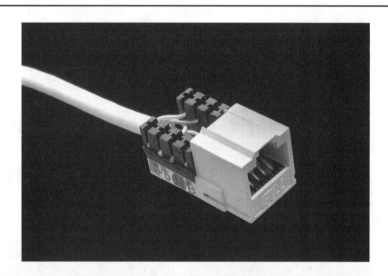

Figure 19-16.   Punch down style modular connector

Stuffer Cap Modular Connector

The stuffer cap style of a modular outlet/connector uses a plastic cap to terminate each wire on the connector (see Figure 19-17). The plastic cap will have eight slots that are col-

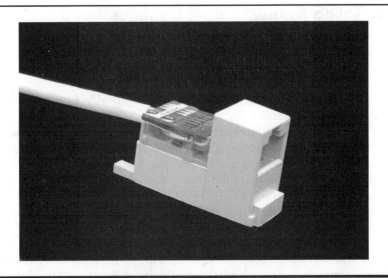

Figure 19-17.   Stuffer cap style modular connector

or coded. The modular connector body makes an IDC connection to the wires inserted in the stuffer cap.

The technician is required to insert all eight wires of the twisted-pair cable into the proper color-coded slots of the stuffer cap. Once the wires are inserted in the plastic cap, the cap is then placed on the modular connector body. The cap is snapped into place with your hands or a pair of channel lock pliers. The pressure will properly seat the wires on the modular connector.

MODULAR OUTLET CONFIGURATIONS

Modular outlets have been used to terminate UTP cables for years. This is the reason there are so many different sizes and styles modular connectors found in many commercial buildings today. Some modular connectors have four connectors, some have six conductors, and new modular connectors support eight conductors.

8P8C modular connectors are typically wired with either a T568A or T568B configuration. These are the two modular outlet configurations supported by industry cabling standards. The USOC configuration is seldom used for eight position modular outlets because this configuration is not supported by either the ANSI/TIA/EIA-568-A or the ANSI/TIA/EIA-568-B.1 structured cabling standards.

T568A versus T568B Modular Outlet Configurations

The T568A configuration is the primary modular outlet configuration for terminating four-pair horizontal UTP cables (see Figure 19-18). The T568A modular configuration is recommended for new cabling installations by both the ANSI/TIA/EIA-568-A and ANSI/TIA/EIA-568-B.1 structured cabling standards.

The T568B configuration is an optional modular outlet configuration that is recognized by both the ANSI/TIA/EIA-568-A and ANSI/TIA/EIA-568-B.1 structured cabling standards. The T568B modular outlet configuration is the recommended standard for the AVAYA Communications (formerly Lucent Technologies) Systimax structured cabling system. The T568B modular outlet configuration is also known as the AT&T 258A modular outlet configuration. This modular outlet configuration is recommended for existing installations that have existing modular outlets wired according to the T568B scheme. It is also used for new Systimax structured cabling installations. The T568B modular outlet configuration is shown Figure 19-19.

The T568A and T568B modular outlet configurations can be used for a communication cable installation. For each installation, one modular outlet configuration must be selected. All connecting hardware termination components must use the selected modular outlet configuration. Using two different modular outlet configurations in the same cabling installation will cause problems.

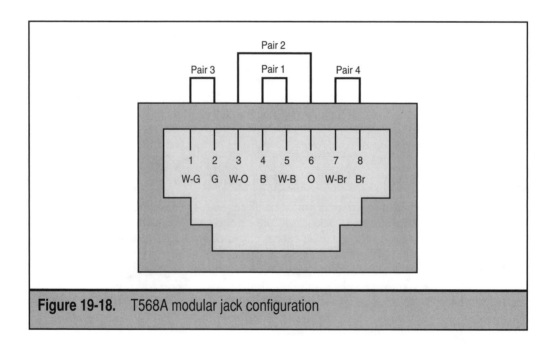

Figure 19-18.   T568A modular jack configuration

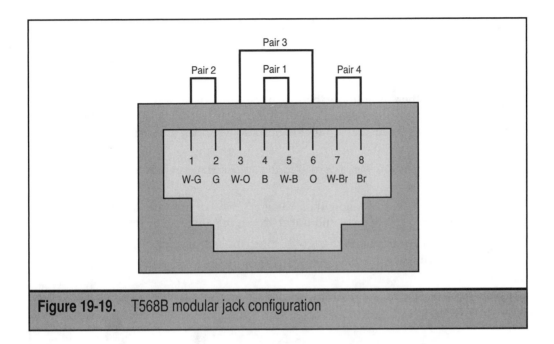

Figure 19-19. T568B modular jack configuration

CABLE SLACK

Twisted-pair cables should always be installed with slack in the cable run. The cable slack will enable the cable to be moved away from the sources of noise along the cable path. When terminating a cable in the work area, allocate the following cable slack for the cable termination:

- 12 to 16 in. in the work area

Avoid leaving too much cable slack after the cable has been terminated. The cable slack in the work area is usually fed back into the outlet box in the wall. Too much cable slack will promote the cable to become kinked as the large amount of slack is shoved into the small outlet box.

TERMINATING PUNCH DOWN STYLE MODULAR OUTLETS

The steps for terminating a twisted-pair cable on a punch down style modular outlet are as follows:

1. Strip the horizontal cable approximately 38 to 50 mm (1.5 to 2.0 in.).

2. Separate each cable pair keeping the individual wires of each pair twisted together.

3. Feed the blue pair into the appropriate retention slots on the modular connector.

4. Verify that there is no more than 13 mm ($^1/_2$ in.) of untwisted wire at the termination point and punch down the wires. This will keep the cable connected to the modular outlet in order to terminate the remaining cable pairs.

5. Feed the remaining three pairs into the appropriate retention slots (see Figure 19-20).

6. Verify that there is no more than 13 mm ($^1/_2$ in.) of untwisted wire for each of the three remaining pairs and punch down the wires on the modular outlet.

7. If required, insert the modular outlet into the faceplate and attach it to the wall (see Figure 19-21).

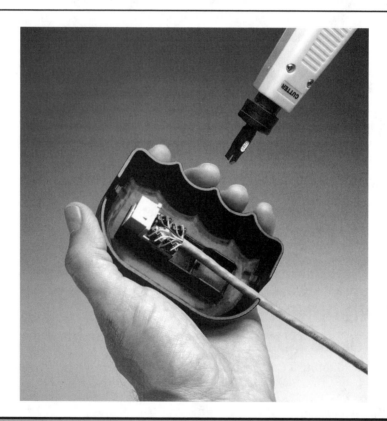

Figure 19-20. Feed remaining cable pairs into the modular connector.

Figure 19-21.   Insert the modular outlet into the faceplate.

TERMINATING STUFFER CAP
STYLE MODULAR OUTLETS

The steps for terminating a twisted-pair cable on a stuffer cap style modular outlet are as follows:

1. Strip the horizontal cable approximately 38 to 50 mm (1.5 to 2.0 in.).

2. Separate each cable pair keeping the pairs twisted together.

3. Untwist the four pairs of the cable until approximately 13 mm ($^1/_2$ in.) of twisted wire remains on each pair up to the cable jacket.

4. Insert each wire into the stuffer cap. Be very careful to follow the color code on the stuffer cap for the modular outlet configuration that you are using on this installation.

5. Slide the wires into the slots of the stuffer cap until the stuffer cap is against the twisted portion of each wire pair (see Figure 19-22).

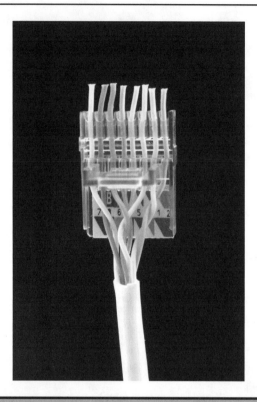

Figure 19-22. Slide the stuffer cap against the pair twists.

6. Verify that each wire is in the proper slot and that there is not more than 13 mm (¹/₂ in.) of untwisted wire up to the stuffer cap.

7. Trim off the excess wire from the edge of the stuffer cap.

8. Place the stuffer cap over the modular outlet and snap into place with a pair of channel lock pliers (see Figure 19-23).

9. If required, insert the modular outlet into the faceplate and attach it to the wall.

STP-A CABLE

The ANSI/TIA/EIA-568-A standard supports installing STP-A cables for the horizontal subsystem. Shielded twisted-pair (STP) cables are terminated with a special type of connector called a data connector. The data connector was created specifically for STP cable. These connectors are designed with grounding bars built into the connector to create a

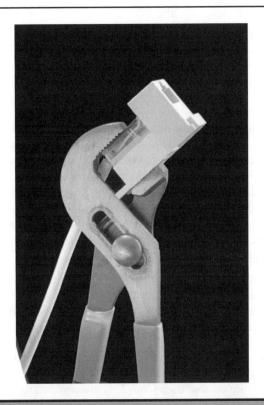

Figure 19-23. Secure the stuffer cap onto the connector body.

physical bond connection to the foil shields surrounding each cable pair and the overall braided shield.

Steps for Terminating a STP-A Cable

The steps for terminating STP-A cable are as follows:

1. Strip the cable jacket to expose the braided cable shield.
2. Undo the braided cable shield and trim to 1 in. in length from the edge of the cable jacket.
3. Trim the foil cable shield for each cable pair approximately 1 in., exposing the cable pairs.
4. Slide the connector ring over the cable.
5. Mate the color-coded wires to the color-coded clear plastic connector cap.

6. Snap the connector cap into the STP-A data connector body and seat firmly with pliers.

7. Snap the data connector housing into place.

COAXIAL CABLE

Coaxial cables are installed in the horizontal subsystem for residential buildings for cable TV applications. RG6 and RG59 cables are used for video, CATV, and private security video surveillance networks. RG-6 coaxial cable is the primary media installed in residential homes to support CATV. RG-59 can also be installed, but the center conductor is smaller in size. These cables must be used for shorter distance installations.

F connectors are the type of connector used with 75 ohm coaxial cable used for cable TV systems or CCTV systems. The F connector is a male connector. These connectors are installed on the end of a 75-ohm, RG59, or RG-6 coaxial cable. Female F connectors are installed on communication equipment.

CAUTION: There are different size F connectors to fit either RG-59 or RG-6 coaxial cable. RG-59 coaxial cable is smaller in diameter than RG-6 coaxial cable. As a result, RG-59 coaxial cable requires a smaller size F connector to correctly terminate the cable.

F connectors are threaded connectors. Male connectors are screwed onto a female F connector on a communication device or onto a female coupler. A coupler enables two coaxial cables to be connected together. Couplers are commonly installed in a wallplate. The coaxial horizontal cable is terminated with an F connector and attached to the back of the coupler on the back side of the wallplate. A coaxial patch cable is terminated with an F connector and attached to the front of the couple on the front of the wallplate. This is usually the configuration for a cable TV connection in a home.

Steps for Installing an F Connector

The steps for installing a coaxial F connector are as follows:

1. Determine the method and length of sheath removal.

2. Make a straight cut in the termination end of the coaxial cable.

3. Place the connector ferrule over the end of the cable.

4. Adjust the two- or three-step stripping tool to meet the desired cable diameter and stripping requirements of the cable.

5. Insert cable end into the coaxial cable stripper.

6. Turn the stripper at least three full turns.

7. Pull the cable out of the stripping tool and inspect the stripped end.

8. Verify that the center conductor and the shield are not nicked.

9. If required, attach the center pin on the center conductor.

10. Install the connector body over the cable.

11. Slide the ferrule up to the connector body to cover the exposed braided shield.

12. Crimp ferrule to the connector body.

13. Inspect the termination for neatness and tightness.

LABELING THE TERMINATED CABLES

The terminated cables must be labeled once the cable termination is complete. Each cable termination must be labeled according to the specifications in the ANSI/TIA/EIA-606 standard. Each faceplate must be clearly labeled with a unique label. The label for each terminated cable should be assigned during the cable design phase. The labeling scheme must be identified in the cable installation documentation. The ANSI/TIA/EIA-606 standard permits handwritten labels provided that they are legible and a permanent marker is used.

SPLICING COPPER CABLES

Splices are another type of copper termination required for multipair UTP cables. Splices are required when cable pairs must be accessed from a multipair cable or when long, direct fiber runs cannot be made between termination locations in a building or a campus. Splices cannot always be avoided because of cable length requirements, raceway congestion problems, or building fire code requirements.

Splices are required for a multipair UTP backbone cable installation when

▼ Large size (high pair count) backbone cables are installed to a centralized location and smaller size (smaller pair count) cables are run from that location.

▲ Outside plant backbone cables are run into a building entrance, the cables must be spliced to a primary protector at the building entrance. Rated backbone cables are spliced from the primary protector and run inside of the building.

As a general planning rule, splices should be minimized if possible. Each copper splice will add additional loss into a backbone cable at each splice point. Splices will also add cost to the backbone cable installation.

SPLICE LOCATIONS

Splice locations should be carefully considered and planned before starting the cable installation. If a splice is necessary, consolidate as many cables as possible at a single splice point. This will minimize the cost of the installation compared to an installation that requires splicing at many different locations.

Multipair copper backbone splice locations are the points where backbone cables must be spliced together. Splice locations must be planned in advance to guarantee that there is enough space to perform the splicing operation. The usual locations where backbone splices are located are

▼ Maintenance holes (MHs)

■ Telecommunications rooms (TRs)

■ Main cross-connects (MCs)

■ Intermediate cross-connects (ICs)

■ Entrance facilities (EFs)

▲ Equipment rooms (ERs)

SETTING UP YOUR WORK AREA

The proper work area must be arranged in order to perform cable pair splicing correctly. The work area is the location where two backbone cables will be spliced together. This space must have

▼ Access to backbone cables to be spliced together

■ A stable work shelf to perform the splicing operation

■ Proper lighting to correctly match cable conductor colors

▲ The proper clearances to work on the cable and install the splice closure correctly

Backbone cable splices are usually required in maintenance holes in a campus environment. These work areas have limited space to perform splicing. The work area for performing cable splicing is usually a temporary location such as a shelf in the maintenance hole.

Safety must always be considered when setting up your work area. The work area must be free of dangerous gases. The work area must also have proper lighting to perform the splice correctly.

PREPARING A BACKBONE CABLE FOR SPLICING

Once the splice location is selected for performing the cable splice and the work area has been set up, the backbone cables must be prepared for splicing. The steps involved in splicing two backbone cables include

▼ Setting up the splicing rig

■ Determining the proper length of the cable jacket to strip from each cable to expose the cable pairs

■ Stripping the cables outer jackets and if necessary the cables inner jackets

■ Removing gel from the binder groups and cable pairs

■ Setting up the splicing heads to splice the cable pairs

■ Bonding the cable shield between the two backbone cables

▲ Organizing the binder groups

Setting up the Splicing Rig

The first step for performing a backbone cable splice is to set up the splicing rig. The *splicing rig* is the hardware where the actual cable splicing is performed. A splicing ring is a metal bar with feet and clamps attached. This hardware has cable clamps that hold the backbone cables in place. The cable rig has a splicing head located in the center. This is where the splice connector is held while the splice is being performed. The splicing rig must be placed on a solid surface when performing the backbone cable splice.

Length Determination

The first step for performing a backbone cable splice is to determine the amount of the cable jacket that must be removed in order to perform the splice. The exact length will be determined by type of hardware closure used to house the splice. The cable pairs must be long enough to fit in the designated termination points in the splice closure once the splice is completed.

The actual length of the cable jacket to remove varies based on the splice hardware and the closure to be used for the splice. The length of the splice closure should be measured. The amount of the jacket to remove must be at least half the length of the splice closure. The optimum amount of the cable jacket to remove will match the length of the splice closure. This will be approximately 1 m (3 ft.) from the end of each cable. This should expose enough of the cable pairs to perform the splice correctly.

Avoid removing too much of the backbone cable jacket. The splice closure fits around the cable jacket with a water proof seal. The cable jacket must extend into the splice closure at least 4 to 6 in. to guarantee that the seal will remain intact and prevent water penetration.

The manufacturer's directions will provide exact cable stripping lengths for the splice closure. Always follow these directions and never deviate from them. The manufacturer instructions will provide the proper specifications to perform the splice correctly.

Stripping a Cable's Jacket

Once the amount of the cable jacket to be removed has been determined, the cable jacket must be stripped from the cable. This procedure must be performed without damaging the cable pairs. The exact amount of the cable jacket should be accurately measured. A permanent marker can be used to indicate the exact removal point for the cable jacket.

The backbone cable jacket can be removed with a cable knife or large ringing tool. The ringing tool or cable knife will be used to score the cable jacket at the marked point. The cable jacket can either be removed by a series of short ring cuts or using a long cut to split the cable jacket lengthwise. Slide the cable jacket off the backbone cable.

The cable jacket should be removed carefully. Care should be taken not to damage the conductors inside the cable. Many outside plant optical fiber cables are stiff. Always cut the cable jacket away from your body and never use a dull ringing tool or cable knife. Once the cable jacket has been cut, the sheath should be discarded.

Multipair UTP backbone cables are constructed with a series of sub units. Each sub unit has a separate cable jacket. The sub unit cable jacket also must be removed in order to access the cable pairs. The low pair numbers are located in the center of the cable and the high pair numbers are located on the outside of the cable. The same cable jacket removal process should be used for each cable sub unit jacket.

Gel Removal

Outside plant backbone cables are manufactured with waterproof gel inside the cable jacket and buffer tubes. This gel material is a waterproofing compound commonly called "icky pick." A cleaning agent must be used to clean the cable pairs. The gel material must be completely removed before the cable pairs can be spliced.

A few companies manufacture products that perform this job easily. Many of these gel removers are a type of petroleum cleaner product. These cleaner products will completely remove the gel or leave a slight residue that can be cleaned with alcohol. All of the gel material should be removed from the cable before starting a splice.

CAUTION: Care should be taken when working with gel-removal compounds. These materials may be harmful to your skin or harmful if inhaled. Gel-removal compounds should only be used in well-ventilated areas. These materials are petroleum-based products and are flammable if exposed to any open flames or fire sources.

Setting up the Splicing Heads

The splice heads must be installed on the splicing rig. The splicing head is attached with a clamp. The splice connector is installed in the splicing head. The two most common types of copper splicing connectors are

▼ **MS2**   Developed by 3M

▲ **710 System**   Developed by AT&T

Bonding the Backbone Cable Shields

The cable shields of the two cables that are to be spliced must be bonded together. This must be done before the splice is started. Bonding the cable shields together will provide a low resistance path for foreign voltages on the backbone cables to move to ground. Not bonding the cable shields presents a serious safety hazard. Foreign voltages introduced on the backbone cables will move through the cable installer and can be fatal.

Organizing the Binder Groups

The individual binder groups in a multipair backbone cable are color coded. The individual 25-pair binder groups must be separated and identified from each cable to be spliced. The identification can be done with color-coded cable ties.

Tape the ends of the entire 25-pair binder group once it has been separated from the other binder groups. This will keep all of the cable pairs for the binder group together. The splice procedure can be started once all of the binder groups have been separated and identified.

STEPS FOR PERFORMING A COPPER CABLE SPLICE

The steps for performing a copper UTP cable splice are as follows:

1. Set up the splicing work area.
2. Set up the splicing rig and clamp each cable in place.
3. Using a multimeter, check for voltages across each backbone cable to be spliced.
4. Measure and mark the amount of the cable jacket to be removed from each cable.
5. Remove the cable sheath from the two cables to be spliced together.
6. Install the bonding bar and connect the two cable shields together.
7. Set up the splicing head on the splicing bar.
8. Start the splice from the center of the cable. Feed the highest count binder group from both cables into the splice head.
9. Layer in each cable pair into the splice head with the tip colors installed on the left and the ring colors installed on the right.
10. Check the cable pair color-coded sequenced in the splice head.
11. Crimp the splice connector.
12. Lift the splice connector out of the splice head and place it aside.
13. Repeat steps 8 through 12 for the remaining binder groups to be spliced.

INSTALLING THE SPLICE CLOSURE

The splice closure must be installed over the cable splice once the splice is completed. The splice closure protects the splice against water entering the splice and damaging the splice connection. The correct splice closure must be selected for the location of the splice. Splice cases are available for the following environments:

▼ Underground

■ Buried

▲ Aerial

Install the cable closure by following the manufacturer instructions. Fill the splice closure with reenterable encapsulant material This material will provide water protection and permit reentry into the splice case at a later date. Encapsulant is a filling compound that expels air and protects the splice.

Steps for Installing the Splice Closure

Perform the following steps to install a splice closure:

1. Insert the splice closure body around the cable splice.
2. Put the splice case cover over the closure body.
3. Put the splice case clamps around the splice case body and cover.
4. Put the end caps on the splice case.
5. Tighten the splice case clamps.
6. Fill up the splice case with reenterable encapsulant.

LABELING THE BACKBONE CABLE SPLICE

The last step for completing the backbone cable splice is to label the spliced backbone cables. The splice and all elements associated with the splice must be accurately labeled according to the ANSI/TIA/EIA-606 standard. Each cable entering the splice closure must have a unique identifier. The binder groups that are spliced together must be uniquely labeled. The splice closure must also be identified with a unique label.

CHAPTER SUMMARY

The new copper cables must be terminated so they can be utilized in a communication system for transmitting signals between system devices. Cable termination involves grouping the communication cables by termination position in the TR, organizing the communication cables into properly dressed cable bundles, labeling the communication cables, and performing the actual termination of the cable conductors on the terminating hardware components.

Terminating copper communication cables requires that the cable pairs be connected properly to the connecting hardware components. The optimum termination occurs when a low resistance connection is established with the wires of the communication cable and the connecting hardware. The termination of the wire must create a gas-tight connection against the metal contact points in the connecting hardware.

Connecting hardware components are the devices that are designed to terminate the conductors of a communication cable. The recommended method for terminating copper communication cables is using an Insulation Displacement Contact (IDC) method. This termination method cuts through the insulation surrounding a wire and creates a connection with the metal contacts of the connecting hardware. Screw down type modular outlets are not recommended by either commercial cabling or residential cabling standards for terminating communication cables.

Connecting hardware is the name given to the cable components used to terminate communication cables. The term connecting hardware can be used to describe termination components in the TR as well as in the work area. Connecting hardware components would include: punch down blocks, patch panels, modular outlets/connectors, and modular plugs.

Punch down blocks, sometimes called connecting blocks, are connecting hardware devices commonly found in a TR. They are used to terminate the conductors for either large multipair backbone cables or the conductors of multiple four-pair horizontal cables. Punch down blocks have slots that terminate cable conductors using IDC style terminations.

Patch panels are connecting hardware components that are used to terminate four-pair horizontal cables. Patch panels have a terminating block on the back of the panel for terminating horizontal cable conductors. Patch panels use IDC termination technology to make a physical connection to the cable pairs.

Modular outlets/connectors are the types of connectors used to terminate horizontal cables in the work area. Modular outlets/connectors are designed to terminate the wires of a horizontal UTP cable using IDC technology. The individual conductors of a UTP cable are inserted into these slots with a punch down tool or a special connector cap.

Equipment patch cords and work area line cords are terminated with modular plugs. Modular plugs are clear plastic connectors that attach to a modular line cord or patch cord. Modular plugs are male connectors. They are designed to attach to a female outlet/connector. Both ends of a modular cord must be configured the same so the wiring is straight through from end to end.

Copper cables only require a few tools to complete the cable termination in the TR and in the work area. The tools for performing a copper cable termination include a cable jacket stripper or ringing tool, a punch down tool, and a crimp tool.

A standard wire stripper or ringing tool is used to strip the copper cable jacket. An 18 or 20 AWG wire stripper can be used to remove the cable jacket. A ringing tool can also be used to cut the cable's jacket. A ringing tool is a specialized stripping tool with a cutter blade. The ringing tool will remove the cable jacket without damaging the optical fibers or cable strength members.

A punch down tool is the tool used to terminate solid conductor cables into IDC style connecting hardware components. The punch down tool is specially designed to perform IDC terminations. Punch down blocks can also be classified as to how they terminate the wires on a connecting hardware device.

The two categories of punch down tools are a high-impact punch down tool and a low-impact punch down tool. A high-impact punch down tool has a spring-loaded mechanism built into the tool. The high-impact punch down tool pushes the wire into the termination slot on the connecting hardware component. A low-impact punch down tool does not have a spring-loaded mechanism built into the tool.

Pretermination functions involve a few steps that prepare each cable for the actual termination procedure. Pretermination functions are very important when termination cables in the TR. The first activity involves organizing the cables by destination. The next pretermination activity is the forming and dressing of the communication cables.

Terminating multipair UTP backbone cables requires that the cable jacket be removed and the cable shield be properly bonded to an approved telecommunications ground in the TR such as the TGB. A #6 AWG bonding conductor must be used to make the bonding connection to the TGB. The cable jacket must be removed to expose the cable pairs. The next step is to separate the 25 binder groups of the cable. Feed each of the 25-pair binder groups into the correct slots on a punch down block. The cable pairs must be terminated in the correct sequence on the punch down block using the correct type of punch down tool.

The ANSI/TIA/EIA-568-A and ANSI/TIA/EIA-568-B.1 standards specify that all horizontal cabling must be installed in a physical star topology. Each horizontal cable must be terminated on a horizontal cross-connect in a TR on the same floor as the work area terminating the opposite end of the cable. The steps for terminating twisted-pair cables are to remove the cable jacket, minimize cable pair untwisting, avoid separating cable pairs, and avoid violating the cable's minimum bend radius.

The ANSI/TIA/EIA-568-A and ANSI/TIA/EIA-568-B.1 standards specify that to remove only as much of the cable jacket as necessary to properly terminate the cable pairs. The ANSI/TIA/EIA-568-A and ANSI/TIA/EIA-568-B standards recommend that all cable pairs should remain twisted up to the point of termination in the TR and in the work area. The cable pair termination should have no more than 13 mm ($^{1}/_{2}$ in.) of untwisted wire. Avoid terminations where the two wires of a cable pair separate. The minimum bend radius of a four-pair UTP cable during installation is four times the outside diameter of the cable while the cable is being pulled.

The ANSI/TIA/EIA-568-A and ANSI/TIA/EIA-568-B standards require that each horizontal cable be terminated with a modular outlet/connector in the work area. Modular outlets/connectors are designed to terminate the wires of a horizontal UTP cable using IDC technology. Modular outlets/connectors can be terminated using either the T568A or T568B modular outlet configurations. The T568A modular configuration is recommended for new cabling installations by both the ANSI/TIA/EIA-568-A and ANSI/TIA/EIA-568-B.1 structured cabling standards. The T568B configuration is an optional modular outlet configuration that is recognized by both the ANSI/TIA/EIA-568-A and ANSI/TIA/EIA-568-B.1 structured cabling standards.

Coaxial cables are installed in the horizontal subsystem for residential buildings for cable TV applications. RG6 and RG59 cables are used for video, CATV, and private security video surveillance networks. F connectors are the type of connector used with 75-ohm coaxial cable used for cable TV systems or CCTV systems.

The terminated cables must be labeled once the cable termination is complete. Each cable termination must be labeled according to the specifications in the ANSI/TIA/EIA-606 standard. Each faceplate must be clearly labeled with a unique label. The label for each terminated cable should be assigned during the cable design phase. The labeling scheme must be identified in the cable installation documentation. The ANSI/TIA/EIA-606 standard permits hand written labels provided that they are legible and a permanent marker is used.

Splices are another type of copper termination required for multipair UTP cables. Splices are required for a multipair UTP backbone cable installation when large size (high pair count) backbone cables are installed to a centralized location and smaller size (smaller pair count) cables are run from that location or an outside plant backbone cables are run into a building entrance; the cables must be spliced to a primary protector at the building entrance. The usual locations where backbone splices are located are: maintenance holes (MHs), telecommunications rooms (TRs), main cross-connects (MCs), intermediate cross-connects (ICs), entrance facilities (EFs), and equipment rooms (ERs).

The steps involved in splicing two backbone cables include: setting up the splicing rig, determining the proper length of the cable jacket to strip from each cable to expose the cable pairs, stripping the cables outer jackets and if necessary the cables inner jackets, gel removal, setting up the splicing heads to splicing the cable pairs, bonding the cable shield between the two backbone cables, and organizing the binder groups for performing the splice. The splice closure must be installed over the cable splice once the splice is completed.

The last step for completing the backbone cable splice is to label the spliced backbone cables. The splice and all elements associated with the splice must be accurately labeled according to the ANSI/TIA/EIA-606 standard. Each cable entering the splice closure must have a unique identifier. The binder groups that are spliced together must be uniquely labeled. The splice closure must also be identified with a unique label.

CHAPTER 20

Installation of Optical Fiber Cable

*O*ptical fiber cable is a very common media installed to support many different types of communication systems. As long as a system's communication signal can be converted to a light signal, then the communication system can be supported using optical fiber cable.

Optical fiber cable is made of glass with strength elements added to the cable to provide strength when installing the cable. Although the light carrying portion of an optical fiber cable is made of glass, the cable is surprisingly strong and difficult to break. The cable can be broken or the cable can suffer from higher than normal losses if it is not installed correctly.

The cabling technician must be aware of the different types of optical fiber cable that are supported by industry cabling standards. They must also understand the different environments for optical fiber cable and the correct installation techniques and applicable codes that must be followed when installing cable in each environment. This chapter will describe the proper installation procedures for installing optical fiber cable.

OPTICAL FIBER CABLE APPLICATIONS

Optical fiber cable can be installed in many different environments such as

▼ Interbuilding backbone (campus backbone)

■ Intrabuilding backbone (building backbone)

▲ Horizontal subsystem

Optical fiber cable is an allowed media type for the horizontal and backbone subsystems in a structured cabling system. Although there is considerable growth for using optical fiber cable as a horizontal media, it is the primary media type for the backbone subsystem. The main reason is that optical fiber cable has extremely high bandwidth and very low loss characteristics. These two characteristics are required for the long distances required in the backbone subsystem.

The ANSI/TIA/EIA-568-A and ANSI/TIA/EIA-568-B.1 standards support the use of optical fiber cable for both interbuilding and intrabuilding backbone applications. The fiber optic backbone cabling is required to follow a hierarchical star topology to conform to industry cabling standards (see Figure 20-1).

The ANSI/TIA/EIA-568-A standard recognizes the following optical fiber media types for the backbone cabling subsystem:

▼ 62.5/125 μm graded index, multimode optical fiber cable

▲ Singlemode optical fiber cable

The ANSI/TIA/EIA-568-B.1 and ANSI/TIA/EIA-568-B.3 standards published in 2001 continue to support the 62.5/125 μm multimode and singlemode optical fiber cable but also enable 50/125 μm multimode optical fiber cable to be supported as well. 50/125 μm

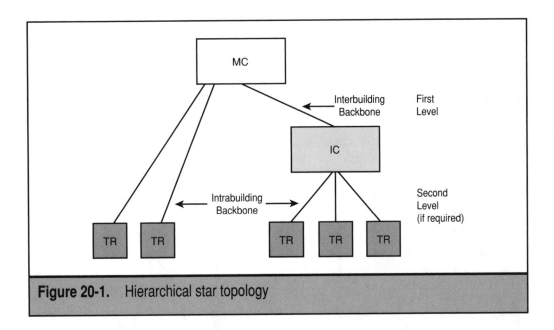

Figure 20-1.   Hierarchical star topology

multimode optical fiber cable has been supported as a recognized media type by the ISO 11801 cabling standard for years. This media has higher bandwidth than 62.5/125 multimode optical fiber cable for gigabit applications.

The maximum distances for each recognized optical fiber cable for the interbuilding backbone is shown in Table 20-1.

Media Type	Maximum Distance from the MC (CD) to IC (BD) Locations
50/125 μm multimode optical fiber cable	1,700 m (5,575 ft.)
62.5/125 μm multimode optical fiber cable	1,700 m (5,575 ft.)
Singlemode optical fiber cable	2,700 m (8,855 ft.)

Table 20-1.   Optical Fiber Interbuilding Cabling Distances

Interbuilding Backbone

The *interbuilding backbone*, sometimes called the campus backbone, is the cabling backbone that connects all of the buildings on a campus to the main cross-connect (MC) (see Figure 20-2).

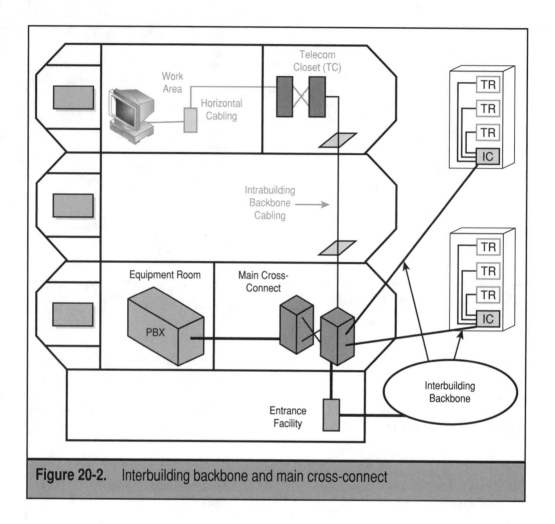

Figure 20-2. Interbuilding backbone and main cross-connect

The ANSI/TIA/EIA-568-A and ANSI/TIA/EIA-568-B.1 standards support the use of optical fiber cable for interbuilding backbone applications. The interbuilding fiber optic backbone cabling shall follow a physical star topology (see Figure 20-3).

The MC is the centralized portion of the backbone cabling. The function of the MC is to mechanically terminate interbuilding backbone cables and to provide a central administration point for the campus backbone cabling. Interbuilding backbone cabling should have only one MC. This provides a single point of administration for the campus cabling.

Ideally, the MC would be co-located in the equipment room with the PBX, data center, security monitoring equipment, and other active equipment. However, this is not required, and physical constraints sometimes make co-location impossible.

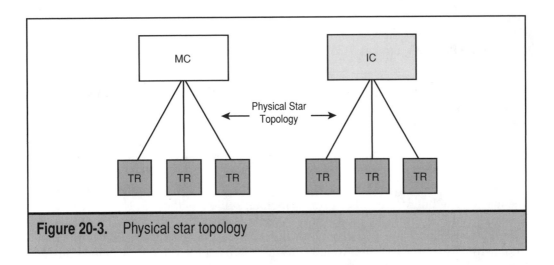

Figure 20-3. Physical star topology

Distributing Interbuilding Optical Fiber Backbone Cables

There are three methods for distributing optical fiber cable between buildings:

▼ Aerial

■ Underground

▲ Direct buried

The choice of a distribution method will depend on many factors such as

▼ Existing facilities having spare capacity for adding new cables

■ Cost of materials for each of the different installation methods

▲ Labor required for each of the different installation methods

Aerial Cable   Interbuilding optical fiber backbone cables can be distributed to other buildings over head using aerial cable. An *aerial cable* is a cable that is run above ground and supported by using poles or being lashed to buildings. This is the most economical method for running cables between buildings in a campus building arrangement.

Aerial cable is exposed to many external forces that can damage the cable such as: wind, ice, and snow. It is also exposed to temperature changes that are more extreme than in other installation environments. As a result, only approved aerial cable should be used for these installations.

Aerial cable should only be installed in environments where the maximum distance between a building and a pole or between poles along the run are less than 100 m (328 ft.). All aerial cables must be secured to a dedicated messenger wire. Aerial cable is also available in self-supporting designs, which do not require a separate messenger wire.

CAUTION: Before attempting an aerial installation, consult the National Electrical Safety Code (NESC) and the Rural Utility Services (RUS) standards for information on aerial safety.

Underground Conduits   Interbuilding optical fiber backbone cables can be distributed to other buildings using underground conduits. Underground conduits provide out-of-sight service between buildings and entering each building. Industry standards recommend installing a minimum of two, trade size 4 conduits between buildings. The size and number of buildings on the campus will usually determine the exact number of conduits to be installed.

Installing optical fiber cable through a conduit is typically the preferred distribution method for interbuilding backbone runs. This distribution method protects the cable from moisture, wildlife, and other forces that can damage the cable. The conduit serves as both a dedicated pathway and a form of protection. Optical fiber cables should be installed in an innerduct within the underground conduit to protect the cable from being damaged when additional cables are installed.

If an underground conduit is used to distribute cables, optical fiber cables must be separated from copper cables. Optical fiber cables should be placed in one conduit and multipair copper cables should be placed in other conduits. Multipair copper backbone cables are very heavy. These cables can tear out an optical fiber cable if they are installed in the same conduit as optical fiber cable.

Buried Cable   The last method that can be used to distribute cable between buildings is to dig a trench and bury the cable directly in the ground without using a conduit. This is called a *buried installation*.

A buried installation requires the use of cable with an armor shield in the cable to provide rodent protection. In addition, specialized cable must be used that can be directly buried in the ground. The cable must be designed to withstand the effects of frost damage and decay.

A buried distribution system for interbuilding backbone cables is not preferred because the cable is more likely to be damaged if there is any future excavation in the trench area. It is also more expensive to add or change interbuilding backbone cables in the future.

Intrabuilding Backbone

The *intrabuilding backbone* is the backbone cabling inside of a building (see Figure 20-4). It is the cabling that connects all telecommunications rooms (TRs) in a building to either the MC or an intermediate cross-connect (IC).

The ANSI/TIA/EIA-568-B.1 standard supports the use of optical fiber cable for intrabuilding backbone applications. The intrabuilding backbone shall follow a physical star topology. Each optical fiber backbone cable must be run from either the IC or MC to each TR in a building. The maximum distance supported for an intrabuilding backbone cable is 300 m (984 ft.).

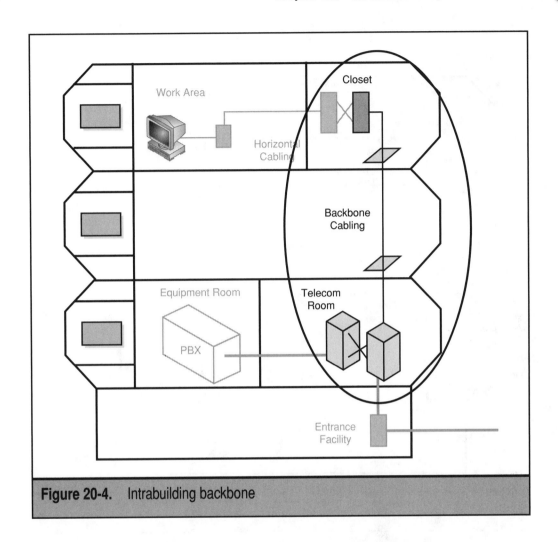

Figure 20-4. Intrabuilding backbone

The ANSI/TIA/EIA-568-B.1 and ANSI/TIA/EIA-568-B.3 standards recognize the following media types for the intrabuilding backbone subsystem:

▼ 50/125 μm graded index, multimode optical fiber cable

■ 62.5/125 μm graded index, multimode optical fiber cable

▲ Singlemode optical fiber cable

Horizontal Subsystem

The *horizontal subsystem* describes the cabling from the telecommunications closet (TC) to the work areas in a building (see Figure 20-5). The ANSI/TIA/EIA-568-B.1 and

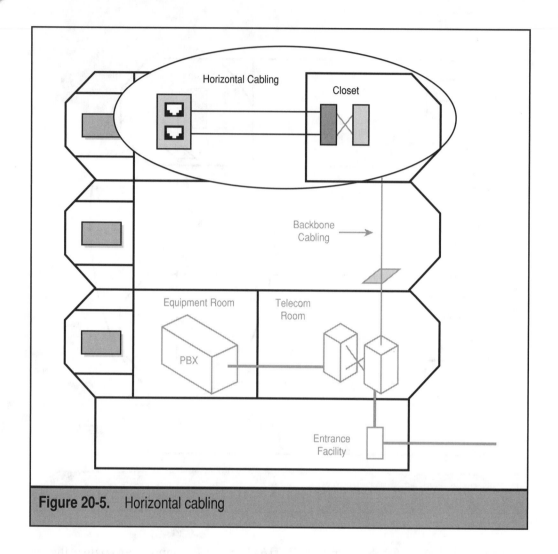

Figure 20-5. Horizontal cabling

ANSI/TIA/EIA-568-B.3 standards also support the use of optical fiber cable for horizontal cabling applications.

The horizontal fiber optic cabling shall follow a physical star topology. The maximum distance supported for horizontal optical fiber cables is 90 m (295 ft.). This is the distance measured from the termination in the TR to the termination in the work area. Industry cabling standards support a provision for 10 m (33 ft.) of work area and equipment patch cords. The maximum channel distance for optical fiber cables is 100 m (328 ft.).

The ANSI/TIA/EIA-568-A standard recognizes the following media types for the horizontal cabling subsystem:

▼   50/125 μm graded index, multimode optical fiber cable

▲   62.5/125 μm graded index, multimode optical fiber cable

NOTE: Singlemode optical fiber cable is currently only a recognized media for the backbone cabling subsystem.

PULLING OPTICAL FIBER CABLE

Pulling optical fiber cable involves the same general steps as pulling copper cables. The cable path must be selected and investigated before the cable is pulled. The optical fiber cable reels must be set up so the cable will pay out freely during the pull. Pull strings or pull ropes are used to pull optical fiber cable through conduits and lubricants.

Optical fiber cables do need to be treated a little differently than copper cables because of the fact that if the glass optical fiber is damaged during the cable pull, the cable is useless and must be replaced. This requires using the proper and industry-recommended installation techniques when installing the cable.

Fiber Optic Installation Tools and Materials

When installing optical fiber cable, many of the tools and materials are the same as those used to install copper cables. Some tools are specific to the installation of optical fiber cable. The tools and materials that will be required for an optical fiber cable installation include all of the following:

▼   **Steel fish tape**   Used when there is not pull rope in an innerduct

■   **Power winch**   Used for interbuilding cable pulls that exceed 100 lbs.

■   **Cable stripper**   Used to strip cable jackets and expose cable strength members

■   **Innerduct**   Used in conduits that have none

■   **Cable lubricant**   Used to reduce the amount of pulling tension on cables pulled through a conduit or innerduct

■   **Meshed wire grip**   Used to attach cable to pull rope

■   **Electrical tape**   Used to attach cable strength members to the pull rope (if a meshed wire grip is not used)

▲   **Innerduct cutter**   Used to cut the innerduct from the reel

Testing the Optical Fiber Cable Before Pulling

It is extremely important to test optical fiber cable for continuity before the installation begins. This simple practice will identify any cable that has been damaged before it is installed. Optical fiber cables are tested at the factory before being shipped by the manufacturer. This test will confirm that the cable was not damaged while it was shipped from the factory.

Optical fiber cable should be tested for continuity while on the reel. This requires having access to both ends of the cable. The cable should be ordered with access to both ends from the cable manufacturer. The fiber cable can be tested for continuity by shining a flashlight into one end of the cable. A more accurate test is to use a power meter or an optical time domain reflectometer (OTDR) to test the cable. These testing devices will identify if the cable has been damaged during transit.

In order to test the fiber cable on the reel with either a power meter or an OTDR, the ends of the cable must be terminated. A temporary connector must be attached to both ends of the optical fiber cable that is being tested. These testers will perform a continuity test and verify that the optical fiber cable has low loss, and light signals are capable of traveling through the entire cable. This practice will save money if an installed optical fiber is deemed defective. The cable manufacturer will usually replace the cable, but in most cases, will not pay for the labor costs to install and remove the damaged cable.

Considerations for Pulling Fiber Optic Cable

Although optical fiber cables are installed like copper cable, there are a few important differences that should be taken into consideration when pulling optical fiber cable. These include the following:

▼ Optical fiber cable is glass and therefore breakable. When pulling the cable, be careful not to bend or flex a fiber cable beyond its minimum bend radius.

▲ The tensile rating of fiber is less than the rating for copper cables. When pulling the cable, be careful not to exceed to maximum tensile rating when pulling the cable.

If during the installation of the cable you exceed the minimum bend radius or maximum tensile rating, the fibers within the cable will break or shatter; the cable will be useless. Violating the cable's minimum bend radius can also cause fractures to the optical fiber, called macrobending, where the optical fiber does not completely break. Macrobending will prevent light rays from traveling freely down the optical fiber. This will result in higher than expected losses in the cable. If the cable run is long or a high-speed application is being supported over the damaged cable, it may not work correctly and need to be replaced.

To avoid damaging the optical fiber cable, it is important to adhere to the following specifications during the cable installation:

▼   Minimum bend radius

■   Maximum tensile rating

▲   Maximum vertical rise

Minimum Bend Radius

The minimum bend radius is probably the most important parameter to be concerned about when pulling optical fiber cable (see Figure 20-6). The primary concern deals with not damaging the glass optical fiber inside of the cable. The second issue deals with additional signal loss the cable will experience if the cable is bent too severely. Light signals travel best in a straight line. Bending a cable will result in light signals hitting the cable's cladding at an angle that prevents them from staying in the cable's core. These signals will be lost as signal attenuation in the cable.

When installing optical fiber cable, it is important not to violate the minimum bend radius allowed for the cable. The minimum bend radius of an optical fiber cable is ten times the outside diameter of the cable when the cable is being pulled or when the cable is terminated. A good rule of thumb when pulling the cable is not to exceed a minimum bend radius of 20 times the outside diameter of the cable.

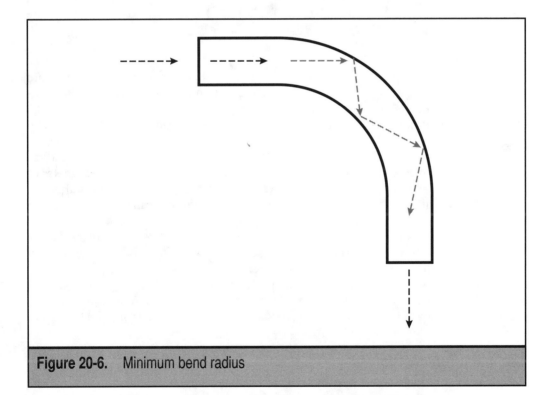

Figure 20-6.   Minimum bend radius

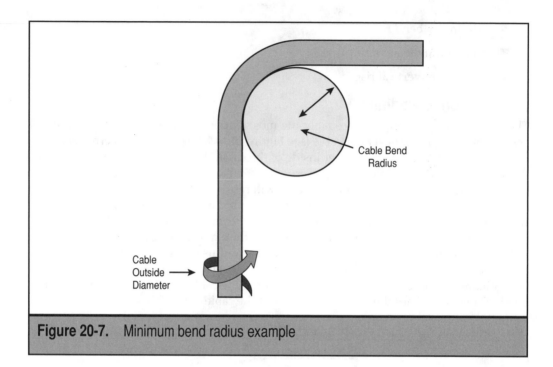

Figure 20-7. Minimum bend radius example

The minimum bend radius of the cable is measured from the center of the bend arc (see Figure 20-7). The actual bending of the cable should not exceed two times the minimum bend radius. This means that an optical fiber cable with an outside diameter of 0.5 in. will have a minimum bend radius of 5 in. The minimum bend of the cable should be no less than 10 in. in diameter.

Larger size and fiber count fiber optic cables will require a larger minimum bend radius than smaller cables. The minimum bend radius is based on the outside diameter of the cable. A cable with a 0.5 in. outside diameter will have a minimum bend radius of 5 in., and a cable with a 0.75 in. outside diameter will have a minimum bend radius of 7.5 in.

Actions, such as kinking the cable or bending the cable in half, will violate the cable's minimum bend radius. Care should also be taken when pulling the cable around sharp corners or in small spaces. These two problems can be easily addressed by placing a person by the cable reel when the cable is being pulled to verify that the cable is not kinked. A second person can also be stationed at each sharp corner or bend in the cabling run to make sure that the cable does not get pressed against the corner, violating the minimum bend radius.

Maximum Tensile Rating

All optical fiber cables have a maximum tensile rating, sometimes called maximum tensile load. The *maximum tensile rating* is the point at which the glass optical fibers will crack or break, resulting in significant signal losses over the cable. This rating is specified by the manufacturer of the fiber cable and should be known for each cable that must be installed.

The *maximum tensile load* is the "maximum" amount of stress or force that can be placed on the cable before the cable becomes damaged. This cable parameter defines the maximum pulling force that can be applied to the cable before the cable is damaged. Excessive pulling forces are exerted on cables that are installed in conduits that are occupied by existing cables. Another common situation is when optical fiber cables are being pulled through long conduits by mechanical pulling equipment. The friction of the cable jacket and conduit walls may require significant pulling force to install the cable.

Never exceed the cable's maximum tensile rating during installation. When a winch or pulling machine is used during installation, it is recommended that a dynamometer (sometimes called a tensiometer) be used to monitor the tension of the cable and break away pulling swivels. The dynamometer will indicate the exact pulling force being placed on the cable at all times. Break away swivels will pull away from the cable if a predesignated amount of pulling force is exceeded during the installation.

Cable lubrication and cable pulleys are devices that can be used to reduce cable friction and reduce the pulling tension on a cable during the installation. Lubricants can be applied to the cable and placed in the conduit to ease the cable past conduit bends. Cable pulleys can be used to feed cables into and out of a conduit. This practice can also reduce the required cable pulling force to install the cable.

After all optical fiber cables are installed, verify that no residual tension remains on the cable. Residual tension will result in the optical fibers stretching over time and possibly resulting in losses due to macrobending. Residual tension can result in the cable's performance deteriorating over time.

Maximum Vertical Rise

The last installation issue that can cause stress on an optical fiber cable is when it is installed in a vertical shaft of a building. If the optical fiber cable is not supported correctly, the cable can be damaged by its own weight pressing against the cable supports. The maximum vertical rise addresses the proper vertical installation of optical fiber cables.

The *maximum vertical rise* is the distance over which the cable is vertically self-supporting. This distance is a function of the weight of the cable and its maximum tensile rating of the cable is defined by the cable's manufacturer. Cable supports must be placed along the vertically installed cable, and the maximum distance between each cable support must not exceed the maximum vertical rise specifications defined by the cable's manufacturer.

If the vertical shaft or pathway for the optical fiber cable is continuous, the use of cable supports is recommended:

▼   At the top of each vertical rise

▲   Every time the vertical rise rating of the cable is exceeded

Many vertical cable pathways connect TRs that are vertically aligned in a multistory commercial building. Optical fiber cables may be run vertically and pass through multiple TRs. Industry cabling standards recommend that each vertically installed optical fiber cable should be supported a minimum of two times as it passes through a TR.

CHOOSING THE BEST CABLE PATH

The shortest distance between two points is always a straight line. When installing fiber optic cabling, circumstances may dictate that the cable be installed in a configuration other than a straight line. Pulling cable in a commercial building requires analyzing the building area between two points and deciding what is the best route for pulling the cable. This may mean running the cable above the ceiling in building hallways because the ceiling above a hall is more accessible than the ceiling in a congested employee work area.

The optical fiber cables should be installed in designated cable pathways. Cable pathways will usually follow building lines and right angles. Many times they are installed above building hallways. If a preestablished pathway is not in place, consider installing the cable along a path that will minimize the cost of materials and labor. Remember, labor costs are typically higher than materials; the path that minimizes labor will typically be considered the best path.

INNERDUCT

Support structures are necessary to properly install or support optical fiber cables once they are installed. Supporting structures usually include

▼ Cable trays

■ Ladder racks

▲ J hooks

The most important supporting structure element for optical fiber cables is innerduct (see Figure 20-8). *Innerduct* is a round, corrugated plastic tubing material this is installed in conduits, cable pathways, supporting structures, and above ceilings. Innerduct is used to provide mechanical protection for optical fiber cables.

It is highly recommended that innerduct be installed in all cable pathways that must support optical fiber cables. The innerduct should extend from one building space location to another through the cable pathway. If innerduct is installed above a ceiling, additional supporting hardware, such as cable trays or J hooks, will be required to suspend the innerduct above the ceiling tiles.

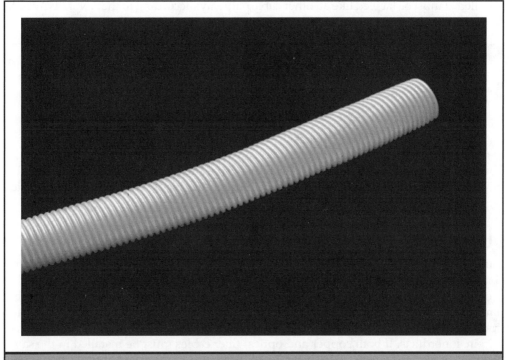

Figure 20-8.   Innerduct

Using Innerduct

Innerduct is used in all environments where optical fiber cable is installed including

▼ In conduits

■ In cable trays

■ On ladder racks

■ Above drop ceilings

■ Under raised floors

▲ Along walls

Innerduct must be installed in conduits and above ceilings if it does not exist. It comes on a large reel and is pulled like cable. If multiple innerducts are required to be installed in a conduit, they should be installed at the same time. Adding a single innerduct can be difficult once two innerducts are already installed in a conduit. Once the innerduct is installed, it must be labeled like all other cable pathways according to the ANSI/TIA/EIA-606-A standard.

> *CAUTION:* If innerduct is required to be installed in a plenum-rated area of a commercial building, both the innerduct and the optical fiber cable installed in the innerduct must be plenum-rated components. Building inspectors and fire marshals can require that nonplenum-rated cables and innerducts be removed from a building.

Occasionally, optical fiber cable is installed without using innerduct. This is generally not recommended. Heavy copper cables can damage or completely rip out an optical fiber that is installed in a conduit. Optical fiber cables may not be installed in innerducts in situations where installing innerduct is either impossible or impractical due to building constraints.

Duct Utilization

Innerducts should be installed in all conduits to support optical fiber cable. The proper size and number of innerducts for any installation varies based on the conduit trade size provided and the cable types that must be supported. Industry cabling standards recommend dedicating an entire conduit for either copper or optical fiber cables. A standard trade size 4 conduit that is dedicated for optical fiber cables is capable of supporting three, 1.25-in. innerducts. If both copper and optical fiber cables must be installed in the same conduit, one innerduct is usually installed in the conduit to support optical fiber cable.

Fill Ratio

When installing optical fiber cable in an innerduct, never exceed the maximum recommended duct fill ratio. The *fill ratio* is the maximum number of cables that can be installed in any cable pathways, such as a conduit or an innerduct.

Industry standards have suggested guidelines on the maximum fill ratio for cable pathway. The maximum fill ratio is based on the number of cables to be installed in the pathway.

The maximum recommended fill ratio is 40 percent of the duct size when three or more cables are installed in the cable pathway. This fill percentage can be applied to straight runs with nominal offsets equivalent to no more than two 90-degree bends. A larger fill percentage can be used for a single cable installation. The actual duct utilization is limited by the maximum allowed pulling tension of the cables.

Installing Innerduct in a Conduit

Innerduct is installed just like cable using a pull rope. The innerduct can either be pulled by hand or by power pulling equipment. If the conduit is straight or has less than two 90-degree bends, it may be possible to push the innerduct through the conduit.

The steps for installing innerduct in a conduit are as follows:

1. If the innerduct was purchased with a pull string, cut off the first 2 to 3 ft. of innerduct without cutting the pull string.

2. Cut a 1-in. notch into the innerduct with a knife.

3. Insert the pull rope into the notch and wrap the pull string around the innerduct and tie the pull string into a knot.

4. Wrap tape around the pull string to prevent it from becoming cut or damaged during the installation.

NOTE: These steps should be performed while the innerduct is still on the roll.

5. Attach the pull rope in the conduit to the innerduct and pull the innerduct through the conduit.

6. Once the innerduct is installed, leave 10 ft. of extra innerduct from the conduit entrance before cutting it from the reel.

7. Cut the innerduct back to the conduit entrance without cutting the pull string.

8. Unwrap the tape at the far end of the innerduct and untie the pull string.

Installing Innerduct Above a Drop Ceiling

There may be situations where innerduct must be installed in a cable tray or above a drop ceiling. This building space may or may not contain a cable pathway for supporting the innerduct.

This situation has the following special considerations:

▼   If the ceiling area is considered a plenum area by local building codes, plenum-rated innerduct, optical fiber cable, and cable ties must be used.

■   Be careful when the innerduct is installed that it does not violate the minimum bend radius of the optical fiber cable.

▲   The innerduct must be supported properly so it meets the requirements of local or national building codes.

LOCATING A PULL STRING

Before starting the optical fiber cable installation, look for a pull string in an innerduct. Innerduct can be purchased with or without a pull string. If the innerduct was purchased with a pull string, you can start with the cable installation. If the innerduct was purchased without a string or the pull string has been pulled out of the innerduct, a new pull string must be installed before the cable installation can begin.

A pull string is usually installed using a fishtape. The fishtape is inserted into the innerduct and fished to the opposite end. The pull string is attached to the end of the fishtape and pulled through the innerduct. Once the new pull string is installed, the cable installation can begin.

Most cable installers leave a pull string in place for future installations. A trailer string is usually attached to the cable being installed so that as the pull string is pulled out the innerduct, the new pull string is installed. The new pull string is used for future cable pulls.

PULLING CABLE SETUP

Before the optical fiber cables are installed, the proper setup must be completed. This usually involves securing the work area and placing the cable reels in the proper location to start the cable pull. Cable reels are usually placed on jackstands. These devices enable the cable reel to spin freely as the cable is being pulled off the reel.

The general procedures for setting up a cable pull are as follows:

1. Secure the work area that will be used for pulling cable. This involves using either orange cones or cones with yellow caution tape.

2. For large cable reels, set the cable reel on a jackstand and anchor the jackstand.

3. For smaller cable reels, set up a cable tree or reel rack.

4. For small horizontal cables, set up cable payout boxes.

5. Install pull string or pull cable, if one doesn't exist.

6. Identify pull points for each horizontal or backbone cable run. A pull point should be set up for each location where the cable must bend tightly and/or a sharp turn exists in the cable run.

UNREELING FIBER OPTIC CABLE

If the optical fiber cable reels cannot be set up to spin freely during the cable pull or if the cable reels are too large to place them on cable jacks, the optical fiber cable must be taken off the cable reel to be pulled.

NOTE: Unreeling optical fiber cable is not recommended and should only be done in situations where the cable reel cannot be set up to spin freely.

If the cable must be unreeled during the installation, use the figure-eight configuration to prevent the cable from kinking or twisting. Avoid coiling the optical fiber cable in a continuous direction for all lengths that exceed 30 m (100 ft.). The preferred size of the figure-eight is about 4.5 m (15 ft.) in length with each loop about 1.5 to 2.5 m (5 to 8 ft.) in diameter. This configuration will accommodate both loose-buffered and tight-buffered cable. The figure-eight for tight buffered cables can be smaller in size. These cables are smaller in diameter and as a result have a smaller minimum bend radius.

ATTACHING THE FIBER OPTIC CABLE TO THE PULL ROPE

Pulling optical fiber cables usually requires attaching the cable to a pull string or multiple cables to a larger pull rope. Optical fiber cable is fragile and can be damaged during the cable pulling stage. The first step in successfully pulling an optical fiber cable is to correctly attach the pull rope to the cable.

The most common methods for attaching the pull rope to the optical fiber cable are

▼   Using a pulling swivel (pulling eye)

■   Using a mesh pulling grip (Kellems grip)

▲   Tying the rope directly to the cable using a rolling hitch knot

Optical fiber cables should be pulled using the strength members of the cable or the strength members and the cable jacket. The strength members facilitate the cable installation and distribute the pulling load. This reduces the stress on the glass optical fibers. The exact method for attaching the pull rope to the optical fiber cable will differ depending on the size and the construction of the cable.

Pulling Swivel

Pulling swivels, sometimes called either a pulling eye or a swivel connector, are commonly used when pulling optical fiber cable with mechanical pulling equipment. Mechanical pulling devices are used for long cable pulls in conduits.

The pulling swivel attaches to the pull rope. These devices prevent the cable from twisting as it is being pulled through the conduit. Pulling swivels are also used to prevent exceeding the maximum pulling force on the cable. Swivels are designed to release if the pulling equipment exceeds the maximum pulling force.

Meshed Pulling Grips

Meshed pulling grips have been used for a long time to pull cables. They attach and grip an optical fiber cable by its jacket. These devices enable the cable to be pulled without the pulling force being placed in the glass optical fibers. Meshed pulling grips are mainly used with power pulling equipment. They help to reduce the chances of snagging or kinking cables.

A meshed pulling grip slides over the end of the optical fiber cable. The pull rope is attached to the looped end of the pulling grip. Pressure from the rope will tighten the pulling grip around the cable jacket.

Pulling grips used for optical fiber cables are slightly different than those used for copper cables. The pulling grips for optical fiber cable are designed for the cable's lighter weight and looser construction. Pulling grips are designed to fit over the cable's jacket. Some manufacturers are designing smaller pulling grips that attach directly to the strength members of an optical fiber cable. The proper pulling grip must be selected to match the cable's diameter so it fits securely. If the wrong grip is selected, the cable can snap or the grip can break loose causing the cable to be repulled.

Lubricants

The use of lubricants is highly recommended during optical fiber cable pulls. Lubricants will reduce friction between the cable jacket and the innerduct or other cables installed in the innerduct. Lubricants should be used regardless of the length or duration of the cable pull.

Most optical fiber cable manufacturers recommend using a water-based pulling lubricant. This type of lubricant will not damage or cause the cable jacket to break down over time. Avoid using detergent-based lubricants such as dish washing detergent or liquid hand soap. Most detergents become sticky when they dry. Detergents have a tendency to dry out the cable jacket, causing it to crack over time.

Lubricants should only be applied to the cable or conduit according to the manufacturer's recommendations. Always take the time to check the lubricant specifications to verify that the lubricant that is being used is approved for use with PE or PVC cable sheaths.

CAUTION: Cable lubricants can be applied liberally to the cable and the conduit. Excess amount of lubricant can spill on the floor causing an unsafe working condition. Always clean up any spilled lubricant before continuing with the cable pull.

Lubricating Innerduct and Pull Rope

Innerducts should be lubricated before optical fiber cable is installed. Friction is created as the cable slides across the plastic walls of the innerduct. The friction causes heat to build up, which in turn creates more friction. Lubricants will reduce the friction of the cable as it is pulled through the innerduct.

Lubricants can be distributed in the innerduct by pulling a swab in front of the cable, or it can be injected with a pump or a gravity device. Conduit bends or conduit off-sets are places that may require large amounts of lubricant to reduce the cable friction at these points in the pathway.

It is also recommended to lubricate the pull rope. The pull rope can cause additional friction especially if a cable is installed in the innerduct. The friction from the pull rope sliding over the cable requires greater pulling force to install the new cable. Using lubricant on the pull rope will reduce friction and pull rope tension as it is pulled through the innerduct.

ATTACHING THE PULL ROPE
TO A SMALL OPTICAL FIBER CABLE

Small optical fiber cables are typically used for horizontal applications. These cables are typically constructed with only two optical fibers, aramid yard strength members, and the cable jacket. The pull rope should be attached to the aramid yarn strength members in the cable. Never attach the pull rope to the glass optical fibers of the cable.

The aramid yarn strength members in the cable can be attached directly to a pull rope or attached to a pulling swivel. The pulling swivel will prevent the cable from twisting as it is installed. The aramid yarn strength members are attached to the pulling swivel by tying them into a knot and using tape to keep the knot secure during the pull.

The aramid yarn strength members should be attached to the pulling swivel using the following steps:

1. Strip back the cable jacket about 4 to 6 in., removing the cable jacket and optical fibers and leaving only the aramid yard strength members.

2. Separate the aramid yarn strength members into two groups.

3. Pass each strand in opposite directions through the pulling swivel.

4. Tie both strands into a knot.

5. Wrap tape around the aramid yarn up to the pulling swivel starting at the cable jacket.

ATTACHING THE PULL ROPE TO A GROUP
OF SMALL OPTICAL FIBER CABLES

Some jobs may require the installation of a group of small optical fiber cables to modular furniture cubicles. The correct method for installing a group of small cables is to directly attach the aramid yarn strength members of these cables to a pulling swivel. The pulling swivel is then attached to the pull rope. This process guarantees that the optical fibers in the cable are free from the pulling forces.

Some cable technicians may simply tie the pull rope around the group of cables using a rolling hitch knot and then wrap tape around the pull rope. This method may save time, but it is not the recommended method for installing a group of cables. Directly tying the pull rope around the group of cables can stretch the cable jackets and possibly damage the optical fibers inside the cables.

The aramid yarn strength members of all the cables should be attached directly to the pulling swivel using the following steps:

1. Strip back the cable jackets about 4 to 6 in., removing each cable jacket and optical fibers and leaving only the aramid yard strength members.

2. Separate the aramid yarn strength members for each cable into two groups.

3. Pass each strand in opposite directions through the pulling swivel.

4. Tie both strands into a knot from each cable.

5. Wrap tape around the aramid yarn for all of the cables up to the pulling swivel starting at the cable jackets.

ATTACHING THE PULL ROPE
TO A LARGE OPTICAL FIBER CABLE

Larger size optical fiber cables are typically used for interbuilding or intrabuilding backbone applications. These cables are typically constructed with 12 to 144 or more optical fibers, aramid yarn strength members, additional strength members, and the cable jacket. Cables with greater than 12 optical fibers will typically have the fibers packaged into groups of 6 or 12 fibers, and a fiberglass rod will separate the groups in the middle of the cable.

Interbuilding optical fiber cables may also have additional elements in the cable such as: fiberglass antibend rods, Kevlar, or steel armoring. These elements provide extra strength to the cable and provide more options for attaching to the pull rope. The additional cable strength members will keep the cable stress from damaging the glass optical fibers.

For larger optical fiber cables, the pull rope is attached to both the cable jacket and the cable strength members. A meshed pulling grip is attached to the cable jacket. Both the meshed pulling grip and the strength members are attached to the pulling swivel using the following steps:

1. Strip back the cable jacket about 12 to 24 in. removing the fiber, antibend rod, and any armor shielding leaving only the aramid yarn strength members.

2. If using a meshed pulling grip, wrap friction tape over 3 to 6 in. of the cable jacket and slide the pulling grip over the cable jacket.

3. Separate the aramid yarn into two strand groups.

4. Pass each strand in opposite directions through the pulling swivel.

5. Attach both the pulling grip and the aramid yard strength members to the pulling swivel.

6. Wrap tape around the pulling grip and aramid yarn up to the pulling swivel starting at the cable jacket.

SERVICE LOOP

Once the optical fiber cable is pulled to the designated location in the building, extra cable slack should be left in the cable run for future moves or changes. This is commonly called a *service loop*. The service loop is used to relieve any tension on the cable and provide cable slack for changes that may be required in the future.

The service loop is usually extra cable stored above the TR. The method of storage is not defined by industry cabling standards, but it is important that the cable for the service loop be stored so it does not get damaged when other cables are added to the TR.

Industry cabling standards do not specify the length required for a service loop. The amount of cable allocated for the service loop will depend on the size of the TR. The extra cable should be long enough to reach the other side of the wiring closet in case the cable run must be relocated or the TR must be reconfigured.

GENERAL PROCEDURES FOR PULLING OPTICAL FIBER CABLE

The steps for pulling optical fiber cable may differ slightly depending on the environment and the type of cable being installed. Although the exact procedures will differ slightly for each environment, most of the general procedures are the same.

The general procedures for pulling optical fiber cable are as follows:

1. Before pulling the cable, test the cable to eliminate any possibility that the cable is damaged.

2. Set up the cable spools so the cable pays off the top of the spools.

3. Reel cable off of the spool to avoid twisting or placing excess strain on the cable.

4. Set the cable spools so they are in a straight line with the cable run.

5. When multiple cables need to be installed, they should be placed in the innerduct at the same time.

6. When applying tension to the cable, always use the cable's strength members and never the optical fibers.

7. Do not pull on the outer jacket. This may temporarily elongate it. When the cable jacket returns to its normal state, the fiber and buffer may be compressed during the retraction of the cable's jacket. This may cause macrobend attenuation in the cable.

8. Pull uniformly on the cable keeping the pulling force below the maximum tensile rating for the cable.

9. Avoid jerking or applying excessive pulling force on the cable even for short periods of time.

10. When pulling multiple cables, pull cables that are the same size and weight together and do not violate the maximum pulling tension of the lowest-rated cable in the group.

11. Never violate the minimum bend radius for the cable. This is usually 20 times the cable's diameter when the cable is being installed.

12. Never use power pulling equipment for inside plant optical fiber cables such as horizontal or intrabuilding backbone cables. These cables should always be pulled by hand.

13. When using power pulling equipment, always use tension monitoring equipment and break away swivels.

14. Always use innerduct to protect the fiber cable from damage by sharp corners or protrusions in the cable pathway.

15. Do not pull optical fiber cables with copper cables.

16. Do not deform the optical fiber cable's jacket with using cable ties or straps to secure the cable.

PLANNING FOR THE PROPER NUMBER OF CABLE TECHNICIANS

Pulling optical fiber cable requires more than one person. The actual number of cable installers will be dependent of the type of installation and the number of cables to be installed. It is very important that there are enough cable installers working on the project so the cable does not get damaged and the installation is performed safely.

The number of cable technicians required for a particular job depends on a number of factors such as

▼ The type of installation

■ The number of cables to be installed

■ The size of the cables to be installed

▲ The need for power pulling equipment

One good rule of thumb is to plan on having enough cable technicians to do the job properly instead of having too few. The following are general guidelines for the number of cable technicians that are required to install optical fiber cable:

▼ Pulling a single cable requires a minimum of one cable technician, but two are recommended. One cable technician should be used for unreeling the cable and the second for feeding the cable into a conduit or plenum area.

■ Pulling multiple cables requires a minimum of two cable technicians. If power equipment is required, a minimum of three cable technicians should be used for the job.

▲ Installing an optical fiber cable in a vertical shaft requires at least three cable technicians and possibly more.

It should be the goal of every optical fiber cable installation to proceed quickly, smoothly, and without risk to personnel or equipment. It is extremely important for all cable technicians to understand

▼   Safety procedures for an optical fiber cable installation

■   Proper use of installation tools and equipment

■   Handling procedures for fiber optic cable

▲   Procedures for pulling optical fiber cable

CHAPTER SUMMARY

Optical fiber cable can be installed in many different environments such as: interbuilding backbone (campus backbone) environments, intrabuilding backbone (building backbone) environments, and horizontal subsystem environments. Optical fiber cable is an allowed media type for the horizontal and backbone subsystems in a structured cabling system. It is the primary media type for the backbone subsystem. The main reason is that optical fiber cable has extremely high bandwidth and very low loss characteristics. These two characteristics are required for the long distances required in the backbone subsystem.

The ANSI/TIA/EIA-568-A and ANSI/TIA/EIA-568-B.1 standards support the use of optical fiber cable for both interbuilding and intrabuilding backbone applications. The fiber optic backbone cabling is required to follow a hierarchical star topology to conform to industry cabling standards.

The ANSI/TIA/EIA-568-A standard recognizes 62.5/125 μm graded index, multimode optical fiber cable, and singlemode optical fiber cable for the backbone cabling subsystem. The ANSI/TIA/EIA-568-B.1 and ANSI/TIA/EIA-568-B.3 standards continues to support the 62.5/125 μm multimode and singlemode optical fiber cable but also enable 50/125 μm multimode optical fiber cable to be supported as well.

The interbuilding backbone, sometimes called the campus backbone, is the cabling backbone that connects all of the buildings on a campus to the main cross-connect (MC). The interbuilding fiber optic backbone cabling follows a physical star topology. There are three methods for distributing optical fiber cable between buildings: aerial, underground, and direct buried.

The intrabuilding backbone is the backbone cabling inside a building. It is the cabling that connects all telecommunications room (TRs) in a building to either the MC or an intermediate cross-connect (IC). The intrabuilding backbone follows a physical star topology. The maximum distance supported for an intrabuilding backbone cable is 300 m (984 ft.).

The horizontal subsystem describes the cabling from the TR to the work areas in a building. The horizontal fiber optic cabling follows a physical star topology. The maximum distance supported for horizontal optical fiber cables is 90 m (295 ft.). Industry cabling standards support a provision for 10 m (33 ft.) of work area and equipment patch cords. The maximum channel distance for optical fiber cables is 100 m (328 ft.).

It is extremely important to test optical fiber cable for continuity before the installation begins. This simple practice will identify any cable that has been damaged before it is installed. Optical fiber cables are tested at the factory before being shipped by the manufacturer. This test will confirm that the cable was not damaged while it was shipped from the factory. Optical fiber cable should be tested for continuity while on the reel.

To avoid damaging the optical fiber cable, it is important to adhere to the following specifications during the cable installation: minimum bend radius, maximum tensile rating, and maximum vertical rise. The minimum bend radius of an optical fiber cable is ten times the outside diameter of the cable when the cable is being pulled or when the cable is terminated. The maximum tensile load is the "maximum" amount of stress or force that can be placed on the cable before the cable becomes damaged. The maximum vertical rise is the distance over which the cable is vertically self-supporting. This distance is a function of the weight of the cable and its maximum tensile rating of the cable defined by the cable's manufacturer.

The optical fiber cables should be installed in designated cable pathways. The most important supporting structure element for optical fiber cables is innerduct. Innerduct is a round, corrugated plastic tubing material that is installed in conduits, cable pathways, supporting structures, and above ceilings. Innerduct is used to provide mechanical protection for optical fiber cables. It is highly recommended that innerduct be installed in all cable pathways that must support optical fiber cables. The innerduct should extend from one building space location to another through the cable pathway. If innerduct is installed above a ceiling, additional supporting hardware, such as cable trays or J hooks, will be required to suspend the innerduct above the ceiling tiles.

Innerduct should be installed in all conduits to support optical fiber cable. The proper size and number of innerducts for any installation varies based on the conduit trade size provided and the cable types that must be supported. When installing optical fiber cable in innerduct, never exceed the maximum recommended duct fill ratio. The fill ratio is the maximum number of cables that can be installed in any cable pathway such as a conduit or an innerduct. The maximum recommended fill ratio is 40 percent of the duct size when three or more cables are installed in the cable pathway. This fill percentage can be applied to straight runs with nominal offsets equivalent to no more than two 90-degree bends. A larger fill percentage can be used for a single cable installation. The actual duct utilization is limited by the maximum allowed pulling tension of the cables.

Before the optical fiber cables are installed, the proper setup must be completed. This usually involves securing the work area and placing the cable reels in the proper location to start the cable pull. Cable reels are usually placed on jackstands. These devices enable the cable reel to spin freely as the cable is being pulled off the reel. If the optical fiber cable reels cannot be set up to spin freely during the cable pull or if the cable reels are too large to place them on cable jacks, the optical fiber cable must be taken off the cable reel to be pulled.

Pulling optical fiber cables usually requires attaching the cable to a pull string or multiple cables to a larger pull rope. Optical fiber cables should be pulled using the strength members of the cable or the strength members and the cable jacket. The strength members facilitate the cable installation and distribute the pulling load. This reduces the stress on the glass optical fibers. The exact method for attaching the pull rope to the optical fiber cable will differ depending on the size and the construction of the cable.

The use of lubricants is highly recommended during optical fiber cable pulls. Lubricants will reduce friction between the cable jacket and the innerduct or other cables installed in the innerduct. Lubricants should be used regardless of the length or duration of the cable pull. Innerducts should be lubricated before optical fiber cable is installed. Lubricant can be distributed in the innerduct by pulling a swab in front of the cable, or it can be injected with a pump or a gravity device. It is also recommended to lubricate the pull rope.

The pull rope should be attached to the aramid yarn strength members in the cable. Never attach the pull rope to the glass optical fibers of the cable. The correct method for installing a group of small cables is to directly attach the aramid yarn strength members of these cables to a pulling swivel. The pulling swivel is then attached to the pull rope. This process guarantees that the optical fibers in the cable are free from the pulling forces.

Once the optical fiber cable is pulled to the designated location in the building, extra cable slack should be left in the cable run for future moves or changes. This is commonly called a service loop. The service loop is usually extra cable stored above the TR. The amount of cable allocated for the service loop will depend on the size of the TR.

CHAPTER 21

Fiber Optic Terminations and Splices

Installing optical fiber cables in a building is the first step to being able to use these cables for a communication system. The next step is terminating the newly installed optical fiber cables. The optical fiber cables must be terminated so they can be utilized in a communication system for transmitting signals between system devices.

Optical fiber cables must be terminated with a fiber optic connector in order to be used by a communication system. Fiber optic connectors provide the means to attach and detach to communication devices. Fiber optic connectors are the mechanical components that align the core of an optical fiber with the optical transmitters and receivers. These components permit light signals to travel through the core of the optical fiber cable.

This chapter will describe the function of a fiber optic connector and a fiber optic splice. It will describe the different methods for attaching fiber optic connectors to optical fiber cable. This chapter will describe the actual steps for performing a fiber optic termination and attaching a fiber optic connector to an optical fiber cable. Finally, this chapter will also describe the steps for performing both a mechanical and fusion fiber optic splice.

LOSS IN A FIBER OPTIC LINK

Fiber optic connections include both fiber optic connector terminations and fiber optic splice terminations. These connection points represent the greatest area of signal loss in most optical fiber links. A fiber optic link will have losses associated with the following:

▼ Optical fiber cable

■ Fiber optic connectors

▲ Fiber optic splices

Transmitted optical signals must be capable of entering an optical fiber cable. The optical fiber signal must remain contained in the core of the optical fiber cable. The fiber connection points must minimize signal losses as the optical signals travel through the fiber link. The losses associated with fiber optic connector terminations and splice terminations must be minimized to the fiber link to work correctly. Losses in a fiber optic link are minimized by using the proper installation and termination techniques.

Optical signal losses will always exist in all fiber links. All optical fiber links are designed with an allowable loss budget. This loss budget defines the maximum amount of signal loss that can occur in the link before the receiver on the opposite end of the link does not have enough signal to interpret the transmitted signal correctly. The loss budget for a fiber optic link is based on the following two factors:

▼ Strength of the transmitted signal

▲ Sensitivity of the optical receiver

Optical transmitters that are very strong will generate a very bright light pulse. The bright light pulse will travel a longer distance in an optical fiber cable than a dim light pulse. The second factor is the sensitivity of the optical receiver. The sensitivity determines the minimum amount of light that must be received for the receiver to decode the signal correctly. The difference between the power of the transmitted optical signal and the minimum signal power that must be received by the optical receiver determines the optical loss budget for the fiber link. The losses for the optical fiber cable and the fiber connections (connectors and splices) must not exceed the allowed loss budget for the fiber link to work correctly.

INTRINSIC AND EXTRINSIC LOSSES

Losses in a fiber optic link are classified as either being intrinsic or extrinsic. Intrinsic fiber optic losses are related to the optical fiber cable itself. They are caused by variations in the glass optical fiber. Intrinsic losses can also occur when two different optical fibers are connected together. Extrinsic fiber optic losses are related to the connection equipment used to terminate optical fiber cable. These losses are caused by attaching a fiber optic connector or a splice to an optical fiber cable.

Intrinsic Loss Factors

It is often assumed that optical fiber cables that are joined together are identical. This is not the case unless two optical fiber cables were manufactured by the same company and came from the same lot. The process of manufacturing optical fiber cable creates cables that are similar but not identical to each other. Slight variances in the cables cause signal loss when two optical fiber cables are joined together.

Light pulses are very sensitive to changes in the transmission medium. If the glass in the core of one optical fiber cable is slightly different than the glass of the core in a second optical fiber cable, light rays will react to this difference. Light rays may bend away from the cable's core into the fiber cladding. This will result in the loss of those light rays. Numerical aperture (NA) mismatch loss is an example of an intrinsic loss. This occurs when the NA of a transmitting fiber is larger than the receiving fiber.

A small amount of intrinsic loss will always exist in every fiber optic link. These losses are typically very small and are not a significant factor in most fiber optic links.

Extrinsic Loss Factors

Extrinsic losses are the most significant losses in a fiber optic link. Extrinsic losses occur when optical fiber cables are terminated. Optical fiber cables that are not perfectly aligned will result in losses in the fiber link.

Extrinsic losses result from using connectors and splices in a fiber optic link. When fiber optic connectors and splices are installed correctly, the resulting extrinsic losses are usually small and acceptable. When fiber optic connectors and splices are installed incorrectly, the resulting losses are usually very large and unacceptable. Large connector and splice losses can cause an optical fiber link to exceed the loss budget of the link and result in the link not working at all.

The four main causes of extrinsic losses from installing fiber optic connectors and fiber optic splices are

▼ Lateral displacement losses

■ End separation losses

■ Angular misalignment losses

▲ Surface roughness losses

Lateral Displacement Losses

Fiber optic connectors are designed to align optical fiber cables along their center axes. When one fiber's axis does not directly align with the other fiber's axis, losses occur. The losses will correlate to the degree of misalignment between the two axes (see Figure 21-1).

Large core optical fiber cables have more tolerance than small core optical fiber cables to misalignment problems. A 10 percent lateral offset is acceptable for an optical fiber cable installation. For example, a 62.5/125 multimode optical fiber cable can have a lateral offset of 6.25 microns. Each side can contribute up to 3.12 microns for the link to remain within acceptable tolerances for link loss.

Smaller core optical fiber cables have very little tolerance for lateral misalignment. The same 10 percent lateral offset for a singlemode optical fiber cable result is a very small acceptable margin. For example, an 8.3/125 singlemode optical fiber cable can have a lateral offset of only 0.81 microns. Each side can only contribute up to 0.4 microns for the link to remain within acceptable tolerances for link loss.

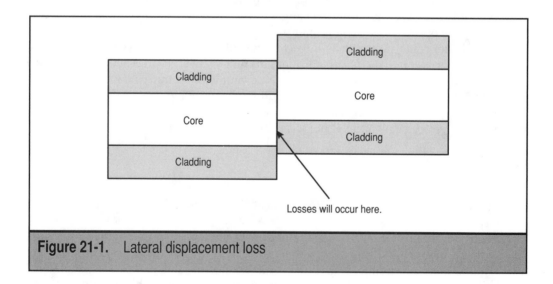

Figure 21-1. Lateral displacement loss

End Separation Losses

Two optical fibers that are separated by an air gap will result in signal loss for the link (see Figure 21-2). Light rays will refract when they travel through the fiber core and hit an air gap. As a result, light rays have difficulty crossing this air gap and entering into another optical fiber. The larger the gap the larger the loss.

Fiber optic connectors and splices are designed to bring the ends of two optical fibers together. In fact, the job of these components is to get the ends of two optical fibers gently touching without causing damage to either optical fiber surface.

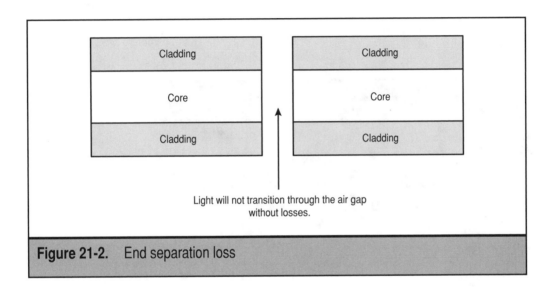

Figure 21-2.   End separation loss

Angular Misalignment Losses

The ends of two mated optical fibers should be perpendicular to the fiber axes and to each other while connected together. When the two optical fiber ends are perpendicular, optical light rays will successfully enter another cable. If the two optical fiber cable surfaces are at an angle, the light rays will reflect off the surface of the second fiber cable (see Figure 21-3).

Fiber optic connectors are designed to avoid angular misalignment for connected optical fiber cables. The fiber optic connect is designed to keep the optical fiber cable cores perpendicular and correctly aligned. This will promote the light rays traveling straight through into the attached fiber cable. Correct cleaving and polishing procedures also prevent angular misalignment from occurring.

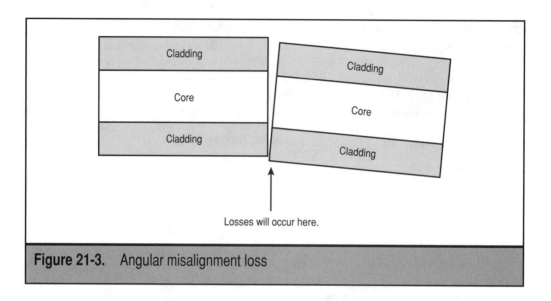

Figure 21-3.   Angular misalignment loss

Surface Finish Losses

The face of an optical fiber surface must be smooth and free from defects. These defects include

▼   Cracks

■   Gouges

■   Scratches

■   Burrs

▲   Chips

Irregularities from a rough optical fiber surface will disrupt the path of a light ray causing them to change direction. Light rays that are blocked or are forced to change direction will be lost. All irregularities to the surface of the optical fiber cable will result in signal losses due to the light rays not entering a mated optical fiber cable.

FIBER OPTIC TERMINATION SAFETY

Installing and working with optical fiber cables can be dangerous. All individuals who work with optical fiber cables must be aware of the following dangers associated with fiber optics:

▼   Glass disposal dangers

■   Chemical dangers

- ■   Eye and skin dangers

- ▲   Laser dangers

In addition, cable technicians must know their company's safety policies and practices. Each employee should consider the possible ramifications to themselves and other employees if company safety procedures are ignored. These procedures should always be followed by all employees.

Glass Disposal

Optical fiber glass fragments are created when optical fiber cables are terminated. Optical fiber glass fragments are very dangerous to all individuals that come in contact with them. They are very difficult to see and can easily become lodged under your skin.

Terminating optical fiber cable requires attaching fiber optical connectors to the glass optical fiber element of an optical fiber cable. Once the fiber optic connector is attached to the glass optical fiber, the excess glass optical fiber must be cut away from the fiber optic connector tip. This glass fragment must be disposed of carefully and correctly.

When doing fiber optic terminations, tweezers should be used to place all glass fragments into an approved container. Glass fragments must never be handled with bare fingers. Fingers contain oils that will cause glass fragments to stick to the oils. Touching other body parts can cause injuries due to the glass fragments. Tweezers will enable the glass fragments to be successfully handled without the possibility of causing injuring to any body parts.

Glass fragments must always be disposed in an approved container. Approved containers will always have a lid to keep the glass fragments secure. Glass fragments should never be left laying around or thrown into an ordinary trash can. These glass fragments may cause an injury to janitors or other workers that must handle the trash.

NOTE: An excellent technique is to attach glass fragments to the sticky side of tape. The tape will secure the glass fragments and prevent them from causing injuries to others.

Chemical Safety

Terminating and splicing optical fiber cables requires working with many different chemicals, solvents, lubricants, and adhesives. Care and caution should always be used when working with these materials. Chemicals and solvents can be harmful and cause skin irritation or burns. These materials should be washed off immediately if they come in contract with you skin. These chemicals may also be harmful if breathed or ingested.

Chemicals, solvents, lubricants, and adhesives should only be used in well-ventilated areas of a building. These building spaces will prevent harmful vapors from building up. The vapors from solvents and adhesives may cause irritation to the soft tissue areas of your body. The effects of breathing in harmful vapors may not be apparent immediately. The symptoms associated with breathing harmful vapors may take days or weeks before they are a problem. Always assume a chemical or adhesive is harmful and prevent unnecessary health problems later.

Chemicals, solvents, lubricants, and adhesive spills should always be cleaned up immediately. One of the immediate dangers is slipping due to the slippery nature of these products. Other dangers are due to either the vapors or making contact with skin of any individuals working near the spill. Rags or paper towels should be used to clean up all chemical spills immediately. Once the spill is cleaned, the rags used to wipe up these spills should be disposed of properly.

Eye and Skin Protection

Cable installers should always wear proper clothing and eye protection when working with optical fiber cables. Proper clothing may prevent stray optical fiber fragments from becoming lodged under your skin. Proper clothing may also provide protection from accidental contact with harmful chemicals or solvents used during the cable installation.

Eye protection should always be worn when installing and terminating optical fiber cables. Glass fibers can crack and easily fly into your eye if proper eye protection is not worn. Safety glasses must always be worn whenever working with or around optical fiber cables.

Laser Safety

Lasers are common light sources used to transmit light signals down optical fiber cables. The light rays generated by lasers are very strong and can be extremely dangerous for individuals that look into the end of an optical fiber cable. The light spectrum used to transmit light signals by lasers cannot be seen by the human eye. The power of a laser light can permanently damage your eyes. Viewing laser light directly does not cause pain. The iris of the human eye will not close involuntary as it does when viewing bright light. Consequently, serious damage to the retina of the eye is possible.

Never look into the end of an optical fiber that may have a laser attached to it. Always assume that there is an active laser light source attached to the opposite end of the cable. The laser light signal is so powerful that it will cause permanent spotting to your vision. If laser light is being used, always wear laser eye protection.

FIBER OPTIC TERMINATION TOOLS

Performing fiber terminations requires using the correct tools (see Figure 21-4). Some of the tools used to cut and strip the cable jacket off optical fiber cables are same as those used for copper cables. The tools used to strip the buffer material from the glass optical fibers and to terminate optical fiber connectors are different than those used to strip and terminate copper cables.

Figure 21-4. Fiber optic termination tools

The tools that are used for terminating optical fiber cables include

▼ Cable jacket stripper

■ Scissors

■ Fiber buffer strippers

■ Cleave tool

■ Scribe tool

■ Alcohol wipes

■ Polishing paper

■ Polishing disk

■ Fiber microscope

▲ Other tools

NOTE: There are many different types of fiber optic connectors sold by different manufacturers. Some fiber optic connectors require specialized tools for cable stripping or connector termination. The most common tools will be discussed in this chapter.

Cable Jacket Stripper

A standard wire stripper or ringing tool is used to strip the optical fiber cable jacket. An 18 or 20 AWG wire stripper can be used to remove the optical fiber cable jacket. This tool will cut the cable's jacket without damaging the optical fibers or cable strength members. There are many types of strippers that will work for this job. The stripper that you use should be sharp and easy to handle.

A ringing tool can also be used to cut the cable's jacket. A ringing tool is a specialized stripping tool with a cutter blade. A ringing tool has different size slots for stripping different size cables. The tool is slid over an optical fiber cable and rotated in a circle to cut the optical fiber cable jacket. The ringing tool will remove the cable jacket without damaging the optical fibers or cable strength members.

Scissors

Once the optical fiber cable jacket is removed, the cable's strength members will be exposed. Scissors should be used to trim the strength members to size. The strength members of an optical fiber cable are attached to the fiber optic connector. The strength members will provide strain relief for the connector assembly and prevent stress from damaging the optical fiber.

Many cable installers carry splicing scissors. These scissors will work fine for a fiber optic installation. Always make sure that the splicing scissors are very sharp. Aramid yarn strength members are very strong and will dull scissors very quickly. Dull scissors may not cut the aramid yarn strength members adequately and could cause an injury.

Fiber Buffer Strippers

Optical fiber cables are manufactured with a plastic buffer applied directly to the glass optical fibers. Loose buffer cables have a loose plastic buffer and a 250-micron primary buffer applied to each optical fiber in the cable. The 250-micron buffer must be stripped off the optical fibers to terminate them. Tight buffered optical fiber cables have a 250-micron primary buffer applied to the optical fibers and a secondary 650-micron buffer applied directly over the 250-micron primary buffer. Both buffers are 900-micron thick. Both the 250- and 650-micron buffers must be removed from tight buffer cables in order to terminate them.

Fiber buffer strippers are special strippers that are designed to strip the 900-micron and 250-micron buffer coatings off the glass optical fiber. Some fiber buffer strippers are designed to remove either the 250- or 900-micron buffers from optical fiber cables. In order to perform fiber terminations, it is helpful to keep two types of fiber buffer strippers in your tool kit:

▼   A 900-micron buffer stripper

▲   A 250-micron buffer stripper

A 900-micron stripper may be able to strip both the 900- and 250-micron buffers. However, this type of stripper tends to leave the 250-micron buffer on the optical fiber. This is the reason for carrying a second buffer stripper in your tool kit. A 250-micron stripper is more precise and will easily remove the 250-micron buffer without damaging or breaking the bare optical fiber.

Cleave Tool

A *cleave tool* is a specialized fiber termination tool that is used to cut a glass optical fiber at a right angle to the core's axis (see Figure 21-5). This is important so an optical fiber link does not suffer from extrinsic losses associated with angular misalignment.

The cleave tool cuts the optical fiber using two steps. First, the cleave tool will scribe the cladding of the glass optical fiber. This will weaken the optical fiber so it can be cut. After the optical fiber is scribed, pressure is applied to optical fiber to break it at the scribe point. The pressure will break the optical fiber at the scribe point. The cleave tool will cut the optical fiber core at or very close to a right angle.

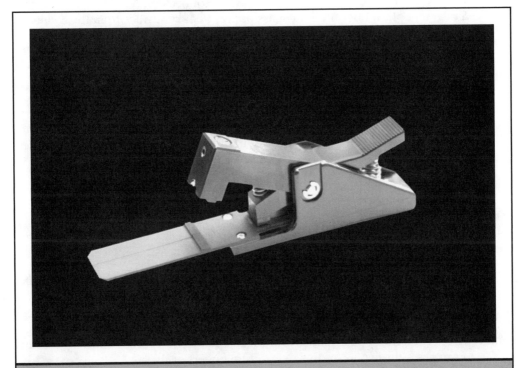

Figure 21-5.   Fiber cleave tool

Low-end cleaving tools will cleave an optical fiber at less than 1 degree from perpendicular. This type of tool is acceptable for fiber terminations. A high-end cleaving tool will cleave an optical fiber at less than 0.24 degree from perpendicular. This type of tool is preferred for performing fiber optic termination. This closer the cleaved optical fiber is to perpendicular, the lower the losses associated with angular misalignment will be. This will result in lower losses to the fiber optic termination.

Scribe Tool

A *scribe tool* is another type of specialized tool for cutting glass optical fibers. Glass optical fiber will fracture if cut with either scissors or a wire cutter. In addition, breaking or cutting optical fibers can cause small glass fragments to fly into the air causing a safety hazard. A scribe tool is used to cut a glass optical fiber.

A scribe tool will typically have a diamond or carbide blade. The blade is used to score the glass optical fiber at the point where the optical fiber is to be cut. Once the glass optical fiber is scored, pressure can be placed on the optical fiber, and it will cleanly break at the scored point.

A scribe tool is used when attaching optical fiber connectors. A fiber optic connector is placed over an optical fiber until the glass optical fiber protrudes from the connector tip. The scribe tool is used to cut the protruding optical fiber so the connector tip can be polished.

Alcohol Wipes

Alcohol wipes are very important when performing fiber optic terminations (see Figure 21-6). In order to transmit light signals, optical fiber cables must be clean from dirt or other substances that will block light rays. Dirty fiber optic connectors are the greatest cause of attenuation in more fiber optic links.

Alcohol wipes are used for cleaning optical fibers from

- ▼ Dirt
- ■ Oils
- ▲ Gels

Optical fibers should always be cleaned with an alcohol soaked wipe after the buffer coating has been stripped off. Alcohol wipes should always be used to clean the tips of optical fiber connectors after the connector has been terminated. Finally, alcohol wipes should always be used to clean optical fiber cable and connector ends any time they are removed from equipment, patch panel, or work area connection ports. Removing the fiber connectors exposes the connector tips to dirt from fingers or the air.

Polishing Paper

Polishing paper, sometimes called polishing film or lapping film, is special paper that is used to polish the tips of optical fiber connectors. Polishing paper grinds away the un-

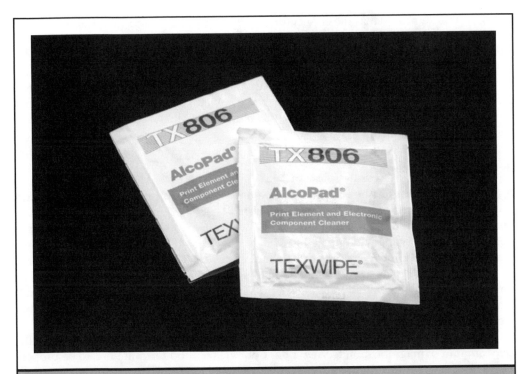

Figure 21-6. Alcohol wipes

even or rough spots on the tip of the optical fiber. The tips of the terminated optical fibers are rubbed on polishing paper to smooth and flatten the optical fiber surface. This process creates a perpendicular and unblemished surface required for transmitting light rays.

Polishing is typically done in either two or three polishing steps. Initial polishing is done with a piece of relatively course 3 μ polishing paper. The second polishing step is done with a piece of smooth 1 μ polishing paper. If a third step is necessary, it is done with a piece of very fine 0.3 μ polishing paper. Every fiber optic tool kit should have at least these three types of polishing paper.

Polishing Disk

A *polishing disk* is a specialized fiber optic termination device. This device is used to polish the tips of fiber optic connectors. A polishing disk is designed with a large, flat polishing surface. The flat polishing surface ensures a perpendicular finish on the connector tip.

The polishing disk has a hole in the center for the fiber optic connector tip. The fiber connector tip is inserted into the polishing disk and locked in place. This keeps the fiber connector tip secure and perpendicular during the polishing procedure. The polishing disk is also designed so that the connector tip remains at the perfect height to make correct contact with the polishing paper. The polishing disk is then rubbed over polishing paper using a figure-eight motion. When the fiber connector is polished, it is removed from the polishing disk.

The polishing disk is necessary to correctly polish the tips of a fiber optic connector. The polishing disk guarantees that the polished connector tip is flat and smooth. If a fiber optic connector was polished without using a polishing disk, the connector tip may have an angled surface, which will cause signal losses.

Fiber Optic Microscope

A *fiber optic microscope* is the tool that will be used to inspect the quality of cleaves and polished fiber connector terminations (see Figure 21-7). Fiber optic terminations must be inspected for scratches or other blemishes that will cause signal loss at the fiber termination. A fiber microscope will enable the optical fiber ends to be inspected once a termination is complete. If the fiber connector tip has scratches, the termination must be redone.

Most fiber optic microscopes are hand held devices that can be used at job sites. These devices have a connector attachment port, which enables the connector tip to be viewed. Many fiber microscopes include a light, which enables them to be used in dark closets or work area locations.

Fiber optic microscopes should provide at least 100× magnification. This is a sufficient amount of magnification to view fiber optic cleaves and terminations to be proper-

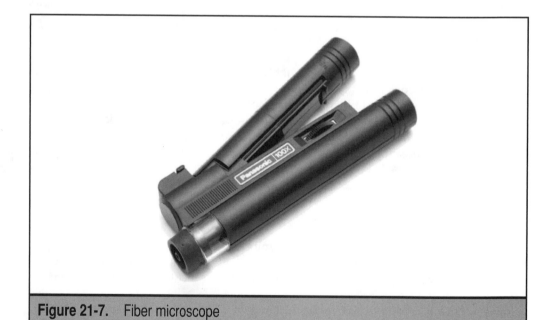

Figure 21-7.   Fiber microscope

ly seen. Fiber microscopes with a larger amount of magnification will enable fiber terminations to be viewed more easily.

Crimp Tool

Many fiber optic connectors require that a crimp tool be used to complete the fiber optic termination (see Figure 21-8). Epoxy fiber optic connectors require that a crimp tool be used to crimp a metal ferrule to the connector body. The metal ferrule holds the strength members of the optical fiber cable to the connector body. Nonepoxy fiber optic connectors are specifically designed to crimp onto an optical fiber cable. These connectors are designed so the crimping procedure will secure the connector body to the optical fiber cable.

The correct size crimp tool should be used when performing fiber optic terminations. The correct size crimp tool will be specified by the fiber optic connector manufacturer. Crimp tools that are too large will not secure the fiber optic connector adequately. Crimp tools that are too small can crush the glass optical fiber rendering the optical fiber cable useless.

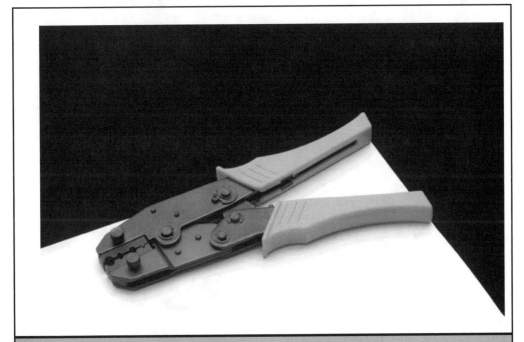

Figure 21-8.   Crimp tool

Other Tools

There are many other tools that are useful for fiber optic terminations and should be included in a fiber optic tool kit (see Figure 21-9). These include

▼   Tweezers for handling optical fiber scraps

■   Safety glasses to wear when working with optical fiber cables

■   Small rulers for measuring optical fiber when performing terminations

■   Large measuring device, such as a measuring tape or ruler, for measuring the correct cable lengths and distances

■   Ink marker for marking optical fibers during terminations

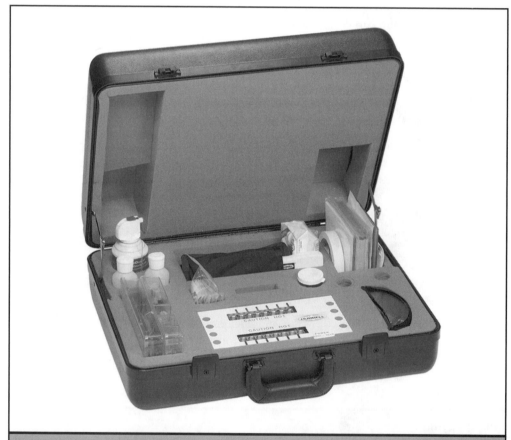

Figure 21-9.   Other fiber tools

■ Fiber waste bottle for holding all optical fiber scraps

▲ Compressed air for cleaning optical fiber connectors

FIBER OPTIC TERMINATIONS TYPES

Terminating optical fiber cable is probably the most important task during a fiber optic cable installation. Fiber optic connectors represent the greatest areas of loss in a fiber optic link. A fiber optic link may fail a certification test or may not function at all if the fiber optic connectors are not installed correctly.

The task of performing a fiber optic termination is further complicated because of the large number of fiber optic connectors and termination methods being used by different connector manufacturers today. It is very common for a customer to have a preference and specify a specific brand of fiber optic connectors that will be used for their building or campus. This means that fiber optic cable technicians must know how to correctly install many different types of fiber optic connectors.

Tight Buffer versus Loose Buffer Cables

Different types of optical fiber cables are terminated using different procedures. Tight buffer optical fiber cables are normally installed inside of commercial buildings (see Figure 21-10). Loose buffer optical fiber cable is typically installed between buildings and used for outdoor applications. Tight buffer and loose buffer optical fiber cables are terminated differently.

Tight buffer optical fiber cables are easier to terminate than loose buffer cables. Tight buffer optical fiber cables have a 900-micron buffer surrounding the optical fibers. This 900-micron buffer enables the fiber optic connectors to be directly attached to the optical fibers without requiring that any special buffers be added.

Loose buffer optical fiber cables are more difficult to terminate compared to tight buffer cables (see Figure 21-11). Loose buffer optical fiber cables typically have a waterproof gel material, called icky pick, in the buffer tubes. This gel material must be completely cleaned off the optical fibers before they can be terminated. In addition, loose buffer optical fibers only have a 250-micron primary buffer coating. In order to terminate loose buffer cables, buffer tubes must be added to the optical fibers for a fiber connector to be attached. A second termination option is to splice the optical fiber to a preterminated pigtail.

Singlemode versus Multimode Fiber Connectors

Singlemode and multimode optical fiber cables are terminated using the same types of fiber optic connectors. The industry-accepted size for multimode optical fiber cables are 50/125 and 62.5/125 microns. The industry-accepted size for singlemode optical fiber cables is 8.3/125. Because both singlemode and multimode optical fibers have a cladding with an outside diameter of 125 microns, then the same type and size connectors can be used.

Figure 21-10. Tight buffer cable

Multimode optical fiber cables are typically used for horizontal and intrabuilding backbone applications. These types of multimode optical fiber cables are usually field terminated by the cable installers. Fiber optic connectors are directly attached to these cables and then the cables are field tested.

Singlemode optical fiber cable is the type of media most commonly installed between buildings in a campus environment. These cables are typically a loose tube construction. As a result, singlemode optical fiber cable is typically terminated using pigtail splices or break-out kits.

Singlemode and multimode optical fiber cables are terminated using the same types of fiber optic connectors. These media types can be terminated using standard: ST or SC fiber optic connectors, or newer fiber optic MTRJ or Volition connector types. Industry cabling standards specify that fiber connectors should be different colors to distinguish the different types of cables once they are terminated:

▼   Fiber optic connectors used to terminate multimode optical fiber cable must be beige in color (see Figure 21-12).

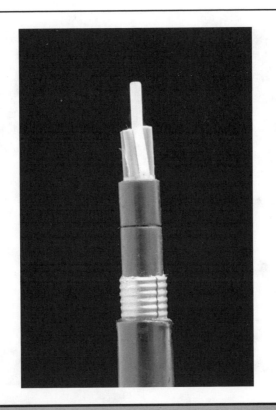

Figure 21-11.   Loose buffer cable

▲   Fiber optic connectors used to terminate singlemode optical fiber cable must be blue in color (see Figure 21-13).

ATTACHING FIBER OPTIC CONNECTORS

Fiber optic connectors must be attached to optical fiber cable for the cable to be used by communication system devices. The exact methods for attaching a fiber optic connector to an optical fiber cable will differ based on the specific connect brand selected. There are two basic categories for fiber optic connector attachment:

▼   **Epoxy**   This method involves using an epoxy type glue to attach fiber optic connects to optical fiber cables.

▲   **Nonepoxy**   This method involves using a crimping procedure to attach a fiber optic connector to an optical fiber cable.

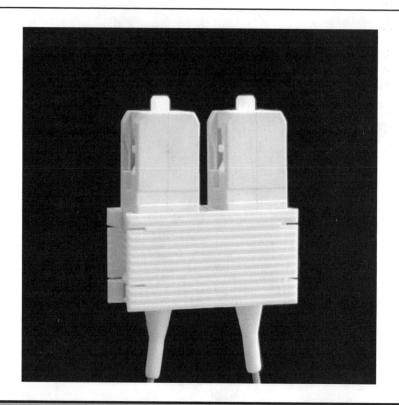

Figure 21-12.   Multimode fiber connector

Epoxy fiber optic connector attachment methods have traditionally been viewed as a more reliable and longer lasting than nonepoxy methods. In recent years, nonepoxy fiber optic connector attachment methods have improved significantly. Nonepoxy connector methods are now viewed by many industry professionals as being just as reliable as epoxy connection methods.

A second consideration when installing fiber optic connectors is whether the fiber optic connector needs to be polished after it is attached to the optical fiber. Fiber optic connectors can be divided into the following categories:

▼   Polish

▲   No polish

Most fiber optic connectors need to be polished after they are attached to the optical fiber. In fact, every type of fiber optic connect that is attached with epoxy requires polishing. Some nonepoxy fiber optic connectors need to be polished after they are termi-

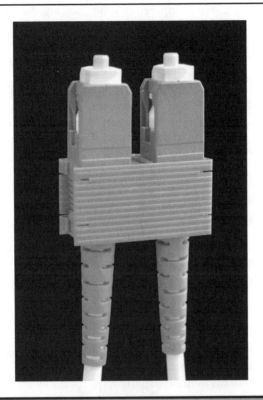

Figure 21-13.   Singlemode fiber connector

nated. Other types of nonepoxy fiber connectors have a prepolished tip. These fiber optic connectors do not need to be polished after the connector is attached to the optical fiber cable.

Epoxy Connectors

The term *epoxy connector* is used to describe fiber optic connectors that are attached to optical fiber cables by means of an adhesive glue. The adhesive glue will hold the optical fiber inside of the fiber optic connector. This secures the optical fiber connector to the glass optical fiber. The connector body is then attached to the strength members in the optical fiber cable to complete the installation.

There are many different methods for using adhesive for attaching fiber optic connectors. These methods differ by how the adhesive is applied to the connector and how the adhesive dries or cures. The traditional method for applying epoxy adhesive to a fiber optic connector is by injecting the epoxy adhesive into the fiber optic connector with a syringe. This method may require mixing epoxy glue, loading the epoxy glue into a syringe, and injecting it into a fiber optic connector. New innovations have simplified the epoxy application procedure by having epoxy adhesive preloaded or built into the fiber optic connector body. The epoxy adhesive stays inactive inside of the connector until it is activated by either heat or a liquid catalyst agent.

All epoxy style connectors must be polished after the epoxy adhesive has cured. There are many different methods used by fiber optic connector manufacturers for drying fiber optic connector epoxy adhesive. Fiber optic connector manufacturers are always trying to create connectors that are easy to handle and take less time to install. The most common methods used for curing epoxy adhesive include

▼ **Air drying**   This is an old method that enables the epoxy adhesive to dry on its own. Drying may take 12 to 24 hours.

■ **UV curing**   This method uses an ultraviolet light to dry epoxy adhesive.

■ **Heat curing**   This method uses an oven to heat the epoxy adhesive in the fiber optic connector. The connector cools to set the epoxy adhesive.

▲ **Anaerobic curing**   This method uses a chemical reaction to set the epoxy adhesive.

Air Drying Connections

The *air drying method* is the traditional method for enabling epoxy adhesive to cure. The adhesive is added to a connector or group of connectors and then enabled to dry without using any special device. This method usually requires between 12 to 24 hours for the epoxy to completely cure.

The air drying methods require a minimum of two days to complete fiber optic connector terminations. The first day is used to add the epoxy to all of the fiber optic connectors to be terminated. The cable technicians would need to leave the connectors to dry for at least a day. They could return the next day to polish the fiber optic connectors and complete the termination.

UV Epoxy Connections

UV epoxy connectors were created to reduce the time required for curing the epoxy adhesive for fiber optic connectors. This method uses an ultraviolet light to cure the epoxy adhesive in the fiber optic connectors. Many UV style connectors have a glass insert in the fiber optic connector. This glass insert propagates the UV light and cures the connector adhesive through the entire fiber optic connector ferrule. This enables the adhesive to cure quickly. The total time under the curing lamp is approximately one minute.

UV epoxy connections enable a group of fiber optic connectors to be terminated and polished in a single business day. The epoxy adhesive can be inserted into the fiber optic connector and cured in about 5 to 15 minutes. Once the epoxy adhesive has completely cured, the fiber optic connected can be polished.

Heat Cured Epoxy Connectors

Heat cured epoxy fiber optic connectors are similar to UV type connectors. Heat cured connectors have epoxy adhesive built into the fiber optic connector body. The most popular heat cured fiber optic connector is the hot melt connector manufactured by 3M. The hot melt connector gets its name from the fact that the epoxy adhesive is activated when the connector is inserted into an oven and exposed to heat.

A hot melt fiber connector is attached to an optical fiber cable by first inserting the stripped end of an optical fiber cable into the connector. The hot melt connector is then inserted into an oven. The oven heats and activates the glue. After a few minutes, the connector is removed from the oven and enabled to cool. The glue will cure and set during the cooling period. Once the connector cools, it is ready to polish. The total time to perform a hot melt termination is approximately 6 to 20 minutes.

Anaerobic Epoxy Connectors

Anaerobic epoxy fiber optic connectors are similar to a hot melt type fiber optic connector. This type of fiber optic connector also has a quick setting epoxy adhesive built into the connector body. The epoxy adhesive is activated, adding a curing agent. The curing agent initiates a chemical reaction to cure the epoxy adhesive built into the fiber optic connector. The adhesive in this type of fiber optic connector will cure very quickly because the curing process is based on this chemical reaction instead of air drying. This reduces the curing time substantially over air dry type methods.

An anaerobic fiber connector is attached to an optical fiber cable by first inserting the stripped end of an optical fiber cable into the connector. The curing agent is then added to the connector. This activates the glue and starts the curing process. The glue will take approximately two to three minutes to cure and completely set. Once the adhesive sets, the connector is ready to polish. The total time to perform an anaerobic termination is approximately three to five minutes.

Nonepoxy Connectors

The second category of fiber optic connectors is the *nonepoxy connector*. This type of fiber optic connector does not use adhesive to attach the fiber optic connector to the optical fiber. The fiber optic connector is crimped to the optical fiber cable and held in place by specialized components in the fiber connector and a crimp attachment.

The nonepoxy type of fiber optic connector was created to reduce the time to attach the fiber optic connector using epoxy adhesives. The process of mixing and adding adhesives in order to perform a fiber optic termination is very time consuming. A crimp termination method reduces the need to use any adhesives during the termination process.

Nonepoxy fiber optic connector terminations can be divided into two categories:

▼ **Nonepoxy, polish**   This type of connector requires polishing after the fiber optic connector is attached to the optical fiber cable.

▲ **Nonepoxy, no polish**   This type of connector does not require polishing after the fiber optic connector is attached to the optical fiber cable.

Nonepoxy, Polish Connectors

Nonepoxy, polish fiber optic connectors are similar to epoxy style connectors. These fiber optic connectors must be polished after the connector has been attached to the optical fiber cable. The optical fiber cable is stripped and then inserted into the fiber optic connector. The fiber optic connector is attached to the optical fiber cable using a simple crimping procedure. After the connector is attached to the optical fiber, the connector must be polished using a standard polishing procedure.

Nonepoxy fiber optic connectors can be more expensive than epoxy style connectors. This style of fiber optic connectors is preferred by some contractors because they save time attaching the fiber optic connectors to the optical fiber cable. These connectors can save money on a cable installation project that requires hundreds of terminations.

Nonepoxy, No Polish Connectors

Nonepoxy, no polish fiber optic connectors are a relatively new technology. These fiber optic connectors have a short optical fiber stub installed in the tip of the fiber optic connector. The fiber optic connector tip is factory polished. This type of fiber optic connector only requires that the optical fiber cable be properly cleaved. The cleaving process creates a perpendicular face to the optical fiber. The cleaved optical fiber is then inserted into the back of the connector until it butts up against the optical fiber stub installed the connector tip.

Many new nonepoxy fiber optic connectors have this design. This type of fiber optic connector substantially reduces the time to install fiber optic connectors. This style of fiber optic connector tends to cost more than the traditional types of fiber optic connectors that require polishing. However, the higher material costs are offset by the cost saved by not having to polish each fiber optic connector for the entire cabling project.

BREAKOUT KITS

Breakout kits, sometimes called fan out kits, are required to terminate the optical fibers in loose buffer cable. The optical fibers in loose buffer cable only have a primary 250-micron coating. This coating alone is insufficient for protecting and supporting optical fibers for fiber optic connector terminations. The purpose of the breakout kit is to add an additional buffer to the 250-micron primary buffer covering the optical fibers in the cable. The breakout kit will enable fiber optic connectors to be attached to these optical fibers in a loose buffer cable.

A breakout kit typically consists of the following items:

▼ 900-micron tubes

■ Main body or tube

▲ Buffer tube ferrule

The breakout kit is installed in order to perform the fire optic termination procedure. The first step is to strip the optical fiber cable jacket to the desired length. The cable strength members must also be removed leaving only the optical fibers. The next step is to remove any gel material from the loose buffer cable and clean the optical fiber strands. Once all of the optical fibers are cleaned, the breakout kit is installed. The optical fiber strands can then be terminated using standard termination procedures.

PIGTAIL SPLICES

Pigtails are the name given to preterminated optical fiber cables. These cables have a fiber optic connector installed on one side and a bare optical fiber on the opposite side of the cable. The fiber optic connectors on pigtail fiber cables are factory installed and polished. These cables are spliced onto the ends of a loose buffer optical fiber cable.

Pigtail splice cables are an alternative to using a breakout kit for terminating loose buffer optical fiber cables. The loose buffered cables would be stripped and cleaned using the same procedure described for using a breakout kit. Pigtail cables are spliced to the ends of the cleaned optical fibers. Once the optical fibers are spliced to the pigtails, the optical fibers can be connected to a fiber optic cross-connect.

FIBER OPTIC TERMINATIONS

Fiber optic termination is the process of attaching a fiber optic connector to an individual optical fiber and then polishing the optical fiber. Attaching a fiber optic connector requires that the connector body be correctly attached to the glass optical fiber. Then the fiber connector tip must be correctly polished. Both of these two steps must be completed before the fiber optic termination in a communication system.

There are many different styles of fiber optic connectors sold today. Each type of fiber optic connector uses a different termination procedure. However, the basic steps for completing a fiber optic termination are the same. The process of performing a fiber optic termination requires performing the following steps:

1. Work area setup
2. Stripping the cable jacket
3. Preparing the aramid yarn
4. Stripping the optical fiber buffer
5. Cleaning optical fibers
6. Cleaving optical fiber, if necessary
7. Attaching fiber optic connectors

8. Polishing fiber optic connectors

9. Inspecting fiber optic connector terminations

Work Area Setup

Fiber optic terminations require setting up the correct work area for performing the terminations. The work area is the work place where the fiber optic terminations will be performed. The work area is a convenient location in the telecommunications room (TR) or in each work area location where the optical cables are terminated.

The work area location must be selected to avoid areas of the building that are considered acceptable due to airborne contaminates or that present a safety hazard. Avoid setting up the fiber optic termination work area in dusty areas of the building. These areas usually cause excessive losses for the fiber optic connectors if the dust or other contaminants are not carefully cleaned from the fiber connector tips. Select the cleanest possible location at the job site that is close to the installed optical fiber cables.

A second location to avoid for a work area is a location that is under ducts or in windy areas of a building. These areas represent a safety hazard when terminating optical fiber cables. The air flow can cause small fiber fragments to become airborne or blown off of the termination work space. These fragments can become lodged in the skin of a worker in the area or for others working in the area at a later date.

The work area should always be set up prior to starting the fiber optic termination procedure. The three steps for setting up your work area are as follows:

1. Verify that you have the correct materials.

2. Verify that you have the correct tools.

3. Verify that you have a well lit and dust-free work environment.

Stripping the Fiber Optic Cable Jacket

The jacket of the fiber cable must be stripped back and removed in order to terminate the optic fibers. The optical fiber cable jacket can be removed using either an 18 or 20 AWG wire stripper or a ringing tool. Avoid damaging the cable's aramid yarn strength members when stripping the cable jacket. In addition, care must be used to avoid damaging the optical fibers in the cable during the cable jacket removal procedure.

When stripping the optical fiber cable, remove approximately 50 mm (2 in.) of the cable's jacket. Measure the amount of the cable's jacket to remove and mark the point with a permanent marker. Remove the cable jacket using a ringing tool or a standard cable stripper. The cable jacket must be cut squarely and cleanly.

Many cable manufacturers provide a rip cord that can be used to remove the cable's jacket. This is another alternative that can remove the cable jacket. Remove enough of the cable jacket to access the rip cord inside the cable jacket. Pull the rip cord until it reaches the designated cable jacket removal point. Carefully remove the cable jacket using either scissors or a straight-edge cutter.

Preparing the Aramid Yarn

The aramid yarn is always used when terminating optical fiber cables. The aramid yarn are the strength members inside of the optical fiber cable. The aramid yarn strength members provide mechanical strength to the entire optical fiber cable. The cable strength members also provide protection for the glass optical fibers inside the cable.

The aramid yarn strength members are attached to the fiber optic connector. This provides strain relief against the optical fiber being pulled out of the connector. The mechanical forces from pulling the connector will be absorbed by the aramid yarn strength members instead of the glass optical fibers.

The exposed aramid yarn strength members must be trimmed to complete the fiber connector termination. The exact length of the strength members will be specified by the fiber optic connector assembly instructions. The scissors in your tool kit should be used for trimming the aramid yarn. Most connector termination procedures require that approximately 25 mm (1 in.) of the aramid yarn be exposed from the edge and should remain in order to correctly terminate the optical fiber connector.

Stripping Optical Fibers

The next step in terminating the optical fibers is to strip the buffer to expose the glass optical fibers in the cable. Each type of optical fiber cable has different buffer removal requirements. The following amount of buffer must be removed for buffer surrounding the optical fiber in order to terminate the fiber cable:

▼ For loose buffer cables, the 250-micron primary buffer coating must be removed.

▲ For tight buffer cables, the 900-micron buffer (this includes the 250-micron primary buffer coating) must be removed.

A fiber optic buffer stripping tool is used to remove the buffer from the optical fibers. Using the fiber buffer stripper, remove approximately 12 to 18 mm ($1/2$ to $5/8$ in.) of the buffer from each optical fiber to be terminated. A ruler and felt tip marker should be used to mark how much of the buffer to remove. It is recommended that the buffer be removed in 5 mm increments. This will help to avoid breaking the optical fiber.

NOTE: The exact amount of buffer to be removed is specified by the fiber optic connector manufacturer. Different types of fiber connectors require different amounts of the buffer to be removed.

Cleaning Optical Fibers

After the buffer has been removed, each optical fiber must be completely cleaned. Dirt particles can cause misalignment to the optical fibers in a connector. Cleaning the optical fibers is required to remove small dirt particles that cannot be seen by the human eye. This process will guarantee that the optical fiber will fit correctly in the fiber optic connector.

Alcohol soaked, lint-free wipes should be used to clean optical fibers. The correct cleaning procedure requires making two or three passes over the optical fiber with a folded over wipe. This will clean all sides of the optical fiber at once.

When cleaning the optical fibers, avoid using cotton or paper wipes. These materials leave lint or other small particles on the optical fibers. These will result in the optical fibers not being seated correctly in the fiber connector and cause misalignment losses in the connector.

Never touch the bare optical fibers after they have been cleaned with an alcohol soaked wipe. Touching the cleaned optical fibers will leave skin oils on the optical fibers. These oils will attach dirt particles and cause them to stick to the optical fibers. Always clean any optical fibers that may have been touched over again.

Cleaving Optical Fibers

Some fiber termination procedures require that the optical fibers be cleaved. The cleaving procedure will cut a glass optical fiber at a right angle to the core's axis. The fiber optic termination procedures that require cleaving are

▼   Fiber optic slice terminations

▲   No polish fiber optic connector terminations

Cleaving a glass optical fiber is performed with a cleaving tool. The resulting cleave should cut the optical fiber to a prescribed length and should provide a flat end face at the end of the optical fiber. The flat end face on the end of the optical fiber will provide the best transfer of light rays through the optical fiber and into the connector tip.

Steps for Cleaving an Optical Fiber

An optical cleave is performed by completing the following steps:

1. Measure the amount of the bare optical fiber to remain after the cleave.
2. Mark the optical fiber at the cleave point.
3. Perform the cleave following the instructions for your cleaver.
4. Discard the end of the cleaved optical fiber with tweezers into a waste bottle.
5. Inspect the cleave with a microscope.

The end of the cleaved optical fiber must be square and free of any chips to the end face of the optical fiber. If the end face of the optical fiber is angled or chipped, the cleave procedure must be redone. Cleaves that are poorly performed or damaged will result in additional losses to an optical fiber link.

Attaching Fiber Optic Connectors

Once the optical fiber cable is stripped and cleaned, the optical fiber connectors are attached to each optical fiber. Attaching a fiber optic connector is the process of securely attaching a fiber optic connector to an optical fiber. The two primary methods of attaching fiber optic connectors are

▼ Using an epoxy adhesive

▲ Crimping (nonepoxy)

The actual method of attaching a fiber optic connect is specified by the connector manufacturer. When attaching fiber optic connectors, always follow the manufacturer's exact instructions and procedures when performing a fiber optic connector termination. Deviating from the exact installation steps may result in the connector being installed in correctly. These connectors will usually exhibit high losses and must be redone.

UV Epoxy Termination

The steps for performing a UV epoxy termination are as follows:

1. Verify that the rubber boot and rear ferrule are on the optical fiber cable before starting the connector termination procedure.

2. Insert the epoxy syringe in the rear of the fiber optic connector and slowly inject epoxy until a bead is visible at the tip of the ferrule.

3. Wipe off any excess epoxy from the connector tip with a lint free wipe.

4. Slide the fiber optic connector over the bare optical fiber until it touches the buffer. Approximately 5 mm of the optical fiber should be sticking out the end of the ferrule.

5. Place the fiber optic connector in the UV curing lamp. This requires about one minute to cure the epoxy adhesive. The epoxy should change color when cured.

6. Using a scribe tool, score the optical fiber where it emerges from the epoxy bead at the ferrule.

7. Use tweezers to remove the excess optical fiber and dispose of it in a waste bottle.

8. Slide the rear ferrule to the back of the fiber optic connector and crimp in place. This will secure the aramid yarn to the connector body.

9. Complete the installation by sliding the boot over the connector and securing it to the connector body.

Once the following steps are completed, the connector is ready to be polished.

Heat Cured Epoxy Termination

The steps for performing a heat cured epoxy termination are as follows:

1. Verify that the rubber boot and rear ferrule are on the optical fiber cable before starting the connector termination procedure.

2. Insert the epoxy syringe in the rear of the fiber optic connector and slowly inject epoxy until a bead is visible at the tip of the ferrule, if necessary.

3. Wipe off any excess epoxy from the connector tip with a lint free wipe.

4. Slide the fiber optic connector over the bare optical fiber until it touches the buffer. Approximately 5 mm of the optical fiber should be sticking out the end of the ferrule.

5. Place the fiber optic connector in the heat oven. This takes between 6 and 20 minutes in the heat oven.

6. Take out of the oven and let cool for the prescribed amount of time to cure the epoxy adhesive. The epoxy should change color when cured.

7. Using a scribe tool, score the optical fiber where it emerges from the epoxy bead at the ferrule.

8. Use tweezers to remove the excess optical fiber and dispose of it in a waste bottle.

9. Slide the rear ferrule to the back of the fiber optic connector and crimp in place. This will secure the aramid yarn to the connector body.

10. Complete the installation by sliding the boot over the connector and securing it to the connector body.

Once the following steps are completed, the connector is ready to be polished.

Nonepoxy Termination

The steps for performing a nonepoxy termination are as follows:

1. Verify that the rubber boot and rear crimp sleeve are on the fiber optic cable before starting the connector termination procedure.

2. Slide the fiber optic connector over the bare optical fiber until it touches the buffer. Approximately 5 mm of the optical fiber should be sticking out the end of the ferrule.

3. Insert the fiber optic connector into the termination tool. Using the tool, lock the optical fiber inside the connector.

4. Remove the fiber optic connector from the termination tool and crimp the bottom of the connect body. Make sure that the cable jacket and aramid yarn are not in the way.

5. Slide the rear crimp sleeve over the aramid yarn until it reaches the bottom of the connector.

6. Crimp the rear crimp sleeve with a crimp tool.

7. Using a scribe tool, score the optical fiber where it emerges from the fiber connector.

8. Use tweezers to remove the excess optical fiber and dispose of it in a waste bottle.

9. Complete the installation by sliding the boot over the connector and securing it to the connector body.

Once the following steps are completed, the connector is ready to be polished.

Nonepoxy, No Polish Termination

The steps for performing a nonepoxy, no polish termination are as follows:

1. Verify that the rubber boot and rear crimp sleeve are on the fiber optic cable before starting the connector termination procedure.

2. Cleave the optical fiber with a cleave tool.

3. Verify the cleave quality with a microscope.

4. Carefully insert the optical fiber into the stem of the fiber optic connector until you feel the optical fibers make contact.

5. Insert the fiber optic connector into the termination tool. Using the tool, lock the optical fiber inside the connector.

6. Remove the fiber optic connector from the termination tool and crimp the bottom of the connect body. Make sure that the cable jacket and aramid yarn are not in the way.

7. Slide the rear crimp sleeve over the aramid yarn until it reaches the bottom of the connector.

8. Crimp the rear crimp sleeve with a crimp tool.

9. Complete the installation by sliding the boot over the connector and securing it to the connector body.

Once the steps are completed, the connector is ready to be polished.

Polishing Fiber Optic Connectors

Polishing the tip of a fiber optic connector is the final step in the fiber connectorization procedure. Polishing a fiber optic connector serves two important functions:

▼ It grinds the connector tip to a precise dimension.

▲ It creates a smooth and perpendicular finish.

Both epoxy and some nonepoxy fiber optic connectors need to be polished before they can be used. The fiber optic connector termination procedure leaves a small piece of the optical fiber protruding from the tip. This tip must be removed using a scribe tool. The fiber tip must be polished to create a smooth surface.

Steps for Polishing Fiber Optic Connectors

The steps for polishing a fiber optic connector are as follows:

1. Rub the fiber connector tip on a 5 micron polishing paper held into a U shape to remove the fiber nub. Make a 25 mm (1 in.) circle on the abrasive side of the polishing paper. Stop when the fiber nub no longer scratches the polishing paper.

2. Place a piece of 3 micron polishing paper, usually gray in color, on the glass polishing surface.

3. Place water on the polishing paper about 25 mm (1 in.) in diameter and wet the entire polishing surface with the polishing disk.

4. Check the connector tip for an epoxy bead. If the epoxy bead is present, proceed to Step 5. If the epoxy bead is not present, proceed to Step 7.

5. Insert the fiber connector into the polishing disk on the 3 micron polishing paper.

6 Make one or two figure-eight patterns on the 3 micron polishing paper using gentle downward pressure (see Figure 21-14). Check the connector tip after

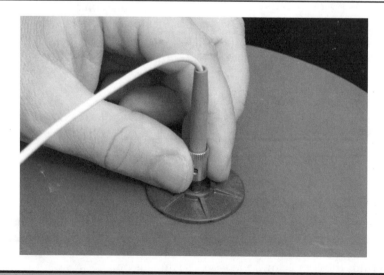

Figure 21-14.   Make one or two figure-eight patterns on the 3 micron polishing paper.

each figure-eight to confirm that the epoxy bead is gone. Once the epoxy bead is gone, remove the connector from the polishing disk and clean the connector tip with a clean, dry wipe.

7. Place a piece of 1 micron polishing paper, usually white in color, on the glass polishing surface.

8. Place water on the polishing paper about 25 mm (1 in.) in diameter and wet the entire polishing surface with a second polishing disk.

9. Make eight to ten figure-eight patterns on the polishing paper using light pressure.

10. Remove the fiber optic connector from the polishing disk and wipe the tip of the polished fiber optic connector with an alcohol soaked, lint-free wipe.

11. Place the dust cap over the fiber optic connector to prevent dust contamination (see Figure 21-15).

NOTE: Two polishing steps are usually sufficient for most fiber optic terminations. Some jobs may require a third polishing step. This is done with .3 micron polishing paper. This can be done by repeating Steps 7 through 9 using the .3 micron polishing paper.

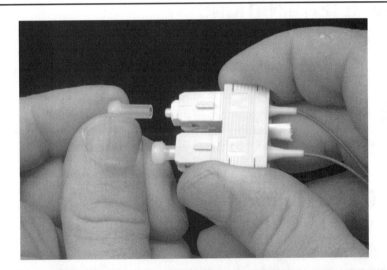

Figure 21-15. Place the dust cap over the fiber optic connector.

Fiber Inspection

Many of the losses in a fiber optic link are attributed to scratches to the end face of the fiber optic connector terminations. Scratches and chips will cause light rays to reflect in different angles. These light rays will usually travel out of the core of the fiber connection and become lost. Close up inspection of the fiber termination is an important quality control procedure for minimizing fiber optic losses.

All completed and polished fiber optic connectors should always be inspected using a fiber microscope. The polished fiber connector termination should be checked for pits, scratches, and polishing patterns. These problems reveal that the polishing procedure was not performed correctly. If the inspection of the fiber optic connector reveals problems, the polishing procedure must be redone.

Fiber Microscope

A *fiber microscope* is the tool used for inspecting either fiber optic cleaves or polished fiber optic connectors. A fiber microscope is a tool that is capable of enhancing the view of a polished fiber optic connector tip. Most fiber optic microscopes are hand held devices providing 100× magnification. This enables the optical fiber terminations to be inspected for quality.

ACCEPTABLE TERMINATIONS

Acceptable fiber optic connector terminations will have a smooth surface. The connector tip must be free from noticeable defects when viewed with a fiber optic microscope. The optical fiber end face of the connector should be polished flat and flush with the fiber optic connector ferrule surface.

Not all fiber optic terminations will be perfect. The core of the optical fiber is the most important area to investigate carefully. Small pits in the end face are acceptable but should be avoided. Scratches on the cladding area of the fiber connector are also acceptable because these will not affect the fiber light rays traveling in the core.

UNACCEPTABLE TERMINATIONS

Fiber optic connections that are scratched or not completely polished smooth will cause light traveling down the optical fiber to be refracted and attenuated. An unacceptable termination would have pits, scratches, cracks, or gouges to the connector end face. These problems are usually associated with either under polishing the fiber optic connector or over polishing the fiber optic connector.

Fiber optic connectors that are not polished enough are caused by not polishing the optical fiber long enough. This results in the optical fiber protruding from the fiber optic connector tip. Another cause of fiber connectors not being polished enough is the result of not using the correct polishing paper. A 3 micron polishing paper will leave the connector end face rough. A 1 or .3 micron polishing paper will yield a smooth surface. The fiber optic connector polishing procedure must result in the optic fiber being flat with the connector tip. Not polishing the optical fiber flat will cause the fiber surface to become scratched or damaged when two fiber optic connectors are mated together at a patch panel port.

Fiber optic connectors that are over polished also result in fiber terminations that must be redone. Over polishing a fiber optic connector will result in grinding way too much of the optical fiber. The end face of the optical fiber will become pitted or concave shaped. This will also result in significant losses in the optic fiber connector. These fiber optic connectors must be reterminated and repolished.

FIBER OPTIC SPLICES

Fiber optic splices are the second type of termination that must be performed during a fiber optic installation. A large fiber optic installation project may require hundreds of splices and thousands of connectors to complete the project.

An *optical fiber splice* is defined as:

"The permanent joining of fiber ends to identical or similar fibers."

There are many times during an optical fiber cable installation project when optical fiber splices must be used. Optical fiber splices are typically required to

- ▼ Extend an existing optical fiber cable

- ■ Join two separate optical fiber cables into one longer cabling run

- ■ Transition one optical fiber cable type to another optical fiber cable type (a nonfire-rated outside plant to a fire rated inside plant cable)

- ■ Conserve duct space by running a larger size fiber cable through a congested duct and splicing to smaller optical fiber cables that are then run to different locations in a building or a campus of buildings

- ▲ Access an individual fiber or fiber strands from a large optical fiber backbone cable (called midspan access)

Splices are not needed in a fiber optic installation when long, direct fiber runs can be made between termination locations in a building or a campus. In most installation projects, this is not possible or economically feasible. Splices cannot always be avoided because of cable length requirements, raceway congestion problems, or building fire code requirements.

Splices are required for fiber optic cabling projects when

- ▼ Large size (high fiber count) optical fiber cables are installed to a centralized location and smaller size (small fiber count) cables are run from that location.

- ▲ Loose buffer optical fiber cable is run into a building entrance; the cable must be spliced to an optical fiber cable that can be run inside the building.

As a general planning rule, splices should be minimized if possible. Optical fiber splices will add additional loss into an optical fiber cable run at each splice point. Splices will also add cost to the optical fiber cable installation.

SPLICE LOCATIONS

Splice locations should be carefully considered and planned before starting the cable installation. If a splice is necessary, consolidate as many cables as possible at a single splice point. This will minimize the cost of the installation compared to an installation that requires splicing at many different locations.

Fiber optic splice locations are the points where optical fiber cables must be spliced together. Splice locations must be planned in advance to guarantee that there is enough space to perform the optical fiber splicing operation. The usual locations where optical splices are located are

▼ Maintenance holes (MHs)

■ Telecommunications rooms (TRs)

■ Main cross-connects (MCs)

■ Intermediate cross-connects (ICs)

■ Entrance facilities (EFs)

▲ Equipment rooms (ERs)

SETTING UP YOUR WORK AREA

The proper work area must be arranged in order to perform optical fiber splicing correctly. The work area is the location where two optical fiber cables will be spliced together. This space must provide the following characteristics:

▼ Access to optical fiber cables to be spliced together

■ A stable work shelf to perform the optical splicing operation

■ Proper lighting to correctly match optical fiber colors

▲ Proper clearances to work on the cable and install the splice closure correctly

Optical fiber splices are usually required in maintenance holes in a campus environment. These work areas have limited space to perform optical fiber splicing. The work area for performing optical fiber splicing is usually a temporary location such as a shelf in the maintenance hole.

Safety must always be considered when setting up your work area. The work areas must be in a well lit location to perform the optical splice correctly. The work area must also be in a wind free location. Optical fiber scraps can be disposed of properly if the work area is well lit and free from wind.

PREPARING AN OPTICAL FIBER CABLE FOR SPLICING

Once the splice location is selected for an optical fiber splice and the work area has been set up, the optical fiber cables must be prepared for splicing. The steps involved in splicing two optical fiber cables include the following:

1. Determining the proper length of the cable jacket to strip from each cable to expose the optical fibers
2. Stripping the cables outer jackets and, if necessary, the cables inner jackets
3. Gel removal, if necessary
4. Removing the cables strength members
5. Stripping the buffer material from the optical fibers
6. Cleaving the stripped optical fibers
7. Cleaning the stripped and cleaved optical fibers

The exact steps required for preparing an optical fiber for splicing will depend on the type of optical fiber cables installed. For example, tight buffer cables have no gel material inside of the cable jacket. These cables do not need the gel material to be removed before removing the strength members and stripping the optical fibers.

Length Determination

The first step for performing an optical fiber splice is to determine the amount of the cable jacket to remove to perform the splice. The exact length will be determined by the type of hardware closure used to house the splice. The optical fibers must be long enough to fit in the designated termination points in the splice closure once the splice is completed.

The actual length of the cable jacket to remove varies based on the splice hardware and the closure to be used for the splice. The length of the splice closure should be measured. The amount of the jacket to remove must be at least half the length of the splice closure. The optimum amount of the cable jacket to remove will match the length of the splice closure. This will be approximately 1 m (3 ft.) from the end of each cable. This should expose enough of the optical fibers to perform the splice correctly.

Avoid removing too much of the optical fiber cable jacket. The splice closure fits around the cable jacket with a waterproof seal. The cable jacket must extend into the splice closure at least 4 to 6 in. to guarantee that the seal will remain intact and prevent water penetration.

The manufacturer's directions will provide exact cable stripping lengths for the splice closure. Always follow these directions and never deviate from them. The manufacturer instructions will provide the proper specifications to perform the splice correctly.

Stripping a Cable's Jacket

Once the amount of the cable jacket to be removed has been determined, the cable jacket must be stripped from the cable. This procedure must be performed without damaging the strength members inside the cable or the optical fibers. The exact amount of the cable jacket should be accurately measured. A permanent marker can be used to indicate the exact removal point for the cable jacket.

Most optical fiber cable jackets can be removed with a standard ringing tool. If the optical fiber cable has a metallic shield under the cable jacket, a cable knife or other type of straight edged cutting tool can be used to cut the cable jacket. The ringing tool or cable knife will be used to score the cable jacket at the marked point. The cable jacket can either be removed by a series of short ring cuts or using a long cut to split the cable jacket lengthwise.

Some fiber optic cables include a rip cord that can be used to cut the cable's jacket. If possible, use the rip cord in the cable to remove the cable's jacket. The rip cord will cut through the cable jacket without damaging any cable elements.

The cable jacket should be removed carefully. Care should be taken not to damage the optical fibers inside the cable. Many outside plant optical fiber cables are stiff. Always cut the cable jacket away from your body and never use a dull ringing tool or cable knife. Once the cable jacket has been cut, the sheath should be discarded.

Many high fiber count cables are constructed with a series of sub units. Each sub unit has a separate cable jacket. The sub unit cable jacket also must be removed in order to access the optical fibers. The same cable jacket removal process should be used for each cable subunit jacket.

Gel Removal

Most outside plant optical fiber cables are manufactured with waterproof gel inside the cable jacket and buffer tubes. This gel material is a waterproofing compound commonly called icky pick. A cleaning agent must be used to clean the optical fibers. The gel material must be completely removed before the buffer can be stripped.

A few companies manufacture products that perform this job easily. Many of these gel removers are a type of petroleum cleaner product. These cleaner products will completely remove the gel or leave a slight residue that can be cleaned with alcohol. All of the gel material should be removed from the cable before starting a splice.

CAUTION: Care should be taken when working with gel-removal compounds. These materials may be harmful to your skin or harmful if inhaled. Gel-removal compounds should only be used in well-ventilated areas. These materials are petroleum-based products and are flammable if exposed to any open flames or fire sources.

Removing the Cable's Strength Members

All optical fiber cables are manufactured with strength members inside the cable jacket. The optical fiber cable's strength members can be aramid yarn, fiberglass rods, or both. These cable components are designed to provide additional mechanical strength to the optical fiber cable. The pull rope must be attached to these strength member components during the cable pull.

The optical fiber cable's strength members must be cut to length and secured to the splice enclosure when performing a fiber optic splice. Aramid yard is fastened to the enclosure by wrapping it around a screw. A fiberglass rod is attached to the enclosure by a set screw lug. The strength members will provide strain relief against damaging the glass optical fibers. This practice will prevent the cable from pulling out of the enclosure and damaging the optical fibers.

Stripping the Buffer Material

The next step in the optical fiber splicing procedure is to strip the buffer material off the cable's optical fibers that must be spliced. The buffer must be removed from each optical fiber. A fiber optic buffer stripping tool is used to remove the buffer from the optical fibers. Using the fiber buffer stripper, remove approximately 12 to 18 mm ($1/2$ to $5/8$ in.) of the buffer from each optical fiber to be terminated. A ruler and felt tip marker should be used to mark how much of the buffer to remove. It is recommended that the buffer be removed in 5 mm increments. This will help to avoid breaking the optical fiber.

NOTE: The exact amount of buffer to be removed is specified by the fiber optic connector manufacturer. Different types of fiber connectors require different amounts of the buffer be removed.

Cleaving the Optical Fibers

The stripped optical fibers should next be cleaved with a cleave tool. Cleaving a glass optical fiber is performed with a cleaving tool. The resulting cleave should cut the optical fiber to a prescribed length and should provide a flat end face at the end of the optical fiber. The flat end face on the end of the optical fiber will provide the best transfer of light rays through the optical fiber and into the connector tip.

Steps for Cleaving an Optical Fiber

An optical cleave is performed by completing the following steps:

1. Measure the amount of the bare optical fiber to remain after the cleave.
2. Mark the optical fiber at the cleave point.
3. Perform the cleave following the instructions for your cleaver.
4. Discard the end of the cleaved optical fiber with tweezers into a waste bottle.
5. Inspect the cleave with a microscope.

The end of the cleaved optical fiber must be square and free of any chips to the end face of the optical fiber. If the end face of the optical fiber is angled or chipped, the cleave procedure must be redone. Cleaves that are poorly performed or damaged will result in additional losses to an optical fiber link.

Cleaning the Optical Fibers

The last step before performing the actual splice is to clean the stripped and cleaved optical fibers. Each optical fiber should be cleaned with an alcohol soaked, lint-free wipe. Each optical fiber must be cleaned before being inserted into the mechanical splice unit or into the fusion splicer. This procedure will clean any dirt or excess oils off of the optical fibers.

Dirt particles on the optical fibers may cause the optical fibers to not be seated correctly in the splice component or in the fusion splicer. This will cause the two cores of the optical fiber to be misaligned when spliced. The misaligned cores will cause lateral displacement losses at the splice in the fiber link.

MECHANICAL SPLICE

Mechanical splicing is the joining of two cleaned and cleaved optical fibers with a mechanical splice component. The mechanical splice component is a device that is designed to accept two optical fibers and splice the two optical fibers together. The mechanical splice mechanism is designed to align the two optical fibers and hold them together. The mechanical splice can then be tuned to reduce the loss between the two optical fiber cables.

There are a number of mechanical splices sold in the market today. Each type of mechanical splice component is unique and requires its own unique procedures for installation. The manufacturer's procedures should be closely followed when performing a mechanical splice. This will guarantee that the splice will be installed correctly and exhibit low losses.

Mechanical Splice Procedures

The basic procedures for a mechanical splice are described as follows:

1. Insert the mechanical splice in the splice assembly tool, if necessary.
2. Verify that the mechanical splice is in the open position.
3. If necessary, wipe off any gel filling compound and clean the optical fiber buffer.
4. Strip the buffer coating off the optical fiber. if not already done. The proper length is determined by the mechanical splice. Most splice components specify that 2 to 5 cm (1 to 2 in.) of the buffer be removed.
5. Cleave both ends of the optical fibers to the prescribed length with a cleaving tool.

6. Discard all broken fiber scraps by depositing them into an approved container.

7. Slide the optical fiber ends into the mechanical splice until they stop. Verify that the ends of the optical fibers are touching inside the splice.

8. Close the splice mechanism.

9. Remove the splice from the splice tool.

10. Secure the splice in the splice tray by following the manufacturer's instructions.

11. Repeat Steps 2 through 9 for additional optical fibers that need to be spliced.

FUSION SPLICE

Fusion splicing is the joining of two cleaned and cleaved optical fibers with an electrical arc. A fusion splice is a procedure that actually melts the ends of two optical fibers together creating a single fiber. The ends of the two optical fiber cables will be fused together by the hot electrical arc. The fused optical fibers will carry light rays between the two optical fibers with very little loss.

A fusion splicer is the device that performs the fusion splice. This device aligns and positions the optical fiber ends for splicing. Alignment can be automatic or manual and is accomplished with either a view scope or a video camera. Once the two optical fiber ends are aligned, the fusion splicer applies a high voltage electrical charge to a pair of electrodes. This procedure generates an arc across the optical fiber ends and fuses the optical fiber strands together.

Fusion Splice Procedures

The basic procedures for a fusion splice are described as follows:

1. Set up the fusion splicer. Specify whether the splicer is to be set up for singlemode or multimode optical fiber cable.

2. Most fusions splicers have V grooves for 900-micron, 250-micron, and bare optical fibers. Verify that the correct V groove is selected.

3. If necessary, wipe any gel material off the optical fibers to be spliced.

4. Strip the buffer coating off the optical fiber, if not already done. The proper length is determined by the fusion splicer. Most splicers specify that 2 to 5 cm (1 to 2 in.) of the buffer be removed.

5. Wipe the optical fibers with an alcohol soaked wipe to clean all dirt from the optical fibers. This will assure that the optical fibers are aligned properly in the V groove of the splicer.

6. Cleave both ends of the optical fibers to the prescribed length with a cleaving tool.

7. Discard all broken fiber scraps by placing them into an approved container.

8. Open the flaps over the electrodes and the fiber holding V grooves.

9. Slide the optical fiber ends into the V grooves of the splicer. Verify that the ends of the optical fibers are inserted until they stop between the upper and bottom electrodes.

10. Close the V groove and electrode flaps.

11. Manually or automatically align the optic fibers.

12. Perform the prefuse of the optical fibers.

13. Perform the splice by applying an electrical arc to the ends of the two optical fibers.

14. Remove the splice from the splicer.

15. Secure the splice in the splice tray by following the manufacturer's instructions.

16. Repeat Steps 1 through 14 for additional optical fibers that need to be spliced.

CHAPTER SUMMARY

Optical fiber cables must be terminated with a fiber optic connector in order to be used by a communication system. Fiber optic connectors provide the means to attach and detach to communication devices. Fiber optic connectors are the mechanical components that align the core of an optical fiber with the optical transmitters and receivers.

Fiber optic connections include both fiber optic connector terminations and fiber optic splice terminations. These connection points represent the greatest area of signal loss in most optical fiber links. A fiber optic link will have losses associated with: optical fiber cable, fiber optic connectors, and fiber optic splices. The losses associated with fiber optic connector terminations and splice terminations must be minimized to the fiber link to work correctly. Losses in a fiber optic link are minimized by using the proper installation and termination techniques.

Losses in a fiber optic link are classified as either being intrinsic or extrinsic. Intrinsic fiber optic losses are related to the optical fiber cable itself. Extrinsic fiber optic losses are related to the connection equipment used to terminate optical fiber cable. These losses are caused by attaching a fiber optic connector or a splice to an optical fiber cable.

The four main causes of extrinsic losses from installing fiber optic connectors and fiber optic splices are: lateral displacement losses, end separation losses, angular misalignment losses, and surface roughness losses.

Installing and working with optical fiber cables can be dangerous. All individuals who work with optical fiber cables must be aware of the following dangers associated with fiber optics: glass disposal dangers, chemical dangers, eye and skin dangers, and laser dangers.

Fiber optic terminations require using the correct tools. The tools that are used for terminating optical fiber cables include: cable jacket strippers, scissors, fiber buffer strippers, cleave tools, scribe tools, alcohol wipes, polishing paper, polishing disks, a fiber microscope, and other tools.

Terminating optical fiber cable is probably the most important task during a fiber optic cable installation. Fiber optic connectors represent the greatest areas of loss in a fiber optic link. A fiber optic link may fail a certification test or may not function at all if the fiber optic connectors are not installed correctly.

Tight buffer optical fiber cables are normally installed inside commercial buildings. Loose buffer optical fiber cable is typically installed between buildings and used for outdoor applications. Tight buffers and loose buffer optical fiber cables are terminated differently.

Singlemode and multimode optical fiber cables are terminated using the same types of fiber optic connectors. Because both singlemode and multimode optical fibers have a cladding with an outside diameter of 125 microns, then the same type and size connectors can be used. Industry cabling standards specify that fiber connectors should be different colors to distinguish the different types of cables once they are terminated. Fiber optic connectors used to terminate multimode optical fiber cable must be beige in color. Fiber optic connectors used to terminate singlemode optical fiber cable must be blue in color.

Fiber optic connectors must be attached to optical fiber cable for the cable to be used by communication system devices. The exact methods for attaching a fiber optic connector to an optical fiber cable will differ based on the specific connect brand selected. There are two basic categories for fiber optic connector attachment called epoxy and nonepoxy.

Epoxy is a method that involves using an epoxy type glue to attach fiber optic connects to optical fiber cables. Nonepoxy is a method that involves using a crimping procedure to attach a fiber optic connector to an optical fiber cable.

The term epoxy connector is used to describe fiber optic connectors that are attached to optical fiber cables by means of an adhesive glue. There are many different methods for using adhesives for attaching fiber optic connectors. These methods differ by how the adhesive is applied to the connector and how the adhesive dries or cures. The most common methods used for curing epoxy adhesive include: air drying, UV curing, heat curing, and anaerobic curing.

A nonepoxy connector does not use adhesives to attach the fiber optic connector to the optical fiber. The fiber optic connector is crimped to the optical fiber cable and held in place by specialized components in the fiber connector and a crimp attachment. A nonepoxy crimp termination method reduces the need to use any adhesives during the termination process.

Fiber optic termination is the process of attaching a fiber optic connector to an individual optical fiber and then polishing the optical fiber. Attaching a fiber optic connector requires that the connector body be correctly attached to the glass optical fiber. Then the fiber connector tip must be correctly polished. The process of performing a fiber optic termination requires performing the following steps: work area setup, stripping the cable jacket, preparing the aramid yarn, stripping the optical fiber buffer, cleaning the optical fibers, cleaving the optical fibers, attaching fiber optics, if necessary, polishing fiber optic connectors, and inspecting the fiber optic connector termination.

Polishing the tip of a fiber optic connector is the final step in the fiber connectorization procedure. Polishing a fiber optic connector serves two important functions of grinding the connector tip to a precise dimension and creating a smooth and perpendicular finish.

All completed and polished fiber optic connectors should always be inspected using a fiber microscope. The polished fiber connector termination should be checked for pits, scratches, and polishing patterns. These problems reveal that the polishing procedure was not performed correctly. If the inspection of the fiber optic connector reveals problems, the polishing procedure must be redone.

Acceptable fiber optic connector terminations will have a smooth surface. The connector tip must be free from noticeable defects when viewed with a fiber optic microscope. The optical fiber end face of the connector should be polished flat and flush with the fiber optic connector ferrule surface. Fiber optic connections that are scratched or not completely polished smooth will cause light traveling down the optical fiber to be refracted and attenuated. An unacceptable termination would have pits, scratches, cracks, or gouges to the connector end face. These problems are usually associated with either under polishing the fiber optic connector or over polishing the fiber optic connector.

Fiber optic splices are the second type of termination that must be performed during a fiber optic installation. Splices are not needed in a fiber optic installation when long, direct fiber runs can be made between termination locations in a building or a campus. In most installation projects, this is not possible or economically feasible. Splices cannot always be avoided because of cable length requirements, raceway congestion problems, or building fire code requirements.

Fiber optic splice locations are the points where optical fiber cables must be spliced together. Splice locations must be planned in advance to guarantee that there is enough space to perform the optical fiber splicing operation. The usual locations where optical splices are located are: maintenance holes (MHs), telecommunications rooms (TRs), main cross-connects (MCs), intermediate cross-connects (ICs), entrance facilities (EFs), and equipment rooms (ERs).

Mechanical splicing is the joining of two cleaned and cleaved optical fiber with a mechanical splice component. The mechanical splice mechanism is designed to align the two optical fibers and hold them together. Fusion splicing is the joining of two cleaned and cleaved optical fibers with an electrical arc. A fusion splice is a procedure that actually melts the end of two optical fibers together creating a single fiber. A fusion splicer is the device that performs the fusion splice. This device aligns and positions the optical fiber ends for splicing.

CHAPTER 22

Cable Testing Devices

Allll communication cables must be properly tested and certified to verify that the cable installation was performed correctly. Testing communication cables will characterize the cables. This process will simulate transmitting communication signals over the installed cables. Measuring the transmitted signals will verify the transmission performance of the installed cables.

Testing communication cables is a systematic approach that verifies that the correct type of communication cables were installed. It also verifies that the installation was performed correctly. Finally, testing will provide baseline information about the performance of the entire cabling system. This information can be used later for troubleshooting cable-related problems.

Cable testing devices are very important to verify that the cabling system was installed correctly. These devices perform tests that determine if the cable pairs are terminated correctly and in the correct position. They can also check the overall performance of the cabling system to confirm that it meets or exceeds industry cabling standards.

This chapter will describe the cable testing process. It will describe the different types of cable testing devices for both copper cables and optical fiber cables.

CABLE TESTING

Testing communications cables is a very important step in the entire cable installation project. The process of testing communications cables is to verify that the cables are terminated correctly. Testing is also required to certify the installed cable's performance. This will guarantee that the installed cables will meet or exceed industry performance specifications.

Testing and certifying communication cabling requires making several basic measurements. Cable field testers and devices are used to verify that the communication cables have been installed and terminated correctly. Proper testing maximizes system longevity, and minimizes system downtime and the time required for troubleshooting and system maintenance.

Historically, the communication cabling used for voice or low-speed data applications required little or no testing. Voice applications just need continuity between the phone and the PBX. Low-speed data applications also require basic continuity between a terminal and a mainframe computer. As a result, either visual inspection or a simple continuity test was sufficient to test these cables.

Today, high performance category 5e UTP cable, category 6 UTP, and optical fiber cables require extensive testing. Testing is required to verify that the cables have been installed correctly and to certify that the cable's performance meets industry performance specifications. The performance testing is required to confirm that the installed cabling will support high-speed network applications over industry supported distances.

CABLE TESTING DEVICES

Cable testing devices are commonly called field testers. *Field testers* are hand held cable testing devices. These devices are used in the field to test installed communication cabling systems. Field cable testers will indicate if the cable passes the certification test once a series of tests are completed. The cable field tester stores the test results, and they can either be printed or downloaded to a floppy disk.

There are many different types of cable field testers to certify communication cables. Communication cable field testers range from very simple to very complex. Usually, these devices are based on what needs to be tested. For example, some installations only need to verify that the cables are terminated properly. Other field testers are very expensive and perform extensive tests on the installed communication cables.

Some common copper testing devices include

▼ Lineman's test set

■ Toner generator and amplifier unit

■ Multimeter

■ Continuity tester

▲ Certification field tester

Some common optical fiber testing devices include

▼ Flashlight

■ Visual cable tracers and fault locators

■ Optical power meter

■ Optical light source

■ Optical loss test sets

▲ OTDR testers

Lineman's Test Set

A *lineman's test set*, sometimes called a butt set, is a simple cable field testing device used to test voice circuits (see Figure 22-1). This testing device enables a voice installation technician to connect to an analog voice circuit. The lineman's test set enables the voice technician to test different parts of the voice communication cable system for a dial tone.

All incoming voice circuits from either a local exchange carrier (LEC) or a service provider (SP) will carry a dial tone. The voice circuits will terminate on the LEC or SP demarcation block. The voice circuits must be connected to the voice switch. The backbone communication cables are typically used to extend the voice circuits from the demarcation point to the voice switch. The lineman's test set is used to confirm that the backbone

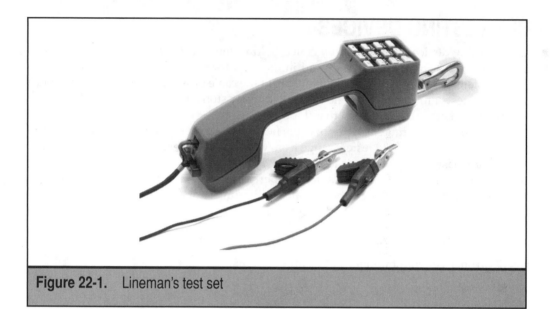

Figure 22-1. Lineman's test set

communication cabling is terminated correctly and that the correct backbone cable pairs are terminated on the voice switch. The lack of dial tone indicates to the voice technician that there is a problem in the backbone cable.

The lineman's test set is a simple device that resembles a telephone hand set. The telephone hand set has buttons that enable telephone numbers to be dialed. The cord on the testing device has two alligator clips on the end. The alligator clips are used to connect to a cable pair directly or to a cable pair terminated on a punch down block. The alligator clips enable the voice technician to connect and check cable pairs very quickly.

The lineman's test set is used by voice technicians to check for a dial tone at any point from the demarcation point to the voice switch. The lineman's test set can be used at each termination point for the voice cabling in the building. All cabling that is terminated correctly will provide dial tone when tested. Lack of a dial tone indicates that there is a cabling problem somewhere in the link.

The lineman's test is used to identify the presence of a dial tone on a cable pair or the lack of a dial tone. This testing device cannot identify the cause of any cabling problems. The voice cable technician must visually check the cable pairs or use another type of cable testing device.

A lineman's test set is used for the following functions:

▼ Identifying analog voice circuits.

■ Simulating a standard analog telephone set for checking dial tone and making calls.

▲ Basic circuit diagnostics and troubleshooting.

NOTE: Analog lineman test sets cannot be used to test digital data or voice circuits. A digital lineman's test set must be used for testing digital circuits.

Tone Generator and Amplifier

A *tone generator* and *amplifier* are common testing devices used by voice and cabling technicians (see Figure 22-2). These devices are simple testing devices used to either identify or locate communication cables. These testing devices are usually part of every cable technician's tool kit.

The tone generator and amplifier are two devices that work together to perform the identification or location function. The tone generator connects to a cable pair and places a low level and distinctive tone on a cable pair. The amplifier is used to amplify the signal and identify the exact cable pair where the tone generator is connected.

The tone generator is connected to a cable pair by inserting the modular jack into an outlet or connecting the alligator clips to a cable pair. Once connected to a cable pair, the tone generator energizes that cable pair.

The amplifier unit has a metal probe on the end that enables the probe to be inserted into the pairs of a multipair backbone cable or on the clips of a punch down block. The probe on the amplifier enables this device to be moved quickly. The metal tip can also be run across the front of a punch down block to find the tone signal.

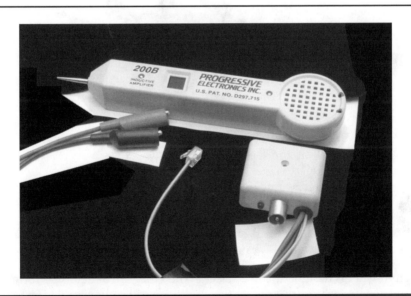

Figure 22-2.   Tone generator and amplifier

> **CAUTION:** The amplifier may detect the distinctive audible tone of more than one cable pair. This is due to the energy from the tone generator being coupled into adjacent cable pairs. The correct pair with the tone generator attached will emit the loudest signal when scanned with the amplifier.

Multimeter

The most common piece of equipment used for cable testing is the volt-ohm-milliampere meter. This device is typically called a multimeter. Many electricians carry a multimeter for performing tests of electrical wiring. These devices are inexpensive and can perform multiple tests quickly.

A *multimeter* is a multipurpose device that can perform multiple test functions (see Figure 22-3). The volt meter enables this testing device to measure voltage of a circuit. The ohm meter enables this testing device to measure resistance on a circuit. The milliampere meter enables this testing device to measure current on a circuit.

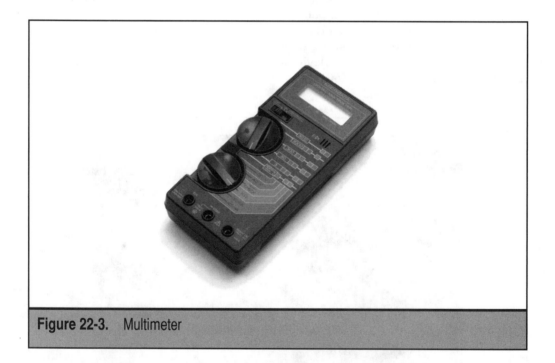

Figure 22-3. Multimeter

The multimeter is designed with a selector knob that can be set to perform a specific test. The multimeter has two test probes that are connected to the circuit to be tested. Once the meter is set correctly, the probes will be used to make a test measurement.

Ohmmeter

The ohmmeter functions of the multimeter can be used to test communication cables. The ohmmeter can provide basic troubleshooting of copper communication cables. The ohm meter function can be used to test resistance in a communication cable. The ohmmeter can be used to indicate if a wire in a horizontal or backbone cable is not terminated properly.

An ohmmeter can be used to identify the following problem conditions in a communication cable:

▼ Shorts

■ Opens

▲ Length of the cable is too long

An ohmmeter can identify an open or short condition of a copper cable. If an ohmmeter tests a cable pair and the cable pair exhibits very low resistance, then the cable pair has a short. If the ohmmeter tests a cable pair and the pair exhibits a very, very high or infinite resistance, then the cable pair is open.

Digital multimeters are able to measure a cable's DC resistance. The measured DC resistance value provides an approximate length measurement for the copper communication cable. The DC resistance test is not a required test for certifying either category 5e or category 6 UTP cables. It is a useful test to indicate if the terminations are correct and tight across the cable link.

A multimeter is a very useful device for testing coaxial cables. A DC resistance test can be a simple way to test the attenuation of coaxial link. The multimeter would be used in conjunction with a shorting plug. The shorting plug will connect the center conductor to the cable shield. The two test probes can be easily connected to the center conductor and the cable shield from the opposite end of the cable link. The ohmmeter can measure the DC resistance and also check for shorts or opens in the coaxial cable link.

Multimeter Disadvantages

The multimeter is a very inexpensive and easy to use testing device. It provides basic cable tests for copper communication cables. This testing device performs tests slower than other types of testing devices that are available for testing copper cables.

A multimeter may not be the best testing device for testing copper UTP cables. This testing device only provides limited tests on copper cables. It cannot perform all of the tests specified by TSB-67, which is the standard to testing and certifying installed UTP cabling systems. A second disadvantage of the multimeter is that this device is very time consuming to use when testing UTP cabling. The multimeter can only test a single cable conductor at a time. Testing four-pair horizontal cables would take a long time because of the large number of these cables installed in commercial buildings. Testing large pairs count backbone cables would also take a long time to test hundreds of cable pairs. This testing device would have to test each individual pair in a cable for opens or shorts with a set of test probes.

Continuity Tester

A *continuity tester* is another simple type of testing device. This device is design to perform simple continuity tests on copper twisted-pair cables. The continuity tester is a device designed specifically to test the continuity of a cable and to perform the test more quickly than using a multimeter.

A continuity tester is made up of two units: the base unit and a remote unit (see Figure 22-4). The base unit is used on one end of the link, and the remote unit is used on the other. The continuity tester performs cable tests by sending a voltage down all of the wires of a twisted-pair cable. The remote unit has an LED light for each cable pair.

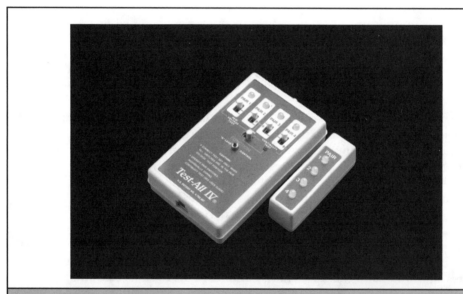

Figure 22-4.   Continuity tester

The continuity tester can indicate the following problems in a twisted-pair cable link:

▼   Opens

■   Shorts

■   Reversed pairs

▲   Poor terminations in the cable link

The continuity tester works by the base unit sending a voltage down each cable pair on the twisted-pair link. A voltage is sent over each cable pair in order for pair 1 to pair

4. If there is continuity on pair 1, the first LED on the remote unit will light up. If the cable has a problem with pair 1, the first LED on the remote unit will not light up indicating an open condition. This sequence repeated for all four pairs of the cable.

The continuity tester can be used to indicate other wiring faults by the activity of the LEDs on the base and remote units. The continuity tester indicates a poor termination on a twisted by cabling link by a dimly lit LED on the remote unit. The dimly lit LED indicates a poor wire connection somewhere in the cable link causing excessive signal loss over the cable pair. The continuity tester indicates a short condition when multiple LEDs on the remote unit light up at the same time. The continuity tester indicates a reversed pair when the base unit lights up the LED for pair 1, but the LED for another pair lights up on the remote. This indicates that two pairs are crossed somewhere in the cable link.

The ANSI/TIA/EIA-568-A and ANSI/TIA/EIA-568-B.1 cabling standards require that horizontal cabling be wired straight through from the telecommunications room to the telecommunications outlet terminated in the work area. Industry cabling standards prohibit using any adaptors or other wiring components that change the configuration of the horizontal wiring.

The advantages of a continuity tester are that they are easy to use and can perform cable tests quickly for twisted-pair cabling links. Continuity testers can provide basic cable tests quickly and easily. Using LEDs, continuity testers are able to verify continuity of installed cabling as well as identify any cabling problems such as: opens, shorts, or reversed cable pairs. Some continuity testers even have a built-in tone generator for cable identification.

The primary disadvantage of a continuity tester is that they do not provide complete testing required by TSB-67. These testers can only perform basic continuity tests. They cannot perform attenuation and NEXT test measurements over a designated frequency range. These tests are required to test and certify high performance category 5e and category 6 twisted-pair cables.

Certification Field Tester

A *certification field tester* is a more comprehensive testing and certification device (see Figure 22-5). This type of testing device can perform basic continuity testing, and it can also perform more comprehensive performance testing. A certification field tester is used to certify installed cabling links to ensure that these cabling links will support high-speed networks.

A certification field tester can perform the following tests required by TSB-67 for a category 5 twisted-pair cable links:

▼ Length

■ Wire map

■ Attenuation

▲ NEXT

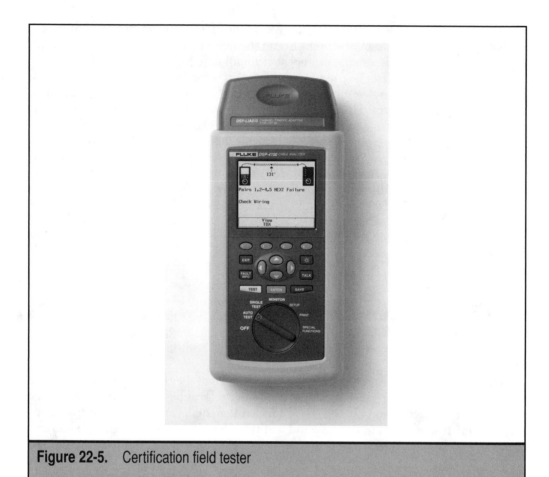

Figure 22-5. Certification field tester

A new certification field tester can perform additional cable tests required for category 5e and category 6 cabling systems. These cabling systems require that the following additional tests be used to test high performance cabling systems:

▼ Return loss

■ Equal level far end crosstalk (ELFEXT)

■ Power sum NEXT

■ Power sum ELFEXT

■ Propagation delay

▲ Delay skew

A certification field tester consists of two components: the base unit and the remote unit. The *base unit* is a device that generates high frequency signals. These signals simulate the signals generated by high-speed LAN equipment. The certification field tester will inject high frequency signals and measure how well these signals travel across the twisted-pair cabling system.

Certification field testers are many times mistakenly referred to as simply TDRs. This is because all certification field testers have TDR functionality built into them. It is the TDR functionality that enables these devices to perform many basic length and continuity tests. TDRs were originally introduced to locate cabling problems such as opens, shorts, or cable damage to telephone company twisted-pair cables or coaxial cables.

TDRs operate by transmitting an electronic pulse down the cable (see Figure 22-6). When the transmitted pulse reaches either a fault in the cable or the end of the cable, part or all of the energy from the transmitted pulse is reflected back to the TDR base unit.

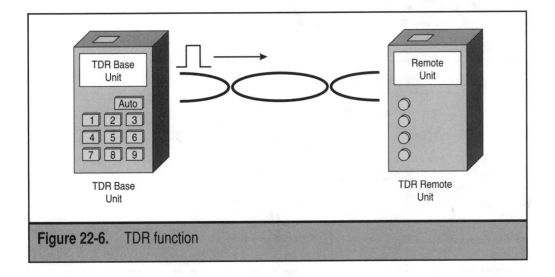

Figure 22-6. TDR function

The TDR then measures the strength of the reflected pulse and the time it took for the pulse to return. The reflected pulse enables the TDR to determine the cabling problem (open, short, and so on) and the location of the fault. If there is no fault identified, the TDR can determine the length of the cable by measuring the time it takes for the reflected pulse to return. This is the reason that a TDR is sometimes referred to as cable radar.

TDRs send out signal pulses and perform basic cable testing by interpreting the returned signal pulses. A short is identified by a TDR when the transmitted signal is returned over the same cable pair, but the signal has changed phase (see Figure 22-7). An open is identified by a TDR when the transmitted signal is returned over the same cable pair, but the signal has not changed phase (see Figure 22-8).

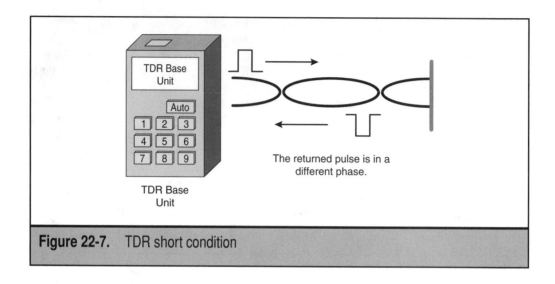

Figure 22-7. TDR short condition

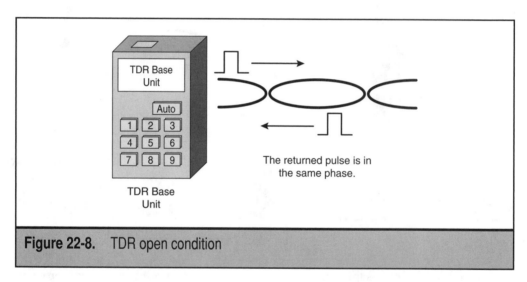

Figure 22-8. TDR open condition

Certification field testers perform more functions than a standard TDR tester. A certification field tester has the ability to inject a high frequency signal and perform an attenuation or NEXT measurements at these high signal frequencies. A TDR cannot perform these tests.

Certification field testers are the most common testing devices for certifying category 5, category 5e, and category 6 cabling systems. These testing devices are useful in the identification of improperly installed or terminated communication cables like a continuity tester (see Figure 22-9). These testing devices are capable of performing all of the

Figure 22-9.   Using a certification field tester

tests specified by TSB-67. Certification field testers are the only devices that can provide complete testing for a high performance cabling system.

FIBER OPTIC TESTING DEVICES

Optical fiber cables must be tested and certified. The testing devices used to perform optical fiber testing and certification are different than the testing devices used for copper cable. Every fiber optic testing device must be capable of generating a light pulse and measuring the light pulse at the opposite end of the optical fiber link.

Some common fiber optic testing devices include the following:

▼ Flashlight

■ Visual cable tracers and fault locators

- ■ Power meters
- ■ Fiber optic test source
- ■ Optical loss test sets
- ▲ Optical time domain reflectometers

These testing devices perform different functions and are used in different situations. Some testing devices perform basic continuity testing while others perform complete performance testing at different light wavelengths.

Flashlight

A *flashlight* is the simplest type of fiber optic testing device (see Figure 22-10). A flashlight is handy for quick identification of an individual optical fiber at a patch panel. This device is also handy for checking the continuity of an optical fiber link segment.

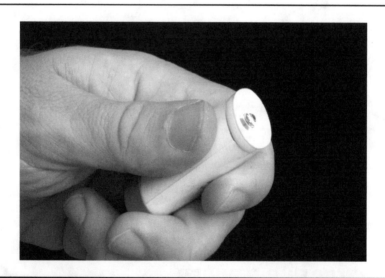

Figure 22-10.   Flashlight

A flashlight is often the first device used before conducting performance testing of an optical fiber link segment. This device can be easily used to verify that both ends of the same optical fiber are being tested. A flashlight is a device that can save time when optical fibers are either incorrectly labeled or installed in the wrong patch panel port.

The disadvantages of using a flashlight for testing optical fiber cable is the low light levels produced by these devices. Very little light actually enters the core of an optical fiber cable. As a result, the light may be difficult or impossible to see on a very long cable run.

Visual Cable Tracers and Fault Locators

Visual cable tracers and *fault locators* are simple fiber optic testing devices. These devices are used to locate unlabeled cable or to identify a fault in an installed cabling link. Visual cable tracers and fault locators can be used on optical link segments that are up to 5 km in length. Both types of fiber optic testing devices will save time locating and fixing optical fiber cabling problems.

The visual cable tracer enables an optical fiber cable to be identified and traced above a ceiling or into a fiber optic patch panel. The device performs a similar function as that performed by a tone generator and amplifier for a copper cable. These testing devices enable a single cable to be identified from a large group of cables.

The visual cable tracer produces a very bright light. The light is capable of illuminating the cable's core and cladding. In fact, the light will shine through the translucent orange or yellow cable jacket enabling the cable to be identified. These devices enable easy tracing of installed optical fiber cables and can provide quick visual identification for an unlabeled optical fiber cable.

A *fiber optic fault locator* is a device that permits faults to be identified in an optical fiber link. This testing device performs a function similar to a continuity tester. It enables a disconnected or broken fiber link to be identified visually. The fault locator produces a light pulse that is significantly more powerful than a flashlight. As a result, a visual cable tracer is more useful for identifying cabling problems in a long cable run.

The fiber optic fault locator produces a light signal in a wavelength that can be seen by the human eye. This permits cabling faults and incorrect patch panel port connections to be visually identified. This enables cabling problems to be fixed quickly saving time and money. The fiber optic signals used in LANs and other types of communication equipment are transmitted in wavelengths that are invisible to the human eye.

Fiber Optic Power Meters

Fiber optic power meters are the primary testing devices for measuring losses in optical fiber cabling links (see Figure 22-11). These devices measure the average optical power that exits an optical fiber cable. Power meters measure the optical loss or attenuation to transmitted light signals in optical fiber link segments.

Most fiber optic power meters are hand held devices that can measure both 850 and 1,300 nm light signals. These are the wavelengths of optical fiber signals used in multimode optical fiber cabling systems. Power meters are the most common testing device to certify optical fiber cables for building or campus environments.

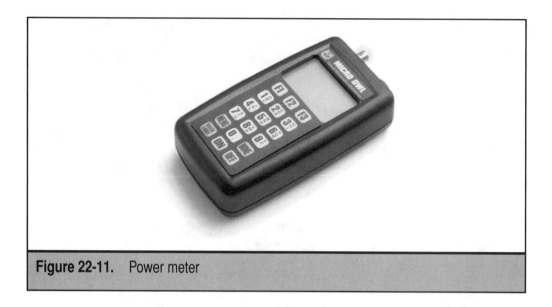

Figure 22-11. Power meter

Power meters used for testing singlemode optical fiber cable can measure both 1,310 and 1,550 nm light signals. These power meters are used with laser light sources. Singlemode power meters are most commonly used for testing outside plant cables.

Fiber Optic Test Sources

Fiber optic test sources are used with fiber optic power meters. A stable light source must be present in order to make power meter measurements. The *fiber optic test source* is the device that generates a stable light signal. The power meter will be used to measure the light loss through the fiber link segment being tested (see Figure 22-12).

A fiber optic test source must be chosen for compatibility with the type of optical fiber cable being tested and the wavelength desired for performing the test. LEDs are the light sources that are typically used for testing multimode optical fiber cable. These light sources operate at 850 and 1,300 nm. Lasers are the light sources that are used for testing singlemode optical fiber cable. These light sources operate at 1,310 and 1,550 nm.

Optical Loss Test Sets

The *optical loss test set* is the name given to the power meter and fiber optic test source together (see Figure 22-13). Optical loss test sets typically include all necessary optical jumper cables, connectors, and couplers to perform optical attenuation losses on an installed optical link segment.

Optical loss test sets are typically sold to test either multimode optical fiber or singlemode optical fiber cable. The optical loss test sets for multimode optical fiber cable will include a LED light source that will generate light signals at 850 and 1,300 nm. The opti-

Figure 22-12.   Fiber light source

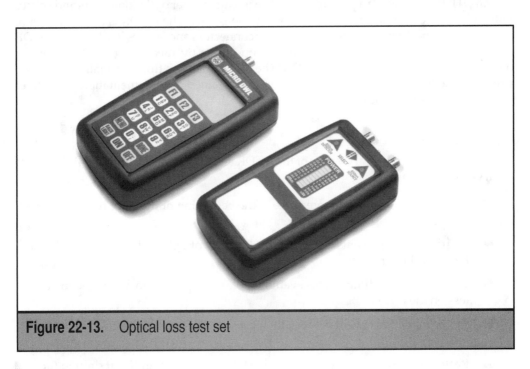

Figure 22-13.   Optical loss test set

cal loss test sets for singlemode optical fiber cable will include a laser light source that will generate light signals at 1,310 or 1,550 nm.

Optical Time Domain Reflectometers (OTDRs)

Optical time domain reflectometers (OTDRs) are the most sophisticated types of fiber optic testing devices. OTDRs are fiber testing devices that can perform optical loss measurements. These devices can also perform length measurements. Finally, OTDRs can also identify the exact location and the probable cause of a fault in an optical fiber cable link.

There are two versions of OTDRs available today:

▼   **Full size OTDRs**   These devices are the highest price but offer the best performance and the most features.

▲   **Mini OTDRs**   These devices are lower in price but have reduced features compared to full size OTDRs.

OTDRs use a laser light source instead of a LED like power meters. These devices inject the light signals and measure the time it takes for the light pulse to reflect back to the testing unit. This time measurement is used to calculate distance measurements in optical fiber links.

An OTDR works using a principle called backscatter. Fiber optic connectors and splices will always reflect some light at these connection points. The OTDR is able to measure that amount of backscatter to detect fiber optic connectors and splices in a link. The OTDR can also determine the distance of these connections by measuring the time for the backscatter signals to return to the OTDR. The OTDR displays this information on a trace printout. The trace printout can be analyzed and retained as documentation of the fiber optic link segment characteristics.

OTDR Trace

An *OTDR trace* is a graphical display of the OTDR test results (see Figure 22-14). The parts of an OTDR trace are

▼   **Initial pulse**   This is a large spike at the beginning of the trace representing the light entering the optical fiber.

■   **Slope**   This represents the optical attenuation of light pulses traveling down the optical fiber.

■   **Connector reflections**   This event is typically represented as a reflection and loss on the trace.

■   **Splice loss**   This event is typically represented as a nonreflective loss on the trace.

▲   **Reflective pulse**   This is a large spike followed by a significant drop in the slope followed by noise. This represents light hitting the end of the optical fiber cable.

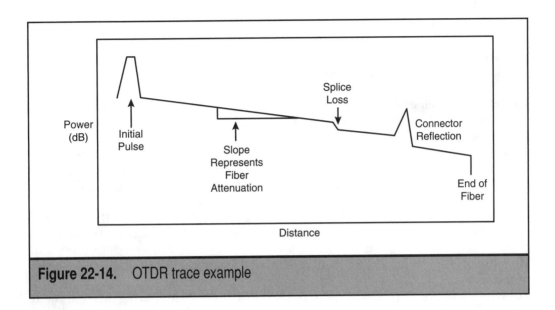

Figure 22-14.   OTDR trace example

CHAPTER SUMMARY

All communication cables must be properly tested and certified to verify that the cable installation was performed correctly. Testing communication cables will characterize the cables. This process will simulate transmitting communication signals over the installed cables. Measuring the transmitted signals will verify the transmission performance of the installed cables.

Testing communications cables is a very important step in the entire cable installation project. The process of testing communications cables is to verify that the cables are terminated correctly. Testing is also required to certify the installed cable's performance. This will guarantee that the installed cables will meet or exceed industry performance specifications.

High performance category 5e UTP cables, category 6 UTP cables, and optical fiber cables require extensive testing. Testing is required to verify that the cables have been installed correctly and to certify that the cable's performance meets industry performance specifications. The performance testing is required to confirm that the installed cabling will support high-speed network applications over industry supported distances.

Cable testing devices are commonly called field testers. These devices are used in the field to test installed communication cabling systems. Field cable testers will indicate if the cable passes the certification test once a series of tests are completed. The cable field tester stores the test results and allows them to either be printed or downloaded to a floppy disk.

There are many different types of cable field testers to certify communication cables. Some common copper testing devices include: lineman's test set, toner generator and amplifier unit, multimeter, continuity tester, and certification field tester. Some common optical fiber testing devices include: flashlight, visual cable tracers and fault locators, optical power meter, optical light source, optical loss test sets, and OTDR testers.

A lineman's test set, sometimes called a butt set, is a simple cable field testing device used to test voice circuits. This testing device enables a voice installation technician to connect to an analog voice circuit. The lineman's test set enables the voice technician to test different parts of the voice communication cable system for dial tone.

A tone generator and amplifier are common testing devices used by voice and cabling technicians. These devices are simple testing devices used to either identify or locate communication cables. The tone generator connects to a cable pair and places a low level and distinctive tone on a cable pair. The amplifier is used to amplify the signal and identify the exact cable pair where the tone generator is connected.

The most common piece of equipment used for cable testing is the volt-ohm-milliampere meter. This device is typically called a multimeter. A multimeter is a multi-purpose device that can perform multiple test functions. The voltmeter enables this testing device to measure voltage of a circuit. The ohmmeter enables this testing device to measure resistance on a circuit. The milliampere meter enables this testing device to measure current on a circuit. An ohmmeter can be used to identify the following problem conditions in a communication cable: shorts, opens, and length of the cable.

A continuity tester is a device that is designed to perform simple continuity tests on copper twisted-pair cables. A continuity tester is made up of two units: the base unit and a remote unit. The base unit is used on one end of the link, and the remote unit is used on the other. The continuity tester can indicate the following problems in a twisted-pair cable link: opens, shorts, reversed pairs, and poor terminations in the cable link.

A certification field tester is a more comprehensive testing and certification device. Certification field tester is used to certify installed cabling links to ensure that these cabling links will support high-speed networks. A certification field tester can perform the following tests required by TSB-67 for a category 5 twisted-pair cable link: length, wire map, attenuation, and NEXT. New certification field testers can perform additional cable tests required by category 5e and category 6 cabling systems. These cabling systems require that the following additional tests be used for testing high performance cabling systems: return loss, equal level far end crosstalk (ELFEXT), power sum NEXT, power sum ELFEXT, propagation delay, and delay skew.

A certification field tester consists of two components: the base unit and the remote unit. The base unit is a device that generates high frequency signals. These signals simulate the signals generated by high-speed LAN equipment. The certification field tester will inject high frequency signals and measure how well these signals travel across the twisted-pair cabling system.

The testing devices used to perform optical fiber testing and certification are different than the testing devices used for copper cable. Every fiber optic testing device must be capable of generating a light pulse and measuring the light pulse at the opposite end of the optical fiber link. Some common fiber optic testing devices include the following: flashlights, visual cable tracers and fault locators, power meters, fiber optic test sources, optical loss test sets, and optical time domain reflectometers (OTDRs).

A flashlight is the simplest type of fiber optic testing device. A flashlight is handy for quick identification of an individual optical fiber at a patch panel. This device is also handy for checking the continuity of an optical fiber link segment.

Visual cable tracers and fault locators are simple fiber optic testing devices. These devices are used to locate unlabeled cable or to identify a fault in an installed cabling link. Visual cable tracers and fault locators can be used on optical link segments that are up to 5 km in length.

The visual cable tracer enables an optical fiber cable to be identified and traced above a ceiling or into a fiber optic patch panel. The visual cable tracer produces a very bright light. The light is capable of illuminating the cable's core and cladding. A fiber optic fault locator is a device that permits faults to be identified in an optical fiber link. It enables a disconnected or broken fiber link to be identified visually. The fault locator produces a light pulse that is significantly more powerful than a flashlight.

Fiber optic power meters are the primary testing devices for measuring losses in optical fiber cabling links. Power meters measure the optical loss or attenuation to transmitted light signals in optical fiber link segments. Most fiber optic power meters are hand held devices that can measure both 850 and 1,300 nm light signals. Power meters used for testing singlemode optical fiber cable can measure both 1,310 and 1,550 nm light signals. Singlemode power meters are most commonly used for testing outside plant cables.

Fiber optic test sources are used with fiber optic power meters. A stable light source must be present in order to make power meter measurements. The fiber optic test source is the device that generates a stable light signal. The power meter will be used to measure the light loss through the fiber link segment being tested.

The optical loss test set is the name given to the power meter and fiber optic test source together. Optical loss test sets typically include all necessary optical jumper cables, connectors, and couplers to perform optical attenuation losses on an installed optical link segment.

OTDRs are the most sophisticated types of fiber optic testing devices. OTDRs are fiber testing devices that can perform optical loss measurements. These devices can also perform length measurements. Finally, OTDRs can also identify the exact location and the probable cause of a fault in an optical fiber cable link.

An OTDR trace is a graphical display of the OTDR test results. The parts of an OTDR trace are: initial pulse, slope, connector reflections, splice loss, and reflective pulse.

CHAPTER 23

Testing and Troubleshooting Copper Cables

The last step in the installation process is the testing and certification of the newly installed cabling system. Every cabling system installation will have some problems. It has been my experience that the best cable installation contractors will experience a 5-percent failure rate on newly installed communication cables. Less experienced contractors and other individuals can experience failure rates of 50 to 90 percent for newly installed cables.

The job of installing communication cabling requires organization and concentration. A 90-percent failure rate on newly installed cables seems high until the entire scope of an average installation project is considered. Most installation teams are made up of many different individuals working on a project. Each new cable installed has multiple cable pairs and must be terminated on both ends. One hundred new four-pair horizontal cables require 800 terminations. The testing will verify that the cables were terminated correctly and that the cables meet minimum industry performance specifications.

Testing is the process of verifying that the cables are installed and terminated correctly. This step checks each cable to confirm that it was terminated correctly. Each wire from each cable pair must be tested to verify that it was terminated in the correct position on each cable termination component.

Testing communication cables will verify the cable's performance specifications. This is called cable certification. Performance testing is required to certify the installed cable's performance through a range of frequencies that different communication systems will use to transmit signals. This will guarantee that the installed cables will meet or exceed industry performance specifications.

Testing communication cables also serves an important role in documenting the cabling system. The test results provide a baseline for the performance of each cable when it was installed. This information can be referenced when a cable experiences problems at a later date. The new test results can be compared to the old test results to identify what has changed that can be causing the problem. This chapter will describe the steps required to test and certify copper communication cables.

CABLE TESTING

Cable testing is an organized and systematic process of verifying that communication cables are installed and terminated correctly. Cable testing is performed with cable testing devices to confirm that the installation complies with the project requirements and industry cabling standards.

Cable testing is required to confirm that the installation was performed correctly and that the installed cables will provide reliable operation. Cable testing confirms that current applications will successfully work over the new cable system. It also provides performance specifications that will verify that the cables will support future applications as well.

The process of testing communication cables includes

▼ Visual inspection of the cables and the cable terminations

■ Continuity testing

▲ Performance testing

VISUAL INSPECTION

Visual inspection is the first step in the testing of the newly installed cabling system. The cabling system must be visually inspected after the installation is completed. The project manager must visually inspect all of the installed communication cables, the cable pathways, and the cable terminations.

The cable runs must be inspected to verify that the communication cables are installed in the cable pathways correctly. The cables must be supported properly in the cable pathways. The cables must also be supported at the correct intervals so the cables do not sag. The cable pathways must be inspected to verify that the communication cables are not pinched or incorrectly installed in these supporting structures. The visual inspection must also confirm that the cable pathways are not overfilled.

The cable terminations must be visually inspected. The visual inspection must confirm that the cables are terminated in the correct location. It must also confirm that the correct color code was followed and the correct termination technique was used for the installation. The termination for all twisted-pair terminations must have no more than 13 mm ($1/2$ in.) of untwisted cable at any termination point in the cabling system.

The visual inspection should include all portions of the cabling system including the following elements:

▼ Cable support structures

■ Cable pathways

■ Grounding and bonding system

■ Placement of cables in conduits, cable trays, and other cable pathways

■ Termination of all cable pairs

■ Connection of work area and equipment patch cords

▲ Labeling of all cabling system elements

CONTINUITY TESTING

The second phase of testing the cabling system is performing complete continuity testing (see Figure 23-1). Communication cables must have continuity to complete an electrical path for communication signals to flow between communication system devices.

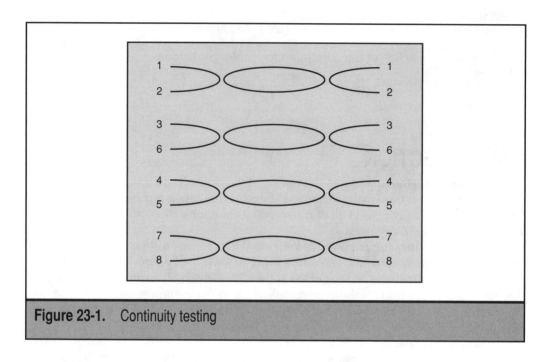

Figure 23-1. Continuity testing

Communication cables are usually multipair cables. Each cable pair is terminated to different pins of a connecting hardware component to conform to a specific modular outlet configuration.

Continuity testing will check the electrical path from one end of the cable to the other. The cable must be capable of enabling electrons or other types of signals to flow across the entire cable. A continuity test will also check to verify that the wires are terminated in the correct position and in the correct order on the connecting hardware components used to terminate the communication cable. Finally, the continuity test will confirm that the required modular outlet configuration is used for all communication cables.

PERFORMANCE TESTING

The last phase of testing the newly installed cabling system is to conduct performance testing on all of the communication cables (see Figure 23-2). Performance testing will determine if the installed communication cables will exhibit low attenuation and crosstalk (NEXT and ELFEXT) resistance.

1	Wire Map	Passed
2	Length	Passed
3	Attenuation	Passed
4	NEXT	**Failed**
5	ACR	Passed

Figure 23-2.   Performance testing

The performance of a new cable installation is determined by the following factors:

▼ **The quality of the connecting hardware components used to terminate the communication cables**   This would include the punch down blocks, patch panels, modular outlets/connectors, and the patch cords used throughout the cable installation.

▲ **The workmanship used to install and terminate the communication cables during the installation**   This would include not exceeding maximum pulling force and minimum bend radii of the cables during the pulling phase of the project. It also includes using the correct termination techniques to terminate the cable pairs at each connecting hardware component.

Performance testing will confirm that the correct components and the proper installation techniques were used during the installation. Performance tests characterize the installed cable. They provide an indication of whether the installed communication cable provides a reliable transmission path for communication signals.

Performance testing must be conducted to conform to the specifications established by the Telecommunications Industries Association (TIA) in the United States and the International Electrotechnical Commission (IEC) internationally. These organizations have developed performance testing standards for structured cabling systems that support many different network applications and vendor equipment. These standards define the electrical performance specifications for a communications cabling link in areas of attenuation, crosstalk, and signal-to-noise ratio. They also provide the measurement specifications and the pass/fail criteria for each cable performance test.

HISTORY OF UTP CABLE TESTING

Communication cables used for voice or low speed data applications historically required little or no testing. Voice applications just need continuity between the phone and the PBX. Low-speed data applications also require basic continuity between a terminal and a mainframe computer. As a result, either visual inspection or a simple continuity test was sufficient to test these cables.

Voice applications and low-speed data applications only required simple continuity testing. These applications operate at very low frequencies and do not require elaborate performance testing to confirm that they will work correctly.

TESTING UTP CABLE

New high-speed networks require that communication cables be thoroughly performance tested. Category 5e and category 6 UTP cables require more comprehensive and stringent testing requirements. Standards and specifications had to be created to define performance testing parameters and methodologies.

The TIA commissioned a task group to develop a comprehensive testing standard for UTP cable systems. The task group created a telecommunications system bulletin to compliment the ANSI/TIA/EIA-568-A standard entitled "Transmission Performance Specifications for Field Testing of Unshielded Twisted Pair Cabling Systems," and referenced the new specification as TIA/EIA TSB-67.

TIA/EIA TSB-67 was published to address field testing specifications for both UTP and ScTP cabling systems. This document was created to address field test specifications for post installation performance measurements of UTP or ScTP cabling installations, designed in accordance with the ANSI/TIA/EIA-568-A standard.

NOTE: The specifications defined in TSB-67 are for 100-ohm cables. ScTP cables are classified as 100-ohm cables. The field testing specifications can therefore be used to test and certify ScTP cabling systems. However, TSB-67 does not address testing shield integrity for ScTP cabling systems.

TSB-67 defines the field test specifications for category 3, category 4, category 5, and category 5e installations. This document relates to the worst case link model described in Annex E of the ANSI/TIA/EIA-568-A standard. It also provides additional information for testing devices, test methods, and interpretation of test results.

NOTE: TSB-67 will define the field test specifications for category 6 installations once they are finalized by the TIA.

TSB-67 STANDARD

The *TIA/EIA TSB-67 standard* is a comprehensive standard that addresses the performance testing of communication cables, the pass/fail performance specifications for each cable test and the requirements for field testing devices.

TSB-67 specifically addresses the following areas for testing and certifying communication cables:

▼ Definition of two testing models: channel and basic link

■ Performance transmission parameters that must be measured for each cabling link

■ Pass/fail performance test limits for each category of cable supported for both the channel and basic link

■ Minimum reporting requirements for field testers

■ Performance requirements of field testers and define how these performance requirements were to be measured

▲ Methods to compare the results of field testers, and it also defines the laboratory setups to perform field tester measurements

Performance Levels

TSB-67 defines four different performance levels for 100-ohm twisted-pair cabling:

▼ Category 3

■ Category 4

■ Category 5

▲ Category 5e

The performance specifications are shown in Table 23-1.

TSB-67 LINK CONFIGURATIONS

TSB-67 defines two horizontal link models. The horizontal cabling link models or configurations are called

▼ Horizontal cabling link

▲ Horizontal cabling channel

Category Rating	Frequency Range	Application Examples
Category 3	1 to 16 MHz	10Base-T Ethernet
Category 4	1 to 20 MHz	16 Mb/s token ring
Category 5	1 to 100 MHz	100Base-TX Ethernet ANSI X3T9 TP-PMD (CDDI) ATM 155
Category 5e	1 to 100 MHz	100Base-TX Ethernet ANSI X3T9 TP-PMD (CDDI) ATM 155

Table 23-1. TSB-67 Performance Levels

Horizontal Cabling Link

The *horizontal cabling link* is the permanently installed horizontal cable from the telecommunications closet to the outlet/connector used to terminate the cable in the work area (see Figure 23-3). A horizontal cabling link is also called the permanent link and the basic link. The horizontal cabling link includes the following components:

▼ Cable between the horizontal cross-connect in the closet

■ Connecting hardware to terminate the horizontal cable in the telecommunications closet

■ An optional TP or consolidation point connector

▲ An outlet/connector to terminate the cable in the work area

The horizontal cabling link does not include the patch cords in the telecommunications room or in the work area. The cabling link starts at the termination in the telecommunications room and ends at the termination at the outlet/connector in the work area.

The testing for the permanent link is slightly different than the basic link (see Figure 23-4). The permanent link defines the cable permanently installed from the termination in the telecommunications room to the termination in the work area. Any tester to test the permanent link must take performance measurements starting at the cable terminations and not including the test patch cords connecting the tester to the permanent link.

The basic link test includes two, 2 m patch cords that are only used for testing the permanent link (see Figure 23-5). The tester typically performs the cable test and includes the losses of the two, 2 m patch cords on both ends of the basic link.

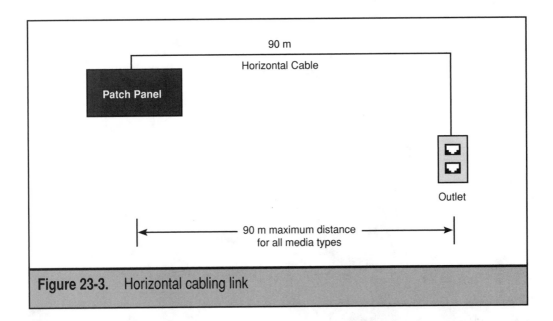

Figure 23-3.   Horizontal cabling link

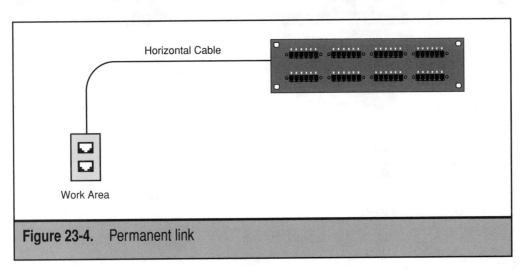

Figure 23-4.   Permanent link

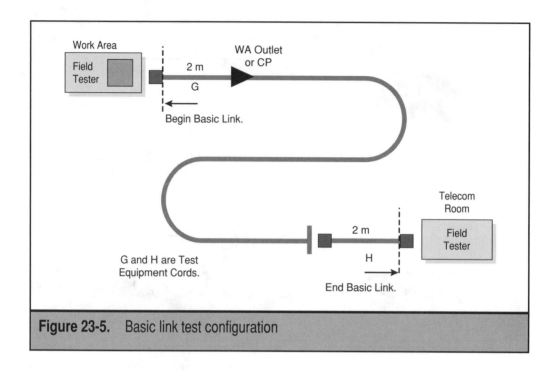

Figure 23-5. Basic link test configuration

Horizontal Cabling Channel

The horizontal cabling channel includes all of the cabling components in the horizontal cabling subsystem (see Figure 23-6). The cabling channel includes the following components:

▼ Cable between the horizontal cross-connect in the closet

■ Connecting hardware to terminate the horizontal cable in the telecommunications closet

■ An optional TP or consolidation point connector

■ A outlet/connector to terminate the cable in the work area

■ Work area patch cords to connect user equipment to the horizontal cable

▲ Equipment patch cords to connect equipment in the telecommunications closet to the horizontal cable or jumper wires to connect the horizontal cable to the backbone cable

The horizontal cabling channel contains the cabling link and also includes the equipment patch cords or jumper wires in the telecommunications closet and the work area

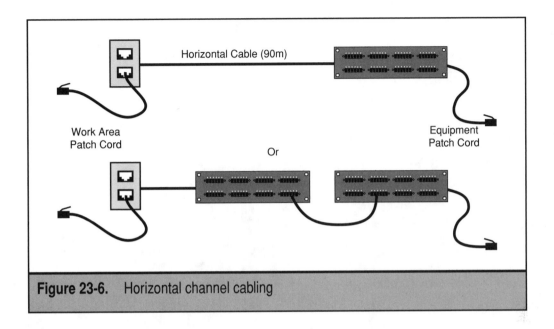

Figure 23-6.   Horizontal channel cabling

patch cords. The channel is the most important of the two horizontal cabling links. Because the horizontal cabling channel included the patch cords on both ends, it will determine if the horizontal cable will support a given application.

Testing the horizontal channel would include testing all of the components in the entire channel including the work area and equipment patch cords. The tester must take cable test measurements starting at the modular plugs of the work area and equipment patch cords (see Figure 23-7).

The reason that TSB-67 defines two different models is to define exactly what components must be included in each type of test. The channel model defines two transitions or connections at each end of the link. It also makes an allowance for stranded patch and equipment cords to be used. The basic link only defines one transition at each end of the link. This link is connected by one, uninterrupted length of solid conductor cable between the two termination points.

The basic link is a subset of the horizontal channel. The test limits for the basic link and the channel are different because of the number of transitions allowed in each configuration. In addition, a special allowance is made in the channel for the attenuation contributed by the work area and equipment patch cords. All individuals performing cable tests must understand the differences between the channel and basic or permanent link because there are significant differences regarding how these links are tested.

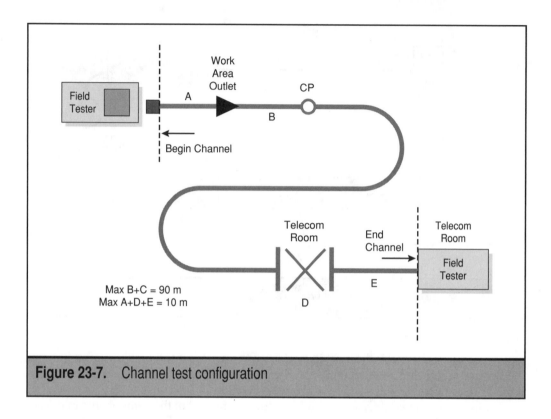

Figure 23-7.   Channel test configuration

TSB-67 FIELD TESTS

The original version of the TSB-67 specification was released in 1997. The original standard specified the following tests must be performed for installed cables:

▼   Wire map test

■   Length test

■   Attenuation test

▲   Near end crosstalk (NEXT) test

The TIA is constantly approving higher qualities of UTP cables. The TIA is also requiring that new, higher performance cables have more extensive performance tests performed to certify the installed cables. As a result, the testing requirements for TSB-67 have been increased to include the following tests for category 5e and higher twisted-pair cables:

▼   Wire map

■   Characteristic impedance

- Length

- Attenuation

- NEXT

- PS NEXT

- Return Loss

- ELFEXT

- PS ELFEXT

- Propagation delay

▲ Delay skew

WIRE MAP TEST

The first requirement for the successful transmission of communication signals over communication cables is end to end continuity of the cable pairs. Correct continuity of the communication cable pairs requires that the pairs are strictly connected across the cable link. This means that the wire connected to pin 1 in the work area should be connected to pin 1 on a patch panel port in the telecommunications room (see Figure 23-8).

The wire map test is intended to verify the end to end electrical continuity for all of the cabling pairs. It is also used to identify installation wiring errors. The wire map test indicates opens, shorts, crossed pairs, and miswires. The horizontal wiring, defined by the ANSI/TIA/EIA-568-A and ANSI/TIA/EIA-568-B.1 standards, is specified as being straight through from the telecommunications room to the work area outlet.

Wire Map—Open

An *open* is a condition where a single wire or multiple wires do not provide continuity from one end of a link to the other (see Figure 23-9). This condition is normally signified by an O next to a pin on a wire map graphic.

Twisted-pair cables should have complete continuity for all eight conductors (four pairs) across the cable link. If an open condition is identified for one wire of a twisted-pair cable, check all of the connection points for the wire showing the open. If all wires of the cable are showing an open condition, verify that the correct cable is being tested. A tone generator and amplifier unit can be used to identify cables that are not labeled. Lastly, confirm that the remote loop back unit is connected to the opposite end of the same cable as the base unit.

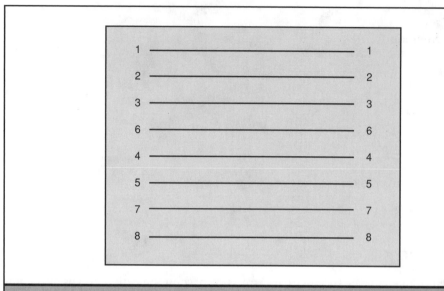

Figure 23-8. Wire map

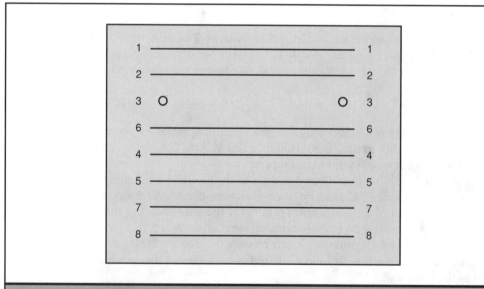

Figure 23-9. Wire map open condition

Wire Map—Short

A *short* is a condition where two or more wires from a cable are connected ahead of where they should normally be connected in the circuit (see Figure 23-10). This condition is normally signified by a line showing more than one pin of the outlet being electrically connected together.

Twisted-pair horizontal cables should not have any shorts in the cable link. If a short condition is identified by your cable testing device, check the terminations at the punch block or patch panel and work area outlets. Two wires may be terminated in the same wire termination slot.

If the problem cannot be identified in the terminations, visually inspect the horizontal cable and all the patch cables in the link. Your visual inspection may identify that a horizontal cable's jacket may be torn or the cable may be pinched. If this is the case, the damaged cable should be replaced.

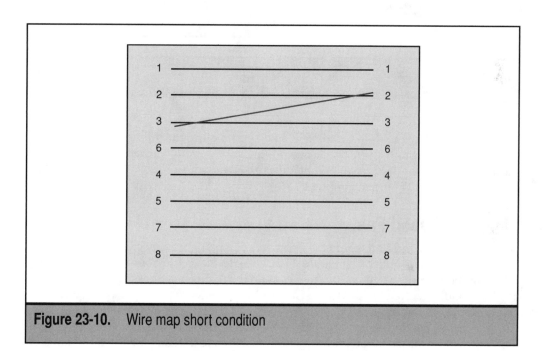

Figure 23-10.   Wire map short condition

Wire Map—Reversed Pair

A *reversed pair* is a condition where the two wires of a pair are connected at the correct location on a modular outlet, but the wires are connected to the wrong pins (see Figure 23-11). A reversed pair condition would mean that a signal transmitted on pin 1 would end up on pin 2 on the opposite end of the cable. The cable tester would show two lines crossed.

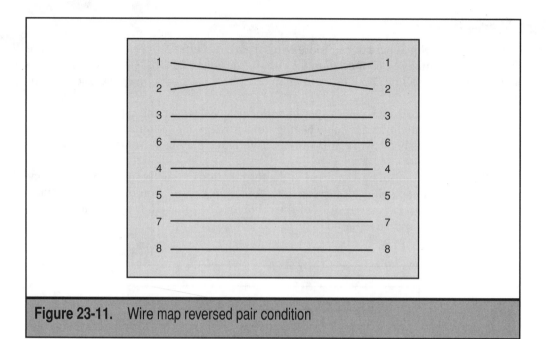

Figure 23-11.   Wire map reversed pair condition

The ANSI/TIA/EIA-568-A and 568B standards require that all horizontal cables be wired straight through from the telecommunications room to the work area outlet. Industry cabling standards require that any crossed or pair transpositions be performed in the work area with special adapters.

Wire Map—Crossed Pair

A *crossed pair* is a condition where the two wires of a pair are connected to the wrong location on a modular outlet (see Figure 23-12). The tester would show the two lines of a cable pair being terminated on different pins on the opposite end of the link.

This condition often happens when a T568A type outlet or patch panel is used on one end of a twisted-pair cable, and a T568B outlet or patch panel is used on the other end of the same cable. This situation would cause the green pair to be terminated on pins 1 and 2 of the T568A component on one end of the cable while the same pair is terminated on pins 3 and 6 of the T568B component at the opposite end of the same cable. The ANSI/TIA/EIA-568-A standard requires that all horizontal cabling be wired straight through from the telecommunications closet to the work area outlet.

Wire Map—Split Pair

A *split pair* is a condition where the wiring is straight through although the two wires that make up a pair are terminated on incorrect pins at both ends of the twisted-pair cable (see

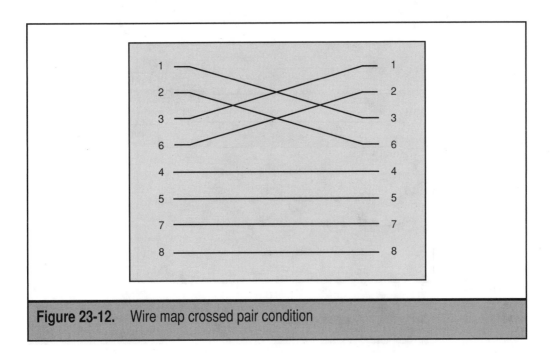

Figure 23-12. Wire map crossed pair condition

Figure 23-13). For example, the T568A modular jack configuration requires that both wires of the green pair are terminated on pins 1 and 2. A split pair condition would result when one wire of the green pair is terminated on pin 1, but the second wire of the pair is terminated on pin 3 at both ends of the cable.

A simple continuity tester cannot identify a split pair condition on a twisted-pair cable. From a continuity perspective, pin 1 is connected to pin 1, and pin 3 is connected to pin 3. This is perfect continuity from end to end of the cable.

A split pair condition is very detrimental for LAN cabling. LAN equipment use balanced signals. The communication cables supporting LAN signals must not have split pairs in order for the transmitted signals to be capable of traveling 100 m (328 ft.) at very high frequencies.

CABLE LENGTH TEST

The length test is used to provide an indication of the length of a cable run. Industry cabling standards specify that the maximum length of the permanently installed horizontal cabling is 90 m (295 ft.) from the termination in the closet to the termination in the work area (see Figure 23-14). An additional 10 m (33 ft.) is allowed for patch cords, jumpers, and equipment cords. The maximum length of the entire horizontal channel is 100 m (328 ft.).

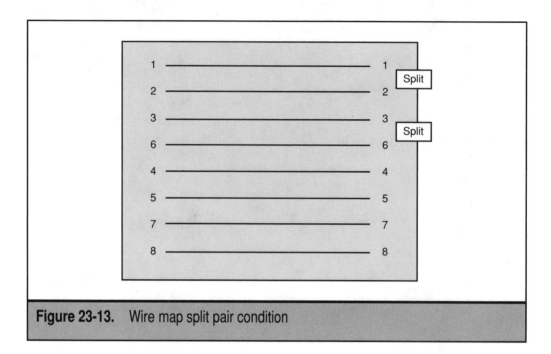

Figure 23-13. Wire map split pair condition

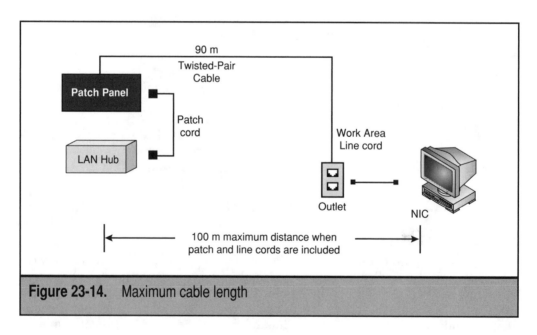

Figure 23-14. Maximum cable length

Cable field testers can measure the length of installed communication cables. Cable field testers will perform an electrical length test. This test is based on the round trip propagation delay of the link. The tester will inject a signal into the cable and measure the time it takes for the signal to return to the tester. To accurately calculate the distance of the cable, the speed of the transmitted signal traveling in the cable must be known. The speed that a signal travels in a cable is known as the Nominal Velocity of Propagation (NVP). The NVP value for the cable will enable a time interval to be calculated to a distance measurement. A transmitted signal travels approximately 8 in. per nanosecond in a category 5 cable. The total time is divided by two and then multiplied by the NVP value for the cable. A typical NVP value for a category 5 cable is 69 percent of the speed of light.

ATTENUATION TEST

Attenuation is defined as the reduction of a transmitted signal due to resistance encountered by the signal as it is traveling down a cable (see Figure 23-15). Attenuation causes signals to shrink as they travel along a cable. In all communication systems (voice system, low-speed data system, or LAN), there needs to be enough of the original signal remaining at the opposite end of the cable so the receiver can determine what the signal was when it was originally sent by the transmitter.

Attenuation is measured in deciBels (dBs). The dB rating is specified per unit length of cable (usually 100 m). Measurements are taken at specified swept/stepped frequency

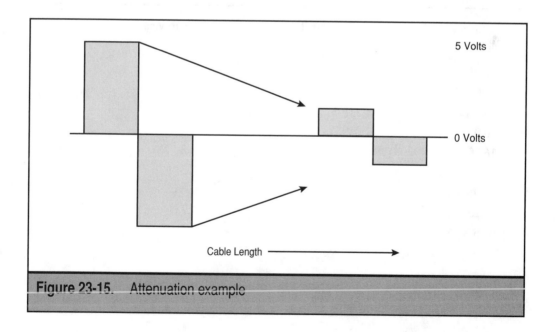

Figure 23-15. Attenuation example

levels. The higher the attenuation dB value, the greater the attenuation (signal loss) and the weaker the received signal.

An attenuation test is a measure of the amount of signal loss in the cable and connecting hardware of a cable link. When measuring for attenuation, the lower the dB values the better.

The two primary causes of attenuation on a twisted-pair cable are the

▼   Length of the cable

▲   Frequency of the transmitted signal over the cable

Cable Length

Simply sending a signal down a cable will cause it to attenuate (shrink). In fact, the cable is the greatest cause of attenuation of a LAN signal. The amount of attenuation that a cable exhibits increases as the length of the cable increases.

Signal Frequency

The amount of attenuation that a cable exhibits is also dependent on the frequency of the signals that are sent over the cable. The higher the signal frequency, the more attenuation a copper cable will exhibit. This is shown in Table 23-2.

Frequency (MHz)	Category 3 (dB)	Category 5e (dB)
1.0	2.6	2.0
4.0	5.6	4.1
8.0	8.5	5.8
10.0	9.7	6.5
16.0	13.1	8.2
20.0	——	9.3
25.0	——	10.4
31.25	——	11.7
62.5	——	17.0
100.0	——	22.0

Table 23-2.   Frequency Attenuation Table

Causes of Attenuation

All cable components, such as modular connectors, modular jacks, patch panels, and punch down blocks, all cause a transmitted signal to attenuate (see Figure 23-16). The attenuation is caused by a transmitted signal traveling over the physical contact points of a cable link. The amount of attenuation at each contact point is small. If there are enough contact points in a cable run, the attenuation can add up to a large amount of signal loss.

Each cabling component will add a small amount of loss in the cabling link. A category 3 component adds more loss into the cabling link than a category 5e component. The cabling components as similar to communication cables. They induce small losses at a lower frequencies and greater losses at higher frequencies. These losses are exhibited in Table 23-3.

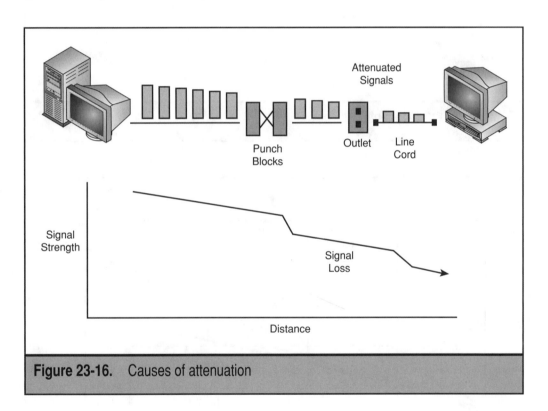

Figure 23-16.   Causes of attenuation

ATTENUATION TESTING

The attenuation test will measure the loss of signal strength from one end of the cable to the other (see Figure 23-17). The attenuation test for category 5e cabling is performed from a frequency of 1 to 100 MHz. A swept frequency measurement is taken to verify the cable's attenuation performance rating. This measurement starts at a low signal frequency and incrementally steps, making measurements at designated frequencies up to 100 MHz.

Frequency (MHz)	Category 3 (dB)	Category 5e (dB)
1.0	0.4	0.1
4.0	0.4	0.1
8.0	0.4	0.1
10.0	0.4	0.1
16.0	0.4	0.2
20.0	——	0.2
25.0	——	0.2
31.25	——	0.2
62.5	——	0.3
100.0	——	0.4

Table 23-3. Component Loss Table

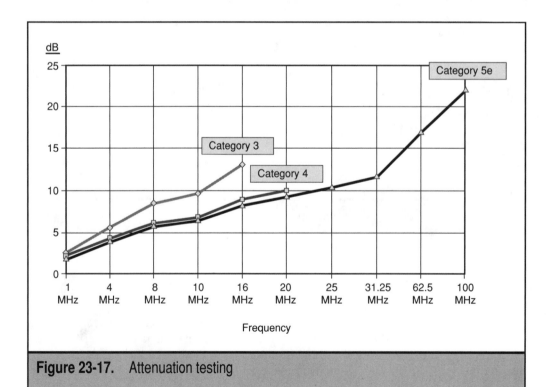

Figure 23-17. Attenuation testing

The attenuation test is a one way test. This means that the test only needs to be performed from one end of the cable. Therefore, this test can be performed from either the work area or the telecommunications room end of a category 5e cable.

The attenuation test is performed on each pair of a category 5e cable. The attenuation of a cable is the highest attenuation rating of the four measured pairs. The attenuation measurements of each pair are reported in dB. The lower the dB rating the better. Once the dB rating starts to increase, more of the transmitted signal is being lost as it is traveling down the cable. TSB-67 defines the maximum allowed attenuation for category 5e cabling at specified frequencies for both the basic link and channel.

The attenuation performance specifications for category 5e are defined for both the basic link and channel. The category 5e attenuation specifications for the basic link and channel are shown in Table 23-4.

Horizontal Link	Maximum Attenuation
Basic Link	21.6 dB @ 100 MHz
Channel	24.0 dB @ 100 MHz

Table 23-4.   Maximum Attenuation for the Basic Link and Channel

NEXT TESTING

NEXT is a measure of the amount of energy that will pass to other pairs within the same cable when a signal is transmitted over a single pair from the same end of the cable. NEXT is also called pair-to-pair NEXT because all pair combinations are measured. The term near end means that the measurement is being taken from the same end of the cable as the transmitted signal. The energy that leaks out from the transmitting cable pair is considered to be noise within that cable because it will interfere with other signals being received over any nontransmitting cable pair (see Figure 23-18).

NEXT is one of the most important parameters for a UTP cable. A UTP cable should have a high NEXT rating. This means that very little energy should be transferred to other cable pairs when a signal is transmitted over another cable pair within the same cable.

This energy that is transferred from the transmitting cable pair to other pairs in a cable is the most significant source of noise in a high-speed network. If enough energy is transferred to a cable pair that is receiving a LAN signal, the receiver may not be able to distinguish between the wanted signal being received and the unwanted energy (noise) from another cable pair.

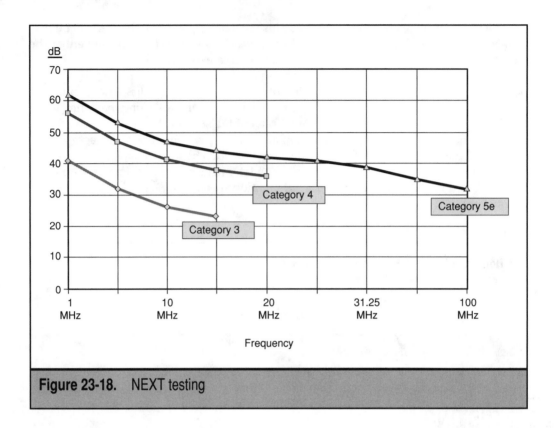

Figure 23-18.   NEXT testing

NEXT is measured in dB. The dB rating is specified for each component individually. Measurements are taken at specified swept/stepped frequency levels. The higher the NEXT dB value the better. A high NEXT dB value means that very little of the signal from the transmitting cable pair can be measured on the nontransmitting pairs of the cable. A low NEXT dB value means that more of the signal from the transmitting cable pair can be measured on the nontransmitting pairs of the cable. For copper cables, the higher the transmitted frequency, the lower NEXT dB values communication cables exhibit.

The formula for measuring NEXT for the cable is

$$\text{NEXT}\ (f) \geq \text{NEXT}\ (0.772) - 15\log\ (f/0.772)$$

The NEXT test for category 5e cabling is performed from a frequency of 1 to 100 MHz.

A swept frequency measurement is taken to verify the cable's NEXT performance rating. This measurement starts at a low signal frequency and incrementally steps, making measurements at designated frequencies up to 100 MHz.

The NEXT test is a two-way test. This means that a NEXT measurement must be performed on both ends of a category 5e cable; therefore, it is often referred to as a two-way test. TSB-67 requires that a NEXT test be performed on both ends of all category 5e cables.

TSB-67 defines the minimum NEXT for category 5e cabling for both the basic link and the channel. The category 5e NEXT specifications for the basic link and channel are shown in Table 23-5.

Horizontal Link	Minimum NEXT Specifications
Basic Link	32.0 dB @ 100 MHz
Channel	30.1 dB @ 100 MHz

Table 23-5.   Minimum NEXT for the Basic Link and Channel

ATTENUATION TO CROSSTALK RATIO (ACR) TESTING

When communication signals are transmitted over communication cable, both attenuation and crosstalk are simultaneously active. The combined effects of these two cable performance parameters is an excellent indicator of the real transmission quality of the cabling link. This combined effect is characterized as the Attenuation to Crosstalk Ratio (ACR) (see Figure 23-19).

ACR is a calculation defining the ratio of the received signal to existing system noise. ACR calculations for a category 5e cable are taken from a frequency range of 1 to 100 MHz for each pair combination. ACR results are reported in dB. The higher the dB rating the better. ACR is the true indication of the quality of the received signal.

As the name implies, the ACR measurement is made up of the components of: total attenuation and NEXT of a link. The formula for determining the ACR is

$$ACR = NEXT - Attenuation$$

A high ACR dB value indicates a strong signal with little noise interference. A high ACR value is derived by having a high NEXT rating and a low attenuation rating for a category 5e cable link.

The ACR test for category 5e cabling is performed from a frequency of 1 to 100 MHz. A swept frequency measurement is taken to verify the cables ACR performance rating. This measurement starts at a low signal frequency and incrementally steps, making measurements at designated frequencies up to 100 MHz.

The ACR test is also a two-way test. This means that the test must be performed on both ends of an installed category 5e cable. This test incorporates a NEXT measurement, and therefore, it must measure the amount of transmitted signal that is coupled into adjacent cable pairs from the transmitted end of the cable. The only way to determine this is by performing the test on both ends of the cable.

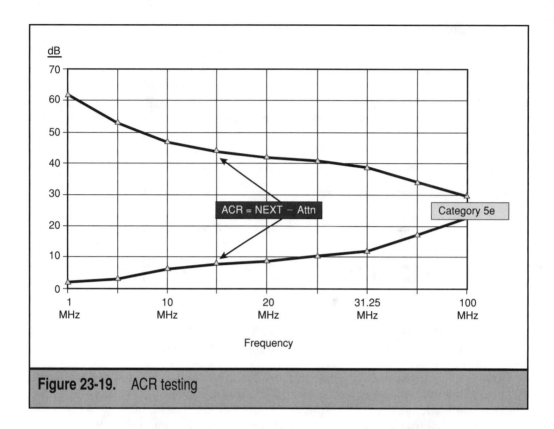

Figure 23-19. ACR testing

The ACR performance specifications for category 5e are defined for both the basic link and channel. The category 5e NEXT specifications for the basic link and channel are shown in Table 23-6.

Horizontal Link	Minimum ACR Specifications
Basic Link	10.4 dB @ 100 MHz
Channel	6.1 dB @ 100 MHz

Table 23-6. Minimum ACR for the Basic Link and Channel

RETURN LOSS

Return loss is a measure of the reflected energy caused by impedance mismatches in the cabling system. Impedance mismatches occur on a communication cable link when the termination impedance (component impedance) does not exactly match the characteristic impedance of the cable. The resulting impedance discontinuity creates a bias in the link. Electrical energy will hit the bias, and extra energy is necessary to overcome the bias in the link. This results in signal loss to the transmitted signal traveling over the bias and a small amount of energy being reflected back to the transmitter. Therefore, impedance mismatches cause both signal loss and reflected noise on the link (see Figure 23-20).

The amount of reflected energy is a direct function of the degree of impedance mismatch between the communication cable and the cable termination components in the link. Ideally, the communication cable and the cable termination components will be closely matched, and very little signal reflections will result. Even small differences between the communication cable and connecting hardware components can result in large differences.

The noise caused from impedance mismatches in the communication cabling system are a significant contributor to the overall noise in the cable link. In order to reduce return loss, cable and connecting hardware must be closely matched. The return loss requirements for a category 5e cabling system is

▼   **1 to 20 MHz**   20 dB

▲   **20 to 100 MHz** $17 - 10 \cdot \log (f / 20)$ dB

The maximum return loss for a category 5e channel tested at 100 MHz is 10 dB.

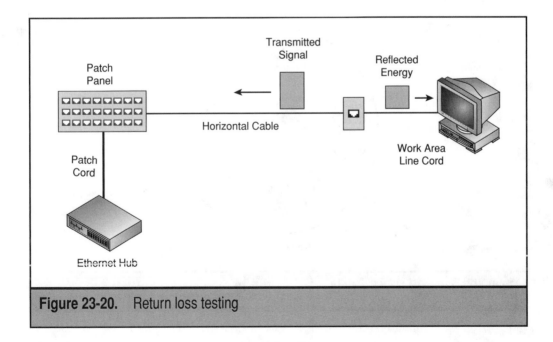

Figure 23-20.   Return loss testing

POWER SUM NEAR END CROSSTALK (PS NEXT)

Power sum near end crosstalk (PS NEXT) is a measure of the total crosstalk energy that can be measured on a nonactive cable pair when more than one pair is active or being used simultaneously. *Power sum* is a formula that totals the crosstalk energy being contributed by each active pair on a nonactive pair measured on the same end of the cable as the transmitted signals (see Figure 23-21).

PS NEXT is a new measurement for UTP cabling systems. The measurement was never specified for category 3, category 4, and category 5 cables. PS NEXT is specified for category 5e and higher UTP cables. This measurement is important for applications that use multiple pairs for sending signals. Many high-speed LAN technologies, such as 100Base-T4 and 1000Base-T, use this signaling technique.

The formula for calculating PS NEXT on a four-pair UTP cable is

$$PSNEXT = -10\log(10^{-x1/10} + 10^{-x2/10} + 10^{-x3/10}) \text{ dB}$$

where X1, X2, and X3 are the pair-to-pair crosstalk measurements in dB between a receive pair and three active transmitting pairs.

The PS NEXT measurements for a category 5e or higher cable are lower than the worst case pair to pair NEXT measurements for the same cable. This is due to multiple active pairs in the cable transferring more measurable energy into a receiving (nontransmitting) cable pair.

The minimum PS NEXT for a category 5e channel at 100 MHz is 27.1 dB.

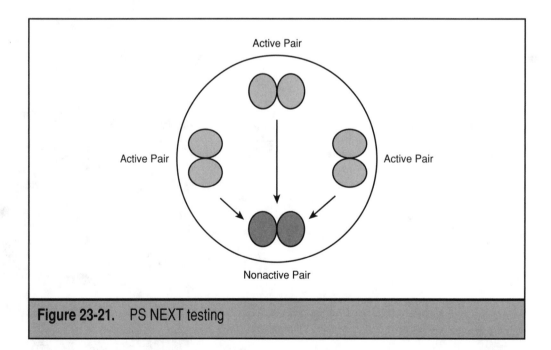

Figure 23-21. PS NEXT testing

EQUAL LEVEL FAR END CROSSTALK (ELFEXT)

FEXT is not a very useful measurement because it is length dependent. Equal level far end crosstalk (ELFEXT) is a more meaningful measurement for UTP cables. ELFEXT is a normalized signal measure. It takes out attenuation length effects from the crosstalk measurement. ELFEXT is a measure of far end crosstalk for any length UTP cable (see Figure 23-22).

ELFEXT is a new transmission parameter for UTP cable. This parameter was never measured for category 3, category 4, or category 5 cables. ELFEXT is specified for category 5e and higher UTP cables. This measurement is important for applications that use multiple pairs simultaneously for full duplex transmission. Many high-speed LAN technologies, such as 100Base-T4 and 1000Base-T, use this signaling technique.

Industry cabling standards require that ELFEXT be measured for all cable pair combinations for components and cabling. The formula for calculating ELFEXT for a four-pair UTP on the channel is

$$\text{ELFEXT pair to pair} \geq -20\log(10^{-\text{ELFEXT cable pair to pair}/20} + 4 \cdot 10^{-\text{FEXT connector pair to pair}/20}) \text{ dB}$$

The minimum ELFEXT for a category 5e channel at 100 MHz is 17.0 dB.

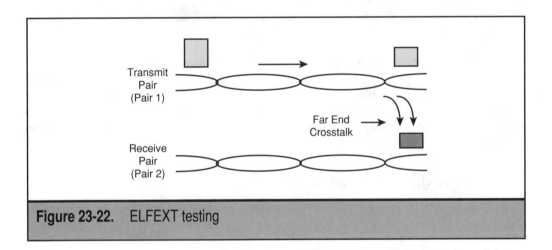

Transmit
Pair
(Pair 1)

Far End
Crosstalk

Receive
Pair
(Pair 2)

Figure 23-22.   ELFEXT testing

POWER SUM EQUAL LEVEL FAR END CROSSTALK (PS ELFEXT)

Power sum equal level far end crosstalk (PS ELFEXT) is a measure of the total crosstalk energy that can be measured on a nonactive cable pair when more than one pair is active or being used simultaneously. Power sum is a formula that totals the crosstalk energy being contributed by each active pair on a nonactive pair measured at the far end of the cable (see Figure 23-23).

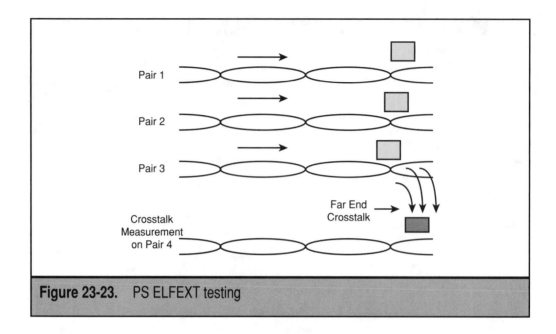

Figure 23-23. PS ELFEXT testing

ELFEXT measurements only looked at energy coupled into passive (receiving) cable pairs when a single pair was active (transmitting). This is the reason that ELFEXT is often called pair to pair ELFEXT. PS ELFEXT measures energy coupled into a single cable pair when multiple cable pairs are active just like PS NEXT. This measurement takes into account the combined crosstalk on a single receive pair from multiple far end disturbers operating at the same time.

The formula for calculating PS ELFEXT on a four pair UTP cable for the channel is

$$\text{PSNEXT}_{\text{channel}} \geq -20\log(10^{-\text{PSELFEXT cable}/20} + 4 \cdot 10^{-\text{PSFEXT connectors}/20})\ \text{dB}$$

The minimum PS ELFEXT for a category 5e channel at 100 MHz is 14.4 dB.

PROPAGATION DELAY SPECIFICATIONS

Propagation delay is defined as the amount of time needed for a transmitted signal to travel over a single pair of a communication cable. Because propagation delay measures the actual signal travel time, the propagation delay of a cable will increase as the length of the cable increases (see Figure 23-24).

The propagation delay will be slightly different for each pair of a communication cable. This is due to the fact that all four pairs have a different twist rate. This means that some cable pairs in a cable are twisted more than other pairs in the same cable. Increasing the twist rate of cable pairs reduces the NEXT within the cable but increases the length

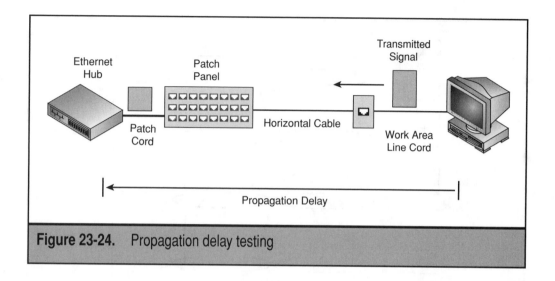

Figure 23-24.   Propagation delay testing

of the cable pairs that are tightly twisted. The cable pairs with more twists are longer, and this results in these cable pairs having a larger amount of propagation delay.

Propagation delay is typically measured in nanoseconds (ns) for 100 meters of cable. The propagation delay of a cable can also be referenced as the minimum of propagation. This is a measure of how fast a signal travels through a cable. This is normally listed as a percentage. This number represents the speed of the signal traveling over the cable pairs compared to the speed of light.

The specifications for category 5e cables require that the maximum propagation delay of a channel must not exceed 538 ns for 100 m (328 ft.) at 100 MHz.

DELAY SKEW SPECIFICATIONS

Delay skew is defined as the difference in the propagation delay between the fastest and slowest pairs of the same UTP cable (see Figure 23-25). Delay skew is becoming an important specification for UTP cable because new high-speed LAN technologies are using multiple cable pairs to transmit data signals. As a result, it is important to have the multiple data signals arrive at the opposite end of the cable at approximately the same time. This is critical for a received signal to be properly decoded. Cables that exceed the maximum delay skew parameter will result in the receiving equipment being mixed up and corrupt.

Industry standards specify that delay skew for a UTP cable not exceed 45 ns for all frequencies between 2 and 12.5 MHz for a 100 m horizontal cable run.

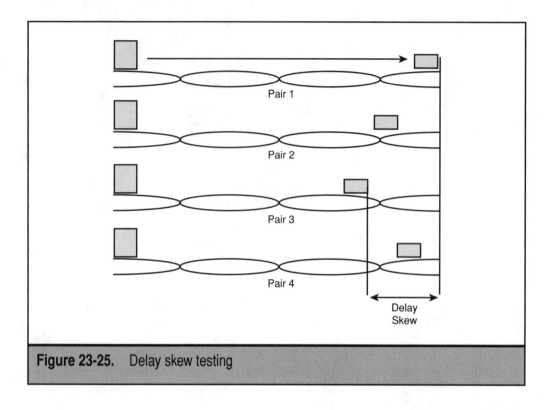

Figure 23-25.   Delay skew testing

SUMMARY OF CATEGORY 5E CHANNEL SPECIFICATIONS

The entire scope of performance specifications for a category 5e channel include the following:

▼   Maximum attenuation at 100 MHz = 24.0 dB

■   Minimum NEXT at 100 MHz = 30.1 dB

■   Minimum PS NEXT at 100 MHz = 27.1 dB

■   Minimum ACR at 100 MHz = 6.1 dB

■   Minimum PS ACR at 100 MHz = 3.1 dB

■   Minimum ELFEXT at 100 MHz = 17.0 dB

■   Minimum PS ELFEXT at 100 MHz = 14.4 dB

■   Minimum return loss at 100 MHz = 10.0 dB

■   Maximum propagation delay = 532 ns

▲   Maximum delay skew = 50 ns

CHARACTERISTIC IMPEDANCE TEST

Characteristic impedance is a test that measures the resistance that opposes the flow of current. The characteristic impedance of a communication cable is a complex property of the cable's inductive, capacitive, and resistive properties. These properties are determined by the construction of the cable. The characteristic impedance of a cable is based on the cable's physical properties including

- ▼ Conductor size
- ■ Distance between the wire of a cable pair
- ▲ Dielectric constant of the wire insulation

Proper signal transmission across a communication cable requires a constant characteristic impedance rating. The characteristic impedance of a communication cable must also remain constant through a range of frequencies. Category 5 and higher UTP cables must have a characteristic impedance of 100 ohms $+/-$ 15 percent from 1 to 100 MHz. TSB-67 does not require that characteristic impedance be checked.

PERFORMING CABLE TESTING

Communication cables can be tested with many different types of testing devices. The most common type of device to perform complete cable testing is a certification field tester. Certification field testers are the most common testing devices for certifying category 5, category 5e, and category 6 cabling systems. These testing devices are useful in the identification of improperly installed or terminated communication cables like a continuity tester. These testing devices are capable of performing all of the tests specified by TSB-67. Certification field testers are the only devices that can provide complete testing for a high performance cabling system.

CERTIFICATION FIELD TESTER

A *certification field tester* is a more comprehensive testing and certification device (see Figure 23-26). This type of testing device can perform basic continuity testing, and it can also perform more comprehensive performance testing. A certification field tester is used to certify installed cabling links to ensure that these cabling links will support high-speed networks.

A certification field tester can perform the following tests required by TSB-67 for category 5 twisted-pair cable links:

- ▼ Length
- ■ Wire map

Figure 23-26. Certification field tester

■ Attenuation

▲ NEXT

New certification field testers can perform additional cable tests required by category 5e and category 6 cabling systems. These cabling systems require that the following additional tests be used to test high performance cabling systems:

▼ Return loss

■ Equal level far end crosstalk (ELFEXT)

■ Power sum NEXT

■ Power sum ELFEXT

■ Propagation delay

▲ Delay skew

Autotest

Certification field tester can perform every required cable test using an autotest feature. The *autotest* is most frequently used for certifying communication cabling systems. The autotest function performs all of the tests necessary to certify a communication cabling system (see Figure 23-27). The autotest will perform every cable test required for a given category of cable. The autotest will provide an overall pass/fail for the cable being tested. The field tester will also provide detailed test results for each test run. Field testers can usually save approximately 500 complete cable test results in the tester memory. The autotest results can either be printed or downloaded to a floppy disk.

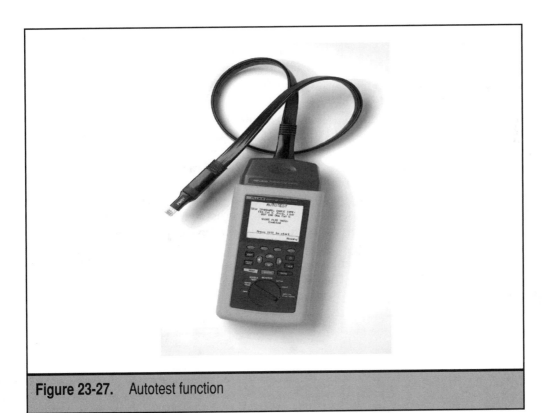

Figure 23-27.   Autotest function

Most certification field testers will perform the following tests during the autotest:

▼ Length

■ Wire map

■ Attenuation

■ NEXT

- Return loss

- Equal level far end crosstalk (ELFEXT)

- Power sum NEXT

- Power sum ELFEXT

- Propagation delay

- Delay skew

- Characteristic impedance

- Attenuation to crosstalk ratio (ACR)

▲ Power sum ACR

TESTER ACCURACY LEVELS

The TIA/EIA TSB-67 standard specifies the required accuracy levels of certification field testers. The standard requires that communication cables be tested with a high degree of accuracy to assure that the pass/fail results given by the tester are correct.

The accuracy levels are defined to identify links that are very close to the pass/fail boundary. Problems can arise if the cable tester provides inaccurate test results. Failing a good cable link requires extra time and material to replace the good cable. Passing a bad link may cause network problems at a later date. The network troubleshooting effort will result in network down time, lost productivity, and extensive troubleshooting to ultimately identify the bad cable.

TSB-67 specifies two different link models and specifies four different accuracy levels for field testing equipment. The field testers are called

▼ Level I

■ Level II

■ Level IIe

▲ Level III

Level I field testers are the least accurate. These testers should be used to test and certify category 3 and category 4 cables. Level II field testers are more accurate. These testers should be used to test and certify category 5 cables. Level IIe field testers should be used to test and certify category 5e cables. Level III field testers are the newest and most accurate testers. These testers should be used to test and certify category 6 cables. Table 23-7 defines the accuracy requirements for field testers for both the basic link and the channel.

Distance from Test Limit in dB	Level I Tester (% Incorrect)	Level II & IIe Testers (% Incorrect)	Level III Tester (% Incorrect)
1.0	30.9	15.9	2.2
2.0	15.9	2.3	0.2
3.0	6.7	0.1	0.0
4.0	2.3	0.0	0.0
5.0	0.6	0.0	0.0

Table 23-7.   Tester Accuracy Levels

Results Within the Accuracy Range

The TIA/EIA TSB-67 standard requires that an asterisk must follow a test result value when the value falls in the tester's range of accuracy (see Figure 23-28). If a pass result is marked with an asterisk, investigate different ways to increase the cable's performance. A fail test result marked with an asterisk should be considered a bad cable.

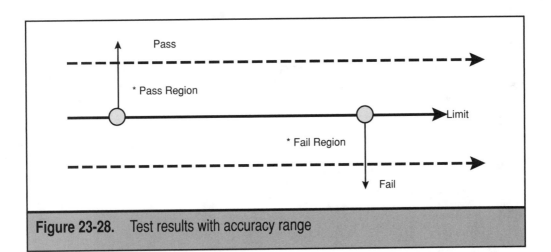

Figure 23-28.   Test results with accuracy range

TROUBLESHOOTING FAILED CABLES

When a communication cable is tested and the test result is a failure, the cause of the failure must be identified and corrected. Many times the cause of a failure for a cable performance test is the result of using an incorrect quality component. Another common cause of cable test failures is untwisting cable pairs. Exceeding 13 mm ($^1/_2$ in.) of untwisted cable at any termination point will cause increased attenuation and greater crosstalk on the link.

The following steps should be followed for troubleshooting communications cables:

1. Determine the exact nature of the cabling problem and verify that it is actually cabling related.
2. Perform a visual inspection looking for anything unusual.
3. Use your cable testing devices and perform cable tests on the cable in question.
4. Break the cable segment into small parts and test each part.
5. Verify that the correct cable and connectors were used.
6. Check for improper installation practices.
7. Replace suspect equipment and work area patch cords.
8. Look for crushed or damaged cable.
9. Look for sources of interference close to the cable.
10. Check for excessive cable distances.

Incorrect Continuity

All wire connections must be terminated correctly and in the correct position on all terminating devices in a cable link.

Wire continuity problems on a twisted-pair link are typically caused by the following conditions:

▼ Opens

■ Shorts

■ Reversed pairs

■ Crossed pairs

▲ Split pairs

Incorrect Length

Cables that are too long will cause communication signal problems. Any cable length that is too long will cause excessive signal attenuation. Devices on the opposite end of the link will not receive enough of the transmitted signal to decode it correctly.

All horizontal cable channels must be limited to a maximum of 100 m (328 ft.).

Causes of High Attenuation

Attenuation is the loss of signal strength. Attenuation occurs as a signal travels down a cable. Attenuation is measured in dB. The lower the dB rating the better.

High attenuation on a twisted-pair cable is typically caused by the following conditions:

▼ Low grade cable are used in the link. Category 3 patch cords are used in a category 5e channel.

■ Flat or untwisted cable is used in the link.

■ Untwisted cable pairs exist in the link

■ Split pairs exist in the link.

▲ Low grade components are used in the link. Category 3 components used in a category 5e channel.

Causes of Low NEXT

NEXT indicates that energy from a transmitting cable pair is interfering with energy on a receiving cable pair. NEXT is measured in dB. The higher the dB rating the better.

Low NEXT is typically caused by the following conditions:

▼ Low grade cable is used in the link. Category 3 patch cords are used in a category 5e channel.

■ Flat or untwisted cable is used in the link.

■ Untwisted cable pairs exist in the link.

■ Split pairs exist in the link.

▲ Low grade components are used in the link. Category 3 components are used in a category 5e channel.

TESTING COAXIAL CABLE

Industry cable standards do not address testing coaxial cable segments. Coaxial cables can be found in both commercial and residential buildings. Fifty-ohm coaxial cable was used extensively for 10Base-2 Ethernet LANs and can still be found in many commercial buildings today.

Many cable testers can perform tests for thin 50-ohm coaxial cable. These testers are equipped with a BNC coaxial connector port on them. Other testers may also be able to perform tests for thin 50-ohm coaxial cable with the correct adapters.

10BASE-2 CABLE TESTS

The following tests should be performed when testing 10Base-2, 50-ohm coaxial cable:

▼ Physical inspection

■ Length test

■ Loop resistance test

▲ Characteristic impedance test

The cable terminators should also be tested to verify that they have the proper resistance of 50 ohms +/− 1 percent. The cable terminators are placed at the ends of each 50-ohm coaxial cable segment.

Physical Inspection

Many problems with 10Base-2, 50-ohm coaxial cable are cable segments that become disconnected, loose connectors, or cable terminators that are removed. During the physical inspection, you should look for the following potential problem areas:

▼ Connectors are attached correctly.

■ The correct terminators are used on both ends of the cable.

■ The correct type of cable (impedance rating) is used.

■ No drop cables are used between the equipment and T connectors.

■ There are no kinked or damaged cable segments.

▲ Cable segment is properly grounded.

Coaxial Cable Maximum Length

To perform a length test on a 10Base-2, 50-ohm coaxial cable, remove the cable terminators on both ends of the cable segment. A cable tester must be attached to one end of the cable segment. A length test should be performed on the entire cable link.

The maximum length allowed for a 10Base-2 coaxial cable segment is 185 m (607 ft.).

Loop Resistance

A loop resistance test will indicate if there is too much attenuation on the cable segment. Loop resistance on a 50-ohm coaxial cable should be no more than 5 ohms per 100 m (328 ft.) of cable.

To measure loop resistance, remove the terminator and install a shorting plug at the opposite end of the cable segment. Using a multimeter, measure the resistance between the center conductor and the cable shield.

Characteristic Impedance

A characteristic impedance test for a 50-ohm coaxial cable should verify that the cable's impedance is 50 ohms +/− 1 percent. The characteristic impedance test is used to identify any impedance discontinuities that can cause signal reflections in the cable segment. Signal reflections will cause collisions on the Ethernet LAN.

CHAPTER SUMMARY

The last step in the installation process is the testing and certification of the newly installed cabling system. Testing is the process of verifying that the cables are installed and terminated correctly. Testing communication cables will verify the cable's performance specifications. This is called cable certification. Performance testing is required to certify the installed cable's performance through a range of frequencies that different communication systems will use to transmit signals.

Cable testing is an organized and systematic process of verifying that communication cables are installed and terminated correctly. Cable testing is performed with cable testing devices to confirm that the installation complies with the project requirements and industry cabling standards. The process of testing communication cables requires performing the following steps: visual inspection of the cables and the cable terminations, continuity testing, and performance testing.

The TIA commissioned a task group to develop a comprehensive testing standard for UTP cable systems. The task group created a telecommunications system bulletin to compliment the ANSI/TIA/EIA-568-A standard entitled "Transmission Performance Specifications for Field Testing of Unshielded Twisted Pair Cabling Systems," and referenced the new specification as TIA/EIA TSB-67. TIA/EIA TSB-67 was published to address field testing specifications for both UTP and ScTP cabling systems. This document was created to address field test specifications for post installation performance measurements of UTP or ScTP cabling installations, designed in accordance with the ANSI/TIA/EIA-568-A standard.

TSB-67 defines two horizontal link models. The horizontal cabling link models or configurations are called the horizontal cabling link and the horizontal cabling channel. The horizontal cabling link is the permanently installed horizontal cable from the telecommunications closet to the outlet/connector used to terminate the cable in the work area. A horizontal cabling link is also called the permanent link and the basic link. The horizontal cabling channel contains the cabling link and also includes the equipment patch cords or jumper wires in the telecommunications closet and the work area patch cords. The channel is the most important of the two horizontal cabling links. Because the horizontal cabling channel included the patch cords on both ends, it will determine if the horizontal cable will support a given application.

The wire map test is intended to verify the end to end electrical continuity for all of the cabling pairs. It is also used to identify installation wiring errors. The wire map test indicates opens, shorts, crossed pairs, and miswires. The horizontal wiring, defined by the ANSI/TIA/EIA-568-A and ANSI/TIA/EIA-568-B.1 standards, is specified as being straight through from the telecommunications room to the work area outlet.

The length test is used to provide an indication of the length of a cable run. Industry cabling standards specify that the maximum length of the permanently installed horizontal cabling is 90 m (295 ft.) from the termination in the closet to the termination in the work area. An additional 10 m (33 ft.) is allowed for patch cords, jumpers, and equipment cords. The maximum length of the entire horizontal channel is 100 m (328 ft.).

An attenuation test is a measure of the amount of signal loss in the cable and connecting hardware of a cable link. Attenuation is measured in deciBels (dBs). When measuring for attenuation, the lower the dB values the better. The two primary causes of attenuation on a twisted-pair cable are the length of the cable and the frequency of the transmitted signal over the cable.

NEXT is measured in dB. The dB rating is specified for each component individually. Measurements are taken at specified swept/stepped frequency levels. The higher the NEXT dB value the better. A high NEXT dB value means that very little of the signal from the transmitting cable pair can be measured on the nontransmitting pairs of the cable. A low NEXT dB value means that more signals from the transmitting cable pair can be measured on the nontransmitting pairs of the cable. For copper cables, the higher the transmitted frequency, the lower NEXT dB values communication cables exhibit.

Attenuation to Crosstalk Ratio (ACR) is a calculation defining the ratio of the received signal to existing system noise. ACR calculations for a category 5e cable are taken from a frequency range of 1 to 100 MHz for each pair combination. ACR results are reported in dB. The higher the dB rating the better. ACR is the true indication of the quality of the received signal.

The ACR test is also a two-way test. This means that the test must be performed on both ends of an installed category 5e cable. This test incorporates a NEXT measurement, and therefore, it must measure the amount of the transmitted signal that is coupled into adjacent cable pairs from the transmitted end of the cable. The only way to determine this is by performing the test on both ends of the cable.

The ACR performance specifications for category 5e are defined for both the basic link and channel. The category 5e NEXT specifications for the basic link is 10.4 dB at 100 MHz, and the NEX specifications for the channel is 6.1 dB @ 100 MHz.

Return loss is a measure of the reflected energy caused by impedance mismatches in the cabling system. Impedance mismatches cause both signal loss and reflected noise on the link. The amount of reflected energy is a direct function of the degree of impedance mismatch between the communication cable and the cable termination components in the link. The maximum return loss for a category 5e channel tested at 100 MHz is 10 dB.

Power sum near end crosstalk (PS NEXT) is a measure of the total crosstalk energy that can be measured on a nonactive cable pair when more than one pair is active or being used simultaneously. PS NEXT is a new measurement for UTP cabling systems. PS NEXT is specified for category 5e and higher UTP cables. This measurement is important for applications that use multiple pairs for sending signals. The minimum PS NEXT for a category 5e channel at 100 MHz is 27.1 dB.

ELFEXT is a measure of far end crosstalk for any length UTP cable. ELFEXT is a new transmission parameter for UTP cable. ELFEXT is specified for category 5e and higher UTP cables. This measurement is important for applications that use multiple pairs simultaneously for full duplex transmission. The minimum ELFEXT for a category 5e channel at 100 MHz is 17.0 dB.

Power sum equal level far end crosstalk (PS ELFEXT) is a measure of the total crosstalk energy that can be measured on a nonactive cable pair when more than one pair is active or being used simultaneously. Power sum is a formula that totals the crosstalk energy being contributed by each active pair on a nonactive pair measured at the far end of the cable. The minimum PS ELFEXT for a category 5e channel at 100 MHz is 14.4 dB.

Propagation delay is defined as the amount of time needed for a transmitted signal to travel over a single pair of a communication cable. The propagation delay of a cable will increase as the length of the cable increases. Propagation delay is typically measured in nanoseconds (ns) for 100 m of cable. The specifications for category 5e cables require that the maximum propagation delay of a channel must not exceed 538 ns for 100 m (328 ft.) at 100 MHz.

Delay skew is defined as the difference in the propagation delay between the fastest and slowest pairs of the same UTP cable. Cables that exceed the maximum delay skew parameter will result in the receiving equipment being mixed up and corrupt. Industry standards specify that delay skew for a UTP cable not exceed 45 ns for all frequencies between 2 and 12.5 MHz for a 100 m horizontal cable run.

Communication cables can be tested with many different types of testing devices. The most common type of device to perform complete cable testing is a certification field tester. Certification field testers are the most common testing devices for certifying category 5, category 5e, and category 6 cabling systems. Certification field testers are the only devices that can provide complete testing for a high performance cabling system.

A certification field tester is more comprehensive testing and certification device. A certification field tester is used to certify installed cabling links to ensure that these cabling links will support high speed networks. A certification field tester can perform the tests required by TSB-67 for a category 5 and higher twisted-pair cable links. Certification field testers can perform every required cable test using an autotest feature. The autotest is most frequently used for certifying communication cabling systems. The autotest function performs all of the tests necessary to certify a communication cabling system.

The TIA/EIA TSB-67 standard specifies the required accuracy levels of certification field testers. The standard requires that communication cables be tested with a high degree of accuracy to assure that the pass/fail results given by the tester are correct.

The accuracy levels are defined to identify links that are very close to the pass/fail boundary. TSB-67 specifies two different link models and specifies four different accuracy levels for field testing equipment called Level I, Level II, Level IIe, and Level III. The TIA/EIA TSB-67 standard requires that an asterisk must follow a test result value when the value falls in the tester's range of accuracy.

When a communication cable is tested and the test result is a failure, the cause of the failure must be identified and corrected. All wire connections must be terminated correctly and in the correct position on all terminating devices in a cable link.

Industry cable standards do not address testing coaxial cable segments. Coaxial cables can be found in both commercial and residential buildings. A 50-ohm coaxial cable was used extensively for 10Base-2 Ethernet LANs and can still be found in many commercial buildings today. Many cable testers can perform tests for thin 50-ohm coaxial cable. The following tests should be performed when testing 10Base-2, 50-ohm coaxial cable: physical inspection, length test, loop resistance test, and a characteristic impedance test. The cable terminators should also be tested to verify that they have the proper resistance of 50 ohms +/− 1 percent.

CHAPTER 24

Testing and Troubleshooting Optical Fiber Cables

The last step in the installation process is the testing and certification of the newly installed optical fiber cables. Testing is the process of verifying that the optical fiber cables are installed and terminated correctly. This step checks each optical fiber cable to confirm that it was terminated correctly. Each optical fiber strand from each cable must be tested to verify that it was terminated correctly and installed in the correct position on the fiber optic patch panel.

Testing fiber optic cabling requires making several basic measurements. Fiber optic cable testing verifies that the optical fiber cable has been installed and terminated correctly. Proper testing maximizes system longevity and minimizes system downtime and the time required for troubleshooting and system maintenance.

Testing the optical fiber cables also serves an important role in documenting the cabling system. The test results provide a baseline for the performance of each cable when it was installed. This information can be referenced when an optical fiber cable experiences problems at a later date. The new test results can be compared to the old test results to identify what has changed that can be causing the problem. This chapter will describe the steps required to test, certify, and troubleshoot optical fiber cables.

TYPES OF FIBER OPTIC TESTS

There are a few different tests that are required to certify a fiber optic cabling system. These tests include the following:

▼ **Attenuation test**   This is the most common type of test after the fiber optic installation to verify that all the cables are installed and terminated correctly.

■ **Bandwidth test**   This is not a very common test performed after a fiber optic installation. It is used to determine the bandwidth of the installed optical fiber cable.

■ **Length test**   This test is typically done after the fiber optic installation for documentation purposes. It will document the length of the installed optical fiber cable segments.

▲ **Fault location test**   This test is done when a problem has been identified in the optical fiber cabling system.

FIBER OPTIC TESTING STANDARDS

Optical fiber cables must be tested to conform to the specifications defined in all industry standards and optical fiber testing standards. The primary standards for fiber optic performance specifications are the ANSI/TIA/EIA-568-A and ANSI/TIA/EIA-568-B.3 standards. These standards define the performance of the optical fiber cables and describe loss specifications for connectors and splices in a fiber optic link.

The standards that address the performance testing of optical fiber cables are

▼ ANSI/TIA/EIA-526-7 standard for measurement of optical power loss of installed singlemode fiber cable plant. This standard addresses the procedures for testing singlemode optical fiber cable systems.

■ ANSI/TIA/EIA-526-14 standard for optical power loss measurements of installed multimode fiber cable plant. This standard addresses the procedures for testing multimode optical fiber cable systems.

■ ANSI/TIA/EIA-455-171A standard for attenuation by substitution measurement for short length multimode and graded index and singlemode optical fiber cable assemblies. This is the proposed revision to the EIA-455-171, FOTP-171 standard.

▲ ANSI/TIA/EIA-455-61 standard for measurement for fiber or cable attenuation using an Optical Time Domain Reflectometer (OTDR) tester. This is the proposed revision to the EIA-455-61, FOTP-61 standard.

FIBER OPTIC TESTING

An optical fiber cabling system should be tested three times. The testing includes the following:

▼ *The optical fiber cable must be tested on the reel for continuity.* This will confirm that the cable has not been damaged when shipped to the job site.

■ *Each fiber optic segment should be tested.* This test will verify that each optical fiber segment is functioning properly and within specifications.

▲ *The entire end-to-end fiber optic link should be tested.* This test will verify that all connected fiber segments are functioning properly and the overall link test results are within specifications. This test should be performed from the work area to the network equipment location.

Testing a Fiber Optic Cable Reel

Every reel of fiber optic cable must be tested when it is first received from the cable manufacturer or stocking distributor. The process of testing the optical fiber cable while it is still on the reel will check the optical fiber for damage. This test must always be performed before the cable is installed. This will prevent installing damaged cable and having to replace the damaged cable at a later date.

Testing Multimode Optical Fiber Cables

Multimode optical fiber cables should be tested at both 850 nm and 1,300 nm wavelengths. These are the two defined wavelengths specified by the ANSI/TIA/EIA- 568-A and

ANSI/TIA/EIA-568-B.3 standards. All tests should be performed using LED light sources.

Testing Singlemode Optical Fiber Cables

Singlemode optical fiber cables should be tested at both 1,310 nm and 1,550 nm wavelengths. These are the two defined wavelengths specified by the ANSI/TIA/EIA- 568-A and ANSI/TIA/EIA-568-B.3 standards. All tests should be performed using laser light sources.

OPTICAL FIBER LINK SEGMENTS

All of the components in an optical fiber link are defined as passive cabling components. Passive cabling components include

▼ Optical fiber cable

■ Fiber optic connectors

▲ Fiber optic splices

An optical fiber segment represents all these components between two end points in a fiber optic cabling system. These end points can be between

▼ A work area outlet and a horizontal patch panel port

■ Two patch panels ports in different telecommunications rooms

▲ A work area outlet and a patch panel port in an equipment room location

LINK SEGMENT PERFORMANCE

Optical attenuation and bandwidth are the most important link performance parameters. Every link segment must be checked for attenuation. This test must be performed on all installed optical fiber segments in order to satisfy the requirements of industry cable testing standards.

Bandwidth is another important performance parameter for a fiber optic link segment. This parameter is seldom checked after the installation of optical fiber cable because the installation procedures do not adversely affect this performance parameter.

OPTICAL FIBER LOSS PARAMETERS

The ANSI/TIA/EIA-568-A standard specifies that 62.5/125 μm multimode optical fiber cable shall exhibit the following losses:

▼ A maximum of 3.75 dB/km at 850 nm

▲ A maximum of 1.5 dB/km at 1,300 nm

The ANSI/TIA/EIA-568-B.3 standard specifies that multimode optical fiber cables (50/125 and 62.5/125 μm) shall exhibit the following losses:

▼ A maximum of 3.50 dB/km at 850 nm

▲ A maximum of 1.5 dB/km at 1,300 nm

The ANSI/TIA/EIA-568-A standard specifies that singlemode optical fiber cable shall exhibit the following losses:

▼ A maximum of 1.0 dB/km at 1,310 and 1,550 nm for tight buffer cable

▲ A maximum of 0.5 dB/km at 1,310 and 1,550 nm for loose buffer cable

CONNECTOR AND SPLICE LOSS PARAMETERS

The ANSI/TIA/EIA-568-A and ANSI/TIA/EIA-568-B.3 standards specify that a mated pair of fiber optic connectors shall exhibit a maximum of 0.75 dB of loss.

The ANSI/TIA/EIA-568-A and ANSI/TIA/EIA-568-B.3 standards also specify that all splices (mechanical or fusion) shall exhibit a maximum of 0.3 dB of loss.

Any fiber optic termination that exceeds these loss specifications must be replaced.

TESTING HORIZONTAL LINKS

Horizontal optical fiber link segments should be installed in a physical star topology and limited to a maximum of 90 m (295 ft.) from the horizontal cross-connect to the work area outlet. The maximum length for an optical fiber channel is 100 m (328 ft.).

Horizontal link segments should only be tested at one wavelength. This wavelength can be either 850 or 1,300 nm. Because of the short segment distances, the attenuation differences based on wavelength are insignificant. The losses associated with fiber optic connectors and splices will be the most significant loss factors in a horizontal link segment.

TESTING MULTIMODE OPTICAL FIBER BACKBONE LINK SEGMENTS

Multimode optical fiber backbone link segments should be installed in a hierarchical star topology and limited to the following distances:

▼ A maximum of 1,700 m (5,575 ft.) from the main cross-connect to an intermediate cross-connect

■   A maximum of 300 m (984 ft.) from an intermediate cross-connect to a horizontal cross-connect

▲   A maximum of 2,000 m (6,560 ft.) from the main cross-connect to a horizontal cross-connect

Multimode optical fiber backbone segments should be tested in one direction at both 850 and 1,300 nm wavelengths.

TESTING SINGLEMODE OPTICAL FIBER BACKBONE LINK SEGMENTS

Singlemode optical fiber backbone link segments should be installed in a hierarchical star topology and limited to the following distances:

▼   A maximum of 2,700 m (8,855 ft.) from the main cross-connect to an intermediate cross-connect

■   A maximum of 300 m (984 ft.) from an intermediate cross-connect to a horizontal cross-connect

▲   A maximum of 3,000 m (9,840 ft.) from the main cross-connect to a horizontal cross-connect

Singlemode optical fiber backbone segments should be tested in one direction at both 1,310 and 1,550 nm wavelengths.

OPTICAL ATTENUATION TESTING

Attenuation testing in a fiber optic cabling system is a test to measure optical power loss (see Figure 24-1). This test is also called an optical power loss test. The attenuation test will determine the loss for all of the passive components in the fiber optic cabling link including

▼   Optical fiber cables

■   Fiber optic connectors

■   Fiber optic splices

▲   Patch cords

Attenuation testing of installed optical fiber cable is measured by the insertion loss method. This method uses a power meter and light source to measure the difference between two optical power levels. The first level is how much light is injected into the optical fiber by the optical light source. The second level is how much light is measured at the opposite end of the cable segment.

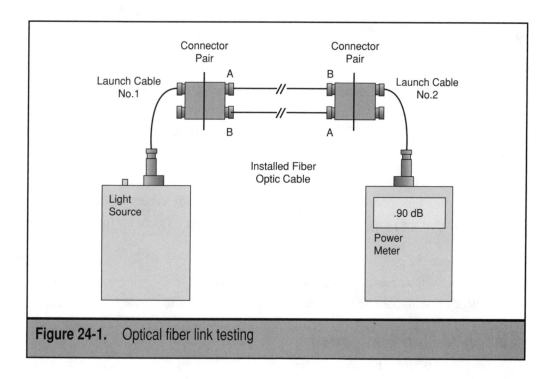

Figure 24-1. Optical fiber link testing

The power meter and light source must be calibrated to determine the amount of light that is put into an optical fiber cable. This provides the starting point for determining optical power loss for all installed cables. Next, power loss measurements can be taken for all installed optical fiber cables. The difference between the two power levels is the optical loss for each optical link.

Optical attenuation or power loss is given in decibels (dBs). Power meters are calibrated to read in linear units. Power meters measure optical power loss in absolute power levels called dBm. A dBm is a referenced loss value to 1 milliwatt of power. Any light that is measured from a cable that is less than 1 milliwatt of power is given as a negative value. As result, power meters will give optical power loss results as negative values.

The formula for calculating optical power loss is

$$\text{Loss (dB)} = \text{P1 (dBm)} - \text{P2 (dBm)}$$

P1 is the referenced light measurement indicating how much light is put into the optical fiber. P2 is the measured light loss at the opposite end of the optical fiber link being tested.

The loss values for an optical link segment are given in dB, which are always positive values. dB values are always positive because of the formula used to calculate dB loss. A negative number subtracted from a larger negative number yields a positive number. This is shown in the following example:

$$-4 \text{ dBm} - -12 \text{ dBm} = +8 \text{ dB}$$

Subtracting two negative numbers is the same as adding a positive number to the negative number. This formula can also be displayed as

$$-4 \text{ dBm} + 12 \text{ dBm} = +8 \text{ dB}$$

Therefore, optical loss results will be listed as positive dB values.

Steps for Performing Optical Attenuation Testing

Testing an optical fiber cable installation for attenuation will include the following steps:

1. Verify that the correct optical fiber cable is to be tested.
2. Verify the type of optical fiber to be tested (multimode versus singlemode).
3. Verify that the power meter and light source are appropriate for the type of optical fiber cable to be tested.
4. Calibrate the power meter.
5. Verify that the power meter and light source are set to the same wavelength.
6. Verify that all fiber optic connectors are cleaned prior to the attenuation test.

Attenuation Testing Equipment

Before you start performing optical attenuation tests, you must have the proper equipment. This will include

▼ A power meter

■ A light source

■ A reference adapter (coupler)

▲ Test jumper cables

All of these components usually are included in an optical fiber test set (see Figure 24-2).

Two-way radios or fiber optic test sets are also highly recommended. These devices will enable two technicians to communicate together during the testing procedure.

Test Jumper Cables

The test jumper cables will be used to test all installed optical fiber link segments. The same jumpers will provide consistent results for all optical loss measurements.

The requirements for optical jumpers are as follows:

▼ They must be the same type of cable as the installed optical fiber cables being tested.

■ They must be a maximum of 1 to 5 m in length.

▲ They must use connectors that match the optical fiber links being tested.

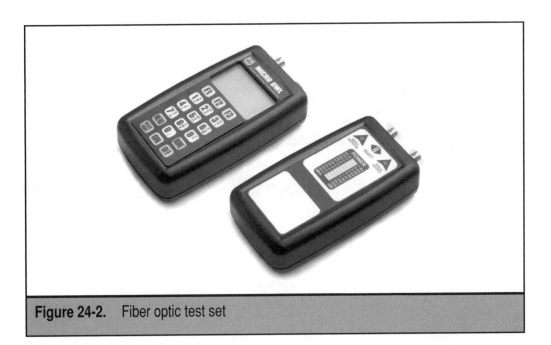

Figure 24-2.   Fiber optic test set

It is highly recommended that test jumper cables be factory manufactured. This will guarantee that these cables are highly reliable.

The TIA FOTP-171 standard requires that the test jumper cable connected to the light source must have a filter device (see Figure 24-3). The filter device specified in the FOTP-171 standard is a smooth, round mandrel that is 17.5 mm (0.7 in.) around. The jumper cable must be wrapped around the mandrel five times creating a fiber loop diameter of 20 mm (0.8 in.).

The mode filter is required to control light launch conditions in the test jumper cable. This configuration will filter out high order modes from being launched into the cable link to be tested. This test configuration yields significantly more consistent results than using a test jumper without the mode filter.

Cleaning Optical Fiber Connections   Always clean the fiber end faces on all optical fiber jumper cables and the installed optical fiber cables before making any connections. Use any of the following to clean the connector end faces:

■   Alcohol soaked, lint free wipes

■   Lint free swabs moistened with alcohol

▲   Cassette style cleaning devices designed for use on optical fiber connectors

Canned air is also a very useful tool for cleaning optical fiber connector end faces. The canned air sprayed on the connector will dislodge any dirt or dust contaminants. Always replace all dust caps after working with an optical fiber connector.

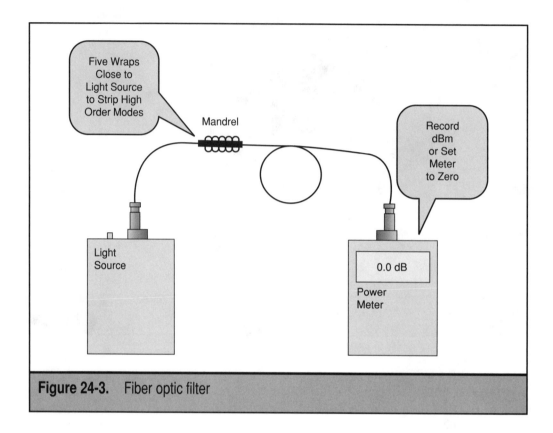

Figure 24-3.   Fiber optic filter

POWER METER CALIBRATION

The first step in performing optical attenuation test measurements is the calibration of the power meter. This step will indicate how much light is launched into the optical fiber cable segment.

In order to perform the power meter calibration, the power meter and light source are connected together with the two test jumper cables. The reference adapter is used to connect the ends of the two test jumper cables together.

Power Meter Calibration Options

The ANSI/TIA/EIA-568-A standard was the first standard document that specified the procedure for performing power meter calibration. This standard specified that an optical fiber power meter must be calibrated using a single reference jumper cable between the power meter and light source. This is shown in Figure 24-4.

TIA/EIA 526-14 standard is a second standard that defines the procedures for performing power meter calibration. This standard requires that the power meter calibration

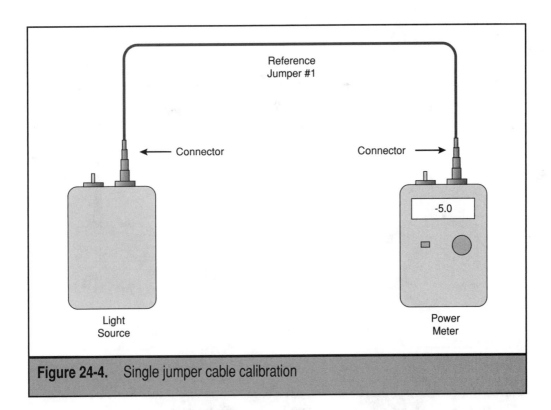

Figure 24-4.   Single jumper cable calibration

procedure be performed with two test jumper cables connected together with a reference adapter. This is shown in Figure 24-5.

The FOTP-171 standard requires that the power meter calibration be performed with a fiber filter attached to the first test jumper cable. This standard requires that the power meter calibration procedure be performed with two test jumper cables connected together with a reference adapter. This is shown in Figure 24-6.

Power Meter Calibration Procedure

The steps for performing the power meter calibration are as follows:

1. Remove the dust cap from the power meter and one end of a test jumper cable. Attach the test jumper cable to the power meter.

2. Remove the dust cap from the opposite end of the test jumper cable connected to the power meter. The end of this cable should be connected to the reference adapter.

3. Remove the dust cap from one port of the light source and one end of the second fiber optic jumper cable and attach the second test jumper cable to the port on the light source.

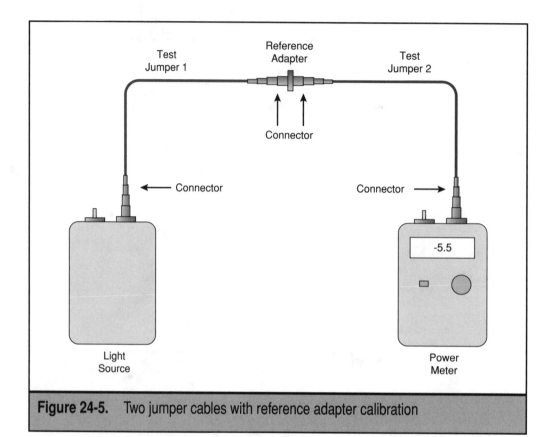

Figure 24-5. Two jumper cables with reference adapter calibration

4. Remove the dust cap from the opposite end of the second test jumper cable connected to the light source. The end of this cable should be connected to the reference adapter.

5. Turn on the light source and measure the optical power. This measurement will typically be a negative value expressed in dBm. This value will be the referenced power level. This should be written down as the reference point for each link to be tested.

ATTENUATION TEST PROCEDURE

Optical attenuation testing can start once the power meter has been calibrated. The steps for performing optical attenuation testing are as follows:

1. Disconnect the two test jumper cables from the reference adapter. These test jumper cables should remain attached to the power meter and light source. Attach the dust caps to the ends of these cables.

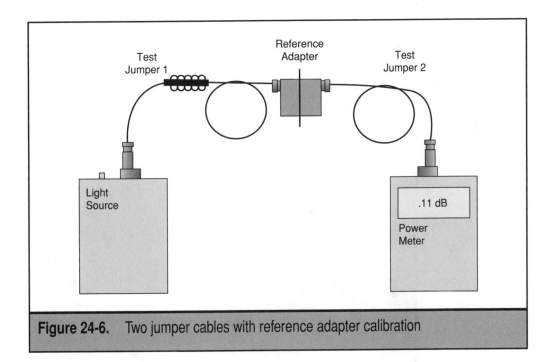

Figure 24-6.   Two jumper cables with reference adapter calibration

2. Two technicians should go to the opposite ends of the cable to be tested.

3. Attach the power meter to the patch panel port.

4. Attach the light source to the work area outlet.

5. The cable technician with the optical light source should turn it on. The cable technician with the power meter should observe and record the power meter reading (see Figure 24-7).

6. The power meter value must be subtracted from the referenced power level value to determine the optical loss in dB.

7. Steps three through five should be repeated for each optical fiber cable to be tested.

8. When all testing is complete, the dust caps must be replaced on all fiber optic connector ports and all test equipment ports. All test equipment must be returned to its carrying case.

OPTICAL TIME DOMAIN REFLECTOMETER (OTDR) TESTING

Optical time domain reflectometer (OTDR) testing is a second important test that can be performed on an optical fiber cabling system. A power meter can measure optical power

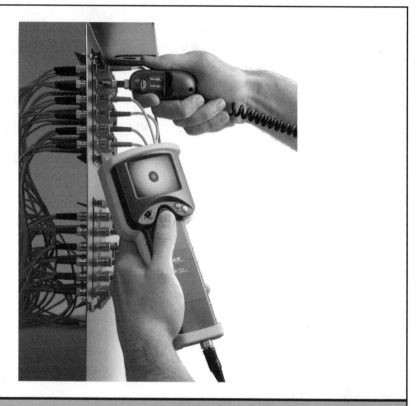

Figure 24-7.   Perform measurement

loss only. An OTDR is a device that can identify the location and cause of losses in a fiber link.

An OTDR is a device that injects light pulses into an optical fiber cable and measures light that reflects back to the OTDR. An OTDR works using a principle called backscatter. Fiber optic connectors and splices will always reflect some light at these connection points. The OTDR is able to measure that amount of backscatter to detect fiber optic connectors and splices in a link. The OTDR can also determine the distance of these connections by measuring the time for the backscatter signals to return to the OTDR.

The OTDR displays this information on a trace printout. The trace printout can be analyzed and retained as documentation of the fiber optic link segment characteristics.

OTDR OPERATION PRINCIPLES

An OTDR injects a laser light pulse into the core of an optical fiber cable. The OTDR measures two effects on the light pulse caused by the optical fiber:

▼ **Rayleigh scattering**   This is the backscatter caused by small particles in the optical fiber cable. This scatter is constant along the entire length of the cable.

▲ **Fresnel reflection**   This is the backscatter caused by connectors and splices. Fresnel reflections are caused by light traveling in one material and hitting a material with a different density. This causes a percentage of light to reflect back the direction it was transmitted. The amount of reflected light is determined by the change in material density. Severe changes in density occur at fiber ends and at fiber break points. Minor changes in density occur at connector and splice points.

Rayleigh scattering is a small reflection of light, while fresnel reflection is a large reflection of light.

OTDR TRACE

An OTDR trace is a graphical display of the OTDR test results (see Figure 24-8). The parts of an OTDR trace are

▼ **Initial pulse**   This is a large spike at the beginning of the trace representing the light entering the optical fiber.

■ **Slope**   This represents the optical attenuation of light pulses traveling down the optical fiber.

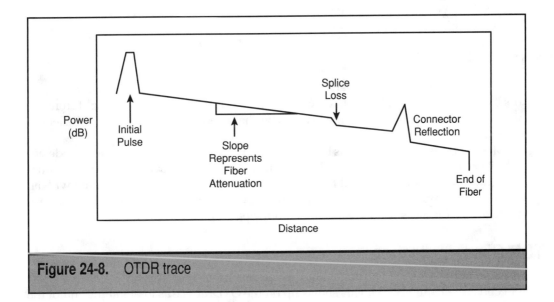

Figure 24-8.   OTDR trace

- ■ **Connector reflections**   This event is typically represented as a reflection and loss on the trace.

- ■ **Splice loss**   This event is typically represented as a nonreflective loss on the trace.

- ▲ **Reflective pulse**   This is a large spike followed by a significant drop in the slope followed by noise. This represents light hitting the end of the optical fiber cable.

OTDR Dead Zone

All OTDRs have a dead zone. This is an area where the device cannot perform accurate measurements. The dead zone occurs in the portion of optical fiber cable closest to the OTDR.

An OTDR cannot make test measurements in its dead zone. The actual length of an OTDR's dead zone is related to the width of the laser pulse injected into the optical fiber cable. An OTDR's dead zone can range in size from 6 to 1,600 m in length.

OTDR Distance Measurements

OTDRs are the primary testing device for measuring the distance of an optical fiber link. OTDRs can be used to determine the distance for an installed length of optical fiber cable or determine the distance for a break in an optical fiber link segment.

An OTDR can determine distances of cables or cable breaks by injecting a light pulse and measuring the amount of time it takes for the pulse reflection to be detected (see Figure 24-9). A calculation is performed based on the speed of light in an optical fiber cable to determine the distance of the cable or cable break.

OTDR Loss Measurements

An OTDR can also be used to perform optical loss measurements. The OTDR measures loss by monitoring the rayleigh backscatter in the optical fiber link. As the light from the rayleigh backscatter is reduced, the loss can be characterized as greater along the length of cable.

Many experts warn that loss is best measured with a power meter for multimode optical fiber cables. OTDRs use a laser light source. These light sources do not fill the entire fiber core of a multimode optical fiber with light. As a result, the loss measured with an OTDR may be different than the loss measured by a power meter. OTDRs are an appropriate device for measuring loss in singlemode optical fiber cables (see Figure 24-10).

OTDR Ghost Reflection

Sometimes OTDRs can yield some unexpected results. One such result is called a ghost reflection (see Figure 24-11). This shows up on the OTDR trace as losses at the end of the cable.

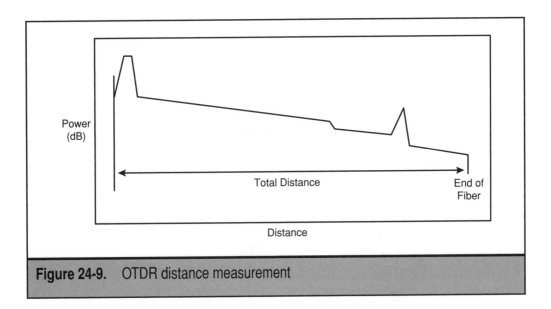

Figure 24-9.   OTDR distance measurement

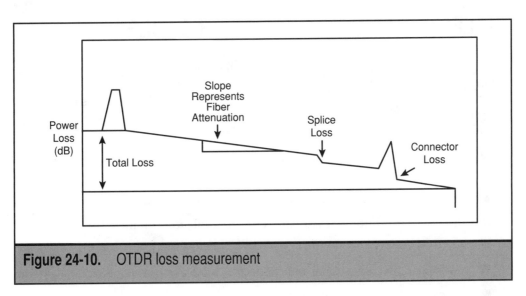

Figure 24-10.   OTDR loss measurement

A ghost reflection is caused by a large reflection in a short optical fiber link. The reflected light can actually bounce back and forth within the optical fiber cable. This can cause one or more false reflections to be seen on the OTDR trace. This reflection will be shown at different distances from the initial reflection on the trace.

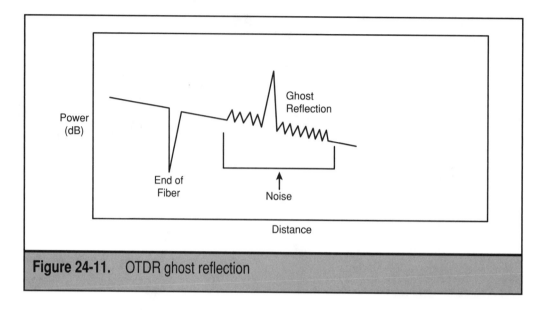

Figure 24-11. OTDR ghost reflection

TROUBLESHOOTING OPTICAL FIBER CABLE

Troubleshooting is the process of locating a broken cable, a bad termination, or a source of loss in an optical fiber link. Troubleshooting is the process of finding and correcting the cabling problem.

The methodology for performing troubleshooting on optical fiber cables is similar to the process for troubleshooting copper communication cables. The following steps should be followed for troubleshooting optical fiber cables:

▼ Determine the exact nature of the cabling problem and verify that it is actually cabling related.

■ Perform a visual inspection looking for anything unusual.

■ Use your cable testing devices and perform cable tests on the cable in question.

■ Break the cable segment into small parts and test each part.

■ Verify that the correct cable and connectors were used.

■ Check for improper installation practices.

■ Replace suspect equipment and work area optical fiber patch cords.

■ Look for crushed or damaged cable.

▲ Check for excessive cable distances.

Steps for Troubleshooting an Optical Fiber Cable

The steps for troubleshooting optical fiber cable are as follows:

1. Perform a visual inspection on the entire cable link looking for the following:

   a. Verify that the proper fiber strands are being used.

   b. Verify that the correct patch panel ports are being used.

   c. Verify that the correct work area ports are being used.

   d. Verify that all cable connectors are properly attached and seated.

   e. Verify that all strands have been terminated properly in the entire cable link (all connections in the link).

   f. Verify that no cables or cable strands are damaged, crushed, or kinked.

2. Disconnect all electronic equipment.

3. Perform cable tests using the appropriate cable tester and perform the following tests:

   a. Continuity test

   b. Length test (maximum length varies per media type and technology) from one end of the link

   c. Attenuation (power loss) test from one end of the cable link:

      - At either 850 or 1,300 nm for horizontal cables
      - Both 850 and 1,300 nm for backbone cables

4. If testing a backbone cable link and problems are indicated, break the cable link into two pieces and test each cable link separately to identify the problem.

5. Record all cable test results.

6. Identify failed cable tests.

7. Perform repairs on the cable link, if necessary.

8. Retest the cable link to verify the cable repair was performed correctly, if necessary.

9. Perform housekeeping as required.

CHAPTER SUMMARY

Testing is the process of verifying that the optical fiber cables are installed and terminated correctly. This step checks each optical fiber cable to confirm that it was terminated correctly. Each optical fiber strand from each cable must be tested to verify that it was terminated correctly and installed in the correct position on the fiber optic patch panel.

Testing fiber optic cabling requires making several basic measurements. Fiber optic cable testing verifies that the optical fiber cable has been installed and terminated correctly.

Proper testing maximizes system longevity and minimizes system downtime and the time required for troubleshooting and system maintenance. There are a few different tests that are required to certify a fiber optic cabling system. These tests include the following: attenuation testing, bandwidth testing, length testing, and fault location testing.

Optical fiber cables must be tested to conform to the specifications defined in all industry standards and optical fiber testing standards. The primary standards for fiber optic performance specifications are the ANSI/TIA/EIA-568-A and ANSI/TIA/EIA-568-B.3 standards. The standards that address the performance testing of optical fiber cables are: ANSI/TIA/EIA-526-7 standard for testing singlemode optical fiber cable systems, ANSI/TIA/EIA-526-14 standard for testing multimode optical fiber cable systems, ANSI/TIA/EIA-455-171A standard for testing short length multimode and singlemode optical fiber cable assemblies, and the ANSI/TIA/EIA-455-61 standard for testing attenuation using an OTDR tester.

An optical fiber cabling system should be tested three times. The optical fiber cable must be tested on the reel for continuity. Each fiber optic segment should be tested. The entire end-to-end fiber optic link also should be tested.

The ANSI/TIA/EIA-568-A standard specifies that 62.5/125 μm multimode optical fiber cable shall exhibit the following losses of a maximum of 3.75 dB/km at 850 nm and a maximum of 1.5 dB/km at 1,300 nm. The ANSI/TIA/EIA-568-B.3 standard specifies that multimode optical fiber cables (50/125 and 62.5/125 μm) shall exhibit the following losses of a maximum of 3.50 dB/km at 850 nm and a maximum of 1.5 dB/km at 1,300 nm. The ANSI/TIA/EIA-568-A and ANSI/TIA/EIA-568-B.1 standards specify that singlemode optical fiber cable shall exhibit the following losses:

▼   A maximum of 1.0 dB/km at 1,310 and 1,550 nm for tight buffer cable

▲   A maximum of 0.5 dB/km at 1,310 and 1,550 nm for loose buffer cable.

The ANSI/TIA/EIA-568-A and ANSI/TIA/EIA-568-B.3 standards specify that a mated pair of fiber optic connectors shall exhibit a maximum of 0.75 dB of loss. The ANSI/TIA/EIA-568-A and ANSI/TIA/EIA-568-B.3 standards also specify that all splices (mechanical or fusion) shall exhibit a maximum of 0.3 dB of loss.

Multimode optical fiber backbone link segments should be installed in a hierarchical star topology and limited to the following distances:

▼   A maximum of 1,700 m (5,575 ft.) from the main cross-connect to an intermediate cross-connect

■   A maximum of 300 m (984 ft.) from an intermediate cross-connect to a horizontal cross-connect

▲   A maximum of 2,000 m (6,560 ft.) from the main cross-connect to a horizontal cross-connect.

Multimode optical fiber backbone segments should be tested in one direction at both 850 and 1,300 nm wavelengths.

Singlemode optical fiber backbone link segments should be installed in a hierarchical star topology and limited to the following distances:

▼   A maximum of 2,700 m (8,855 ft.) from the main cross-connect to an intermediate cross-connect

■   A maximum of 300 m (984 ft.) from an intermediate cross-connect to a horizontal cross-connect

▲   A maximum of 3,000 m (9,840 ft.) from the main cross-connect to a horizontal cross-connect.

Singlemode optical fiber backbone segments should be tested in one direction at both 1,310 and 1,550 nm wavelengths.

Attenuation testing of installed optical fiber cable is measured by the insertion loss method. This method uses a power meter and light source to measure the difference between two optical power levels. The power meter and light source must be calibrated to determine the amount of light that is put into an optical fiber cable. This provides the starting point for determining optical power loss for all installed cables. Optical attenuation or power loss is given in decibels (dB).

Performing optical attenuation tests requires having the proper equipment. This will include a power meter, a light source, a reference adapter (coupler), and test jumper cables. All of these components usually are included in an optical fiber test set. Always clean the fiber end faces on all optical fiber jumper cables and the installed optical fiber cables before making any connections.

The first step in performing optical attenuation test measurements is the calibration of the power meter. This step will indicate how much light is launched into the optical fiber cable segment. Optical attenuation testing can start once the power meter has been calibrated.

OTDR testing is a second important test that can be performed on an optical fiber cabling system. An OTDR is a device that can identify the location and causes of losses in a fiber link. The OTDR is able to detect fiber optic connectors and splices in a link. The OTDR displays this information on a trace printout. The trace printout can be analyzed and retained as documentation of the fiber optic link segment characteristics.

APPENDIX

Glossary of Terms

10Base2   An IEEE specification for 802.3 Ethernet networks using thin 50-ohm coaxial cable, also called Thinnet.

10Base5   An IEEE specification for 802.3 Ethernet networks using thick 50-ohm coaxial cable, also called Thicknet.

10BaseT   An IEEE specification for 802.3 Ethernet networks using UTP cable of category 3 or higher for station connections to the hub.

A

Ablative   The development of a hard char when exposed to fire or flames. Ablative materials resist erosion due to fire and flames; ablative is a characteristic of a nonmechanical firestop when exposed to fire.

Acceptance angle   The half-angle of the cone within which incident light is totally internally reflected by the fiber core. The light within the acceptance cone is coupled into the core of an optical fiber cable.

Acceptance tests   A test used to determine if the transmission characteristics of a cable and components meet a predefined performance specification. This is also called certification testing.

Access floor   A system consisting of completely removable and interchangeable floor panels that are supported on adjustable pedestals or stringers (or both) to enable access to the area beneath the floor for installing communication cables.

Access provider (AP)   The operator of any facility that is used to convey communication signals to and from a customer premises.

Attention-to-Crosstalk Ratio (ACR)   Defined as the difference between attenuation and crosstalk measured in decibels (dB) at a given frequency for a circuit or cable. This difference is critical to ensure that the signal sent down the twisted-pair cable is stronger at the receiving end of the cable than any interference signals (crosstalk) from other cable pairs.

Active circuit   A voice/data/video channel that is currently in use by a customer, access provider (AP), or a communication system or device. A circuit that is actively being used to transmit information between two communication devices.

Administration   The method for labeling and documentation all the components of a communication cabling system defined by the ANSI/TIA/EIA-606 standard. The act of managing communication cabling to accommodate moves, additions, and changes of the telecommunications infrastructure.

Aerial cable   Telecommunications cable installed between buildings or poles and supported using structures such as poles, sides of buildings, and other like structures.

Aerial cable plant   Wires and cables installed on poles. Aerial cables are supported with the assistance of guys, anchors, and pole attachment hardware to support aerial cables.

Air bottle   A compressed air source used to clean fiber optic connectors.

Alternating current (ac)   A continuously varying and changing current that changes polarity at a uniformly repetitious rate (such as 120 Hz).

American National Standards Institute (ANSI)   An organization that formalizes standards recognized in the United States. ANSI is also the U.S. representative to the International Organization for Standardization (ISO), and through the U.S. National Committee, to the International Electrotechnical Commission (IEC).

American wire gauge (AWG)   A system used to specify wire size in the United States. The greater the wire diameter, the smaller the AWG value.

Ampere   Unit of electric current. One ampere is equal to the current produced by one volt acting through a resistance of one ohm.

Analog   A format that uses continuous physical variables, such as voltage amplitude or frequency variations, to transmit information.

Analog signal   Information in the form of a wave that varies continuously over its duration.

Anchor   A device inserted into a prepared hole that will secure a screw or bolt that has been inserted. This component usually affixes itself to the wall and usually does not come out without the removal of the screw or bolt.

ANSI/TIA/EIA-570-A   The telecommunications standard titled *Residential and Light Commercial Telecommunications Wiring Standard.*

ANSI/TIA/EIA   Trade associations involved in developing telecommunications cabling standards in the United States.

ANSI/TIA/EIA-568-A   The telecommunications standard titled *Commercial Building Telecommunications Cabling Standard.*

ANSI/TIA/EIA-568-A-1   The telecommunications standard titled *Propagation Delay and Delay Skew Specifications for 100-ohm, 4-pair Cable.*

ANSI/TIA/EIA-569-A   The telecommunications standard titled *Commercial Building Standard for Telecommunications Pathways and Spaces.*

ANSI/TIA/EIA-606   The telecommunications standard titled *Administration Standard for the Telecommunications Infrastructure of Commercial Buildings.*

ANSI/TIA/EIA-607   The telecommunications standard titled *Commercial Building Grounding and Bonding Requirements for Telecommunications.*

TIA/EIA TSB-67   The Telecommunications Systems Bulletin titled *Transmission Performance Specifications for Field Testing of Unshielded Twisted-Pair and Screened Twisted Pair Cabling Systems.* This TSB defines field test parameters for category 3, 4, 5, and 5e UTP and ScTP cabling systems.

TIA/EIA TSB-72   The Telecommunications Systems Bulletin titled *Centralized Optical Fiber Cabling Guidelines.*

TIA/EIA TSB-75   The Telecommunications Systems Bulletin titled *Additional Horizontal Cabling Practices for Open Offices.*

Application   Communication system and associated system devices that are required to transmit information at a certain speed or using a certain format. Communication systems are applications that are supported by telecommunications cabling.

Application specific cabling   Cabling installed to meet the requirements of a specific transmission system and not guaranteed to support other transmission systems.

Approved ground   An intentional ground that has been approved for use by the authority having jurisdiction.

Aramid   A liquid crystal polymer material with exceptional tensile strength and coefficient of thermal expansion near that of glass. Widely used as a strength member in optical fiber cables. Also referred to as aramid yarn strength members.

Armoring   Cable protection, usually made of corrugated steel and installed inside of the cable jacket. Armoring provides protection against severe outdoor environments and rodents.

As-built   Documentation that indicates cable routing and connections. As-built drawings can be specially drawings or modified building blueprints. As-built drawings are finalized upon job completion. These drawings reflect the changes to the cable runs from the original project drawings.

Attenuation The decrease in strength of transmitted signals. Attenuation is expressed as the ratio of output to input. Usually measured in decibels (dB) at a specific frequency for copper or wavelength for fiber, the signal strength may be power or voltage.

Attenuation-to-crosstalk ratio (ACR) A ratio comparing the received signal with the near-end crosstalk noise coupled into the cable pair from the transmitting cable pair.

Authority having jurisdiction (AHJ) The building official, electrical inspector, fire marshal, or other individuals or entities responsible for interpretation and enforcement of local building and electrical codes.

Autotest A function used by field cable test equipment to automatically run all the required tests and certify the cabling installation to a recognized cable test standard.

B

Backboard A sheet of plywood used for mounting connecting hardware and equipment. Backboards are usually 8 ft. high and 4 ft. wide.

Backbone A pathway or cable between telecommunications rooms (TRs), the entrance facility (EF), and the equipment room (ER) within or between buildings. Backbone cables are also known as riser cables. It is the main (primary) cable pathway between floors and buildings. Multistrand optical fiber and multipair copper cables are commonly used backbone cables.

Backbone cable A cabling that connects the entrance facility (EF), the equipment room (ER), and telecommunications rooms (TRs) in a building or between buildings.

Backbone cabling Cable and connecting hardware used in the backbone subsystem that provides interconnections between telecommunications rooms (TRs), equipment rooms (ERs), and entrance facilities (EFs).

Backbone pathway The portion of the building pathway system that permits the placing of backbone cables between the entrance facility (EF), equipment room (ER), and all telecommunications rooms (TRs) within a building and between buildings.

Backscatter The scattering of light into a direction it was transmitted. Cable impurities and loss components in a fiber optic link will cause light to backscatter. The method that an OTDR uses to identify cable losses and identify the magnitude of the losses in a fiber optic link.

Balun   A balanced-to-unbalanced cabling component. A balun is used to convert from unbalanced coaxial cable to balanced twisted-pair cable. A balun also performs an impedance matching function between twisted-pair to coax cables.

Balanced copper cable   A cable consisting of one or more copper symmetrical cable pairs. Balanced cables have the wire twisted together to support differential signaling.

Bandwidth   A range of frequencies, usually the difference between the upper and lower limits of the range, expressed in hertz (Hz). It is used to describe the information-carrying capacity of a medium. In copper and optical fibers, the bandwidth decreases with increasing length. Optical fiber bandwidth is specified in megahertz for one kilometer (MHz-km).

Basic link test configuration   Horizontal cable of up to 90 m (295 ft.) plus up to 2 m (6.5 ft.) of test equipment cord from the main unit of the tester to the local connection, and up to 2 m (6.5 ft.) of test equipment cord from the remote connection to the remote unit of the tester. Maximum length is 94 m (308 ft.).

BNC connector   Bayonet Neil-Concelman (BNC). The name for a coaxial cable connector used for thin Ethernet coaxial cable (10Base-2). BNC connectors are named for the designers of these coaxial connectors. BNC connectors are a bayonet locking connector, which attaches to T-connectors on thin 50-ohm coaxial cable.

Bel   A measure of analog signal strength named in honor of telephone pioneer Alexander Graham Bell.

Bend radius   Maximum radius that a cable can be bent to avoid physical or electrical damage or cause adverse transmission performance.

BICSI®   A telecommunications association, formerly known as Building Industry Consulting Service International.

Bill of materials   A list of the quantity and specific types of materials to be utilized on a project.

Binder group   A group of 25 cable pairs found in large multipair backbone cables. Groups can be distinguished from one another through the use of colored threads. Standard color-coding provides for 25 pairs per binder group.

Block (connecting)   Device used to connect one group of wires to another.

Blueprint   A reproduction of an architectural plan and/or technical drawing that provides details of a construction project or an existing structure. These drawings are printed on special paper that enables the graphics and text to appear as blue on a white background.

Bonding The permanent joining of metallic parts to form an electrically conductive path that will assure electrical continuity, the capacity to safely conduct any current likely to be imposed, and the ability to limit differences in potentials between the joined parts.

Bonding conductor A conductor used specifically for the purpose of bonding.

Braid A group of noninsulated conductors interwoven to surround one or more insulated conductors. A cable shield that consists of metallic strands. Braided shields provide superior structural integrity, while maintaining good flexibility and flex life.

Branch splice A type of splice used with copper cables. This type of splice permits one cable to be spliced to multiple smaller pair-count cables.

Break-out cable A fiber buffer assembly that permits a larger buffer material to be added to an optical fiber. The break out cable permits the optical fiber to be terminated with an optical fiber connector.

Bridged tap The multiple appearances of the same cable pair at several different points in the cable run.

Bridging clips Metal clips utilized to couple cable conductors on a 66-series connecting block.

Bridle ring A ring that is circular in shape but is open rather than closed. It has a pointed shaft at its apex that is threaded for installation into wood or prethreaded devices. It is available in various sizes.

Buffer A protective material coating extruded directly over an optical fiber. A tube placed around coated optical fiber(s) to enable isolation of the fibers from stress on the cable.

Buffer coating A protective thermoplastic material that is applied to the optical fiber during manufacturing to protect against environmental hazards.

Buffer tube Loose-fitting thermoplastic material used to cover the optical fibers in loose-tube construction, used for protection and isolation.

Buffering	A protective material extruded directly on the fiber coating to protect the fiber from the environment (tight-buffered). Extruding a tube around the coated fiber to enable isolation of the fiber from stresses on the cable (loose-buffered).
Building entrance	The building space or room inside a building where telecommunications cables enter and leave the building.
Building entrance protector	An electrical protection device or devices used to terminate cables entering or leaving buildings. It provides housing for the voltage and current modules protecting the cable pairs from lightning and foreign voltage.
Building grounding electrode system	A network of grounded building components (that is, metal underground water piping, metal building frame, concrete-encased electrode, a ground ring and rod, and pipe electrodes).
Bullwheel	Large wheel used to maintain an arc when feeding large cables into a backbone pathway.
Bundle	Many individual fibers contained within a single jacket or buffer tube. Also, a group of buffered fibers distinguished in some fashion from another group in the same cable.
Bundled cable	An assembly of two or more cables continuously bound together to form a single unit, also known as a hybrid cable.
Bundled fiber	Many fibers contained within a single jacket or buffer tube. A group of buffered fibers distinguished in some fashion from another group in the same manner.
Buried cable	A cable installed under the surface of the ground (not in a conduit) in such a manner that it cannot be removed without disturbing the soil.
Bus topology	A linear configuration where all network devices are placed on a single segment of cable. Ethernet 10Base2 and 10Base5 cables are examples of a bus topology.
Butt set	A device used by telephone technicians to test telephone circuits. Also known as a lineman's test set.
Butt splice	A copper splice technique in which cables enter the same endcap of the splice closure.

C

Cabinet Cabinets are enclosed relay racks. They are normally equipped with two sides, a front door, and a rear door. They are available in various sizes with a wide variety of miscellaneous equipment mounted inside them (such as fans, power strips, connection devices, terminations, apparatus, wiring, and equipment, and so on).

Cable An assembly of one or more conductors, cable pairs, or optical fibers within an enveloping sheath.

Cable assembly A short, premanufactured cable that has connectors installed on one or both ends.

Cable labeling system Scheme adapted for labeling cables to identify them based on ANSI/TIA/EIA-606, *Administration Standard for the Telecommunications Infrastructure of Commercial Buildings*. The scheme employed when identifying cable or its associated hardware.

Cable rack The vertical or horizontal open support structure (usually made of aluminum or steel) that is attached to a ceiling or wall to support cable-supporting hardware.

Cable reel The wooden spool that cable is wrapped around.

Cable reel brake A device used to control the rate of removal of a cable from a cable reel.

Cable run A length of installed cable (copper or optical fiber) that may include other cable termination components along its path.

Cable sheath A covering over the copper, optical fiber, or conductor assembly that may include one or more metallic members, strength members, or cable jackets.

Cable support system A combination of conduits, cable trays, support hooks, tie wraps, and any other hardware pieces used in a cabling installation to support copper and optical fiber cables. The cable support system keeps excess stress off the cables and provides mechanical protection for the cables being supported.

Cable termination Item used for attaching the pairs of a cable to enable for connecting the cable to other cables or devices. Examples of cable termination hardware are: patch panels, punch down blocks, and modular outlets/connectors.

Cable tray   A metal tray (ladder, trough, solid-bottom, or channel) used to route and support communication cables. Typically equipped with sides that enables cables to be placed within the sides over its entire length. It is usually supported by threaded rods suspended from the ceiling structure or from wall-mounted brackets fastened to the wall structure.

Cable tree   A movable rack with multiple arms for holding small reels of cable.

Cable trough   A raceway consisting of metal trough and fittings, formed and constructed so that insulated conductors and cables may be readily installed or removed without injury either to conductors or their coverings.

Cabling   A combination of all copper and optical fiber telecommunications cables, equipment/patch cords, and connecting hardware that can support the attachment of communication devices and equipment.

Cabling system   A specific system of telecommunications cables, cords, and connecting hardware and other components that is assembled as a single system to support the connection of communication equipment and devices.

Calibration   Task of verifying that a testing device will measure and cable tests correctly. Calibration is performed against a reference signal level to ensure proper operation of the tester.

Campus   A group of buildings, such as a college, university, industrial park, or military base, having legal contiguous interconnection.

Capacitance   The tendency of an electronic component to store electrical energy. Pairs of wires in a cable tend to act as a capacitor, which has two conductors or plates that are separated by a dielectric.

Category   A classification for communication cables that describes mechanical properties and transmission characteristics of unshielded twisted-pair (UTP) cables and screened twisted-pair (ScTP) cables and assigns a unique number classification. Common category classifications include: category 3, category 4, and category 5, category 5e, and category 6.

Category 3 UTP   100-ohm unshielded twisted-pair copper cable that meets or exceeds specifications in ANSI/TIA/EIA-568-A, *Commercial*

Building Telecommunications Cabling Standard, for transmissions up to 16 megahertz (MHz).

Category 4 UTP   100-ohm unshielded twisted-pair copper cable that meets or exceeds specifications in ANSI/TIA/EIA-568-A, *Commercial Building Telecommunications Cabling Standard*, for transmissions up to 20 megahertz (MHz).

Category 5 UTP   100-ohm unshielded twisted-pair copper cable that meets or exceeds specifications in ANSI/TIA/EIA-568-A, *Commercial Building Telecommunications Cabling Standard*, for transmissions up to 100 megahertz (MHz).

Category 5e UTP   100-ohm unshielded twisted-pair copper cable that meets or exceeds specifications in ANSI/TIA/EIA-568-A-5, *Commercial Building Telecommunications Cabling Standard*, for transmissions up to 100 megahertz (MHz).

Category 6 UTP   100-ohm unshielded twisted-pair copper cable that meets or exceeds proposed specifications in the, *Commercial Building Telecommunications Cabling Standard*, for transmissions up to 250 megahertz (MHz).

Ceiling distribution system   A communication cable distribution system that utilizes the space between a suspended or drop ceiling for running and supporting communication cables.

Centralized cabling   A cabling configuration from the work area to a centralized cross-connect using pull through cables, an interconnect, or splice in the telecommunications room (TR). A cabling configuration defined in the TIA/EIA TSB-72 specification.

Certification field tester   A cable test set designed specifically to measure the electrical properties of a communication cable and to determine whether the cable's electrical properties meets minimum industry certification standards.

Channel   A path between two telecommunications devices that includes the patch cords at the device location and at the telecommunications closet. TIA/EIA TSB-67 defines a channel as up to 90 m (295 ft.) of horizontal cable with connectors, plus up to 10 m (33 ft.) of patch and equipment cords.

Characteristic impedance   Characteristic impedance is defined as the total opposition to the flow of electrons imposed by a communications cable, and it is measured in ohms. All copper communication cables have a defined characteristic impedance rating. The characteristic impedance rating for a communication cable is a function of the diameter of the cable conductors and dielectric constant of the insulation material covering the cable conductors.

Characteristic Impedance Test   Characteristic impedance test measures the resistance that opposes the flow of current. The characteristic impedance of a communication cable is a complex property of the cable's inductive, capacitive, and resistive properties. These properties are determined by the construction of the cable.

Chase nipple   A conduit fitting usually consisting of a plastic ring that is threaded onto the sharp ends of a conduit that reduces cable sheath damage during pulling operations.

Chromatic dispersion   The effect of optical pulses spreading out due to the transmission of light rays at different wavelengths.

Circuit   The electrical or optical path used for communication signals to travel between two communication devices.

Cladding   The outer concentric glass layer that surrounds the fiber core and has a lower index of refraction than the core. The portion of the optical fiber that provides total internal reflection and protects light rays from scattering.

Cleave   The process of breaking an optical fiber by a controlled fracture of the glass to obtain a fiber end that is flat, smooth, and perpendicular to the fiber core's axis.

Cleaver   A fiber optic termination tool that square-cuts the ends of glass fibers.

Closet   An enclosed building space for housing telecommunications equipment, cable terminations, and cross-connect cabling that is the recognized location of the cross-connect between the backbone and horizontal facilities. Also known as a telecommunications room (TR).

Coating   A plastic material applied on an optical fiber during the manufacturing process to protect it from the environment.

Coax   An abbreviated name for coaxial cable.

Coaxial cable   A cable consisting of a central metallic core surrounded by a layer of insulating material. This insulating (dielectric) material may be a solid material or air spaced. The entire assembly is covered with a metallic mesh or solid metallic shield and is protected by a cable jacket.

Conduit	A rigid or flexible metallic or nonmetallic raceway of circular cross-section through which cables can be pulled. A conduit can either be metallic or plastic.
Conduit stub-out	A short section of conduit that is installed from an outlet box installed in a wall. The short conduit is run from the outlet box into the ceiling space above a hallway. The conduit stub out provides a pathway for communication cables to the outlet box.
Conduit stub-up	A short section of conduit that is installed from an outlet box installed in a wall. The short conduit is run from the outlet box into the ceiling space above the wall. The conduit stub-up provides a pathway for communication cables to the outlet box.
Conduit system	Any combination of ducts, conduits, maintenance holes, handholes, and/or cable vaults joined together to form an integrated cable pathway system.
Cone	A safety marker, usually orange in color, that is used to designate a secure off limits area for nonworkers.
Connecting hardware	A device providing mechanical cable terminations. Connector A mechanical device used to provide a means for aligning, attaching, and achieving continuity between conductors or fibers. A device used to terminate a cable. Connectors may mate with other connectors in an adapter, or mate with sources and detectors in a receptacle.
Consolidation point	A location for interconnection between horizontal cables extending from building pathways and horizontal cables extending into furniture pathways.
Continuity test	A test that validates whether a cable can carry a signal, current, or light pulse without significant interruption or degradation.
Core	The light-carrying part (central region) of an optical fiber strand through which light pulses generated by a laser or LED are transmitted. It has an index of refraction higher than that of the surrounding cladding. The core is typically 50 or 62.5 micron in diameter for multimode and 9 micron for singlemode fiber.
Coupler	A device for connecting two other devices, such as connectorized cables, together. This device must provide low losses between the two cables.

Crimp	The act of clamping connectors or connector components to a cable for the purpose of securing the connector to the cable.
Cross-connect	A facility of punch down blocks that enables the termination of cable conductors their interconnection or cross-connection using jumper wires or patch cords.
Cross-connection	A connection scheme between cabling runs, subsystems, and equipment using patch cords or jumpers that attach to connecting hardware on each end.
Crossed pairs	An error condition in twisted-pair cabling where two cable pairs are crossed (terminated in the wrong position).
Crosstalk	The unwanted reception of signals on a communications channel or cable pair from another channel or cable pair. These unwanted signals are the result of an electromagnetic fields that produce a signal on the adjacent circuit or cable pair. These induced signals are strong enough to be measured and can affect communication signals traveling over adjacent circuits or cables.
Curing	A chemical process of drying epoxy glue expected over time.
Current	Flow of electrons in a conductor measured in amperes.
Cutover	The process of switching from old network cables and termination components to new network cables and termination components. This term is used when describing the switching of old cabling or communication equipment to new cabling or communication equipment.
Cutsheet	A listing of cable pair assignments used to specify desired circuit connections in a splice or cross-connect. This listing can also serve as the as-built of a splice or cross-connect field.
D	
Daisy-chained	The practice of wiring devices in a series. This is a common cabling configuration in a 10Base-2 wiring configuration.
Dark fiber	Fiber that is not in use. Fiber optic cables that are not terminated and have no light signals being transmitted through them. Excess fiber installed in anticipation of system expansion.
dBm	Decibel referenced to one milliwatt of power; 0 dBm is equal to 1 milliwatt of power.

DC loop resistance Cable conductor resistance with the far end of the cabling shorted. This is the resistance for both conductors of a coax cable (center conductor and the shield).

Dead zone A space on a fiber link where no fiber optic measurement can be made. The dead zone is related to the width of the transmitted signal pulse.

DeciBel (dB) A standard logarithmic unit for the ratio of two values of power, calculated by 10 log (P1/P2) where P1 is the power input level and P2 is the power output level. The unit of measure for relative signal strength for signals transmitted in a communication cable.

Delay skew The difference in the propagation delay between any two pairs within the same cable sheath.

Demarcation point (demarc) A point where the operational control or ownership changes for a communication circuit or service. This point is usually where the access provider's facilities stop and the customer-owned structured cabling begins at a designated demarcation point defined by the FCC part 68 standard.

Dielectric The nonconducting properties of an insulating material to resist the passage of electric current. The insulation surrounding a copper conductor is known as a dielectric.

Direct-buried cable A communications cable specifically designed to be installed under the surface of the earth and in direct contact with the soil. This cable is manufactured to protect the cable conductors from moisture damage and rodents.

Dispersion The broadening or widening of transmitted light pulses along the length of an optical fiber cable.

Divestiture The term used to describe the break up of AT&T and the bell system of companies. Divestiture broke up AT&T and its 22 telephone operating companies and reorganized into them into seven regional Bell operating companies (RBOCs).

Drain wire A noninsulated conductor placed in electrical contact with a cable shield that may be used to bond the cable shield to ground.

Dressing Placing cables into a neat and symmetrical pattern for proper alignment and positioning the cables for termination in the telecommunications room (TR).

Dressing block   A plastic connector cap that is used to hold cable conductors in a modular connector for termination.

D-ring   Wire management ring made of metal or plastic, shaped like the letter D for routing and supporting distribution cables and/or cross-connections on a plywood backboard in a telecommunications room (TR).

Drop cable   The name for a cable dropped from a main trunk cable. Sometimes called a branch cable.

E

Earth ground   An electrical connection to earth obtained by a grounding electrode system.

Effective ground   A low-resistance ground such as the power multigrounded neutral. Electrical connection to a low-resistance ground permits current to discharge to the ground without the buildup of hazardous voltages on the telecommunications cabling in the event of power contact.

Electromagnetic compatibility (EMC)   The ability of a device, equipment, or system to function satisfactorily in its electromagnetic environment without introducing intolerable electromagnetic disturbances to anything in that environment.

Electromagnetic disturbance   An electromagnetic interference that may be superimposed on a telecommunications signal.

Electromagnetic emission   The phenomenon by which electromagnetic energy emanates from a source. Emissions can be either radiated or conducted.

Electromagnetic immunity   The ability of a device, equipment, or system to perform without degradation in the presence of an electromagnetic disturbance.

Electromagnetic induction   Current flow in communications conductors produced by the coupling of a magnetic field and producing an electrical current or flow of electrons.

Electromagnetic interference (EMI)   Any electrical or electromagnetic interference that causes undesirable signals in electronic equipment. Optical fibers are immune to EMI. A more general term than radio frequency interference (RFI).

Encoding   The conversion of transmitted signals to a format suitable for reliable transmission over a communication cable.

Entrance facility (EF) An entrance to a building for both public and private network service cables that provides the entrance point at the building wall and continues to the entrance room or space.

Equal level far-end crosstalk (ELFEXT) A measure of the unwanted signal coupling from a transmitter at the near-end into a neighboring pair measured at the far-end, and normalized to the received signal level.

Equipment patch cord A cable or cable assembly used to connect telecommunications equipment to horizontal or backbone cabling.

Equipment grounding conductor The conductor used to connect the non-current carrying metal parts of equipment raceways and other enclosures to the system grounded conductor, the grounding electrode conductor, or both, at the service equipment.

Equipment room (ER) A centralized space for telecommunications equipment that serves the occupants of a building. Equipment housed in this building space is considered common equipment serving multiple users.

Exothermic weld A method of permanently bonding two metals together by a controlled heat reaction, resulting in a molecular bond.

F

F connector The 75-ohm RF connector used to terminate coaxial cables. The F connector does not have center pins. The F connector uses the solid copper center conductor of the coaxial cable itself as the center pin to establish the connection. These connectors are usually crimp connectors and are widely known as CATV connectors and are also used for video connections.

Fan out Used to describe the physical preparation of wire pairs exiting the jacketed cable to facilitate placement and termination in a splice or connecting block. A termination technique to avoid for terminating twisted pair cables.

Far-end crosstalk (FEXT) Crosstalk measured in decibels at the opposite end from which the source signal is transmitted. The unwanted reception or coupling of signals by one wire pair from another wire pair at the opposite end of a link or circuit. See near-end crosstalk (NEXT).

Ferrule A mechanical fixture, generally a rigid tube, used to confine and align the stripped end of an optical fiber into a connector.

Fiber Thin filament of glass or plastic that conducts light signals.

Fiber optics   A communications system that uses optical fiber glass or plastic as its transmission medium.

Fiber optic cable   A cable containing one or more optical fibers. Other components of the cable usually include the sheath, strength members, and buffer. The purpose of these components is to protect the fiber or fibers from mechanical and environmental damage.

Firestopping   The process of installing specialty materials into penetrations in fire-rated barriers to reestablish the integrity of the barrier.

Firestop system   A specific construction consisting of the material(s) that fill an opening in a fire-rated barrier, such as a wall or floor, and around and between any items that penetrate the wall or floor, such as cables, cable trays, conduit, ducts, pipes, and any termination devices, such as electrical outlet boxes, along with their means of support.

Fishtape   A flexible metal or fiberglass tool that can be extended from the beginning of a pathway to the other end to assist in installing a pull line or to pull in a cable.

Flexible conduit   A type of conduit, usually made of flexible metal that enables it to be bent in different directions. Flexible conduit is normally used to connect rigid pathways to other pathways where they may not join in exact alignment.

Floor plan   A scaled diagram of a building floor in plan or other structure shown as if seen from above. Floor plans are usually drawn to scale and include all of the information associated with the type of architectural view it represents.

Frequency   The measure of the number of cycles (waves) per second, expressed in hertz (Hz).

Fresnel reflection   The backscatter caused by connectors and splices. Fresnel reflections are caused by light traveling in one material and hitting a material with a different density. This causes a percentage of light to reflect back the direction it was transmitted. The amount of reflected light is determined by the change in material density. Severe changes in density occur at fiber ends and at fiber break points. Minor changes in density occur at connector and splice points.

Fusion splice   A permanent joint accomplished by applying localized heat sufficient to fuse or melt the ends of two optical fibers together, forming a continuous single fiber.

G

GANTT chart	A chart used to indicate a task associated with a job. It is generally used to check progress or delay of a project.
Gopher pole	Telescoping pole for lifting and moving cable in open ceiling distribution system.
Ground	A conducting connection, intentional or accidental, between an electrical circuit (such as telecommunications) or equipment and earth, or to some conducting body that serves in place of earth. *See* earth ground.
Grounded	Connected to earth or to some conducting body that serves in place of the earth.
Grounded conductor	A system or circuit conductor that is intentionally connected to a ground electrode. A conductor, usually a rod, pipe, or plate (or group of such conductors), in direct contact with the earth providing a connection to the earth.
Ground potential	The zero reference level used to apply and measure voltages in a system.
Grounding conductor	A conductor used to connect the grounding electrode to the building's main grounding busbar.
Grounding electrode	A conductor, such as a metal water pipe, building steel, metal frame, bare copper conductor, rod, pipe, or plate (or group of conductors), in direct contact with the earth for the purpose of providing a low-resistance connection to the earth.
Grounding electrode conductor	The conductor used to connect the grounding electrode to either the equipment grounding conductor and/or to the grounded conductor (neutral) of the circuit at the service equipment or at the source of a separately derived system.
Grounding electrode system	One or more grounding electrodes bonded to form a single reliable ground for a building. The specifications for a grounding electrode system are defined in the NEC, Article 250, Part H.
Grounding system	A system of hardware and wiring that provides an electrical path from a specified location to an earth ground point.

H

Hand trace	Physically hand trace a cable from the workstation to its termination to determine the path of the cable.

Hanger A device that is used to hold a communication cable or supporting structure in an elevated position.

Hermaphroditic connector A four-contact connector that is neither male nor female and is designed for token ring applications. This connector is used to terminate STP cables. Sometimes called a data connector.

Hertz (Hz) A unit of frequency equal to one cycle per second.

Hierarchical star An extension of the star topology utilizing a central hub. It is the required topology for structured cabling backbone systems in buildings and in campus environments.

High pair-count cable Cables consisting of multipair conductors formed into binder groups of 25 pairs. Sometime called a multipair backbone cable.

Horizontal cable Cables that run from the telecommunications room (TR) to a work area location. It may be installed in either a horizontal or vertical plane.

Horizontal cabling The cabling between and including the work area telecommunications outlet/connector and the horizontal cross-connect (HC) in the telecommunications room (TR).

Horizontal cross-connect (HC) A cross-connect of horizontal cabling to backbone cabling in the telecommunications room (TR).

Hybrid cable An assembly of two or more cables, of the same or different types or categories, covered by one overall sheath. Also referred to as a bundled cable.

I

Impedance A unit of measure, expressed in Ohms, of the total opposition that a circuit offers to the flow of current.

Impulse noise Discrete noise spikes that occur on a regular or irregular basis having random amplitude and spectral content. Noise that is measured on a communication cable from environmental or other system energy.

Index-matching gel A material used at optical fiber interconnections or mechanical splices that has a refractive index close to that of the fiber core; used to reduce reflections from the residual air gap between two optical fiber cables.

Index of refraction The ratio of the velocity of propagation of an electromagnetic wave in a vacuum to the velocity in a given transmitting medium.

Inductance   The opposition to change in current flow in an alternating current (ac) circuit.

Inductive amplifier   Test device used to detect a signal placed on a cable for the purpose of tracing and identification. Sometimes referred to as a wand, amplifier, or probe.

Infrared   The electromagnetic spectrum having wavelengths between 0.75 to 1 mm. A light spectrum used to transmit control or communication signals. A light spectrum that is not visible to the naked eye.

Infrastructure   Permanently installed cable plant and cable-supporting components.

In-line splice   A type of copper splice where the cable enters one endcap and, after splicing the cable, exits the other endcap of the closure.

Innerduct   A nonmetallic raceway (conduit) placed within a larger raceway (usually conduit) to support and protect optical fiber cables.

Insertion loss   The loss resulting from the insertion of a device in a transmission line, expressed as the reciprocal of the ratio of the signal power delivered to that part of the line following the device to the signal power delivered to that same part before insertion.

Insulation   The material that physically separates wires and prevents electrical conductivity.

Insulation displacement connection (IDC)   A wire termination technology that penetrates the insulation of a copper wire when it is being punched-down into a metal contact, creating a gas tight contact.

Interbuilding backbone   A backbone network providing communications between more than one building on a campus.

Interbuilding backbone cable   Cable that runs between buildings in a campus environment. Commonly called campus cabling or customer owned outside plant (OSP) cabling.

Interconnection   A connection scheme that provides for the direct connection of a cable to another cable or to an equipment cable without a patch cord or jumper.

Intermediate cross-connect (IC)   The connection point between a backbone cable that extends from the main cross-connect (MC) (first-level backbone) and the backbone cable from the horizontal cross-connect (HC) (second-level backbone).

Intrabuilding backbone A backbone cable or pathway within a building.

Intrabuilding backbone cable Cable that runs between telecommunications rooms (TRs) inside of a commercial building. The cables can be installed vertically or horizontally in physical orientation. These cables connect TRs together in the building.

J

Jacket The outer layer of a cable. Sometimes called the cable sheath.

Jackstand A device for holding a large cable reel off the floor so the cable reel can spin freely as the cable is being installed.

J-hook A cable-supporting device for horizontal cables that is shaped like the letter *J*. This device is attached to some building structures. Horizontal cables are laid in the opening formed by the *J* to provide support for the cables.

Job change order A written request from the customer, another contractor, a subcontractor, or other person or company on the project to add, delete, or change some work operation on the project. This document must be signed by the customer prior to starting the work described therein.

Job plan A comprehensive outline of all aspects of the project. It includes all work operations and scheduling, how and when the work is to be performed, how each aspect of the work will affect the remaining areas, and how the work will fit into the general contractor's construction schedule.

Job site The physical location where work is to be performed during the installation of a telecommunications system.

Jumper A cable pair or an assembly of twisted pairs without connectors, used to join telecommunications circuits/links at the cross-connect. Sometimes called a jumper wire.

Jumper wire Typically, 24 AWG twisted-pair wire terminated on type 66 or other types of termination blocks. Used to join telecommunications feeder and backbone cables to other backbone or horizontal cables at a cross-connect facility or location.

K

Key system   An electronic telephone system where telephones have multiple buttons permitting the user to manually select outgoing or incoming central office phone lines. The system can operate using unshielded twisted-pair (UTP) category 3, 4, or 5 cabling.

Keyed   A jack, outlet, or connector is considered keyed when it requires a specific orientation in order to insert the connector plug into an outlet. Prevents mismating incompatible cables or communication devices together.

Keying   The mechanical feature of a connector system that guarantees correct orientation of a connection or prevents the connection to a jack or to an optical fiber adapter of the same type intended for another purpose.

L

Labor list   A complete list of all major units of labor to be employed on the project.

Ladder rack   A cable-supporting device used in a telecommunications room (TR). This device is similar to a cable tray but more closely resembles a single section of a ladder. It is constructed of metal with two sides affixed to horizontal cross-members.

Laser diode   Laser transmitter for optical fiber applications. Laser diodes produce brighter light signals and provide higher performance than LEDs. Laser diodes are also more expensive than LEDs. Laser diodes are commonly used with singlemode fiber.

Lashing   Attachment of a communication cable (copper or optical fiber) to a supporting cable by wrapping thin steel or dielectric strands about them.

Launch cable   Length of optical fiber cable used to condition the launch of the transmitted light pulse.

Legend   A definition of symbols used on a blueprint.

Light amplification by stimulated emission of radiation (LASER)   A device that produces coherent, highly directional light with a narrow range of wavelengths used in a transmitter to convert information from electric to optical form.

Light-emitting diode (LED)	A semiconductor diode that spontaneously emits incoherent light from the p-n junction when forward current is applied. It converts information from electrical to optical form. A LED typically has a large spectral width. LEDs give moderate performance at lower prices than laser diodes. LEDs are commonly used with multimode fiber in data enterprise and industrial applications.
Light source	A piece of test equipment used to create a light stable light source for testing optical fiber cable.
Link	A transmission path between two points, not including terminal equipment, work area cables, and equipment cables.
Local exchange carrier (LEC)	The telecommunications company that provides public switched network access service for local phone service.
Loop	In telephone systems, the wire pair that connects the customer to the switching equipment in the central office. This path is called a loop because it is generally two wires electrically tied together through the customer terminal set when the customer goes off hook.
Loop diversity	The placing of alternate facilities to back up the main system in case of failure.
Loop resistance	A measurement of the resistance of both conductors in a pair of conductors connected in a series.
Loose tube	A type of optical fiber cable construction where one or more fibers are laid loosely in a larger tube.
Loose-tube fiber	Optical cable constructed of fiber strands individually covered with a 250 μm primary buffer coating, usually encased in bundles of 6 or 12 strands.
Loss	Attenuation of a communication signal (electrical or optical), usually measured in decibels (dB).
Loss budget	The total allowable loss between source and detector allocated among fiber, connectors, splices, and safety margin.
Loss resolution	Setting on an optical time domain reflectometer (OTDR) to determine data points.
Low intensity laser	Also known as a hot red light, this device operates in the visible light range. It is used to identify individual fibers and will glow red at the point of a fiber break.

M

Macrobend
The bending of an optical fiber cable causing signal loss. Results in greater stress, leading to shorter lifetime. At a smaller radius, it may lead to extra attenuation.

Main building ground electrode
The designated point to which all utilities in a building are connected as a single ground point to earth.

Main cross-connect (MC)
The cross-connect normally located in the (main) equipment room for cross-connection and interconnection of entrance cables, first level backbone cables, and equipment cables.

Mandrel
A rod or a shaft.

Manhole (MH)
A hole through which a person may go to gain access to an underground or enclosed structure. This term is being replaced by the term maintenance hole.

Materials list
A complete list of all materials to be ordered and received for the project.

Measured tape
A calibrated tape used to measure and pull lengths of conduits.

Measurement resolution
Setting on the optical time domain reflectometer (OTDR) to determine spacing of data points.

Mechanical splicing
Mechanical splicing is the joining of two cleaned and cleaved optical fibers with a mechanical splice component. The mechanical splice component is a device that is designed to accept two optical fibers and splice the two optical fibers together. The mechanical splice mechanism is designed to align the two optical fibers and hold them together.

Media
Wire, cable, or conductors used to transmit communication signals from communication devices.

Megabits per second (Mb/s)
A unit of measure used to express the data transfer rate of a system, device, or communications channel.

Megahertz (MHz)
A unit of frequency equal to 1 million Hertz (Hz).

Megger
A device that can be used to measure electrical resistance in a grounding system.

Mesh grip
A device attached to the end of a cable to facilitate pulling the cable. Attaches to the cable jacket and tightens around the cable jacket as the end of the grip is pulled.

Microbend	Imperfections in the glass core of an optical fiber cable. Usually the result of the cable construction. Results in increased attenuation.
Micron (μ)	One millionth of a meter (0.000001 meter). Also denoted micrometer. Abbreviation is μm.
Modal dispersion	The spreading out of light pulses resulting from the different optical path lengths in a multimode fiber.
Mode	A ray or path of light in a multimode or singlemode optical fiber cable.
Modem	An acronym for modulator/demodulator. A modulator-demodulator device that converts between analog signals and digital signals for transmission over telephone networks.
Modular connector	Modular, multipair connector consisting of a base, body, and cover.
Modular furniture	Groups of low-wall partitions, desks, and furniture assembled in the field in open spaces within an office.
Modular jack	A female telecommunications connector that may be keyed or unkeyed and may have six or eight contact positions, but not all the positions need be equipped with jack contacts.
Modular plug	A male telecommunications connector for cable or cords that may be keyed or unkeyed and may have six or eight contact positions, but not all the positions need be equipped with contacts. Sometimes called an ice cube.
Modulation	A process whereby certain characteristics of a wave, often called the carrier, are varied or selected in accordance with a modulating function. This includes amplitude, frequency, or phase, and other modulation techniques. The carrier is the modular to carry information.
Multimeter	Test equipment that can be set up to perform a variety of electrical property measurements, usually including resistance, voltage, and current.
Multimode optical fiber	A graded-index or step-index optical fiber cable that supports the propagation of more than one bound light mode. Typical core/cladding sizes are 50/125 μm and 62.5/125 μm.
Multiuser telecommunications outlet assembly (MUTOA)	A group of telecommunications outlets that are arranged together in a single assembly housing. They may be located within the confines of a group of modular, low-wall, partitioned furniture and serve only that group. A line cord is

extended from the MUTOA to the work area contained by the modular partitions and is plugged directly into a device at that location.

Mushroom	A plastic cable-supporting device in the shape of a mushroom, used for routing jumper wires on a backboard in a telecommunications room (TR).
Mutual capacitance	Effective capacitance between the two conductors of a pair.

N

Nanometer (nm)	A unit of measurement equal to 1 billionth of a meter, abbreviated nm. The most common unit of measurement for optical fiber operating wavelengths.
National Electrical Code® (NEC)	A safety code written and administered by the National Fire Protection Association (NFPA®).
National Fire Protection Association (NFPA)	This association writes and administers the National Electrical Code (NEC).
N-connector	Used as a connector for RG-8A/U, Thicknet, and RG-11U coaxial cables. N-type connectors are used at the ends of these coaxial cables. These connectors have a center pin that must be installed over the cable's center conductor.
Near-end crosstalk (NEXT)	The unwanted signal transfer between pairs at the near end of a cable nearest the point of transmission.
Noise	Unwanted signal on a wire that provides a random or persistent disturbance that interferes with the clarity or quality of the expected signal.
Nominal velocity of propagation (NVP)	Refers to the speed or velocity of the signal traveling inside of a cable relative to the speed of light in a vacuum.
Nonreflective break	A cut or break in a fiber cable that may shatter so that the angle at which the light hitting the end may not reflect at all.
Numerical aperture (NA)	A number that expresses the light-gathering ability of a fiber. The NA defines the maximum angle to the fiber axis at which light will be accepted and propagated through the fiber core.

O

Occupational Safety and Health Administration (OSHA)	This U.S. agency develops and enforces safety and health standards that apply to work conditions, practices, means, methods, operations, installations, and processes performed in U.S. workplaces.

Offset	Degree to which the cable or conduit changes direction.
Ohm	Unit of measurement for the opposition to the flow of current, called resistance. The abbreviation for an ohm is Ω.
Ohm's law	The relationship of voltage, amperage, or resistance in any circuit can be determined by using the formula for Ohm's law. If two of these values are known, the third can be determined. The formula for Ohms law can be expressed using any of the following equations: $V = I \cdot R$, or $R = V / I$, or $I = V / R$ Where: V = voltage, I = current flow (amperes), and R = resistance.
Ohm-meter	A device used to measure voltage and resistance.
Open	A break in the continuity of a circuit, preventing signal from traveling over the transmission medium.
Open office	An area of floor space with division provided by furniture, moveable partitions, or other temporary means instead of by building walls.
Open office cabling	The cabling that distributes from the telecommunications room (TR) to the open office area utilizing a consolidation point (CP) or multiuser telecommunications outlet assembly (MUTOA).
Optical fiber	Transmission medium using glass or plastic to transmit pulse light signals. Its bandwidth is higher than copper and is not subject to EMI. The optical fiber consists of a central core consisting of either glass or plastic and an outer cladding.
Optical fiber cable	Cable made up of one or more strands of optical fiber, strength members, and an outer jacket.
Optical fiber cladding	The outer layer of glass surrounding the light-carrying core of the optical fiber. It has a lower refractive index than the core, which serves to confine and refract the light into the core.
Optical fiber core	The central part of an optical fiber that is used to carry the light pulses, made of glass or plastic.
Optical fiber duplex adapter	A mechanical cable termination device designed to align and join two duplex optical fiber connectors.
Optical fiber duplex connection	Mated assembly of two duplex optical fiber connectors and a duplex adapter.
Optical fiber flashlight	A device utilizing a light-emitting diode (LED) to check for fiber continuity.

Optical power meter A fiber optic test device that measures the strength of light signals leaving an optical fiber cable. This device measures in decibel milliwatts (dBm) the strength of a light wave over a fiber cable.

Optical time domain reflectometer (OTDR) A device for measuring optical fibers based on detecting backscattered (reflected) light. Used to measure attenuation of fiber, splices, connectors, and locate faults. It can be used as a measure of splices and connector locations.

Outside plant (OSP) Telecommunications infrastructure designed for installation outside of or between buildings. Also called interbuilding backbone cable.

Outlet box A metallic or nonmetallic box mounted within a wall, floor, or ceiling used to hold telecommunications outlets/connectors or transition devices.

Outlet/connector Mechanical cable termination device for horizontal cables. Installed in the work area.

Outside plant Telecommunications infrastructure designed for installation exterior to buildings.

P

Pair Two insulated wires twisted around each other to form a cable unit.

Pair count Indicates how many pair of wires are in a cable or the pair identification serving a location.

Pair scanner A simple cable testing device for checking the continuity of cable pairs.

Pair twists The uniform twist of an insulated copper pair that helps to improve the effects of capacitance imbalance and electromagnetic induction. Higher performance cables have greater pair twists compared to low performance cables.

Passive cross-connect A facility enabling the termination of cable elements and their interconnection or cross-connection by means of jumpers or patch cords.

Patch cord A length of cable with connector plugs on one or both ends used to join telecommunications links at the cross-connect or at the work area connecting the outlet to the station equipment.

Patch panel   A connecting hardware device consisting of multiple jacks that facilitates cable termination and cabling administration using patch cords.

Pathway   A sequence of cable-supporting structures that provides the route for communication cables to be installed between devices on a network or between networks on an internetwork.

Payout box   A container for communication cables. The container has a hole for cable distribution directly from the box.

Pedestal   A protective above-ground enclosure used most commonly to house a splice point or administrative terminal location.

Penetrations   Openings made in fire-rated barriers. There are two kinds of penetrations: 1. Membrane penetrations pierce or interrupt the outside surface of only one side of a fire-rated barrier; 2. Through-penetrations completely transmit a fire-rated barrier, piercing both outside surfaces of the barrier.

Personal protective equipment (PPE)   Any number of safety devices or apparatuses worn or used that shields against possible injury while performing tasks. Examples include: goggles, gloves, or clothing.

PERT chart   A network chart or logic diagram. Generally used by the project manager to see how one change in the project affects the remaining tasks. The PERT chart defines the critical path for the project.

Photon   A fundamental unit of light. Photons are to optical fiber what electrons are to copper wires.

Physical topology   The physical layout of a network as defined by its cabling architecture, as opposed to the logical topology that is the path that the signal travels.

Picofarad   One-trillionth of a farad. Used to designate capacitance unbalance between pairs and capacitance unbalance of the two wires of a pair to ground.

Pigtail   A copper or optical fiber cable that has a factory-installed connector on one end and no connector on the other. The unterminated end is connected to another cable.

Pinout   A wiring scheme for the individual conductors in a telecommunications connector/outlet.

Plaster ring   A metal or plastic plate that attaches to a wallboard for the purpose of mounting a telecommunications outlet box.

Plastic insulated conductor (PIC)	A conductor that is insulated with a plastic material.
Plenum	A designated area, closed or open, used for transport of environmental air, as part of the air distribution system. Because it is part of the air distribution system, cables installed in this space require a plenum fire rating such as MPP, CMP, or OFNP.
Plenum cable	A cable with flammability and smoke characteristics that enable it to be routed in a plenum area without being enclosed in a conduit, meeting the flammability requirements of Underwriters Laboratory (UL) as defined by the National Electrical Code (NEC).
Plenum rated	Meeting the flammability requirements of Underwriters Laboratory (UL) as defined by the National Electrical Code (NEC).
Point of demarcation (demarc)	A point at which two services may interface and identify the division of responsibility. An example would be the point inside a commercial building where the location service provider stops and the customer's cabling begins.
Point-to-point	A direct connection established between two specific locations, as between two buildings or devices.
Poke-thru	A penetration through the fire-rated floor structure to permit the installation of communications cables.
Poke-thru system	A systemic approach to penetrations through a fire rated floor structure to permit the installation of horizontal telecommunications cables.
Polyvinyl chloride (PVC)	A tough, nonflammable, water-resistant insulator on the individual wires of a communication cable.
Power pole	Correctly termed a utility column. It is a vertical pathway used to support cables that run from above a drop ceiling to the termination location in a work area.
Power sum near end cross talk (PS NEXT)	A measure of the total crosstalk energy that can be measured on a nonactive cable pair when more than one pair is active or being used simultaneously. Power sum is a formula that totals the crosstalk energy being contributed by each active pair on a nonactive pair measured on the same end of the cable as the transmitted signals.

Power sum equal level far-end crosstalk loss (PS ELFEXT)	A computation of the unwanted signal coupling from multiple transmitters at the near-end into a pair measured at the far-end and normalized to the received signal level.
Power sum near-end crosstalk loss (PS NEXT)	A computation of the unwanted signal coupling from multiple transmitters at the near-end into a pair measured at the near-end.
Prefusing	The process of applying an electrical charge to the end of two optical fibers for the purpose of cleaning them prior to performing a fusion splice.
Premises	A generic term that includes a building or set of buildings on common property that are owned by a single tenant or landlord.
Premises wiring	A generic term that includes interbuilding, intrabuilding, and horizontal cabling that is owned by a single tenant or landlord.
Prime contractor	The master contractor on a job site that may be serviced by several general contractors.
Project log	A written log of everything that happens on a project, hour-by-hour, day-by-day, and item-by-item. It should contain any information relating to events that occur on the project that can affect the project. The project manager or job foreman usually maintains this log.
Project schedule	A chronological order of events that will be accomplished on a project and in the order that they must occur. This device can be manually generated on paper or can be developed using any of the software packages available on the market.
Propagation delay	Propagation delay is defined as the amount of time needed for a transmitted signal to travel over a single pair of a communication cable. Because propagation delay measures the actual signal travel time, the propagation delay of a cable will increase as the length of the cable increases.
Proposal	An offer of services or resources, usually in exchange for other services or monies.
Protector	A device used to limit damaging foreign voltages on metallic telecommunications conductors.
Pull	The act of placing cable in a building or cable pathway by pulling.

Pull box (PB)   A device to access a raceway used to facilitate placing of wire or cables.

Pull cord   A cord or wire placed within a raceway and used to pull wire and cable through the raceway.

Pull point   Location where it is possible to physically access the cables to pull them.

Pull rope   A rope attached to large communication cables or between a pull string and a cable. Used to obtain an increased amount of strength for pulling or moving high-pair-count cable.

Pull strength   The pulling force that can be applied to a cable without affecting specified characteristics for the cable.

Pull string   Line attached to a cable to pull it through conduit trays or open ceiling supports.

Pulling eye   A factory-installed device on a length of cable to which a swivel eye and pull rope are attached.

Pulling sheave   A pulley having a grooved rim for retaining a rope or cable.

Pulling technique   Collectively refers to the methods and materials employed to install cables.

Punch down   The process of terminating copper cable conductors on insulation displacement connection (IDC) terminals by use of a handheld punch down tool.

Q

Quad cable   A four-conductor nontwisted pair cable with a red, green, black, and yellow conductor. Used extensively before twisted-pair cable.

Quote   A response to a request for price of services and/or materials.

R

Raceway   Any enclosed channel designed for holding wires, cables, or busbars.

Rack   Also called communication rack. A hardware device used to support patch panels, punch down blocks, and communication devices.

Radio frequency interference (RFI)   A disturbance in the reception of radio and other electromechanical signals due to conflict with undesired signals.

Rat   Lightweight object that can be sent into a conduit to aid in installing a pull string.

Rayleigh scattering   Rayleigh scattering is the backscatter caused by small particles in the optical fiber cable. This scatter is constant along the entire length of the cable. Optical attenuation due to scattering from small fluctuations in the index of refraction. These may be due to the molecular structure and variations in that structure.

Rearrangement   An action taken to replace, add, adapt, or remove existing premises wiring system components.

Receiver, optical (RX)   An optoelectronic circuit that converts an optical signal to an electrical signal. It contains a photo detector, amplifier, discriminator, and pulse-shaping electronics.

Record drawing (as-built)   A plan on paper that graphically documents and illustrates the installed telecommunications infrastructure in a building or portion thereof.

Reel brake   A device used to control the rate of removal of a cable from a cable reel.

Reel dolly   A jackstand with wheels used to assist in carrying out and paying out cable.

Reflection   The abrupt change in direction of light as it travels from one material into a dissimilar material. In optical fibers, some of the light at a core-air interface is reflected back to the source. A critical phenomenon for optical time domain reflectometer (OTDR) operation.

Reflective break   The amount of reflection at the location of a break.

Reflection coefficient   The degree of reflection caused by a mismatch between the line and the load or between two cables connected together.

Refraction   The angular change in direction of a beam of light at an interface between two dissimilar media or a medium whose refractive index is a continuous function of position (graded index medium).

Refractive index   The ratio of the velocity of light in a vacuum to the velocity of light in a given material.

Relay rack   A vertical metallic frame that is equipped with threaded holes that will accept screws at a predefined spacing on the front and rear of the rack. They are used to mount termination hardware, electronic equipment, or a combination of both.

They can be floor-mounted (free standing) or wall-mounted. They are generally available in 0.6 m (2 ft.), 1 m (3 ft.), 1.2 m (4 ft.), 2 m (6.5 ft.), and 2.1 m (7 ft.) heights.

Request for proposal (RFP) A detailed document of requested services and equipment of a buyer submitted to others for responses.

Request for quotation (RFQ) A document that solicits quotes for telecommunications projects or equipment and provides vendors with all the information necessary to prepare a quote.

Resistance Resistance is a property of a copper communication cable's conductors. Resistance is a term that indicates the amount of opposition of a given conductor to the flow of electricity. Resistance in a communication conductor results in heat being generated. Resistance is expressed in a measurement called ohms. One ohm of resistance enables one ampere of current to flow through a conductor when one volt of electricity is supplied.

Resistance unbalance The difference in resistance, expressed in ohms, between the conductors of a pair. May also be expressed in terms of percentage by the ratio of unbalance in ohms to the lowest conductor resistance.

Retrofitting To modify systems that are already in service using parts made available after the time of original installation.

Return loss Return loss is a measure of the reflected energy caused by impedance mismatches in the cabling system. Impedance mismatches occur on a communication cable link when the termination impedance (component impedance) does not exactly match the characteristic impedance of the cable. The resulting impedance discontinuity creates a bias in the link.

Reversed pair When the tip and ring wires of a cable pair are crossed.

Rigging A system of ropes or pulleys used to move material and equipment.

Ring A means for identification of one conductor of a pair. Historically associated with the wire connected to the ring portion of an operator's telephone plug.

Ringing tool A device used to remove cable sheaths.

Riser cable Obsolete term, replaced by backbone cable. Cables intended for use in vertical shafts between floors in a building.

S

Safety margin	A power loss (dB) value used to assure optical fiber cable performance criteria will be satisfied over the life of the network. Includes expected losses in source power, splice losses, and wear and tear of the optical fiber connectors.
SC	A type of optical fiber connector identified by the square cross-section of its plastic housing. The type of fiber optic connector required for new installation by the ANSI/TIA/EIA-568-A standard.
Scanner	A device that checks cables for opens, shorts, crossed pairs, and sometimes, cable length; however, it does not measure cable performance.
Scattering	A property of a fiber that causes light to deflect from the fiber contributing to losses.
Screen	An element of a cable formed by a shield surrounding the cable conductors. A foil shield surrounding the cable pairs located inside the cable jacket.
Screened twisted-pair cable (ScTP)	A cable with one or more pairs of twisted copper conductors covered with an overall metallic shield and insulating jacket.
Scribe tool	A fiber optic tool used to score an optical fiber so it can be cleanly cut and removed for a fiber optic connector.
Section throw	Splicing of a new section of cable at both ends into an existing cable plant.
Segment	A portion of a network sharing an electrically continuous length of cable.
Sheath	The outer covering of a cable. Also called the cable jacket.
Shield	Metallic layer placed around a conductor or group of conductors to prevent electrostatic or electromagnetic coupling between the enclosed wires and external fields.
Shield (screen)	A metallic layer placed around a conductor or group of conductors.
Shielded twisted-pair (STP) cable	Cable made up of two twisted copper pairs with an additional metallic shield covering individual pairs. Both shield cable pairs are surrounded by a braided shield. The entire assembly is covered with an insulating sheath (cable jacket).

Short   A low-resistance contact between conductors of a circuit. Two wires are connected ahead of where they should be connected in a circuit.

Shorting bar   An element in a STP data connector that maintains continuity of the ring after removal of a hermaphroditic connector. The shorting bar connects pairs 1 and 2 together after the connector is disconnected.

Shorting plug   A device to create a direct-connect between two or more conductors at one end of a cable for test purposes.

Signal generator   Test equipment that generates a distinctive tone(s) that is placed on a cable pair for identification purposes. Sometimes referred to as a toner.

Signal-to-noise ratio (SNR)   The ratio between the detected signal power and noise in a receiver, expressed in decibels (dB). The prime determining factor in bit error rate (BER). *See* bit error rate.

Simplex signaling   A signaling method in which data transfer can take place in only one direction. *See* full-duplex signaling and half-duplex signaling.

Sine wave   The variation of a wave from zero to maximum (positive), back through zero to minimum, and back to zero (negative).

Sleeve   An opening, usually circular through a wall, ceiling, or floor with a metal or nonmetalic conduit inserted to allow the passage of cables.

Slot   An opening (usually rectangular) through a wall, floor, or ceiling to allow the passage of cables and wires.

Space   An area used for housing the installation and termination of telecommunications equipment and cables. Common building spaces include: telecommunications room (TR), equipment room (ER), and entrance facility (EF).

Spike   An instantaneous surge of energy on a cable or wire.

Spine cable tray   Open tray with a central rigid spine with cable support ribs along the length at 90° angles.

Splice   The permanent or temporary joining of conductors from different cables.

Splice bank   Placement of 25-pair modules in a symmetrically spaced configuration within a splice enclosure.

Splice box	A box, located in a pathway run, intended to house a cable splice.
Splice case	A metal or plastic housing with a semicyclindrical cavity used in identical pairs to clamp around a cable splice to provide a closure.
Splice closure	A device used to protect a cable or splice.
Splice tray	A container used to organize and protect splices and spliced fibers.
Splicing	The permanent joining of bare copper conductors or fiber strands to another cable.
Splicing head	A section of a splicing rig that supports the crimp head. It can be either single or dual head.
Splicing rig	A specific manufacturer's tool kit for terminating modular splice connectors.
Split grip	A wire mesh grip that is open on one side.
Split pairs	When the physical pairs are separated, but pair continuity is maintained.
ST	A straight tip fiber optic connector. A type of optical fiber connector identified by its bayonet housing. The housing may be metallic or plastic.
Star topology	A topology in which telecommunications cables are installed from a central point to each work location.
Station	Telecommunications end-user location. Usually dedicated to a single-user location and function such as a telephone or computer hook-up work area outlet.
Step-index fiber	An optical fiber, either multimode or singlemode, in which the core refractive index is uniform throughout so that a sharp step in refractive index occurs at the core-to-cladding interface.
STP-A	A high performance shielded twisted-pair cable consisting of two individual shielded pairs capable of supporting transmission to 300 megahertz (MHz).
Strand	A single string of wire used to make up a larger wire or cable by twisting a number of strands together. Galvanized steel stranded cable is used as support strand and guy wires. Support strand is listed by strength. For example, a 6M strand is rated at 6,000 pounds of strength.

Strength member That part of an optical fiber cable composed of aramid yarn, steel strands, fiberglass filaments, or a fiberglass-reinforced epoxy composite rod that increases the tensile strength of the cable.

Structural return loss Measurement of the distance between the test signal amplitude and the amplitude of the signal reflections returned by the cable.

Stub-out Conduit installed from a wall outlet to a raceway. It provides physical and electrical protection for communication cables to an outlet box.

Support strand (messenger wire) A strength element used to carry the weight of the telecommunications cable usually installed for aerial cables.

Surface mounted raceway Plastic or metallic raceway that is installed on the surface of a wall, floor, or ceiling for supporting communication cables.

Surge arrestor A device used to prevent transient voltage surges from reaching electronic equipment.

Susceptibility The inability of a device, equipment, or system to resist an electromagnetic disturbance.

Suspended ceiling A ceiling that creates an area or space between the ceiling material and the structure above.

Sweep Bend that has a gentle arc rather than a sharp bend.

T

Telecommunications Any transmission, emission, and reception of signs, signals, writings, images, and sounds. Information of any nature by cable, radio, optical, or other electromagnetic systems.

Telecommunications grounding busbar (TGB) The single grounding point for all communications equipment, cabling, and cable-supporting structure devices in a telecommunications room (TR). The TGB must be installed inside each TR. Each TGB must be connected to the TMGB using the TBB.

Telecommunications bonding backbone (TBB) A conductor that interconnects the telecommunications main grounding busbar (TMGB) to the telecommunications grounding busbar (TGB).

Telecommunications room (TR) An enclosed space for housing telecommunications equipment, cable terminations, and cross-connects. The TR is the recognized cross-connect between the backbone cable and horizontal cabling.

Telecommunications Industry Association (TIA)	A standards association that publishes telecommunications criteria.
Telecommunications main grounding busbar (TMGB)	A busbar placed in a convenient and accessible location and bonded, by means of the bonding conductor for telecommunications, to the building service equipment (power) ground.
Temporary cabling	Cables and equipment that are installed to provide service on a temporary basis for short-term equipment locations.
Termination	The connection of cable pairs to cable-connecting hardware components.
Termination hardware	The components used to terminate communication cable pairs.
Termination point	A cable connection point, such as a terminal block, wall plate, or unshielded twisted-pair (UTP) modular plug.
Termination position	A discrete element of connecting hardware where telecommunications conductors are terminated.
Terminator	An impedance matching component or connector placed at the end of a coaxial cable installed in a bus topology.
Thicknet	An IEEE specification for an 802.3 Ethernet network using thick 50-ohm coaxial cable.
Thinnet	An IEEE specification for an 802.3 Ethernet network using thin 50-ohm coaxial cable.
Through penetration	A continuous opening that passes through both surfaces of a fire-rated barrier.
Tie wraps	Plastic or hook and loop strips used for binding and dressing cable.
Tight buffer	A cable construction where each fiber is tightly buffered by a protective thermoplastic coating to a diameter of 900 microns.
Tight-buffered cable	Type of cable construction whereby each glass fiber is tightly buffered by a protective thermoplastic coating to a diameter of 900 micrometers. The tight buffer provides ease of handling and makes connectorization easier.
Time domain reflectometer (TDR)	A device that sends a signal down a cable, then measures the magnitude and the amount of time required for the reflection of that signal to return. TDRs are used to measure the length of cables as well as locate cable faults.

Toner	A device used to apply an electrical signal to a circuit to assist in cable or circuit identification.
Trade size	Nominal name given to materials to identify a nominal size.
Transition point	Location of a change in facilities or means. Used to transition round horizontal cable to flat cable.
Transmission media	The physical carriers of electromagnetic energy (such as copper, fiber, and air) radiation.
Transmitter (TX)	An optoelectronic circuit that converts an electrical logic signal to an optical signal. In fiber optics, using a source such as light-emitting diode (LED) or laser.
Trapeze	A cable-supporting device using a threaded rod and channel stock to hold up cable trays and conduits.
Trench	A furrow dug into the earth for the direct placement of direct-buried cable. A duct installed under the floor of a building.
Trench duct	An interior or exterior trough embedded in concrete that has removable cover plates that are level with the top of the surrounding surface.
Tugger	Device that acts as an assist mechanism for advancing a cable or groups of cables during installation.
Twisted-pair	Two individually insulated copper wires physically twisted together. Each wire pair acts as a single telecommunications path.
Twisted-pair cable	A multiconductor cable comprising of two or more copper conductors twisted in a manner designed to cancel electrical interference.

U

Underfloor raceway	A pathway placed within the floor and from which wires and cables are installed from the telecommunications room (TR) to work area locations on a floor.
Underground	Any conduit or maintenance hole spaces installed below the surface of the ground.
Underground cable	A telecommunications cable designed to be installed under the surface of the earth in a trough or duct that isolates the cable from direct contact with the soil.

Underwriters Laboratory (UL)	A U.S.-based independent testing laboratory that sets safety tests and standards for electrical equipment.
Unshielded twisted-pair (UTP)	Cable containing one or more pairs of twisted copper covered by a cable jacket. These cables do not have a metallic cable shield.
Usable floor space	Floor space that is capable of being used as a work area.
Utility column	An enclosed pathway extending from the ceiling to furniture or to the floor that forms a pathway for electrical wiring, telecommunications cable, or both.
Utility pole	An enclosed pathway extending from the ceiling to furniture or to the floor, that forms a pathway for electrical wiring, telecommunications cable, or both.
Utility tunnel	An enclosed passageway, usually placed between buildings, for the distribution of utility services.

V

Vault	Also called a maintenance hole.
Velocity of propagation	The speed of transmission along a cable relative to the speed of light in a vacuum.
V-groove	Position in a fusion splicer where fiber strand is placed.
Volt	A unit of electromotive force or potential difference that will cause a current of one ampere to flow through a resistance of one ohm.
Volt ohm-meter (VOM)	An instrument used to measure electrical characteristics.

W

Wall mount brackets	Support devices that are constructed at a right angle, having a diagonal brace between the vertical section and the horizontal section, and mounted to a wall. They support sections of conduits, ladder racks, cable tray shelving, equipment racks, or equipment.
Wand	Test device used to detect a signal placed on a cable for the purpose of identification. Also called an induction amplifier.
Wavelength	The length of a wave measured from any point on one wave to the corresponding point on the next wave, such as from crest to crest.
Wire	An individually insulated solid or stranded metallic conductor.

Wire management	Components placed on racks or walls to support the routing of cables.
Wire map tester	An instrument used to determine circuit opens, shorts, crossed pairs, improper wiring, and the determination of proper pin configuration; additionally, some units indicate cable length.
Wiring closet	*See* telecommunications closet.
Wireway	A supported pathway for cables.
Work area	A building space where the occupants interact with telecommunications terminal equipment.
Work area cable	A cable connecting the telecommunications outlet/connector to the terminal equipment.
Work area outlets	A device placed at user workstations for the termination of horizontal media.
Workstation	A telecommunications device used in communicating with another telecommunications device.

Z

Zero-dispersion wavelength	Wavelength at which the chromatic dispersion of an optical fiber is zero. Occurs when waveguide dispersion cancels out material dispersion.
Z-gap	Spacing in fusion splicing.
Zone cabling	*See* open office cabling.

REFERENCES

ANSI Information Infrastructure Standards Panel, Information Infrastructure Glossary

BICSI Telecommunications Dictionary, 1999

Federal Standard 1037C, Telecommunications Glossary, 1996

CTech Solutions Telecommunications Dictionary

Global Technologies Inc. Glossary

Lantronix Glossary

Federal Communications Commission, A Glossary of Telecommunications Terms

INDEX

▼ **B**

C

▼ J–K

▼ L

▼ M

▼ N

O

Q–R

INTERNATIONAL CONTACT INFORMATION

AUSTRALIA
McGraw-Hill Book Company Australia Pty. Ltd.
TEL +61-2-9417-9899
FAX +61-2-9417-5687
http://www.mcgraw-hill.com.au
books-it_sydney@mcgraw-hill.com

CANADA
McGraw-Hill Ryerson Ltd.
TEL +905-430-5000
FAX +905-430-5020
http://www.mcgrawhill.ca

GREECE, MIDDLE EAST,
NORTHERN AFRICA
McGraw-Hill Hellas
TEL +30-1-656-0990-3-4
FAX +30-1-654-5525

MEXICO (Also serving Latin America)
McGraw-Hill Interamericana Editores S.A. de C.V.
TEL +525-117-1583
FAX +525-117-1589
http://www.mcgraw-hill.com.mx
fernando_castellanos@mcgraw-hill.com

SINGAPORE (Serving Asia)
McGraw-Hill Book Company
TEL +65-863-1580
FAX +65-862-3354
http://www.mcgraw-hill.com.sg
mghasia@mcgraw-hill.com

SOUTH AFRICA
McGraw-Hill South Africa
TEL +27-11-622-7512
FAX +27-11-622-9045
robyn_swanepoel@mcgraw-hill.com

UNITED KINGDOM & EUROPE
(Excluding Southern Europe)
McGraw-Hill Education Europe
TEL +44-1-628-502500
FAX +44-1-628-770224
http://www.mcgraw-hill.co.uk
computing_neurope@mcgraw-hill.com

ALL OTHER INQUIRIES Contact:
Osborne/McGraw-Hill
TEL +1-510-549-6600
FAX +1-510-883-7600
http://www.osborne.com
omg_international@mcgraw-hill.com